SUSTAINABLE DEVELOPMENT IN PRACTICE
Sustainomics Methodology and Applications

This book provides a comprehensive, rigorous and practical analysis of sustainable development prospects today by applying the innovative sustainomics framework. Developed over the past 18 years by the eminent environmental scientist and development expert, Mohan Munasinghe, sustainomics shows us the first practical steps in making the transition from the risky business-as-usual scenario to a safe and sustainable future. Its main message is optimistic: although the problems are serious, an effective response can be mounted to make development more sustainable if it is initiated immediately.

The book explains the key principles underlying sustainomics cogently, concisely and with a minimum of technical jargon, with mathematical and other details being provided in annexes. It illustrates the methodology with empirical case studies that are practical and policy-relevant over a wide range of time and geographic scales, countries, sectors, ecosystems and circumstances. The extensive bibliography is useful to researchers of specific issues within sustainable development. This book appeals to a wide audience, including students, researchers from many disciplines, policy analysts, public and private decision makers, and development practitioners.

PROFESSOR MOHAN MUNASINGHE is co-winner of the 2007 Nobel Prize for Peace, as Vice Chair of the UN Intergovernmental Panel on Climate Change (IPCC-AR4). He is the Chairman of the Munasinghe Institute of Development (MIND), Sri Lanka, Director General of the Sustainable Consumption Institute (SCI), University of Manchester, UK, and Honorary Senior Advisor to the Sri Lankan Government. During 35 years of distinguished public service, he has served as Senior Energy Advisor to the President of Sri Lanka, Advisor to the United States Presidents Council on Environmental Quality, and Senior Advisor/Director at the World Bank.

PROFESSOR MUNASINGHE has earned graduate degrees in engineering, physics and development economics from Cambridge University (UK), Massachusetts Institute of Technology (USA), and McGill University and Concordia University (Canada). He has also received several honorary doctorates (honoris causa). He is a Fellow of several internationally recognized Academies of Science and serves on the editorial board of 12 academic journals. He has authored 92 books and over 300 technical papers on economics, sustainable development, climate change, power, energy, water resources, transport, environment, disasters, and information technology.

MUNASINGHE INSTITUTE FOR DEVELOPMENT (MIND) SERIES ON
GROWTH AND SUSTAINABLE DEVELOPMENT

Series Editor

Mohan Munasinghe
Chairman, Munasinghe Institute for Development, Sri Lanka
Vice Chair, Intergovernmental Panel on Climate Change (IPCC), Switzerland
Honorary Advisor to the Government, Sri Lanka
Visiting Professor, United Nations University, Japan

This series of volumes deals with the interaction between conventional economic growth and the more recent paradigm of sustainable development. A distinguished group of international experts drawn from a broad range of disciplines examine this nexus, and suggest ways for making development more sustainable in the future. The volumes cover both theory and practical applications at global, national and local levels:

1. *The Sustainability of Long-term Growth: Socioeconomic and Ecological Perspectives*, Mohan Munasinghe, Osvaldo Sunkel and Carlos de Miguel (Cheltenham: Edward Elgar, 2001).

2. *Sustainable Energy in Developing Countries: Policy Analysis and Case Studies*, Peter Meier and Mohan Munasinghe (Cheltenham: Edward Elgar, 2005).

3. *Primer on Climate Change and Sustainable Development: Facts, Policy Analysis and Applications*, Mohan Munasinghe and Rob Swart (Cambridge: Cambridge University Press, 2005).

4. *Macroeconomic Policies for Sustainable Growth: Analytical Framework and Policy Studies of Brazil and Chile*, Mohan Munasinghe, Raul O'Ryan, Ronaldo Seroa da Motta, Carlos de Miguel, Carlos Young, Sebastian Miller and Claudio Ferraz (Cheltenham: Edward Elgar, 2006).

5. *Global Agenda for Sustainable Governance of Ecosystems: Lessons from the Millennium Ecosystems Assessment*, Janet Ranganathan, Mohan Munasinghe and Frances Irwin (Cheltenham: Edward Elgar, 2007).

SUSTAINABLE DEVELOPMENT IN PRACTICE

Sustainomics Methodology and Applications

Mohan Munasinghe

Munasinghe Institute for Development (MIND), Sri Lanka

Foreword by James Gustave Speth

Munasinghe Institute for Development (MIND)
Colombo, Sri Lanka • Montreal, Canada • Gaithersberg MD, USA

The University of Manchester
Sustainable Consumption Institute

Munasinghe Institute for Development
'making development more sustainable-MDMS'

CAMBRIDGE UNIVERSITY PRESS
Cambridge, New York, Melbourne, Madrid, Cape Town, Singapore, São Paulo, Delhi

Cambridge University Press
The Edinburgh Building, Cambridge CB2 8RU, UK

Published in the United States of America by Cambridge University Press, New York

www.cambridge.org
Information on this title: www.cambridge.org/9780521895408

First published 2009

Printed in the United Kingdom at the University Press, Cambridge

A catalogue record for this publication is available from the British Library

Library of Congress Cataloguing in Publication data
Munasinghe, Mohan, 1945–
Sustainable development in practice : sustainomics methodology and applications /
Mohan Munasinghe ; foreword by James Gustave Speth.
p.   cm. – (Munasinghe Institute for Development (MIND) Series
on growth and sustainable development ; 6)
ISBN 978-0-521-89540-8
1. Sustainable development – Economic aspects.   2. Sustainable development – Social aspects.
3. Sustainable development – Environmental aspects.   I. Title.
HC79.E5M8675   2009
338.9′27–dc22
2009004021

ISBN 978-0-521-89540-8 hardback
ISBN 978-0-521-71972-8 paperback

To my granddaughter Linara (Lena) and her progeny – in the fond hope that they will inherit a world that is more sustainable than ours

Contents

Foreword

Sustainable development is the foremost challenge to humanity in the twenty-first century. It affects every human being on the planet, and therefore we are all stakeholders. Traditional development has focused on material-based economic growth to overcome problems such as poverty, hunger, sickness and inequality. However, despite impressive progress during the last century, especially in the OECD and middle-income countries, these issues have grown worse in most of the poorest countries, and even among poorer communities in the industrial world. New challenges, such as environmental degradation, violent conflicts, climate change and runaway globalization, could exacerbate problems and make them unmanageable.

At the global level, several thousand leading scientists in the United Nations Inter-governmental Panel on Climate Change (IPCC) have clearly confirmed that human activities that emit greenhouse gases are leading to potentially catastrophic global warming. Similarly, the recent Millennium Ecosystem Assessment, commissioned by UN Secretary General Kofi Annan and written by foremost ecologists, has chronicled the steady decline of ecosystem services, which support all life on the planet. They have urged early action to reverse this alarming trend. Yet, the alleviation of poverty among billions (who eke out their existence on less than one dollar a day) will require continued economic growth in those areas. Maintaining this balance among economic, social and environmental needs is the essence of sustainable development.

The powerful technologies and forces we have unleashed may have increasingly unforeseeable and unmanageable consequences. We need to act with the prudence and wisdom suggested in Antoine de Saint Exupery's *The Little Prince*:

The fox said to the little prince: Men have forgotten this truth, but you must not forget it. You remain responsible, forever, for what you have tamed.

Therefore, Professor Munasinghe should be commended for writing a comprehensive, concise and clear volume that offers an immediate and practical path for making current development more sustainable, by applying the sustainomics framework. He demystifies the complexities of sustainable development with a critical and probing analysis. This book is unique in not only presenting an easily understandable and rigorous conceptual framework, but also in illustrating its practical applications using a wide range of empirical case studies.

Professor Mohan Munasinghe first set out the basic principles of sustainomics at the 1992 Earth Summit in Rio de Janeiro. This volume expands on that base, and describes the careful analysis and rigorous testing of the framework during the past 15 years. Key elements of sustainomics include the fundamental approach of 'making development more sustainable' (MDMS); the balanced applications of Mohan's widely recognized sustainable development triangle (with social, economic and environmental dimensions); better integration by transcending conventional boundaries (imposed by discipline, space, time, stakeholder viewpoints and operational needs); and practical application of innovative methods and tools throughout the full cycle (from data gathering to policy implementation and feedback). The methodology is elucidated with a number of practical case studies that are relevant over a wide range of geographic and time scales, countries, sectors, ecosystems and circumstances.

In this book, Mohan brings together a wide range of skills. As a respected and award winning researcher, his analysis is rigorous and well documented. As a senior decision maker and manager with over 35 years of experience in the development arena, his advice is eminently practical. Finally, as a veteran university professor with an enviable record of publications, he presents his arguments lucidly and convincingly.

To conclude, this text, written by a leading world authority on sustainable development, is an invaluable resource for students, researchers, development practitioners, policy analysts, public and private sector decision makers and, indeed, all concerned citizens.

Professor James Gustave Speth
Dean, School of Forestry and Environmental Studies,
Yale University, and former Administrator,
United Nations Development Program

Preface

This book is the sixth major volume in the Munasinghe Institute of Development (MIND) series on growth and sustainable development. Earlier volumes are listed at the front of this publication.

A range of ideas about addressing the complex problems of sustainable development and poverty are set out in this text. Therefore, the reader may find some relevant background information helpful in understanding and interpreting my viewpoint. Physics and engineering were my first loves, and they sustained me all the way through a Ph.D. However, the lure of development was hard to resist, and this led me to pursue concurrently a post-graduate degree in development economics. This focus on the issues of poverty and development has continued ever since, and I have had no cause to regret the choice.

Early work in the development area, during the early 1970s, helped me to concentrate on development planning and natural-resource management (especially energy and water) – amidst the 'limits to growth' debate and the first oil crisis. Although the concept of sustainable development was not known at the time, much of this initial work on marginal cost pricing, integrated resource planning and macroeconomic modelling was not only based on sound economic principles, but also included important social and environmental considerations, including poverty, equity and externalities. From the mid 1980s, my efforts shifted more towards environmental and natural-resource issues and their links with macro-economic policies and poverty. With the publication of the Bruntland report in 1987, I began to focus on forming a better understanding of the new concept of sustainable development.

The core framework of sustainomics was developed from around 1990, and now draws on more than 15 years of direct applications. Thus, the bulk of this book relies on work carried out since 1990. At the same time, sustainomics also makes use of previous research, where the issues, principles and policy options involved are still relevant. Some of the broader development insights, concepts and case studies in this volume are based on over 35 years of professional work. During this period, hands-on involvement in designing and implementing projects and policies in a variety of countries helped to build up practical experience in development activities. Meanwhile, continuing research and teaching sharpened my analytical insights. The basic foundation for intellectual growth was, of course, the preceding two decades of formal education, as well as the subconscious absorption of knowledge whilst growing up amidst the problems of development in Sri Lanka. To summarize, I have learned about development whilst playing many roles – be it as a student or teacher, researcher or field practitioner, policy analyst or decision maker.

Two major international events (i.e. the 1992 UN Earth Summit in Rio de Janeiro and the 2002 UN World Summit on Sustainable Development (WSSD), in Johannesburg) provided major impetus for two seminal publications (Munasinghe, 1992a, 2002a). The first paper set out the conceptual framework for sustainomics, based on the results of a major World Bank research programme that I led. At this time, the Vice Presidency for Environmentally and Socially Sustainable Development was established in the Bank, with the sustainable development triangle as its official logo. Shortly afterwards, some senior colleagues and I presented an important policy paper on Economy-wide Policies and the Environment to the Bank's Board of Executive Directors, proposing policy remedies to address the adverse environmental and social impacts of structural adjustment programmes. The findings were then presented to the world's finance ministers at a special seminar during the World Bank–International Monetary Fund 50th anniversary celebrations in Madrid, in 1994. Subsequently, my 2002 paper at WSSD elaborated on the initial sustainomics framework – based on a range of practical applications and lessons learned during the intervening decade.

Clearly, sustainomics is not the creation of one person. Isaac Newton's classic remark about 'seeing further by standing on the shoulders of giants', is most appropriate.[1] Thus, sustainomics is a practical transdisciplinary framework (or 'transdiscipline') that makes use of my own ideas as well as many existing concepts, methods and tools developed by others – gladly acknowledged in the text. Such an eclectic approach is necessary because sustainable development is so broadly defined and vast in scope that it cannot possibly be dealt with by any single traditional discipline. Furthermore, there is no need to 're-invent the wheel', when practical techniques and solutions are already at hand. Chapter 1 describes the main current rationale for writing this book. However, the original motivation that led to the neologism 'sustainomics' was more basic – simply the lack of a discipline or practical framework that focused explicitly on sustainable development problems in a policy-relevant manner.

The first basic principle of sustainomics – making development more sustainable – was a practical reaction to the endless (and ongoing) theoretical debate on the ultimate definition of sustainable development. It motivates and validates those who wish to address urgent issues such as poverty and hunger immediately. The second core element – balanced treatment of the sustainable development triangle – was prompted by the lively discussions that took place in the run-up to Rio 1992, about how the 'three pillars' (environment, economy and society) might be integrated within development policy. It emphasizes that the sides and interior of the triangle (representing interaction among the three pillars) are as important as the three vertices. The third basic idea of transcending traditional boundaries (of discipline, space, time, etc.) has been around for many years, and proved quite appropriate for sustainomics. Finally, the kitbag of sustainomics methods and models includes some key policy-focused tools, such as the Action Impact Matrix (AIM), Issues-Policy Transformation Mapping (ITM) and Policy Tunnelling, which were developed specifically in the context of sustainomics. Others, such as sustainable development assessment (including cost–benefit analysis and environmental and social assessment), environmental valuation, green accounting, various macroeconomic

---

[1] Lohne, J. (1965). 'Isaac Newton: the rise of a scientist', *Notes and Records of the Royal Society London*, **20**, 125–39.

and sectoral models, etc., were borrowed from other disciplines, or adapted from existing material. The empirical case studies are designed to be not only rigorous applications of the theory, but also practical and policy-focused. The extensive reference list should be useful to those who wish to research specific topics further.

A brief word is appropriate here about the creation of the Munasinghe Institute for Development (MIND) in the year 2000. Working many years abroad within the UN system provided me with unique opportunities and insights. Nevertheless, I felt that I could improve my understanding of development problems and contribute more by taking early retirement and returning to live and work in Sri Lanka. This is a key decision I do not regret, because the view from Colombo is refreshingly different from the 'Washington Consensus' perspective. The outcome was MIND, a small non-profit research centre based in Sri Lanka, whose official logo is the sustainable development triangle, and whose motto is 'making development more sustainable'. A balanced South–North partnership, built on mutual respect and cooperation, is essential to save the planet. To facilitate this process, MIND is building capacity in the South, and fostering both South–South and South–North collaboration to address sustainable development issues.

During the course of this intellectual journey, I have benefited from my association with a wide range of people, each of whom has contributed generously to my understanding of development issues in his (or her) own way. While the core framework presented in the first few chapters of this book are based mainly on my own papers, the case studies have benefited greatly from ideas in selected co-authored publications.

The list of names of the many erudite colleagues I have collaborated with over the years is far too numerous to set out here, but among them special thanks are owed to those with whom I have had the privilege of co-authoring journal articles and books that are the sources of material on which parts of this volume are based. They range from young students and researchers to eminent experts and Nobel prize winners. Working with them has enriched my professional growth and deepened my insights into the problems of development. Their valuable contributions are explicitly acknowledged in the relevant chapters. The honour list includes: Kenneth Arrow, Caroline Clarke, Matthew Clarke, William Cline, Wilfrido Cruz, Carlos de Miguel, Chitrupa Fernando, Claudio Ferraz, Sardar Islam, Susan Hanna, Paul Kleindorfer, Randall Kramer, Karl-Goran Maler, Jeffrey McNeely, Peter Meier, Robert Mendelsohn, Sebastian Miller, Risako Morimoto, Raul O'Ryan, Annika Persson, Walter Reid, Niggol Seo, Ronaldo Seroa da Motta, Narendra Sharma, Walter Shearer, Joseph Stiglitz, Osvaldo Sunkel, Rob Swart, Jeremy Warford and Carlos Young.

I am equally grateful for the kind courtesies and good wishes extended by the following international journals in which relevant papers have appeared: *Ambio, Conservation Ecology, Ecological Economics, Ecological Economics Encyclopedia, Encyclopedia of Earth, Environment and Development Economics, International Journal of Ambient Energy, International Journal of Environment and Pollution, International Journal of Global Energy Issues, International Journal of Global Environmental Issues, Land Use Policy, Natural Resources Forum, Natural Resources Journal, Proceedings of the IEEE, The Energy Journal, World Bank Economic Review* and *World Development*.

Thanks are also due to the following institutions who have published books and monographs I have authored, from which material is drawn: Asian Development Bank (ADB), Asian Pacific Economic Cooperation (APEC), Beijer International Institute of Ecological Economics, Cambridge University Press, Butterworths-Heinemann Press, Edward Elgar Publishing, Intergovernmental Panel on Climate Change (IPCC), International Decade for Natural Disaster Reduction (IDNDR), International Society of Ecological Economics (ISEE), Johns Hopkins University Press, Organization for Economic Cooperation and Development (OECD), Sri Lanka Association for the Advancement of Science (SLAAS), United Nations Development Programme (UNDP), United Nations Environment Programme (UNEP), United Nations University (UNU), Westview Press, World Bank (WB) and International Union for Conservation of Nature (IUCN).

Generations of students have helped to sharpen my concepts and logical thinking over the years. I would like to express my gratitude for the valuable feedback provided by students and faculty from the following academic and research institutions where I have given courses or lectures on various aspects of sustainable development in recent years: American University, USA; Asian Institute of Technology, Thailand; Boston University, USA; Cambridge University, UK; China Meteorological Administration, China: Colombo University, Sri Lanka; Concordia University, Canada; Federal University of Rio de Janeiro, Brazil; Gotenberg University, Sweden; Groningen University, Netherlands; Harvard University, USA; Indian Institute of Management (Calcutta), India; Indira Gandhi Institute of Development Research, India; Institute of Economic Growth, India; Institute of Social and Economic Research, India; Japan Development Bank, Japan; Massachusetts Institute of Technology, USA; Moratuwa University, Sri Lanka; Oxford University, UK; Peking University, China; University of Pennsylvania, USA; Peradeniya University, Sri Lanka; Ritsumeikan Asia Pacific University, Japan; Sorbonne University, France; State University of New York, USA; Tellus Institute, USA; TERI University, India; Tsinghua University, China; United Nations University, Japan; Wuppertal Institute, Germany; Yale University, USA.

I am deeply indebted to the following, who provided detailed and insightful comments and helpful material: Johannes Opschoor, Rob Swart and Harald Winkler.

I also thank the following for useful suggestions and advice: Michael Chadwick, Nazli Choucri, Cutler Cleveland, Shelton Davis, Surendra Devkota, Sytze Dijkstra, Chitru Fernando, Prasanthi Gunawardene, Anders Hansen, Jochen Jesinghaus, Steven Lovink, Risako Morimoto, Eric Neumayer, John O'Connor, Paul Raskin, Terry Rolfe, Fereidoon Sioshansi, Nimal Siripala, Jeremy Warford and Robin White.

The MIND team who helped to prepare this manuscript provided invaluable assistance, for which I am most grateful. They include: Nishanthi De Silva, Yvani Deraniyagala, Irusha Dharmaratna, Priyangi Jayasinghe and Sudarshana Perera.

Last, but not least, my wife Sria deserves special praise for her advice and steadfast support, and for putting up with the many impositions and pressures arising from the preparation of this book. Support provided by my children Anusha and Ranjiva and my mother Flower Munasinghe were also much appreciated.

All my generous benefactors deserve full credit for their valuable contributions to the ideas expressed in this book. Any errors, omissions, shortcomings and misinterpretations are my own responsibility. I hope that the book will appeal to a wide audience, including students, researchers, teachers, policy analysts, development practitioners, public- and private-sector decision makers, concerned citizens and all stakeholders.

To conclude, sustainomics is a preliminary framework and is, as yet, incomplete. It is like a giant jigsaw puzzle, with some gaps and pieces that do not quite fit. Nevertheless, it does seem to provide a promising and practical start, which is allowing the bigger picture to emerge. My earnest hope is that other practicing and potential 'sustainomists' will step forward to correct any errors, reconcile inconsistencies and fill in the empty spaces in the framework, in the process of moving towards the ultimate goal of sustainable development. The final take-home message is optimistic: although the problems are serious, an effective response can be mounted, provided we begin immediately. Sustainomics can help to show us the first practical steps in making the transition from the risky business-as-usual scenario to a safer, and more sustainable, future.

Part I

Framework and fundamentals

1

Overview and summary

This book recognizes that sustainable development is a primary challenge of the twenty-first century (with poverty alleviation as the main goal), and sets out a framework called 'Sustainomics' developed over the past 15 years to meet that challenge. Sustainable development is broadly defined here as 'a process for improving the range of opportunities that will enable individual human beings and communities to achieve their aspirations and full potential over a sustained period of time, while maintaining the resilience of economic, social and environmental systems'.

The main message of this volume is optimistic – although the problems are serious, an effective response can be mounted, provided we begin immediately. Sustainomics seeks to show us the first practical steps in making the transition from the risky business-as-usual scenario to a safer and more sustainable future.

Sustainomics is 'a transdisciplinary, integrative, comprehensive, balanced, heuristic and practical framework for making development more sustainable'. Unlike other traditional disciplines, it focuses exclusively on sustainable development. Thus, the main principle of the framework seeks to make ongoing and future development efforts more sustainable, as a first step toward the ultimate goal of sustainable development. Other key principles stress: (a) balanced consideration of the three dimensions of the sustainable development triangle (social, economic and environmental); (b) better integration by transcending conventional boundaries imposed by discipline, space, time, stakeholder viewpoints and operational needs; and (c) practical application of innovative methods and tools throughout the full cycle from data gathering to policy implementation and feedback.

This volume also seeks to illustrate clearly the methodology with empirical case studies that are practical and policy-relevant over a wide range of geographic and time scales, countries, sectors, ecosystems and circumstances. Every application does not necessarily give equal weight to all elements of the triangle (i.e. social, environmental and economic). Many cover all three aspects, while others primarily address two aspects (e.g. economic and environmental), or a single aspect (e.g. economic cost–benefit analysis, social multistakeholder consultative process, etc.), with the other aspects covered less prominently. In general, the book shows how a broad array of sustainomics-compatible methods and tools could be applied simply and practically to a variety of problems, to make development more sustainable.

I have tried to make the book both accurate and readable. However, because of its wide coverage and length, some parts may seem complex and others too simple, depending on the academic training and disciplinary background of the reader. A fair balance is maintained between theory and applications, recalling the famous rebuke by Nobel Laureate Wassily Leontief (Leontief, 1982): 'Page after page of professional economic journals are filled with mathematical formulas leading the reader from sets of more or less plausible but entirely arbitrary assumptions to precisely stated but irrelevant theoretical conclusions.' Generally, the analytical sections are rigorous but relatively free of technical jargon, while mathematical and other details are provided in appendixes. The case studies have been simplified to show, as clearly as possible, the practicality and policy-relevance of the underlying principles involved. They are presented in decreasing order of geographic scale – from global to local applications. The extensive bibliography should be useful to those who wish to research specific topics further. I hope that the book will appeal to a wide audience, including students, researchers, teachers, policy analysts, development practitioners, public and private sector decision makers, concerned citizens and all stakeholders.

To conclude, sustainomics is put forward as an innovative transdisciplinary framework (or transdiscipline), based on a holistic set of key principles, theories and methods. It draws on many other approaches and techniques, because no single traditional discipline can cover the vast scope and complexity of sustainable development issues. The advantages and shortcomings of sustainomics are frankly laid out, with the expectation that future contributions by other potential 'sustainomists' will rapidly build on the strengths, remedy gaps and inconsistencies, and further flesh out the initial framework and applications.

1.1 Outline of the book

Part I of the book contains four chapters covering the introduction and fundamentals. Chapter 1 provides a broad overview of the entire volume. The first section outlines the various chapters and provides a road map for the reader. Next, we set out the rationale and motivations for the book, including key sustainable development challenges (especially poverty), major global agreements on sustainable development, lessons of history and future scenarios and a vision for a practical way forward. A brief history and introduction to the fundamental elements of sustainomics are provided, followed by a review of key ideas. The chapter ends with selected information on the status of modern development.

Chapter 2 lays out the basic principles, concepts and methods of sustainomics in greater detail. A practical approach based on *making development more sustainable*, or MDMS, is described as an alternative to pursuing abstract definitions of sustainable development. The sustainable development triangle, comprising the social, economic and environmental domains, is introduced, and the driving forces and concepts of sustainability underlying each viewpoint are explained. The integration and synthesis of these three viewpoints is facilitated by two complementary approaches, based on the concepts of optimality and durability. The poverty–equity–population nexus and linkages between economic efficiency and social equity are discussed. A variety of practical analytical tools are outlined to implement the sustainomics framework – including the Action Impact Matrix (AIM), sustainable development assessment (SDA), cost–benefit analysis (CBA), multicriteria analysis (MCA), etc. It is important to select relevant, time and location specific indicators of sustainable development. The need to harmonize development with nature, and restructure the pattern of growth is explained, especially in developing countries, where poverty alleviation will require continued increases in income and consumption.

In Chapter 3, we explore the economy–environment interface (and related social linkages). Economic CBA is a key element of SDA and the project cycle. Basic concepts of CBA are set out, including decision criteria, efficiency and social shadow pricing and measurement of costs and benefits. Practical techniques for economic valuation of environmental assets and services play a key role in incorporating externalities into traditional CBA. When such economic valuation is difficult, MCA helps to make trade-offs among disparate objectives. Key issues, such as discounting, risk and uncertainty, are discussed. The two-way links between economy-wide (macroeconomic and sectoral) policies and environment (and social) issues are outlined. The incorporation of environmental considerations into the conventional system of national accounts is explained.

Chapter 4 expands on the social and ecological interlinkages that play a key role in determining the use of natural resources. The Millennium Ecosystem Assessment (MA) conceptual framework and cyclic interaction between the ecological and socioeconomic domains is summarized, including the main ecosystem services which sustain key components of human well-being. Ecological cycles involving birth–growth–decay–death–regeneration help us understand ecosystem dynamics. Property rights regimes determine how socioeconomic forces interact with environmental resource, especially in the case of traditional societies and native peoples, who are heavily dependent on ecological resources, as well as the landless poor, who subsist in degraded areas. Finally, environmental and social assessments are described as important tools that complement economic assessment (CBA) – all three are key elements of SDA.

Next, we turn to applications of sustainomics at various scales: global and transnational, national and macroeconomic, sub-national sectoral and system, project and local. Part II of the book contains two chapters (5 and 6) with case studies covering the global and transnational levels.

In Chapter 5 the sustainomics framework is applied to study the circular linkage between two global-level issues – climate change and sustainable development. The role of adaptation and mitigation are analysed, and several applications are provided. First, alternative climate change mitigation response strategies are assessed in terms of optimality and durability. Next, we examine the interplay of equity and efficiency in joint implementation (JI) and emissions trading, between Annex 1 and non-Annex 1 countries. The final case study describes how climate change might interact with sustainable development at the national level – by analysing greenhouse gas (GHG) mitigation prospects in Sri Lanka.

Chapter 6 examines a unique transdisciplinary, international scientific dialogue within the Intergovernmental Panel on Climate Change (IPCC), describing how researchers are analysing climate change and sustainable development links. Then, the AIM tool is used to explore two-way linkages between two international activities – the millennium development goals (MDGs) and the findings of the MA. Finally, we examine the practical functioning of a transnational, multistakeholder, multilevel consultative process, involving the UNEP Dams and Development Programme (DDP).

Part III of the book comprises three chapters (7, 8 and 9), covering case studies of sustainomics at the country-wide and macro levels, which deal with a wide range of countries, policy issues and models.

Chapter 7 reviews past research on the sustainability of long-term economic growth, including economy–environment linkages. Some stylized facts about environmental and social impacts of growth-oriented macroeconomic policies are summarized. Unforeseen economic imperfections can interact with growth to cause environmental and social harm. An environmental-macroeconomic analysis confirms that second-best remedial measures could help to limit the damage. Environmental concerns may be introduced into the standard static IS-LM macroeconomic model. The role of green accounting and concepts such as genuine savings are discussed. The AIM approach plays a key role in environmental-macroeconomic analysis. A 'policy-tunnelling' model shows how elimination of economic imperfections permits continued growth while limiting environmental and social harm. Finally, some of these ideas are illustrated through a case study of Brazil. A combination of sectoral and macroeconomic models are used to examine the effects of the growth-oriented strategy pursued by the Brazilian government during the past decades, on a range of sustainable development issues including poverty, employment, urban pollution and deforestation in the Amazon region. Ideas for future research are discussed.

Chapter 8 explores two different theoretical approaches to making development more sustainable at the national macroeconomic level. The literature on the relationship between optimization and sustainability in growth models is reviewed. First, a sustainomics-compatible mathematical model examines the conditions under which development paths, focusing on optimal economic growth, might also be made more sustainable. The model is solved numerically using stylized data. Second, a theoretical model looks at the circumstances that may justify the use of second-best adjustments to macroeconomic policies, to compensate for pre-existing economic distortions that give rise to environmental harm. Three developing world examples (Botswana, Ghana and Morocco) show how macroeconomic polices might combine with local imperfections to harm the environment, and appropriate remedial measures are discussed.

Chapter 9 focuses on computable general equilibrium (CGE) models. First, we apply the ECOGEM model to assess economic, environmental and social policy linkages in Chile. The model systematically and holistically analyses different economy-wide policies and their impact on the Chilean economy. It combines different environmental and social policies so as to enhance positive cross-effects or to mitigate the negative side effects of any single policy. Complex interrelations between the diverse sectors and agents of the economy are captured. Winners and losers are identified, but the results obtained are not always obvious, i.e. indirect effects are also relevant. In the second example, a static CGE model is applied to study the effects of macroeconomic policies on deforestation in Costa

Rica. The results support the more conventional partial equilibrium approach that establishing property rights tends to decrease deforestation, because such rights allow forest users to capture the future benefits of reduced logging damage today. Findings about effects of discount-rate changes also parallel results of partial equilibrium models – higher interest rates promote deforestation, and vice versa. The CGE approach also identifies the indirect effects of intersectoral links, and shows the importance of pursuing sectoral reforms in the context of growth. A dynamic CGE model of Costa Rica, where the value of forest conservation, capital accumulation and interest rate are endogenized, gives the same results as the static CGE model.

Part IV of the book contains five chapters (10 to 14) describing case studies and applications of sustainomics at the sub-national and meso levels within several countries – involving energy, transport, water, ecological and agricultural systems and resource pricing policies.

In Chapter 10, we begin with a general review of links between energy and sustainable development, including a worldwide assessment of energy sector status and issues. Next, the sustainomics approach is used to develop a comprehensive and integrated conceptual framework for an energy-related decision-making framework called sustainable energy development (SED), which identifies practical sustainable energy options by taking into account multiple actors, multiple criteria, multilevel decision making and policy constraints. The methodology is applied to demonstrate how social and environmental externalities could be incorporated into traditional least-cost power-system planning in Sri Lanka, using both CBA and MCA. The study is relatively unique in its focus on assessing environmental and social concerns at the system-level planning (including technology choices among hydro, oil, coal and renewable-energy-based generation), as opposed to the more usual practice of carrying out such analyses only at the project level. Sustainable energy policies for Sri Lanka are identified. Another case study applies SED to the South African energy sector, using MCA to assess the social, economic and environmental trade-offs arising from policy options relating to electricity supply and household energy use. Finally, long-term UK electricity expansion options are examined, to show that decentralized energy may be more sustainable than centralized generation.

Chapter 11 starts by reviewing generic sustainable transport priorities. Then we examine how transport policy could be made more sustainable in Sri Lanka, including the analysis of fuel pricing policy, alternative fuel choices and a range of transport projects. Two classic externalities are discussed. First, the detrimental impact on health from local air emissions are estimated using the benefit transfer method, and the specific health benefits of introducing unleaded petrol are assessed. Second, the effects of traffic congestion in the city of Colombo are studied, including estimation of the cost of time wasted. Several specific infrastructure projects and other measures for reducing congestion are analysed, and an overview is provided of sustainable transport policy options for Sri Lanka.

Chapter 12 explores how to make water resource management more sustainable. The first section describes the natural hydrological cycle and how interventions have affected it. Next, water and development linkages are examined, including a review of the global status of water resources, water shortages and rising costs, poverty issues and sustainable live-lihoods. A comprehensive framework for sustainable water resources management and policy (SWAMP) is outlined, which parallels the SED approach of Chapter 10. The SWAMP methodology is practically applied to a typical water resources project involving groundwater for urban use in Manila, Philippines. The case study analyses the effects of environmentally harmful externalities like aquifer depletion, saltwater intrusion along the coast and land subsidence, and then identifies remedial policy measures. Finally, another case study demonstrates a simple, low-cost, socially acceptable and environmentally desir-able approach to purifying drinking water and reducing waterborne diseases that has yielded significant economic, social and environmental gains to poor villagers in Bangladesh.

Chapter 13 sets out case studies dealing with both natural and managed ecological systems – i.e. forests and agriculture, respectively. First, we analyse the management of megadiverse natural ecosystems in rainforests to identify generic policies that make forest management more sustainable. Next, a case study of Madagascar is presented to achieve a better understanding of the specific environmental and socioeconomic impact of national parks' management policies on tropical forests. Relevant policy implications are drawn. Various techniques are used to value damage economically to forests and watersheds, timber and non-timber forest products, impact on local inhabitants and biodiversity and ecotourism benefits. In a second case study, we examine the potential impact of climate change on managed ecosystems (agriculture) in Sri Lanka. A Ricardian model is used to estimate the past effects of natural variations in both temperature and precipitation. Several scenarios of future climate change are imposed to assess future agricultural production. The harmful impact of rising temperatures generally dominate the beneficial effects of increased precip-itation. Policy conclusions are drawn for sustainable agricultural policy in Sri Lanka.

Chapter 14 examines natural-resource pricing policy issues within a national economy – the economics of both renewable and non-renewable resources are discussed. The principles of sustainable pricing policy (SPP) are explained and applied to energy, based on the sustainable energy development framework (Chapter 10). First, economic principles are used to determine efficient energy prices, which lead to economically optimal production and consumption of energy. Second, environmental aspects may be incorporated by eco-nomically valuing relevant impacts (Chapter 3). Finally, efficient prices may be made more sustainable by adjusting for economic second-best distortions, social consideration, such as affordable (subsidized) prices to meet the basic needs of the poor, and other general policy objectives such as regional or political considerations. The closing section describes how the SPP framework might be used for pricing of other natural resources, such as water, and examines water-specific issues.

Part V of the book contains two chapters (15 and 16) dealing with case studies and applications of sustainomics at project and local levels, which cover topics such as hydro-power, solar energy, water supply, sustainable hazard reduction and disaster management and urban growth.

Chapter 15 commences with the SDA of small hydro-projects in Sri Lanka, by applying MCA to economic, social and environmental indicators. The second case study analyses new and renewable energy projects and national energy policy in a typical developing country. It highlights the use of different policy tools (including the interlinked shadow and market prices) to influence human behaviour and ensure more sustainable energy use – based on solar photovoltaic (PV) energy for agricultural pumping. Then, rural electrification projects in Sri Lanka are analysed with a focus on new and renewable energy technologies, and rural energy priorities are set out.

Chapter 16 explains how natural hazards become major disasters because of heightened vulnerability, often due to prior damage inflicted by unsustainable human activities. A practical framework is presented for mainstreaming sustainable hazard reduction and management (SHARM) into national development – involving the stages of relief, rehabilitation and reduction (planning, preparedness and prevention). The two-way linkages between hazards and sustainable development are analysed. These ideas are illustrated by a case study that assesses the impacts of the 2004 Asian Tsunami in India, Indonesia, Maldives, Sri Lanka and Thailand. A comparison of the Tsunami impacts on Sri Lanka and Hurricane Katrina on New Orleans raises important questions about the role of social capital in coping with disasters. Issues concerning the sustainability of long-term growth in Asian cities are described, including policy options to address these problems – especially in the rapidly expanding mega-cities. The vulnerability of cities to natural hazards and environmental degradation is analysed and illustrated through a case study of floods in Rio de Janeiro. Finally, we examine two examples of how urban development is becoming more sustainable in developed nations – in Canada and the European Union.

1.2 Rationale and motivations

This section summarizes several important motivations underlying this book.

1.2.1 Addressing key sustainable development challenges today

The first and main rationale is the urgent need to address key sustainable development challenges of the twenty-first century.

Poverty, inequity and human well-being

The key sustainable challenges that arise are as follows (see also Box 1.1).

- Alleviating *poverty* for the 1.3 billion people who live on less than $1 per day and the 3 billion people who live on less than $2 per day.
- Providing adequate *food*, especially for the 800 million people who are malnourished today – this will require food production to double in the next 35 years without further land and water degradation.
- Supplying *clean water* to the 1.3 billion people who live without clean water, and providing *sanitation* for the 2 billion people who live without sanitation.
- Supplying adequate *energy* for basic needs, and providing access to the 2 billion people who live without electricity.

- Providing a *healthy environment* for the 1.4 billion people who are exposed to dangerous levels of outdoor pollution and the even larger number (especially women and children) exposed to dangerous levels of indoor air pollution and vector-borne diseases.
- Providing *safe shelter* for those who are vulnerable to natural disasters and those that live in areas susceptible to civil strife.

The extreme poverty and deprivation captured by these statistics are further highlighted by high levels of global inequality. For example, the richest 20% of the world population currently consumes about 60-fold more than the poorest 20%. Highly inequitable income

---

Box 1.1 Summary of Millennium Development Goals (MDGs)

The UN Millennium Development Goals provide a basis for measuring global progress toward sustainable development. In 2000, all countries agreed on eight development goals that would serve as targets for 2015.

Goal 1: **Eradicate extreme poverty and hunger**, by halving the population (1) whose income is less than a $1/day and (2) who suffer from hunger, between 1990 and 2015.

Goal 2: **Achieve universal primary education**, by ensuring that all children will complete full primary schooling by 2015.

Goal 3: **Promote gender equality and empower women**, by eliminating gender disparity in primary and secondary education, preferably by 2005 and in all levels of education no later than 2015.

Goal 4: **Reduce child mortality**, by lowering the under-five mortality rate by two-thirds between 1990 and 2015.

Goal 5: **Improve maternal health**, by reducing maternal mortality rates by 75% between 1990 and 2015.

Goal 6: **Combat HIV/AIDS, malaria and other diseases**, by reversing the spread of HIV/AIDS and the incidence of malaria and other major diseases by 2015.

Goal 7: **Ensure environmental sustainability**, by (1) integrating sustainable development into country policies and programmes and reversing the loss of environmental resources; (2) halving the population without sustainable access to safe drinking water and basic sanitation by 2015; and (3) achieving a significant improvement in the lives of at least 100 million slum dwellers by 2020.

Goal 8: **Develop a global partnership for development**, by (1) improving trading and financial systems; (2) addressing the special needs of the least-developed countries; (3) addressing the special needs of landlocked countries and small island developing states; (4) dealing comprehensively with the debt problems of developing countries; (5) developing and implementing strategies for decent and productive work for youth; (6) providing access to affordable, essential drugs in developing countries; and (7) making new technologies available in cooperation with the private sector, especially information and communications.

Energy services, although not explicitly identified, are essential to achieve the MDGs (UNDP, 2005c).

distributions also persist within many countries (World Bank, 2000). In Brazil and South Africa, the ratios of national income received by the richest and poorest 10% of the population are 53% and 42%, respectively. Corresponding figures for India and the USA are 10% and 14%.

Globalization

Globalization is a major sustainable development challenge. There are many benefits, but the focus here is on identifying potential risks in order to address the underlying problems. This phenomenon has been driven by two fundamental forces – underlying technological change, which has accelerated the integration of markets, and the freer movement of raw materials, goods, services, labour, capital, information and ideas. For example, during 1950 to 1998, world exports of goods increased 17-fold (from $311 billion to $5.4 trillion); the global economy expanded six-fold; international tourist arrivals increased 25-fold (from 25 million to 635 million); during 1970 to 1998 the number of transnational corporations grew eight-fold (from 7000 to 54 000); and during 1960 to 1998 the number of non-cellular telephone lines linked directly to the global phone network grew eight-fold (from 89 million to 838 million) (French, 2000).

Globalization also implies a gradual weakening of the influence of individual national governments. While this process may improve opportunities for economic growth, recent research has pointed out that it fails to provide equal opportunities either across or within nations (Ehrenfeld, 2003). In addition, globalization is associated with significant social and environmental costs that are rarely assigned monetary values and often fall on the poor and disadvantaged, while the benefits accrue mainly to the wealthy.

The environmental costs of globalization (due to pollution of air, land and water and the depletion of natural resources) are mostly associated with increased free trade across borders and industrial activities. Pollution may shift to (mainly developing) countries where environmental protection laws and property rights are not adequately enforced or do not exist. Meanwhile, the burden of global environmental issues like climate change will fall disproportionately on poorer countries that have contributed least to the problem. Furthermore, these countries are less well equipped to deal with such impacts due to lack of financial and technical resources (IMF, 2002). Biodiversity loss has worsened due to the wave of globalization and stimulation of unsustainable development activities, reduction of forests, over-fishing, land degradation, etc. (MA, 2005a). Loss of biodiversity in turn impacts on sustainable development, as it undermines ecosystem health and reduces resilience (Munasinghe, 1992a). For example, globalization has promoted monoculture agricultural practices that favour commercially successful crops and reduce the diversity of less successful crop varieties.

The social costs of globalization often remain hidden and indirect before surfacing suddenly (Ahmad, 2005). Among many such social issues are growing inequity, social unrest, unemployment, dissolution of families and communities and instability of socio-economic systems (Stiglitz, 2002). The widening of the gap between rich and poor is a frequent issue that is raised by many critics of globalization. Open borders for flow of capital and finished products combined with technological advancement has increased the power of multinational corporations and has given them enormous economic profits. However, these profits may not be fairly distributed between multinational corporations and workers (especially in developing countries). Inequity is worsened when seemingly borderless multinationals externalize costs of production in order to increase profits, while jeopardizing social and environmental resilience within borders.

One of the main challenges that globalization poses concerns the inadequacy of current systems of governance to manage this new integrated world. Globalization permits positive as well as negative economic, environmental or social activity in one country to be transmitted to another – for example, an economic downturn or an upturn in the USA is easily felt in Latin America, or the economic 'footprint' of Japan may have a heavy influence on deforestation in South East Asia. At the same time, advances in information sharing and international communications may help to make development more sustainable. For example, the Global System for Sustainable Development based at MIT[1] seeks to map information on sustainable development and make it widely accessible as a dynamic, distributed global knowledge network operating on the Internet (Choucri, 2003). Another example is the open source philosophy of Linux,[2] which provides free operating system software.

On the positive side, the rise of the General Agreement on Tariffs and Trade and the World Trade Organisation has led to a dramatic increase in world trade and a corresponding jump in standards of living. Elimination of trade barriers would generate global gains in economic growth in excess of US $750 billion per year (Commonwealth of Australia, 1999). The beneficial effects of competition stemming from globalization improve the position of all parties, with the potential for increased output as a result of the rationalization of production on a global scale, the spread of technology and competitive pressures for continual innovation on a worldwide basis (Micklethwait and Wooldridge, 2000) and economies of scale that can potentially lead to reductions in costs and prices. The result is a potential for greater human well-being throughout the world. Countries that have grown prosperous through extensive trade interactions are less likely to use armed conflict to resolve their differences. Trade and investment, and the economic growth they encourage, are very positive forces in reducing international tension. For less-developed countries, globalization offers access to foreign capital, global export markets and advanced technology, while breaking the monopoly of inefficient and protected domestic producers. Faster growth, in turn, promotes poverty reduction, democratization and higher labour and environmental standards (Lukas, 2000).

In brief, globalization is not an inanimate process – it is controlled by people. Reform of the global institutional framework is needed, especially the World Bank, the International Monetary Fund, and the World Trade Organisation. Changes include better voting structures and representation (Stiglitz, 2006). Reforms should also increase transparency, limit conflicts of interest, improve accountability, enforce the international rule of law and enhance the ability of developing countries to participate meaningfully in decision making. The

---

[1] See http://gssd.mit.edu/   [2] See http://www.linux.org/

sustainomics approach suggests that it will be possible to shape the forces of globalization for the greater good, based on rational analysis, good governance and ethics.

Private–public balance

Between 1985 and 1994, $468 billion worth of state enterprises were sold off to private investors, globally. However, with a few notable and highly controversial exceptions, governments have not been as eager to sell off their vast natural resource holdings, including forest lands, parks and waterways (Cole, 1999). Some economists argue that natural resources would be better managed economically and environmentally by the private owners than by governments. However, since non-use values of the resource have no monetary value, this may discourage owners from conserving the resource, leading to unsustainable overexploitation of the resource without considering the long-term benefits of conservation.

Privatization of state property may provide a unique opportunity to address not only existing financial issues, but also environmental ones that are neglected due to a lack of investments or poor knowledge of new technology. However, unless a clear legislative framework is set up to deal with the problems under the new system, the profit-maximizing private sector may not invest the required amount of capital to minimize environmental impact and acquire environmentally friendly technology. Inadequate regulation may also cause social problems by permitting privatized providers of basic needs such as energy and water services to raise prices to levels that are not affordable by the poor (Chapter 14).

Multinational organizations usually transfer modern, environmentally friendly technology and install advanced pollution control equipment in their plants. However, this may not be the latest technology, even though it is in compliance with the (lower) environmental standards in developing countries. These lower standards are due to two reasons. One is to attract more foreign capital from the international investment market, and the other is due to the delay in identifying and introducing new standards.

Another problem may arise if the government agency usually involved in privatization of state-owned enterprises (SOEs) is mainly interested in generating a higher income from the transaction, rather than in solving any environmental problems. Lack of transparency in the privatization process will exacerbate such problems.

Environmental damage

Global environmental trends have reached a dangerous crossroads as the new century begins (Ayensu *et al.*, 2000; IPCC, 2001d; Baille *et al.*, 2004; MA, 2005a; UNEP, 2006; Worldwatch, 2001; WRI, UNDP, UNEP and World Bank, 2000). Signs of accelerated ecological decline have coincided with a loss of political momentum on environmental issues. This failure calls into question whether the world will be able to reverse these trends before the economy suffers irreversible damage.

New scientific evidence indicates that many global ecosystems are reaching critical thresholds. The Arctic ice has already thinned by 42%, and 27% of the world's coral reefs have been lost in the last 100 years, suggesting that some of the planet's key ecological systems are in decline. Environmental degradation is also leading to more severe natural disasters, which have cost the world $608 billion over the last decade – as much as in the previous four decades combined. One sign of ecological decline is the risk of extinction that hangs over dozens of species of frogs and other amphibians around the globe, due to pressures that range from deforestation to ozone depletion. With many life-support systems at risk of long-term damage, decisions need to be made whether to move forward rapidly to build a sustainable economy or to risk allowing the expansion in consumption, the increase in greenhouse gas emissions and the loss of natural systems that undermine future development.

Even after a decade of declining poverty in many nations, 1.2 billion people lack access to clean water and hundreds of millions breathe unhealthy air. Poor people in developing countries are pushed to destroy forests and coral reefs in a desperate effort to raise living standards. Environmental degradation is increasing vulnerability to natural disasters – mainly among the poor. In 1998 to 1999 alone, over 120 000 people were killed and millions were displaced in regions such as India and Latin America, due to their inability to withstand disasters. Lack of land has led people to settle in flood-prone valleys and unstable hillsides, where deforestation and climate change have increased their vulnerability to disasters such as Hurricane Mitch, which produced economic losses of $8.5 billion in Central America in 1998 – equal to the combined GNPs of Honduras and Nicaragua. Unless fossil fuel use slows dramatically, the Earth's temperature could rise as high as 6 degrees above the 1990 level by 2100, according to the latest climate models. Such an increase could lead to more extreme events, acute water shortages, declining food production and the proliferation of deadly diseases such as malaria and dengue fever, which will especially harm the poor.

Conflict and competition for resources

Violent conflict blights the lives of hundreds of millions of people. It is a source of systematic violations of human rights and a barrier to progress toward the MDGs. Poverty and the lack of progress toward the MDGs may themselves exacerbate conflicts.

For many people in rich countries the concept of global insecurity is linked to threats posed by terrorism and organized crime. Meanwhile, the interaction between poverty and violent conflict in many developing countries is destroying lives on an enormous scale. Failure to build human security by ending this vicious cycle will have global consequences. In an interdependent world the threats posed by violent conflict do not stop at national borders. Development in poor countries is a key element in achieving global peace and collective security. The current approach may be overemphasizing military strategy and not paying adequate attention to addressing poverty and human security concerns.

The nature of conflict has changed, and new threats to collective security have emerged. The twentieth century was defined first by wars between countries and then by cold war fears of violent confrontation between two superpowers. Now these fears have given way to fears of local and regional wars fought predominantly in poor countries within weak or failed states, and with small arms as the weapon of choice. Most of the victims in today's wars are civilians. There are fewer conflicts in the world today than in 1990, but the share of those conflicts occurring in poor countries has increased – often arising from the struggle for valuable resources (like water, oil, gold, diamonds, etc.), and exacerbated by foreign interests. In an increasingly interconnected world, local conflicts could spread quickly. More effective international cooperation could help to remove the barrier to MDG progress created by conflict, creating the conditions for sustainable development and real human security.

The human development costs of violent conflict are not sufficiently appreciated. In the Congo deaths attributable directly or indirectly to conflict exceed the losses sustained by Britain in the First and Second World Wars combined. In the Darfur region of Sudan, nearly two million people have been displaced because of conflict. Conflict undermines nutrition and public health, destroys education systems, devastates livelihoods and retards prospects for economic growth. Of the 32 countries in the low human development category as measured by the UNDP Human Development Index (HDI), 22 have had some conflict since 1990. Countries that have experienced violent conflict are far more likely to be performing well below the MDG projections for 2015 (Section 1.4). Of the 52 countries that are failing to reduce child mortality, 30 have experienced conflict since 1990. Such costs underline the need for conflict prevention, resolution and post-conflict reconstruction as three basic requirements for building human security, accelerating progress toward the MDGs and making development more sustainable.

As indicated earlier, globalization and privatization could intensify competition for resources and lead to conflicts. Both international and national mechanisms need to be strengthened to prevent and manage conflicts. Due to the rising demand for goods and services, along with economic development, the level of extraction or utilization of natural resources increases. Higher demand and competition for oil, coal, water, land, forest products, recreational areas and other natural resources lead to long-run depletion of, and competition for, those resources – especially when there are no appropriate policies for sustainable utilization.

Competition for scarce natural resources will intensify in the future due to the unsustainable present usage of natural resources. This issue is linked to the environmental harm problem discussed above. It will be necessary to invest more in research and development to identify more efficient methods of resource use to fulfil human requirements and find effective conservation measures. Furthermore, greater efforts need to be devoted to enhancing both international and national institutional mechanisms and management capacities to respond to the competition for natural resources and harm to fragile ecosystems. Promoting pluralistic, multistakeholder, multilevel consultation is important for resolving differences and avoiding conflicts (see Section 1.2.4 and Chapter 6).

Poor governance

Poor governance has caused the massive waste of resources which has hampered efforts to address sustainable development problems such as poverty, hunger and environmental degradation (Section 4.2). Corruption, inefficiency, greed, rape of natural resources and other manifestations of bad governance abound. Overcoming them is a major challenge for those who govern and are governed. Good governance needs to be participatory, consensus-oriented, accountable, transparent, responsive, effective and efficient, equitable, inclusive and must follow the rule of law. Among the key outcomes are that corruption is minimized, the views of minorities are taken into account, the most vulnerable in society participate in decision making and policy becomes responsive to the present and future needs of society.

Where there is poor governance, there is more scope for corruption. An overview of corruption around the world demonstrates that its most common causes are economic in nature. Corruption thrives in the presence of excessive government regulation and inter-vention in the economy, substantial exchange and trade restrictions and complex tax laws. Corruption is further favoured by lax spending controls and when the government provides goods, services and resources at below-market prices (e.g. foreign exchange, credit, public utilities and housing, access to education and health facilities and access to public land). There is potential for corruption when officials take decisions that are potentially costly to private individuals or companies – e.g. tax incentives, zoning laws, timber rights and rights to extract mineral resources, investment permits, privatizations and monopoly rights over exports and imports or domestic activities (Abed and Davoodi, 2000; Tanzi, 1998). Factors that contribute indirectly to corruption include the quality and remuneration of the civil service, the effectiveness of deterrents, the example set by the country's leadership, the nature of meritocratic recruitment and promotion in civil service, the quality and effective-ness of legal enforcement and the degree of transparency in government operations (Haque and Sahay, 1996; Van Rijckeghem and Weder, 1997).

Poor governance can have a major negative impact on economic performance by reduc-ing investment and economic growth. It diverts public resources toward private gains and away from needed public spending; it reduces public revenues, misallocates talent to rent-seeking activities and distorts the composition of government expenditures and of tax revenues (Mauro, 1995). Empirical evidence suggests that corruption reduces spending on publicly provided social services (Tanzi and Davoodi, 1997) and results in lower spending on healthcare and education services, such as medicine and textbooks (Gupta, Davoodi and Tinogson, 2000). Higher levels of corruption also tend to be associated with rising military spending (Gupta, Mello and Saran, 2000). Corruption can worsen poverty and equity (see Section 2.3.5) because it exacerbates an unequal distribution of wealth and unequal access to education and other means to increase human capital (Gupta, Davoodi and Alonso-Terme, 1998; Hindriks, Keen and Muthoo, 1999).

Given the high costs of corruption, why do governments not eliminate it? Because, when corruption is endemic, the likelihood of detection and punishment decreases and incentives are created for corruption to increase further. Individuals at the highest levels of government may have no incentives to control corruption or to refrain from taking part in rent-seeking activities. At the same time, eradication of corruption may be costlier in countries where the level of institutional development and the general economic environment is weak (Dabla-Norris and Freeman, 1999). Empirical evidence suggests that the rule of law (including effective anticorruption legislation), the availability of natural resources, the economy's degree of competition and trade openness and the country's industrial policy affect the breadth and scope of corruption (Leite and Weidmann, 1999).

1.2.2 Fulfilling major global agreements on sustainable development

A second powerful motivation for developing the sustainomics framework is provided by the need to meet the many major global targets, relating to sustainable development, widely agreed by world leaders in recent years (see Section 1.3.1).

The Stockholm Conference on the Human Environment in 1972 was a watershed gathering that brought the international community together to focus on development and environment issues. It focused on benefits of science and technology on economic growth. After 15 years, the report of the World Commission on Environment and Development (WCED, 1987) served as another important milestone, which brought the concept of sustainable development into the mainstream. The report succinctly paraphrased sustainable development, as 'meeting the needs of the present generation without jeopardizing the ability of future generations to meet their needs'. However, due to lack of an operational definition and experience, little success was realized in practice.

The next step was the Agenda 21 document agreed at the UN Earth Summit (UNCED) in Rio de Janeiro in 1992 (UN, 1992), which was intended as a blueprint for putting sustainable development into practice. Although the conference was able to generate worldwide enthusiasm, funding for the ambitious Agenda 21 targets never materialized. The UN Commission for Sustainable Development (CSD) was established to monitor progress on Agenda 21, but many indicators of sustainable development declined, particularly the environment indicators. Greater progress was made on other important agreements pro-duced in Rio – e.g. the framework convention on climate change (UNFCCC) and the convention on biodiversity (CBD). Modest progress was also achieved after Rio with several new international agreements, including the Montreal Protocol (ozone), the Kyoto Protocol (climate) and the UN convention on desertification.

In 2000, the UN Millennium Summit produced the Millennium Development Goals (MDGs), universally accepted by world leaders as a practical benchmark for measuring progress toward sustainable development (see Box 1.1 and Section 1.4). Supplementary targets were also agreed at the World Summit on Sustainable Development (WSSD) in Johannesburg in 2002. The WSSD focused on the shortcomings of the post-Rio develop-ment process, and sought to reinvigorate sustainable development activities worldwide. It yielded the goal-oriented and comprehensive Johannesburg Plan of Implementation, includ-ing targets relating to poverty and WEHAB (water, energy, health, agriculture and biodiver-sity). Most recently, in 2005 the UN Millennium Development Project was endorsed to press forward with the MDGs. In summary, there have been several international agreements on sustainable development during the past decades, but with progressively declining targets. At the same time, implementation of these goals has generally fallen short of their aims (see Section 1.4). Many international conferences and reports have helped to bring about a paradigm shift in development thinking. However, the linkages among scientific evidence, policy making and practical application need to be strengthened (see Section 1.3). In addition, scientific evidence and analysis are still inadequate on new global trends such as globalization and privatization, which implies that the achievement of MDG and WSSD targets will require dynamic implementation processes that adapt to new knowledge. Therefore, ongoing discussions and consensus-building among scientific experts, decision makers and other stakeholders need to be intensified.

1.2.3 Avoiding worst-case future scenarios and learning from past experience

The third major motivation arises from the need to avoid disastrous future outcomes and learn the lessons of history relating to human development. Several ancient civilizations have shown remarkable durability by lasting 4000 years or more, including those located in the Yellow river basin in China, the Nile river basin in Egypt, and the Saraswati river basin in India. Other regions, such as the Sahel and the dust bowl in the USA, have demonstrated the fragility and collapse of carrying capacity in marginal lands exposed to the pressure of unsustainable human activity over time.

Building on this historical experience and using modern analytical tools, a number of scenarios of future world development have emerged – see Table 1.1. While a range of optimistic and pessimistic futures are considered, we are especially concerned about avoiding the more disastrous scenarios. Among the undesirable and alarming outcomes are the 'barbarization' scenario of the Global Scenarios Group, the IPCC A2 scenario projecting dangerously high growth of GHG emissions, and the Millennium Ecosystem Assessment 'order from strength' scenario. These scenarios provide ample motivation for renewed efforts to address the major global problems and prevent the potential deterioration of society into chaos and anarchy. One particular extrapolation of past experience serves as a powerful rationale for this book. Two catastrophic famines or holocausts during the late nineteenth century killed tens of millions in the developing world (Davis, 2001). They were the outcome of negative synergies between adverse global environmental factors (i.e. the El Niño droughts of 1876–1878 and 1898–1901) and the inadequate response of socioeconomic systems (i.e. vulnerability of tropical farming forcibly integrated into world commodity markets). In the eighteenth century, the quality of life in countries like Brazil, China and India was comparable with European standards. However, colonial dictates and rapid expansion of world trade reoriented production in developing countries (from food to cash crops) to service distant European markets. By the time the El Niño droughts struck in the nineteenth century, the domination of commodity and financial markets by Britain forced developing country small-holders to export cash crops at ever deteriorating terms of trade. This process undermined local food security, impoverished large populations and culminated in holocausts, on an unprecedented scale, which have been identified as one major cause of the present state of underdevelopment in the third world. From a sustainomics perspective, the corollary is clear, based on the precautionary principle (see Chapter 5). The future vulnerability of developing country food production systems to a combination of climate change impact and accelerated globalization of commodity and financial markets, poses significant risks to the survival of billions, especially in the poorest nations (Munasinghe, 2001a).

Table 1.1 *Summary of some recent global scenario exercises*

Name	Description
Global Scenario Group (GSG)	global scenarios based on three classes – conventional worlds, barbarization (bad), great transitions (good) (Gallopin, 1997; Raskin *et al.*, 1998, 2002)
Global Environment Outlook 3 (GEO-3)	similar to GSG with emphasis on regional texture (UNEP, 2002)
World Energy Council (WEC)	multiple global energy scenarios to year 2100 (Nakicenovic, Grubler and McDonald, 1998)
IPCC Emission Scenarios (SRES)	GHG emission scenarios to year 2100; axes of change are sustainable versus unsustainable and globally integrated versus fragmented (IPCC, 2000)
Millennium Ecosystem Assessment (MA)	four scenarios based on future status of ecosystems (2003); axes of change are globally integrated versus regional and environmentally proactive versus reactive

1.2.4 Vision for a practical way forward

The fourth and final motivation is to set down some ideas which might serve as the first steps along a practical path toward the ultimate goal of sustainable development. This transition is depicted in Figure 1.1.

(1) The top row shows that the extrapolation of current trends driven by forces like globalization and conventional market-oriented policies based on the so-called 'Washington Consensus' will pose significant risks. While policy reforms are proposed to correct for market deficiencies, issues arising from both the immediate drivers and underlying pressures are not being addressed systematically within a framework aimed at long-term sustainability (see Section 3.7). The main current policies tend to be reactive and defensive. Poverty, inequity, exclusion, conflict, poor governance and environmental damage could worsen sharply under such a business-as-usual approach and lead to a breakdown of global society.

(2) The middle row depicts the practical contribution of the sustainomics approach. It offers an intermediate, but practical, step which takes us forward via proactive measures that make current development more sustainable. Society moves gradually toward the ultimate goal of sustainable development by influencing key immediate drivers of change, including consumption patterns, population, technology and governance – and thereby shaping global trends and managing market forces. Some aspects of the sustainomics framework also facilitate direct manipulation of underlying pressures. There is emphasis on early action to overcome the huge inertia of 'supertanker Earth', to begin steering it away from its risky current path toward safer waters using existing experience and tools. Co-evolving socioeconomic and ecological systems need to be guided by rational human foresight, at a moment in history where a major global transition might lead to disastrous results (see Section 4.1.3).

(3) The bottom row indicates the long-term goal of making the transition to a new global sustainable development paradigm and sustainable lifestyle. Proponents seek deep changes, via a networked, multistakeholder, multilevel global citizens' movement, responsive governance structure,

Main issues	poverty, inequity, exclusion, conflict, environmental harm, etc.	Human interventions business-as-usual risks from unrestrained market forces at work ('Washington consensus', globalization, etc.)
Immediate drivers	consumption patterns, population, technology, governance	Intermediate practical step making development more sustainable (MDMS), using existing knowledge and lessons learned to manage market forces (sustainomics)
Underlying pressures	basic needs, social power structure, values, choices, knowledge base	Long-term goal fundamental global sustainable development transition through multilevel, multistakeholder, citizens' networks, advanced policy tools, responsive governance and better technologies (new sustainable development paradigm)

Figure 1.1. Role of sustainomics in the long-term transition to global sustainable development.

improved policy tools, advanced technologies and better communications (including the Internet), which will work on underlying pressures linked to basic needs, social power structure, values, choices and knowledge base. The World Social Forum (Leite, 2005) and the Global Transition Initiative (Raskin, 2006) are two such efforts to build pluralistic global citizens' networks. Chapter 6 describes some multilevel, multistakeholder, transdisciplinary dialogues, where networks of experts and practitioners play a key role.

1.3 Brief history and summary of sustainomics

1.3.1 Evolution of the sustainomics approach

This section provides a brief overview, from an institutional perspective, of how sustainomics evolved. The Preface provides a more personal viewpoint. The sustainomics framework draws together two broad streams of thought – i.e. development (focused on human well-being) and sustainability (systems-science-oriented), as described below.

Development stream (focused on human well-being)

Current approaches to sustainable development draw on the experience of several decades of development efforts. Historically, the development of the industrialized world focused on material production as the basis of human well-being. Not surprisingly, most industrialized and developing nations have pursued the economic goal of increasing output and growth during the twentieth century. While the traditional approach to development was strongly associated with economic growth, it had important social dimensions as well.

By the early 1960s, the large and growing numbers of poor in the developing world, and the lack of 'trickle-down' benefits to them, resulted in greater efforts to improve income distribution directly. The development paradigm shifted toward equitable growth, where social (distributional) objectives, especially poverty alleviation, were recognized as being distinct from, and as important as, economic efficiency in contributing to well-being.

Protection of the environment has now become the third major objective of sustainable development. By the early 1980s, a large body of evidence had accumulated that environmental degradation was a major barrier to human development and well-being, and new proactive safeguards were introduced (such as the environmental assessments).

Some key milestones relating to the evolution of recent thinking on sustainable development include: the 1972 United Nations Environmental Summit in Stockholm, the 1987 Bruntland Commission report, the 1992 United Nations Conference on Environment and Development (UNCED) in Rio de Janeiro, the 1995 World Summit on Social Development in Copenhagen, the UN Millennium Summit and Millennium Development Goals (MDGs) in 2000, the 2002 World Summit on Sustainable Development (WSSD) in Johannesburg, the UN Millennium Development Project approved as a follow-up to the MDGs in 2005 and the UN Decade on Education on Sustainable Development (1995–2014); see Section 1.2.2.

Sustainability stream (systems-science-oriented)

Meanwhile, the scientific community became more interested in exploring the concept of sustainability. During the 1980s a number of relevant international scientific research initiatives dealing with nature emerged, including the World Climate Research Programme (WCRP) in 1980, the International Geosphere and Biosphere Programme (IGBP) in 1986 and DIVERSITAS (on biodiversity and ecology) in 1990. The United Nations Intergovernmental Panel on Climate Change (IPCC) was also established in 1988 (by WMO and UNEP), with global scientific expertise to assess periodically information on climate change. However, global sustainability issues like climate change were mainly framed by natural scientists as problems involving bio-geophysical systems, largely divorced from their social context. Although the social aspects have received increasing attention in the scientific debate, it was considered an 'add-on' rather than a fundamental element.

In the 1990s, it was recognized that human activity was a major factor influencing global changes – e.g. in the work of existing scientific bodies such as the IPCC (Bruce, Lee and Haites, 1996; IPCC, 2001a) and in the creation of new bodies such as the International Human Dimensions to Global Environmental Change (IHDP) in 1996. In 1995, the IGBP GAIM (Global Analysis, Integration and Modelling) Task Force was established to integrate the knowledge generated in the various IGBP core projects. Since then, a series of international conferences and initiatives have called for (i) a more integrated approach between the natural and the social sciences and (ii) a better link between scientific activities and sustainable development problems – especially the human dimension. Among the significant outcomes of this trend was the Millennium Ecosystem Assessment (MA) launched by UN Secretary General Kofi Annan in 2001, which linked ecosystems, human communities and development.

Emergence of sustainomics

Amongst these multiple initiatives, the first ideas about sustainomics were outlined from 1990 onwards in several conference presentations by Mohan Munasinghe, culminating in a formal paper presented at the Rio Earth Summit in 1992, which set out key elements of the framework (Munasinghe, 1992a). These ideas were further elaborated for practical application (Munasinghe, 1994a). The aim was a more holistic and practical synthesis that would help to make development more sustainable by integrating the concerns of the development community (who focused on pressing development issues such as poverty, equity, hunger, employment, etc.) and the interests of the scientific community (who emphasized research on sustainability science, environment, etc.). The neologism 'sustainomics' was coined to project a more neutral image by focusing attention on sustainable development, so avoiding any disciplinary bias or hegemony. Sustainomics also seeks to balance people-oriented Southern Hemisphere priorities, including promotion of development, consumption and growth, poverty alleviation and equity, with environment-oriented Northern Hemisphere concerns about issues like natural resource depletion, pollution, the unsustainability of growth and population increase.

Sustainable development is broadly described as 'a process for improving the range of opportunities that will enable individual human beings and communities to achieve their aspirations and full potential over a sustained period of time, while maintaining the resilience of economic, social and environmental systems' (Munasinghe, 1992a). Adapting this general concept, a more focused and practical approach toward making development more sustainable sought 'continuing improvements in the present quality of life at a lower intensity of resource use, thereby leaving behind for future generations an undiminished stock of productive assets (i.e. manufactured, natural and social capital) that will enhance opportunities for improving their quality of life'.

The sustainomics framework is described in greater detail in Chapter 2. In particular, it encourages decision making based on the balanced and consistent treatment of the economic, social and environmental dimensions of sustainable development, and draws on a sound but evolving body of scientific knowledge, including the natural and social sciences, engineering and humanities. A decade or more of experience in further developing and practically applying the sustainomics framework in the field was described at the 2002 World Summit on Sustainable Development (GOSL, 2002; Munasinghe, 2002a). Meanwhile, the approach has been cited and used in the work of many world bodies (e.g. ADB, CSD, EC, OECD, UNDP, UNEP, World Bank, etc.), governments (e.g. Canada, Netherlands, Philippines, Sri Lanka, UK, etc.) and individual researchers – specific references are given throughout the text. This book seeks to provide a comprehensive assessment of sustainomics today.

1.3.2 Summary of basic principles and methods

The sustainomics framework draws on the following basic principles and methods (Munasinghe, 1992a, 1994a, 2002a); details are given in Chapter 2.

(a) Making development more sustainable

The step-by-step approach of 'making development more sustainable' (MDMS) becomes the prime objective, while sustainable development is defined as a process (rather than an end point). Since the precise definition of sustainable development remains an elusive, and perhaps unreachable, goal, a less ambitious strategy that merely seeks to make development more sustainable does offer greater promise. Such a gradient-based method is more practical and permits us to address urgent priorities without delay, because many unsustainable activities are easier to recognize and eliminate. Although MDMS is incremental, it does not imply any limitation in scope (e.g. restricted time horizon or geographic area – see (c) below). MDMS also seeks to keep future options open and identify robust strategies which meet multiple contingencies and increase resilience. Thus, while implementing short- and medium-term measures, we also follow a parallel track by continuing efforts to define and achieve the long-term goal of sustainable development.

(b) Sustainable development triangle and balanced viewpoint

Sustainable development requires balanced and integrated analysis from three main per-spectives: social, economic and environmental. Each view corresponds to a domain (and system) that has its own distinct driving forces and objectives. The economy is geared toward improving human welfare, primarily through increases in the consumption of goods and services. The environmental domain focuses on protection of the integrity and resilience of ecological systems. The social domain emphasizes the enrichment of human relationships and the achievement of individual and group aspirations. Interactions among domains are also important.

(c) Transcending conventional boundaries for better integration

The analysis transcends conventional boundaries imposed by discipline, space, time, stake-holder viewpoints and operationality. The scope is broadened and extended in all domains to ensure a comprehensive view. Transdisciplinary analysis must cover economics, social science and ecology, as well as many other disciplines. Spatial analysis must range from the global to the very local, while the time horizon may extend to decades or centuries. Participation of all stakeholders (including government, private sector and civil society), through inclusion, empowerment and consultation, is important. The analysis needs to encompass the full operational cycle from data gathering to practical policy implementation and monitoring of outcomes.

(d) Full-cycle application of practical and innovative analytical tools

A variety of practical and novel analytical tools facilitate governance over the full cycle from initial data gathering to ultimate policy implementation and feedback.

Two complementary approaches based on 'optimality' and 'durability' may be used to integrate and synthesize across economic, social and environmental domains, within an integrated assessment modelling framework. An issues-implementation transformation map

(IITM) helps to translate issues in the environmental and social domains into the conventional national economic planning and implementing mechanisms within line ministries and departments.

Restructuring the pattern of development to make economic growth more sustainable is explained through a 'policy-tunnelling' model, especially useful in poor countries, where poverty alleviation will require continued increases in income and consumption. Other practical tools include the Action Impact Matrix (AIM), integrated national economic–environmental accounting (SEEA), sustainable development assessment (SDA), environmental valuation, extended cost–benefit analysis (CBA), multicriteria analysis (MCA), integrated assessment models (IAMs) and so on. A range of sustainable development indicators help to measure progress and make choices at various levels of aggregation.

The AIM process is the key link from initial data gathering to practical policy application and feedback. Critical sustainable development concerns are included in conventional national development strategy and goals in two main ways: an upward link, where sustainable development issues are embedded in the macrostrategy of a country via the medium- to long-term development path; and a downward link, where such issues are integrated into the national development strategy in the short- to medium-term, by carrying out SDAs of microlevel projects and policies.

Brief review of key ideas

The principle conclusion of this book is that we have made significant progress toward understanding and implementing the concept of sustainable development since the 1990s. The way forward is by taking practical steps toward MDMS, as set out in the sustainomics framework. Many unsustainable practices are obvious and may be addressed incrementally today, as we progress toward the long-term (and less clear) goal of sustainable development. Sufficient examples exist of good (and bad) practices, and the lessons learned permit us to address immediate problems such as poverty, hunger and environmental degradation in a more sustainable manner, while concurrently seeking to define better and attain the ultimate goal of sustainable development.

The core principles underlying the sustainomics framework provide a good starting point for systematic analysis of sustainable development problems: (a) making development more sustainable; (b) sustainable development triangle (economic, social and environmental dimensions) and balanced viewpoint; (c) transcending conventional boundaries (discipline, space, time, stakeholder viewpoint and operationality) for better integration; and (d) full-cycle application of practical and innovative analytical tools (including the AIM).

Furthermore, the case studies in this book (and elsewhere) demonstrate that the approach of making development more sustainable has already yielded encouraging practical results and shows increasing promise for the future. Specific examples described here begin with global problems such as climate change and the analysis of international- and national-level policy responses. Next, we learn from the experience of transnational institutions like the World Commission on Dams (WCD), the Intergovernmental Panel on Climate Change (IPCC), the Millennium Ecosystems Assessment (MA) and the Millennium Development

Goals (MDGs), which work through multistakeholder, multilevel, multidisciplinary processes involving governments, business, civil society and scientists. At the national macroeconomic level, a wide range of country applications involving a variety of models are presented, which provide useful insights for practical economy-wide policies.

Within countries, case studies cover sustainable development of key sectors like energy, transport and water, as well as important ecological systems involving forests and agriculture. Resource pricing policy could be used as a practical and flexible tool for making development more sustainable. Finally, the book shows how the sustainomics framework may be applied at the project and local levels, in areas such as hydropower, solar energy, water supply, sustainable hazard reduction and disaster management and urban growth.

We accept that sustainomics is incomplete – there are both gaps in knowledge and problems of implementation. Nevertheless, our hope and expectation is that the important contributions of other potential 'sustainomists' will rapidly help to further flesh out the initial framework and applications set out in this volume.

1.4 Millennium development prospects and worldwide status

This section reviews recent trends and prospects in relation to the MDGs as an appropriate backdrop for the subsequent chapters.

One yardstick for measuring the progress of civilization is the ability of humans to manipulate energy, matter and information. We may distinguish four eras (De Vries and Goudsblom, 2002; Munasinghe, 1987, 1989). The first was the nomadic hunter–gatherer phase starting several million years ago, including the domestication of fire and use of stone tools. Around 8000 BC a second transition to the agricultural period began, associated with farming settlements and agricultural implements. The advent of the industrial age in the eighteenth century was even more rapid, and was characterized by increasingly crowded and polluted urban centres and machines. The twentieth century marks the fourth transition to a planetary civilization, increasingly linked together by fast communications, rapid transportation, information technology and computers. During this process, both *extensive* and *intensive* development took place. With each transition, extensive development and growth in the scale of activities expanded the footprint of humanity (see Figure 2.8). At the same time, intensive development increased the internal complexity, interlinkages and ability to process information within society. Nevertheless, human beings are still utterly dependent on the bio-geosphere for their existence and, thus, extensive growth makes us more vulnerable to environmental degradation. Meanwhile, intensive development improves resilience due to greater complexity, interconnections and redundancy, but also increases vulnerability to harmful disturbances that are quickly transmitted to all parts of the globe (e.g. financial and market instabilities or new diseases).

Many recent books have set out key sustainable development problems and potential remedies – taking optimistic, pessimistic or intermediate viewpoints (Easterbrook, 1995; Environment and Development Economics, 1998; IPCC, 2001a; Jodha, 2001; Lomborg, 2001; MA, 2005a; Maddison, 2001; McNeill, 2000; MDG, 2005; Munasinghe and Swart,

2005; Myers and Simon, 1994; Speth, 2004; UNDP, 2005b; World Bank, 2006; Worldwatch, 2003). While it is difficult to generalize, environmentalists and natural scientists have tended to see the glass half empty, while economists and technological optimists have perceived the glass half full – reflecting a range of opinions. This book takes the middle path, arguing that the problems are serious enough to warrant urgent attention, while noting that existing and emerging remedies could provide adequate solutions if early action is taken.

Below, we summarize the disappointing progress on the MDGs – the most widely accepted set of global sustainable development targets today.

Poverty and hunger

More than 1 billion people survive on less than $1 a day. More than 800 million people have too little to eat to meet their daily energy needs. Over 25% of children under the age of five in developing countries are malnourished, retarding their physical and mental development and threatening their survival. In Asia, the number of people living on less than $1 a day dropped by nearly a quarter of a billion from 1990 to 2001. In over 30 countries, hunger was reduced by at least 25% during the last decade. Sub-Saharan Africa is the hardest hit by hunger and malnutrition.

The proportion of people lacking the food needed to meet their daily needs is on the decline (see Section 13.3). The percentage of people with insufficient food was lower in 2000–2002 than in 1990–1992 in all regions except Western Asia. However, progress has slowed, and the number of hungry people increased between 1997 and 2002, probably due to growing populations and poor agricultural productivity. Hunger tends to be concentrated among the landless or among farmers whose plots are too small to provide for their needs.

Efforts to eradicate poverty and hunger are frequently set back by conflict and natural disasters. The average income of the extremely poor in Sub-Saharan Africa has declined. Reversing this negative trend requires faster economic growth that reaches the poor – a challenging task in the face of disease and armed conflicts. Hunger and poverty, in turn, can provide fertile ground for conflict (especially when combined with factors such as inequality) and make it more difficult to cope with disasters. Strategies to combat child malnutrition include breastfeeding for the first six months, increasing the use of micro-nutrient supplements, reducing infectious diseases and improving access to clean water and sanitation.

Primary education

More than 115 million children of primary school age do not go through proper schooling. These are mostly children from poor households, whose mothers often have no formal education either. Education, especially for girls, has social and economic benefits for society as a whole. Achieving this goal will require dramatically scaled-up efforts in Sub-Saharan

Africa, Southern Asia and Oceania. In these regions and elsewhere, increased enrolment must be accompanied by efforts to ensure that all children remain in school and receive a high-quality education.

In five regions, 90% of children or more are enrolled in primary school. Sub-Saharan Africa has made progress, but still has over one-third of its children out of school. In Southern Asia, Oceania and Western Asia, enrolment is also lagging, with about 20% of children out of school.

Gender equality

Achieving parity in education is critical if women are to engage fully in society and the global economy. Although women have increased their share in paid non-agricultural employment, they remain a small minority in salaried jobs and are overrepresented in the informal economy. Having an equal voice in decisions is a key element of women's empowerment.

Countries with the widest gender gap in primary education have made progress in increasing the proportion of girls enrolled in school. This gap still remains a serious concern in Southern Asia, Sub-Saharan Africa and Western Asia. In countries where resources and school facilities are lacking, only boys are sent to school. However, in countries where overall enrolments are high, girls are well represented in both primary and secondary education (e.g. in Latin America).

Women's access to paid employment is lower than men's in most of the developing world. Women in Southern Asia, Western Asia and Northern Africa still hold only about 20% of paying jobs in sectors outside of agriculture. In Latin America and the Caribbean, women now hold over 40% of paying jobs. Over 60% of people working in family enterprises without pay are women.

Child mortality

Every year, almost 11 million children below the age of five die (about 30 000 children a day). Most live in developing countries and die from a disease or a combination of diseases that can be prevented or treated by existing inexpensive means. Malnutrition contributes to over half these deaths. Improvements in public-health services are key, including safe water and better sanitation. Education, especially for girls and mothers, saves children's lives. Raising incomes can help, but little will be achieved unless services reach those who need them most.

In 1960, more than one child in five died before the age of five in the developing regions. By 1990, the rate decreased to one in ten. Only in Northern Africa, Latin America and the Caribbean and South-Eastern Asia has this pace been maintained. In these regions, economic growth, better nutrition and access to healthcare have spurred improvements in child survival. Almost half of all deaths among children under five occur in Sub-Saharan Africa, where progress has slowed owing to weak health systems, conflicts and AIDS. More than one-third of all deaths occur in Southern Asia, despite the reduction in poverty. Countries that have experienced conflict, including Cambodia and Iraq, have seen sharp increases or no improvement in child mortality since 1990. Countries reeling from AIDS, especially in Southern Africa, have also seen an increase in child mortality.

Most of these lives could be saved by expanding low-cost prevention and treatment measures. These include exclusive breastfeeding of infants, antibiotics for acute respiratory infections, oral rehydration for diarrhoea, immunization and the use of insecticide-treated mosquito nets and appropriate drugs for malaria. Proper nutrition is part of prevention, because malnutrition increases the risk of dying from these diseases. Better care for mothers and babies before and after birth would reduce the one-third of these deaths that occur in the first days of life.

Maternal health

Currently, 200 million women have an unmet need for safe and effective contraceptive services; 20 times as many women suffer serious injuries or disabilities. Countries with already low levels of maternal mortality have made progress. Reductions in the worst-affected countries will require additional resources to ensure that the majority of births are attended by doctors, nurses or midwives who are able to prevent, detect and manage obstetric complications. When problems do arise, women must be able to reach a fully equipped medical facility in time. Universal access to reproductive healthcare, including family planning, is the starting point for maternal health.

In 2000, the average risk of dying during pregnancy or childbirth in the developing world was 450 per 100 000 live births. The chances of dying during pregnancy or childbirth over a lifetime are as high as one in 16 in Sub-Saharan Africa, compared with one in 3800 in the developed world. This risk could be substantially reduced if women had adequate family planning services, good medical care and access to emergency obstetric-care facilities in case of unexpected complications.

Advances were made in most developing regions between 1990 and 2003 in providing medically skilled attendants at birth. Major improvements were achieved in South-Eastern Asia, Northern Africa and Eastern Asia, but there was no change in Sub-Saharan Africa, where maternal mortality is highest.

HIV/AIDs, malaria and other diseases

More than 20 million people have died around the world since the epidemic began (in the 1980s), it being the leading cause of premature death in Sub-Saharan Africa and the fourth largest killer worldwide; by the end of 2004, an estimated 39 million people were living with HIV. Thailand and Uganda have shown that infection rates can be reversed with vision and leadership. Historically, malaria has been a far greater scourge. It currently claims the lives of a million people a year and is estimated to have slowed economic growth in African countries by 1.3% a year. Tuberculosis, once thought defeated, is making a comeback, helped by the emergence of drug-resistant strains and the vulnerabilities created by HIV and AIDS. Not surprisingly, all three of these diseases are concentrated in the poorest countries. They can be largely controlled through education, prevention, treatment and care.

Globally, 4.9 million people were newly infected with HIV in 2004 and 3.1 million died. HIV is spreading fastest in the European countries of CIS and in parts of Asia. In countries where the epidemic is still at an early stage, programmes targeted at the most vulnerable are effective.

Because there is no cure for AIDS, prevention is essential. But millions of young people know too little about HIV to protect themselves. Surveys in Sub-Saharan Africa and South-Eastern Asia show low knowledge about the basics about how to avoid infection. During the second half of 2004, the number of people receiving antiretroviral therapy in developing regions increased from 440 000 to 700 000, but that figure is only about 12% of those who would benefit from these medications. Treatment and care need to be expanded to reach millions more.

Malaria is endemic in many of the world's poorest countries, affecting 350–500 million people a year; 90% of the one million malaria deaths each year occur in Sub-Saharan Africa, where more than 2000 children die each day from malaria. Tuberculosis kills 1.7 million people a year, most of them in their prime productive years. The number of new tuberculosis cases has been growing by about 1% a year, with the fastest increases in Sub-Saharan Africa and CIS. In 2003, there were nearly 9 million new cases, including 674 000 among people living with HIV.

Environmental sustainability

Land is becoming degraded at an alarming rate. Plant and animal species are being lost in record numbers. The climate is changing, bringing with it threats of rising sea levels and worsening droughts and floods. Fisheries and other marine resources are being over-exploited. The rural poor are most immediately affected because their day-to-day subsistence and livelihoods more often depend on the natural resources around them. Though the exodus to urban areas has reduced pressure on rural lands, it has increased the number of people living in unsafe and overcrowded urban slums. In both urban and rural areas, billions of people lack safe drinking water and basic sanitation. Overcoming these and other environmental problems will require greater attention to the plight of the poor and an unprecedented level of global cooperation.

Forests cover one-third of the Earth's surface and constitute one of the richest ecosystems. In the last decade alone, 940 000 square kilometres of forest were converted into farmland, logged or lost to other uses. Some 19 million square kilometres (over 13% of the Earth's land surface) have been designated as protected areas. This represents an increase of 15% since 1994. Loss of habitats and biological diversity continues, with more than 10 000 species considered to be under threat.

The transfer of new energy-efficient technologies to developing countries is not happening fast enough. In poor nations, the lack of clean fuels has a direct impact on rural households, which depend on wood, dung, crop residues and charcoal for cooking and heating. Indoor air pollution caused by these fuels is estimated to cause more than 1.6 million deaths per year, mostly among women and children.

The fraction of population using safe sources of drinking water in the developing world increased from 71% in 1990 to 79% in 2002. However, over 1 billion people have yet to benefit, with lowest coverage in rural areas and urban slums. In Sub-Saharan Africa, 42% of the population is still unserved. The obstacles to progress (which include conflict, political instability and low priority for investments in water and sanitation) are especially daunting because of high-population-growth rates.

Much slower progress has been made globally in improving sanitation. About 2.6 billion people (representing half the developing world) lack toilets and other forms of improved sanitation. Sanitation coverage in the developing world rose from 34% in 1990 to 49% in 2002. If present trends continue, close to 2.4 billion people worldwide will still be without improved sanitation in 2015. A dramatic increase in investment is needed to meet the sanitation target.

The urban population of developing countries is growing at over 3% per year, or three times faster than in rural areas. Thus, including migration to the cities and additional births, about 100 million people are added to urban communities of the developing world each year. By 2008, the urban population will exceed the rural population in developing regions. Nearly one in three city dwellers (almost one billion people) live in slums, in conditions characterized by overcrowding, few jobs or security of tenure, poor water, sanitation and health services and widespread insecurity, including violence against women. Not surprisingly, disease, mortality and malnutrition are much higher in slums than in planned urban areas. Surveys suggest that in some African cities the death rate of children under five who live in slums is about twice as high as that of children in other urban communities.

2

Sustainomics framework[1]

In this chapter, the elements of the sustainomics framework are set out in greater detail. Section 2.1 describes the fundamental principles and methods. Sustainable development, traditional development and growth are defined. A practical approach based on *making development more sustainable*, or MDMS, is described as an alternative to pursuing abstract definitions of sustainable development. The sustainable development triangle (comprising social, economic and environmental dimensions) is introduced, and the driving forces and concepts of sustainability underlying each viewpoint are explained. Sustainomics also promotes methods which transcend conventional boundaries of thinking and full-cycle analysis from data gathering to practical policy implementation. In Section 2.2, the dimensions of the sustainable development triangle, their interactions and different concepts of sustainability are explained. Methods for integrating these three dimensions are described in Section 2.3, including the complementary concepts of optimality and durability. The poverty–equity–population–natural-resources nexus, and linkages between economic efficiency and social equity, are discussed. Section 2.4 describes a variety of practical methods and tools for applying sustainomics principles to the real world, including the Action Impact Matrix, sustainable development assessment, cost–benefit analysis, multicriteria analysis and so on. It is important to select relevant time- and location-specific indicators of sustainable development. Section 2.5 outlines approaches for restructuring long-term growth and development to make them more sustainable by harmonizing development with nature, while pursuing poverty reduction in developing countries that require continued growth of incomes and consumption.

2.1 Basic concepts and principles

World decision makers are facing traditional development issues (such as economic stagnation, persistent poverty, hunger and illness) as well as new challenges (like environmental damage and globalization). One key approach that has emerged is the concept of sustainable development or 'development which lasts'. Following the 1992 Earth Summit in Rio de Janeiro and the adoption of the United Nations Agenda 21, this idea has become well

---

[1] Some parts of the chapter are based on material adapted from Munasinghe (1992a, 1994a, 2002a, 2004a).

accepted worldwide (UN, 1992; WCED, 1987). Subsequently, international events like the 2000 Millennium Development Goals (MDGs) and the 2002 World Summit on Sustainable Development (WSSD) in Johannesburg have helped to maintain the impetus.

The Bruntland Commission's original definition of sustainable development was succinctly paraphrased as 'meeting the needs of the present generation without jeopardizing the ability of future generations to meet their needs' (WCED, 1987). As a contribution to define, analyse and implement sustainable development better, Munasinghe (1992a, 1994a) proposed the term *sustainomics* to describe 'a transdisciplinary, integrative, comprehensive, balanced, heuristic and practical framework for making development more sustainable'. Many other definitions have been proposed, but it is not the purpose of this book to review them.

Sustainomics broadly describes sustainable development as 'A process for improving the range of opportunities that will enable individual human beings and communities to achieve their aspirations and full potential over a sustained period of time, while maintaining the resilience of economic, social and environmental systems.' This definition recognizes that the *development* of economic, social and ecological systems depends on expanding the set of opportunities for their improvement. Meanwhile, the *sustainability* of systems will be enhanced by improving their resilience and adaptive capacity. Based on this approach, a more focused and practical approach toward making development more sustainable also emerged, which sought 'continuing improvements in the present quality of life at a lower intensity of resource use, thereby leaving behind for future generations an undiminished stock of productive assets (i.e. manufactured, natural and social capital) that will enhance opportunities for improving their quality of life' (Munasinghe, 1992a). This evolution of ideas takes us beyond traditional 'development' (which relates to improving broadly the well-being of individuals and communities) and growth (which refers to increases in economic output or value added in goods and services, conventionally measured by gross national product, etc.).

The heuristic element in sustainomics underlines the need for continuous adaptation and rethinking of the framework based on new research, empirical findings and current best practice, because reality is more complex than our incomplete models. The current state of knowledge is inadequate and does not provide a comprehensive definition of sustainomics. Sustainomics must provide a dynamically evolving learning framework to address rapidly changing sustainable development issues.

The basic ideas about sustainomics sketched out below have benefited greatly from the post-Bruntland discussions and the work of other researchers. They also provide a fresh start. The intent is to stimulate discussion and further research that will help to flesh out further the basic framework. Many authors (cited throughout the text) have already contributed significantly to this effort with work that is related to the sustainomics approach and the sustainable development triangle.

The core framework rests on several basic principles and methods:

(a) making development more sustainable (MDMS);
(b) the sustainable development triangle and balanced treatment;

(c) transcending conventional boundaries for better integration; and

(d) full-cycle application of practical analytical tools and methods, from data gathering to policy implementation and operational feedback.

2.1.1 Making development more sustainable

Since the precise definition of sustainable development remains an elusive goal, a less ambitious strategy might offer greater promise. Thus, the step-by-step approach of 'making development more sustainable' (MDMS) becomes the prime objective, while sustainable development is defined as a process rather than an end point (see Section 2.2). Such an incremental (or gradient-based) method is more practical and permits us to address urgent priorities without delay, while avoiding lengthy philosophical debates about the precise definition of sustainable development. However, this approach does not eliminate the need to have a practical metric to measure progress toward sustainable development.

MDMS suggests a pragmatic, systematic process. We start with the many unsustainable activities that are easiest to recognize and eliminate – for example, reducing land degradation through improved farming practices, or conserving energy by switching off unnecessary lights. Section 2.1.2 argues that an appropriate measurement framework should cover the economic, social and environmental dimensions of sustainable development. Especially critical is the choice of appropriate indicators to suit the application (see Section 2.4.2). Conventional economic evaluation attempts to measure all such indicators (economic, social and environmental) in monetary units and then use economic cost–benefit analysis criteria to test for viability (see Section 3.2). However, problems arise because cost–benefit analysis is based on the concept of optimality, which differs from sustainability (see Section 2.3), and such economic valuation is often difficult to do. In that case, our MDMS metric will need to rely on indicators that have different units of measurement (monetary, biophysical, social, etc.) and corresponding sustainability criteria. Multicriteria analysis is more suitable to assess indicators that cannot be directly compared (see Section 3.6). If an activity results in an improvement of all sustainability indicators, it clearly satisfies the MDMS requirement – also called a 'win–win' outcome. For other actions, some sustainability indicators may improve while others worsen. In such cases, judgement is required to trade-off one indicator against another, and practical ways of addressing such issues are discussed in the case studies (Chapters 5 to 16). This process needs to adapt continuously and improve itself, as scientific knowledge about sustainable development improves.

Instead of criticising the shortcomings of other disciplines, sustainomics takes a positive and practical viewpoint by borrowing appropriate methods and tools. Reliance on an eclectic set of concepts and methods does not imply lack of rigour, but rather underlines the value of diversity in cross-disciplinary thinking. However, concepts drawn from different disciplines may not be mutually consistent, and thus require more efforts to ensure transdisciplinary integration (see Sections 2.1 to 2.2).

Although MDMS is incremental, it does not imply any limitation in scope (e.g. restricted time horizon or geographic area; see Section 2.1.3). Thus, the effects of specific near-term actions on long-run sustainable development prospects need to be analysed within the sustainomics framework. While pursuing the MDMS approach to deal with current problems, we also follow a parallel track by seeking to define better the ultimate goal of sustainable development (see Section 1.3). In particular, it is important to avoid sudden catastrophic ('cliff edge') outcomes, in case our MDMS analysis is too restricted and 'myopic'. Similarly, incremental analysis may fail to detect serious consequences of large-scale changes (see Section 2.5.1). Finally, MDMS encourages us to keep future options open and seek robust strategies that could meet multiple contingencies, thereby increasing resilience and durability (see Section 2.3).

2.1.2 Sustainable development triangle and balanced treatment

Current thinking on the concept has evolved to encompass three major points of view: economic, social and environmental, as represented by the sustainable development triangle in Figure 2.1 (Munasinghe, 1992a). Each viewpoint corresponds to a domain (and system) that has its own distinct driving forces and objectives. The economy is geared mainly toward improving human welfare, primarily through increases in the consumption of goods and services. The environmental domain focuses on protection of the integrity and resilience of

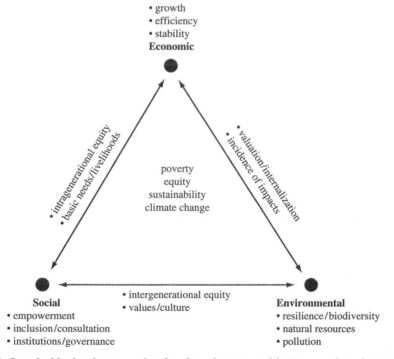

Figure 2.1. Sustainable development triangle – key elements and interconnections (corners, sides, centre).

ecological systems. The social domain emphasizes the enrichment of human relationships and the achievement of individual and group aspirations.

During the preparations for the 1992 Earth Summit in Rio de Janeiro, there was a lively debate on how the 'three pillars' (environment, economy and society) might be integrated within development policy. The sustainable development triangle was presented at Rio to emphasize that the sides and interior of the triangle (representing interaction among the three pillars) are as important as the three vertices – e.g. placing an issue like poverty or climate change in the centre reminds us that it should be analysed in all three dimensions (Munasinghe, 1992a). There was considerable resistance to the idea, mainly due to disciplinary rivalries. However, by the time of the 2002 World Summit on Sustainable Development (WSSD) in Johannesburg, the approach had become widely accepted (e.g. GOSL, 2002). Several versions of the triangle are in operational use today (e.g. Hinterberger and Luks, 2001; Odeh, 2005; World Bank, 1996a). For some specialized applications, a fourth vertex such as 'institutions' or 'technology' has been proposed, converting the triangle into a pyramid. While these additions are useful in specific cases, the original triangle retains its advantages of simplicity and versatility.

Key features of the three vertices of the sustainable development triangle (economic, social and environmental) are elaborated upon in Section 2.2. The linkages represented by the sides of the triangle are explained in Section 2.3.5 and Box 2.4 (mainly social–economic, dealing with poverty and equity), Chapter 3 (economic–environmental) and Chapter 4 (environmental–social). Methods of integrating all three dimensions are introduced in Section 2.3. The case studies in Chapters 5 to 16 explore the three dimensions and their interactions – not always comprehensively or symmetrically, because the relative emphasis varies according to the circumstances and policy-relevance. These applications chapters are structured on a spatial scale, from global to local.

The substantive transdisiplinary framework underlying sustainomics should lead to the balanced and consistent treatment of the economic, social and environmental dimensions of sustainable development (as well as other relevant disciplines and paradigms). Balance is also needed in the relative emphasis placed on traditional development versus sustainability. For example, Southern Hemisphere priorities include continuing development, consumption and growth, poverty alleviation and equity, whereas much of the mainstream literature on sustainable development which originates in the Northern Hemisphere tends to focus on pollution, the unsustainability of growth and population increase.

2.1.3 Transcending conventional boundaries for better integration

Sustainable development encompasses all human activities, including complex interactions among socioeconomic, ecological and physical systems. Accordingly, sustainomics encourages practitioners to synthesize novel solutions by transcending conventional boundaries imposed by discipline, space, time, stakeholder viewpoint and operational focus.

Discipline

The neologism 'sustainomics' underlines the fact that the emphasis is explicitly on sustainable development, and emphasizes a neutral approach free of any disciplinary bias or hegemony. Several authors suggest that sustainomics represents a new discipline, paradigm or science (e.g. Markandya *et al.*, 2002; Vanderstraetten, 2001). We stress that sustainomics is a practical, transdisciplinary framework (or 'transdiscipline') that seeks to establish an overarching, 'holistic' design for analysis and policy guidance, while the constituent components (principles, methods and tools drawn from many other disciplines) provide the rigorous 'reductionist' building blocks and foundation. It complements rather than replaces other approaches to addressing sustainable development issues.

The multiplicity and complexity of issues involved cannot be covered fully by a single discipline. Hitherto, *multidisciplinary* teams, involving specialists from different disciplines, have been applied to sustainable development issues. *Interdisciplinary* work goes a step further by seeking to break down the barriers among various disciplines. However, what is now required is a truly *transdisciplinary* framework, which would bridge and weave the scientific knowledge from diverse disciplines into new concepts and methods, while facilitating a full information exchange among all stakeholders that could address the many facets of sustainable development – from concept to policy and actual practice (Box 2.1). Thus, sustainomics would provide a more comprehensive framework and eclectic knowledge base to make development more sustainable.

The sustainomics approach seeks to integrate knowledge from both the sustainability and development domains (see Chapter 1). Thus, it draws on information from other recent initiatives such as 'sustainability transition' and 'sustainability science' (Parris and Kates, 2001; Tellus Institute, 2001). Such a synthesis needs to make use of core disciplines such as ecology, economics and sociology, as well as anthropology, botany, chemistry, demography, ethics, geography, law, philosophy, physics, psychology, zoology, etc. Technological skills such as engineering, biotechnology and information technology also play a key role.

Spatial and temporal scales

The scope of analysis needs to extend geographically from the global to the local scale, cover time spans extending to centuries (e.g. in the case of climate change) and deal with problems of uncertainty, irreversibility and non-linearity. Multiscale analysis (Box 2.2) and multistakeholder involvement are especially important with growing globalization of economic, social and environmental issues. The case studies in Chapters 5 to 16 are ordered on a spatial scale (global to local).

Stakeholder viewpoints and operational focus

Sustainomics encourages multistakeholder participation through inclusion, empowerment and consultation in analysis and decision making (see Chapter 6). Such processes not only help to build the consensus, but also promote ownership of outcomes and facilitate implementation of agreed policies. Three basic groups – government, civil society and the business community – need to collaborate to make development more sustainable at the

---

Box 2.1 Transdisciplinary methods

Sustainomics is a neutral expression – the neologism focuses attention on sustainable development without any disciplinary bias. It has much in common with other transdisciplinary methods that attempt to bridge the economy–society–environment interfaces. Distinctive features of sustainomics include the focus on making development more sustainable, discipline neutrality, applications orientation and policy-relevance. It prefers to draw on other disciplines to use the most practical and appropriate methods available (with relevant caveats and cautions), rather than to criticize them.

One closely related field is ecological economics, which combines ecological and economic methods to address a range of problems and emphasizes the importance of key concepts such as the scale of economic activities (Costanza *et al.*, 1997). Environmental and resource economics attempts to incorporate environmental concerns into traditional neoclassical economic analysis (Freeman, 1993; Tietenberg, 1992). Newer areas related to ecological science, such as conservation ecology, ecosystem management, industrial ecology and political ecology, have birthed alternative approaches to the problems of sustainability, including crucial concepts such as system resilience and integrated analysis of ecosystems and human actors (Holling and Walker, 2003). Key papers in sociology have explored ideas about the integrative glue that binds societies together, while drawing attention to the concept of social capital and the importance of social inclusion (Grootaert, 1998; Putnam, 1993).

The literature on systems, energetics and energy economics has focused on the relevance of physical laws such as the first and second laws of thermodynamics (covering mass/energy balance and entropy, respectively). This research has yielded valuable insights into how stocks and flows of energy, matter and information link physical, ecological and socioeconomic systems together, and has analysed the limits placed on ecological and socioeconomic processes by laws governing the transformation of 'more available' (low-entropy) to 'less available' (high-entropy) energy (Boulding, 1966; Georgescu-Roegen, 1971; Hall, 1995; Munasinghe, 1990a). Recent work on cultural economics, environmental psychology, economics of sociology, environmental sociology, social psychology, sociological economics and sociology of the environment are also relevant. The literature on environmental ethics has explored many issues, including the weights to be attached to values and human motivations, decision-making processes, consequences of decisions, intra- and intergenerational equity, the 'rights' of animals and the rest of nature and human responsibility for the stewardship of the environment (Andersen, 1993; Sen, 1987; Westra, 1994; see also various issues of the Elsevier journal *Environmental Ethics*).

Understanding human behaviour is a challenge to all disciplines. For example, both biology and sociology can provide important insights into this problem that challenge the 'rational actor' assumptions of neoclassical economics (see Box 2.2). Thus, recent studies seek to explain phenomena such as hyperbolic discounting (versus the more conventional exponential discounting), reciprocity and altruistic responses (as opposed to selfish, individualistic behaviour) (Gintis, 2000; Robson, 2001). Siebhuner (2000) defines '*homo sustinens*' as a moral, cooperative individual with social, emotional and nature-related skills, as opposed to the conventional '*homo economicus*', who is motivated primarily by economic self-interest and competitive instincts. Neoclassical economics has been criticized both for ignoring fundamental physical limitations (Georgescu-Roegen, 1971) and for being mechanistically (and mistakenly) modelled on classical thermodynamics (Sousa and Domingo, 2006).

Box 2.2 Multiscale spatial and temporal aspects of sustainable systems

An operationally useful concept of sustainability must refer to the persistence, viability and resilience of organic, biological and social systems, over their 'normal' lifespan (see Section 2.2.2). Sustainability is linked to both spatial and temporal scales, as shown in Figure B2.1. The x-axis indicates lifetime in years and the y-axis shows linear size (both in logarithmic scale). The central circle represents an individual human being – having a longevity and size of the order of 100 years and 1.5 metres, respectively. The

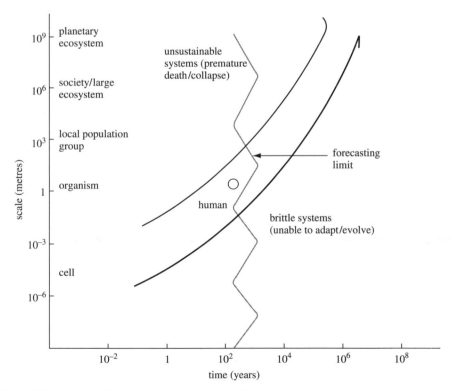

Figure B2.1. Transcending spatial and temporal scales.

diagonal band shows the expected or 'normal' range of lifespans for a nested hierarchy of living systems (both ecological and social), starting with single cells and culminating in the planetary ecosystem. The bandwidth accommodates the variability in organisms and systems, as well as longevity.

We may argue that sustainability requires living systems to be able to enjoy a normal lifespan and function normally within the range indicated in the figure. Environmental changes that reduce the lifespan below the normal range imply that external conditions have made the system unsustainable. For example, the horizontal arrow might represent an infant death – indicating an unacceptable deterioration in human health and living conditions. Thus, the regime above and to the left of the normal range denotes premature death or collapse. At the same time, no system is expected to last forever. Indeed, each sub-system of a larger system (such as single cells within a multicellular organism) generally has a shorter lifespan than the larger system itself. If sub-system lifespans increase too much, the system above it is likely to lose its plasticity and become 'brittle' – as indicated by the region below and to the right of the normal range (Holling, 1973). Gunderson and Holling (2001) use the term 'panarchy' to denote such a nested hierarchy of systems and their adaptive cycles across scales (see Section 4.1.3).

Forecasting over a timescale of several hundred years is rather imprecise. Thus, it is important to improve the accuracy of scientific analysis to make very long-term predictions about sustainability more convincing – especially in the context of persuading decision makers to spend large sums of money to reduce unsustainability. The precautionary approach is one way of dealing with uncertainty, especially if potential risks are large – i.e. avoiding unsustainable behaviour using low-cost measures, while studying the issue more carefully.

local, national and global levels. This multistakeholder, multilevel breakdown may be further tailored to suit location-specific circumstances (see Chapter 6). The principle of subsidiarity is especially important for good governance, whereby decentralized decisions are taken and implemented at the lowest practical and effective level.

The analytical process is operationally focused. The full cycle includes purposeful data gathering and observations, concepts and ideas, issues, models and analysis, results, remedies, policies and plans, implementation, monitoring, review and feedback.

2.1.4 Full-cycle application of practical analytical tools

Sustainomics includes a set of analytical tools that facilitate practical solutions to real-world problems over the full operational cycle, from data gathering to policy implementation. These elements are described below, including optimality and durability, issues–policy mapping, policy tunnelling, the Action Impact Matrix, sustainable development assessment, environmental valuation, extended cost–benefit analysis, multicriteria analysis, etc. Practical applications and case studies are provided in Chapters 5 to 16.

2.2 Key elements of the sustainable development triangle

Chapter 1 described the past evolution of economic, social and environmental thinking within the development paradigm. We elaborate on current ideas in this area and the need for an integrated approach.

2.2.1 Economic aspects

Economic progress is evaluated in terms of welfare (or utility) – measured as willingness-to-pay for goods and services consumed. Thus, economic policies typically seek to increase conventional gross national product (GNP) and induce more efficient production and consumption of (mainly marketed) goods and services. The stability of prices and employment are among other important objectives. At the macrolevel, some researchers have highlighted the role of economic forces such as world trade to explain differences in affluence and growth rates of nations (Frankel and Romer, 1999; World Bank, 1993d). Mainstream (neoclassical) economics provides the concepts underlying this framework (Box 2.2).

However, human well-being also depends on bodily and mental health status. Often, economic, physical and psychological aspects of well-being support each other. For example, good physical health enhances income-earning capacity and psychological satisfaction. Most religions emphasize non-material aspects. Typically, Buddhist philosophy (over 2500 years old) classified a comprehensive list of human desires and stressed that contentment is not synonymous with material consumption (Narada, 1988). More recently, Maslow (1970) and others have identified hierarchies of needs that provide psychic satisfaction, beyond mere goods and services. Alkire (2002) reviews the widely varying dimensions of human development (see Section 2.4.2 on indicators).

Economic sustainability

The modern concept underlying economic sustainability seeks to maximize the flow of income that could be generated while at least maintaining the stock of assets (or capital) which yield this income (Maler, 1990; Solow, 1986). Fisher (1906) defined *capital* as 'a stock of instruments existing at an instant of time' and *income* as 'a stream of services flowing from this stock of wealth'. Hicks (1946) argued that people's maximum sustainable consumption is 'the amount that they can consume without impoverishing themselves'. Economic efficiency plays a key role in ensuring optimal consumption and production (Box 2.2).

Many argue that unrestrained economic growth is unsustainable, and point out practical limitations in applying the economic sustainability rule without additional environmental and social safeguards (see weak and strong sustainability in Section 2.3.2). Problems arise in defining the kinds of capital to be maintained (e.g. manufactured, natural, human and social capital have been identified) and their substitutability (see Section 2.2.2). Often, it is difficult to value these assets and the services they provide, particularly in the case of ecological and social resources (Munasinghe, 1992a). Even key economic assets may be overlooked,

Box 2.3 Key concepts in mainstream economics

Mainstream economics today is basically neoclassical economics, although less known alternatives exist, including Austrian, classical, evolutionary, institutional, Marxist and socialist economics. Neoclassical economics is based on several fundamental assumptions.

(1) Individual consumers maximize their utility (or welfare) by making rational choices among goods and services available in the market – this is known as the consumer theory.
(2) Individual producers maximize their profits by making rational choices about what outputs to produce, what inputs to use and what technologies to adopt – this is the producer theory.
(3) Individuals act independently, using full and accurate information – known as market behaviour.

These ideas underlie the concept of 'general equilibrium' (associated with Walras), where supply and demand for goods and services balance in all markets. Another key concept involves Pareto (economic) efficiency or optimality, which is a (Walrasian) equilibrium state where no further actions are possible that could make any single person better off (i.e. welfare improvement) without making someone else worse off. Economic efficiency in the real world is measured in relation to the ideal of Pareto optimality (Bator, 1957).

Within the neoclassical economics framework, one intellectual foundation of 'capitalism' is the assumption of 'perfect competition'. Here, large numbers of consumers compete for homogeneous goods and services, which are produced by many small firms. Neither consumers nor producers have market control – i.e. they must accept the market price. Under certain restrictive conditions, perfect competition could lead to a Pareto efficient outcome, which has become a major argument in favour of 'free markets'. In this economist's ideal world, (efficient) prices reflect the true marginal social costs and ensure both efficient allocation of productive resources to maximize output and efficient consumption choices that maximize consumer utility.

Neoclassical assumptions underlie standard microeconomics – e.g. consumer theory, producer theory and cost–benefit analysis (see Chapter 3). Mainstream macroeconomic models (e.g. the simple IS-LM analysis described in Section 7.3), are also based on the neoclassical synthesis. The latter combines classical models (based on long-term Walrasian market equilibrium, characterized by full employment and price stability) with Keynesian theory (which focuses on short-run disequilibrium phenomena such as unemployment and inflation).

A serious issue arises because the existing income distribution is ignored when strict efficiency criteria are used to determine economic welfare. The result may be unethical, socially inequitable and politically unacceptable, especially if there are large income disparities. For example, the cost-benefit criterion (see Section 3.2) accepts all projects whose net benefits are positive (i.e. aggregate benefits exceed costs). It is based on the weaker 'quasi'-Pareto condition, which assumes that net benefits could be redistributed from the potential gainers (based on their willingness-to-pay) to the losers (based on their willingness-to-accept), so that no one is worse off than before. Such transfers are rarely practical. More generally, interpersonal comparisons of (monetized) welfare are difficult to make – both within and across nations, and over time. Cost–benefit analysis assumes that the marginal utility of each unit consumed is the same for a given individual and across individuals (irrespective of the levels of consumption).

Perfectly competitive conditions rarely exist in the real world. Distortions due to monopoly practices, externalities (e.g. environmental impacts that are not internalized; see Chapter 3), interventions in the market process through taxes and duties and subsidies all result in market prices for goods and services that diverge from efficient values. Thus, neither consumption nor production decisions may be efficient. Moreover, the rational actor assumption is also questionable (see Box 2.2).

Neoclassical economists have responded to such criticisms, e.g. with 'second-best' changes, when ideal (first-best) conditions do not apply. One example relevant to sustainomics is the use of shadow prices (instead of market prices) to determine optimal investment decisions (via cost–benefit analysis) and pricing policies (see Chapter 3). Chapters 7 to 9 also describe examples which seek to incorporate environmental and social concerns into macroeconomic models.

e.g. where non-market transactions dominate. Uncertainty, irreversibility and catastrophic collapse also pose difficulties (Pearce and Turner, 1990).

Many commonly used microeconomic approaches rely heavily on marginal analysis based on small perturbations (e.g. comparing incremental costs and benefits of economic activities). From the viewpoint of resilience theory (see Section 2.2.2), such a mildly perturbed system soon returns to its dominant stable equilibrium and thus there is little risk of instability. Thus, marginal analysis assumes smoothly changing variables and is not appropriate for analysing large changes, discontinuous phenomena and rapid transitions among multiple equilibria. Economic system resilience is better judged by the ability to deliver key economic services and allocate resources efficiently in the face of major shocks (e.g. the 1973 oil price shock or severe drought). More recent work is exploring the behaviour of large, non-linear, dynamic and chaotic systems in relation to system vulnerability and resilience.

2.2.2 Environmental aspects

Unlike traditional societies, modern economies have only recently acknowledged the need to manage scarce natural resources in a prudent manner – because human welfare ultimately depends on ecological services (MA, 2003). Ignoring safe ecological limits will increase the risk of undermining long-run prospects for development. Munasinghe (2002b) reviews how economic development and the environment have been linked in the literature since Malthus. Dasgupta and Maler (1997) point out that, until the 1990s, the mainstream development literature rarely mentioned the topic of environment (Chenery and Srinivasan, 1988–1989;

Dreze and Sen, 1990; Stern, 1989). More recent examples of the growing literature on the theme of environment and sustainable development include books by Faucheux, Pearce and Proops (1996), describing models of sustainable development, and Munasinghe, Sunkel and de Miguel (2001), addressing the links between growth and environment. Several researchers argue that environmental and geographic factors have been key drivers of past growth and development (Diamond, 1997; Sachs, 2001).

Environmental sustainability

The environmental interpretation of sustainability focuses on the overall viability and health of living systems – defined in terms of a comprehensive, multiscale, dynamic, hierarchical measure of resilience, vigour and organization (Costanza, 2000). These ideas apply to both natural (or wild) and managed (or agricultural) systems, and cover wilderness, rural and urban areas. Resilience is the potential of a system state to maintain its structure/function in the face of disturbance (Holling and Walker, 2003; Ludwig, Walker and Holling, 1997; Pimm, 1991). An ecosystem state is defined by its internal structure and set of mutually re-enforcing processes. Holling (1973) originally defined resilience as the amount of change that will cause an ecosystem to switch from one system state to another. Resilience is also related to the ability of a system to return to equilibrium after a disruptive shock (Pimm, 1984). Petersen, Allen and Holling (1998) argue that the resilience of a given ecosystem depends on the continuity of related ecological processes at both larger and smaller spatial scales (Box 2.2). Adaptive capacity is an aspect of resilience that reflects a learning element of system behaviour in response to disturbance. Natural systems tend to be more vulnerable to rapid external changes than social systems – the latter may be able to plan their own adaptation. Vigour is associated with the primary productivity of an ecosystem. It is analogous to output and growth as an indicator of dynamism in an economic system. Organization depends on both complexity and structure of an ecological or biological system. For example, a multicellular organism like a human being is more highly organized (having more diverse subcomponents and interconnections among them) than a single-celled amoeba. Higher states of organization imply lower levels of entropy. Thus, the second law of thermodynamics requires that the survival of more complex organisms depends on the use of low-entropy energy derived from their environment, which is returned as (less useful) high-entropy energy. The ultimate source of this energy is solar radiation.

In this context, natural resource degradation, pollution and loss of biodiversity are detrimental because they increase vulnerability, undermine system health and reduce resilience (Munasinghe and Shearer, 1995; Perrings and Opschoor, 1994). Ciriacy-Wantrup (1952) introduced the idea of safe thresholds (also related to carrying capacity), which is important – often to avoid catastrophic ecosystem collapse (Holling, 1986; Ekins, Folke and de Groot, 2003). Sustainability may be understood also in terms of the normal functioning and longevity of a nested hierarchy of ecological and socioeconomic systems, ordered according to scale (see Box 2.2).

Sustainable development goes beyond the static maintenance of the ecological status quo. A coupled ecological–socioeconomic system may evolve so as to maintain a level of biodiversity that will ensure long-term system resilience. Such an ecological perspective supercedes the narrower economic objective of protecting only the ecosystems on which human activities directly depend. Sustainable development demands compensation for opportunities foregone by future generations, because today's economic activity changes biodiversity in ways that will affect the flow of vital future ecological services.

The linkage between, and co-evolution of, socioeconomic and ecological systems also underlines the need to consider their joint sustainability; see Section 2.3.1. In brief, what ecological (and linked socioeconomic) systems need is improved system health and the dynamic ability to adapt to change across a range of spatial and temporal scales, rather than the conservation of some 'ideal' static state (see Box 2.2).

2.2.3 Social aspects

Social development usually refers to improvements in both individual well-being and the overall social welfare that result from increases in social capital – typically, the accumulation of capacity for individuals and groups of people to work together to achieve shared objectives (Coleman, 1990; Putnam, 1993). Social capital is the resource people draw upon in pursuit of their aspirations and is developed through networks and connectedness, membership of more formalized groups and relationships of trust, reciprocity and exchanges. The institutional component of social capital refers mainly to the formal laws as well as traditional or informal understandings that govern behaviour, while the organizational component is embodied in the entities (both individuals and social groups) that operate within these institutional arrangements. For our purposes, we assume that human capital (e.g. education, skills, etc.) and cultural capital (e.g. social relationships and customs) are also included within social capital – although fine distinctions do exist.

The quantity and quality of social interactions that underlie human existence, including the level of mutual trust and extent of shared social norms, help to determine the stock of social capital. Thus, social capital tends to grow with greater use and erodes through disuse, unlike economic and environmental capital, which are depreciated or depleted by use. Furthermore, some forms of social capital may be harmful (e.g. cooperation within criminal gangs may benefit them, but impose far greater costs on the larger community).

Equity and poverty alleviation are important; see Section 2.3.5. Thus, social goals include protective strategies that reduce vulnerability, improve equity and ensure that basic needs are met. Future social development will require sociopolitical institutions that can adapt to meet the challenges of modernization – which often destroy traditional coping mechanisms that disadvantaged groups have evolved in the past.

From the poverty perspective, social capital may be classified into three basic types that overlap in practice: bonds, bridges and links (discussed later in Box 16.1). Bonding social capital is centred on relations of trust and common activities among family, friends and groups within the same community. It helps to create broad-based social solidarity, meet the daily needs of the poor and reduce their risk vulnerability. Bridging social capital relies on individuals and local groups building connections with nearby communities, as well as regional and national organizations that share similar values or interests (e.g. credit organizations and livelihood networks, which provide social protection and job opportunities). Such bridging has facilitated the emergence of many non-governmental and civil society organizations. Linking social capital is built on influential associations – e.g. having access to powerful people or organizations such as government ministries and international agencies. Such links are useful to facilitate access to benefits (e.g. loans, jobs, help with small enterprise development, etc.) and to lift people out of poverty.

Trust, power and security are also important elements of cognitive social capital. Levels of trust in individuals, groups or institutions provide an indication of the extent of cooperation. Where networks are weak, people generally have lower levels of trust. Power is usually equated with influence and connections. If leaders are distant and do not deliver beneficial changes, people do not recognize them as powerful. Leaders often fail to link with the poorest groups, thereby disempowering them further. Secure relationships play a key role in good governance. Analysis of the dynamics of community relations provides a social map that allows practitioners to tailor specific programmes to targeted groups, thereby creating better opportunities for the poor to participate in decision making.

Recent research has emphasized the role of institutions in explaining differences among nations in terms of economic growth or stagnation; i.e. how behavioural norms govern social conduct, which ultimately determines economic behaviour (Acemoglu, Johnson and Robinson, 2001; North, 1990).

Social sustainability

Social sustainability parallels the ideas discussed earlier regarding environmental sustainability (UNEP, IUCN and WWF, 1991). Reducing vulnerability and maintaining the health (i.e. resilience, vigour and organization) of social and cultural systems, and their ability to withstand shocks, is important (Bohle, Downing and Watts, 1994; Chambers, 1989; Ribot, Najam and Watson, 1996). Enhancing human capital (through education) and strengthening social values, institutions and equity will improve the resilience of social systems and governance. Many such harmful changes occur slowly, and their long-term effects are overlooked in socioeconomic analysis. Preserving cultural capital and diversity across the globe is important – there are about 6000 cultural groups with different languages worldwide, while indigenous cultures (as opposed to state cultures) may represent over 90% of global cultural diversity (Gray, 1991). Munasinghe (1992a) drew parallels between the respective roles of biodiversity and cultural diversity in protecting the resilience of ecological and social systems and the interlinkages between them. Several subsequent reports from international organizations have highlighted cultural diversity (UNDP, 2004; UNESCO, 2001). Strengthening social cohesion and networks of relationships, and reducing destructive conflicts, are also integral elements of this approach. An important aspect of empowerment and broader participation is subsidiarity – i.e. decentralization of decision making to the lowest (or most local) level at which it is still effective.

Understanding the links that radiate out from poor communities, and their interface with agencies and government, is critical for building connections and channelling resources more directly to make social development more sustainable. Emphasis has sometimes been placed on the formation of new community-level organizations, which occasionally undermine existing networks and local groups – ultimately causing the locals to feel that they have no stake or ownership in the project. Thus, the focus is shifting toward improving governance by giving poor people the right to participate in decisions that affect them. Working with existing community-based social capital generates pathways to lever people upward from poverty. It also results in a more sustainable link with communities and creates opportunities for more meaningful participation.

2.3 Integration of economic, social and environmental elements

2.3.1 Need for integration

It is important to integrate and reconcile the economic, social and environmental aspects within a holistic and balanced sustainable development framework. Economic analysis has a special role in contemporary national policy making, since many important decisions fall within the economic domain. Unfortunately, mainstream economics, which is used for practical policy making, has often ignored the environmental and social dimensions of sustainable development. However, there is a small but growing body of literature which seeks to address such shortcomings – e.g. the journals *Ecological Economics* and *Conservation Ecology.*

As a prelude to integration, it is useful to compare the concepts of ecological, social and economic sustainability. One useful idea is that of the maintenance of the set of opportunities, as opposed to the preservation of the value of the asset base (Githinji and Perrings, 1992). In fact, if preferences and technology vary through successive generations, merely preserving a constant value of the asset base becomes less meaningful. By concentrating on the size of the opportunity set, the importance of biodiversity conservation becomes more evident for the sustainability of an ecosystem. The preservation of biodiversity allows the system to retain resilience by protecting it from external shocks, while the maintenance of stocks of manufactured capital protects future consumption. Differences emerge because economics indicates that a society that consumes its fixed capital without replacement is not sustainable, whereas, using an ecological approach, unsustainable loss of biodiversity and resilience implies a reduction in the self-organization of the system, but not necessarily a loss in productivity. In the case of social systems, resilience depends, to a certain extent, on the capacity of human societies to adapt and continue functioning in the face of stress and shocks. Thus, linkages between sociocultural and ecological sustainability emerge through their interactions, organizational similarities between human societies and ecological systems and the parallels between biodiversity and cultural diversity. From a longer-term perspective, the concept of co-evolution of social, economic and ecological systems within a larger, more complex, adaptive system, provides useful insights regarding the harmonious integration of the various elements of sustainable development; see Figure 2.1 and Chapter 4 (Costanza *et al.*, 1997; Munasinghe, 1994a; Norgaard, 1994).

Optimality and *durability* are two broad approaches that help to integrate the economic, environmental and social dimensions of sustainable development. While there are overlaps between the two methods, the main thrust is somewhat different in each case. Uncertainty often plays a key role in determining which approach would be preferred. For example, a system modeller expecting relatively steady and well ordered conditions may pursue an optimal solution that attempts to control, and even fine-tune, theoretical outcomes. Meanwhile, a subsistence farmer facing chaotic and unpredictable circumstances might opt for a more durable and practical response that simply enhances survival prospects.

2.3.2 Optimality

The optimality-based approach has been widely used in economic analysis to generally maximize welfare (or utility), subject to the requirement that the stock of productive assets (or welfare itself) is non-decreasing in the long term This assumption is common to most sustainable economic growth models, as reviewed by Pezzey (1992) and Islam (2001b). The essence of the approach is illustrated by the simple example of maximization of the flow of aggregate welfare (*W*), cumulatively discounted over infinite time (*t*), as represented by the following expression:

$$\text{Max} \int_0^\infty W(C,Z)\mathrm{e}^{-rt}\,\mathrm{d}t,$$

where *W* is a function of *C* (the consumption rate) and *Z* (a set of other relevant variables), and *r* is the discount rate. Further side constraints may be imposed to satisfy sustainability needs, e.g. non-decreasing stocks of productive assets (including natural resources). The welfare-maximizing optimality-based approach underlies commonly used economic techniques such as shadow pricing and cost–benefit analysis (see Section 3.2).

Some ecological models also optimize variables such as energy use, nutrient flow or biomass production – giving more weight to system vigour as a measure of sustainability. In economic models, utility is measured mainly in terms of the net benefits of economic activities, i.e. the benefits minus the costs (see Chapter 3 and Freeman (1993) and Munasinghe (1992a)). More advanced economic optimization methods seek to include environmental and social variables (e.g. by valuing environmental externalities, system resilience, etc.) However, given the difficulties of valuing such 'non-economic' assets, the costs and benefits associated with market-based activities dominate in most economic optimization models.

Within this framework, the optimal growth path maximizes economic output, while sustainability rules are met by ensuring non-decreasing stocks of assets (or capital). Some analysts support a 'strong sustainability', which requires separate preservation of each type of critical asset (e.g. manufactured, natural, sociocultural and human capital), assuming that they are complements rather than substitutes (Pearce and Turner, 1990). Others have argued for 'weak sustainability', which seeks to maintain the aggregate monetary value of total stocks of all assets, assuming that various asset types may be valued and that there is some degree of substitutability among them (Nordhaus and Tobin, 1972).

Side constraints are often necessary, because the underlying basis of economic valuation, optimization and efficient use of resources may not be easily applied to ecological objectives such as protecting biodiversity and improving resilience, or to social goals such as promoting equity, public participation and empowerment. Thus, such environmental and social variables cannot be easily combined into a single-valued objective function with other measures of economic costs and benefits (see Section 2.4.2 and Chapter 3). Moreover, the price system (which has time lags) might fail to anticipate reliably irreversible environmental and social harm and non-linear system responses that could lead to catastrophic collapse. In such cases, non-economic measures of environmental and social status would be helpful, e.g. area under forest cover and incidence of conflict (Hanna and Munasinghe, 1995a, 1995b; Munasinghe and Shearer, 1995; UNDP, 1998; World Bank, 1998). The constraints on critical environmental and social indicators are proxies representing safe thresholds, which help to maintain the viability of those systems. Multicriteria analysis facilitates trade-offs among a variety of non-commensurable variables and objectives (see Chapter 3). Risk and uncertainty will also necessitate the use of decision analysis tools. Recent work has underlined the social dimension of decision science by pointing out that risk perceptions are subjective and depend on the risk measures used as well as other factors, such as ethnocultural background, socioeconomic status and gender (Bennet, 2000).

2.3.3 Durability

The second broad integrative approach focuses primarily on sustaining the quality of life, e.g. by satisfying environmental, social and economic sustainability requirements. Such a framework favours 'durable' development paths that permit growth, but are not necessarily economically optimal. There is more willingness to trade-off some economic optimality for the sake of greater safety, in order to stay within critical environmental and social limits, e.g. among increasingly risk-averse and vulnerable societies or individuals who face chaotic and unpredictable conditions (see the precautionary principle in Chapter 5). The economic constraint might be framed in terms of maintaining consumption levels (defined broadly to include environmental services, leisure and other 'non-economic' benefits), i.e. per capita consumption that never falls below some minimum level or is non-declining. The environmental and social sustainability requirements may be measured by indicators of 'state' relating to the durability or health (resilience, vigour and organization) of ecological and socioeconomic systems. For example, consider a simple durability index (D) for an ecosystem measured in terms of its expected lifespan (in a healthy state) as a fraction of the normal lifespan (see Box 2.2). We might specify $D = D(R, V, O, S)$ to indicate the dependence of durability on resilience (R), vigour (V), organization (O) and the state of the external environment (S) – especially in relation to potentially damaging shocks. Further interaction between the sustainability of social and ecological systems may be relevant, e.g. social conflict could exacerbate damage to ecosystems and vice versa. For example, long-standing social norms in many traditional societies have helped to protect the environment (Colding and Folke, 1997).

Durability encourages a holistic systemic viewpoint, which is important in sustainomics analysis. The self-organizing and internal structure of ecological and socioeconomic systems makes 'the whole more durable (and valuable) than the sum of the parts' (see Chapter 4). A narrow measure of merit based on marginal analysis of individual components may be misleading (Schutz, 1999). For example, it is more difficult to value the integrated functional diversity in a forest ecosystem than the individual species of trees and animals. Therefore, the former is more likely to fall victim to market failure (as an externality). Furthermore, use of simple environmental shadow prices could lead to homogenization and reductions in system diversity (Perrings, Maler and Folke, 1995). Systems analysis helps to identify the benefits of cooperative structures and behaviour, which a more partial analysis may neglect. Durability is also linked to the well known concept of 'satisficing' behaviour, where individuals seek to reach a *minimum* level of satisfaction, without striving to achieve the *maximum* possible value (Simon, 1959).

The possibility of many durable paths favours simulation-based methods, including consideration of alternative world views and futures (rather than one optimal result). This approach is consonant with recent research on integrating human actors into ecological models (Ecological Economics, 2000). Key elements include multiple-agent modelling, to account for heterogeneous behaviour, recognition of bounded rationality, leading to different perceptions and biases, and emphasis on social links, which give rise to responses such as imitation, reciprocity and comparison.

In the durability approach, sustainability constraints could be met by maintaining stocks of assets (as for optimality). Here, the various forms of capital are viewed as a bulwark that decreases vulnerability to external shocks and reduces irreversible harm, rather than mere accumulations of assets that produce economic outputs. System resilience, vigour, organization and ability to adapt will depend dynamically on the capital endowment as well as on the magnitude and rate of change of a shock.

2.3.4 *Complementarity and convergence of optimality and durability*

National economic management provides good examples of how the two approaches complement one another. For example, economy-wide policies involving both fiscal and monetary measures (e.g. taxes, subsidies, interest rates and foreign exchange rates) might be optimized on the basis of quantitative macroeconomic models. Nevertheless, decision makers inevitably modify these economically 'optimal' policies before implementing them, to take into account other sociopolitical considerations based more on durability (e.g. protection of the poor, regional factors), which facilitate governance and stability. Setting an appropriate target for future global greenhouse gas (GHG) emissions (and corresponding GHG concentration) provides another useful illustration of the interplay of the durability and optimality approaches (see Chapter 5 and Munasinghe (1998a)).

The complementarity and convergence of the two approaches may be practically realized in several ways. First, waste generation should be limited to rates less than or equal to the assimilative capacity of the environment. Second, the utilization of scarce renewable resources should be limited to rates less than or equal to their natural rate of regeneration. Third, non-renewable resources need to be managed in relation to the substitutability between these resources and technological progress. Both wastes and natural-resource-input use might be reduced by moving from the linear throughput to the closed-loop mode. Thus, factory complexes could be designed in clusters – based on the industrial ecology concept – to maximize the circular flow of materials and recycling of waste among plants. Finally, additional aspects should be considered (at least in the form of safe limits or constraints), including inter- and intragenerational equity (poverty alleviation), pluralistic and consultative decision making and enhanced social values and institutions.

Greenhouse gas mitigation provides one example of how such an integrative framework could help to incorporate climate change policies within a national sustainable development strategy. The rate of total GHG emissions (G) may be decomposed by means of the following identity:

$$G = [Q/P] \times [Y/Q] \times [G/Y] \times P, \tag{2.1}$$

where $[Q/P]$ is quality of life per capita; $[Y/Q]$ is the material consumption required per unit of quality of life; $[G/Y]$ is the GHG emission per unit of consumption; and P is the population. A high quality of life $[Q/P]$ can be consistent with low total GHG emissions $[G]$, provided that each of the other three terms on the right-hand side of the identity could be minimized (see 'tunnelling' in Section 2.5.2). Reducing $[Y/Q]$ implies 'social decoupling' (or 'dematerialization'), whereby satisfaction becomes less dependent on material consumption through changes in tastes, behaviour and values – more sustainable consumption. Similarly, $[G/Y]$ may be reduced by 'technological decoupling' (or 'decarbonization'), which reduces the intensity of GHG emissions in both consumption and production. Finally, population growth needs to be reduced, especially where emissions per capita are already high. The links between social and technological decoupling need to be explored (IPCC, 1999) – changes in public perceptions and tastes could affect the directions of technological progress and influence the effectiveness of mitigation and adaptation capacity and policies. A range of economic and social policy instruments may be used to make both consumption and production patterns more sustainable. Policy tools include market incentives and pricing, legislation and controls, improved technological alternatives and consumer education (see Chapters 5 and 14).

Climate change researchers are currently exploring the application of large and complex integrated assessment models, or IAMs, which contain coupled submodels that represent a variety of ecological, geophysical and socioeconomic systems (IPCC, 1997). Both optimality and durability might be appropriately applied to the various submodels within an IAM.

2.3.5 Poverty, equity, population and sustainable natural resource use

This section examines key issues in the nexus of poverty–equity–population–natural resources from a holistic sustainomics perspective.

Dimensions of equity and poverty

Equity and poverty are two important issues, which have mainly social and economic dimensions, and also some environmental aspects (see Figure 2.1). Compelling worldwide statistics were given in Section 1.2. Meanwhile, income disparities are worsening – the per capita ratio between the richest and the poorest 20 percentile groups was 30 to 1 in 1960 and over 60 to 1 by 2000.

Equity is an ethical and people-oriented concept with primarily social and some economic and environmental dimensions. It focuses on the fairness of both the processes and outcomes of decision making. The equity of an action may be assessed in terms of several approaches, including parity, proportionality, priority, utilitarianism and Rawlsian distributive justice. Rawls (1971) stated that 'Justice is the first virtue of social institutions, as truth is of systems of thought.' Societies seek to achieve equity by balancing and combining several of these criteria.

Economic policies aiming to increase overall human welfare have been used for poverty alleviation, improved income distribution and intragenerational (or spatial) equity (Durayappah, 1998; Sen, 1981, 1984). Brown (1998) points out shortcomings in the utilitarian approach, which underlies the economic approach to equity. Broadly speaking, economic rules provide guidance on producing and consuming goods and services more efficiently, but are unable to choose the most equitable outcome among alternative patterns of efficient consumption. Equity principles provide better tools for making judgements about such choices.

Social equity is also linked to sustainability, because highly skewed or unfair distributions of income and social benefits are less likely to be acceptable or lasting in the long run. Equity will be strengthened by enhancing pluralism and grass-roots participation in decision making, as well as by empowering disadvantaged groups (defined by income, gender, ethnicity, religion, caste, etc.) (Rayner and Malone, 1998). In the long term, considerations involving intergenerational equity and safeguarding the rights of future generations are key factors. In particular, the economic discount rate plays a key role with respect to both equity and efficiency aspects (Arrow *et al.*, 1995b). Box 2.4 reviews links between social equity and economic efficiency within the sustainomics framework.

Equity in the environmental sense has received more attention recently because of the disproportionately greater environmental damages suffered by disadvantaged groups. Thus, poverty alleviation efforts (that traditionally focused on raising monetary incomes) are being broadened to address the degraded environmental and social conditions facing the poor. Martinez-Allier (2004) argues that the poor who rely more directly on natural resources are often good environmental managers, whereas the rich impose a more harmful environmental footprint through the indirect effects of their consumption. Munasinghe (1997)

Box 2.4 Interactions between social equity and economic efficiency

Conflicts between economic efficiency and equity may arise during the definition, comparison and aggregation of the welfare of different individuals or nations. For example, efficiency implies maximization of output subject to resource constraints, assuming that increases in average income per capita will make most or all individuals better off. However, if the income distribution becomes less equitable, overall welfare might drop, depending on how welfare is defined in relation to income distribution. Conversely, total welfare may increase if policies and institutions ensure appropriate resource transfers – typically from rich to poor.

Aggregating and comparing welfare across and within different countries is also a disputable issue. Gross National Product (GNP) is a measure of the total economic output of a country and does not represent welfare directly. Aggregating GNP within a nation may not be a valid measure of total welfare. However, national economic policies frequently focus more on GNP growth rather than its distribution, implying that additional wealth is equally valuable to rich and poor alike, or that there are mechanisms to redistribute wealth in an equitable way. Attempts have been made to incorporate equity considerations within an economic framework, by weighting costs and benefits so as to favour the poor. Although systematic procedures exist for determining such weights, often the arbitrariness in assigning weights has caused practical problems.

At the same time, it should be recognized that all decision-making procedures do assign weights (arbitrarily or otherwise). For example, progressive personal income taxes are designed to take proportionately more from the rich. On the other hand, traditional cost–benefit analysis based on economic efficiency assigns the same weight to all monetary costs and benefits – irrespective of income levels. More pragmatically, in most countries the tension between economic efficiency and equity is resolved by keeping the two approaches separate, e.g. by maintaining a balance between maximizing GNP and establishing institutions and processes charged with redistribution, social protection and provision of basic needs. The interplay of equity and efficiency at the international level is shown later, in the climate change case study.

---

challenges the common belief that poverty and population growth per se are harmful to nature, which conceals a crucial equity issue – the poor, although more numerous, consume far less than the rich (see below). Ethics and equity in relation to climate change are discussed in Section 5.2.2.

In summary, both equity and poverty have not only economic, but also social and environmental dimensions, and therefore they need to be assessed using a comprehensive set of indicators (rather than income distribution alone). From an economic policy perspective, emphasis needs to be placed on expanding employment and gainful opportunities for poor people through growth, improving access to markets and increasing both assets and education. Social policies would focus on empowerment and inclusion, by making institutions more responsive to the poor and removing barriers that exclude disadvantaged groups. Environmentally related measures to help poor people might seek to reduce their vulnerability to disasters and extreme weather events, crop failures, loss of employment, sickness, economic shocks, etc. Thus, an important objective of poverty alleviation is to provide poor people with assets (e.g. enhanced physical, human and financial resources) that will reduce their vulnerability. Such assets increase the capacity for both coping (i.e. making short-run changes) and adapting (i.e. making permanent adjustments) to external shocks (Moser, 1998).

The foregoing ideas merge quite naturally with the sustainable-livelihoods approach to poverty alleviation. We identify three key aspects of livelihoods that are important for the sustainability of poverty programmes (Munasinghe, 2003). First, there are gainful activities that people engage in, ranging from formal, full-time employment to seasonal, informal and ad hoc jobs, which provide only a bare subsistence income in both urban and rural settings. Second, access to productive assets and the services they provide are important. Economic assets consist of familiar manufactured capital such as machines and buildings. Key environmental assets, which draw on the base of natural capital, are often overlooked. Social capital is equally important and includes social, political and other processes and institutions that facilitate human interactions; they are linked to values, culture and behavioural norms. Third, there are rights and entitlements, which are especially important for poor and destitute groups to meet basic needs for survival (Sen, 1981). Other authors have identified five types of assets that are important for sustainable livelihoods: human, social, natural, physical and financial (Carney, 1998).

An even broader non-anthropocentric approach to equity involves the concept of fairness in the treatment of non-human forms of life or even inanimate nature. One view asserts that humans have the responsibility of prudent 'stewardship' (or 'trusteeship') over nature, which goes beyond mere rights of usage (Brown, 1998).

Population and natural resource use

The linkage between population and natural resource use is also complex and needs to be studied in the context of poverty and equity (Munasinghe, 1995a). Sustainomics encourages us to take a balanced view, where people are seen as a resource, not necessarily an unsustainable burden. One general belief is that the growth of poor population is harmful to natural resources, starting with Malthus (1798); see Section 7.1.1. For example, a widely cited article on the conservation of wild living resources (Mangel *et al.*, 1996) asserts provocatively that 'the only practicable way to reduce human per capita resource demand is to *stabilize* and then *decrease* the human population' (our emphasis) . This proposition is misleading and detracts from the overall content of an otherwise authoritative and comprehensive paper. No convincing evidence exists to link per capita natural-resource demand with population size. Even the link between *total* resource use and population is complex and cannot be captured adequately by a simple statement.

Consider the earlier equation (2.1), rewritten to show total natural-resource use as follows: $N = [N/P] \times P$, where P is the population and $[N/P]$ is per capita natural-resource use. An exclusive focus on population control is one-sided, because high levels of per capita consumption are as much to blame for resource depletion as simple population growth. Currently, a mere 15% of the world's rich population consume over 16 times as much as the almost 60% of the poor population (and will do so for the foreseeable future). A more equitable and balanced viewpoint would recognize the implications of both population and per capita consumption for sustainability. Furthermore, the growth rates of per capita consumption and population among the rich should be matters of greater concern than the same indices among the poor.

Environmental degradation, population and poverty are known to form a nexus with complex interactions (see Section 4.2.6). The poor are the most frequent victims of both pollution and resource degradation usually caused by the rich – which is inequitable. At the same time, there are macrocircumstances in which the landless poor are forced to encroach on fragile lands, eventually degrading their own environment (Munasinghe and Cruz, 1994). A comprehensive multiagency report argued recently that poverty alleviation requires environmental protection, and that both objectives should be pursued simultaneously (DFID *et al.*, 2002). Grima, Horton and Kant, (2003) discuss reconciliation of the opposing viewpoints of ecologists favouring natural-resource sustainability and economists promoting development and poverty alleviation, under four different themes – institutions, ecotourism, measurement indicators and fragile lands. Meanwhile, population growth itself depends on many factors, including not only the highly visible elements such as family planning programmes, but also deeper underlying factors such as education level (especially of women), the status of women, family income, access to basic needs and financial security (Dasgupta, 1993).

A simple mathematical exposition suggests that the common wisdom linking population growth with natural resource depletion is not necessarily as straightforward as it seems (Munasinghe, 1997). Consider a society which has a population P and a stock of natural resources N. One useful indicator of the sustainability of natural-resource stocks would be the ratio $R = N/P$. More specifically, one might seek a development path in which this ratio was non-decreasing. Thus, sustainability would require that $dR/dt \geq 0$. A more convenient sustainability rule may be defined as follows:

$$S = (dR/dt) / R = [(d/dt) (W/P)]/[W/P]0.$$

It is possible to decompose the measure S to show the distinct effects of growth in natural resource stocks and growth in population. Assuming that $N = N(P, t)$ and $P = P(t)$, we obtain

$$S = [(\partial W/\partial t)/N] - \{[(dP/dt)/P][1 - e]\}, \text{ where } e = (\partial N/\partial P)/(W/P).$$

Clearly, the first term $[\cdots]$ is positive if $(\partial W/\partial t) > 0$; that is, S rises as natural-resource stocks increase over time, holding the population constant. However, the sign of the second term $\{\cdots\}$ depends on the sign of both (dP/dt) and $(1 - e)$. Thus, reducing the population $(dP/dt < 0)$ will increase sustainability S only if $e < 1$. The opposite condition $e > 1$ is more likely to prevail if N/P is low to begin with and $\partial N/\partial P$ is relatively high, e.g. if mild population growth stimulates greater efforts toward protecting and increasing resource stocks. One example might be a community living in an arid area. If the human population dwindles, the natural progress of desertification could well proceed unimpeded. By contrast, a growing and thriving population (with increasing income levels) is likely to devote more efforts toward environmental protection, ensuring that the condition $e > 1$ is maintained.

Rapid declines in population growth rates have serious demographic implications – as many countries are discovering today. The base of the population pyramid shrinks as birth rates drop and the population ages, leaving a smaller group of productive young people to support an increasing fraction of elderly and dependent persons. Some countries have responded by encouraging immigration to increase the labour force. The policy implications of an aging population include a radical rethinking of many serious issues, including the retirement age, encouraging more productive activity among the elderly, rebalancing social insurance contributions and pension payments, etc.

The foregoing argument may be summarized as follows. While it is 'fashionable' to assume automatically that people are a threat to natural resources and sustainability, a good case may be made for considering human beings as a valuable resource for sustainable development (see Section 4.3.2). Human and natural resources are complementary. Furthermore, human attitudes toward the environment and their patterns of economic activity are at least as important as the number of people. From a sustainomics perspective, if scarce environmental resource stocks are at risk, building human and social capital through enhanced education, training, health and other social services could be the key to unlocking the potential of poor people and converting a perceived liability into an asset. The third element of the sustainable development triangle (economic resources) could also play a role through improved technology to reduce the pressure on mineral and living wild resources.

To conclude, if both per capita resource demand and population are examined more even-handedly, some promising options for the conservation of natural resources will emerge. A background factor that cannot be ignored is that economic growth is a prime imperative for developing countries, especially ones with large numbers of poor and destitute people. Section 2.5 shows how growth could be re-structured to make development more sustainable and how policies might be tailored to find a more sustainable path or 'tunnel' (see Figure 2.4).

2.4 Tools and methods for integrated analysis and assessment

Some important tools and methods that may be used for integrated analysis and assessment are summarized below. Given the vast scope of sustainable development, the 'tool kit' is eclectic and by no means exhaustive. The idea is to provide the sustainomics practitioner with a selection of key methods. Later chapters provide practical applications, indicating tools that are appropriate under various circumstances.

2.4.1 Action Impact Matrix

The Action Impact Matrix (AIM) is a multistakeholder consultative approach that facilitates the integration of the social, economic and environmental dimensions of development, identifies and prioritizes key interactions among them and determines policies and projects that make development more sustainable. The method has been widely used since the early 1990s, and was originally presented as part of the sustainomics framework at the 1992 Rio Earth Summit (Munasinghe, 1992a). Initially, it was used to integrate a range of environmental and social concerns into development planning (Munasinghe, 1994a, 1997, 2002a; Munasinghe *et al.*, 2006) and later was adapted to address specific issues such as climate change, energy and water (MIND, 2004; Munasinghe, 2002b; Munasinghe and Swart, 2005).

Basic procedure

Typically, the AIM is used as a strategic tool to understand better the interlinkages among critical elements, at the country-specific level: (a) major national development policies and goals and (b) key sustainable development vulnerabilities and issues, e.g. relating to economic sectors, ecological systems and social factors.

The AIM process begins with an *ex-ante* analysis of the two-way linkages between the fundamental elements (a) and (b), i.e. the effects of (a) on (b) and vice versa. By explicitly linking development goals with key economic–environmental–social issues, the AIM identifies potential barriers to sustainable development and helps to determine the priority strategies that will overcome them.

The approach uses a fully participative multistakeholder exercise to generate the AIM itself. Up to 50 analysts and experts are drawn from government, academia, civil society and the private sector; they represent various disciplines and sectors relevant to both sustainable development and other issues relevant to the exercise. Initially, the stakeholders interact intensively over a period of about two days to build a preliminary AIM. This participative process is as important as the product (i.e. the AIM), since important synergies and cooperative team-building activities emerge. The collaboration helps participants to under-stand better opposing viewpoints, resolve conflicts, build ownership and facilitate imple-mentation of agreed policy remedies. On subsequent occasions, the updating or fine-tuning of the initial AIM can be achieved quickly by the same group, since they are already conversant with the methodology.

For maximum effectiveness, the AIM workshop needs to be prepared carefully by trained instructors who conduct the exercise, documentation (e.g. AIM Guide), screening and pre-selection of a balanced group of participants and advance gathering of relevant background data.

The AIM methodology draws on the basic principles and methods of the sustainomics framework described earlier in this chapter, including a focus on making development more sustainable (MDMS), balanced consideration of the sustainable development triangle, emphasis on transcending boundaries and full-cycle application of integrative tools – where the AIM plays a key role. Thus, the AIM is the key link from initial data gathering to practical policy application and feedback.

The AIM process consists of the following key steps.

Screening and problem identification

(a) Determine the most important development goals and policies (DG) – matrix rows.
(b) Determine key sustainable development vulnerabilities and issues (VI) – matrix columns.
(c) Determine the current status of VI – the matrix cells.
(d) Identify how DG might affect VI (matrix DEV) – the matrix cells.
(e) Identify how VI might affect DG (matrix VED) – the matrix cells.

Analysis, prioritization and remediation

(f) Analyse and prioritize most important interactions and determine appropriate remedial policies and measures.
(g) Perform more detailed studies and analysis of key interactions and policy options identified in step (f) above.
(h) Update and refine steps (c)–(f) above.

Two matrices are derived, representing the two-way links:

(1) matrix DEV – effects of development goals and policies on vulnerabilities and issues (DG → VI);
(2) matrix VED – effects of vulnerabilities and issues on development goals and policies (VI → DG).

To summarize, AIM rows show national development goals and policies (DG) and columns indicate sustainable development vulnerabilities and issues (VI). The cells of the two preliminary matrices identify broad relationships between DG and VI, provide a quantitative and qualitative idea of the magnitudes of the key interactions, help to prioritize the most important links and facilitate formulation of appropriate policy responses. Meanwhile, the organization of the overall matrices facilitates the tracing of impacts, as well as the coherent articulation of the links among development activities (policies and projects).

The AIM process is flexible and may be adapted in various ways to address different problems. Typical examples include the following.

(1) Once the preliminary AIM is prepared, priority linkages may be pursued in two complementary ways:
  (a) upward link, where sustainable development vulnerability concerns are embedded in the macroeconomic and sectoral development strategy of a country via the medium- to long-term sustainable development path;
  (b) downward link, where sustainable development vulnerability concerns are integrated into the sub-national-level development strategy in the short- to medium-term, by carrying out sustainable development assessments aimed at making specific projects and policies more sustainable.
(2) After completing a national-level AIM exercise, it is possible to apply the process at a sub-national or community level to fine-tune the analysis.
(3) In a subsequent step, the impacts of other major external factors (such as climate change, natural disasters, rising oil prices, etc.) may be overlaid on the primary interaction between national development goals and policies (DG) and sustainable development vulnerabilities and issues (VI).

A practical application of the AIM procedure is provided in Section 6.3.

2.4.2 Other methods and indicators

Sustainable development assessment

Sustainable development assessment (SDA) is an overarching methodology (with many components), which is used in evaluating investment projects (as well as programmes and policies) to ensure balanced analysis of both development and sustainability concerns. The 'economic' component of SDA is based on conventional economic and financial analysis (including cost–benefit analysis, as described below and in Chapter 3). The other two key components are environmental assessment (EA) and social assessment (SA); see Chapter 4 (World Bank, 1998). However, many other more specialized types of assessments may be included within an integrated SDA.

Economic, environmental and social analyses need to be integrated and harmonized within SDA. Historically, EAs and SAs developed as separate processes. However, a full appreciation of all impacts requires a thorough understanding of all biophysical and social changes invoked as a result of planned interventions. Biophysical impacts have social impacts, and social changes also affect the biophysical environment. Recent work attempts to integrate biophysical and social impacts using a conceptual framework that is consistent with sustainomics, and this has led to a better understanding of the full extent of human impacts as well as the impact pathways that result from such interventions (see, e.g., Lee and Kirkpatrick, 2000). Green (2001) shows a practical application to mining.

There is increasing interest in exploring various integrated approaches for SDA to facilitate research, policy planning and decision making (Boulanger and Brechet, 2002). Among the growing list of more specialized forms of appraisal are social assessment, health assessment, risk assessment, climate assessment, development impact assessment, poverty assessment, environmental assessment and gender impact assessment.

This increase in the number of different components within the SDA framework has brought about an increasing number of difficulties. At the procedural level it has become more difficult to coordinate the timings of separate appraisals and to synchronize this with decisions made about the project. At the methodological level, there is an increasing likelihood of inconsistencies between the appraisal methods used, of interdependencies between certain types of impacts and of increasing difficulties in constructing an overall appraisal for use in decision making. At the organizational level, the workload has increased considerably, due to the burdens of managing and coordinating separate appraisals and multidisciplinary teams as part of the project planning and management process. The weaknesses in this aspect-by-aspect approach include the risk of misjudgement of impacts and overlooking of better alternative solutions based on taking cross-cutting issues into account (Brown, 1998). Projects appraised in this manner risk failure as their formulation is biased or incomplete. In an ideally integrated SDA approach, different assessments are no longer required, and the project officer would be presented with an integrated overall picture, covering all choices that can be made.

Various degrees of integration could be done. For example, procedural tuning of the various sectoral assessments may create sufficient overlap in the timing of assessments so that different assessment teams have the opportunity to communicate and exchange findings. Assefa (2005) argues that SDA may be combined with traditional technology assessment (TA) and systems analysis to provide an integrated, holistic approach.

Development cooperation has resulted, so far, in less than optimal project quality. Initially, development cooperation targeted only economic and technical goals. As awareness grew, policy themes relating to culture, equity, gender, environment and institutional capacity emerged. An integrated approach would overcome the weaknesses of an aspect-by-aspect approach, leading to a more optimal project formulation and that would simplify project decision making.

Since the sustainable development goal has independent economic, social and environmental components, it is argued that appraisal procedures and methodologies should use interconnected economic, social and environmental appraisal criteria which are consistent with achieving this goal. There is a clear need to strengthen SDA methods to use at a more strategic level of decision making relating to development policies, plans and programmes (see Section 3.4).

Traditional decision making relies heavily on economics. Thus, an initial practical step toward integration would be the systematic incorporation of environmental and social issues into the economic policy framework of human society – e.g. using the 'issues–policy transformation mapping' method.

Issues–policy transformation mapping

Issues–policy transformation mapping (ITM) is a method of integrating and applying various components of SDA (such as EAs and SAs) within the policy process. Figure 2.2 provides an example of how environmental issues are transformed and mapped into

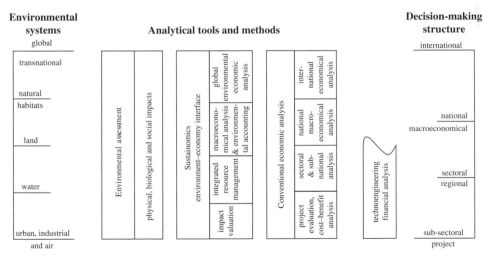

Figure 2.2. Issues–policy transformation mapping to incorporate sustainable development issues into conventional decisions.

implementable actions and policies in the decision-making domain. The right-hand side of the diagram indicates the hierarchical nature of conventional decision making and implementation in a modern society.

The global and transnational level consists of sovereign nation states. In the next level are individual countries, each having a multisector macroeconomy. Various economic sectors (such as industry and agriculture) exist in each country. Finally, each sector consists of different sub-sectors and projects. The usual decision-making process on the right-hand side of the figure relies on technoengineering and financial and economic analyses of projects and policies. In particular, conventional economic analysis has been well developed in the past and uses techniques such as project evaluation/cost–benefit analysis, sectoral/regional studies, multisectoral macroeconomic analysis and international economic analysis (finance, trade, etc.) at the various hierarchic levels.

Unfortunately, environmental and social analysis cannot be carried out readily using the above decision-making structure. We examine how environmental issues might be incorporated into this framework (with the understanding that similar arguments may be made with regard to social issues). The left side of Figure 2.2 shows one convenient environmental breakdown in which the issues are:

- global and transnational (e.g. climate change, ozone layer depletion);
- natural habitat (e.g. forests and other ecosystems);
- land (e.g. agricultural zone);
- water resource (e.g. river basin, aquifer, watershed); and
- urban–industrial (e.g. metropolitan area, airshed).

In each case, a holistic environmental analysis would seek to study an integrated bio-geophysical system in its entirety. Complications arise when such natural systems cut across the structure of human society. For example, a large and complex forest ecosystem (like the Amazon) could span several countries and also interact with many economic sectors within each country.

The causes of environmental degradation arise from human activity (ignoring natural disasters and other events of non-human origin) and, therefore, we begin on the right-hand side of Figure 2.2. The ecological effects of economic decisions must then be traced through to the left-hand side. The techniques of EA have been developed to facilitate this difficult analysis (World Bank, 1998). For example, destruction of a primary moist tropical forest may be caused by hydroelectric dams (energy sector policy), roads (transport sector policy), slash and burn farming (agriculture sector policy), mining of minerals (industrial sector policy), land clearing encouraged by land-tax incentives (fiscal policy) and so on. Disentangling and prioritizing these multiple causes (right-hand side) and their impacts (left-hand side) needs a complex analysis.

Figure 2.2 also shows how sustainomics could play its bridging role at the ecology–economy interface by transforming and mapping the EA results (measured in physical or ecological units) onto the framework of conventional economic analysis. A variety of environmental and ecological economic techniques, including valuation of environmental impacts (at the local/project level), integrated resource management (at the sector/regional level), environmental macroeconomic analysis and environmental accounting (at the economy-wide level) and global/transnational environmental economic analysis (at the international level), facilitate this process of incorporating environmental issues into traditional policy making. Since there is considerable overlap among the analytical techniques described above, this conceptual categorization should not be interpreted too rigidly. Furthermore, when economic valuation of environmental impacts is difficult, techniques such as multicriteria analysis would be useful (see below).

Once the foregoing steps are completed, projects and policies must be redesigned to reduce their environmental impacts and shift the development process toward a more sustainable path. Clearly, the formulation and implementation of such policies is itself a difficult task. In the deforestation example described earlier, protecting this ecosystem is likely to raise problems of coordinating policies in a large number of disparate and (usually) non-cooperating ministries and line institutions (i.e. energy, transport, agriculture, industry, finance, forestry, etc.).

Analogous reasoning may be readily applied to SA at the society–economy interface, in order to incorporate social considerations more effectively into the conventional economic decision-making framework. In this case, the left-hand side of Figure 2.2 would include key elements of SA, such as asset distribution, inclusion, cultural considerations, values and institutions. Impacts on human society (i.e. beliefs, values, knowledge and activities) and on the bio-geophysical environment (i.e. both living and non-living resources) are often interlinked via second- and higher-order paths, requiring integrated application of SA and EA. This insight also reflects current thinking on the co-evolution of socioeconomic and ecological systems (see Chapter 4).

In the framework of Figure 2.2, the right-hand side represents a variety of institutional mechanisms (ranging from local to global) that would help to implement policies, measures and management practices to achieve a more sustainable outcome. Implementation of sustainable development strategies and good governance would benefit from the transdisciplinary approach advocated in sustainomics. For example, economic theory emphasizes the importance of pricing policy to provide incentives that will influence rational consumer behaviour. However, cases of seemingly irrational or perverse behaviour abound, which might be better understood through findings in areas such as behavioural and social psychology and market research. Such work has identified basic principles that help to influence society and modify human actions, including reciprocity (or repaying favours), behaving consistently, following the lead of others, responding to those we like, obeying legitimate authorities and valuing scarce resources (Cialdini, 2001).

Cost–benefit analysis and multicriteria analysis

Cost–benefit analysis (CBA) is the main tool for economic and financial assessment. It is a single-valued approach based on neoclassical economics (Box 2.2), which seeks to assign monetary values to the consequences of an economic activity. The resulting costs and benefits are combined into a single decision-making criterion such as the net present value (NPV), the internal rate of return (IRR) or the benefit–cost ratio (BCR). Useful variants include cost-effectiveness and least-cost-based methods. Both benefits and costs are defined as the difference between what would occur *with and without* the project being implemented. The economic efficiency viewpoint usually requires that shadow prices (or opportunity costs) be used to measure costs and benefits. All significant impacts and externalities need to be valued as economic benefits and costs. However, since many environmental and social effects may not be easy to value in monetary terms, CBA is useful mainly as a tool to assess economic and financial outcomes. Chapter 3 provides further details.

Multicriteria analysis (MCA), or multiobjective decision making, is particularly useful in situations when a single criterion approach like CBA falls short – especially where significant environmental and social impacts cannot be assigned monetary values (see Chapter 3). In MCA, desirable objectives are specified and corresponding attributes or indicators are identified. Unlike in CBA, the actual measurement of indicators does not have to be in monetary terms; i.e. different environmental and social measures may be developed, side by side with economic costs and benefits. Thus, more explicit recognition is given to the fact that a variety of both monetary and non-monetary objectives and indicators may influence policy decisions. MCA provides techniques for comparing and ranking different outcomes, even though a variety of indicators are used.

Other specific models and methods

The subsequent chapters contain several other methods and models which are specific to particular applications and adapted to the sustainomics approach, including:

- integrated assessment models (IAMs);
- macroeconomic models (simulation, growth, computable general equilibrium (CGE), etc.);
- green accounting (e.g. integrated national economic-environmental accounting or SEEA);
- sectoral approaches (sustainable energy development (SED), sustainable transport development (STD), sustainable water resources management (SWARM), sustainable hazard reduction and management (SHARM), etc.);
- shadow pricing and costing methods (economic efficiency, social equity, environmental externalities, separable costs remaining benefits allocation (SCRB), etc.);
- integrated resource pricing (energy – LRMC-based, water, etc.).

Indicators and measures

The practical implementation of sustainomics principles and application of integration tools will require the identification of specific economic, social and environmental indicators that are relevant at different levels of aggregation, ranging from the global/macro to local/micro. It is important that these measures of sustainable development be comprehensive in scope, multidimensional in nature (where appropriate) and account for spatial differences. If we wished to apply the full-cycle analysis approach of sustainomics (see Sections 2.1.3 and 2.1.4) to trace causal linkages, one useful classification of indicators would be by pressure, driver, state, impact and response. For example, consider the following chain (see Chapter 5): underlying *pressure* – societal values and tastes; immediate *driver* – greater use of sport utility vehicles (SUVs); *state* – increased GHG concentrations; *impact* – global warming; *policy response* – tax on SUVs and consumer education to encourage more sustainable behaviour.

A wide variety of indicators are described in the literature (Adriaanse, 1993; Alfsen and Saebo, 1993; Azar, Homberg and Lindgren, 1996; Bergstrom, 1993; Eurostat, 2006; Gilbert and Feenstra, 1994; Holmberg and Karlsson, 1992; Kuik and Verbruggen, 1991; Liverman *et al.*, 1988; Moffat, 1994; Munasinghe and Shearer, 1995; OECD, 1994; Opschoor and Reijnders, 1991; UN, 1996; UNCSD, 2005; UNDP, 1998; World Bank, 1998). We discuss briefly below how measuring economic, environmental (natural), human and social capital raises various problems. In the economic dimension, the word 'capital' or 'asset' implies stock of wealth to produce economic goods and services. Social and environmental assets have a broader meaning, as discussed below.

Manufactured capital may be estimated using conventional neoclassical economic analysis. As described later in the section on cost–benefit analysis, market prices are useful when economic distortions are relatively low, and shadow prices could be applied in cases where market prices are unreliable (see, e.g., Squire and van der Tak, 1975).

Natural assets need to be quantified in terms of key biophysical attributes. Typically, damage to natural capital may be assessed by the level of air pollution (e.g. suspended particulates, sulphur dioxide or GHGs), water pollution (e.g. biological-oxygen demand (BOD) or chemical-oxygen demand (COD)) and land degradation (e.g. soil erosion or deforestation). Then the physical damage could be valued using a variety of techniques based on environmental economics (Chapter 3; Freeman, 1993; Munasinghe, 1992a; Tietenberg, 1992).

Social capital is the one that is most difficult to assess (Grootaert, 1998). Putnam (1993) described it as 'horizontal associations' among people, or social networks and associated behavioural norms and values, which affect the productivity of communities. A somewhat broader view was offered by Coleman (1990), who viewed social capital in terms of social structures, which facilitate the activities of agents in society – this permitted both horizontal and vertical associations (like firms). An even wider definition is implied by the institutional approach espoused by North (1990) and Olson (1982), which includes not only the mainly informal relationships implied by the earlier two views, but also the more formal frameworks provided by governments, political systems, legal and constitutional provisions, etc. Recent work has sought to distinguish between social and political capital (i.e. the networks of power and influence that link individuals and communities to the higher levels of decision making). Human resource stocks may be measured in terms of the value of educational levels, productivity and earning potential of individuals. Chopra (2001) argues that one key measure of social capital especially relevant to development of poor communities is the cooperation between individuals across the traditional divides separating state, market and non-market institutions.

Currently, there is no universally accepted aggregate measure of sustainable development to rival economic indicators of welfare such as GDP (whose shortcomings are discussed in Chapters 3 and 7). While many alternative indicators have been suggested by individual researchers, measures proposed by UN organizations are more widely known, including the human development index (UNDP, 2005b), wealth stocks (World Bank, 2006) and environmentally adjusted national accounts (UN, 2003); see Section 3.7.5. The UN

Commission on Sustainable Development proposes a set of social, economic, environmental and institutional indicators. Data for most nations are available through the 'Dashboard of Sustainability' – a versatile and effective tool that allows users to select various sustainable development indicators, aggregate them appropriately and apply them at different geographic scales and for specific years (CGSDI, 2006). This tool also contains the MDG indicators, currently the most important framework for development policy. IISD (2006) provides further information on indicators.

2.5 Restructuring development and growth for greater sustainability

A wide range of recent ideas on long-term growth and sustainable development was introduced in Section 1.4. The same theme is pursued further in this section, with a focus on restructuring to make development more sustainable. Growth is a major objective of almost all developing countries – especially the poorest ones. This promise cannot be fulfilled unless economic growth is sustained into the long term. The developing countries need to ensure that their endowments of natural resources are not taken for granted and squandered. If valuable resources such as air, forests, soil and water are not protected, development is unlikely to be sustainable – not just for a few years, but for many decades. Furthermore, on the social side, it is imperative to reduce poverty, create employment, improve human skills and strengthen institutions.

2.5.1 *Harmonizing development with nature*

Let us examine the alternative growth paths available and the role of sustainomics principles in choosing options. Lovelock (1979) made a pioneering contribution with his Gaia hypothesis. He proposed that the totality of life on Earth might be considered an integrated web which works together to create a favourable environment for survival. As a corollary, the unregulated expansion of human activity might threaten the natural balance. In this spirit, Figure 2.3(a) shows how the socioeconomic sub-system or 'anthroposphere' (shaded

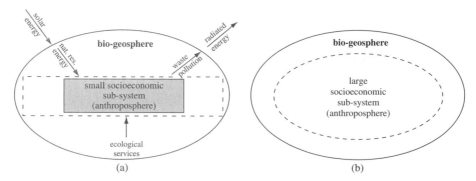

Figure 2.3. Restructuring development to make the embedded socioeconomic sub-system (anthroposphere) more sustainable within the broader bio-geosphere. (a) Unsustainable; (b) sustainable. Source: Munasinghe (1992).

rectangle) has always been embedded within a broader bio-geophysical system or 'bio-geosphere' (large oval). National economies are inextricably linked to, and dependent on, natural resources – since everyday goods and services are in fact derived from animate and inanimate resources that originate from the larger bio-geosphere. We extract oil from the ground and timber from trees, and we freely use water and air. At the same time, such activities have continued to expel polluting waste into the environment, quite liberally. The broken line in Figure 2.3(a) symbolically shows that, in many cases, the scale of human activity in the anthroposphere has increased to the point where it is now impinging on the underlying bio-geophysical system (see Chapter 3). This is evident today if we consider that forests are disappearing, water resources are being polluted, soils are being degraded and even the global atmosphere is under threat. Consequently, the critical question involves how human society might contain or manage this problem of scale?

One traditional view that has caused confusion among leaders around the world is the assumption that concern for the environment is not necessarily good for economic activity. Thus, until recently, the conventional wisdom held that it was not possible to have economic growth and a good environment at the same time, because they were mutually incompatible goals. However, the more modern viewpoint (embodied also in sustainomics) indicates that growth and environment are indeed complementary. One key underlying assumption is that it is often possible to devise so-called 'win–win' policies, which lead to economic as well as environmental gains (Munasinghe *et al.*, 2001). As illustrated in Figure 2.3(a), the traditional approach to development would certainly lead to a situation where the economic system would impinge upon the boundaries of the ecosystem in a harmful manner. On the other hand, Figure 2.3(b) summarizes the modern approach that would allow us to have the same level of prosperity without severely damaging the environment. In this case, the oval outer curve is matched by an oval inner curve – where economic activities have been restructured in a way that is more harmonious with the ecosystem.

2.5.2 Changing the structure of growth

Another way of depicting the importance of changing the structure of development and growth is illustrated in Figure 2.4, which shows how environmental risk in a country (e.g. represented by GHG emissions per capita) might vary with its level of development (e.g. measured by GNP per capita).

One would expect carbon emissions to rise more rapidly during the early stages of development (along *AB*) and begin to level off only when per capita incomes are higher (along *BC*). A typical developing country may be at a point such as *B* on the curve and an industrialized nation may be at *C*. Ideally, industrial countries (exceeding safe limits) should increase environmental protection efforts and follow the future growth path *CE*. Munasinghe (1995a, 1999a) proposed the idea of developing countries adopting policies to 'tunnel' through (along *BDE*) by learning from past experiences of the industrialized world – the tunnel would lie below the safe limit at which environmental damage (such as climate change or biodiversity loss) could become irreversible.

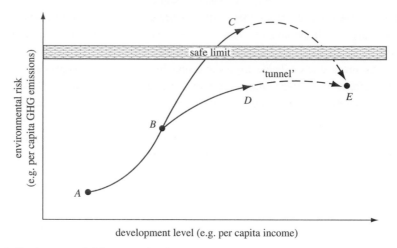

Figure 2.4. Environmental risk versus development level.

Such a tunnel also corresponds to a more economically optimal path and resembles 'turnpike' growth paths, which appeared in past literature (Burmeister and Dobell, 1971). The highly peaked path *ABCE* could result from economic imperfections that make private decisions deviate from socially optimal ones. Corrective policies would help to reduce such divergences and permit movement through the tunnel *BDE*. Developing countries could thereby avoid severe environmental degradation along conventional development paths of industrial economies (*ABCE*). This approach is not concerned with the related issue of the existence of the so-called environmental Kuznets curve for any single country or group of nations. Instead, 'tunnelling' focuses on identifying policies to delink environmental degradation and economic growth (Munasinghe, 1995a, 1999a; Opschoor 1998b).

Chapter 7 describes several ways to find such a policy 'tunnel'.

(1) Actively seek 'win–win' policies that simultaneously yield both economically and environmentally (and socially) sustainable paths.
(2) Use complementary policies. Growth-inducing economy-wide policies could combine with imperfections in the economy to cause environmental and social harm. Rather than halting economic growth, complementary measures may be used to remove such imperfections and thereby prevent excessive environmental and social harm. Such measures include *ex-ante* environmental (and social) assessment of projects and policies, introducing remedies that eliminate imperfections (such as policy distortions, market failures and institutional constraints) and strengthening capacity for environmental and social protection.
(3) Consider the fine-tuning of growth-inducing economy-wide policies (e.g. altering their timing and sequencing), especially where severe environmental and social damage could occur.

It would be fruitful to encourage a more proactive approach whereby the developing countries could learn from the past experiences of the industrialized world – by adopting sustainable development strategies and climate change measures that would enable them to follow development paths such as *BDE* in Figure 2.4 (Munasinghe, 1998b). Thus, the emphasis is on identifying policies that will help delink carbon emissions and growth, with the curves in Figure 2.4 serving mainly as a useful metaphor or organizing framework for policy analysis.

This representation also illustrates the complementarity of the optimal and durable approaches discussed earlier. It has been shown that the higher path *ABC* in Figure 2.4, could be caused by economic imperfections that make private decisions deviate from socially optimal ones (Munasinghe, 1999a). Thus, the adoption of corrective policies that reduce such divergences from optimality, and thereby reduce GHG emissions per unit of output, would facilitate movement along the lower path, *ABD*. Concurrently, the durability viewpoint also suggests that flattening the peak of environmental damage (at *C*) would be especially desirable to avoid exceeding the safe limit or threshold representing dangerous accumulations of GHGs (shaded area).

Several authors have econometrically estimated the relationship between GHG emissions and per capita income using cross-country data and found curves with varying shapes and turning points (Cole, Rayner and Bates, 1997; Holtz-Eakin and Selden, 1995; Sengupta, 1996; Unruh and Moomaw, 1998). One reported outcome is an inverted U-shape (called the environmental Kuznet's curve, or EKC) – like the curve *ABCE* in Figure 2.4. In this case, the path *BDE* (both more socially optimal and durable) could be viewed as a sustainable development 'tunnel' through the EKC (Munasinghe, 1995a, 1999a).

In the above context, it would be fruitful to seek specific interventions that might help to make the crucial change in mindset, where the emphasis would be on the structure of development, rather than the magnitude of growth (conventionally measured). Sustainomics promotes environmentally and socially friendly technologies, which use natural-resource inputs more frugally and efficiently, reduce polluting emissions and facilitate public partic-ipation in decision making. Box 2.5 shows how science and technology (S&T) policy may be better integrated into a national sustainable development strategy.

One example is information technology (IT), which could make development more sustainable by increasing economic productivity (Munasinghe, 1987, 1989, 1994a). From an environmental perspective, it would make modern economies more services oriented – by shifting activities away from highly polluting and material intensive types of manufacturing and extractive industries. If properly managed, IT might also promote social sustainability, by improving access to information, increasing public participation in decision making and empowering the poor. The correct blend of market forces and regulatory safeguards are required.

2.5.3 Long-term growth and sustainable development

We conclude the chapter with some recent ideas about growth and development. The three dimensions of the sustainable development triangle (see Section 2.2), are reflected in contemporary thinking on the fundamental determinants of the developmental status of countries. Some researchers have emphasized the economic engine of trade as the main driver of growth and development (Frankel and Romer, 1999; World Bank, 1993c). Others

Box 2.5 Science and technology for making development more sustainable

Making development more sustainable (MDMS) will require science and technology
(S&T) and research methods that are in harmony with the new sustainable development
paradigm, human values and social institutions (see Section 1.2). Sustainomics encourages a more holistic, transdisciplinary analysis and solutions. This view is confirmed by
findings in basic areas such as quantum physics and complexity theory, as well as
applied disciplines such as economics, sociology and ecology, which show that every-
thing is interdependent. Many of our current problems have arisen because we have
ignored increasingly important interconnections – given the rapidly growing scale of
human activity and consequent impacts on both natural and socioeconomic systems.
A new synthesis is needed that combines the dominant Cartesian analytical, reductionist methods of modern science (which have made great advances in knowledge
possible) with the more holistic philosophies of the past (which stress interdependence
at all levels). Sustainomics seeks to use S&T to address current major world issues and
make development more sustainable (see Section 1.2), rather than to reverse progress
and go back to some pre-technological state. Ultimately, we wish to make a fundamental long-term transition to a global sustainable society (see Figure 1.1).

Worldwide investments in R&D (both public and private) are large and growing. For
example, the largest R&D spenders, USA and China, allocated US $330 and 136 billion
for this purpose in 2006 (FT, 2006a, 2006b). Meanwhile, Ford and Samsung spent about
US $8 and 5.5 billion, respectively, on R&D during 2005 and 2006. Figure B2.2 shows

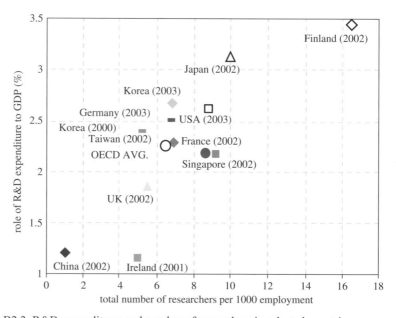

Figure B2.2. R&D expenditures and number of researchers in selected countries.

R&D expenditures and the number of researchers in scientifically advanced countries. In some cases, the north–south S&T divide is narrowing, with the growing capabilities and accomplishments of scientists and more effective policies in scientifically advanced developing nations (Hassan, 2005). Typically, China and India invest 1 to 1.5% of GDP on S&T and are emerging as world leaders in key areas. However, there is a disturbing south–south gap emerging between the scientifically proficient countries (e.g. Brazil, China, India) and lagging ones (e.g. Sub-Saharan Africa). It is widely agreed that building S&T capacity is critical to harnessing knowledge for development. S&T innovation may be promoted by strengthening S&T capacity that focuses on (1) solving priority problems; (2) supporting key sectors; and (3) improving decision making (Watkins *et al.*, 2007). Sustainomics provides the framework for such actions.

Sustainomics promotes an S&T policy that is better integrated into national sustainable development strategy and objectives. Such a mainstreaming approach enables scientists to make clear to decision makers and senior officials what the key linkages and priorities might be, and how to identify practical options and implement solutions. Ultimately, national policies should not only guide public investments in research and development (especially education and capacity building), but also provide incentives to encourage corresponding activity in the private sector and make effective use of market forces. It would require developing strategic policy tools (such as Action Impact Matrix, AIM) and applying them through multidisciplinary, multistakeholder teamwork and consultations.

The AIM methodology (see Section 2.4) has been used to identify and prioritize impacts of investments in key S&T areas (such as agroenergy, bioenergy, information, medical, micro- and nano, technologies and indigeneous sciences and knowledge) on major national sustainable development goals and policies (such as growth, poverty alleviation, food security, employment, health, etc.). A more sophisticated two-stage AIM process is also possible, where the first matrix identifies impacts of S&T on key economic sectors and the second determines effects of sectoral developments on national sustainable development goals and policies (MIND, 2004). The convolution of the two AIMs yields the desired links between S&T areas and sustainable development goals and policies.

While sensible public policy interventions could be very beneficial, prudence suggests that such policy should be flexible, encourage innovation and avoid locking-in specific technologies for long periods – because future scientific discoveries and their outcomes are unpredictable. Every innovation that solves one set of problems is likely to create new ones. One example is nuclear technology, which has both peaceful and military uses. Another key example is the race between S&T progress (which improves resource productivity and reduces costs) and problems caused by the greater consumption it stimulates. Almost 150 years ago, Jevons (1865) set out his famous paradox concerning energy use: 'It is wholly a confusion of ideas to suppose that the economical use of fuel is equivalent to diminished consumption. The very contrary is the truth… every improvement of the engine…accelerates anew the consumption of coal.' In this same vein, at the turn of the nineteenth century, transport experts warned that the streets of London would soon be knee-deep in horse droppings because of the growth of traffic. This issue was resolved with the advent of the 'horseless carriage' (motor car) in the early twentieth century. However, rising oil use, traffic jams and urban air pollution from cars again caused pessimism in the post-World War 2 period. In recent decades, mobility management and more energy efficient and less polluting vehicles have eased the problem, and new technologies (such as hydrogen-fuelled cars) offer further hope. This type of cycle will undoubtedly continue, unless we focus more on MDMS.

feel that natural environment, climate and location represented broadly by geography and resource endowments are the dominant influences that explain the difference between development and stagnation (Diamond, 1997; Sachs, 2001). Finally, a third argument has been advanced that social forces are important in explaining wide income variations between rich and poor countries. They emphasize the role of institutions – i.e. how explicit and implicit behavioural norms govern social conduct and ultimately determine economic behavior (Acemoglu *et al.*, 2001; North, 1990). A more integrated viewpoint is provided by the concept of long-term co-evolution of socioeconomic and ecological systems within a more complex adaptive system (see Section 2.3.1). Munasinghe *et al.* (2001) provide a wide range of current ideas on the complex links between long-term growth and sustainable development by leading researchers in the world.

Growth and sustainability

Opschoor (2001) explores the negative relationships between economic growth and environmental sustainability, while proposing institutional and moral reforms to promote sustainable development. Norgaard (2001) illustrates some basic problems with rapid growth, discusses some myths concerning economic growth and finally outlines an agenda based on ecological economics to go beyond growth and globalization. Hinterberger and Luks (2001) deal with competitiveness (economic development), employment (social development) and dematerialization (environmental sustainability) in a rapidly globalizing world. A fourth 'corner' is added to the sustainable development triangle (institutions – which was embedded within the social dimension in Figure 2.1), forming a pyramid. Ocampo (2001) advocates consolidation of strong institutions for sustainable development in Latin America and the Caribbean, and argues that price reforms are less effective than technical change.

General analytical frameworks

Daly (2001) shows how traditional marginal analysis in microeconomics, which fails to internalize environmental and social externalities, will lead to overestimation of macroeconomic GNP. Globalization is pushed by powerful transnational corporations to weaken the nation state, leading to uneconomic growth, increased population, greater inequality, increased unemployment and environmental harm. Sachs (2001) seeks to integrate development (economic), human rights (social) and environment. He disputes the usefulness of valuing ecosystems, since it may promote unbalanced agreements on intellectual property rights and the unsustainable privatization of all natural capital and ecosystem services. Because ecological economics addresses social issues inadequately, a new discipline is proposed, along the lines of sustainomics. Naredo (2001) argues that even recent valuation methods, such as the pollution analysis, life-cycle analysis and the new System of National Accounts (SNA), are inadequate for sustainable development because they mainly incorporate the monetary values but not the underlying physical information. He proposes a complementary approach that would allow more accurate calculations of the physical cost of recovering mineral resources from the Earth's crust.

Modelling applications

Kadekodi and Agarwal (2001) show that the shape of the EKC depends upon the capital intensity of the energy-based natural-resource-using sectors, during the process of economic development (see Section 2.5.2). Factor price changes that favour labour-intensive goods will affect the shape of the curve. Tsigas *et al.* (2001) use a modified global, applied general equilibrium model to suggest that trade liberalization in the Western Hemisphere coupled with harmonization of environmental policy will benefit all countries, although environmental quality may decline in Mexico and Brazil. Batabyal, Beladi and Lee (2001) explain how developing countries have attempted to improve their balance of payment positions and develop manufacturing industries, by actively following a policy of encouraging import-substituting industrialization. Brazil, Mexico, Pakistan and the Philippines have used the infant industry argument to apply trade policies that systematically protect the manufacturing sectors. Baer and Templet (2001) use the Greenhouse Limitation Equity Assessment Model (GLEAM) to analyse global climate mitigation policies (see Chapter 5). They conclude that per capita allocations of GHG emissions permits produce the greatest average welfare levels – with feasible emission scenarios that stabilize CO_2 at less than twice pre-industrial levels. Hansen (2001) compares the merits of five different methods for estimating the capital consumption of non-renewable resource rents and shows how the discount rate, depletion period and depletion path influence the outcome. Neumayer (2001) criticises the World Bank 'genuine savings' method, which appears to show that many Sub-Saharan, North African, Middle Eastern and other countries have failed to pass the test of weak sustainability (see Section 2.3.2). These results are reversed if the alternative El Serafy method is used, with a relatively low discount rate of 4%. The genuine savings concept is unreliable because it depends on a dynamic optimization framework, whereas most economies develop along non-optimal paths.

3

Economics of the environment[1]

This chapter explores how economics relates to environmental (and related social) concerns. Section 3.1 outlines how environmental degradation is impeding economic development, while human activity is harming the environment. Sections 3.2 and 3.3 expand on economic cost–benefit analysis – a key element of SDA and the project cycle. Important details are explained, including economic decision criteria, efficiency and social shadow pricing, economic imperfections (market failures, policy distortions and institutional constraints), methods of measuring costs and benefits and qualitative considerations. Types of environmental assets and services, and practical techniques of valuing them, are described in Section 3.4. Section 3.5 outlines multicriteria analysis, which is useful for decision making when economic valuation is difficult. Key issues relating to discounting, risk and uncertainty are set out in Section 3.6. Finally, Section 3.7 explains links between economy-wide policies and environmental (and social) issues, as well as environmentally adjusted national accounts.

3.1 Human activities and the environment

Mankind's relationship with the environment has gone through several stages, starting with primitive times, in which human beings lived in a state of symbiosis with nature. Human interactions were primarily within the biotic sphere. This phase was followed by a period of increasing mastery over nature up to the industrial age, in which technology was used to manipulate physical laws governing the abiotic sphere. The outcome was the rapid material-intensive and often unsustainable growth patterns of the twentieth century, which damaged the natural-resource base. The initial reaction to such environmental harm was a reactive approach characterized by increased clean-up activities. Recently, a more proactive attitude has emerged, including the design of projects and policies that will help to make development more sustainable (see Chapter 2).

Both environmental and resource economics and ecological economics are useful to address these issues (see Boxes 2.1 and 2.3). They have been defined comprehensively by other authors (e.g. Costanza *et al.*, 1997; Freeman, 1993; Gowdy and Ericson, 2005; Opschoor, Button and Nijkamp, 1999; Tietenberg, 1992; Van den Bergh, 1999). These

---

[1] Some parts of the chapter are based on material adapted from Munasinghe (1992a, 1993a, 1999b, 2002b, 2004b).

two disciplines overlap (Turner, 1999). Instead of highlighting the differences, we focus on the common elements that support the sustainomics framework. A recent training textbook issued by the World Bank and European Commission provides an excellent review of the subject – starting with sustainomics and the sustainable development triangle (Markandya *et al.*, 2002)

The environmental assets that are under threat due to human activities provide three main types of services to society – provisioning, regulation and aesthetic–cultural (details given in Chapter 4). Environmental and ecological economics help us incorporate ecological concerns into the conventional human decision-making framework (see Figure 2.2). More generally, the process for improving policies and projects to make development more sustainable involves: (1) identifying biophysical and social impacts of human activities; (2) estimating the economic value of such impacts; and (3) modifying projects and policies to limit harm.

3.2 Conventional project evaluation

A development project involves several steps. The systematic approach used in a typical project cycle includes identification, preparation, appraisal, negotiations and financing, implementation and supervision and post-project audit (see Box 3.1). The economic basis of project evaluation, including cost–benefit analysis and shadow pricing are described in what follows. Practical applications are given in Chapters 11 and 15.

3.2.1 Cost–benefit analysis and economic assessment

Cost–benefit analysis (CBA) is the economic assessment component of overall sustainable development assessment (SDA) in the project appraisal stage (see Section 2.4.2). CBA assesses project costs and benefits monetarily. Benefits are defined by gains in human well-being. Costs are defined in terms of their opportunity costs, which is the benefit foregone by not using resources in the best available alternative application.

SDA also requires us to consider a number of non-economic aspects (including financial, environmental, social, institutional and technical criteria) in project appraisal. In particular, the *economic* analysis of projects differs from *financial* analysis. The latter focuses on the money profits derived from the project, using market or financial prices, whereas economic analysis uses shadow prices rather than financial prices. Shadow prices (including valuation of externalities) reflect economic opportunity costs and measure the effect of the project on the *efficiency objectives* in relation to the whole economy. Criteria commonly used in CBA may be expressed in economic terms (using shadow prices) or financial terms (using market prices) – our emphasis will be on economic rather than financial evaluation.

The most basic criterion for accepting a project compares costs and benefits to ensure that the net present value (NPV) of benefits is positive:

$$\mathrm{NPV} = \sum_{t=0}^{T} (B_t - C_t)/(1+r)^t,$$

Box 3.1 The project cycle

A typical project cycle involves: identification, preparation, appraisal, financing, implementation, supervision and evaluation (World Bank, 2006).

Identification – involves the preliminary selection of potential projects that appear to be viable in financial, economic, social and environmental terms, and that conform to national and sectoral development goals.

Preparation – lasts up to several years, and includes systematic study of economic, financial, social, environmental, engineering–technical and institutional aspects of the project (including alternative methods for achieving the same objectives).

Appraisal – consists of a detailed review that comprehensively evaluates the project, in the context of the national and sectoral strategies, as well as the engineering–technical, institutional, economic, financial, social and environmental issues. Environmental and social assessments are also key elements that may affect the project design and alter the investment decision. The economic evaluation itself involves several well defined stages, including the demand forecast, least-cost alternative, benefit measurement and cost–benefit analysis.

Financing – if outside financial assistance is involved, the country and financier negotiate measures required to ensure the success of the project and the conditions for funding (usually included in loan agreements).

Implementation and supervision – implementation involves putting into effect in the field all finalized project plans; supervision of the implementation process is carried out through periodic field inspections and progress reports. Ongoing reviews help to update and improve implementation procedures.

Evaluation – the final stage, involving an independent project performance audit to measure the project outcome against the original objectives. This analysis can yield valuable information to improve processing of future projects.

---

where B_t and C_t are the benefits and costs, respectively in year t, r is the discount rate and T is the time horizon.

Both benefits and costs are defined as the difference between what would occur *with* and *without* project implementation. In economic analysis B, C and r are defined in economic terms and shadow priced using efficiency prices (Munasinghe, 1990a). Alternatively, in financial analysis, B, C and r are defined in financial terms.

If projects are to be compared or ranked, the one with the highest (and positive) NPV would be preferred. Suppose NPV_i = net present value for project i. Then if $\text{NPV}_\text{I} > \text{NPV}_\text{II}$, project I is preferred to project II, provided also that the scale of the alternatives is roughly the same. More accurately, the scale and scope of each of the projects under review must be altered so that, at the margin, the last increment of investment yields net benefits that are equal (and greater than zero) for all the projects. Complexities may arise in the analysis of interdependent projects.

The internal rate of return (IRR) is another project criterion given by

$$\sum_{t=0}^{T} (B_t - C_t)/(1 + \text{IRR})^t = 0.$$

Thus, the IRR is the discount rate which reduces the NPV to zero. The project is acceptable if IRR > r, which in most cases implies NPV > 0 (ignoring projects where multiple roots could occur, because the annual net benefit stream changes sign several times). Problems of interpretation occur if alternative projects have widely differing lifetimes, so that the discount rate plays a critical role. If economic (shadow) prices are used, then the terminology internal economic rate of return (IERR) may be used, while the application of financial (market) prices yields the internal financial rate of return (IFRR).

Another frequently used criterion is the benefit–cost ratio (BCR):

$$\text{BCR} = \left(\sum_{t=0}^{T} B_t/(1+r)^t \right) \bigg/ \left(\sum_{t=0}^{T} C_t/(1+r)_t \right).$$

If BCR > 1, then NPV > 0 and the project is acceptable.

Each of these criteria has its strengths and weaknesses, but the NPV is probably the most useful. It may be used to derive the least-cost rule, when the benefits of two alternative projects are equal (i.e. both serve the same need or demand). Then the comparison of alternatives is simplified, since the benefit streams cancel out. Thus,

$$\text{NPV}_\text{I} - \text{NPV}_\text{II} = \sum_{t=0}^{T} \left[C_{\text{II},t} - C_{\text{I},t} \right]/(1+r)^t.$$

Therefore, $\text{NPV}_\text{I} > \text{NPV}_\text{II}$ if

$$\sum_{t=0}^{T} C_{\text{II},t}/(1+r)^t > \sum_{t=0}^{T} C_{\text{I},t}/(1+r)^t.$$

In other words, the project with the lower present value of costs is preferred. This is called the least-cost alternative (when benefits are equal). However, even after selecting the least-cost alternative, it is still necessary to ensure that this project has a positive NPV.

3.2.2 Shadow pricing

Shadow pricing of economic inputs and outputs is used in project analysis when some idealized assumptions of neoclassical economics are violated in the real world (see Box 2.3). Conceptually, one may capture all the key economic relationships in a comprehensive 'general equilibrium' model of the economy. In such a model, the overall national development goal might be embodied in an objective function, such as aggregate consumption. Usually, analysts seek to maximize this consumption subject to constraints, including limits on scarce resources (such as capital, labour and environmental assets), structural distortions in the economy and so on – see the optimality-based approach in Chapter 2. Then, the shadow price of a scarce economic resource is the change in value of the objective function, caused by a marginal change in the availability of that resource. In a mathematical programming macroeconomic model, the optimal values of the dual variables (corresponding to the binding resource availability constraints in the primal problem) have dimensions of price, and could be interpreted as shadow prices (Luenberger, 1973). While the general equilibrium approach is conceptually important, it is too cumbersome and data-intensive to use. In practice, partial equilibrium methods are used to evaluate shadow prices of key economic resources in a few sectors or areas (Squire and van der Tak, 1975).

Efficiency and social shadow prices

Two basic types of shadow prices exist, depending on how sensitive society is to income distribution considerations. Consider the national goal of maximizing the present value of aggregate consumption over a long period. If the consumption of different individuals is added directly, regardless of their income levels, then the resulting shadow prices are efficiency prices because they reflect the pure efficiency of resource allocation. Alternatively, if the consumption of low-income groups needs to be raised, shadow prices may be adjusted by income group to give greater weight to the poor in aggregate consumption. Such prices are called social prices. In practice, such formal weighting schemes are seldom used in project evaluation. Instead, distributional and other social issues are addressed by direct targeting of beneficiaries and similar ad hoc methods.

In brief, efficiency shadow prices try to establish the economic values of inputs and outputs, while social shadow prices take account of the fact that the income distribution between different societal groups or regions may be distorted in terms of overall national objectives. Our analysis will place primary emphasis on efficiency shadow pricing.

Common property resources and externalities

Non-priced inputs and outputs, such as common property resources and externalities (especially those arising from environmental impacts), must be shadow-priced to reflect their economic opportunity costs. Access to common property resources is unrestricted, and thus exploitation tends to occur on a first come, first served basis, often resulting in (unsustainable) overuse. Public goods are environmental resources (e.g. scenic view) that are freely accessible and indivisible (i.e. enjoyment by one individual does not preclude enjoyment by others). These properties lead to 'free-riding' – a situation in which one user (either knowingly or unknowingly) uses the resource at a price less than the efficient cost and thereby takes advantage of greater contributions by others (Samuelson, 1954). For example, wastewater discharge taxes may be paid by users of a transnational water source in one nation, while the benefits of cleaner water are shared with users in another country who draw from the same source, but do not pay such taxes. The JDB international symposium involving leading economists (Arrow *et al.*, 1996) highlighted and analysed such problems affecting both local and global communities.

Externalities are defined as beneficial or adverse effects imposed on others for which the originator of these effects cannot charge or be charged (Coase, 1960). If a (damaging) externality can be economically valued or shadow-priced, then a charge or tax may be levied on the perpetrator, to compensate for and limit the damage. This is the so-called 'Pigouvian' or 'price-control' approach to environmental regulation. The basic concepts and techniques for economic valuation of environmental impacts underlying this approach are discussed later in this chapter.

Unfortunately, many externalities are difficult to measure, not only in physical terms, but also in monetary equivalents (i.e. willingness-to-pay). Quite often therefore, the 'quantity-control' approach is taken by imposing regulations and standards expressed in physical measurements only that try to eliminate the perceived external damages (e.g. safe minimum standards for pollution). Especially when environmental pollution is severe and obvious, setting standards could serve as a useful first step to raise consciousness and limit excessive environmental damage, until more accurate valuation studies can be carried out. In such cases, the initial emphasis is on cost-effectiveness (i.e. achieving pollution targets at the lowest cost), rather than valuing the benefits of control measures. For example, quantity controls on air pollution that limit the aggregate emission level may be combined with an initial allocation of emission rights among existing and potential polluters (which collectively do not exceed the total emission limit). This is analogous to defining property rights to an open access resource – in this case, the airshed over a particular region. Next, it would be logical to encourage schemes such as marketable pollution permits (which may be competitively traded among polluters) to achieve an economically efficient redistribution of 'pollution rights' within the overall emission limit. However, minimum quantity controls may not be an efficient long-term solution if no attempt is made to compare the marginal costs of compliance with the real benefits provided (i.e. marginal damages avoided) – especially as environmental conditions improve over time.

In practice, a mix of price and quantity controls is used to protect the environment (Pearce and Turner, 1990). A mixed system allows the various policy instruments to be adjusted flexibly depending on marginal clean-up costs. Thus, an optimal outcome can be approached even without full information concerning control costs (Baumol and Oates, 1988).

Practical considerations

Shadow prices are location- and time-specific, and their computation may be tedious. Key elements, such as the numeraire, border-priced conversion factors, shadow wage rates, accounting rate of interest (or discount rate), social shadow prices and distribution weights, are described in the appendix, Section 3.8. Applications to resource pricing policy are given in Chapter 14.

3.3 Measuring costs and benefits

In CBA, economic costs and benefits of a project are measured by differences in outcome between two alternative scenarios – *with* and *without* the project. This process is explained below for a typical resource – water (see also Chapter 12). The same analysis may be easily generalized to other areas such as energy, agricultures, etc.

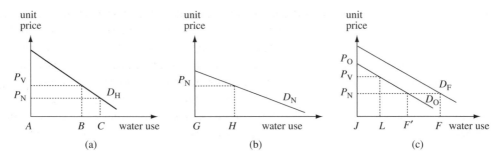

Figure 3.1. Effects of a water investment project on water use. (a) Same supply quality: D_H = demand for household water; P_V = cost of water from old source; P_N = cost of water from new supply. (b) New use of water: D_N = demand for new uses of water. (c) Higher supply quality: D_O = demand for water from old source; D_F = demand for water from new supply.

3.3.1 Patterns of resource use

Figure 3.1 shows the likely effects on water use when piped water is supplied to an area that had no such service previously available. In practice, the effects of introducing piped water will be felt over a number of years, as users gradually make the necessary investments in water-using appliances to take full advantage of the new water system.

There are three main reasons why demand for water will shift because of the development of a water supply system (see also Section 14.7):

- cost difference between the new supply and the old supply (price shift);
- consumers find new uses of water, unrelated to any shift in price (greater availability and quantity);
- consumers switch to a more acceptable source (improved quality).

The first demand effect is illustrated in Figure 3.1(a). It indicates the demand for household water where the new water supply (e.g. pipeborne supply) can substitute for another source of water that was previously used (e.g. water vendor), with little significant change in quality of the useful output. The horizontal axis represents water consumed per unit time, while the vertical axis shows the effective total cost per unit to the customer. Since piped water is usually much cheaper than water from a vendor, consumption will increase from AB to AC. The second demand effect, shown in Figure 3.1(b), arises from new uses of water (e.g. watering a vegetable garden) that were previously not thought of, or considered infeasible, because of the limited quantity available or prohibitively high costs. Thus, the consumption GH represents an entirely new or induced market for water. The third demand effect is shown in Figure 3.1(c). Here, new piped water also displaces an old source, such as contaminated surface water. There is an improvement in quality, which results in the demand curve shifting out from D_O to D_F. If there was no such shift, demand would have increased from JL to JF' because of the lower price of water, but, with the additional displacement of the demand curve, the overall consumption would be JF (see Chapter 14).

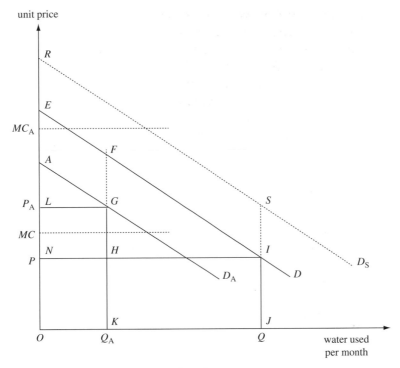

Figure 3.2. Measuring the net costs and benefits of water use.

3.3.2 Basic economics of cost and benefit measurement

Consider Figure 3.2, which is a static picture of the likely water use by a typical consumer, both with and without the project. This case is similar to the one shown in Figure 3.1(c). The symbols are given in the following.

Without project condition

D_A = demand curve for an alternative source of water;
Q_A = quantity of alternative water consumed, in litres per month of water required to produce the equivalent output;
MC_A = marginal cost of supplying alternative water;
P_A = price of alternative water (subsidized below MC).

With project condition

D = demand curve for water, shifted outward due to higher quality of piped water provided;
Q = quantity of piped water consumed, in litres per month;
MC = marginal cost of supplying piped water;
P = price of piped water (subsidized below MC).

The benefit of consuming water is given by the area under the demand curve. Therefore, in the 'without project' situation, $[OAGK]$ is the user benefit of consuming an amount of water Q_A, where the string of capitals in brackets indicates the boundary of the area. The corresponding cost of supplying this water is $MC_A \cdot Q_A$. In the same way, the benefit and cost in the 'with project' condition are $[OEIJ]$ and $MC \cdot Q$, respectively.

The project's incremental benefit (or change in benefit) is given by

$$IB = [OEIJ] - [OAGK] = [AEFG] + [FHI] + P(Q - Q_A).$$

Similarly, the incremental cost is given by

$$IC = MC \cdot Q - MC_A \cdot Q_A.$$

Finally, the net benefit due to the water supply project is given by

$$NB = IB - IC = \{P(Q - Q_A) + MC_A \cdot Q_A + [FHI] + [AEFG]\} - [MC \cdot Q].$$

The final term above indicates the project costs, and we may write this as follows:

$$C = [MC \cdot Q].$$

The remaining part of the expression is usually called the project benefit:

$$B = \{P(Q - Q_A)) + MC_A \cdot Q_A + [FHI] + [AEFG]\}.$$

In the expression for C, the marginal cost element MC is the long-run marginal cost (LRMC) per unit of water supplied. The LRMC is the incremental system cost of supplying one unit of sustained future water consumption (see Chapter 14); Q is the total quantity of new water supplied.

The expression for B is more complicated. The first term is the sales revenue corresponding to additional water used, while the second is the cost saving due to alternative water not used. The final two terms are areas representing consumer surplus. In general, these demand curves will shift and consumption levels (as well as the LRMC) will change over time. The present value of the stream of (shadow-priced) net benefits must be evaluated, year by year, over the lifetime of the project, to calculate the NPV and other cost–benefit criteria described earlier.

3.3.3 Estimation of project costs and benefits

Total cost

The total cost of the new water supply system is given by the least-cost solution. Alternatively, we may use the equations MC = LRMC per unit of water supplied and Q = total quantity of new water.

First benefit term: $P(Q - Q_A)$

The benefit component involving revenues from incremental consumption is the price times the quantity (from the demand forecast). When there is uncertainty concerning future price trends, the 'neutral' assumption of the constant real future price of water may be used. If this water supply price is well below the level of the LRMC, then the consumer surplus portion of benefits [*FHI*] will be relatively large and its estimation becomes more important, as discussed below. On the other hand, in the event that price is not very different from the LRMC, then the incremental revenues will approximate the full benefits more closely. Revenues are evaluated in market prices; they must be converted into shadow-priced values (see Section 3.2.4).

Second benefit term: $MC_A \cdot Q_A$

The second term in the expression for *B* represents cost savings from not using water derived from previous sources, measured in shadow prices. The rate at which this substitution takes place has to be predicted and also reflected consistently in the demand forecast. Additional cost-saving benefits may arise due to substitution of hypothetical new water sources that might have emerged in the absence of the water supply project, but these benefits must be carefully justified.

Third and fourth benefit terms: [FHI] and [AEFG]

The third term in the benefit expression, [*FHI*], is the consumer surplus associated with incremental water consumed. Additional output due to increased productivity in new activities may be used to approximate some of this willingness-to-pay for water. For example, the availability of more water for irrigation might increase farm yields significantly. The shadow-priced economic value of additional output, net of all input costs including expenditures on water, is the appropriate measure of consumer surplus to be used. Similarly, higher net output derived by replacing an existing water source may be used to estimate consumer surplus [*AEFG*]. The benefit [*FHI*] is over and above the cost-saving benefit arising from the replacement of alternative water described earlier.

3.3.4 Benefits that are difficult to value monetarily

Non-monetary gains are difficult to value. Analysts must be careful to avoid using such supposed benefits to justify a water supply project that otherwise may not have been viable. Such benefits may be included in the analysis through qualitative judgement.

First, improved water supply supports and stimulates modernization and growth. Most of the productivity gains by households, agriculture and industry may be quantified as shown earlier. However, if water supply acts as a catalyst, there may be further unrecognized benefits, for example due to changes in attitudes of the entire community.

Second, social benefits could accrue due to overall improvements in the quality of life. For example, clean and accessible water would improve health and sanitation and free up people's time. Other intangible benefits might include increased personal satisfaction, family welfare and reduced social discontent and unrest.

Third, water supply may be viewed by governments as a tool for improving social equity and income distribution (Munasinghe, 1988). Often, the benefits of water supply may accrue mainly to the rich. Weighting benefits to favour the poor is problematic because it is difficult to identify poverty groups and determine the correct social weights. Therefore, targeting the benefits of water supply, especially through connections policy and price subsidies, is often a more practical method.

Fourth, there may be significant employment and other gains as a result of the water project. The direct employment effects due to greater productive uses of water will be captured by analysing incremental output, as described earlier. In the case of rural water supply, another benefit is reduced rural to urban migration, due to better opportunities for employment and advancement, or improvements in the quality of life.

Fifth, it is sometimes argued that better water supply may provide a number of other benefits, from the broad national viewpoint, such as improved political stability, national cohesion and reduced urban–rural and interregional tensions and inequalities.

In Figure 3.2, the 'social' demand curve D_S captures the social surplus benefits or willingness-to-pay of society [*ERSI*], not directly internalized within demand curves of individual users.

3.4 Basic concepts for valuing environmental costs and benefits

This section describes methods of valuing environmental impacts. Little and Mirrlees (1990) noted that from the mid 1970s to the 1990s, there had been a rise and decline of project appraisal in development community. Our view is that natural-resource and environmental issues may be critical for making development more sustainable. Therefore, environmental economic analysis should be pursued, preferably early in the project cycle. Even where the valuation is difficult, techniques like multicriteria analysis are useful to make decisions (see Section 3.5).

The first step in the analysis is to determine the environmental (and social) impacts of the project or policy, by comparing the 'with project' and the 'without project' scenarios (see Section 3.3). Transdisciplinary work is essential (see Section 2.1). The quantification of impacts in non-monetary units is a prerequisite, not only for accurate economic valuation, but also for the use of other analytical methods such as multicriteria analysis. Such biophysical impacts are themselves complex and often poorly understood.

The second step in considering environmental effects involves valuing project impacts. Several practical valuation techniques are described below, based on extensions of the framework of Section 3.3.

3.4.1 Categories of economic value

Conceptually, the *total economic value* (TEV) of a resource consists of its (i) use value (UV) and (ii) non-use value (NUV). *Use values* may be broken down further into the direct use

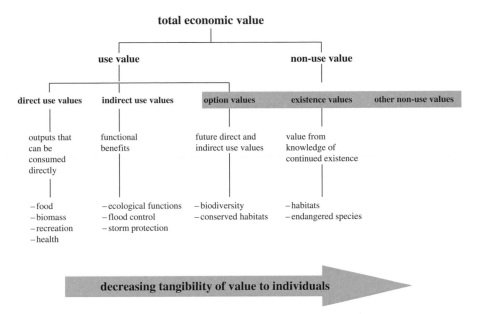

Figure 3.3. Categories of economic values attributed to environmental assets (examples from a forest).

value (DUV), the indirect use value (IUV) and the option value (OV) (potential use value). One needs to be careful not to count both the value of indirect supporting functions and the value of the resulting direct use. We may write the following:

$$TEV = UV + NUV$$

or

$$TEV = [DUV + IUV + OV] + [NUV].$$

Figure 3.3 shows this disaggregation of the TEV in schematic form. A short description of each valuation concept, and a few typical examples of the underlying environmental resources, are provided:

- *direct use value* is the contribution to current production/consumption;
- *indirect use value* includes benefits from functional services that the environment provides to support current production/consumption (e.g. ecological functions such as nutrient recycling);
- *option value* is the willingness-to-pay for an unutilized asset, simply to avoid the risk of not having it available in the future (see Section 3.6.2); and
- *non-use value* is the willingness-to-pay for perceived benefits not related to use value, e.g. *existence value*, which is based on the satisfaction of merely knowing that an asset exists, even without intending to use it.

Economic theory clearly defines the TUV, but there is considerable overlap and ambiguity in the breakdown categories, especially with regard to non-use values. Thus, option values and non-use values are shaded in Figure 3.3. These categories are useful as an indicative guide, but the goal of practical estimation is to measure the TUV rather than its components.

The distinction between use and non-use values is not always clear. The latter tend to be linked to more altruistic motives. Differing forms of altruism include: intergenerational altruism, or the bequest motive; interpersonal altruism, or the gift motive; stewardship (which has more ethical than utilitarian origins); and q-altruism, which states that the resource has an intrinsic right to exist. This final definition is outside conventional economic theory and incorporates the notion that the welfare function should be derived from something more than purely human utility (Quiggin, 1991).

For the practitioner, the precise conceptual basis of economic value is less important than the various empirical techniques that permit us to estimate a monetary value for environmental assets.

3.4.2 *Practical valuation techniques*

The economic concept underlying all valuation methods is the willingness-to-pay (WTP) of individuals for an environmental service or resource, which is itself based on the area under the demand curve (Freeman, 1993).

In Figure 3.4, $IHFD_0$ is the demand curve for an environmental good (e.g. litres per day of water used); $AJFS$ is the supply curve or marginal cost (MC) for each unit supplied. The demand curve is generally downward sloping because each succeeding unit consumed has less value. However, we might expect MC to increase (e.g. as water sources become scarcer and less accessible). At any price p_1, the quantity demanded is Q_1 and the total economic

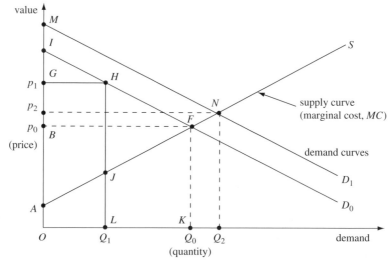

Figure 3.4. Economic value of an environmental good.

benefit of consumption is the WTP represented by the area OIHL (mathematically, $\int p \, dQ$). The corresponding total cost of supply is area OAJL (i.e. $\int MC \, dQ$). The net benefit (NB) of water use is given by benefit – cost = area *AIHJ*, which is the economic surplus (or net value) from this activity. NB has two components: areas *IHG* (consumer surplus) and *AGHJ* (producer surplus). Net benefits (*AIF*) are maximized at point *F*, when the optimal price price p_0 is set equal to marginal cost *MC* and the optimal quantity Q_0 is used.

Next, we examine how a change in quality of the same environmental good might affect its value. Suppose the curve D_0 indicates the demand for an environmental resource in its original condition (e.g. polluted river water). The point *I* represents the choke price, at which demand falls to zero. Suppose the water quality is improved by environmental clean-up activity. Then the demand curve shifts upward to the new position D_1. With the new price and quantity combination (p_2, Q_2), the new net benefit increases to *AMN*. Therefore, there is an incremental increase in net value given by the area *IFNM*, due to the water quality improvement – provided water and water quality are weak complements (Maler, 1974).

Theoretically, the compensated or Hicksian demand function should be used to estimate value, since it indicates how demand varies with price while keeping the user's utility level constant. The change in value of an environmental asset could also be defined by the difference between the values of two expenditure (or cost) functions. The latter are the minimum amounts required to achieve a given level of household utility or firm output, *before* and *after* varying the quality of, price of, or access to the environmental resource, while keeping all other aspects constant.

Measurement problems arise because the commonly estimated demand function is the Marshallian one – which indicates how demand varies with the price of an environmental good, while keeping the user's income level constant. In practice, it has been shown that the Marshallian and Hicksian estimates of the WTP are in good agreement for a variety of conditions, and in a few cases the Hicksian function may be derived from the estimated Marshallian demand functions (Braden and Kolstad, 1991; Willig, 1976).

People's willingness-to-accept (WTA) in the way of compensation for environmental damage is another measure of economic value that is related to the WTP; the WTA and the WTP could diverge as discussed below (Cropper and Oates, 1992). In practice, both measures are used in the valuation techniques described below.

Empirical evidence indicates that WTP questions yield higher answers than WTA questions about people's willingness-to-pay to retain the same amenity. Some argue that WTA questions need more time to be understood properly and assimilated, and that the gap between WTA and WTP narrows with successive iterations. Others suggest that people are less willing to pay actual income than to receive 'hypothetical' compensation (Knetsch and Sinden, 1984). It may also be the case that individuals are more cautious when weighing the net benefits of changing assets than when no change is made. Generally, WTP is considered to be more consistent and credible a measure than WTA. However, when significant discrepancies exist between the two measures, then the higher values may be more appropriate when valuing environmental losses.

	Type of market		
Behaviour type	**Conventional market**	**Implicit market**	**Constructed market**
Actual behaviour	effect on production	travel cost	artificial market
		wage differences	
	effect on health	property values	
	defensive or preventive costs	proxy/marketed goods	
		benefit transfer	
Intended behaviour	replacement cost shadow project		contingent valuation

Figure 3.5. Techniques for economically valuing environmental impact.

In developing countries, the ability to pay is a concern. In low-income areas, money values placed on environmental goods and services are traditionally low, and income weights may be used (see Section 3.2.2). Alternatively, other social and ethical measures might be used to protect the poor (see Section 13.2.3).

Practical valuation methods are categorized in Figure 3.5.

3.4.3 Direct effects valued on conventional markets

The methods considered in this section are directly based on changes in market prices or productivity due to environmental impacts.

Change in productivity

Projects can affect production. Changes in marketed output can be valued by using standard economic prices.

Loss of earnings

Environmental quality affects human health. Ideally, the monetary value of health impacts should be determined by the WTP for improved health. In practice, proxy measures such as foregone net earnings may be used in case of premature death, sickness or absenteeism (and higher medical expenditures, which can be considered a type of replacement cost). One may avoid ethical controversies, associated with valuing a single specific life, by costing the statistical probability of ill health or death (like the actuarial values used by life insurance firms).

Actual defensive or preventive expenditures

Individuals, firms and governments undertake 'defensive expenditures' to avoid or reduce unwanted environmental effects. Defensive expenditures may be easier to obtain than direct valuations of environmental harm. Such *actual* expenditures indicate that individuals, firms or governments judge the resultant benefits to exceed the costs. Defensive expenditures can then be interpreted as a minimum valuation of benefits.

3.4.4 *Potential expenditure valued on conventional markets*

Replacement cost

In this section, the costs to be incurred in order to replace a damaged asset are estimated. The actual damage costs may be higher or lower than the replacement cost. However, it is an appropriate method if there are compelling reasons for restoring the damage. This approach is especially relevant if there is a sustainability constraint that requires certain assets stocks to be maintained intact (see Chapter 2).

Shadow project

This approach is based on costing one or more 'shadow projects' that provide for substitute environmental services to compensate for environmental assets lost under the ongoing project. Further, this approach is often an institutional judgement of replacement cost, and its application would be most relevant when 'critical' environmental assets at risk need to be maintained.

3.4.5 *Valuation using implicit (or surrogate) markets*

The techniques described in this section use market information indirectly. Each method has advantages and disadvantages, including specific data and resource needs.

Travel cost

The travel cost method has been used to measure benefits produced by recreation sites. It determines the demand for a site (e.g. number of visits per year) as a function of variables such as consumer income, price and various socioeconomic characteristics. The price is usually the sum of observed cost elements such as (a) entry price to the site, (b) costs of travelling to the site and (c) foregone earnings or opportunity cost of time spent. The consumer surplus associated with the estimated demand curve provides a measure of the value of the recreational site in question. More sophisticated versions include comparisons across sites, where environmental quality is also included as a variable that affects demand.

Property value

This is a hedonic price technique based on the more general land value approach, which decomposes real estate prices into components attributable to different characteristics such as proximity to schools, shops, parks, etc. The method seeks to determine the increased WTP for improved local environmental quality, as reflected in housing prices in cleaner surroundings. It assumes a competitive housing market, and its demands on information and tools of statistical analysis are high.

Wage differential

This method is also a hedonic technique, which assumes a competitive market, where the demand for labour equals the value of the marginal product, and labour supply varies with working and living conditions. Thus, a higher wage is necessary to attract workers to locate in polluted areas or undertake more risky occupations. This method relies on private valuation of health risks, not necessarily social ones. Data on occupational hazards must be good for private individuals to make meaningful trade-offs between health risks and remuneration. Finally, the effects of other factors, such as skill level, job responsibility, etc., that might influence wages must be eliminated to isolate the impacts of environment.

Marketed goods as proxies for non-marketed goods

In situations where environmental goods have close substitutes that are marketed, the value of an environmental good may be approximated by the observed market price of its substitutes.

Benefit transfer

Values determined at one place and time are used to infer values of similar goods at another place and time (where direct valuation is difficult), with adjustments for differences in incomes, prices, quality, behaviour, etc. (ADB, 1996; *Ecological Economics*, 2006).

3.4.6 Valuation using constructed markets

Contingent valuation

When market prices do not exist, this method basically asks people what they are willing to pay for a benefit and/or what they are willing to accept by way of compensation to tolerate a cost. This process of asking may be either through a direct questionnaire/survey, or by experimental techniques in which subjects respond to stimuli in 'laboratory' conditions. The contingent valuation method has certain shortcomings, including problems of designing, implementing and interpreting questions. However, in some cases, it may be the only available technique for estimating benefits. It has been applied to common property resources, amenity resources with scenic, ecological or other characteristics and to other situations where market information is not available. Caution should be exercised in seeking to pursue some of the more abstract benefits of environmental assets, such as existence value.

Artificial market

Such markets could be constructed for experimental purposes to determine consumer willingness-to-pay for a good or service. For example, a home water purification kit might be marketed at various price levels, or access to a game reserve might be offered on the basis of different admission fees, thereby providing an estimate of the value placed on water purity or on the use of a recreational facility, respectively.

3.5 Multicriteria analysis

Projects, policies and their impacts are embedded in a system of broader (national) objectives. If the impacts of projects and policies on these broader objectives can be valued economically, all such effects may be incorporated into the conventional decision-making framework of cost–benefit analysis. However, some social and biophysical impacts cannot be easily quantified in monetary terms, and multicriteria analysis offers a complementary approach that facilitates decision making.

Multicriteria analysis (MCA) or multiobjective decision making differs from CBA in three major areas. While CBA focuses on efficiency (although incorporation of income distribution objectives may be attempted), MCA does not impose limits on the forms of criteria, allowing for consideration of social and other forms of equity. Second, while CBA requires that effects be measured in quantitative terms, to allow for the application of prices, MCA can be broken down into three groups: one that requires quantitative data; a second that uses only qualitative data; and a third that handles both simultaneously. Finally, MCA does not require the use of prices, although they might be used to arrive at a score. CBA uses prices which may sometimes be adjusted according to equity weighting. MCA uses weighting involving relative priorities of different groups as opposed to pricing. If efficiency is the only criterion, and prices are available to value efficiency attributes, CBA is preferable. However, in many cases, a paucity of data and the need to incorporate social and biophysical impacts make the use of MCA a more practicable and realistic option.

MCA calls for desirable objectives to be specified. These often exhibit a hierarchical structure. The highest level represents the broad overall objectives (e.g. improving the quality of life), which are often vaguely stated and, hence, not very operational. They may be broken down into more operational lower-level objectives (e.g. increased income) so that the extent to which the latter are met may be practically assessed. Sometimes only proxies are available (e.g. if the objective is to enhance recreation opportunities, the number of recreation days can be used). Although value judgements may be required in choosing the proper attribute, measurement does not have to be in monetary terms (like the single-criterion CBA). More explicit recognition is given to the fact that a variety of concerns may be associated with planning decisions.

An intuitive understanding of the fundamentals of MCA can be provided by a two-dimensional graphical exposition, such as in Figure 3.6. Assume that a scheme has two non-commensurable and conflicting objectives, Z_1 and Z_2. For example, Z_1 could be the additional project cost required to protect biodiversity and Z_2 could be some index indicating the loss of biodiversity. Assume further that alternative projects or solutions to the problem (A, B and C) have been identified. Clearly, point B is superior to (or dominates) A in terms of both Z_1 and Z_2 because B exhibits lower costs as well as biodiversity loss relative to A. Thus, alternative A may be discarded. However, we cannot make such a simple choice between solutions B and C since the former is better than the latter with respect to objective Z_1 but worse with respect to Z_2. In general, more points (or solutions) such as B and C may be

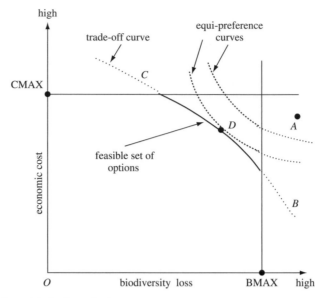

Figure 3.6. Simple multicriteria analysis.

identified to define the set of all non-dominated feasible solution points that form an optimal trade-off curve or curve of best options.

For an unconstrained problem, further ranking of alternatives cannot be conducted without the introduction of value judgements. Specific information has to be elicited from the decision maker to determine the most preferred solution. In its most complete form, such information may be summarized by a family of equi-preference curves that indicate the way in which the decision maker or society trades off one objective against the other – typical equi-preference curves are shown in Figure 3.6. The preferred alternative is the one that yields the greatest utility, which occurs (for continuous decision variables as shown here) at the point of tangency *D* of the best equi-preference curve with the trade-off curve.

Since the equi-preference curves are usually not known, other practical techniques have been developed to narrow down the set of feasible choices on the trade-off curve. One approach uses limits on objectives or 'exclusionary screening'. For example, in the figure the decision maker may face an upper bound on costs, CMAX (i.e. a budgetary constraint). Similarly, ecological experts might set a maximum value of biodiversity loss, BMAX (e.g. a level beyond which the ecosystem collapses). These two constraints define a more restricted portion of the trade-off curve (darker line), thereby reducing and simplifying the choices available.

Pearce and Turner (1990) describe five main forms of multicriteria evaluation methods: aggregation, lexicographic, graphical, consensus- maximizing and concordance. Among the various types of MCA, the most suitable method depends upon the nature of the decision situation (Petry, 1990). For instance, interactive involvement of the decision maker has proved useful for problems characterized by a large number of decision variables and complex causal interrelationships. Some objectives may be directly optimized, while others will need to meet a certain standard (e.g. level of biological oxygen demand (BOD) not below 5 mg/litre).

The major accomplishment of MCA models is that they allow for more accurate representation of decision problems, by accounting for several objectives. However, a key question concerns whose preferences are to be considered. The model only aids a single decision maker (or a homogeneous group). Various stakeholders will assign different priorities to the respective objectives, and it may not be possible to determine a single best solution via the multi-objective model. Also, the mathematical framework imposes constraints upon the ability to represent the planning problem effectively. Non-linear, stochastic and dynamic formulations can assist in better defining the problem, but impose costs in terms of complexity in formulation and solving the model (Cocklin, 1989). In constructing the model, the analyst communicates information about the nature of the problem by specifying why factors are important and how they interact. There is value to be gained in constructing models from differing perspectives and comparing the results. MCA, used in conjunction with a variety of models, and effective stakeholder consultations, could help to reconcile the differences between individual versus social and selfish versus altruistic preferences.

In addition to facilitating specific trade-off decisions at the project level, MCA could also help in selecting strategic development paths.

3.6 Discount rate, risk and uncertainty

In this section, some key issues that arise in the sustainable development assessment of projects and policies are briefly reviewed.

3.6.1 Discounting and intergenerational choices

Discounting is the process by which costs and benefits that occur in different time periods may be compared. It has been a general problem in cost–benefit analysis and is particularly important with regard to long-term environmental issues (Harberger, 1976; Marglin, 1963).

In standard analysis, past costs and benefits are treated as 'sunk' and are ignored in decisions about the present and future. Future costs and benefits are discounted to their equivalent present value and then compared. In theory the interest rate in a perfect market reflects both the subjective rate of time preference (of private individuals) and the rate of productivity of capital. These rates are equated at the margin by the market, so that the rate at which individuals are willing to trade present for future values is just equal at the margin to the rate at which they are able to transform present goods, in the form of foregone consumption, into future goods (through capital investment).

Often, the rate of time preference and the rate of capital productivity are not equal, because of imperfect financial markets and government distortions introduced by taxation. Also, individual decisions differ from social decisions in that individuals are relatively short-lived, whereas societies persist for longer periods. The community usually discounts the future less than individuals. These considerations give rise to the concept of social rate of discount (Box 3.2).

Box 3.2 Social rate of discount and long-term concerns

Social rate of discount

The social rate of discount (SRD) is appropriate for determining public policy. Basic issues of value and equity are involved in the choice of such a social discount rate. Sustainable development provides a broad guideline – each generation has the right to inherit economic, social and environmental assets that are at least as good as the those enjoyed by the preceding generation (see Chapter 2).

Even in traditional CBA used in project evaluation, the choice of discount rates is not clear cut (Munasinghe, 1992a). They vary across countries, depending on behavioural preferences and economic conditions. Furthermore, it is considered prudent to test the sensitivity of project results by using a range of discount rates (usually about 4 to 12% per annum), even within one country.

Starting from the theoretically ideal (or first best) situation of perfectly functioning, competitive markets and an optimal distribution of income (see Box 2.3), it is possible to show that the discount rate should be equal to the marginal returns to investment (MRI), which will also equal the interest rate on borrowing by both consumers and producers (Lind, 1982). There are three conditions to ensure an efficient (or optimal) growth path. First, the marginal returns to investment between one period and the next should equal the rate of interest (i) charged from borrowing producers. Second, the rate of change of the marginal utility of consumption (or satisfaction derived from one extra unit consumed) from one period to the next should be equal to the interest rate (r) paid out to lending consumers. Third, and finally, the producer and consumer rates of interest are equal (i.e. $i = r$) throughout the economy and over all time periods.

As we deviate from ideal market conditions and the optimal income distribution, the choice of discount (or interest) rates becomes less clear. For example, taxes (subsidies) may increase (decrease) the borrowing rate to producers above (below) the interest rate paid to consumers on their savings (i.e. i differs from r). More generally, if the three conditions do not hold because of economic distortions, then efficiency may require project-specific discount rates with corrections to compensate for the economic imperfections. In some cases, no theoretical basis exists to link market interest rates to the social discount rate, but market behaviour could still provide useful data to estimate the latter.

Declining or negative discount rates (in the long term)

Traditional discount rate analysis may be used to derive declining (and even negative) discount rates for evaluating costs and benefits over very long (or multigenerational) time periods, when welfare and returns on investment may be falling. Consider the consumer rate of time preference (CTP), which is the subjective discount rate of individuals (as opposed to the MRI, which is market-derived). It has several components:

CTP $= \alpha + \beta g$. Here, α represents the preference of an individual for consumption today rather than in the future – it may be based on the myopic notion of 'pure' preference, as well as the risk perception that future consumption may never be realized; β is the elasticity of marginal welfare; and g is the growth rate of consumption.

Assuming that welfare (W) depends on consumption (c), we may write $W = W(c)$. Then, by definition,

$$\beta = -\left\{ \frac{c(\mathrm{d}^2 W/\mathrm{d}c^2)}{(\mathrm{d}W/\mathrm{d}c)} \right\}$$

and

$$g = \frac{(\mathrm{d}c/\mathrm{d}t)}{c}.$$

Marginal welfare increases with consumption, $(\mathrm{d}W/\mathrm{d}c) > 0$, but at a declining rate, $(\mathrm{d}^2 W/\mathrm{d}c^2) < 0$, as consumers become satiated. Therefore $\beta > 0$, so that the sign of the term (βg) is the same as sign of g. The term (βg) shows that the declining marginal welfare of consumption combined with higher expected future consumption will make the latter less valuable than present-day consumption; i.e. since we are likely to be richer in the future, consumption today is more valuable.

The general consensus is that α is close to zero, usually 0–3%, and β may be in the range of 1 to 2. Thus, if g is large (i.e. high expected economic growth rates), then the CTP could be quite large too. On the other hand, if we consider a long-range scenario, in which growth and consumption are falling (e.g. catastrophic global warming in 100 years), then g could become negative and consequently the CTP may be small or even negative. In this case, with the CTP as the discount rate, future costs and benefits would loom much larger in present-value terms than if the conventional opportunity cost of capital (say 8%) were used, thereby giving a larger weight to long-term, intergenerational concerns. The key point is that it may be misleading to choose discount rates without assuming some consistent future scenario; Uzawa (1969) shows how discount rates may be endogenized to reflect future consumption. Thus an optimistic future would favour higher discount rates than a gloomy one, which is consistent, since the risk of future catastrophes should encourage greater concern for the future. Hansen (2006) and Winkler (2006) further discuss the pros and cons of declining (hyperbolic) discount rates.

Source: Munasinghe (1992a).

The rate of productivity is higher in many developing countries, because of capital scarcity. In poor countries, the rate of time preference may also be elevated, because of the urgency of satisfying immediate basic needs rather than ensuring long-term sustainability.

The neoclassical discounted utility model implies that the rate of time preference is independent of time frames and the amounts of commodities – this is not always true. Furthermore, the lack of properly developed capital markets in many developing economies often causes investment decisions to be linked to consumption and to depend on preferences.

Higher discount rates may discriminate against future generations. This is because projects with social costs occurring in the long term, and net social benefits occurring in the near term, will be favoured by higher discount rates. Projects with benefits accruing in the long run will be less likely to be undertaken under high discount rates. Thus, future generations will suffer from market discount rates determined by high rates of current generation time preference and/or productivity of capital.

The foregoing arguments suggest that discount rates could be lowered to reflect long-term environmental concerns and issues of intergenerational equity – see Section 5.2.3 for a discussion relating to climate change. Yet, this may lead to a problem. Although ecologically sound activities would pass the cost–benefit test more frequently, many more projects would also generally pass the test, and the resulting increase in investment could lead to additional environmental stress (Krautkraemer, 1988).

Many environmentalists believe that a zero discount rate should be employed to protect future generations. However, employing a zero discount rate is inequitable, since it would imply a policy of high current sacrifice, which would discriminate against the poor of today. Non-constant (and declining) discount rates may be more relevant to deal with long-term multigenerational issues (see Section 5.2.3), especially where the future productivity of capital is expected to decrease. The discount rate could be determined on a country-specific basis, and be regularly updated, as is the case with other shadow prices.

Arbitrary manipulation of discount rates to facilitate intergenerational transfers could distort resource allocations. A better alternative might be to impose sustainability constraints to ensure that the overall stock of capital is preserved or enhanced for future generations (see Chapter 2). Even simple rules that limit specific environmental impacts (e.g. pollution standards) may be a useful first step. Another alternative is to ensure that irreplaceable environmental assets command a premium value in CBA.

In summary, the following practical guidance is useful within the context of sustainomics. (a) The standard opportunity cost of capital (e.g. 4–12%) may be used as a benchmark for net present value calculations and as the comparator when the internal rate of return (IRR) is computed. (b) Efforts should be made to ensure that compensating investments offset capital stock degradation within a framework of policy and project decisions. (c) In the case of projects leading to irreversible damage, the CBA should be adapted, to the extent possible, to include a measurement of the foregone benefits of preservation in the computation of costs. (d) Where valuation of environmental and social impacts is difficult, and large irreversible damage might occur, restrictions might be set to limit the damage within acceptable biophysical or social norms. (e) Declining or negative discount rates may be considered for pessimistic long-term scenarios.

3.6.2 *Risk and uncertainty problems*

All projects and policies entail risk and uncertainty. Risks are usually measured by the probabilities assigned to the likelihood of occurrence of an undesirable event (e.g. a natural disaster). Uncertainty describes a situation where little is known about future impacts. Therefore, no probabilities can be assigned because the outcomes are undefined.

Risk can be treated probabilistically on the basis of estimated data, and therefore it may be insured against and treated like any other project cost. However, uncertainty defies actuarial principles because the future is undefined. As projects and environmental impacts grow larger, uncertainty looms larger than risk. The proper response to risk is to count it as a cost in expected value computations. However, the use of a single number (or expected value of risk) does not capture the risk variability or the range of values to be expected. Additionally, it does not allow for individual perceptions of risk. Precaution is one response to uncertainty – if the future cannot be perceived clearly, then the speed of advance should be tailored to the distance over which the clarity of vision is acceptable.

In practice, the way risk and uncertainty are included in project appraisal work is through sensitivity analyses, which determine how the IRR is dependent on different variables. Using optimistic and pessimistic values for different variables can indicate which ones will significantly affect benefits and costs. Sensitivity analysis need not reflect the probability of occurrence of the upper or lower values. In project appraisal, deterministic point estimates of value could be quite misleading, whereas ranges of value help identify more robust options (Anderson and Quiggin, 1990). Various criteria, such as mini-max and minimum-regret may also be used (Friedman, 1986).

The issue of uncertainty plays an important role in environmental valuation and policy formulation. Option values and quasi-option values are based on the existence of uncertainty (see Section 3.4.1). Option value (OV) is essentially the premium that consumers are willing to pay to avoid the risk of not having something available in the future. Among the definitions of OV, one useful measure is the difference between the *ex-ante* and *ex-post* welfare associated with the use of an environmental asset. The sign of OV depends upon the presence of supply or demand uncertainty, and on whether the consumer is risk-averse or risk-loving (Pearce and Turner, 1990).

The quasi-option value (QOV) is the value of preserving options for future use in the expectation that knowledge will grow over time. If a project causes irreversible environmental damage, the opportunity to expand knowledge through scientific study of that asset is lost. Uncertainty about the benefits of preservation to be derived through future knowledge expansion (which is independent of development) yields a positive QOV. Thus development might be postponed until increased knowledge facilitates a more informed decision. If information growth itself depends on the development taking place, then the QOV is positive when the uncertainty concerns preservation benefits and negative when the uncertainty is about development benefits (Pearce and Turner, 1990).

If calculations are performed in terms of the option price (valuing what a person would pay for future benefits today), then the OV may be redundant. The OV is added to expected future benefits to bring total value up to the option price. Most contingent valuation methods (CVMs) estimate the option price directly. Thus, the OV may be practically redundant if it is captured in other measures, although conceptually valid (Freeman, 1993).

Environmental policy formulation is complicated by the presence of numerous forms of uncertainty. As an illustration, Bromley (1989) identified six different aspects of uncertainty in the case of air pollution resulting from acid deposition. They are (1) identification of the sources of particular pollutants; (2) ultimate destination of particular emissions; (3) actual physical impacts at the point of destination; (4) human valuation of the realized impacts at the point of destination; (5) the extent to which a particular policy response will have an impact on the abovementioned factors; and (6) the actual cost level and the incidence of those costs that are the result of policy choice.

Policy makers address these uncertainties based on their perception of the existing entitlement structure. The interests of the future may be protected by an entitlement structure that imposes a duty on current generations to consider the rights of future generations – since unborn generations are unable to enter bids in today's markets – to protect their interests. There are three policy instruments to ensure that future generations are not made worse off: mandated pollution abatement; full compensation for future damages (e.g. by taxation); and an annuity that will compensate the future for costs imposed in the present. In the face of uncertainty, the first option would appear to be the most practical.

3.7 Economy-wide policies and the environment

Next, we turn to larger-scale issues that show how economy-wide policies (both macro-economic and sectoral) may cause significant environmental and social harm. More details, including a historical review of ideas and recent case studies, are given in Chapters 7, 8 and 9.

Fiscal and monetary policies, structural adjustment programmes and stabilization measures all affect the natural-resource base. Unfortunately, interactions among the economy, society and environment are complex, and our understanding of them is limited. Ideally, one would wish to trace the effects of economy-wide policy reforms (both macroeconomic and sectoral) through the socioeconomic and ecological systems. Time and data limitations generally preclude such comprehensive approaches in developing countries. Practical policy analysis is usually limited to a more partial approach, which traces the key impacts of specific economy-wide policies, at least qualitatively, and, wherever possible, quantitatively.

No simple generalizations are possible as to the likely environmental and social effects of broad policy measures. Nevertheless, opportunities have been missed for combining poverty reduction- or efficiency-oriented reforms with the complementary goal of environmental protection – i.e. 'win–win' outcomes (Munasinghe, 1992a). For example, addressing problems of land tenure, as well as access to financial and social services, not only yields economic gains, but also are essential for promoting environmental stewardship. Similarly, improving the efficiency of industrial or energy-related activities would reduce both economic waste and environmental pollution (World Bank, 1992b–e).

Many instances of excessive pollution or resource overexploitation are due to market distortions. Broad policy reforms, which usually promote efficiency or reduce poverty, could be made more beneficial for the environment. The challenge is to identify the complicated paths by which such policy changes ultimately influence conservation at the firm or household level. Some changes can have either beneficial or harmful environmental and social effects, depending on the nature of intervening conditions. The objective is not necessarily to modify directly the original broader policies (which have other conventional, non-environmental goals), but rather to design more specific complementary policy measures that would help mitigate negative effects or enhance the positive impacts of the original policies on the environment.

3.7.1 Macroeconomic policies

During the economic crisis of the early 1980s, many developing countries that had been running substantial budget and trade deficits (and financing these by increasing external debt) were forced to adopt emergency stabilization programmes. These programmes often had unforeseen social and environmental consequences.

One important environmental impact of the crisis was related to poverty and unemployment. The stabilization efforts often necessitated currency devaluations, controls on capital and interest rate increases. When income levels dropped, tax revenues decreased accordingly. As unemployment increased, governments fell back upon expansionary financing policies, which led to increases in consumer prices. The effect of such policies on the poorest population groups often drove them onto marginal lands, resulting in soil erosion or desertification. Fuel price increases and lowered incomes also contributed to deforestation and reductions in soil fertility, as the poor were forced to use fuelwood and animal dung for heating, lighting and cooking.

Aside from the contractionary aspects of short-term stabilization measures, many macroeconomic policies also have potentially important effects on resource use and the environment. Unfortunately, no easy generalizations as to the directions of these effects are possible; they can be either beneficial or negative, depending on specific conditions. For example, real currency devaluations have the effect of increasing international competitiveness and raising production of internationally tradable goods (e.g. forestry and agricultural products). If the agricultural response occurs through crop substitution, environmental impact would depend on whether the crop being promoted tended to be environmentally benign (such as tea, cocoa, rubber) or environmentally damaging (such as tobacco, sugar cane, corn). Environmental impacts would also depend on whether increased production led to farming on new land (which could result in increased deforestation) or to more efficient use of existing farmland. Another possibility is that overvaluation of the exchange rate (and resulting negative terms of trade, decreased competitiveness of products and lower farm-gate prices) may well push small cultivators onto more environmentally fragile marginal lands, in an attempt to absorb the effects of the price changes.

The output from a natural-resource stock such as a forest or fishery will be affected by other factors, such as property rights (see Section 4.2). Thus, if trade policy increased the value of output (e.g. timber or fish exports), then the degree of ownership would influence how production and resource stocks were managed. Reactions might range from more investment in, and maintenance of, assets (if environmental costs were internalized by owner–users) to rapid depletion (when the users had no stake in the resource stock). Thus,

Capistrano and Kiker (1990) propose that increasing the competitiveness of world exports would also increase the opportunity cost of keeping timber unharvested. This could lead to forest depletion that significantly exceeds natural regenerative capacity. Another study (Kahn and McDonald, 1995) used empirical evidence to suggest that a correlative link exists between debt and deforestation. They propose that debt burdens cause myopic behaviour that often results in overdepletion of forest resources – through deforestation rates that may not be optimal in the long run, but are necessary to meet short-term needs.

Munasinghe and Cruz (1994) explicitly traced how economy-wide policy reforms to promote economic development could have numerous unanticipated environmental and social effects Table 3.1 summarizes some typical results. The first column lists only a few of the many economy-wide policy issues addressed through macroeconomic reforms. The policies in the second column are usually designed to address these issues, and the corresponding economic development objectives or direct impacts are given in the third column. The fourth column shows important second-order environmental and social impacts that may not be anticipated. While policy reforms could improve natural-resource management, some potential negative environmental impacts that concern us are given in this column. Thus, to evaluate such reforms properly, it would be necessary to assess their direct and indirect effects as well as the trade-offs between their conventional development contribution and their environmental effects. Relevant defensive measures or modifications may then be analysed for each policy. This systematic process is captured in the Action Impact Matrix (AIM) methodology (see Section 2.4.1).

The key influence of macroeconomic policies on agriculture has already been shown by early studies (Johnson, 1973; Schuh, 1974). Krueger, Schiff and Valdes (1991) also show that economy-wide factors may be more important than sectoral policies in agriculture. When a broad assessment perspective is adopted, direct output price interventions by government have less effect on agricultural incentives than indirect, economy-wide factors, such as foreign exchange rates and industrial protection policies.

The impact of economy-wide policies may also be important for the environment. For example, Hyde, Newman and Sedjo (1991) cite studies in Brazil and in the Philippines that demonstrate how economic policy spillovers constitute an important source of deforestation. Agricultural subsidies in Brazil probably contribute to half of the forest destruction in Amazonia (Binswanger, 1989; Mahar, 1988). A general equilibrium simulation for the Philippines suggests that foreign exchange rate changes, although motivated by general balance of payments concerns, have major implications for the demand for wood products, therefore influencing logging rates. The case of fuelwood may be as interesting, since fuelwood shortages have been identified as the major forestry problem in many developing countries. National price policies on fuel and investment policies on alternative energy sources may be important for addressing the fuelwood problem.

3.7.2 *Structural adjustment*

Structural adjustment programmes address a well defined set of reform areas (see Section 7.2.1). These will generally include establishing an appropriate macroeconomic

Table 3.1 *Typical examples of direct and indirect environmental and social impacts of economy-wide policies*

Policy issue	Policy reform	Direct economic objectives/effects	Indirect (environmental and social effects)
Trade deficits	flexible exchange rates	promote industrial competitiveness, exports; reduce imports	export promotion might promote more deforestation for export and lead to substitution of tree crops for annual crops; industrial job creation may reduce pressure on land resources
Food, security and unemployment	agricultural intensification in settled lands and resettlement programmes for new areas	increase crop yields and acreage; absorb more rural labour	may reduce spontaneous migration to ecologically fragile areas; however, there is potential for overuse of fertilizers and chemicals
Industrial protection, due to inefficient production	reduce tariffs and special investment incentives	promote competition and industrial efficiency	more openness may lead to more energy-efficient or less polluting technologies; it may also attract hazardous industries

framework for growth, introducing a set of supporting sectoral policies and investment efforts and integrating the domestic economy into the world economy (Fischer and Thomas, 1990).

Adjustment lending in the early 1980s addressed problems of maintaining growth caused by the worldwide economic crisis. The crisis was triggered by the second round of energy price hikes, the collapse of export markets and increased international interest rates. These external conditions, combined with lack of competitiveness of local industries, lagging employment generation and persistent budget deficits, led to unsustainable current account deficits.

Thus, trade-oriented reforms, including tariff reductions and devaluation, became key components of adjustment lending. Adjustment implications for managing external debt also received much attention. In turn, this led to concern for stimulating domestic savings, increasing the role of taxation in resource mobilization, decreasing the extent of government expenditures and making investments more productive.

The benefits and costs of such programmes are country-specific. In a review of the Latin American experience, Birdsall and Wheeler (1992) conclude that there is no evidence to show that open developing country economies are more prone to pollution. The inflow of foreign technology and capital would tend to bring in better pollution standards. At the same time, it is the pollution-intensive heavy industries sector that has benefited from protective industrial and trade policies. Nevertheless, some concern persists that encouraging foreign investment and privatization might lead to the growth of 'pollution havens', given the weakness of environmental regulations in most developing countries. Trade liberalization also could encourage the growth of energy-intensive and/or highly polluting industry. However, pollution caused by industrialization could be offset by afforestation (although this does not necessarily compensate residents of polluted areas) and limited by appropriate taxation policies that encouraged the use of pollution-abatement technologies.

The environmental relevance of structural adjustment reforms was reviewed by Cruz, Munasinghe and Warford (1997). The reforms included (l) relative price changes in agricultural outputs, inputs, energy and export taxes; (2) trade and industry policy reform; (3) changes in public expenditure programmes; and (4) institutional reforms by sector. In the early to mid l980s, environmental aspects were relatively neglected in adjustment lending operations, with few environmental loan components or conditionalities. The review also found that programmes from FY88–FY92 included more on the environment. For example, about 60% of the 58 countries reviewed had adjustment programmes whose loan components or conditionalities were environmentally related, compared with 37% during FY79–FY87. Sectoral adjustment programmes have also included environmental policy reforms.

In the 1990s, international donor agencies, non-governmental organizations and academic institutions contributed to the debate on the environmental effects of structural adjustment and stabilization programmes. Several good studies exist of environmental and social impacts of country-wide policies (Abaza, 1995; Cruz *et al.*, 1997; *Environment and Development Economics*, 1999; Kessler and Van Dorp, 1998; Munasinghe, 1992a; Munasinghe, 1996b; Munasinghe and Cruz, 1994; Opschoor and Jongma, 1996; Panayotou and Hupe, 1996; Reed, 1992, 1996; Warford, Munasinghe and Cruz, 1997; Young and Bishop, 1995) – see Chapter 7 for details.

3.7.3 Public investment/expenditure reviews

Reductions in public expenditure are an integral part of many structural adjustment loans, and usually emerge from recommendations on spending priorities made in Public Investment/Expenditure Reviews (PI/ERs). The main purpose of PI/ERs is to provide recommendations to governments on the size and composition of their spending programmes and on ways to strengthen local institutions in ways that enhance country capabilities to design and implement such programmes. They have also been used to carry out basic sector work and to identify projects appropriate for World Bank support. PI/ERs facilitate expenditure decisions by the core planning and finance agencies, which are central to the key objectives of structural adjustment, poverty alleviation and sound management of natural resources.

Public investment programmes often do not give adequate weight to environmental objectives as compared with efficiency and poverty alleviation. The potential exists for investment reviews to elevate environmental concerns appropriately and thereby help to avoid making investments that have some of the serious long-term environmental consequences. While the expenditure reviews are perhaps less crucial, these could be used to ensure, for example, that environmental agencies and their programmes receive a fair share of current government expenditures.

3.7.4 Sectoral policies

While adjustment is inherently a macroeconomic effort, involving macroeconomic policy reform, it also requires specific sectoral reforms (Munasinghe and Cruz, 1994). The key macroeconomic variables in adjustment programmes are the investment–savings gap, the fiscal deficit, the trade deficit, the exchange rate and the rate of inflation. The microeconomic or sectoral reforms relevant to adjustment include industrial promotion and investment incentives, tax incidence, import liberalization and trade and energy pricing. These are undertaken to improve resource allocation, but they also have important implications for macroeconomic *stability* and *growth* (Fischer and Thomas, 1990). The first is primarily a microeconomic goal, while the second is an adjustment goal.

For example, taxation and government expenditures are the prime microeconomic mechanisms for resource allocation. However, they also comprise the basic elements of fiscal policy. In turn, fiscal policy has a critical macroeconomic impact because it directly determines the fiscal deficit, and therefore affects the current account deficit and, after a lag, investment levels. Tax reform issues are particularly relevant from an environmental management perspective because they can have a wide range of potential impacts on resource use. The choice of the tax or tariff base can lead to substantial changes in the level of pollution-related activities. However, such environmental implications are not considered in conventional assessments that focus on fiscal effectiveness. Other sectoral reforms, such as those dealing with energy pricing and industrial exports, also affect macroeconomic stability, and have thus played a regular role in adjustment programmes (World Bank, 1989).

Beyond their role in contributing to a stable macroeconomic environment, sectoral policies also have economy-wide relevance in terms of promoting growth from the supply side. These include sectoral investment and pricing policies, as well as sectoral regulation and institutional development. As noted by Fischer and Thomas (1990), the traditional approach to development was through investment in agriculture, industry, infrastructure and human resources. However, the contribution of these sectoral investments also depended largely on macroeconomic policies and the presence of enabling institutions. Some countries subsidize urban consumers by placing price ceilings on food. In such cases, the environmental consequences will be the same as for currency overvaluation, as both result in lowered incentives to increase production of internationally tradable crops.

In the case of Brazil, Binswanger (1989) showed that general tax policies, special tax incentives, the rules of land allocation and the agricultural credit system all accelerate deforestation in the Amazon. These policies also increase landholding size and reduce the land available to the poor. Mahar (1989) traced many problems in the Amazon in Brazil to the decision in the mid 1960s to provide overland access to Amazonia. Further examples of sectoral work that address issues of environmental concern through economy-wide policy reform are given in Chapter 7, Munasinghe (1997) and Munasinghe and Cruz (1994).

3.7.5 *National income accounts and macroeconomic performance*

In order to recognize accurately and include environmental concerns in macroeconomic analyses, standard national income accounting techniques must be re-examined. Performance is currently measured by the growth in gross domestic product (GDP), and policy reforms are justified routinely on the basis of their short-, medium- or long-term contribution to such growth. While GDP measures market activity reasonably well, it has been criticized for its neglect of other key aspects, such as non-market value added, income distribution and so on. Further, GDP does not consider depreciation of manmade capital (although the less quoted net domestic product, or NDP, does); it also leaves out the degradation of 'natural capital'. Thus, GDP is an inaccurate measure of true, sustainable income.

In terms of the environment, there are several shortcomings in the widely used traditional system of national accounts framework.

(1) Natural and environmental resources are not fully included in balance sheets; therefore, national accounts represent limited indicators of national well-being, since they are a poor, or even 'perverse', measure of changes in environmental and natural-resource conditions.

(2) Conventional national accounts fail to record the true costs of using natural resources in economic activity. The depletion or degradation of natural capital stocks (water, soil, air, minerals and wilderness areas), which occur due to productive activity, is not included in current costs or depreciation of natural wealth. Thus, resource-based goods are underpriced – the lower the value added, the larger is the extent of underpricing of the final product. Some countries promote primary product exports by subsidizing them, often with disproportionately large adverse impacts on the poor (who are less able to protect themselves) – the small cultivator, the forest dweller, the landless peasant and so on. If such hidden costs or 'subsidies' were estimated, the GDP of many countries could well be significantly lower. In addition, natural-resource depletion raises inter-generational equity issues, since productive assets available to future generations may be unfairly diminished (see Section 3.6.1).

(3) Clean-up or abatement activities (e.g. expenditures incurred to restore environmental assets) often serve to inflate national income, while the offsetting environmental damages are not considered. For private firms, defensive environmental expenditures are netted out of final value added. In contrast, such clean-up costs are considered as productive contributions to national output if they are incurred by the public sector or households. GDP calculations are distorted in two ways, because undesirable outputs (like pollution) are overlooked, while beneficial environment-related activities are often implicitly valued at zero.

Such deficiencies in the accounting techniques employed up to the 1980s pointed to the need for a system of national accounts (SNA), which permits the computation of an environmentally adjusted net domestic product (EDP) and an environmentally adjusted net income (EDI). National-level decision makers and macroeconomic planners (typically in a ministry of finance or planning) routinely rely on the conventional SNA to formulate economic

policies. Thus, a supplementary environmentally adjusted SNA and corresponding performance indicators would encourage policy makers to reassess the macroeconomic situation in
light of environmental concerns and to trace the links between economy-wide policies and
natural-resource management (Munasinghe and Cruz, 1994).

Based on work carried out during the 1980s (Bartelmus, Stahmer and van Tongeren,
1989), the System for Environmentally adjusted Economic Accounts (SEEA) was created as
an interim measure. Its objective was to integrate environmental data sets with existing
national accounts information, while maintaining SNA concepts and principles insofar as
possible. Environmental costs, benefits and natural-resource assets, as well as expenditures
for environmental protection, were presented as satellite accounts in a manner consistent
with the accounting framework of the SNA. The method involved disaggregation of the
conventional SNA to highlight environmental relationships, linked physical and monetary
accounting, imputations of environmental costs and extensions of the SNA production
boundary – without modifying the core accounts.

The SEEA framework received further impetus through the UN interim handbook on
environmental accounting (UN, 1993), which outlined the possibilities for computing
various national accounts aggregates such as 'green GNP' – that are adjusted downward
to reflect the costs of net resource depletion and environmental pollution. Green net national
product is a Hicks–Lindahl measure of *potentially* sustainable income (Hicks, 1946).
However, it cannot indicate whether the saving rate can maintain this income indefinitely,
and typically does not measure potential consumption if the economy were actually on a
constant-utility path. 'Genuine savings' is a better measure of macrosustainability (Atkinson
et al., 1997). Further work is outlined in Section 7.1.5.

Following this, an operational handbook was published (UN, 2000b), and finally the
Integrated Environmental and Economic Accounting Handbook was issued in 2003 (UN,
2003). The revisions provide methods to estimate environmental and natural-resource-
related expenditures, which were not effectively captured in conventional SNA. Features
include: (1) natural-resource asset accounts, which include natural-resource stock depletion
and improve the balance sheets of the conventional SNA; (2) pollutant and material flow
accounts, which report the use of energy and materials, and the generation of pollutants and
wastes in the production process and the final demand: these accounts are linked to the
supply and use tables of the IO table described in SNA; (3) environmental protection and
resource management expenditures are shown more explicitly, and this data may be used for
policy analysis and other research on sustainable development; and (4) better macroeconomic aggregates, such as environmentally adjusted net domestic product, have been
developed.

Natural-resource accounts have a balance sheet flavour, with their emphasis on opening
and closing stocks in quantity and values of natural resources, including both commercial
natural resources and non-commercial or environmental resources. Thus, resource accounts
underlie the expanded national balance sheet accounts in the revised SNA. The principal
policy and analytical uses of these accounts include: measuring physical scarcity, resource
management, assessing the balance sheet of the resource sectors, productivity measurement,

portfolio analysis and management, valuing depletion and identifying effects of environmental degradation. Natural-resource accounts, and their counterparts in the national balance sheet accounts, can therefore have wide use with regard to resource-management policies and broader environmental policies.

Several countries have explored various environmental adjustments to the SNA (World Bank, 2006). Various measures of national product and wealth are under consideration, including natural resource (stock) accounts, resource and pollutant flow accounts, environmental expenditure accounts, and alternative national accounts aggregates (Atkinson *et al.*, 1997). However, no countries have formally altered their SNA to reflect the environmental concerns in the 2003 revision to the SNA (UN, 2003), although pilot studies have been done.

The simple measure introduced in Section 2.3.5 to indicate the sustainability of natural-resource stocks may be extended to cover total wealth per capita. The latter would be a useful indicator of sustainability, if the SNA aimed to measure total national wealth (including the value of stocks of manufactured capital, as well as living and non-living resources). For total wealth W and population P, development is (weakly) sustainable when

$$S = [\mathrm{d}(W/P)/\mathrm{d}t]/[W/P]0.$$

This index has several desirable properties – e.g. separately accounting for changes in natural assets having low substitution possibilities.

Evolution of practical applications

The World Bank, together with the UN Statistical Office (UNSO), completed early case studies in Mexico (van Tongeren *et al.*, 1991) and Papua New Guinea (Bartelmus, Stahmer and van Tongeren, 1991) to determine how such accounts can be prepared. The Papua New Guinea study demonstrates the feasibility of applying the SEEA framework in a country with relatively weak institutional capacities and limited data availability (a scenario that would exist in many resource-rich developing countries). Depreciation of produced assets was calculated to be 9–11% of GDP, resulting in a conventional NDP of between 89 and 91% of GDP. Environmental impacts were assessed for the agriculture, forestry, mining and energy sectors.

The authors estimated that these impacts were about 2% of NDP on average, for the 1986–1990 time period. First, the environmentally adjusted net domestic product 1 (EDP1) was calculated, which incorporates the 'economic' depletion costs of natural-resource use (but does not account for the degradation of environmental quality and corresponding losses of non-marketed environmental services that is reflected in EDP2). Next, EDP2 was estimated after subtracting the costs of degradation of environmental quality from EDP1; EDP2 was estimated to range from 90 to 97% of NDP. The final results showed that consumption exceeded net environmentally adjusted domestic production in most years. However, lack of physical data made it extremely difficult to obtain accurate estimates. Significant fluctuations in commodity prices also reflect the difficulties for governments in attempting to maintain sustainable development policies.

Additionally, contrary to findings, Papua New Guinea is not necessarily depleting its capital base, as the capital gain from erosion of external debt (caused by inflation reducing the value of the debt) is about 4% of GNP in real terms. The substitutability of capital is therefore an issue to be considered in the definition of 'income'. In addition to these World Bank-supported studies, a few examples exist of the application of environmental accounting in developing countries (and even less in the developed world). The UN Economic Commission for Latin America and the Environment (ECLAC) and UNEP performed two case studies in Latin America that apply environmental accounting methodologies to limited areas within countries (CIDIE, 1992). The Argentina study valued a forest ecosystem by estimating the costs of improving productive functions and of maintaining ecosystem functions. Results gained were employed in modelling alternative management and exploitation scenarios. The Mexico study calculated adjustments to the gross product, due to a biological corridor, using market valuation of replacement cost in the agricultural and forestry sectors, and constructed physical balance sheets for individual resources. The Hicksian concept of income was utilized to provide a revised measure of the region's income.

Gilbert (CIDIE, 1992) did a study of Botswana using an environmental accounting framework within a larger modelling and information system. The approach used stock accounts (describing natural-resource stocks in physical units); resource user accounts (describing stocks in physical and monetary units); and socioeconomic accounts (focusing on resource use, demographics and environmental policy). However, full implementation of the framework has not been possible because of severe data constraints.

An early application of environmental accounting in a developing country was performed by Repetto *et al.* (1989) for the World Resources Institute. The study collected data on petroleum, timber and soil resources. The approach used is based upon physical stock and flow accounts of natural resources and the valuation of these stocks. It has been suggested that the valuation method used in forestry overestimates the true resource depreciation, but has nevertheless proved extremely useful as an indicator of the magnitudes involved in adjustments to GDP through environmental accounting (CIDIE, 1992). A later study (WRI, 1991) utilized the same valuation methodology for forestry, but focused on providing detailed methods for the technical estimates of deforestation, soil erosion and coastal fishery overexploitation in Costa Rica.

Recent work suggests that Bolivia may be on an unsustainable development path (World Bank, 2006). When depletion of natural resources is included, the genuine national savings rate became minus 3.8% of gross national income (GNI) in 2003, although the traditionally computed national savings rate was 12% of GNI. In this estimate, depletion of energy, metals and minerals was 9% of GNI and pollution damage was almost 7%, while the net forest depletion was zero.

Some researchers have computed more composite indices of human welfare to show that the relationship between 'true' welfare and conventional income per capita is positive in the early development stage but becomes negative later – in contrast to the EKC effect (Daly and Cobb, 1989; Max-Neef, 1995). One such measure, called the index of sustainable economic welfare (ISEW), has already peaked in the 1970s or 1980s and is now declining for the USA, the UK, Germany, Austria and Netherlands. Poverty alleviation remains a dominant social objective (Sen, 1984). Lawn (2005) examines the valuation methods used to calculate the ISEW, the Genuine Progress Indicator and the Sustainable Net Benefit Index. He argues that a consistent and more robust set of valuation techniques is required in order for these alternative indexes to gain broad acceptability as a means of comparing the costs and benefits of growth. Recent work seeks to expand the social accounting matrix (SAM) to include the distributional impacts of environmental damage across income groups (Munasinghe, 2002a).

3.8 Appendix: Estimating and using shadow prices

3.8.1 Numeraire

To derive a consistent set of economic shadow prices for goods and services, a common yardstick or numeraire to measure value is necessary. The same nominal unit of currency may have a different value depending on the economic circumstances in which it is used. For example, 1 rupee-worth of chocolate purchased in a duty free shop is likely to be more than the quantity of chocolate obtained for 1 rupee from a retail store (after import duties and taxes have been levied). Therefore, it is possible to distinguish intuitively between the border-priced rupee, which is used in international markets free of import tariffs, and a domestic-priced rupee, which is used in the domestic market subject to various distortions.

The choice of the numeraire, like the choice of a currency unit, should not change the outcome of an economic decision – provided the same consistent framework and assumptions are used in the analysis. For example, only one difference exists between a cost–benefit study that uses 'cents' as units and another that uses 'rupees' (1 rupee is equal to 100 cents). In the analysis using cents, all quantities will be numerically 100 times larger than in the one using rupees. Since the analytical results will not be changed by this linear scale factor, one may choose the numeraire according to convenience.

A most appropriate numeraire in many instances is a unit of uncommitted public income at border shadow prices (Little and Mirrlees, 1974). This unit is the same as freely disposable foreign exchange available to the government, but expressed in terms of units of local currency converted at the official exchange rate (OER). The border-priced numeraire is particularly relevant for the foreign exchange-scarce developing countries. It represents the set of opportunities available to a country to purchase goods and services on the international market.

3.8.2 Economic efficiency shadow prices

The estimation and use of efficiency shadow prices is facilitated by dividing economic resources into tradable and non-tradable items. Tradables are directly imported or exported goods and services, and their values are already known in border prices – i.e. foreign exchange costs converted at the OER. Non-tradables are local goods whose values are known only in terms of domestic market prices, which must be converted to border prices by applying conversion factors (CFs). Hence, border (shadow) price = conversion factor × domestic (market) price,

$$BP = CF \times DP.$$

For tradables with infinite elasticities (of world supply for imports and world demand for exports), the cost, insurance and freight (CIF) border price for imports and the free-on-board (FOB) border price for exports may be used (with a suitable adjustment for the marketing margin). If the relevant elasticities are finite, then the change in import or export costs, as well as any shifts in other domestic consumption or production levels or in income transfers, should be considered. The free trade assumption is not required to justify the use of border prices since domestic price distortions are adjusted by netting out all taxes, duties and subsidies.

To clarify this point, consider a household where a child is given an allowance of 20 pesos a month as pocket money. The youngster may purchase a bag of sweets from a store at a price of 2 pesos. If the parents want to discourage consumption of sweets, they may impose a fine of 1 peso on each bag. The fine is exactly like an import duty, and the child must surrender 3 pesos for every bag of candy (valued at its domestic price, inside the household). From the family's perspective, the total external payment for the item is only 2 pesos, because the 1 peso fine is a net transfer within the household. Therefore, the true economic cost (or shadow price) of the bag of lollipops to the household is 2 pesos (i.e. its border price), when the impact of the fine on the distribution of the income between parent and child is ignored.

A non-tradable is conventionally defined as a commodity whose domestic supply price lies between the FOB export price and CIF import price. Items that are not traded at the margin because of prohibitive trade barriers, such as bans or rigid quotas, are also included within this category. If the increased demand for a given non-tradable good or service is met by the expansion of domestic supply or imports, the associated border-priced marginal social cost (MSC) of this increased supply is the relevant resource cost. If decreased consumption of other domestic or foreign users results, the border-priced marginal social benefit (MSB) of this foregone domestic consumption, or of reduced export earnings, would be a more appropriate measure of social costs.

The socially optimal level of total consumption for the given input (Q_{opt}) lies at the point where the curves of MSC and MSB intersect. Price and non-price distortions lead to non-optimal levels of consumption, $Q \neq Q_{opt}$, where MSB $\neq$ MSC. More generally, if both effects are present, a weighted average of MSC and MSB should be used. The MSB is more important in a short-run, supply-constrained situation, while the MSC dominates in the longer run, when expansion of output is possible.

The MSC of non-tradable goods and services from many sectors can be determined through appropriate decomposition. For example, suppose 1 peso-worth of the output of the construction sector (valued in domestic prices) may be broken down successively into components – such as capital, labour, materials, etc., which are valued at pesos $C_1, C_2,\ldots, C_n$ in border prices. Then the construction conversion factor (CCF, defined as the ratio of the border price to the domestic price) is given by

$$\text{CCF} = \sum_{i=1}^{n} C_i.$$

The standard conversion factor (SCF) may be used with non-tradables that are not important enough to merit individual attention, or lack sufficient data. The SCF is equal to the OER divided by the more familiar shadow exchange rate (SER), appropriately defined. Using the SCF to convert domestic-priced values into border-price equivalents is conceptually the inverse of the traditional practice of multiplying foreign currency costs by the SER (instead of the OER) to convert foreign exchange to the domestic-price equivalent. The SCF is approximated by the ratio of the official exchange rate to the free trade exchange rate (FTER), when the country is moving toward a freer trade regime:

$$\text{SCF} = \frac{\text{OER}}{\text{FTER}} = \frac{eX + nM}{eX(1 - t_x) + nM(1 + t_m)},$$

where X = FOB value of exports, M = CIF value of imports, e = elasticity of domestic supply of exports, n = elasticity of domestic demand for imports, t_x = average tax rate on exports (negative for subsidy) and t_m = average tax rate on imports.

The foregone output of workers is the dominant component of the shadow wage rate (SWR). Consider unskilled labour in a labour surplus country, e.g. rural workers employed in an urban factory. Complications arise in estimating the opportunity cost of labour, because the original rural income earned may not reflect the marginal product of agricultural labour. Furthermore, for every new urban job created, more than one rural worker may give up former employment. Adjustments are also needed for seasonal activities, such as harvesting, and overhead costs, such as transport expenses. Then, the efficiency shadow wage rate (ESWR) is given by

$$\text{ESWR} = a \cdot m + c \cdot u,$$

where m and u are the foregone marginal output and overhead costs of labour in domestic prices, respectively, and a and c are corresponding conversion factors to convert these values into border prices.

The appropriate shadow value placed on land depends on its location. Usually, the market price of urban land is a good indicator of its economic value in domestic prices, and the application of an appropriate conversion factor (such as the SCF) to this domestic price will yield the border-priced cost of urban land inputs. Rural land that can be used in agriculture may be valued at its opportunity costs – the net benefit of foregone agricultural output. The marginal social cost of other rural land depends on potential uses such as recreation (see Section 3.4).

The shadow price of a capital is usually reflected in the discount rate or accounting rate of interest (ARI), which is defined as the rate of decline in the value of the numeraire over time (see Sections 3.2 and 3.6). In terms of pure efficiency, one practical proxy for the ARI is the opportunity cost of capital (OCC) – defined as the expected value of the annual stream of consumption, in border prices net of replacement, which is yielded by the investment of one unit of public income at the margin.

3.8.3 Adjustments for social (and environmental) shadow prices

If social pricing is important, it is necessary to include the effect of changes on consumption patterns. Starting with the efficiency shadow wage rate (ESWR), suppose a worker receives a wage W_n in a new job and that the income forgone is W_o (both in domestic prices). We note that W_n may not necessarily be equal to the marginal product foregone m. It could be assumed, quite plausibly, that low-income workers consume the entire increase in income $(W_n - W_o)$. Then this increase in consumption will result in a resource cost to the economy of $b(W_n - W_o)$. The increased consumption also provides a benefit given by $w(W_n - W_o)$, where w represents the MSB, in border prices, of increasing domestic-priced private sector consumption by one unit.

Thus, we may estimate the following social shadow wage rate (adjusted for consumption effects):

$$\text{SSWR} = a \cdot m + c \cdot u + (b - w)(W_n - W_o).$$

Here b represents the MSC of increased consumption. If all new income is consumed, then b is the consumption conversion factor or resource cost (in units of the numeraire) of supplying consumers with one unit worth (in domestic prices) of the marginal basket of goods they would purchase:

$$b = \sum_{i=1}^{n} g_i \cdot \text{CF}_i,$$

where, g_i is the proportion or share of the ith good in the marginal consumption basket and CF_i is the corresponding conversion factor.

The corresponding MSB of increased consumption is given by: $w = d/v$. Here, $1/v$ is the value (in units of the numeraire) of a one-unit increase in domestic-priced consumption accruing to someone at the average level of consumption (c_a). Therefore, v may be roughly thought of as the premium attached to public savings, compared to 'average' private consumption. Under certain simplifying assumptions, $b = 1/v$.

Note that d is a form of 'social weighting' that favours the poor. If $\text{MU}(c)$ denotes the marginal utility of consumption at some level c, then $d = \text{MU}(c) / \text{MU}(c_a)$. Assuming that the marginal utility of consumption is diminishing, d would be greater than unity for 'poor' consumers who are below the average level of income (i.e. $c < c_a$), and vice versa.

A simple form of marginal utility function could be as follows: $\text{MU}(c) = c^{-n}$. Thus, $d = \text{MU}(c)/\text{MU}(c_a) = n(c_a/c)$. Making the further assumption that the distribution parameter $n = 1$ yields

$$d = c_a/c = i_a/i,$$

where i_a/i is the ratio of net incomes, which may be used as a proxy for the corresponding consumption ratio. In this simple case, the social weight d is equal to the income ratio.

The consumption term $(b-w)$ in the expression for SSWR disappears if, at the margin, (a) society is indifferent to the distribution of income (or consumption), so that everyone's consumption has equivalent value $(d=1)$ and (b) private consumption is considered to be as socially valuable as uncommitted public savings $(b=1/v)$.

A simple formula for the Social ARI or social shadow price of capital, which also includes consumption effects, is given by

$$\text{SARI} = \text{OCC}[s + (1 - s)w/b],$$

where s is the fraction of the yield from the original investment that will be saved and reinvested.

Adjustments for environmental shadow prices are based on environmental externalities (see Section 3.4). Since the rigorous estimation of shadow prices is a long and complex task, it is advisable to use whatever shadow prices have already been calculated. Alternatively, one might estimate a few important items, such as the standard conversion factor, opportunity cost of capital and shadow wage rate. When the data are not precise enough, sensitivity studies may be made over a range of values of such key national parameters.

4

Ecological and social aspects[1]

This chapter provides an in-depth discussion of the linkages between the environmental and socioeconomic domains of sustainable development, institutional settings and environmental and social assessments. Some ideas underlying the sustainability of ecological and social systems were discussed earlier in Chapter 2. The basic role of ecosystems in supporting human society and economic activities, and methods of assessing this contribution (including monetary valuation), were explained in Chapter 3. These ideas are extended in Section 4.1, which summarizes the comprehensive conceptual framework based on the Millennium Ecosystem Assessment (MA), including the cyclic interactions between ecological and socioeconomic systems, and the main ecosystem services which sustain human well-being. The MA highlights the precarious situation of many critical ecosystems. The idea of 'panarchy' of living systems, and dynamic ecological cycles involving birth, growth, adaptation, decay, death and regeneration, help us understand ecosystem behaviour. Section 4.2 describes the key mediating role played by property rights regimes in determining how societies exploit natural resources. Property rights regimes play an important role in designing and implementing sustainable environmental management measures. Their effectiveness largely depends on the congruency of well specified property rights regimes with ecological and social factors, especially in the case of traditional societies and native peoples who are heavily dependent on ecological resources, as well as the landless poor who subsist in degraded areas. Finally, in Section 4.3, environmental and social assessments are described as important elements of sustainable development assessment, which complement cost–benefit analysis (or economic assessment).

4.1 Conceptual framework linking ecological and socioeconomic systems

The Millennium Ecosystem Assessment (MA) was launched by United Nations Secretary-General Kofi Annan in 2000 (UN, 2000a). Conducted during 2001–2005, the goal of the MA was to assess the impacts of ecosystem change on human well-being and then identify

---

[1] The valuable contributions of S. Hanna, W. Reid and W. Shearer to this chapter are gratefully acknowledged. Some parts of the chapter are based on material adapted from Hanna and Munasinghe (1995c), Munasinghe (1992c), Munasinghe and Reid (2005) and Munasinghe and Shearer (1995).

the actions needed to enhance the conservation and sustainable use of those systems and their contribution to human well-being. Briefly, an ecosystem is a 'dynamic complex of plant, animal and micro-organism communities and their non-living environment interacting as a functional unit' (CBD, 1992).

The MA results provide valuable inputs to the work of four international environmental treaties – the UN Convention on Biological Diversity, the Ramsar Convention on Wetlands, the UN Convention to Combat Desertification and the Convention on Migratory Species. The work was supported by 22 of the world's leading scientific bodies and involved more than 1360 experts from 95 countries. Their findings on the condition and trends of ecosystems, scenarios for the future, possible responses and assessments at a sub-global level are set out in technical reports (MA, 2005c, d, e, f). Several synthesis reports draw on these detailed studies to answer questions posed by specific groups of users.

4.1.1 *Ecosystem services and human well-being*

Figure 4.1 summarizes the complex, circular and dynamic relationship between the ecological and socioeconomic (development) domains. The large horizontal arrows at the top and bottom indicate the cyclic relationship. Starting from the top, ecosystem services have social, economic and environmental impacts, from which alternative future development paths will emerge, with different consequences for human well-being. The alternative development scenarios affect indirect drivers of change, which in turn influence direct drivers of change (two downward arrows). The two upward vertical arrows also indicate key feedback effects between both indirect and direct drivers and human well-being. Finally, the direct drivers have important impacts on ecosystems and their services.

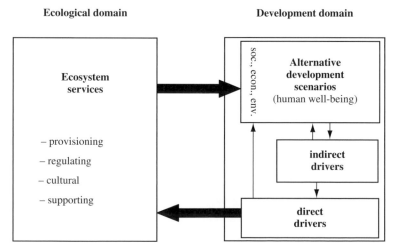

Figure 4.1. Circular interaction between ecological and development (socioeconomic) domains.

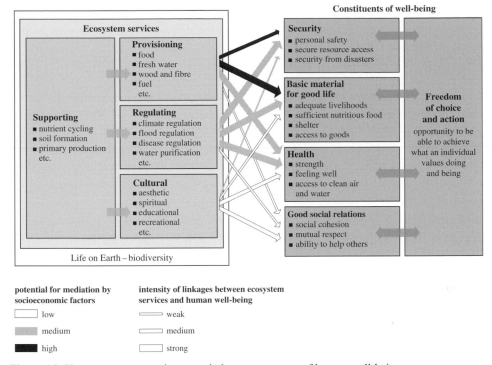

Figure 4.2. How ecosystem services sustain key components of human well-being.

Indirect drivers include the following major components: demographic; economic (globalization, trade, market and policy framework); sociopolitical (governance and institutional framework); science and technology; cultural and religious.

Direct drivers include the following main elements: changes in land use; species introduction or removal; technology adaptation and use; external inputs (e.g. irrigation); resource consumption; climate change; bio-geophysical drivers (e.g. volcanoes).

Figure 4.2 further elaborates the basic linkages in Figure 4.1, by providing an overview of the key ways in which ecosystems and their services support and affect human well-being (see also Chapter 3 and MA (2005c)).

Overall supporting services

The left-hand side of Figure 4.2 shows that all other ecosystem functions (provisioning, regulation and cultural) ultimately depend on a set of broad supporting services, which include soil formation, nutrient cycling, primary production, etc.

Provisioning services

Ecosystems provide products to support human activities and consumption, including food, fresh water, fuelwood, fibre, biochemicals and genetic resources.

Regulating services

Ecosystems regulate natural processes and purify natural resources, affecting areas such as climate, disease and water.

Cultural services

Ecosystems yield non-material benefits, including spiritual and religious support, recreation and ecotourism, aesthetic pleasure, inspiration, education, sense of place and cultural heritage.

We note that provisioning, regulating and cultural ecosystem services correspond roughly to the respective categories of economic value – direct-use value, indirect-use value and non-use value, defined in Chapter 3.

The right-hand side of Figure 4.2 summarizes the elements of human well-being which are supported by ecosystem services, with the width and shading of each arrow indicating the intensity of the linkage and the potential for human mediation, respectively. The expansion of freedoms and options intrinsic to the sustainable development process (Chapter 2) is associated with the following constituents of human well-being: security; basic material needs; health; good social relations.

In Section 4.2, this underlying conceptual framework is used to study how property rights regimes embedded in the fabric of human communities influence the way in which environmental resources are used.

4.1.2 Main findings of the Millennium Ecosystem Assessment

Based on the foregoing framework, the MA arrived at a number of key conclusions (MA, 2005a, 2005b).

Major issues

All human beings depend on nature and ecosystem services for their well-being (Figure 4.3). We have made unprecedented changes to ecosystems in recent decades to meet growing demands for food, fresh water, fibre and energy, and to improve the lives of billions. These changes have weakened nature's ability to deliver other key services, such as purification of air and water, protection from disasters and the provision of medicines.

About 60% of the ecosystem services that support life on Earth (e.g. fresh water, capture fisheries, air and water regulation and the regulation of regional climate, natural hazards and pests), are being degraded or used unsustainably. Specific problems include: the dire state of many of the world's fish stocks; great vulnerability of two billion people living in dry regions to the loss of ecosystem services (especially lack of water resources); growing pressure on ecosystems from climate change and nutrient pollution. The loss of services derived from ecosystems is a significant barrier to the achievement of the Millennium Development Goals (MDGs), especially the reduction of poverty, hunger and disease.

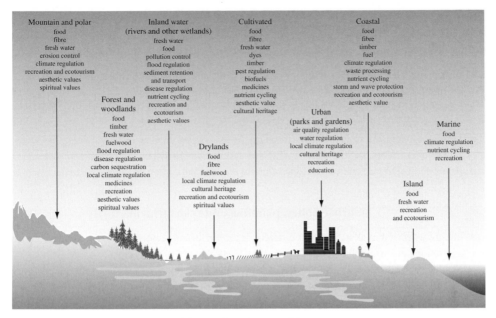

Figure 4.3. Ecosystems and some of the services they provide.

A further threat to our well-being has arisen from human activities that have taken the planet to the edge of a massive new wave of species extinctions. Fossil records indicate that the historical extinction rate was less than one species per 1000 every 1000 years. In recent years, this extinction rate has increased between 100- and 1000-fold. Projected future extinction rates are likely to be ten times higher.

The degradation of ecosystems will increase globally in coming decades, unless human attitudes and actions change. The current status and continuing decline of 15 of the 24 ecosystem services examined in the MA has increased the likelihood of abrupt changes that will seriously affect human well-being. Such changes include the emergence of new diseases, sudden loss of water quality, creation of 'dead zones' along the coasts, the collapse of fisheries and shifts in regional climate. Only provisioning services such as crops, livestock and aquaculture show gains.

Policy options and remedies

Some important steps to protect and manage ecosystem services more sustainably are summarized in Box 4.1. Measures to conserve natural resources will be more successful if local communities are empowered by giving them ownership of these resources, a fair share of the benefits and a greater role in decision making. Even the technology and knowledge available today could considerably reduce human impacts on ecosystems. However, such measures are unlikely to be deployed fully until the full value of ecosystem services is taken into account.

Box 4.1 Measures taken to manage ecosystem services more sustainably

Change the economic background to decision making

- Ensure the value of all ecosystem services, not just those bought and sold in the market, are taken into account when making decisions.
- Remove subsidies to agriculture, fisheries and energy that cause harm to people and the environment.
- Introduce payments to landowners in return for managing their lands in ways that protect ecosystem services, such as water quality and carbon storage, which are of value to society.
- Establish market mechanisms to reduce nutrient releases and carbon emissions cost-effectively.

Improve policy, planning and management

- Integrate decision making between different departments and sectors, as well as international institutions, to ensure that policies are focused on protection of ecosystems.
- Include sound management of ecosystem services in all regional planning decisions and in the poverty-reduction strategies being prepared by many developing countries.
- Empower marginalized groups to influence decisions affecting ecosystem services, and recognize in law the local communities' ownership over natural resources.
- Establish additional protected areas, particularly in marine systems, and provide greater financial and management support to those that already exist.
- Use all relevant forms of knowledge and information about ecosystems in decision making, including the knowledge of local and indigenous groups.

Influence individual behaviour

- Provide public education on why and how to reduce consumption of threatened ecosystem services.
- Establish reliable certification systems to give people the choice to buy sustainably harvested products.
- Give people access to information about ecosystems and decisions affecting their services.

Develop and use environment-friendly technology

- Invest in agricultural science and technology aimed at increasing food production with minimal harmful trade-offs.
- Restore degraded ecosystems.
- Promote technologies to increase energy efficiency and reduce greenhouse gas emissions.

Source: Taken from MA (2005f).

Better protection of natural assets will require coordinated efforts across governments, businesses, civil society and international institutions. The state of ecosystems will depend, *inter alia*, on critical policy choices concerning investment, trade, subsidies, taxation and regulation.

4.1.3 Dynamics of interlinked living systems

Chapters 2 and 3 indicated that socioeconomic and ecological systems are closely linked and have co-evolved dynamically within a larger complex adaptive system over a long span of time. In this section, we briefly summarize the dynamics of such a 'panarchy' of systems, using the cycle of growth, adaptation, transformation, collapse and regeneration described by Gunderson and Holling (2001).

Box 2.2 introduced panarchy as a nested hierarchy of living systems and their adaptive cycles across scales. Figure 4.4 shows how a system at a given level is able to operate in its stable (sustainable) mode, because it is protected by the slower and more conservative changes in the super-system to which it belongs. At the same time, the system will be invigorated and energized by the faster cycles taking place in the many sub-systems within it. In brief, both conservation and continuity from above, and innovation and change from below, are integral to the panarchy-based approach, helping to maintain the dynamic balance between the twin requirements for stability and for change.

The dynamic path of a given system (ranging in scale from a cell to a biome) is shown in Figure 4.5. The cycle shows four phases: (1) entrepreneurial exploitation (r); (2) conservation and organizational consolidation (K); (3) release and creative destruction (Ω); and (4) reorganization and destructuring (α). Each phase is characterized by different degrees of potential (ability to develop and grow) and connectedness (internal linkages and structure). Using the example of the centuries-long evolution of a forest, the first part of the cycle shows exploitation of novelty to grow and evolve from pioneer species (r) to climax species (K). Accumulation of biomass and wealth results in reduced resilience and increased vulnerability, raising the risk of destruction due to major disturbances such as fire, storm or pest (Ω). This is followed by the release of accumulated nutrients and biomass, which may be reorganized into the start of a new cycle (α). Each phase of the cycle creates the conditions for the next phase.

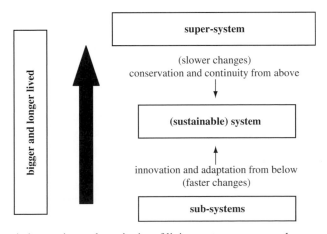

Figure 4.4. Dynamic interaction and continuity of living systems across scales.

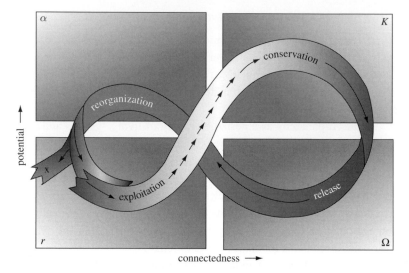

Figure 4.5. Cycle of growth and reorganisation for living systems.

The slower and steadier 'forward loop' consists of the first two 'growth' phases, while the less predictable 'backward loop' includes the second two 'reorganization' phases.

Resilience is a key concept, which indicates the ability of a system to continue functioning within normal limits when externally perturbed and maintain the component elements needed to renew or reorganize if a large shock significantly changes system structure and function (Walker *et al.*, 2002). The more resilient the system, the more sustainable it is.

If a third axis of resilience is included in the analysis, the figure-eight shape in Figure 4.5 becomes the twisted but non-intersecting loop shown in Figure 4.6. Each system is still a part of the panarchy shown earlier in Figure 4.4. Thus the exploitation phase (r) of a smaller system could trigger change or revolt in the larger system to which it belongs, while the consolidation phase (K) of a larger system will stabilize and facilitate reorganization of a subordinate system.

Holling (2004) argues that the concept of panarchy could be extended also to study how social systems grow, adapt, transform and collapse. The backward loop (usually involving abrupt change) is a critical time when opportunities arise for experimentation and learning – systems face risk and their resilience is tested and established. As we consider the long-term co-evolution of socioeconomic and ecological systems, it would be useful to determine if we are entering into a phase of higher risk, during such a backward loop, by assessing the changes brought about by the challenges described in Chapter 1.

4.2 Property rights, governance and ecological–social linkages

Next, we examine the institutional dimensions of environmental–social sustainability. Humans interact with their environment through systems of property rights and governance

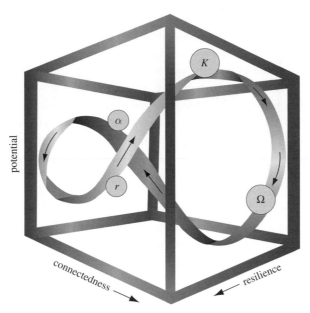

Figure 4.6. Adding the third dimension of resilience unravels the twist in the two-dimensional figure-eight shape of Figure 4.5.

(that are embedded in social, political, cultural and economic context), and thereby affect both the quantity and quality of environmental resources. While national and international economic policies have often ignored the environment, institutions could play a key role in reconciling economic development and the maintainance of environmental-carrying capacity and resilience (Arrow *et al.*, 1995a; Grima *et al.*, 2003). *Ecology and Society* (2006) and *Environment and Development Economics* (2006) describe recent research on resilience in social–ecological systems. Folke and Gunderson (2006) identify several papers that explain how better ecological–social research can help to address global environmental issues. We explain in the following how the functioning of property rights regimes, in relation to human use of the environment, is critical to the design and implementation of sustainable environmental management measures (Hanna and Munasinghe, 1995c).

4.2.1 Sustainability, sustainable development and property rights regimes

Property rights regimes consist of *property rights*, bundles of entitlements defining rights and duties in the use of natural resources, and *property rules*, the rules under which those rights and duties are exercised (Bromley, 1991). Property rights regimes influence the use of environmental resources, a fact that has long been well established, if not well practiced. Anderson (1983) wrote of the dangers of fisheries overexploitation without ownership, an argument already noted by Gordon (1954). In 'The tragedy of the commons', Garrett Hardin (1968) focused widespread attention on the problem of environmental degradation in the absence of rules governing use. For many years, the general interpretation of Hardin's argument was that collectively owned property was the culprit, and that private property was necessary to sustain environmental resources. However, a rapidly expanding body of scientific evidence indicates that sustaining environmental resources is not dependent on a particular structure or type of property regime, but rather on a well specified property rights regime and a congruency of that regime with ecological and social factors.

In this ecological and social context, sustainability is a difficult concept to interpret because it has a wide range of meanings based on different disciplines and world views. What is being sustained, how it is to be sustained, and for how long, are all open to interpretation. Regardless of the specific meaning used, it is clear that, to some extent, sustainability is a human construct. Humans use their environment for a range of objectives (see Section 4.1.1), which leads to different expectations as to what is to be sustained and who is to have claims on environmental services. Cochrane (2006) argues that social (cultural) capital determines the sustainability of environmental capital by influencing management objectives, efficiency of use and demand relating to natural-resource use (see Chapter 2).

The question of sustainability is a complicated one, the answer to which involves more than the generic application of a property rights regime. Property rights regimes need to reflect both general principles and specific social and ecological contexts, in order to be effective in modulating the interaction between humans and their environment. General principles include the structural and functional attributes of property rights regimes that transcend a particular context (Hanna, Folke and Maler, 1996). General principles are the necessary conditions for effective property rights regimes, because a property rights regime cannot succeed over the long run without them. They include several key elements, such as congruence of ecosystem and governance boundaries; specification and representation of interests; matching of governance structure to ecosystem characteristics; containment of transaction costs; monitoring, enforcement and adaptation processes at the appropriate scale (Bromley, 1991; Eggertsson, 1990; Hanna, 1992; Ostrom, 1990).

General principles are necessary, but not sufficient in themselves, for effective property rights regimes. In addition, specific attributes of social and ecological context must be represented. Social contexts contain all the dimensions of the human relationship to environmental resources, including social arrangements, cultural practices, economic uses and political constraints. Ecological contexts contain the structure of ecosystems in which humans live and work, as well as the particular functional properties of those ecosystems. The particular details of the social and ecological context are what give a human social–environmental interaction its variety and detail. The match between a property rights regime and the contextual characteristics of the affected humans and ecosystems will determine success or failure in terms of sustainability.

Better economic valuation of environmental and sociocultural assets (see Chapter 3), and their internalization in the price system, is one means of ensuring that market forces lead to more sustainable resource use. The more equitable distribution of resources and assets is a step toward poverty reduction and social sustainability, as is greater participation and empowerment of disadvantaged groups. Clearly, property rights regimes that specify access to the natural-resource base and rights of use have a crucial role to play in this context.

The literature addressing questions of property rights and natural-resource use is growing, but there are large gaps in knowledge (Hanna and Munasinghe, 1995c). Five of these areas are explored below.

4.2.2 Governance systems

Questions of governance over environmental resources have to do with the ability to predict and oversee probabilistic ecosystem responses to human behaviour and management, and to external drivers such as climate. Complexity of the human systems and ecosystems affects the ability to extract consistent objectives, design meaningful control systems and monitor response. The scale of the ecosystem in comparison with scales of social organization or legal jurisdiction determines the extent of the match between the human and environmental systems. The delineation and coordination of authority over environmental decisions is critical to relating actions to outcomes. The way in which governance is coordinated between authorities at different levels determines consistency across scales. The success of decentralized governance systems may be improved by applying the principle of subsidiarity, which requires that each decision is made and implemented at the lowest practical and effective level.

Most studies assume that the manager is outside the system being managed (Walker *et al.*, 2002). However, in the context of long-term sustainability, linked socioeconomic and ecological systems (SESs) behave as complex adaptive systems, with the managers as integral components of the system. Ostrom (1995) argues that, since many biological processes occur at small, medium and large scales, governance arrangements that can cope with this level of complexity also need to be organized at multiple scales and linked together effectively. The importance of nested institutional arrangements is emphasized, with quasi-autonomous units operating at very small, up to very large, scales. The concept of distributed governance is analysed by Townsend and Pooley (1995a) using competing models of cooperative management, co-management and rights-based management in the context of fisheries. They pay attention to both internal and external governance issues. Fitzpatrick (2000) also looks at distributed governance in Canada. He emphasizes that there is a need for partnership arrangements, especially between multiple sectors and levels of governance to meet shared objectives. Distributed authority affects governance efficiency, in particular through the role played by user participation in lowering management costs (Hanna, 1995). The contribution of user participation to governance efficiency may be analysed in terms of the structure and function of user participation and its effect on management costs. Kaitala and Munro (1995) address the question of governance coordination over multiple jurisdictions, as exemplified by transboundary fishery resources categorized as highly migratory fish stocks and straddling fish stocks. The high-seas portion of the stocks are exploited by both coastal states and distant-water fishing nations. The difficult issue of managing such resources (characterized by ill defined property rights over the high-seas portion of the resources) is the focus of a major United Nations intergovernmental conference.

Several case studies illustrate the application of the various principles of governance to the environmental challenges of air pollution, fishery management and pesticide use. Tietenberg (1995) examines the question of governance design and scale through an analysis of the use of market-based mechanisms on the transferable permits approach to pollution control problems in the United States. From the various examples described, he extracts lessons for both the implementation process and programme design. Townsend and Pooley (1995b) consider the question of appropriate levels of authority – through a potential application of the distributed governance concept to the lobster fishery of the northwestern Hawaiian Islands. Gren and Brännlund (1995) show that, although geographic differences in environmental impacts may call for region-specific environmental regulations, regional differences in enforcement costs will lead to different levels of cost-effective regulation. Grima, Horma and Kant (2003) discuss the role of institutions at the international, national and community levels (including property rights) in making the forestry sector development more sustainable.

4.2.3 *Equity, stewardship and environmental resilience*

Generally, the degree of equity represented by a property rights regime helps to create the incentive structure which either promotes or inhibits stewardship of environmental resources. In turn, the degree of stewardship practiced affects the level of ecosystem resilience. Exactly how equity affects stewardship, and how specific stewardship practices affect resilience, are still matters of research. Definitions of equity, stewardship practices and environmental resilience reflect a combination of local context, appropriate incentive structures and adaptation to environmental change. The goals of equity and stewardship are commonly considered to be inconsistent with efficiency in environmental management. In a departure from the usual approach, Young and McCay (1995) look at efficiency-driven, market-based property rights systems and evaluate them for their ability to accommodate equity, stewardship and resilience in the design of adaptive and flexible management regimes – after considering a number of different types of property rights systems for a variety of resources. Chichilnisky and Heal (2000) emphasize that the most attractive feature of markets is efficient allocation of resources, requiring minimal intervention once an appropriate legal infrastructure is in place.

Several studies demonstrate the difficulties of crafting equitable schemes that promote better stewardship and resilience for the conservation of natural resources. Gadgil and Rao (1995) examine the incentives for managing biodiversity contained in India's folk traditions of nature conservation. They focus on the efficiency and equity gains possible through re-establishing conservation approaches based on positive incentives to local communities. This attractive option is contrasted with current unsuccessful regulatory methods that are too centralized, sectoral and bureaucratic. Zylicz (1995) analyses the conflict between conservationists and a municipality in northeastern Poland, in which (i) areas of national parks are being claimed by previous landowners who feel they were not reimbursed fairly, (ii) there are private or communal enclaves left within park boundaries and (iii) neighbouring land-owners protest against development constraints due to the park's existence. The fate of nature depends on the ability of conservationists to demonstrate economic benefits from investing in natural capital to prevent degradation.

Parks and Bonifaz (1995) examine the joint use of environmental resources by looking at the inconsistencies of short-term commodity production with long-term environmental sustainability in open-access Ecuadorian mangrove–shrimp systems. They identify incentives to maximize short-term profits through shrimp mariculture, which have led to destruction of larval-shrimp habitats as mangrove ecosystems were converted to shrimp ponds. Gottret and White (2001) describe integrated natural-resource management (INRM) in Latin America. The complexity of INRM interventions requires a more holistic approach to impact assessment, which combines the traditional 'what' and 'where' factors of economic and environmental priorities, with newer 'who' and 'how' aspects of social actors and institutions.

4.2.4 Traditional knowledge

The documentation and use of traditional ecological knowledge is now an internationally accepted practice. At an even deeper level, many 'modern' concepts such as 'Gaia' and 'deep ecology' have basic roots in ancient philosophies – e.g. the contribution of eastern thinking is documented in Daniels (2005), Hall (1989) and Hargrove (1989).

Here we focus on how long-standing systems of environmental-resource management and their use of traditional ecological knowledge are yielding insights into current resource-management problems. Cicin-Sain and Knecht (1995) review data on reconciling systems of traditional knowledge with modern approaches to the management of natural resources. They analyse implementation challenges that both regional- and national-level entities will face as they endeavour to enhance the role of indigenous knowledge and participation.

Ecosystems are complex adaptive systems, and their governance requires flexibility and a capacity to respond to environmental feedback (Berkes, Colding and Folke, 2000; Dietz, Ostrom and Sten, 2003; Levin, 1998). Carpenter and Gunderson (2001) stress the need for continuously testing, learning about and developing knowledge and understanding in order to cope with change and uncertainty in complex adaptive systems. Knowledge acquisition about complex systems seems to require institutional frameworks and social networks nested across scales to be effective (Berkes, Colding and Folke, 2003).

Knowledge of resource and ecosystem dynamics and associated management practices exists among people of communities that, over long periods of time, interact for their benefit and livelihood with ecosystems (Berkes *et al.*, 2000; Fabricius and Koch, 2004). The way such knowledge is being organized and culturally embedded, its relationship to institution-alized, professional science and its role in catalysing new ways of managing environmental resources have all become important subjects (Armitage, 2003; Brown, 2003; Davis and Wagner, 2003; Gadgil *et al.*, 2000; Kellert *et al.*, 2000). It has been suggested that the management and governance of complex adaptive systems may benefit from the combination of different knowledge systems (Johannes, 1998; Ludwig, Mangel and Haddad 2001; McLain and Lee, 1996). Some attempt to import such knowledge into the realm of scientific knowledge (Mackinson and Nottestad, 1998), while others argue that these knowledge systems are culturally evolved and exist as knowledge–practice–beliefs complexes that are not easily separated from their institutional and cultural contexts (Berkes, 1999). There are those who question the role of traditional and local knowledge systems in the current situation of pervasive environmental change and globalized societies (Du Toit, Walker and Campbell 2004; Krupnik and Jolly, 2002), while others argue that there are lessons from such systems for complex systems management, which also need to account for interactions across temporal and spatial scales as well as organizational and institutional levels (Barrett *et al.*, 2001; Pretty and Ward, 2001), and in particular during periods of rapid change, uncertainty and system reorganization (Berkes and Folke, 2002).

The use of traditional and non-technical knowledge by itself, in combination with modern scientific knowledge and in the restoration of previously established property rights, is explored in several case studies. Pálsson (1995) considers the use of practical knowledge obtained by Icelandic fishing skippers in the course of their work, exploring how fishermen's knowledge differs from that of fishery scientists, and how the former could be brought more systematically into the process of resource management for the purpose of ensuring resilience and sustainability. A study of Cree Indians from the Canadian subarctic is presented by Berkes (1995), who analyses the evidence regarding the distinctions of the local indigenous knowledge from Euro-Canadian, science-based wildlife and fishery management knowledge. The understanding of traditional knowledge for resource management has remained elusive, not only for development policy makers, but also for scholars engaged in such research. Traditional knowledge may be used to re-establish claims to former rights (Ruddle, 1995). For the New Zealand Maori, traditional property rights have been recognized by customary law. The codification of existing rights and customary laws within a system of statutory law in various cultural settings is a contemporary process in many nations in the Pacific Basin, which might provide useful precedents for application worldwide.

Long, Tecle and Burnette (2003) reveal that myths, metaphors, social norms and knowledge-transfer between generations of the White Mountain Apache tribe facilitate collective action and understanding of ecosystem dynamics, and provide a cultural foundation for adaptive management and modern ecological restoration. Watson, Alessa and Glaspell (2003) argue that traditional ecological knowledge serves an important function in the long-term relationships between indigenous people and vast ecosystems in the circumpolar north, and that it can contribute to understanding the effects of management decisions and human-use impacts on long-term ecological composition, structure and function. Ghimire, McKey and Thomas (2004) assess variation in knowledge relating to the diversity of medicinal plant species, their distribution, medicinal uses, biological traits, ecology and management within and between two culturally different social groups living in villages in northwestern Nepal. Devkota (2005) describes how traditional knowledge embedded in Nepalese forest communities enhances natural, social and economic systems simultaneously, and provides a practical example of strong sustainability. These local groups are not only meeting their present demand for natural-resource services, but also seeking to increase their socioeconomic and environmental resources for the future.

Becker and Ghimire (2003) show the important role of organizations such as NGOs, in bridging traditional knowledge and scientific insights, and in providing social space for mobilizing a synergy between traditional knowledge and western knowledge for sustaining ecosystem services and biodiversity in Ecuadorian forest commons. Milestad and Hadatsch (2003) analyse the potential for organic farming in the Austrian Alps to flourish under the Common Agricultural Policy of the European Union in relation to the farmers' perspectives on sustainable agriculture, and whether or not organic farming and traditional practices are capable of building social–ecological resilience in the area.

4.2.5 Mechanisms linking humans and environmental resources

Linkages between humans and environmental systems operate in different ways according to their structure, the systems they link and the process by which the linkage is made. Some linkages are constructed by the informal observation of environmental characteristics on the part of users and the gradual evolution of behavioural response. Others are established as more rapid responses to change. In cases of environmental overuse, linking mechanisms are often weak or absent, cutting off the interaction between environmental condition and human response. The particular structure of a linking mechanism reflects the economic, social and ecological context in which it is established. The structure determines what information will be monitored, how it will be monitored and what will be done with the information once it is acquired. The key question is whether the governance system promotes, or even allows, behavioural adaptation to environmental change. Linkages affect both ecosystem and human system adaptation and evolution through the type of feedback allowed.

Folke and Berkes (1995) present a systems view of social and ecological interactions, which stresses the need for active social adaptation to environmental feedback and the use of traditional ecological knowledge. Particular attention is paid to the lessons that can be learned to assist in the design of more sustainable resource management systems – improving their adaptiveness and resilience. Chopra (2001) describes the management of natural resources and the environment for livelihoods and welfare based on three empirical studies in India, to show that the endowment of social capital may be measured by how well individuals cooperate across the traditional division of institutions (state, market and non-market).

Berke and Folke (1998) look at management practices based on local ecological knowledge and offer the following guiding principles for designing management systems that build resilience in social–ecological systems: (1) 'flow with nature', (2) enable the development and use of local ecological knowledge to understand local ecosystems, (3) promote self-organization and institutional learning and (4) develop values consistent with resilient and sustainable social–ecological systems.

Nested forest tenure systems, fisheries and joint farming–forestry systems help to determine the function of linkages. Mexican resource tenure systems function as 'shells' that
provide the super-structure within which activities are developed and operate (Alcorn and
Toledo, 1995). Such shells are linked in very specific ways to the larger 'operating system'
in which the shell is embedded. The best course of action for promoting ecologically
sustainable resource management is to support existing structures. Hammer (1995) focuses
on the links between ecological and social systems in Swedish fisheries, especially in the
Baltic Sea. He compares traditional small-scale and current large-scale management systems in terms of how they promote linkages between social and ecological systems, and
finds that large-scale systems are more vulnerable because of their failure to process
ecosystem feedbacks.

Social–ecological linkages help to analyse the broader parametric effects of fishing on the
whole biotic and environmental system (Wilson and Dickie, 1995). The fundamental cause
of overfishing lies in the social institutions that either cannot grasp the complexities of
biological interactions, or have insufficient means to control the inputs. This institutional
difficulty, combined with the uncertainty characterizing marine systems, suggest the appropriateness of a multilevel governance system that captures the social–ecological linkages on
different scales. Pradhan and Parks (1995) look at how the interactions between forests and
subsistence agricultural systems in Nepal's villages are influenced by the activities of rural
farming communities that depend on the forest for various subsistence products. Past
government efforts to protect forest resources by excluding local communities have resulted
in the opposite effect. Destruction of the social–ecological linkages at the local level has
resulted in village residents perceiving forests as open-access resources, and this has led to
further environmental degradation. Sastry (2005) examines the spatial dimensions of making development more sustainable in the mountainous Western Ghats region of India, from
the economic, social and environmental perspectives. He proposes an integrated model,
which promotes three distinct forest ecosystems to operate at three different altitudes where
three separate socioeconomic systems operate. The model helps to rejuvenate forests while
maintaining ecological balance – based on the 'unity in diversity' approach. Satake and
Iwasa (2006) use a Markov model of social–ecological coupling to show that myopic
decisions by private landowners will push entire landscapes toward agricultural use,
although the forested state is more socially optimal. A long-run management view and
enhanced forest recovery is the remedy.

4.2.6 *Poverty, population and natural-resource use*

Linkages among poverty, population and natural-resource use are discussed here in the
context of property rights. A broader discussion is provided in Section 2.3.5. The population
policy literature reflects the current view that previous successes in family planning, directed
at the supply side of population growth, cannot be sustained without paying serious attention
to reducing both the demand for births and the momentum of population growth (Bongaarts,
1994). Proposed policies include establishing formalized systems of property rights to

resources, education of women to enhance economic standing and incentives to postpone child-bearing to later years (Bongaarts, 1994; De Soto, 1993).

Dasgupta (1995) finds that population growth is, in varying degrees, linked to poverty, to gender inequalities in the exercise of power, to communal sharing of child-rearing and to an erosion of the local environmental-resource base. These linkages suggest that population policy should contain, not only measures such as family planning programmes, improved female education and employment opportunities, but also other measures to alleviate poverty and provide basic household needs.

Jodha (1995) shows how poverty affects resource-use behaviour based on desperation. He argues that the current unsustainable pattern of resource use in the Himalayas is due to the replacement of traditional conservation-oriented resource-management systems with more recent extractive systems. He examines the driving forces underlying this shift and discusses ways to restore some of the beneficial properties of the traditional systems.

Munasinghe (1997) shows that oversimplifying the complexities of the poverty–population–resource-use linkage could lead to inequitable and unwarranted conclusions. He argues that, under appropriate circumstances, people may be considered a social resource that would complement and strengthen the natural-resource base, so enhancing economic prosperity – see Section 2.3.5. Grima *et al.* (2003) examine agricultural practices in fragile lands and hill areas in order to understand better the trade-offs among development, poverty alleviation and sustainable use of natural capital.

4.2.7 Lessons learned and conclusions

Both general principles and specific social and ecological context play a crucial role in the design, implementation and maintenance of property rights regimes for environmental resources.

Governance systems

General principles of governance were discussed in relation to matching the scale and complexity of ecological systems with property rights regimes, ensuring that sets of rules are consistent across different levels of authority, distributing authority to achieve representation and contain transactions costs and coordinaing between jurisdictions. Specific properties of governance were presented for limiting air pollution, managing a fishery and enforcing regional environmental regulations.

Equity, stewardship and environmental resilience

General principles were discussed in terms of the relationship between equity, stewardship, environmental resilience and efficiency in property rights regimes designed for a range of environmental resources. Specific interactions were analysed in the contexts of traditional systems for maintaining biodiversity in India, changing property rights to national parks in Poland and mangrove–shrimp production systems in coastal Ecuador.

Traditional knowledge

General principles of traditional knowledge were discussed in terms of the interaction between international environmental policy on the use of traditional knowledge and the implementation of local-level resource-management systems that use traditional knowledge. Specific properties of traditional knowledge were presented in the contexts of practical knowledge about fishing in Iceland and Canada and the restoration of Maori property rights in New Zealand.

Mechanisms linking humans and environmental resources

General principles of mechanisms that link humans to their environment were discussed in terms of their structures and the processes by which they allow humans to observe environmental change, adapt their behaviour to reflect environmental change and create knowledge in the process. Specific properties of linking mechanisms were presented in the contexts of forest tenure systems in Mexico, fisheries management in Sweden and elsewhere and the interaction between agriculture and forestry in Nepal.

Poverty, population and natural-resource use

General principles of the connection between population and poverty were discussed in terms of the intermediate linkages of gender equality, child-rearing practices, women's education and general employment opportunities. Specific properties of the population–poverty connection were presented in the context of the relationship of population growth to poverty and unsustainable forest use. Simple generalizations may lead to wrong conclusions because the poverty–population–resource-use nexus is complex.

The diverse papers discussed in this section are woven together by a common thread – the interaction of social and ecological systems through property rights to produce environmental outcomes. They show how the ecological context shapes human organization and behaviour, and how the human context in turn shapes ecological organization and response. The structure of governance, values of equity and stewardship, traditional knowledge, linking mechanisms and conditions of poverty and population all form a part of that context. The analysis of property rights regimes confirms that the co-evolutionary path that humans and their environment follow (see Section 2.3) is indeed determined by the interaction of socioeconomic and ecological contextual elements.

4.3 Environmental and social assessment

Sustainable development assessment (SDA) used in the project cycle includes economic, social and environmental elements (see Chapter 2). Economic (and financial) assessment relies on cost–benefit analysis (CBA) – see Sections 2.4.2 and 3.2.1. Below, we examine the other two key components of SDA: environmental and social assessment (EA and SA).

4.3.1 Environmental assessment

Most nations and donor agencies now incorporate EA into their decision making.

EA process

The EA process is a part of the SDA to ensure that development options under consideration are environmentally sound and sustainable and that any environmental consequences are taken into account early in project design. In recent decades, EA has been adopted by most countries and international agencies, and it has evolved into a comprehensive instrument for making development more sustainable.

The breadth, depth and type of analysis in an EA depend on the nature, scale and environmental impacts. The process (a) evaluates the potential environmental risk and impacts of a project in its area of influence; (b) examines project alternatives; (c) identifies ways of improving project selection, siting, planning, design and implementation by minimizing, mitigating or compensating for adverse environmental impacts, as well as by enhancing positive impacts; and (d) follows up on managing environmental impacts during project implementation (World Bank, 1998).

EA examines the natural environment (air, water and land); human health and safety; social aspects (involuntary resettlement, indigenous peoples and cultural property); and transboundary and global environmental aspects, in an integrated way. It also takes into account the variations in project and country conditions; the findings of country environmental studies; national environmental action plans; the country's overall policy framework, national legislation and institutional capabilities related to environment and social aspects; and obligations of the country under relevant international environmental treaties and agreements.

An EA should be initiated as early as possible in the project processing and should be integrated closely with the economic, financial, institutional, social and technical analyses of a proposed project (see Box 3.1). EA is most effective when preliminary findings are made available early in the preparation process. At that time, environmentally desirable alternatives (sites, technologies, etc.) may be considered, and implementation and operating plans can be designed to respond to critical environmental issues in a cost-effective manner. Later actions, such as making a major design change, selecting an alternative proposal or deciding not to proceed at all with a project, can become very expensive. Even more costly are delays in implementation of a project because of environmental issues that were not considered during the design stage.

A range of instruments can be used to supplement the EA requirement: an environmental audit, strategic environmental assessment (SEA), hazard or risk assessment, and an environmental management plan (EMP). Other complementary approaches, such as environmental-cost accounting and life-cycle assessment, are used mainly in the private sector. EA procedures may also be applied to development activities broader than specific projects – e.g. an SEA can be adapted to regional or sectoral scales and used to assess impacts of sector-wide programmes, multiple projects or development policies and plans. A regional or sectoral EA can reduce the time and effort required for many project-specific EAs by identifying issues and existing data in advance, or by eliminating the need for a project-specific EA.

The process involves an analysis of the likely effects of a project or policy on the environment, recording these effects in a report, undertaking a public consultation exercise on the report, taking into account the comments on the report when making the final decision and informing the public about that decision. The EA implementation plan should provide for frequent coordination meetings and information exchange between EA and feasibility study teams. Most successful EAs have thorough mid-term reviews. Most major concerns arise within the first months, and the rest of the EA period focuses on mitigating measures.

Implementation and supervision

Supervision ensures that measures to mitigate anticipated environmental impacts, to monitor programmes, to correct unanticipated impacts and to comply with any environmental conditionalities, are implemented adequately. Procedures for startup and continuing operation of the project will normally specify these agreements as well as measures to protect the health and safety of staff. Proper staffing, staff training and procurement of spare parts and equipment to support preventive, predictive and corrective maintenance are also necessary elements of implementation.

Supervision could be carried out through a combination of the following:

(1) reports required on compliance with environmental conditionalities; status of mitigating measures, results of monitoring programmes and other environmental aspects of the project;
(2) oversight by line agency with responsibility for the sector, and/or by environmental management, land use control, resource conservation or permit-issuing agencies at the local, regional or national level;
(3) early warning about impending unforeseen impacts;
(4) supervision missions to review implementation of environmental provisions, corrective actions taken to respond to impacts and compliance with environmental conditionalities, including institutional strengthening components;
(5) site visits by environmental specialists or consultants as required to supervise complex environmental components or respond to environmental problems.

Reporting on the environmental aspects should cover key data (e.g. violations of pollution standards), descriptions of impacts observed, progress on mitigating measures, the status of monitoring programmes (especially those for detecting new impacts), progress on institutional strengthening and adherence to environmental conditionalities.

At the conclusion of a project, a completion report is prepared and submitted, including a description of impacts that actually occurred, whether or not it was anticipated in the EA report, and evaluations of the effectiveness of mitigating measures and of institutional strengthening and training. The World Bank (1998) provides a checklist of major items.

Environmental auditing

Environmental audits have been developed as an instrument to analyse existing conditions at and around a specific site, the environmental risk it may cause, the environmental liabilities and the degree of compliance with environmental standards and legislation. Users of such information are the companies themselves, customers, commercial banks, other lending institutions, local and national governments and the general public. Environmental audits help to reduce environmental and public health risks and assist in improving environmental management.

Environmental audits provide reliable environmental information on industries and other types of enterprises in response to increasing public concern over the quality of the environment and stricter environmental legislation. It can be viewed as a 'snapshot' of the environmental situation at a given site. Audits can provide important input to the EA's analysis of baseline conditions, consideration of alternatives and development of a mitigation plan for the existing impacts. Criteria may be based on local, national or international environmental standards, national laws and regulations, permits and concessions, internal management system specifications, corporate standards or guidelines of organizations such as the World Bank (World Bank, 1995).

The environmental audit primarily uses existing documentation of the institution being audited, interviews with managers and personnel and observation of practices at the facility. Spot checks, in the form of tests and samples, are often included in the audit to verify that a company is in compliance and that information provided by the company is correct.

Strategic environmental assessment

Strategic environmental assessment (SEA) is a promising approach to ensure that strategic-level policy making takes account of sustainability principles (Wood and Djeddour, 1992). A number of countries have recently introduced elements of this approach, and more appear likely to do so. To date, however, practical experience with SEA of policies, plans and programmes is limited, with critical issues yet to be resolved, such as the proposed scope of the approach, its role and relationship to other policy instruments in decision making and the appropriateness of relying on the methods and procedures of project EAs. SEA overlaps with the analysis of economy-wide policies and the environment (see below).

Wood and Djeddour (1992) review the advantages of introducing SEAs from two viewpoints: overcoming the limitations of conventional project EAs and promoting more integrated approaches for assessing and evaluating the sustainability of development policies, programmes and plans.

Ecological and economic considerations must be treated on the same level and at the same time in decision making. To promote the sustainomics principle of making development more sustainable (MDMS), all development options and activities must be adjusted to and be consistent with the 'carrying capacity' of the global biosphere and regional ecosystems. Often, scientific understanding is inadequate to permit predictions of whether and when significant thresholds will be crossed (i.e. the point at which cumulative stress of use and activity will cause irreversible change or structural breakdown in natural systems; see Kay (1991)).

SEA extends the principles of EA to cover the development policies and plans that govern the conversion and depletion of natural capital. This basic approach must be coordinated with other strategies and instruments for environment–economy integration, including analysis of links between economy-wide policies and the environment (see Chapters 3, 7, 8 and 9).

SEA may be seen as a vector for incorporating sustainability. Specifically, this process can help to instill and integrate environmental goals and principles into the highest levels of policy making, ensure that economic and fiscal agencies are responsible and accountable for the environmental consequences of their choices and actions and promote long-term changes in attitudes and assumptions about economic growth.

Economy-wide policies and the environment

Since economy-wide policies (both macroeconomic and sectoral) have pervasive, powerful and long-lasting effects throughout a national economy, their environmental impacts need to be assessed. This is a complex exercise, described in Chapters 3 (see Section 3.7), 7, 8 and 9.

4.3.2 Social assessment

Social assessment (SA) is an important element of SDA – see Section 2.4.2. SA focuses on people, who are both the reason and a resource for sustainable development. Culture, societies and organizations are the foundation on which development programmes rest. People's varied needs, beliefs and expectations are factors which shape their response to development activities. In the past, these factors were often analysed separately, and some key issues were overlooked.

The sustainomics framework recognizes that integrated, systematic social analysis can help ensure that projects are more sustainable and feasible within their social and institutional context. The sustainable development triangle in Figure 2.1 emphasizes that stakeholder participation in the selection and design of projects can improve decision making, strengthen ownership and include poor and disadvantaged groups.

SAs first emerged in the 1970s as a means to assess the impacts on society of development schemes and projects before they went ahead. It has since been incorporated into the formal planning and approval processes in many countries, in order to assess how major schemes may affect population, groups and settlements (Barrow, 2000).

IAIA (2003) states the following: 'Social assessment includes the processes of analysing, monitoring and managing the intended and unintended social consequences, both positive and negative, of planned interventions (policies, programmes, plans, projects) and any social change processes invoked by those interventions. Its primary purpose is to bring about a more sustainable and equitable biophysical and human environment.'

SA provides a framework for incorporating participation and social analysis into the design and delivery of projects (World Bank, 1995). SAs are carried out in order to: (a) identify key stakeholders and facilitate participation in project selection, design, implementation and monitoring and evaluation; (b) ensure that project objectives and incentives are acceptable to all the people intended to benefit, and that social differences are taken into account in project design; (c) assess the social impact of investment projects, and determine how adverse impacts can be avoided, minimized or substantially mitigated, and positive impacts maximized; (d) develop capacity to enable participation, resolve conflict, permit service delivery and carry out socially sound mitigation measures; and (e) make projects more sustainable, whereby the right institutions are strengthened, constraints are overcome and micro–macro links are made.

SAs may also be included in poverty assessments and other economic and sector studies; they involve consultations with stakeholders and affected groups and other forms of data collection and analysis. Formal studies need to be carried when social factors are complex and social impacts are significant. Where there is considerable uncertainty, due to lack of awareness, commitment or capacity, SAs can contribute to the design of projects that build on experience and are responsive to change.

The degree of stakeholder involvement needed also influences assessment design. In some cases, stakeholders simply provide information and no further interaction is foreseen, but often projects are improved when issues are jointly assessed and agreed, or beneficiaries are given the responsibility for identifying problems and empowered to find solutions. Where local participation in project design and implementation is expected, participatory data collection and analysis can help build trust and mutual understanding early in the project cycle. Stakeholder analysis involves the identification of key stakeholders, interests, influence and power, liability and risks and plans for stakeholder participation. It is important that findings be discussed with affected people to ensure that conclusions and recommendations are appropriate. Many methodological tools can be used when conducting SAs, including quantitative surveys, qualitative methods, such as beneficiary assessment, and participatory processes and workshops (World Bank, 1996b). It is the task of the SA team to identify which concepts apply and what methods and tools should be used to provide decision makers with operationally relevant information.

Part II

Global and transnational applications

5

Global analytical applications[1]

In this chapter, applications of key elements of the sustainomics framework are illustrated through several examples dealing with two critical global problems – climate change and sustainable development, and how they are best addressed together. Section 5.1 provides a general analysis of the circular linkages between these two issues. In Section 5.2, challenges posed to the social, economic and environmental dimensions of sustainable development, and relevant principles for formulating a policy response, are described. Ethical and equity considerations play an important role, especially in addressing the unfair and disproportionately large share of the burden imposed on the poor and vulnerable. Section 5.3 defines and analyses the principal potential human responses – adaptation and mitigation. Several practical applications are provided. Three international-level case studies are described in Section 5.4. First, alternative climate-change-mitigation response strategies are assessed in terms of the optimality and durability approaches. Next, we examine the interplay of equity and efficiency in joint implementation, as well as in emissions trading, especially between Annex 1 and non-Annex 1 countries. Sections 5.5 and 5.6 discuss how a global problem such as climate change might interact with sustainable development at the national level through a case study that examines greenhouse gas (GHG) mitigation prospects in Sri Lanka. National energy-sector responses are analysed, and a real options framework for carbon options trading under uncertainty is described.

5.1 Climate change and sustainable development

Comprehensive assessments by the Intergovernmental Panel on Climate Change (IPCC, 2001a, b, c, d, 2007a, b, c, d) state that climate change is unequivocal and very likely caused by human activities. Changes in important climate variables, such as global average temperature, are driving changes in natural and managed ecosystems (see Box 5.1). Serious, and possibly irreversible, future impacts are projected for a broad set of socioeconomic scenarios. Climate-change-response options include, primarily, adaptation and mitigation. Adaptation

[1] The valuable contributions of K. J. Arrow, W. Cline, C. Fernando, K. G. Maler, P. Meier, J. Stiglitz and R. Swart to this chapter are gratefully acknowledged. Some parts of the chapter are based on material adapted from Arrow *et al.* (1995b), Munasinghe (2000a, 2001a), Munasinghe, Meier and Fernando (2003) and Munasinghe and Swart (2005).

Box 5.1 Key IPCC findings on climate change

(1)   The global climate is changing and human actions are partly to blame.

(2)   Many physical and biological systems have already been affected.

(3)   Non-linear, large-scale and possibly irreversible changes in climate system components may occur, but probably not in this century.

(4)   Poor people and poor countries are the most vulnerable to climate-change impacts because they have the lowest capacity to adapt.

(5)   Inertia in both natural and socioeconomic systems requires a long time perspective and safety margins in designing climate responses.

(6)   Many technological and biological options are known that can enable us to meet short-term emissions reduction targets (e.g. the Kyoto Protocol) and to stabilize long-term GHG concentrations.

(7)   Additional measures related to changes in economic structure, institutional arrangements and behaviour can provide important opportunities to adapt to or mitigate climate change.

(8)   There are many cultural, political, institutional, economic and technological barriers to the adoption of the various options, but also many types of policy instruments that can overcome these barriers.

(9)   For most countries, mitigation costs will be less than a percentage point of projected annual macroeconomic growth rates, depending on how measures are combined and implemented. However, for particular sectors (e.g. energy-intensive industries) and countries (e.g. oil-exporting countries), costs can be higher.

(10) For GHG emissions, the general socioeconomic pathways that countries will follow are as important as specific climate policies.

(11) While mitigation and adaptation options can be effective individually, it is better to integrate them into a sustainable development strategy that deals holistically with complex linked human and natural systems.

(12) Sustainable development can be mutually reinforcing with climate-change adaptation and mitigation at national, regional and local levels.

Source: Munasinghe and Swart (2005).

---

involves measures that will reduce the impacts of climate change (without necessarily altering the probability that it will occur), whereas mitigation includes actions that will reduce the likelihood of climate change (e.g. by reducing GHG emissions or removing them from the atmosphere). Stern (2006) reviews economic issues in detail.

Figure 5.1 shows an integrated assessment modelling (IAM) framework, including the full cycle of cause and effect between climate change and sustainable development (IPCC, 2001a). Each socioeconomic development path in the bottom right-hand quadrant (driven by the forces of population, economy, technology and governance) gives rise to different levels of GHG emissions (carbon dioxide, halocarbons, methane and nitrous oxide).

These gases accumulate in the atmosphere, disturbing the natural balance between incident solar radiation and energy re-radiated from the Earth, as shown in the climate-domain box on the left-hand side. Such changes underlie the enhanced greenhouse effect that increases

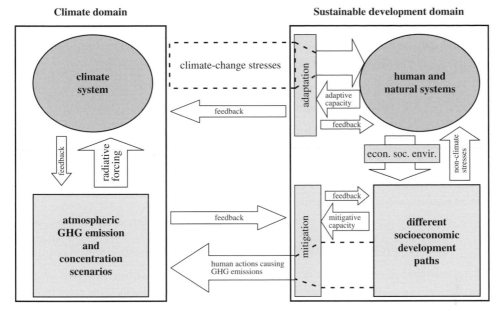

Figure 5.1. Circular interaction between climate change and sustainable development.

radiative forcing, which will change the climate well into the future and impose stresses on the human and natural systems shown in the top right-hand quadrant (sustainable development domain). Such impacts on human and natural systems will ultimately have effects on socio-economic development paths, thus completing the cycle. The development paths also have direct effects on the natural systems in the form of non-climate stresses, such as changes in land use, leading to deforestation and land degradation.

Development paths strongly affect the capacity to adapt to and mitigate climate change. The adaptive capacity (of both human and ecological systems) will enhance adaptation and reduce the severity of impacts. Analogously, superior mitigative capacity in human society could enhance prospects for future GHG mitigation. Thus, adaptation and mitigation response strategies are dynamically connected with changes in the climate system and the prospects for ecosystem adaptation, food production and long-term economic development. Finally, the sustainable development triangle (see Chapter 2) provides a useful framework for analysing the effects of climate change on future socioeconomic development scenarios. Feedback occurs throughout the cycle, and changes in one part affect other parts dynamically via multiple paths.

Material- and energy-intensive lifestyles and continued high levels of consumption, as well as rapid population growth, are inconsistent with sustainable development paths. Further, extreme socioeconomic inequality within and between nations undermines the social cohesion that would promote sustainability and make policy responses more effective. Socioeconomic and technology policy decisions made for non-climate-related reasons have significant implications for climate-change impacts and policy, as well as for other environmental issues. In addition, vulnerability to climate-change impacts is directly connected to environmental, social and economic conditions, as well as to institutional capacity. Kok and de Coninck (2004) and Swart, Robinson and Cohen (2003) review options for broadening climate policy by linking it with sustainable development.

5.2 Applying the sustainomics framework to climate change

The climate-change problem fits in quite readily within the broad conceptual framework of sustainomics described in Chapter 2. Responding to concerns of decision makers, the IPCC is analysing climate issues within the framework of the sustainable development triangle (IPCC, 2001d; Munasinghe, 2000a; Munasinghe and Swart, 2000). Relevant sustainomics-related principles that could be applied are outlined below.

5.2.1 Economic, social and environmental risks and opportunities

Global warming poses a significant potential threat to the future economic well-being of most human beings. Both monetarily quantifiable and non-quantifiable costs arise from the impacts of climate change and the measures people take to mitigate and adapt to it. Basically, the efficient economic response will be to maximize the net benefits derived from the use of the global atmospheric resource (see Section 2.3.2). This implies that the stock of atmospheric assets, which provide a sink function for GHGs, needs to be maintained at an optimum target level, defined by the point where the marginal GHG abatement costs are equal to the marginal avoided damages (see Section 5.4.1).

Climate change could also undermine social welfare and equity in an unprecedented manner. More attention needs to be paid to the vulnerability of social values and institutions, which are already stressed due to rapid technological changes (Adger, 1999). Especially within developing countries, erosion of social capital is undermining the basic glue that binds communities together – e.g. the rules and arrangements that align individual behaviour with collective goals (Banuri et al., 1994). Existing mechanisms to deal with transnational and global problems are fragile and unable to cope with worsening climate-change impacts – e.g. more 'environmental' refugees (Lonergan, 1993; Westing, 1992).

Both intra- and intergenerational equity will be worsened, among and within countries, due to the uneven distribution of the costs of damage, as well as adaptation and mitigation efforts (Bruce *et al.*, 1996); see Section 5.2.3. The poor are especially vulnerable to disasters (Banuri, 1998; Clarke and Munasinghe, 1995). Inequitable distributions are not only ethically unappealing, but also unsustainable in the long run (Burton, 1997). More generally, inequity undermines social cohesion and worsens conflicts over scarce resources.

Historical evidence on large-scale disasters such as El Niño provides useful insights into future climate-change impacts. Food insecurity, exacerbated by rapid global trade expansion, combined with two massive El Niño droughts in the late nineteenth century, killed tens of millions in the developing world and set back their development for many decades (Davis, 2001); see Section 1.2.3. There are disturbing parallels today, with rapid globalization of commodity and financial markets and increasing risks to food supplies of the poor due to climate change (Munasinghe, 2001a).

Yohe and Van Engel (2004) have analysed the potential trade-off between equity (measured by the convergence of per capita GDP between rich and poor countries) and sustainability (measured by the contraction in fossil-fuel consumption compared with current levels) over a 50-year horizon. They seek to resolve the conflict between sustainability and equity, by using the very transfers of international capital that would promote relative 'income equity' between rich and poor countries to facilitate 'burden sharing' equity – by spreading the cost of achieving any emissions reduction target more evenly across their boundaries.

The environmental viewpoint draws attention to the fact that increasing anthropogenic emissions and accumulations of GHGs might significantly perturb a key global sub-system – the atmosphere (UNFCCC, 1993). Changes in the global climate (e.g. mean temperature, precipitation, etc.) could also threaten the stability of a range of critical, interlinked physical, ecological and social systems and sub-systems (Watson, Zinyowera and Moss, 1996). This view is related to the durability approach (see Section 2.3). Environmental sustainability (see Section 2.2.2) will depend on several factors, including (a) climate-change intensity (e.g. incidence of extreme events); (b) system vulnerability (e.g. exposure and sensitivity to climate impacts); and (c) system resilience (i.e. the ability to recover from impacts).

On the more positive side, climate-change response also provides some opportunities for furthering sustainable development. The international acknowledgement of climate change as a risk for current and future generations has also highlighted the current vulnerability of populations and ecosystems to a broad range of existing environmental issues (of which climate change is only one); see Chapter 4. Reducing vulnerability of socioeconomic and ecological systems to climate change could also reduce their vulnerability to a broader set of unsustainable practices, improve resilience, increase the efficiency of resource use, reduce pressures on the environment and enhance human well-being.

To summarize, climate change and sustainable development issues are best addressed together; for example, using the sustainomics principle of making development more sustainable (see Chapter 2).

5.2.2 Relevant principles for policy formulation

When considering climate-change responses, several economic principles and ideas are useful, including the 'polluter pays' principle, economic valuation, internalization of externalities and property rights. The polluter pays principle argues that those who are responsible for damaging emissions should pay the corresponding costs. The market-based rationale is that this provides an incentive for polluters to reduce their emissions to optimal (i.e. economically efficient) levels. Quantification and economic valuation of potential damage from polluting emissions is a key prerequisite. The atmosphere is a common property resource, which GHG emitters can freely pollute without penalties. Such 'externalities' (defined in Section 3.2.2) need to be internalized by imposing costs on polluters that reflect the damage caused. Pigou (1932) originally defined and treated externalities in rigorous fashion. Here, the notion of property rights is also relevant to establish that the atmosphere is a valuable and scarce resource that cannot be used freely and indiscriminately.

An important social principle is that climate change should not be allowed to worsen existing inequities – although climate-change policy cannot be expected to address all prevailing equity issues. Some special aspects include: (a) the establishment of an equitable and participative global framework for making and implementing collective decisions about climate change; (b) reducing the potential for social disruption and conflicts arising from climate-change impacts; and (c) protection of threatened cultures and preservation of cultural diversity.

From the social equity viewpoint, the polluter pays principle is based not only on economic efficiency, but also on fairness. An extension of this idea is the principle of recompensing victims – ideally by using the revenues collected from polluters. There is also the ethical issue concerning the extent of the polluters' obligation to compensate for past emissions. Weighting the benefits and costs of climate-change impacts according to the income levels of affected persons is also one way of redressing inequities (see Section 3.2.2). Equal per capita GHG emission rights (i.e. equal access to the atmosphere) is consistent with both conventional justice principles (Kverndokk, 1995) and the UN human rights declaration underlining the equality of all human beings.

Traditional economic analysis has addressed efficiency and distributional issues separately – i.e. the maximization of net benefits is distinct from who might receive such gains (see Box 2.3). Equity aspects of climate change are discussed in Section 5.2.3.

Several concepts from contemporary environmental and social analysis are relevant for developing climate-change-response options, including the concepts of durability, optimality, safe limits, carrying capacity, irreversibility, non-linear responses and the precautionary principle. Broadly speaking, durability and optimality are complementary and potentially convergent approaches (see Section 2.3). Under the durability criterion, an important goal would be to determine the safe limits for climate change, within which the resilience of global ecological and social systems would not be seriously threatened. In turn, the accumulations of GHGs in the atmosphere would have to be constrained to a point that prevented climate change from exceeding these safe margins (see Section 5.4.1). Some bio-geophysical and socioeconomic systems may respond to climate change in a non-linear fashion, with the potential for catastrophic collapse. Thus, the precautionary principle argues that lack of scientific certainty about climate-change effects should not become a basis for inaction, especially where relatively low-cost steps to mitigate climate change could be undertaken as a form of insurance (UNFCCC, 1993).

5.2.3 *Equity, ethics and climate change*

Equity is an important element of the collective decision-making framework needed to respond to global climate change (see Box 5.2).

Box 5.2 Why is equity important in climate change?

Equity considerations are important in addressing global climate change for a number of reasons, including: (a) moral and ethical concerns; (b) effectiveness; (c) sustainable development; and (d) the UNFCCC itself.

First, the principles of justice and fair play are important in human interactions. Most modern international agreements, including the UN Charter, enshrine moral and ethical concerns relating to the basic equality of all human beings and the existence of inalienable and fundamental human rights. Equity is also embodied, explicitly or implicitly, in many of the decision-making criteria used by policy makers.

Second, equitable decisions carry greater legitimacy and encourage all parties to cooperate better in carrying out mutually agreed actions. A successful collective human response to climate change will require the sustained collaboration of all sovereign nation states and many billions of human beings over long periods of time. While penalties and safeguards have a role, decisions that are perceived as equitable will be implemented more willingly than those enforced under conditions of mistrust or coercion. Thus, a future scenario that restricts per capita carbon emissions in the South to 0.5 tonnes per year, while permitting a corresponding Northern level of over 3 tonnes, will not facilitate the cooperation of developing countries, and therefore is unlikely to be durable.

Third, as explained earlier, equity and fairness are extremely important elements of the social dimension of sustainable development. Thus, the impetus for sustainable development provides another crucial reason for finding equitable solutions to the problem of global warming.

Fourth, the UNFCCC has several specific references to equity in its substantive provisions. To begin with, Article 3.1 states that 'The Parties should protect the climate system for the benefit of present and future generations of humankind, on the basis of equity and in accordance with their common but differentiated responsibilities and respective capabilities. Accordingly, the developed country Parties should take the lead in combating climate change and the adverse effects thereof.' Other equity-related principles emphasized in Article 3 include: (a) the right to promote sustainable development; (b) the need to take into account the specific needs and special circumstances of developing-country and vulnerable parties; (c) the commitment to promote a supportive and open international economic system; and (d) the precautionary principle.

According to Article 4.2 (a), all developed-country parties are required to take the lead in mitigating climate change. Further, they should transfer technology and financial resources to developing-country parties that are particularly vulnerable to the adverse effects of climate change in meeting the costs of adaptation (Article 4.4). Article 4.2 (a) also requires developed-country parties to commit themselves to 'adopt national policies and take corresponding measures on the mitigation of climate change ... These policies and measures will demonstrate that developed countries are taking the lead in modifying longer-term trends in anthropogenic emissions consistent with the objective of the Convention ... taking into account the difference in the Parties' starting points and approaches, economic structures, available technologies and other individual circumstances, as well as the need for equitable and appropriate contributions by each of the Parties to the global effort regarding that objective.' Finally, Article 11.2 requires the Convention's financial mechanism to 'have an equitable and balanced representation of all Parties within a transparent system of governance'.

The foregoing provisions of the UNFCCC provide important guidance on how equity considerations should influence or modify the achievement of the Convention's goals. While protecting the climate system is a 'common concern of humankind', the Annex 1 countries are expected to take a lead in initiating actions and assume a greater share of the burden. Furthermore, in burden sharing, emphasis is also placed on applying equity considerations among developed countries. The responsibilities of the present generation with respect to those of future generations are also referred to. Finally, equity is mentioned in the context of governance, to emphasize the importance of including procedural elements that guarantee distributive outcomes that are perceived to be equitable.

Procedural and consequential equity

The requirements of the UNFCCC indicate that equity principles must apply to: (a) procedural issues – how decisions are made and (b) consequential issues – the outcomes of those decisions. Both aspects are important because equitable procedures need not guarantee equitable decisions, and vice versa. Support for the convention and its implementation will depend largely on widespread participation by the global community and on how equitable it is perceived to be.

Procedural equity has two components. First, equity implies that those who are affected by decisions should have some say in the making of these decisions, either through direct participation or representation. Second, the process must ensure equal treatment before the law – similar cases must be dealt with in a similar manner, and exceptions must be made on a principled basis.

Consequential equity also has two elements, relating to the distribution of the costs and benefits of: (a) impacts and adaptation to climate change and (b) mitigating measures (including the allocation of future emissions rights). Both elements (a) and (b) have implications for burden sharing among and within countries (intragenerational and spatial distribution) and between present and future generations (intergenerational and temporal distribution). The equity of any specific outcome may be assessed in terms of a number of generic approaches, including parity, proportionality, priority, classical utilitarianism and Rawlsian distributive justice. Societies normally seek to achieve equity by balancing and combining several of these criteria. Self-interest also influences the selection of criteria and the determination of equitable decisions. Consequential equity as applied in the international arena is derived mainly from these principles, which were developed originally in the context of human interactions within specific societies.

A human response to climate change requires the application of equity at an even more elevated (global) level, where there is far less practical experience. Cultural and societal norms and views about ethics, the environment and development complicate efforts to achieve a worldwide consensus (Pinguelli-Rosa and Munasinghe, 2002). Even the urgency of a response to climate change is subject to dispute. Given the different meanings, philosophical interpretations and policy approaches associated with equity, judgement plays an important role in resolving potential conflicts. Ultimately, any global response strategy will be a compromise between different views. As an example, the practical difficulties of allocating future emissions rights among nations are explored in a case study – see below (Munasinghe, 1998a).

Nevertheless, from a pragmatic viewpoint, significant progress toward a global consensus would be made if the decision-making framework could harness enlightened self-interest to support equitable or ethical goals. Thus, developed countries will have a self-interest in shouldering the major burdens of addressing climate-change issues because their own citizens have shown greater willingness-to-pay to solve environmental problems. Similarly, developed nations would enjoy greater opportunities for trade and export if developing-country markets grew without being disrupted by climate change. All countries would also prefer to avoid the significant negative spillover effects of worldwide instability arising from climate change. At the same time, the higher risks and vulnerability faced by developing countries provides them with an incentive to seek common solutions to the climate-change problem.

Equity and economic efficiency

General problems of reconciling equity and economic efficiency were discussed earlier (see Box 2.4). In the specific context of climate change, the lack of proper institutions to make equity-related assessments and play a redistributive role on an international scale compounds the problems of comparing national welfare levels across countries. The extreme viewpoints are that: (a) welfare levels should be compared as though all countries value each others' welfare equally (i.e. equivalent welfare functions exist across countries and equal weights might be assigned to each) and (b) that each country is concerned primarily with its own welfare and bears no responsibility for the welfare of any other. Since GHG emissions in one country affect others, a convention on climate change must arrive at some compromise between these two extremes.

Intragenerational (spatial) equity

While equity is not synonymous with equality, differences between countries clearly affect issues of international equity. International response strategies will eventually translate into actions adopted at the national level, and therefore should reflect equity concerns within countries as well. Several categories of differences between countries that are relevant to the question of equity are discussed next.

Wealth and consumption

Wealth is perhaps the most obvious and prevalent difference between (and within) countries. Measured in terms of GNP, the World Bank estimates that about 2.4 billion of the world's population (41%) live in low-income countries (World Bank, 2001). These countries have an average per capita GNP of $420. In contrast, 15% of the world's population live in 'high-income economies', which have an average per capita GNP of $26 440. The remaining 44% of the population live in the 'middle-income economies' and 'low- and middle-income economies', which have an average per capita GNP of $1500. Such wide variations in per capita income between countries imply that simply comparing this measure of welfare may be inappropriate (see Chapter 2).

These differences have direct implications for the way climate change is addressed. For instance, activities in developing countries that produce GHGs are generally related to fulfilling 'basic needs'. They may result from generating energy for cooking or keeping tolerably warm, engaging in agricultural practices, consuming energy to provide barely adequate lighting and occasionally for travel by public transport. In contrast, emission of GHGs in developed countries is likely to result from activities such as operating personal vehicles and central heating or cooling and energy embodied in a wide variety of manufactured goods and the use of such goods. Therefore, the level of personal wealth is directly related to the welfare impacts of reducing GHG emissions (WCED, 1987). Furthermore, wealth has a direct bearing on the vulnerability to the impacts of climate change. By virtue of being richer, some countries will be able to adapt more effectively to climate change. A similar relationship between poor and rich also exists within countries.

Poorer countries are less prepared to adopt mitigation and adaptation strategies due to several reasons. First, poverty has implications for urgency of other national priorities and of time scales used in policy planning. Wealth has a direct correlation to personal discount rates (i.e. discount rates decline with rising wealth). The more affluent have a greater share of disposable wealth to invest in the future, and therefore are able to conceptualize longer planning time horizons. The poor are forced to focus on shorter-term objectives, such as basic survival necessities.

A similar phenomenon applies to national-level economic and political systems. Consequently, interest rates are higher in poorer countries, capital is scarcer and the emphasis of policy planning is on the short-term needs, such as poverty alleviation and employment generation. The focus of government may be to keep up with infrastructure needs due to rapidly rising demands. They may not have the luxury to consider optimal development strategies, as some richer countries may be able to. Thus, national wealth affects both actual investment decisions as well as broader public policy planning capability.

The IPCC Special Report on Developing Countries addresses this concern by stating that 'the priority for the alleviation of poverty continues to be an overriding concern of the developing countries; they would rather conserve their financial and technical resources for tackling their immediate economic problems than make investments to avert a global problem which may manifest itself after two generations'. Similarly, Article 4.7 of the

UNFCCC states that 'economic and social development and poverty eradication are the first and overriding priorities of the developing country Parties', and thus their climate change responses will be influenced by these considerations. Even though concerns about climate change will grow in the developing countries (especially the most vulnerable), they are likely to lack the resources to address the issue.

Contributions to climate change

Given the range of sources and sinks, different ways of aggregating and presenting data can have implications for equity. The developed countries accounted for over 85% of cumulative worldwide GHG emissions up to 1990. On a per capita basis, the contrasts are even more stark, with North America and all developed countries, respectively, emitting over 20 times and 11 times the total cumulative carbon dioxide emissions of the developing countries. Thus, some authors have argued that the industrialized countries owe the developing world a 'carbon debt', due to disproportionately high GHG emissions in the past (Jenkins, 1996; Munasinghe, 1993a). The developing countries also need considerable 'headroom' to allow for the future economic growth and energy consumption, since they are starting from a much lower base (see Box 3.1). Meanwhile, differentiating along the lines of developed and developing countries may be too simple, because they vary. Winkler, Brouns and Kartha (2006) have assigned mitigation burdens and financial transfers among non-Annex 1 countries, based on responsibility for climate change, capability and potential to mitigate.

Incidence of impacts and vulnerability

The incidence of impacts may bear no relationship to the pattern of GHG emissions, which violates equity principles and is inconsistent with the 'polluter pays' and 'victim is recompensed' approach. In particular, the negative effects of climate change are likely to be most pronounced in tropical regions, where developing countries lie. In addition to asymmetries in incidence, many developing countries are more vulnerable to the effects of global warming because of fewer resources, weaker institutional capacity and scarcer skilled human resources. The plight of poor and subsistence-level communities, or low-lying small island nations subject to sea-level rise, will be quite bleak. Therefore, such groups need special attention, based on humanitarian and equity principles and procedures already established to deal with disasters (see Chapter 16).

Equity within countries

Most of the above arguments relating to equity across countries also apply to equity within individual nations. Fortunately, there are many existing mechanisms within countries (such as subsidized food, healthcare and schooling, social security or progressive taxation) to achieve a fairer redistribution of resources. Equity issues, especially views about social justice, will influence the formation, decisions and credibility of such policies. Although the capacity and legitimacy of these institutions may vary, they provide a useful framework within which climate-change issues can begin to be addressed at the national and sub-national levels.

Intergenerational (temporal) equity and discounting

Most of the earlier points relating to spatial equity also affect equity across time, and in very similar ways. First, future generations may be richer or poorer than the present generation. Second, past and present human actions will determine future climate-change impacts. Third, while future generations will have to bear the consequences of past GHG emissions, they will also benefit from sacrifices and investments made by their forbears. At the same time, it is unclear whether our descendants will be more or less vulnerable to climate-change impacts.

There are two additional issues relating to intergenerational equity. First, to the extent that future generations are not represented in the ongoing decision-making process that will affect climate change, particular care needs to be exercised to protect their rights. Second, once events unfold, it will be difficult to compensate future generations for past mistakes. Once again, extra prudence is required to avoid imposing future burdens that are both irreversible and impossible to compensate. Nevertheless, generations do overlap in practice (e.g. parents and children) and will facilitate the incorporation of some intergenerational concerns into the discount rate and decision making in general.

Social rate of discount

From an economic viewpoint, one of the principle instruments available to influence the allocation of resources across time is the social rate of discount (see Section 3.6). Indeed, the conclusions derived from any long-term analysis of climate-change policy will depend crucially on the discount rate that is selected – i.e. the real discount rate, net of inflation. The conceptual mirror image of the discount rate (at which future expenditures are discounted to the present) is the interest rate (at which present-day capital will grow into the future).

Since discounting compares economic costs and benefits that occur at different times, it will have a direct bearing on intergenerational equity. In climate-change analysis, the effects of discounting will be pronounced for two reasons: (a) the relevant time horizons are extremely long and (b) many of the costs of mitigation occur relatively early, while potential benefits lie in the distant future. Lower, present-day discount rates favour future generations by increasing the importance of future benefits (of avoided harm), relative to near-term costs (of mitigation).

The two main approaches to determining a value for the social rate of discount are based on the consumer rate of time preference (CTP), and the (risk-free) marginal returns to investment (MRI) – see Box 3.2. While the concepts underlying these two approaches may appear to diverge, in practice both the CTP and MRI produce comparable estimates for the social rate of discount. Thus, estimates for the CTP vary from 1 to 4% and for the MRI from 3 to 6% per annum (Arrow *et al.*, 1995b).

Climate change negotiations, ethics and equity

Equity and ethical considerations will play an important role in determining an effective climate-change response strategy. Ongoing climate-change negotiations are based on several factors, including risk, fear and the precautionary principle. Current approaches favour mitigation efforts via a global market that is driven by profits derived from trading in emission reductions, rather than through more deep rooted alterations in social attitudes – as suggested in the sustainomics vision (see Section 1.2.4).

Many climate-change initiatives were undertaken in both the public and private sectors, ahead of the ratification of the Kyoto Protocol. Some of them exemplify the speculative nature of global climate issues and clearly reflect the motivations of stakeholders striving to acquire future economic advantages through dealing in GHG emissions. The brokering of carbon credits over the Internet is one example of current pressures driving emissions-reduction mechanisms in the international marketplace. The Prototype Carbon Fund (PCF) run by the World Bank is the semi-government version of such trading in carbon credits, influencing emerging criteria for certification projects. The International Emissions Trading Association (IETA) further exemplifies the involvement of leading world enterprises using market-based efforts to reduce emissions in the oil and power sectors. It seems easier and cheaper to speculate on mitigation projects relating to land use (forestry, agriculture, etc.) than to invest in new energy sources or effective alterations in lifestyles and consumption standards that will reduce GHG emissions.

Climate-change negotiations are strongly influenced by the capacity and potential of countries to articulate their viewpoints. The developing countries are especially handicapped in this regard. The sustainomics approach suggests that they would be able to place themselves in a more favourable position in these global talks by focusing on the linkages among climate change, poverty and sustainable development and by clearly explaining the strategic and sociopolitical importance of the more humanistic aspects, such as equity and ethics. A recent book sets out the views of several experts with diverse disciplinary, sectoral and geographic backgrounds, on six relevant issues: economics, morality, politics, rights and law, philosophy and science (Pinguelli-Rosa and Munasinghe, 2002).

Miguez (2002) argues that the largest share of historical and current global GHG emissions has originated in industrial countries. Per capita emissions in developing countries are still relatively low, and must grow to meet their future social and development needs. The Brazilian Proposal emphasizes the very deep gap between Annex I and non-Annex I countries with respect to the atmospheric concentration of GHGs, rather than their emissions. The appropriate variable to measure climate change is the change in global mean surface temperature. Full support must be given to the least-developed countries to adapt to climate change.

Estrada-Oyuela (2002) stresses that ethics and equity require common but differentiated responsibility among countries. To stabilize GHG concentrations, industrialized countries will have to reduce their emissions, while developing countries are permitted to increase emissions. The high cost of mitigation in Annex I countries decreases the possibility of equalizing per capita emissions among all nations. The main question then is How does the burden of emission reduction compare with other internationally imposed burdens? Market prices that distort real values are the cause of frequent assertions about lower emission-reduction costs in developing countries. Emission reductions would be more effective if the production volume of sectors and their projections were considered. The mechanism recognizes the specific needs of each country, while being equitable for both industrialized and developing countries.

Banuri and Spanger-Siegfried (2002) point out that, while equity appears strongly as a foundational principle of the UNFCCC, it has gradually taken a back seat to considerations of cost-effectiveness and efficiency, as set out in the Kyoto Protocol. A long-term perspective should ensure that developing countries are able to grow economically and eradicate poverty. In the short run, this means identifying win–win policies, providing financial and technical assistance, and helping poor and vulnerable communities. If long-term capacity building for carbon-free growth is not fostered now, future mitigation costs will harm poor countries and deepen inequities. To ensure equity in mitigation, it is necessary to stimulate developing-country mitigative capacity. Clean development mechanism (CDM) projects that align equity and efficiency concerns help to make development more sustainable.

Muylaert and Pinguelli-Rosa (2002) critically contrast the emphasis on ethics and equity in approaches used by the environmental community with the low priority accorded to these issues in approaches based on 'power-politics'. They argue that 'ethics' may be understood better in terms of conduct – as behaviour without previous moral linkages. From this viewpoint, everyone has the power to decide what is fair, or not, and to negotiate the outcome on a case-by-case basis, depending on time and circumstances. Equity is not defined in the documents of the UNFCCC or the IPCC, and there is no formal requirement to implement this concept under international agreements on climate change. Since climate-change issues cannot be addressed without considering equity, the authors propose a more quantitative 'equity index'.

Ott and Sachs (2002) discuss important aspects of emissions trading. Under the UNFCCC, developed countries are requested to take the lead in combating climate change. Meanwhile, the CDM would assist developing countries financially and technologically in dealing with climate change. It should focus strictly on assisting non-Annex I countries in the transition to a non-carbon economy. Under such a scheme, only carbon-free energy, such as solar, biomass, wind and hydro, would be promoted by the CDM.

5.3 Climate-change adaptation and mitigation

5.3.1 Sustainable development and adaptation to climate change

Adaptation refers to the adjustments in human and natural systems as a response to climate-change stresses and their effects, which moderate damage and exploit opportunities for benefit (e.g. building higher sea walls or developing drought- and salt-resistant crops). Different types of adaptation include anticipatory versus reactive adaptation, private versus public adaptation and autonomous versus planned adaptation. Clearly, sustainable development and adaptation to climate change are interlinked. Most sustainable development strategies are unrelated to climate change, but they could make adaptation more successful. Similarly, many climate-change-adaptation policies could make development more sustainable.

Vulnerability, resilience and adaptive capacity

Durability criteria or constraints focus on maintaining the quality and quantity of asset stocks (see Chapter 2). The various forms of capital are a bulwark that decreases vulnerability to climate change and reduces irreversible harm, rather than mere accumulations of assets that produce economic outputs. System resilience, vigour, organization and ability to adapt will depend dynamically on the capital endowment and magnitude and rate of change of a shock. In the context of climate change, *vulnerability* is the extent to which human and natural systems are susceptible to, or unable to cope with, the adverse effects of climate change (IPCC, 2001a, 2007b). It is a function of the character, magnitude and rate of climate variation, as well as the sensitivity and adaptive capacity of the system concerned. *Resilience* is the degree of change a system can undergo, without changing state. *Adaptive capacity* is the ability of a system to adjust to climate change. Strengthening adaptive capacity is a key policy option, especially for vulnerable and disadvantaged groups. Adaptive capacity itself will depend on the availability and distribution of economic, natural, social and human resources; institutional structure and decision-making processes; information, public awareness and perceptions; menu of technology and policy options; ability to spread risk, etc. (Yohe and Tol, 2001). These variables are linked to location-specific patterns of socioeconomic and social development.

Adaptation options

Adapting to climate change can be spontaneous or planned. Planning is needed to minimize the costs of negative impacts and maximize the benefits of positive impacts. Adaptation efforts must be combined with mitigation, since controlling of emissions is vital to minimize future impacts.

The most vulnerable ecological and socioeconomic systems are those with the greatest sensitivity, the greatest exposure and the least ability to adapt to climate change. Ecosystems already under stress are particularly vulnerable. Social and economic systems tend to be more vulnerable in developing countries with weaker institutions and economies (e.g. high population density and low-lying coastal, flood prone and arid areas).

Strategies for adapting to climate change include preventing losses (e.g. barriers against sea-level rise); reducing losses (e.g. changing the crop mix); spreading or sharing losses (e.g. government disaster relief); changing land use (e.g. relocating away from steep slopes) or restoring a site (e.g. historical monument prone to flood damage). Better strategies need advances in technology, management and law, finance and economics, public education, training and research and institutional changes. Incorporating climate-change concerns into development plans can help ensure that new investments in infrastructure reflect likely future conditions. While uncertainty complicates the crafting of adaptation policies, many such policies will make development more sustainable (e.g. by improving natural-resource management or social conditions). Recent work has focused on formulating and assessing such adaptation strategies (Corfee-Morlot, Berg and Caspary, 2002; Niang-Diop and Bosch, 2004).

5.3.2 *Sustainable development and mitigation of climate change*

Sustainable development and mitigation are also interlinked. Most sustainable development strategies are unrelated to climate change, but they could make mitigation more successful. Similarly, many climate-change mitigation policies could make development more sustainable.

The IPCC recently elaborated six different reference scenarios that show a wide variety of alternative development pathways over the next century, each yielding a very different pattern of GHG emissions (IPCC, 2000). Lower-emission scenarios require less carbon-intensive energy-resource development than in the past. Emission-reduction technologies have developed faster than anticipated. Improved methods of land use (especially forests) offer significant potential for carbon sequestration. Such methods might allow time for more effective mitigation techniques to be developed. Ultimately, mitigation options will depend on differences in the distribution of natural, technological and financial resources, as well as mitigation costs across nations and generations (IPCC, 2001c, 2007c).

Although future low-emission paths will vary by country, the IPCC results indicate that appropriate socioeconomic changes combined with known mitigation technology and policy options could help to achieve atmospheric CO_2 stabilization levels around 550 ppmv, or less, by 2100.

Mitigative capacity

The effectiveness of future mitigation could be improved by strengthening *mitigative capacity* (i.e. the ability to reduce GHG emissions or enhance sinks), which depends on social, political and economic structures and conditions. More research and analytic capacity is needed to build mitigative capacity in developing countries. Increases in mitigative capacity could allow climate-change considerations to be more effectively integrated with broader sustainable development strategy in a manner that effectively limits GHG emissions over time, while maximizing the developmental co-benefits of mitigative actions.

Social learning and innovation, and changes in institutional structure, could strengthen mitigative capacity. Policy options that yield 'no-regrets' outcomes will help to reduce GHG emissions at no or negative social cost. However, the incremental costs of stabilizing almospheric CO_2 concentrations over the next century rise sharply as the target concentration level falls from 750 ppmv to 450 ppmv. There are many technical, social, behavioural, cultural, political, economic and institutional barriers to implementing mitigation options within countries.

Mitigation options

Like adaptation, mitigation has cost and benefits. Many variables need to be considered in the cost equation, including: (a) internationally agreed timetables and targets for emissions reductions; (b) global population and economic trends; (c) development of new technologies; (d) rate of capital replacement; (e) discount rates; (f) co-benefits of mitigation actions that address non-climate issues; and (g) actions of industry and consumers in response to climate-change-related policy.

Policies to minimize the risk by reducing GHG emissions will also come with a price tag and vary widely due to uncertainty. Although immediate action may seem more expensive, delays could lead to greater risks and therefore greater long-term costs. An early effort toward controlling emissions would increase the long-term flexibility of human responses to work toward stabilizing atmospheric GHG concentrations.

Many cost-effective technologies and policies are available (e.g. hybrid engine cars, wind turbines, advances in fuel cell technology, end-use energy efficiency in building, transport, manufacturing and industry to reduce emissions, etc.), which not only mitigate GHG emissions, but also address other development objectives by increasing resource efficiency and decreasing environmental pressure. Governments need to promote these solutions actively, by addressing institutional and other barriers first. Economic incentives can be used to influence investors and consumers. For example, deposit funds could encourage people to trade in their cars and appliances for more energy-efficient models; manufacturers could be rewarded for selling climate-friendly goods, or penalized if they do not. Prices could incorporate climate-change concerns by changing taxes or subsidies. For example, a tax on oil, coal or gas would discourage fossil-fuel use and help reduce CO_2 emissions. Tradable emission permits could also offer a cost-efficient, market-driven approach to controlling emissions. Caspary and O'Connor (2002) provide a useful review of such options.

Energy policy is a key to enhancing the cost-effectiveness of decreasing emissions (e.g. optimal energy mix). Incentives for investing in cost-effective and energy-efficient technologies are essential, e.g. improved building design, new chemicals for refrigeration and insulation, more efficient refrigerators and cooling/heating systems. Power plant emissions of both air pollutants and GHG will fall if renewable sources are used. Technology innovation, energy efficiency and more renewable energy will be essential to stabilize GHG concentrations in the next 50–100 years, while also providing other co-benefits. Governments need to remove barriers that slow the spread of low-emission technologies.

The transport sector is the most rapidly growing source of GHG emissions in most countries (see Chapter 11). Heavy reliance on fossil fuels makes controlling GHG emissions particularly difficult. In urban areas air pollutants, such as particulate matter and ozone precursors, also cause problems. New technologies can increase the efficiency of automobiles and reduce the emissions per kilometre travelled. Switching to less-carbon-intensive fuels will reduce local and regional air pollution, which is of serious concern in most cities in the developing world as well as in industrialized countries, but it will also help reduce carbon emissions (e.g. biofuels, fuel-cell-powered vehicles, etc.). Some policies to reduce emissions from transport include: (a) use of renewable energy technologies; (b) better maintenance and operating practices; (c) policies to reduce traffic congestion; (d) urban planners to encourage low-emission transport (e.g trams and trains, bicycles, walking); and (e) imposing user fees. Climate-friendly transport policies can promote development while minimizing the local costs of traffic congestion, road accidents and air pollution.

Deforestation and agriculture account for increases in local and regional air pollution as well as GHG emissions. Forests need to be protected and better managed (see Chapter 13). Deforestation may be controlled by decreasing pressures of agriculture on forestry, slowing down population growth, involving local people in sustainable forest management, harvesting commercial timber sustainably and reducing migration into forest areas. Sustainable forest management can generate renewable biomass as a substitute for fossil fuels. Improved management to increase agricultural productivity could enable soils to absorb more carbon, at the same time leading to higher organic-matter content and enhanced productivity. Methane emissions from livestock could be reduced with new feed mixtures that improve the efficiency of digestion and also increase the overall efficiency of livestock management. Methane emissions from wet rice cultivation can be reduced significantly through changes in irrigation practices and fertilizer use, while improving or safeguarding current productivity and reducing environmental pressures. Nitrous oxides from agriculture can be minimized with new fertilizers and practices, some of which not only reduce nitrous oxide emissions, but also reduce nitrogen losses (in the form of polluting nitrates, nitrogen oxides and ammonia) and enhance fertilizer efficiency.

Thus, it is possible to decrease emissions while generating environmental and economic benefits. 'No-regrets' emissions-reduction strategies are most effective in minimizing the costs of climate-change policies. Their benefits exceed costs, even excluding the benefits of avoided climate change, e.g. removing market imperfections like fossil-fuel subsidies or generating double dividends by using tax revenues to reduce other distortionary taxes. Public participation (i.e. by stakeholders, individuals, communities, businesses) is important for effective policies. Education and training is also vital (e.g. the importance of conserving energy, introducing building codes to maximize sunlight and use solar power, etc.). Equity aspects of policy need to be considered (i.e. cost-efficiency and fairness).

Climate-change responses should aim to combine mitigation and adaptation. Developing country researchers have reiterated that development will remain the first priority while mitigation needs to pursued in this context (Munasinghe and Swart, 2005; Winkler *et al.*, 2002). Coordinated actions across countries and sectors could reduce mitigation costs and limit concerns about competitiveness, conflicts over international trade regulations and carbon leakage. To summarize, early actions, including mitigation measures, technology development and better scientific knowledge about climate change, will increase the possibilities for stabilizing atmospheric GHG concentrations and make development more sustainable.

5.4 Global-level interactions between climate change and sustainable development

Three simplified examples are presented below, to illustrate the application of some of the sustainomics-based concepts discussed earlier.

5.4.1 *The interplay of optimality and durability in determining appropriate global GHG-emission target levels*

Optimal and durable approaches can help to determine target GHG-emission levels (Munasinghe, 1998a). Using economic optimization, the ideal solution is to estimate the

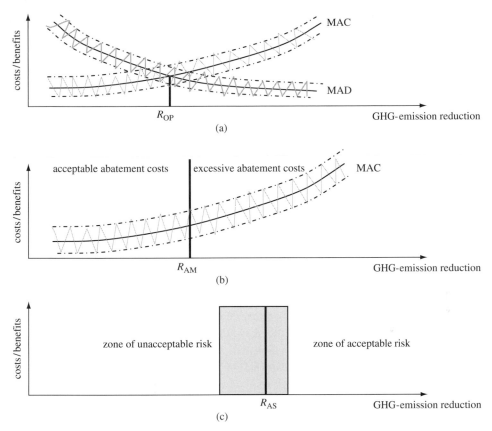

Figure 5.2. Setting mitigation targets: (a) cost–benefit optimum; (b) affordable safe minimum standard; (c) absolute standard.

long-run marginal abatement costs (MACs) and the marginal avoided damages (MADs) associated with different GHG-emission profiles – see Figure 5.2(a), where the error bars on the curves indicate measurement uncertainties (Bruce *et al.*, 1996). The optimal emission levels would lie at the point where future benefits (in terms of climate-change damage avoided by reducing one unit of GHG emissions) are just equal to the corresponding costs (of mitigation measures required to reduce that unit of GHG emissions), i.e. MAC = MAD at point R_{OP}.

Durable strategies become more relevant when MAC and/or MAD might be poorly quantified and uncertain. Figure 5.2(b) assumes that MAC is better defined than MAD. First, MAC is determined using technoeconomic least-cost analysis (an optimizing approach), while MAD is ignored. Next, the target emissions are set, based on an affordable but safe minimum standard (at R_{AM}). This value is the upper limit on mitigation costs that will still avoid unacceptable socioeconomic disruption. This choice is more consistent with the durability approach.

Finally, Figure 5.2(c) indicates an even more uncertain world, where neither MAC nor MAD is defined. Here, the emission target is established based on an absolute standard

(R_{AS}). Typically, such a safe limit could seek to avoid an unacceptably high risk of damage to ecological (and/or social) systems, without necessarily valuing any costs in monetary terms. This last approach is based mainly on the durability concept.

5.4.2 *Combining efficiency and equity to facilitate South–North cooperation for climate-change mitigation*

Figure 5.3 clarifies the basic rationale for greater North to South cooperation through resource and technical transfers, and highlights how the sustainomics approach elucidates the complex interaction of economic efficiency and social equity in addressing the climate-change problem. The vertical bars indicate the marginal abatement costs for two countries (X is a developing or southern country and Y is an industrialized or northern nation). In other words, the bars show the net additional costs per unit of GHG emissions reduced by mitigation schemes (over and above the costs of conventional technologies, and including all ancillary costs and benefits). The figure assumes that GHG-emission reduction options are cheaper in the developing country than in the industrialized nation.

The global benefit of mitigation is shown by the upper horizontal line representing the MAD accruing to the entire global community due to GHG-emission reductions. The MAD realized by the developing country alone would be negligibly small, since abatement measures undertaken by any given nation will yield predominantly worldwide benefits well beyond its borders. Clearly, if the developing country acted just in its own interests, it

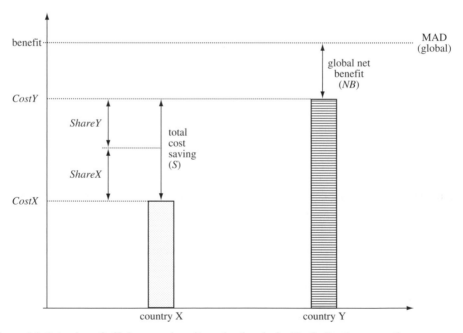

Figure 5.3. Interplay of efficiency and equity and rationale for North–South cooperation.

would be unwilling to incur any incremental costs of mitigation. In such a situation, only so called 'win–win' or 'no-regrets' options would be pursued – such as energy-efficiency schemes where there is a net economic gain, even without considering GHG-abatement benefits. Global mitigation benefits would be considered an 'externality' by the developing country.

From the strict economic efficiency perspective of the entire world community (see Box 2.3) and ignoring equity issues, mitigation options need to be pursued in all countries, up to the point where additional costs of a marginal unit of emissions curtailed are equal to the corresponding benefits of avoided global-warming damages. In this case, the avoided damages that are 'external' to the mitigating country should be 'internalized' from the global viewpoint.

First, we explore how such an efficiency-based approach might support resource transfers from North to South. Consider a representative GHG mitigation project (e.g. re-afforestation) in the developing country X, where the additional costs of GHG-emission reduction is less than the global avoided damage. From the perspective of the global development community (i.e. rich countries), it would be *economically efficient* for them collectively to finance any additional costs (e.g. on a grant basis) in the developing country. They would thereby 'internalize' and capture the worldwide net mitigation benefits equivalent to $NB + S$ (see Figure 5.3).

Second, we make the case for a bilateral transfer of resources from an industrialized to a developing country. Consider the cost of a project (e.g. the conversion of coal plants), which seeks to reduce GHG emissions in the industrialized country Y. This country could realize a cost saving if it persuaded the developing country X to undertake the mitigation measure, while still achieving the same global-emissions-reduction benefit. The minimum compensation acceptable to country X would be its *CostX*. The maximum payment country Y would be willing to make is S (*CostY* – *CostX*). This could be the basis for cooperative schemes, such as joint implementation (JI) and the clean development mechanism (CDM). If the net benefits, *NB*, and cost savings, *S*, are adequate, it would be both *equitable* and *efficient* for the industrial nation to give the developing country more resources than the break-even reimbursement *CostX*. For example, the cost saving could be shared in the proportions *ShareY* and *ShareX* between the industrial and developing nations, respectively (*ShareX* + *ShareY* = *S*). Sustainomics would favour such an equitable sharing of potential cost savings between the two cooperating nations (see Section 5.2.3). This would also provide more incentives for developing countries to participate in such a scheme. Munasinghe and King (1992) made the same proposal in the case of South–North cooperation to reduce ozone-depleting substances under the Montreal Protocol.

5.4.3 Equity and efficiency in emissions trading

Equity and efficiency principles may be applied usefully in allocating the mitigation burden among various countries to achieve a future target level of desirable worldwide GHG emissions (see Section 5.2.3). Suppose there is international agreement to aim for stabilization

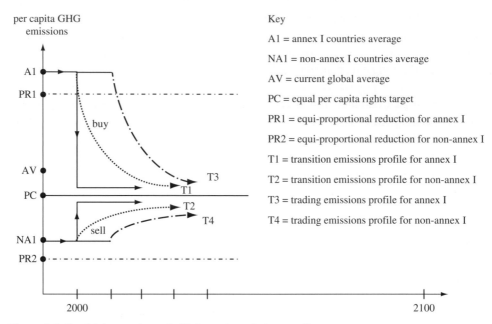

Figure 5.4. Combining equity and efficiency in emissions trading.

of GHG concentrations, say in the range 550 ppmv in the next 200 years. This would determine the total global-emissions budget in the future.

Consider two contrasting rules for allocating rights to the fixed global level of future emissions, year by year among the different nations.

(1) Equal per capita (PC) emission rights for all human beings, based on ethics and human rights. The total national 'right to emit' would be the product of the population and the basic per capita emissions quota, with all national quotas summing to the desired global-emissions target.
(2) Equi-proportional reductions (PR) of emissions, based on so-called 'grandfathering'. In this case, all countries would reduce emissions by the same percentage amount relative to some pre-agreed baseline year, to achieve the desired global-emissions target.

The dynamics of this allocation process are shown in Figure 5.4. The line PC indicates the constant level of per capita emissions if the total global-emissions target were allocated equally to all human beings during the decision-making time horizon. The points A1 and NA1 represent the average current per capita GHG emissions of the Annex I (industrialized), and non-Annex I (developing) countries, respectively; A1 is considerably larger and NA1 is somewhat less than PC. Thus, the industrialized countries would need to incur economic costs to cut back GHG emissions significantly, if they were to meet the PC criterion. On the other hand, the developing countries have some 'headroom' to increase their per capita emissions, as incomes and energy consumption grow.

The alternative allocation rule is based on equi-proportional reductions (PR) of emissions. Assuming that the global average emission rate per capita per year is slightly higher than PC; this implies that all countries would need to curtail carbon emissions by a small amount (say about 10%) to meet the PR criterion (as shown by the broken lines PR1 and PR2 in Figure 5.4). Clearly, such an outcome is highly inequitable, since it would severely restrict growth prospects in the developing world – where per capita energy use is still quite low (Munasinghe, 1995a).

Thus, both developed and developing countries would have reasons to oppose strict enforcement of the PC and PR approaches. Meanwhile, the developing countries argue that responsibility for past emissions should be considered when future rights are allocated. Clearly the industrialized countries have used up a significant share of the 'global carbon space' available to humanity while driving up atmospheric CO_2 concentrations from the pre-industrial norm of 280 ppmv to the current level of over 380 ppmv. On the other hand, it would be in the industrialized countries' interests to use a fixed-base-year population (e.g. in the year 2000) as the multiplier of the per capita emissions right (e.g. PC) to determine total national emission quotas. This would effectively penalize countries which had high-population-growth rates, since their allowed national quota (determined by the base-year population) would have to be divided up among more people in the future.

In practice, it is possible that some intermediate requirement that falls between PC and PR might eventually emerge from the collective decision-making process. For example, PC may be set as a long-term goal. In the shorter run, pragmatic considerations suggest that both the industrialized and transition countries be given a period of time to adjust to the lower GHG-emissions level, in order to avoid undue economic disruptions and hardship – especially to poorer groups within those countries (see transition emissions paths T1 and T2 in Figure 5.4). While some industrialized nations might argue that the goal of equal per capita emissions is too idealistic or impractical, the direction of adjustment is clear. Net CO_2 emissions per capita in industrialized countries should trend downwards, while such emissions in developing countries will increase with time. This result will emerge even if the objective is a more equitable distribution of per capita emissions, rather than absolute equality (the so-called 'contraction and convergence' scenario).

Another adjustment option could be the facilitation of an emissions-trading system. For example, once national emissions quotas have been assigned, a particular developing country may find that it is unable to utilize its allocation fully in a given period. Meanwhile, an industrialized country might find it cheaper to buy such 'excess' emissions rights from the developing nation, rather than undertaking a much higher cost emissions-abatement pro-gramme to meet its own target (see Section 5.5.2). More generally, the emissions-trading system would permit quotas to be bought and sold freely on the international market – thus establishing an efficient current price and a futures market for GHG emissions. In Figure 5.4, new transition emission profiles T3 and T4 might emerge, creating potential space for adjustment through the buying and selling of carbon rights.

5.5 Greenhouse-gas-mitigation prospects in Sri Lanka

In this section, we discuss how a global problem like climate change might interact with sustainable development prospects at the national level – through a case study that examines

GHG-mitigation prospects in Sri Lanka. Furthermore, in Section 5.6 we develop a basic real options analytical framework to deal with significant uncertainties facing Sri Lankan decision makers in responding to opportunities offered by the Kyoto Protocol's flexibility instruments (i.e. CDM, JI and emissions trading).

The following procedure is used in this 'bottom-up' case study: (a) estimate GHG emissions for the reference (business-as-usual) scenario; (b) estimate GHG emissions for a reform scenario to assess the impact of pricing and other policy interventions typically undertaken by the government; (c) identify, evaluate and screen a range of GHG-mitigation options; (d) formulate alternative mitigation scenarios and estimate the GHG impacts of each scenario; and (e) compare them to the reform scenario to gauge the cost-effectiveness of the GHG-emissions-reduction options.

First, power-sector GHG emissions are estimated for a reference (or business-as-usual) scenario. The least-cost capacity expansion programme is developed to satisfy the growth of electricity demand for 20 years, while meeting acceptable levels of reliability and environmental protection standards. Next, the GHG emissions associated with a reform scenario (including various policy options) are estimated. Several mitigation options are screened and then combined within alternative GHG mitigation scenarios, which are compared to the reference and reform scenarios. The modelling was achieved with ENVIROPLAN used in the 1990s to study environmental issues in the Sri Lanka power sector (Meier and Munasinghe, 1994), and subsequently applied in many other countries (BC Hydro, 1995; USAID, 1995; World Bank, 2004).

5.5.1 Baseline emissions

Biomass still accounts for the largest share of primary energy (see Table 5.1), although the share of commercial energy has grown steadily since 1984. The corresponding changes in GHG emissions are shown in Table 5.2 (Ratnasiri, 1998). However, the increases in power-sector emissions from 1990 to 1992 are due solely to the variation of hydro generation (1991 and 1992 were dry years), rather than any change in generation capacity.

Table 5.1 *Shares of total primary energy*

	1984		1996		1984–1996 change
	1000 TOE	%	1000 TOE	%	(%/year)
Biomass	4203	71	3925	57	−0.6
Commercial	1700	29	2952	43	4.71
Total	5903	100	6877	100	1.28

TOE = tonnes of oil equivalent; 'Commercial' includes hydro and oil; 1996 was a drought year, in which the share of hydro was lower than normal.
Source: Energy Conservation Fund (1996).

Table 5.2 *Estimates of CO_2 emissions by source, 1990–1992 (thousand tonnes)*

	1990	1991	1992
Power (CEB)	8.5	226.6	643.2
Transport	2214	2317	2334
Energy generation in industry	559	485	561
Commercial (fisheries, agriculture)	172	161	166
Domestic (LPG, kerosene)	550	578	651
Cement/lime production	249	244	436
Refinery own use	0.7	0.6	0.7
Total energy and industrial processes	3899	4120	4894
Biomass	21 261	20 095	21 498
Emissions from agriculture, land-use and waste	8435	8370	8098

CEB = Ceylon Electricity Board.
Source: Ratnasiri (1998).

This situation is changing since the share of hydroelectricity in Sri Lanka's energy mix continues to decline, and almost all new power plants over the next two to three decades will be fossil-fuelled. Wind power, mini-hydro and demand side management will also increase in importance in the near future. Consequently, in the business-as-usual case, the share of GHG emissions from the power sector will increase from 18% of energy-sector emissions in 1998 to 45% in 2018; in absolute terms, the power sector will account for 20.1 million tonnes per year (mtpy) by 2018, compared with 1.7 mtpy in 1997, a more than tenfold increase.

Emission coefficients and conversions

GHG-emission coefficients are calculated by stochiometry, and where these data are unavailable, IPCC emission coefficients are used. To convert non-carbon dioxide GHGs to carbon equivalents, the IPCC 100-year equivalent global-warming potentials are applied (IPCC, 2001a, 2007a).

5.5.2 Base case or business-as-usual scenario

The 'base case' in the Ceylon Electricity Board (CEB) annual long-term generation expansion planning study is used here as the business-as-usual case (CEB 1988, 1999). GDP growth is the dominant determinant of demand (CEB, 1988). In the business-as-usual demand forecast, the tariff is assumed to rise with inflation (constant in real terms).

By 2018, the busbar peak demand is estimated to grow to 4292 MW (compared with 1136 MW in 1998); the corresponding 2018 energy demand is 20 678 GWh, up from 5683 GWh in 1998. Total T&D loss rates, and the system load factor (SLF), are

Table 5.3 *Generation capacity expansion for wind power case*
All values are in megawatts; negative values indicate retirement

	1999	2001	2003	2005	2007	2009	2011	2013	2015	2017
Hydro			70	150						
Coal			300		300		300	300	300	300
Liquid fuels Gas		106	300			105	105	105	105	300
Diesel	100					−36		−13		

taken as 17.6% (of generation) and 55%, respectively, which are their 10-year average values (both have stayed remarkably constant over the past decade). Of the total T&D loss, 15.3% is technical loss, and the balance of 2.3% is non-technical (commercial) loss. Table 5.3 shows the resulting capacity expansion plan for the business-as-usual (BAU) case.

5.5.3 Reform scenario

In Sri Lanka, the specific components of a comprehensive reform initiative are still evolving. Nevertheless, the following elements might be part of a power-sector reform programme: (a) greater T&D loss reduction (e.g. due to distribution privatization); (b) implementation of the remaining cost-effective DSM options; (c) improvements to time-of-day tariff; and (d) tariff reforms (higher average price).

T&D losses are assumed to fall steadily from 17.8% of generation (15.5% technical and 2.3% non-technical) in 1999, to 12.5% (11% technical and 1.5% non-technical) in 2007, and then to remain constant.

It is assumed that, in the first stage of reform, DSM-1 would be limited to lighting. Energy-efficient motors and AC systems are considered later under DSM-2. By 2007, lighting DSM-1 reduces the peak evening demand by 330 MW, about 15% of the total evening peak load.

As shown in Table 5.4, the combination of reduced T&D losses and the peak-shaving impact of the lighting DSM-1 programme reduces the generation requirement compared with the base case. Baseload coal units decline from six to five, and thermal peaking units decline from six to two 105 MW open cycle combustion turbines (OCCTs) from 2010 to 2018. There is a corresponding 15% reduction in GHG emissions, from 118 million tonnes over the planning horizon in the base case to 98 million tonnes under reform (Figure 5.5). This is a win–win outcome. By contrast, in the Indian state of Haryana, the economic benefits of reform are six times larger than in Sri Lanka, but this results in a 25% increase in GHG emissions – due to major inefficiencies such as T&D losses of 35% (World Bank, 1997b).

The impact of reforms on system costs and GHG emissions can be displayed as a trade-off plot in Figure 5.6. The impacts of T&D loss reduction and DSM-1 are shown separately

Table 5.4 *Generation capacity expansion for reform case*

All values are in megawatts; negative values indicate retirement

	1999	2001	2003	2005	2007	2009	2011	2013	2015	2017
Hydro			70	150						
Coal				300		300		300	300	300
Liquid fuels		106	300						105	105
Gas										
Diesel	100			−36		−36				
Renewables										

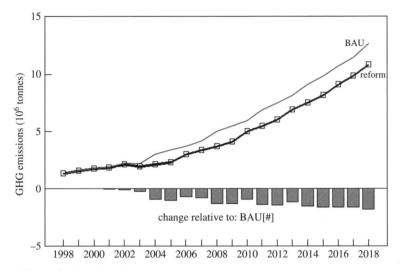

Figure 5.5. GHG-emission reductions.

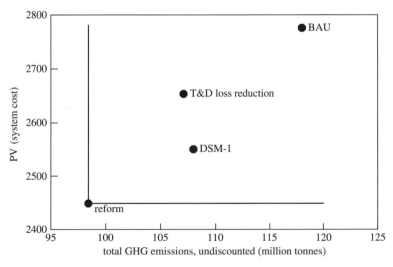

Figure 5.6. Impact of reform on system costs and GHG emissions.

(each as perturbations of the BAU case). Reform is clearly 'win–win'; indeed, reform is also win–win with respect to other environmental attributes for local air emissions.

5.5.4 *Mitigation options*

We next analyse individual mitigation options separately, as an increment to the reference (reform) case. The goal is to compare the cost of avoided carbon for individual options and construct GHG-mitigation scenarios. Individual options are combined to generate a GHG-mitigation option supply curve that includes interactions among individual programmes. The focus is on the economic costs and magnitude of the physical GHG-emission-reduction benefits – expressed as the price of avoided carbon.

Many alternative-energy options have upward-sloping supply curves; this is attributable to two main reasons. The first applies to situations where capital costs are likely to be relatively constant across individual projects, but where energy output between the best and worst sites shows large differences (e.g. wind power). The second applies to the converse case – where plant factors might show relatively small differences, whereas construction costs may show high variation (e.g. small hydro).

Alternative-energy options

Small hydro

Grid-connected small hydro is the largest single component of the IDA/Global Environment Facility Energy Services Delivery Project (ESDP), comprising US$ 14.4 million of US$ 24.2 million (World Bank, 1997a). Four such small hydro plants, totalling about 1.3 MW, were connected to the CEB grid in 1996 and 1997.

Based on studies by Posch and Partners (1994) and Fernando (1998), we divide the mini-hydro potential into two tranches: a first tranche of 10 MW of the larger projects with capital costs of less than US $1100/kW, implemented in 2000–2002 (mini-hydro I) and a second tranche of 35 MW of smaller projects costing US $1100–US $1500/kW, implemented between 2001 and 2007 (mini-hydro II).

One of the main constraints to small-hydro development is the adequacy of the tariff. Presently, the CEB tariff is based solely on avoided energy costs, with no capacity credit – which is disputed by developers. The main CEB argument against a capacity benefit is that results from their WASP model show little or no impact of small hydro on the optimal capacity expansion plan. On the other hand, even in the driest months, there is still some mini-hydro generation. As more mini-hydro plants are built, the diversity effect is likely to increase the capacity value to CEB. In other words, while the capacity benefit of any single plant may be small because of the water flow variation of a particular site, the aggregate outputs of all small-hydro-projects provide more firm capacity.

In some locations, while individual technologies cannot be diversified, combinations of different renewable technologies may provide diversification and increase the capacity credit for the renewables portfolio as a whole. For example, just such a combination may

Table 5.5 *Generation capacity expansion for wind-power case*

All values are in megawatts; negative values indicate retirement

	1999	2001	2003	2005	2007	2009	2011	2013	2015	2017
Hydro			70	150						
Coal					300			300		300
Liquid fuels		106	300				105	105 105	105 105	105
Gas										
Diesel	100			−36		−36				
Renewables	3 30	30 30	60 60	75 75	75 75	150 150	150 150	150 150	150 150	150 150

be possible in the Eastern China province of Zhejiang, where small hydro peaks in summer and wind peaks in winter.

Wind power

Sri Lanka's wind climate is characterized by two monsoon systems – the stronger southwest monsoon, lasting from May to early October, and the northeast monsoon, from December to late February. With strong to moderate winds prevailing for about eight months of the year, Sri Lanka has a modest potential for wind-power generation. A 3 MW wind-power demonstration is underway with the support of the Extending Service Delivery (ESD) project, with an estimated capital cost of US $1175/kW.

Sri Lanka lacks good quality historical wind data to make a reliable assessment of wind-energy potential. Nevertheless, some tentative conclusions regarding windy regions in Sri Lanka could be drawn from existing wind data and also natural indicators. About 3600 MW of potential generation have been identified, mainly in the southern and southeastern lowland regions (CEB, 1992). The WASP model was used to examine the maximum amount of wind power that could be absorbed by the system while meeting the CEB planning criteria (loss-of-load probability, LOLP, of less than 0.1%). These studies reveal that up to 2000 MW could be absorbed into the system over the planning horizon.

The CEB capacity expansion plan for the maximum-wind-power scenario is shown in Table 5.5. Uncertainties in both costs and wind data underline the need for caution and better data. We assume a decrease in capital costs from the present US $1175/kW to US $1000/kW over the planning horizon. Far lower capital costs may be achieved if the rate of progress in wind-turbine technology achieved over the past decade continues into the future. On the other hand, a Danish study of 1080 wind-power sites over a period of six years showed that the actual annual production is 12% lower than predicted at the time of wind-farm design. Reasons for this discrepancy may be overoptimistic estimates of future turbine costs, lower reliability of machines and overestimates of wind availability.

Dendro-thermal power

The main rationale for dendro-thermal generation is its potential to displace costly fossil-fuel imports, while generating employment (Wijewardene and Joseph, 1999). Such power

Table 5.6 *Generation capacity expansion for dendro-thermal case*

All values are in megawatts; negative values indicate retirement

	1999	2001	2003	2005	2007	2009	2011	2013	2015	2017
Hydro			70	150						
Coal										
Liquid fuels		106	300						105	105 105
Gas										
Diesel	100		−36		−36					
Renewables			10	100 0	100 100 150	150		200 200	200 0	200 0

Table 5.7 *Assumptions for dendro-thermal power plants*

	Dendro (gasifier)	Coal plant
Unit size (MW)	10	2 × 300
Capital cost (US$/kW)	1200	899
Fixed O&M (US$/kW/month)	1.8	0.64
Variable O&M (non-fuel) (US$/MWh)	2.5	3.54
Heat rate (Kcal/kWh)	4560	2162
Sulphur content (%)	0.02	0.6
Heat value as received[a] (Kcal/kg)	3800	6300
Fuel cost (at plant gate) (US $/tonne)	22	48
Land area for fuelwood plantation (Ha/MW)	360	

[a] Assuming 20% moisture for fuelwood.

Source: Based on information provided by P. G. Joseph of the Sri Lanka Energy Conservation Fund.

plants require substantial land for the necessary fuelwood plantations – in Sri Lanka, advocates argue that 1000 MW of dendro-thermal would use only 360 000 hectares of scrub and chena lands (20% of total available).

Increments of dendro-thermal (50 MW) power for GHG mitigation were tested as an alternative to baseload coal plants. This results in the capacity expansion plan indicated in Table 5.6 – fuelwood costed at US $22/tonne.

Cost assumptions for dendro- versus coal-fired power are summarized in Table 5.7. It is assumed that gasifier rather than combustion (steam-cycle) technology is employed. The fuel cost of US $22/tonne is based on the present price of fuelwood delivered in Colombo. Fuelwood produced in properly managed plantations near the power plants may reduce this cost. Therefore, an alternative dendro-thermal fuel-cost price of US $14/tonne was also analysed.

Solar photovoltaic systems

Solar photovoltaic (PV) systems for remote rural homes ('solar homes') represent another component of the ESD project with Global Environment Faculty (GEF) support to overcome institutional and financing constraints – the ESD programme provides a US $100 grant per solar home module of 30 W or greater.

In the solar homes scenario, we assume that, by 2018, about 85% of the then remaining unelectrified homes would be served by solar systems, representing about 500 000 systems in place. This is significantly greater than the present estimate of between 100 000 to 215 000 homes considered by private vendors as the present potential market, taking into account affordability criteria (Jayewardene and Perera, 1991). Given the GDP growth assumed for the power demand forecast, a doubling of real income is possible over the 20-year planning period. We also assume that the present cost of US $6000/kW will decrease over time, reaching US $1000/kW by 2018, and the unit output per system would increase from the present 30–50 W to 200 W by 2018. These mildly optimistic assumptions seem warranted in order to determine the bounds of potential cost-effectiveness for GHG mitigation.

Fuel substitution options

Oil steam-cycle plants

For this GHG assessment we assume that 3.5% high-sulphur fuel oil would be imported from the Gulf, and that flue gas desulphurization (FGD) would be required. The plant characteristics are taken from Electrowatt (1996).

Liquid nitrogen gas (LNG)

The LNG price delivered to the plant gate is taken as US $5/MMBtu. This includes the cost recovery of the up-front infrastructure costs (terminal, gas storage, regasification facility, etc.) Capital and operating costs of the power-generation plant, heat rate, etc., may be taken as the same as for diesel-fuelled combined-cycle plants.

Conventional hydro

In addition to the Kukule and Upper Kotmale projects already in the least-cost generation expansion plan, additional plants (see Table 5.8) were forced into the plan to produce a maximum hydro development scenario (MaxHy) for GHG mitigation.

Table 5.8 *Additional hydro-projects for the maximum hydro scenario*

	Start-up year	MW	Capital cost ($/MW)[a]
Broadlands	2005	40	2548
Gin Ganga	2005	49	2127
Moragolla	2007	27	3002
Uma Oya	2010	150	2152

[a] Pure (overnight) project cost, without interest during construction, customs or duties.

Biomass co-firing

Biomass co-firing at the proposed coal-fired plants was considered. Supplying 15% of the energy input from fuelwood should be feasible at minimal modification of the coal plant (about US $75/kW) – based on the EPRI Technical Assessment Guide.

DSM

In addition to the lighting DSM-1 in the reform case, further GHG mitigation may be achieved by DSM-2 through energy-efficient motors (EEMs) and DSM-3 with energy-efficient air conditioning (EEAC).

5.5.5 Results

The screening analysis is summarized in Table 5.9. Note that the reductions in emissions in columns [4] and [5] cannot be added, since the individual data points represent perturbations of the reform scenario, one at a time (and some are mutually exclusive, such as LNG, oil steam-cycle with FGD, or the dendro-thermal options at different delivered wood costs). Negative costs of avoided carbon indicate 'win–win' options.

Figure 5.7 shows these data differently, plotting system cost against GHG emissions (undiscounted CO_2), with the four quadrants defined by the reform case. The slope of the line connecting any point with the reform case defines the cost of avoided carbon (see column [6] of Table 5.9).

These results are unsurprising. The most expensive option is the solar homes programme at US $184/tonne of carbon. However, this result is a good example of the hazards of conducting the analysis in terms of changes in system costs rather than changes in net benefits. When benefits of providing lighting and TV in off-grid areas are properly assessed, the solar home option brings significant net benefits (see Section 15.7.1).

Impact on local air emissions

Implementation of GHG emission reduction measures also reduces local air emissions (SO_2, NOx, particulates). However, the monetized value of these local environmental benefits is small in comparison to the cost of avoided carbon.

GHG emission reduction scenarios

Starting with BAU, individual mitigation measures are brought into the solution cumulatively. The criterion for introducing the next measure could be the next lowest cost of avoided carbon, or the measure most likely to be implemented. For example, starting with BAU, the first step could be either DSM (which has the best cost of avoided carbon) or T&D rehabilitation. In Figure 5.8, T&D loss reduction is the first step.

Table 5.10 shows the order in which the measures are brought into solution, reaching the least-cost scenario (step [8]) after introduction of all of the DSM, mini-hydro and further

Table 5.9 *Cost of avoided carbon*

	System cost (million $)	Cost difference (relative to reform)	CO$_2$ emissions (million tonnes)	CO$_2$ difference (relative to reform)	Carbon difference	Cost of avoided carbon ($/tonne C)
	[1]	[2]	[3]	[4]	[5]	[6]
Reform	2449		98.4			
+DSM-2: EEM	2430	−18.5	96.6	−1.8	−0.5	−37.6
Oil–steam (resid.)	2325	−123.7	83.1	−15.3	−4.2	−29.7
Oil–steam (resid.) + FGD	2362	−87.2	83.1	−15.3	−4.2	−20.9
+DSM-3: EEAC	2441	−7.6	96.4	−2.0	−0.6	−13.6
Oil–steam + FGD	2416	−33.2	88.5	−9.9	−2.7	−12.3
+T&D (to 10%)	2440	−9.2	95.2	−3.2	−0.9	−10.4
Mini-hydro: I	2448	−0.8	97.5	−1.0	−0.3	−3.2
Mini-hydro: II	2450	1.5	95.7	−2.7	−0.7	2.1
Dendro-thermal ($14/tonne)	2492	42.7	39.2	−59.3	−16.2	2.6
Oil–steam (0.3%S)	2465	16.5	88.6	−9.8	−2.7	6.1
Dendro-thermal ($22/tonne)	2580	131.1	39.6	−58.8	−16	8.2
Diesel ($800/kW)	2494	45.3	83.8	−14.6	−4	11.4
LNG	2545	96.3	77.3	−21.1	−5.8	16.7
Diesel ($1140/kW)	2580	130.9	83.8	−14.6	−4	32.8
MaxHy	2553	104.0	88.3	−10.1	−2.8	37.7
Wind (max.)	2870	421.2	74.8	−23.7	−6.5	65.3
Solar homes	2490	41.6	97.6	−0.8	−0.2	184.5

T&D loss reduction. Any further measures to reduce GHG emissions would then begin to increase costs.

By the time we reach the economic least-cost scenario (all the DSM, mini-hydro and further reduction of T&D losses), which is the lowest point on the curve, the number of coal plants over the planning horizon has reduced further from the five in the reform scenario to four.

5.5.6 Developing the standard abatement cost curve (SACC)

Table 5.11 shows the avoided costs of carbon and the percentage reductions (relative to the BAU case) achievable in each scenario. Win–win options, when considered as a stand-alone perturbation of the reform case, may not remain win–win when combined with other win–win options. In Table 5.11, introducing oil–steam + FGD *after* the last tranche of mini-hydro increases costs, and is therefore no longer win–win.

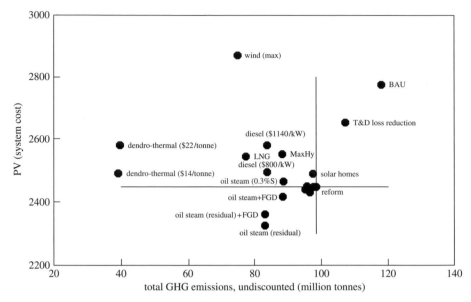

Figure 5.7. System cost versus GHG emissions.

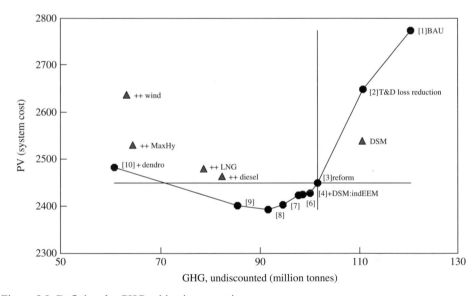

Figure 5.8. Defining the GHG-mitigation scenario.

The corresponding GHG-mitigation supply curve – where we introduce each measure in order of avoided cost – is shown in Figure 5.9. Here we draw the SACC in tonnes of carbon (rather than tonnes of CO_2). In such a standard deterministic framework, all the steps that lie below the emission-trading price should be pursued if decision makers seek to maximize the

Table 5.10 *Definition of mitigation scenarios*

		Measure								Mutually exclusive options						
		CBB base case	T&D >12.5%	DSM lighting	DSM ind EEM	DSM comm AC	MiniHy I	T&D >10%	MiniHy II	Oil–steam + FGD	Dendro	Diesel	LNG	MaxHy	Wind	Solar homes
Cost of avoided carbon, $/tonne		C>	−82	−35	−50	−20	−16	−14	−0.5	−21	8	11	16	38	66	150
Scenarios																
1	BAU	X														
2	+T&D > 12.5%	X	X													
3	Reform	X	X	X												
4	DSM:indEEM	X	X	X	X											
5	+DSM:commAC	X	X	X	X	X										
6	+MiniHy I	X	X	X	X	X	X									
7	+T&D >10%	X		X	X	X	X	X								
8	+MiniHy II	X		X	X	X	X	X	X							
9	Oil–steam (+FGD)	X		X	X	X	X	X	X	X						
10	Dendro-thermal	X		X	X	X	X	X	X		X					
11	Diesel	X		X	X	X	X	X	X			X				
12	LNG	X		X	X	X	X	X	X				X			
13	+MaxHy	X		X	X	X	X	X	X		X			X		
14	+Wind	X		X	X	X	X	X	X		X			X	X	
15	+Solar homes	X		X	X	X	X	X	X		X			X	X	X

Table 5.11 *GHG-mitigation scenarios*

Scenario	System cost	Cost difference	CO_2	CO_2 difference	$/tonne C	% reduction (BAU)
BAU	2775	382	118.0			
T&D loss reduction	2653	260	107.1	19	−49.5	9
Reform	2449	56	98.4	11	−19.4	17
DSM:indEEM	2430	38	96.6	9	−15.7	18
DSM:commAC	2425	32	95.3	7	−15.7	19
Mini-hydro I	2423	30	94.6	7	−16.2	20
T&D > 10%	2403	10	90.5	3	−13.8	23
Mini-hydro II = least-cost	2393		87.8			26
Oil–steam ++FGD	2402	10	79.6	−8	4.4	33
Dendro	2481	89	46.2	−42	7.8	61
Diesel	2500	107	75.4	−12	31.6	36
LNG	2465	73	70.2	−18	15.2	41
MaxHy	2540	147	49.8	−38	14.2	58
Wind	2639	246	50.1	−38	23.9	58

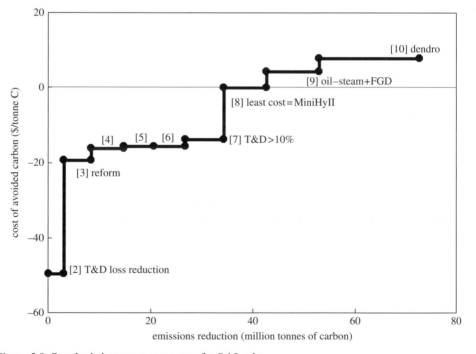

Figure 5.9. Standard abatement cost curve for Sri Lanka.

net benefits of abatement. However, uncertainty introduces complications that require a more dynamic framework, as shown below.

5.6 Real-options framework for carbon trading under uncertainty

The results of the previous section help to identify an appropriate GHG strategy for Sri Lanka. However, there are large uncertainties, including the value of carbon in international trading – which could range from zero, if a market for carbon reductions does not develop, to values in excess of US $20/tonne if evidence of global warming begins to appear.

5.6.1 Sources of uncertainty and the real-options approach

Uncertainty calls for the options-based approach to be used to enhance the traditional net present value (NPV) rule used in CBA. Jepma and Munasinghe (1998) classify uncertainty related to climate change into two broad categories. First, scientific uncertainty arises due to limited knowledge of rates of natural emission and absorption, and of environmental consequences of GHGs. Second, socioeconomic and technological uncertainty linked to human actions arises from the difficulty of predicting the future rates of emissions, the inability to value in monetary terms the future impact of climate change and other forms of environmental degradation, lack of knowledge about human responses to environmental changes and lack of knowledge about the development of technological options, which would affect all aspects of the environmental equation. Climate change has a long time frame, with forecast periods of over 100 years. Even small uncertainties can lead to a wide range of outcomes over such long time periods (Munasinghe and Swart, 2005).

Standard and dynamic abatement cost curves

In this section, we follow the model developed in Fernando and Munasinghe (1998). An important first step in the bottom-up approach to mitigation is the identification of the options available for reducing emissions. A standard abatement cost curve (SACC) for GHG mitigation options (as in Figure 5.9) is obtained by deterministically ranking specific GHG mitigation projects in the order of cost (or benefit in the case of 'win–win' projects) of reducing a unit of carbon emissions. The costs and benefits of GHG mitigation are obtained by discounting future streams of value back to the present time. Projects with a lower cost per unit of carbon reduction should be implemented prior to higher-cost projects.

This static approach can yield misleading results, especially in the case of GHG mitigation projects, which can vary widely with regard to time frame, the cost of reversal and the uncertainty associated with future costs and benefits. This is because the SACC, which is based on the assessment of future costs and benefits at a particular instant in time, disregards the value of the options embedded in specific projects associated with changing the timing of their implementation. Taking such options into account may lead to a reversal in the ordering of projects along the SACC or control-cost staircase.

For example, higher-cost (but lower-option-valued) projects might be undertaken prior to their lower cost (but higher-option-valued) counterparts. This option value will arise, in part, from the fact that the control-cost curve is itself dynamic, with changes brought about due to the evolution of science and technology, as well as socioeconomic conditions. Developing a dynamic abatement cost curve (DACC) would require taking account of each of the above drivers of option value, for each of the GHG mitigation options that have been identified in the SACC.

To show how risk and uncertainty might affect the SACC, consider a deterministic case where the cheapest mitigation option (step A) would be to increase energy prices, while the next best option (step B) is energy conservation. In a riskless analysis, the decision maker would first carry out step A, then go to step B. However, in reality, public reaction against energy-price increases may involve a greater political risk – it may be preferable to undertake step B first and defer step A until later. Thus, political uncertainty and risk could change the decision-making process.

Uncertainties in future technology costs or carbon offset values could also result in the transposition of steps, compared to the deterministic case. This decision problem can be analysed using a real-options framework, which has been used extensively in other fields. Box 5.3 illustrates the basic concept using a simple numerical example. Fernando and Munasinghe (1998) provide a detailed description.

5.6.2 *Applying the real-options approach*

Oil–steam (+FGD)

In Table 5.12, we examine the use of oil–steam (+FGD) as a mitigation measure, starting from the least-cost scenario. As shown in panel A, this increases the system cost by US $9.7 million and decreases GHG emissions by 8.1 million tonnes, with a discounted cost of avoided carbon of US $21.2/tonne (which falls to US $4.4/tonne when undiscounted).

Panel B shows the probability distribution for the value of the carbon offset, expressed as US $/tonne C. The expected value of the carbon offset, $E\{V(C)\}$, is US $22. The corresponding expected value of carbon offset revenue, $E\{R(C)\}$, is US $10.1 million when discounted at 10%; $E\{R(C)\}$ is given by

$$E\{R(C)\}d = \Sigma Vj \cdot P\{j\} \cdot \Delta C,$$

where ΔC is the avoided carbon (8.1 million tonnes in this case) and $P\{j\}$ is the probability of the carbon offset having value Vj.

Panel C of Table 5.12 then derives the expected value of implementing this mitigation option today, which is the cost given in Table 5.12, panel A (NPV of US $2402.3 million), less the expected value of revenue from carbon offsets (US $10.1 million). This is US $0.4 million less than the least-cost case (US $2392.6 million). This reduction in cost (though only about 4% of the expected value of the carbon offset revenue) would normally justify undertaking the mitigation measure (given the expected value of US $22/tonne for carbon offsets).

Box 5.3 Calculation of option values

Consider an environmental project that requires an investment of US $100 million. Based on the information available today (time 0), this project will yield an environmental credit valued at US $200 million (good state) or US $50 million (bad state), with equal probability, a year from now (time 1). The project terminates at time 1. With a discount rate of 10%, the NPV is given by

$$NPV = 0.5\,\{200/1.1\} \quad + \quad 0.5\{50/1.1\} \quad - \ 100 \qquad = \text{US \$13.6 million}$$

return in year 1   return in year 1   cost of

$\times$ Pr{good state} $\times$ Pr{bad state}   investment

The standard NPV rule would recommend that this project be undertaken in order to realize the expected positive net present value of US $13.6 million.

  Suppose the project can be postponed at a cost of US $5 million, and that one year from now it will be known whether the state is good or bad. If the good state is observed, the investment will be made, with a return of US $200 million at time 2. If the bad state is observed, the investment will not be made. Therefore the NPV of postponing the investment decision until time 1 is given by

$$NPV = 0.5\,\{200/1.1^2\} \ + \ 0.5\{100/1.1\} \ + \ 0.5^*\text{zero} \quad - \quad 5 \qquad = \text{US \$32.2 million}$$

return in year 2   cost of   Pr{bad state}   cost of

$\times$Pr{bad state}   investment   [no investment]   delay

Thus, although the NPV is positive, it will be suboptimal to invest in this project at time 0, since investors can gain by waiting until time 1, when the uncertainty is resolved and the expected value increases to US $32 million. Thus, the option value of delaying a decision by one year is $32.2 - 13.6 = $ US $18.6 million.

Panel D shows the implications of delaying a decision by five years. This delay is not costless, for instead of building the coal baseload plant now, one must build other interim capacity, such as diesels, to meet the demand. The capacity expansion plan is recalculated with the first coal unit delayed by five years and 300 MW of diesels (at US $1100/kW) built over the five-year period. Then, five years from now, one would reconsider whether to build a coal plant or to implement the mitigation measure. The new costs and GHG emissions are noted in Panel D. Because the interim diesels have some impact on the merit order dispatch, GHG emissions are different from those shown in Panel A, with a slightly higher cost of avoided carbon (US $21.9/tonne, row [7] of panel D).

  In panel E we show the impacts of delay. The costs increase in both cases by a roughly similar amount. The least-cost case requires a first coal plant in 2006. It follows that if the coal plant were delayed and some other interim plant were built, costs will rise by US $41.6 million. However, GHG emissions decrease by 3.1 million tonnes, since emissions from a

Table 5.12 *Oil–steam (+FGD) compared to least-cost solution*
All costs are in US $

A Cost and avoided carbon if implemented today

		Baseline: least cost	Mitigation measure ++oil–steam+FGD	Δ cost
[1]	System cost (US $ million)	2392.6	2402.3	9.7
Undiscounted				
[2]	GHG (CO_2) (million tonnes)	87.8	79.6	−8.1
[3]	Cost of avoided CO_2 ($/tonne CO_2)			1.2
[4]	Cost of avoided carbon ($/tonne C)			4.4
Discounted				
[5]	GHG (CO_2) (million tonnes)	25.4	23.8	−1.7
[6]	Cost of avoided CO_2 ($/tonne CO_2)			5.8
[7]	Cost of avoided carbon ($/tonne C)			21.2

B Expected value of revenue from carbon offsets

	$/tonne	Pr{j}	$R(C)$ ($ million)	$E\{R(C)\}$ ($ million)
[1]	0	0.025	0.00	0.0
[2]	10	0.150	4.58	0.7
[3]	20	0.500	9.15	4.6
[4]	30	0.250	13.73	3.4
[5]	40	0.075	18.31	1.4
[6]	Discounted value			10.1

C Expected value of implemeting measure today ($ million)

[1]	Cost with mitigation measure (from A, [1])	++oil–steam+FGD	2402.3
[2]	Less expected value of carbon offsets (from B, [8])		−10.1
[3]	Expected cost of mitigation measure = [1] + [2]		2392.3
[4]	Cost without mitigation measure (from A, [1])	least cost	2392.3
[5]	Cost reduction		0.4
[6]			benefit: proceed

D Cost and avoided carbon if measure ++oil–steam+FGD is implemented in year 5

		Baseline: reform + 5 diesel	Interim measure Mitigation measure ++dendro	Δ cost
[1]	System cost (US $million)	2434	2441	7.1
Undiscounted				
[2]	GHG (CO_2) (million tonnes)	84.7	78.5	−6.3
[3]	Cost of avoided CO_2 ($/tonne CO_2)			1.1
[4]	Cost of avoided carbon ($/tonne C)			4.1

Table 5.12 (*cont.*)

| | Interim measure | | |
	Baseline: reform + 5 diesel	Mitigation measure ++dendro	Δ cost
Discounted			
[5] GHG (CO_2) (10^6 tonnes)	24.6	23.5	−1.2
[6] Cost of avoided CO_2 ($/tonne CO_2)			6.0
[7] Cost of avoided carbon ($/tonne C)			21.9

E Impact of delay

	Baseline: reform +5	Mitigation measure ++dendro
[1] System cost (US $million)	41.6	39.0
[2] GHG (CO_2), undiscounted (million tonnes)	−3.1	−1.2

F Decision if uncertainty resolved: calculation of option value

$/tonne	Pr{j}	PV[$E\{R(C)\}$] ++Dendro	Reform+5	Δ cost	Decision	Benefit	E{benefit}
[1] 0	0.025	0	2441	2434	7	do not build	0	0
[2] 10	0.150	3.2	2438	2434	4	do not build	0	0
[3] 20	0.500	6.5	2435	2434	1	do not build	0	0
[4] 30	0.250	9.7	2432	2434	−3	build	2.6	0.7
[5] 40	0.075	12.9	2428	2434	−6	build	5.8	0.4

[6] Total expected value of carbon offsets	1.1
[7] Benefit if implemented today (from C, [5])	0.4
[8] Option value of delay ([6]–[7])	0.7

diesel plant are lower than from the corresponding coal plant. Similarly, because diesels are more efficient than steam-cycle plants, replacing the first oil plant by diesels also reduces GHG emissions relative to no delay, and so GHG emissions decrease by 1.2 million tonnes per year.

In panel F we now recalculate the expected values, given resolution of the uncertainty at $t + 5$. If the actual value of the offset is less than the cost of avoided carbon (US $21.9/tonne), then the mitigation measure is not undertaken. The converse holds with the discrete probability distribution assumed here and actual offset values of US $30/tonne and US $40/tonne. The expected value of benefits is calculated at US $1.09 million, which is greater than the US $0.37 million calculated if the decision is made today. Thus, the option value is US $1.09 − 0.37 = US $0.72 million. Although the numbers are small, the option value of delay is almost twice the expected value of the benefit of making the commitment to the mitigation measure today – representing about 7% of expected carbon offset revenues.

Equally important is the illustration of the importance of proper discounting. Since undiscounted carbon emissions over some given planning horizon will always be greater than the corresponding discounted sum, it necessarily follows that the apparent cost of avoided carbon will be lower than if discounted. However, the economic flows that result from carbon offset payments must be discounted for valid analysis, which effectively increases the cost of avoided carbon (from US $4.4/tonne to US $21.2/tonne in this example). End effects are included by deducting salvage values from system costs.

Liquid nitrogen gas

A similar analysis for LNG (measured against the reform option) shows that a commitment to LNG today has an expected value of −US $69.5 million. Here, the costs of carbon offsets (US $22/tonne) are insufficient to compensate for the higher estimated cost of avoided carbon (US $79.2/tonne). Waiting for five years does not change the attractiveness of LNG, and there is no option value. In this case, the avoided cost of carbon is US $66/tonne, and even if the uncertainty is resolved and the actual value of the carbon offset rises to US $40/tonne, the LNG option would remain unattractive.

Dendro-thermal

When the option value is applied to dendro-thermal power, the expected value of a commitment today is a benefit of US $31.4 million, because the cost of avoided carbon (US $10.9/tonne) is less than the expected value of the carbon offset (US $22/tonne).

However, the impact of delay is quite different for dendro-thermal than for the previous two cases. As before, forcing diesels into the least-cost solution for the interim period reduces GHG emissions. But, in the case of the dendro-thermal option, diesels will significantly increase GHG emissions – by 9.1 million tonnes. This results in an aggregate cost of avoided carbon that jumps to US $42.6/tonne. Hence, given the maximum value of US $40/tonne in the discrete probability distribution assumed for carbon offset revenue, dendro-thermal would not be implemented at $t+5$. Clearly, there is no option value in this case.

This counter-intuitive result arises because the economic life of diesels extends well beyond the five-year interim period. Thus, new dendro-thermal plants at $t+5$ must compete against only the low variable cost of diesel plant operation, since capital costs are sunk and are no longer relevant at $t+5$. However, one of the advantages of dendro-thermal is that it can be built in small increments of 1–5 MW, unlike coal plant, where the capacity increment would be 600–900 MW to capture economies of scale. Therefore, instead of the intermediate five-year commitment to diesels before choosing coal or dendro-thermal, we make a five-year commitment to a dendro-thermal demonstration programme, and then decide whether to go to coal or continue with a full-scale dendro-thermal programme.

The corresponding option value calculation shows that the expected value for a present permanent commitment to dendro-thermal is unchanged at US $31.4 million. However, if the interim dendro-thermal demonstration is undertaken, the delay creates a win–win situation – the mitigation measure costs US $2482 million, which is lower than the least-cost solution (with the interim dendro-thermal demonstration) of US $2515 million, but still higher than the least-cost solution alone of US $2448 million. Nevertheless, the calculated option value is US $59.4 million, indicating the significant benefit of being able to abandon the dendro-thermal option at $t+5$, regardless of the value of the carbon offset.

6

International process applications: multilevel, multistakeholder, transdisciplinary dialogues[1]

The case studies in this chapter focus on participatory-consultative processes relating to the social dimension of sustainable development. They describe a variety of global multilevel, multistakeholder, transdisciplinary dialogues that are crucial for making development more sustainable (see Sections 1.2.4 and 2.1.3). Within the conventional categories of government, business and civil society, epistemic communities of experts and practitioners could play a key catalytic role in cross-linking and stimulating pluralistic participation (Munasinghe, 2001b, 2004c; Sneddon, Howarth and Norgaard, 2006). The involvement of young people is also important (Focus the Nation, 2007). Section 6.1 describes how climate change and sustainable development (see Chapter 5) are handled in the Intergovernmental Panel on Climate Change (IPCC) writing process. The case study examines how this unique international dialogue among thousands of scientists is transcending barriers of discipline, space, time, stakeholder viewpoints and operationality, in addressing complex, interlinked, large-scale, long-run issues. In the second case study, Sections 6.2 and 6.3 explore two-way linkages between two other complex global initiatives – the millennium development goals (MDGs) and millennium ecosystem assessment (MA) findings. The Action Impact Matrix (AIM), a key sustainomics tool, is used to explore linkages between the two at both national and global levels. Finally, in Sections 6.4 to 6.6, we examine how a uniquely successful multistakeholder, multilevel process has been organized by the UNEP Dams and Development Programme (DDP), as a follow-up to the World Commission on Dams (WCD). It deals with key water resource issues at the international, regional and national levels (see Chapter 12).

6.1 Global transdisciplinary scientific dialogue on climate change and sustainable development

The following example describes how the IPCC is addressing the complicated issues linking climate change and sustainable development, through a unique transdisciplinary international dialogue among several thousand scientists. They have developed effective modes of consultation and collaboration to assess the latest research and identify policy-relevant issues and

---

[1] Some parts of the chapter are based on material adapted from Munasinghe (1998a, 2001b, 2002c, 2004c, 2007a).

remedial options. This study shows the practical interplay of key elements of the sustainomics approach in the IPCC process that help to transcend barriers of discipline, space, time, stakeholder viewpoints and operationality, to deal with large-scale, long-term, complex and interlinked issues such as sustainable development and climate change (see Sections 5.1 to 5.4)

6.1.1 Introduction to the IPCC

The work of the IPCC addresses the twin challenges of climate change and sustainable development (see Chapter 5). The IPCC was established in 1988 by the World Meteorological Organization (WMO) and the United Nations Environment Program (UNEP), to assess scientific information on climate change, as well as its environmental and socioeconomic impacts, and to formulate response strategies. Under the aegis of the United Nations, the world's foremost climate experts were engaged in a multiyear process to carry out this task. In 1990, the IPCC's First Assessment Report (FAR) focused on the science of climate change, concluding that continued accumulation of anthropogenic GHGs in the atmosphere would lead to climate change whose rate and magnitude were likely to have important impacts on both socioeconomic and natural systems. The Second Assessment Report (SAR), in 1995, deepened the analysis on ecological impacts and provided rough estimates of future economic damage as well as mitigation measures. Confirming the FAR findings, the SAR stated that 'the balance of evidence suggests a discernible human influence on the global climate,' and predicted a 1–3.5 °C increase in global mean temperature and 15–95 cm rise in mean sea level by 2100.

In 2001, the Third Assessment Report (TAR) further confirmed that climate change is inevitable and estimated that the global mean temperature will increase by 1.5–6 °C. The report examined the interlinkages between climate change and sustainable development. This section describes the lessons learned from the multidisciplinary interactions involved during the writing of the TAR, and shows how the integrative, transdisciplinary approach promoted in the sustainomics framework has contributed to the IPCC process.

The TAR has three parts, dealing with (1) the science of climate change; (2) adaptation; and (3) mitigation. These parts were prepared by working groups WG1, WG2 and WG3, respectively. Over 500 'lead authors' from a large variety of disciplines and many countries were organized into chapter-writing teams. Climate scientists were in the majority in WG1; natural scientists predominated in WG2; and economists and energy experts were more common in WG3. Furthermore, many thousands of other experts reviewed several drafts of the TAR before it was approved by all national governments.

6.1.2 Guidance paper on development, equity and sustainability

The IPCC Bureau (managing the TAR) commissioned guidance papers on several key issues that cut across the working groups and chapters, to ensure consistent treatment. The guidance paper on climate change and sustainable development proved to be a real challenge. Most authors had little prior exposure to the complex sustainable development literature.

Furthermore, the paper had to be prepared within a few months, to feed into the IPCC process before the writing teams began to draft their chapters. The paper was entitled 'Development, equity, and sustainability (DES) in the context of climate change' (Munasinghe, 2000a).

The DES paper was built on the sustainomics framework (see Chapter 2). It posed three questions to TAR authors: (1) How will future development patterns and scenarios affect climate change? (2) How will climate-change impacts, adaptation and mitigation affect future sustainable development prospects? (3) How could climate-change responses be integrated better into sustainable development strategies?

To examine the circular interaction between climate change and sustainable development, the guidance paper outlined the analytical framework that has already been described in Sections 5.1 and 5.2. Climate-change interactions with sustainable development (including alternative response strategies) could be assessed in a risk management framework, considering long-term effects on: (1) human welfare and equity; (2) the durability and resilience of ecological, geophysical and socioeconomic systems; and (3) the stocks of different kinds of capital (e.g. manufactured, natural, human and sociocultural assets).

Specific economic, social and environmental indicators are needed at different levels of aggregation ranging from the global/macro to local/micro. Indicators must be comprehensive, multidimensional, practical and account for regional and scale differences. Among the large array of indicators already available, TAR authors should carefully select those indicators that focus on key attributes of sustainable development. They need to engage in a transdisciplinary, integrative process, which systematically searches beyond the mainstream journals, for the growing volume of literature that addresses the nexus of climate change and sustainable development, especially interdisciplinary.

The social, economic and environmental approaches to sustainability must be recognized and reconciled wherever possible (see Chapter 2). Two methods based on *optimality* and *durability* are useful in providing an integrated and balanced treatment of these viewpoints (see Section 5.4). Even though a climate strategy cannot address all poverty- and equity-related problems, it would be useful to assess whether climate change will worsen existing poverty and inequity.

Climate change and other global environmental issues, such as loss of biodiversity, desertification and stratospheric ozone depletion, are inextricably linked with each other, as well as with more localized environmental problems. One important challenge is to identify 'win–win' strategies, which would favour development paths that reduce GHG emissions without undermining prospects for reducing poverty and improving human welfare. Institutional and governance issues would be crucial in implementing adaptation and mitigation measures. It was also emphasized that the TAR would be more useful to decision makers if it was able to incorporate the viewpoints of all stakeholders, including governments, business, civil society and non-governmental organizations.

6.1.3 *The internal debate, outcome and lessons learned*

The first draft of the DES paper was circulated via e-mail to all TAR authors in late 1999, and a spirited debate ensued, unprecedented in IPCC history. It involved natural scientists, economists, sociologists, climate scientists, developmental specialists, environ-mentalists, geographers, political scientists, general policy analysts and others with mixed backgrounds. The first phase began with a heavily critical e-mail jointly signed by six neoclassical economists, urging that the paper be discarded. They claimed that the role of economics had been diminished, while a new framework was being intro-duced (linking economic, social and environmental concepts), which did not reflect consensus opinion.

In the second phase, many others responded individually (1) broadly supporting the main thrust of the paper; (2) offering specific but constructive criticisms; and (3) rebutting the original six critics. There was general support for the need to bridge disciplinary approaches via the holistic, balanced framework combining economic, social and environmental view-points, and for reconciling optimality/efficiency with durability/resilience. Most agreed that the paper outlined a flexible approach, rather than being a straightjacket to force consensus, because it drew attention to the main issues and suggested options to address them.

Other comments on the paper included requests for more specific practical guidance to apply the new framework, more details on economic, ecological and social indicators, to assess the sustainability of alternative futures, and many minor technical corrections. Contradicting the neoclassical economists' criticism, many other authors felt that the paper was overly oriented toward economic efficiency, and that it should focus more on poverty, equity and sustainability issues.

The original six critics were also faulted for selectively misrepresenting arguments presented in the paper, exaggerating the role of economics while overlooking its short-comings and failing to accept the importance of key sustainable development issues relating to poverty, equity and sustainability. They were further criticized for 'ganging up' early, to pre-empt and choke off further discussion, and for adopting a 'hegemonistic,' confronta-tional and harsh tone inappropriate for effective scientific dialogue within the IPCC.

The final phase was marked by much milder exchanges, many involving second thoughts. A deeper dialogue took place among participants, and many points of agree-ment emerged. The original six critics withdrew their objections and the DES paper was revised and finalized (Munasinghe, 2000a). Subsequent discussions continued in a collegial and convergent manner, within and across the writing teams of specific chapters of the TAR.

Judging the success of this exercise is best left to readers of the TAR. One outcome was that the IPCC process has been further strengthened. Participating scientists ended up with a better idea of each others' viewpoints, and there was surprisingly little rancour at the end. Minds became more open and the transdisciplinary dialogue improved. Despite differences in academic training, culture and outlook, an underlying sense of fellowship prevailed – that the unique, and hitherto highly successful, IPCC process was indeed worth protecting. Sustainable development issues were explicitly introduced into the TAR and associated documents. However, treatment of sustainable development across chapters remains uneven. Even greater progress could have been made if the early selection process for lead authors had recognized the need for experts with a better grasp of these issues. One key outcome was that the IPCC Bureau and the main governing body (the IPCC Plenary) decided to incorporate fully sustainable development as a major theme cutting across all three working groups of the next (fourth) assessment report.

What are the key lessons learned from this experience? The sustainomics-based approach proposed in the guidance paper was clearly preferred by the majority of lead authors (except for initial reservations of the small group of neoclassical economists). Thus, transdisciplinary work was considered essential to deal with large-scale, long-term, complex and interlinked issues such as sustainable development and climate change. However, crossing disciplinary and cultural boundaries requires sound knowledge of one's own discipline (especially its limitations), open-mindedness, great patience and sincere effort on all sides. A heuristic approach is essential to maintain the delicate, dynamic balance between the twin objectives of promoting holistic integration across disciplines and preserving the rigour of individual disciplinary models.

The continuing IPCC process has greater value than any single result, because our knowledge is far from complete and constantly evolving. Thus, building good faith and trust (i.e. social capital) among diverse colleagues and understanding different viewpoints are more important longer-term goals than being correct on some specific point.

E-mail proved to be a powerful, but potentially risky, tool for quick, broad-based reviews. It was a necessity, given the international scope of exchanges within severe time and resource constraints. However, face-to-face meetings are far less likely to cause ill-feeling in a multidisciplinary, multicultural debate, in which modes of expression vary widely. Often, the 'tone' of e-mail dialogues could be misperceived as abrasive, especially when it is not among close friends and colleagues. In such circumstances, *how* something is said could be as important as *what* is said, to ensure effective communication. Nevertheless, fair-mindedness and good-will finally prevailed, despite some difficult moments.

What insights did the debate provide about the resilience of the IPCC intellectual community? This network has already proved to be quite cohesive in the face of determined attacks by powerful and well financed 'anti-climate-change' lobbies. The strong pressure to include sustainable development concerns within the TAR was a different kind of external stress. Adaptation and learning within the IPCC community took place in several ways. First, fresh ideas were brought in to catalyse change. Second, the disciplinary mix evolved to meet the challenge (and continues to do so). Third, IPCC internal processes adjusted to facilitate beneficial changes, while limiting harmful dissension. Scientists were able to accommodate different ways of thinking about the problem, as well as new modes of communication (e.g. e-mail), while re-enforcing desirable codes of conduct and behavioural norms (i.e. building social capital).

6.2 Multilevel integration of millennium ecosystem assessment results and millennium development goals

In this case example, we examine how a key sustainomics tool, the Action Impact Matrix (AIM), might be used to explore the linkages between two important international initiatives – the millennium development goals (MDGs) and millennium ecosystem assessment (MA) – see Chapters 1 and 4.

6.2.1 *Mainstreaming the environment into a sustainable development strategy*

An important follow-up of the MA is to apply the results and promote sustainable development in the twenty-first century, by generating recommendations on policy, institutional design and governance at the local, national and global scales. Developing linkages and synergies with other international processes, such as the MDGs and multilateral environmental agreements (e.g. UNFCCC, CBC, CMS, CCD, Ramsar, etc.), is especially important.

We start from the fundamental premise that measures to protect ecosystems and ecosystem services ultimately must be mainstreamed into conventional development strategy. The comprehensive and far-reaching recommendations proposed by the MA are rather generalized, and exist mainly at the global and regional levels. Recognizing the multiscale dimensions of protecting ecosystem services (ranging from the local to the global levels), and the need to strengthen in-country activities, we should seek to mainstream the broad MA results by integrating them into sustainable development (SD) strategy at the national and local levels, and implementing them on a more disaggregate basis through local communities and individuals. As a parallel second step, the MA findings will also receive more favourable attention from the development community if one could explicitly identify their linkages with global development concerns – e.g. the MDGs.

These mainstreaming objectives could be achieved by using the AIM to identify and prioritize key MA–SD policy linkages at both national and global levels (see Chapter 2).

National-level mainstreaming through MA–SD linkage

National decision makers normally pay attention to conventional development strategies that seek to achieve objectives such as economic growth, poverty alleviation, food security, improved human health and employment. As shown in Figure 6.1, sustainable development is considered a poorly understood aspect of conventional development. In turn, the environment is one component of sustainable development, and finally ecosystems are a single element of the environment. The horizontal arrow shows that the key step in practical implementation of the MA results within a country is to show the interaction between conventional development activities and key ecosystem services, identify priority issues and determine appropriate policy responses in the development domain.

Global-level mainstreaming through MA–MDG linkage

Figure 6.2 shows how to link key ecosystems identified in the MA report with all the MDGs. These are multiple, two-way interactions. The common pitfall is that the development community tends to restrict linking ecosystems and their services with just one MDG – i.e. MDG 7 dealing with the environment. A recent review of 100 country-level MDG reports concludes that 'An assessment of the extent to which environmental considerations

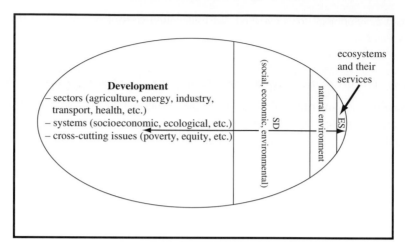

Figure 6.1. National-level ecosystems–sustainable development nexus. Ecosystems are a minor element of development strategy. Source: Munasinghe (1992a).

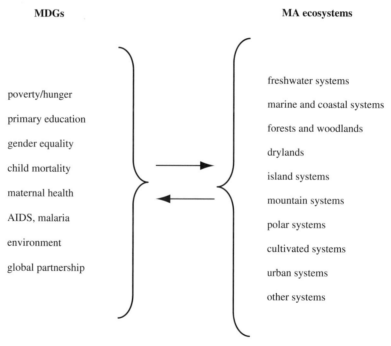

Figure 6.2. Global-level mainstreaming. Key MA ecosystems should be linked to all MDGs, not only MDG 7 on environment.

are integrated into MDG reports other than Goal 7 shows that environmental issues do not receive much attention outside of MDG7…the causal link between environment and other goals is not well recognized or articulated and response systems are not developed' (UNDP, 2005a). Establishing the MDG–MA integration at the global level will facilitate efforts to make the same linkage at the national level (Schmidt-Traub and Cho, 2005).

6.2.2 Implementing the MA results

Key policy-relevant issues

Two policy-relevant questions reinforce the main theme of this paper; i.e. the MA results need to be interpreted and incorporated within a broader sustainable development framework. First, is the balance between humans and nature appropriate? It appears that the MA favours the anthropocentric viewpoint, and gives prominence to the relevance of ecosystems for human well-being. This will be helpful in convincing decision makers and stakeholders to undertake some of the difficult policy remedies.

Second, is the south–north balance appropriate? The MA process devoted considerable effort to incorporate the southern perspective fairly (e.g. in the recruitment of managers, lead authors and reviewers, case study material, etc.). Nevertheless, more effort is required in the dissemination and implementation phase, to reassure the developing countries. The broad results suggest that: (1) ecosystems and their services are under threat globally, and the poor are most vulnerable to loss of ecosystem services; (2) policy options and measures are available to manage ecosystems, but they will require radical changes; and (3) such management will yield significant benefits for human well-being.

The MA highlights an additional fact, which is relevant for the billions of poor people in the developing world – the bulk of the world's biodiversity resides in the developing countries. Here, two key poverty–equity related questions arise: (1) Who bears the costs and reaps the benefits of exploiting ecosystem services? (2) Who will bear the burden of preserving ecosystem services and benefit from it?

On the first issue, the MA states: 'In many cases, it is the poor who suffer the loss of services caused directly by the pressure put on natural systems to bring benefits to other communities, often in different parts of the world' (MA, 2005a). If the rich in distant places exploit ecosystem services, and the local poor have to pay the costs, there are obvious equity implications – both international (south–north) and within countries (and, indirectly, inter-generational, as well).

On the second issue, poor countries hardly have resources to address more urgent priorities such as poverty and hunger. If preserving ecosystems and biodiversity have global benefits, both efficiency and equity considerations argue in favour of resource transfers to poor countries that will help them to manage their ecosystems better (see Section 5.4.2). Existing mechanisms (e.g. Global Environment Faculty) are not adequate for this purpose.

These questions need to be addressed in order to help the international development community and developing country decision makers respond to the urgent MA challenge of better ecosystem management, while simultaneously addressing existing priority issues, such as poverty alleviation, against a general backdrop of resource scarcity.

Role of the MA conceptual framework

Starting from the global framework provided by the MA, specific strategies, policies and measures for implementation need to be generated at the level of individual communities and sovereign nations. Thus, assessing the advantages and disadvantages of ecosystem management, within a national decision-making framework, will be an essential prerequisite for establishing the balance between ecosystem management and other urgent development priorities, and for identifying and mainstreaming key policies for implementation.

The MA conceptual framework (see Figure 4.1) clearly shows the circular linkages between human well-being and ecosystem services. The impacts of ecosystem services on development (upper horizontal arrow) may be better understood in terms of effects on the three major elements of sustainable development – i.e. economic, social and environmental. At the global, national and community levels, we need to determine more specifically if these interactions make development more or less sustainable. Then, specific remedial policy options may be determined and implemented to minimize negative effects and enhance positive ones.

Win–win policy options that yield both ecosystem and development benefits (social, economic and environmental) are the most desirable. In other cases, scarce resources may need to be shared between ecosystem management measures and other sustainable development needs, through a careful assessment of trade-offs. Key trade-offs may be needed between the present and future, among ecosystem services, among constituents of human well-being and among stakeholders (MA, 2005b).

Such a process will also require the engagement of a broad range of stakeholders, through multilevel mechanisms, to build both ownership and consensus for following up on the MA results within specific countries and communities – the AIM is a useful instrument for this purpose.

6.2.3 *Applying the Action Impact Matrix methodology*

The AIM is an integrating and linking tool (see Section 2.4.1), which has several desirable properties identified in the MA – e.g. the deliberative, information-gathering and planning elements (MA, 2005b). It will help mainstream ecosystem issues to make development more sustainable, at both global and national levels. Globally, we could link MDGs with key MA ecosystem services. At the national level, the AIM will: (1) embed ecosystem concerns in the macrolevel national development strategy of a country via the medium- to long-term sustainable development path and (2) integrate ecosystem concerns into the sub-national-level development strategy in the short- to medium-term, by making specific ecosystem projects and policies more sustainable. Furthermore, by linking the global, macroeconomic and microlocal aspects of decision making, the AIM approach helps us to coordinate implementation across scales.

The AIM approach may be used to understand better two-way interactions between (a) development policies and goals and (b) key ecosystem areas relevant to sustainable development. First, the effects of development policies and goals on ecosystems are explored, and then the reverse effects of ecosystems on sustainable development prospects are identified. The AIM approach analyses key economic–environmental–social interactions to identify potential barriers to making development more sustainable (MDMS), including degradation of ecosystem services. It also helps to determine the priority strategies, policies and projects that facilitate implementation of measures to manage ecosystems and restore damaged ecosystem services. A national-level AIM may be generated through a fully participative, consensus-building, multistakeholder, multidisciplinary exercise (see Section 2.4.1). The process may be repeated at a sub-national or community level to fine-tune the analysis. Thus, the AIM process addresses key implementation issues that are recognized in the MA, such as insufficient participation and transparency in planning and decision making, poor integration across decision-making agencies and inadequate access of stakeholders to information (MA, 2005b).

6.3 Using the AIM to analyse MA–MDG links at the national and global levels

6.3.1 Sample application to Sri Lanka at the national level

We illustrate this approach by sketching out a preliminary application to Sri Lanka at the national level. The examples provided below are only indicative, and need to be validated by a full AIM stakeholder exercise.

The AIM process involves several key practical steps as follows.

Step (a): Determine the most important national goals and policies

The following goals and policies are important in Sri Lanka: economic growth, poverty alleviation, food security, employment, trade and globalization, budget deficit reduction and privatization (see Section 2.4.1).

Step (b): Determine critical ecosystems and services relevant
to sustainable development

Starting from the broad generic areas identified by the MA under the supporting, provisioning, regulating and cultural categories of ecosystem services (MA, 2003), we use Sri Lanka data to identify the following critical ecosystem-related areas: forests, managed ecosystems 1 (grain), managed ecosystems 2 (tree crops), coastal and marine systems, wetlands and water resources.

Step (c): Identify how development goals/policies might affect ecosystems
(DE-AIM)

The two lists determined by consensus in steps (a) and (b) are used to establish the basic AIM framework (see Figure 6.3). For convenience of presentation, the row and column

	Critical ecosystems and services					
	(1) Forests	(2) Managed ecosyst. 1 (grain)	(3) Managed ecosyst. 2 (tree crops)	(4) Coastal and marine systems	(5) Wetlands	(6) Water resources
(S) Status	−2	−1	0	−1	−1	−1
Dev. goals/policies						
(A) Growth				−2		
(B) Poverty alleviation	+2					
(C) Food security						
(D) Employment					+1	
(E) Trade and globalization						
(F) Budget deficit reduction						
(G) Privatization						

Figure 6.3. Sri Lanka sample AIM. Development effects on ecosystems (DE-AIM). Key: 3 = high; 2 = moderate; 1 = low; minus(−) = negative impact/status; plus (+) = positive impact/status.

headings are given concisely, but the full spreadsheet will contain detailed notes describing each category in further detail. Thus, within each column, all relevant ecosystem services would be considered as sub-categories (not shown for brevity).

The row (S) marked 'status' is a useful benchmark indicating the current condition of each ecosystem. For example, cell S1 has a value −2 (moderately negative status), because deforestation has reduced forest cover significantly in Sri Lanka and has decreased all associated services. Next, we identify the impacts of national goals and policies on vulnerable ecosystems, as indicated by the direction of the arrows in the top left hand corner. A few shaded cells are selected to show some key effects. The qualitative numbers represent net outcomes due to various impacts, including trade-offs among different ecosystem services. Brief explanations are provided for each cell. Typical examples include the following.

(1) Cell B1 = +2: moderate positive effects of poverty alleviation on forests. The poor may exploit forests unsustainably for their survival (e.g. slash and burn agriculture). Poverty programmes promoting sustainable livelihoods will encourage poor people, who depend on natural resources such as forests, to become less dependent, by moving away from marginal lands into other areas. Helping the rural poor through community forestry projects would also restore some forest ecosystem functions.

(2) Cell A4 = −2: moderate negative effects of economic growth on coastal and marine systems. Growth may lead to destruction of coastal ecosystems for industry and urbanization, intensive coastal construction, coral and sand mining, depletion of fish stocks, etc. On the positive side, growth may divert population away from vulnerable coastal resources (e.g. increased employment from tourism decreases coral mining), while higher incomes and awareness could encourage conservation.

(3) Cell D5 = +1: low positive effects of employment on wetlands. Greater employment opportunities in sectors that do not depend directly on natural resources and biodiversity, especially for the poor rural folk, would decrease their dependence on marginal natural resources, thus helping to preserve wetlands.

	Critical ecosystems and services					
	(1)	(2)	(3)	(4)	(5)	(6)
	Forests	Managed ecosyst. 1 (grain)	Managed ecosyst. 2 (tree crops)	Coastal and marine systems	Wetlands	Water resources
(S) Status	−2	−1	0	−1	−1	−1
Dev. goals/policies						
(A) Growth						
(B) Poverty alleviation	−2					
(C) Food security						−3
(D) Employment				−2		
(E) Trade and globalization						
(F) Budget deficit reduction						
(G) Privatization						

Figure 6.4. Sri Lanka sample AIM. Ecosystems effects on development (ED-AIM). Key: 3 = high; 2 = moderate; 1 = low; minus (−) = negative impact/status; plus (+) = positive impact/status.

Step (d): Identify how ecosystems might affect development goals/policies (ED-AIM)

Next, we identify impacts of vulnerable ecosystems on national goals and policies, as indicated by the direction of the arrows in the top left hand corner of Figure 6.4. Again, a few shaded cells provide examples of key issues, and brief summaries of the relevant links are provided in each cell.

(1) Cell B1 = −2: moderate negative effects of forest degradation on poverty alleviation. Deforestation would lead to land degradation, causing further negative impacts on poorer groups who depend on natural resources for their livelihoods. A vicious cycle might be established, as evidenced in recent studies of sustainable livelihoods in Sri Lanka.
(2) Cell D4 = −2: moderate negative effects of coastal and marine habitat destruction on employment. Employment provided through activities like fishing, prawn cultivation and tourism would decrease due to coastal and marine system degradation.
(3) Cell C6 = −3: high negative effects of water resource degradation on food security. Many crops are highly dependent on the availability of water. Decreases in both quantity and quality of water (e.g. due to over-extraction of groundwater or pollution) will undermine food production.

All cell summaries in steps (c) and (d) are usually supplemented by several pages of text giving details of mechanisms involved and citing relevant reports and research studies.

Step (e): Prioritize the most important interactions and determine appropriate remedial policies and measures (preliminary AIM)

The list of 78 response options in the MA serve as a useful generic starting point. Other Sri Lanka documents, such as the Poverty Reduction Strategy Paper (PSRP), the National Environmental Action Plan (NEAP) and relevant multilateral environmental agreements (MEAs), will help to develop consensus and provide national and sub-national entry points, which facilitate the implementation of measures to address both development and ecosystem issues. Practical and political constraints that limit the range of policy options need to be factored in here.

Step (f): Perform more detailed studies and analyses of key interactions and policies options identified in step (e)

The critical issues, policy options and measures identified in step (e) may be subject to further analysis and research to identify better remedial measures for implementation. A variety of macro-, regional or local models are usually applied to focus on specific questions (Munasinghe, 1994a, 1997, 2002a). This procedure helps us to evaluate country-specific ecosystem management options, selected from the broad response categories listed in the MA – institutions and governance, economic measures and incentives, social and behavioural responses, technological response and knowledge and cognitive responses (MA, 2005b).

Step (g): Update and refine steps (c) to (e) – revised AIM

The results of the detailed research and analysis in step (f) are introduced into the AIM process to update and refine the information in the cells and begin the next stage of implementing remedial actions (see Section 2.4).

6.3.2 *Application to global and sub-global levels*

The procedure outlined in Section 6.3.1 could be applied to provide a summary of the key two-way interactions between global-level policy goals and ecosystem services. Thus, the AIM rows become the MDGs (global policy objectives), while the columns are the key MA ecosystems, with ecosystem services included as sub-categories (see Figure 6.2).

MA and MDG documents provide information to build two preliminary matrices: (1) the effects of MDG on critical ecosystem services and (2) the impacts of critical ecosystem services on MDG. This process will help to prioritize issues, determine and implement policy options, identify areas for further research and ultimately mainstream the MA findings into the MDG implementation process. It is also possible to consider the effects of further stresses imposed by a variety of global-level drivers, such as globalization, trade expansion and climate change, to identify appropriate international policy responses.

Furthermore, similar matrices may be constructed to mesh the MDGs with other MEAs, such as climate change (UNFCCC), desertification (UNCCD) and biodiversity (CBD). A recent UNEP sponsored 'brainstorming' meeting concluded: 'Modalities for greater co-operation should include combining Millennium Project Programmes and MEA programmes to bear upon specific ecosystems identified as country priorities … A matrix should be created in order to identify where environmental concerns intersect with initiatives to reduce poverty' (UNEP, 2005).

Analogous exercises may be conducted at the regional and continental levels, as appropriate. For transboundary ecosystems (e.g. Amazon, multicountry rivers, etc.), the AIM application needs to be tailored to fit the relevant resource basin and stakeholder objectives, which may span many countries and communities.

6.3.3 Conclusions and recommendations

The MA has achieved the major objective of bringing to the world's attention the serious global threats faced by ecosystems and their services, and the potential adverse consequences for human well-being – especially the world's poor. The following actions are therefore justified:

(1) Further dissemination and implementation of the MA results need to focus on interpreting the generic global- and regional-level findings at more geographically disaggregate levels, especially the assessment of the advantages and disadvantages to specific stakeholders, resulting from ecosystem management measures.
(2) One key step in this process would be the incorporation and mainstreaming of ecosystem management measures into sustainable development strategy at the global, national and community levels.
(3) The AIM methodology is a useful tool for better integrating policy-relevant MA findings within sustainable development strategy, and implementing them at multiple scales (global to local) – especially within specific countries. The AIM may also be applied to integrate issues arising from other MEAs. The AIM participative process will help to build human resource capacity that facilitates practical implementation of the MA results.
(4) A number of case studies should be carried out to test and validate the AIM approach in a range of countries. Based on these case studies, the existing MA multiscale sub-global assessments, and other recent literature, an action programme may be developed. The latter will provide practical guidance to decision makers, policy analysts and other stakeholders, in interpreting, mainstreaming and ultimately implementing the far-reaching MA findings, both globally and on a country-specific basis.

6.4 Dams and development: multilevel, multistakeholder dialogue

Large dams have traditionally been analysed and justified on the basis of comparing economic costs and benefits. Among their multiple purposes, hydroelectric power generation and irrigation have tended to provide the dominant benefits. Potable water, fisheries, downstream regulation, flood control and navigation are some of the frequent additional benefits. On the cost side, engineering expenditures have dominated, although environmental and social costs have been highlighted in recent years.

One largely neglected social dimension of dam development has arisen from the absence of stakeholder consultations, especially among those who have been most affected – e.g. families that have faced involuntary resettlement due to inundation of their traditional home areas.

Accordingly, this case study focuses on the participative (social) aspects of the sustainable development triangle (see Chapter 2), and on transcending boundaries (geographic, stakeholder and operational). The study is based on the follow up to the World Commission on Dams (WCD) and describes a rather unique multistakeholder, multilevel consultative process for dams. We will examine efforts to: (a) promote dialogue to improve decision making on dams and their alternatives at the global, regional and country levels among a wide range of stakeholders; (b) carry out information networking; (c) disseminate WCD materials; and (d) facilitate exchange of ideas on good practices.

6.4.1 The World Commission on Dams

Institutional framework and process

The WCD was established in May, 1998, by the World Bank and the International Union for the Conservation of Nature (IUCN), with two major goals: (1) to review the development effectiveness of large dams and assess alternatives for water resources and energy development and (2) to develop internationally acceptable criteria, guidelines and standards for the planning, design, appraisal, construction, operation, monitoring and decommissioning of dams.

The Commission used extensive public consultation and funding based on contributions from 54 public, private and civil society organizations. A consultative forum with 68 members from 36 countries, representing a cross-section of interests, views and institutions, assisted the WCD's efforts. A variety of inputs ensured the comprehensiveness and independence of the review, including: (1) in-depth case studies of eight large dams in five continents, with three country papers; (2) a cross-check survey of 125 large dams in 56 countries; (3) 17 thematic reviews on five dimensions of the debate and a number of working papers; (4) four regional consultations; and (5) 950 inputs submitted by interested individuals, groups and institutions.

The report published by the WCD in November 2000 (WCD, 2000) was widely acknowledged as a major contribution, not only to the debate on the benefits and costs of large dams, but also to current rethinking of development decision making in a world deeply affected by accelerating global change. One key recommendation was that decisions on major infrastructure developments like large dams should take place within a framework that recognizes the rights of all stakeholders and the risks that each stakeholder group is asked, or obliged, to sustain. Consequently, when the Commission had completed its work, a WCD Stakeholders' Forum was convened as a transitional body. The Forum concluded that maximizing the impact of the WCD report required many actions beyond the initiatives of individual stakeholder groups. Accordingly, at the request of the WCD Forum, UNEP set up the Dams and Development Project (DDP) in July, 2001, to promote a multilevel, multistakeholder dialogue that would facilitate the implementation of the WCD findings, especially at the national and local levels.

Main WCD findings

While the WCD report did not settle all issues surrounding water and energy development, there was general agreement that the rights and risks approach, the five core values and the seven strategic priorities provide a good framework. The five core values stressed are: equity, efficiency, participatory decision making, sustainability and accountability.

Based on these core values, the following seven strategic priorities were set out to serve as a framework for the multilevel, multistakeholder dialogue: (1) gaining public acceptance; (2) comprehensive options assessment; (3) addressing existing dams; (4) sustaining rivers and livelihoods; (5) recognizing entitlements and sharing benefits; (6) ensuring compliance; and (7) sharing rivers for peace, development and security. These priorities echo the key role of consultative mechanisms in sustainable development assessment, like the AIM and environmental and social assessment (see Sections 2.4 and 4.3).

6.4.2 Dams and Development Project goals and organization

This section describes the DDP structure and activities that help to organize and manage such a large global consultative process more systematically.

Goal

The broad goal of the DDP is to promote a worldwide dialogue on improving decision making, planning and management of dams and their alternatives based on the WCD's core values and strategic priorities.

Objectives

The mandate of the DDP excludes it from taking positions or making judgements on individual projects. The specific objectives of the DDP are to: (1) support country, regional and global dialogues, building on issues addressed in the WCD report and aiming to engage all stakeholders with emphasis on those not currently involved; (2) strengthen interaction and networking among participants in the dams debate; (3) support the wide dissemination of WCD findings and other stakeholders' responses; and (4) facilitate the flow of information and advice concerning initiatives relevant to dams and development.

General institutional structure

The DDP is a UNEP project directed by the Division of Environmental Policy Implementation (DEPI), with its office based in Nairobi, Kenya. The internal structure of the DDP is shown in Figure 6.5.

Steering Committee

A 14-member multistakeholder Steering Committee (drawn from the Dams and Development Forum) provides advice to UNEP on policy issues, the work programme and activities of the DDP. UNEP is a 'non-voting' member and facilitator of the Committee.

Dams and Development Forum

The Dams and Development Forum (DDF) comprises approximately 120 organizations. The broad range of constituencies represented include the following main categories: affected peoples groups, government agencies (policy), government agencies (projects/basins), intergovernmental organizations, indigenous peoples groups, non-governmental organizations, NGOs (advocacy), non-governmental organizations (international), organizations working on options/alternatives, professional associations, private sector/industry, research organizations and utility owners/operators. The DDP Forum serves as a sounding board for the work of the DDP and assists in implementation of its activities.

DDP Secretariat

During 2001–2003, the DDP Secretariat was based in Cape Town, South Africa, with IUCN acting as the implementation agency. From April 2003, the Secretariat was relocated to

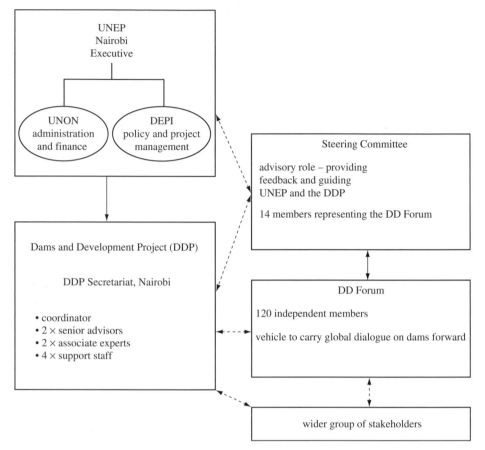

Figure 6.5. Structure of the Dams and Development Project (DDP). Solid arrows show the responsibility links; dashed arrows show the communication links. Source: Munasinghe (2004c).

UNEP in Nairobi. Five professional staff and four support staff currently work in the DDP Secretariat.

Financing

The original budget of the project was US $3.4 million, drawn from a number of multilateral and bilateral donors, anchored by UNEP. The current aim is to broaden the financial base through other bilateral agencies, industry and the private sector, foundations and NGOs.

Partners and network

The DDP continues to interface and build contacts with more than 7000 organizations and individuals on the WCD database and to interact with the development partners. In particular, new partnerships are being continuously forged to promote dialogue at national and local levels.

6.4.3 DDP work programme

The work programme contains four main elements, which are being implemented according to documented and established criteria. In executing the work programme, the DDP consults many stakeholders to understand their reactions and incorporate their views.

Promoting dialogue

The project seeks to catalyse and support efforts by the different stakeholders to consider and discuss the WCD findings and recommendations. Such support is being provided according to criteria established by UNEP with guidance from the Steering Committee.

Multilevel, multistakeholder actions undertaken in this area focus on: (1) servicing the DDF in a dialogue at a global level on issues related to dams and the WCD report and supporting the role of the DDF in encouraging the involvement of all stakeholders, including those with reservations on the report; (2) assisting broad-based national or intersectoral processes, workshops and dialogues; (3) supporting such dialogues through financial resources, access to expertise, information materials and examples of approaches used successfully elsewhere; (4) facilitating the financing of multistakeholder processes; and (5) building on the dialogues and assisting in improving guidelines and criteria for dams and their alternatives in accordance with the WCD core values and strategic priorities.

Information network

The DDP disseminates information, on new or ongoing initiatives undertaken by others, to help interested parties in participating in initiatives relevant to the WCD report, and in gaining access to information, technical support and funding. The project is focusing on: (1) establishing a communications and networking strategy with clearly defined priorities; (2) maintaining and updating an active website on WCD follow-up with appropriate links to other websites; (3) producing newsletters and other information updates to keep abreast of the status of WCD follow-up and implementation and results of various dialogue processes surrounding the report; (4) establishing a 'help desk' for stakeholders to find information on issues related to the WCD report and keeping a record of the source and nature of the requests; and (5) documenting reactions to the report.

Dissemination

This activity ensures that the WCD results are disseminated as broadly as possible and made available in local languages and in formats that would enhance its impact. Key tasks include: (1) distributing the WCD report, overview, CD-ROM, knowledge base and related products, including the views expressed at the Third WCD Forum and other stakeholder responses; (2) overseeing and assisting the translation of WCD materials into different languages; and (3) communicating and coordinating information dissemination at meetings, and facilitating attendance by former Commissioners, senior advisors, etc. as resource persons.

Facilitating exchange of ideas on good practice

The DDP disseminates information on experiences, practices and tools relevant to the use of the WCD report.

6.5 Evaluation of the Dams and Development Project (2001–2004)

6.5.1 Objectives, scope and methodology

A comprehensive evaluation of the DDP was conducted by an independent, external evaluator,[2] with the objective of determining to what extent the project has been successful in fulfilling its objectives and achieving expected results in a cost-effective manner – by reviewing project impact and the implementation of planned project activities, outputs and outcomes. The evaluation provided the fundamental basis for extending the DDP into a second phase beyond July 2004.

The findings of the evaluation were based on the following.

(a) A comprehensive survey questionnaire sent to all DD Forum members, the Steering Committee and other key stakeholders.
(b) Desk review of the project document and work programme outputs (such as information sheets, forum proceedings, Steering Committee meetings notes, assisted national multistakeholder processes, translations, databases, websites, reports).
(c) Twenty-five interviews (in person, by telephone and by e-mail), including 11 Steering Committee members, the Director of the UNEP Division of Environmental Policy Implementation, the Coordinator of the Dams and Development Secretariat, key stakeholders involved in the national dialogue processes and former Commissioners of the World Commission on Dams, DD Forum Members and other staff of the DDP Secretariat.
(d) Interviews with key stakeholders involved in a representative case study of the national multi-stakeholder process on dams and development in South Africa.

6.5.2 Survey results

The assessment of the DDP is provided in the following, according to specific performance indicators. The overall evaluation is based on the survey responses, supplemented by information from interviews and written documents. Of the 147 surveys sent out, 42 responses were received – i.e. a high response rate of almost 30%. The findings and rating of specific achievement categories are based on the following approximate weights – survey (50%), interviews (25%), written documents (25%). The final results are quite robust. Changing the relative weights did not significantly alter the pattern of results, since the three main sources of information (survey, interviews and reports) were generally

---

[2] Full and independent access to information was ensured through the cooperation of UNEP's Chief of Evaluation and Oversight Unit (EOU), the Director of UNEP's Division for Environmental Policy Implementation (DEPI) and the Coordinator, Dams and Development Project, in Nairobi, Kenya. Criteria for selecting the evaluator included the following: (a) no prior direct involvement with the WCD and/or the DDP; (b) good expertise on the subject matter; (c) good experience with projects of a global nature; and (d) good project evaluation experience.

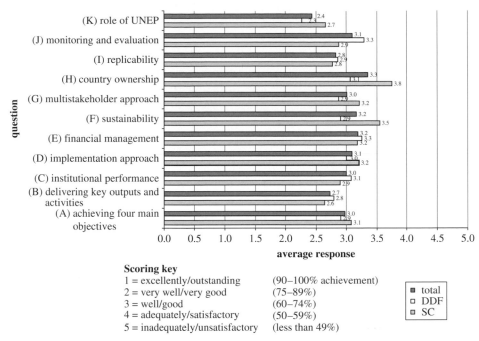

Figure 6.6. Averaged results of respondents in the Steering Global and Forum Committee (scale of 1 to 5, with lower values indicating more favourable ratings). Source: Munasinghe (2004c).

consistent. However, some differences of viewpoint among various stakeholder categories were found. Survey results given in Figure 6.6 are explained below.

(A) How well has DDP achieved planned results with regard to the four broad project objectives? – Good (3).

(B) How well has DDP delivered key outputs and activities set out in the project document? – Good (3).

(C) How well have different parts of the institutional and administrative framework performed? – Good (3).

(D) How successful was the implementation approach? – Good (3).

(E) How good is the financial management (to be answered by SC members only)? – Good (3).

(F) How sustainable are DDP activities? – Good (3).

(G) How well has the multistakeholder approach succeeded? – Good (3).

(H) How well has country ownership of activities, policies and processes progressed? – Satisfactory (4)

(I) Can the DDP process, multistakeholder approach and institutional setting be replicated? – Good (3).

(J) How well have DDP activities been monitored and evaluated, *ex-post*? – Good (3).

(K) How helpful was the role of UNEP in supporting and facilitating DDP activities? – Very good (2).

Averaged survey responses, grouped by different stakeholder categories, are shown in Table 6.1. Overall, the various groups of stakeholders had similar views about the success of DDP. However, there were some divergent opinions. With respect to the success of the implementation approach, research organizations found this aspect to be very good, whereas

Table 6.1 *Responses to survey questions (A) to (K), by stakeholder category*

Stakeholder category	No of replies	A	B	C	D	E	F	G	H	I	J	K
Affected peoples groups	4	2.9	2.3	2.7	2.7	2.8	2.6	2.7	3.2	1.8	3.0	2.7
Govt agencies (policy)	3	3.3	2.6	2.9	3.7	3.0	3.7	3.8	3.5	3.8	2.0	2.0
Govt agencies (proj/basins)	3	2.7	2.7	3.3	2.5	2.3	2.8	3.2	3.5	2.0	3.0	1.7
Intergovernmental orgs	4	2.7	2.8	2.6	2.8	3.2	3.5	3.3	3.8	3.7	3.3	2.3
Indigenous peoples groups	3	3.5	3.7	4.1	3.7	3.0		2.8	2.1	4.5	3.0	4.5
NGOs (advocacy)	4	3.2	2.9	3.2	3.5	3.6	2.7	1.9	4.2	1.9	2.9	3.7
NGOs (int)	5	2.9	2.9	3.0	3.2	4.3	2.8	2.2	3.1	2.6	3.2	2.8
Orgs working on options	2	3.0	1.5	2.1	3.0	3.0	3.3	3.5	3.7	1.5	4.0	2.0
Professional associations	3	2.6	2.2	3.1	4.0	4.3	4.2	3.4	2.0	4.0	3.0	1.3
Private sector/industry	4	3.1	2.9	3.4	2.7	3.3	2.6	2.6	3.5	4.0	3.0	1.0
Research orgs	2	3.3	2.8	2.0	2.0	3.0	3.7				3.0	3.0
Utility owners/operators	5	2.9	3.0	2.7	3.0	4.2	4.1	3.8	4.3	2.8	3.3	2.0
Average	**42**	**3.0**	**2.7**	**3.0**	**3.1**	**3.2**	**3.2**	**3.0**	**3.3**	**2.8**	**3.1**	**2.4**

professional associations indicated a rating of satisfactory. Regarding country ownership of activities, policies and processes, professional organizations found that this aspect was very good, whereas NGOs, private sector/industry and utility owners/operators felt that progress was only satisfactory.

Further, views on the replicability of the multistakeholder approach also varied between stakeholder groups. Organizations working on options, NGOs, government agencies (projects/basins) and affected peoples groups found that this approach could be very well replicated, whereas private sector/industry, professional associations and indigenous peoples groups found little potential for replication. Private sector/industry and government agencies (policies) found that DDP activities had been very well monitored and evaluated, whereas organizations working on options rated this aspect as only satisfactory.

The role of UNEP in supporting and facilitating DDP activities was found to be very helpful by all stakeholder groups, with the sole exception of indigenous peoples groups, who found it to be bordering on unsatisfactory.

6.6 Dams and Development Project evaluation, conclusions and results

6.6.1 Key lessons learned

Multistakeholder process

The DDP has sought to disseminate and build on the WCD findings. The core of this effort has been the multistakeholder, multilevel consultative process. After some initial successes, the perception is that this process is now experiencing diminishing returns and delays. Some key trade-offs involve time and substantive content.

Time requirements

Care and patience are needed to ensure the inclusion of all stakeholders and the creation of a balanced and non-confrontational atmosphere for conducting the dialogue. However, this may increase the risk of unduly lengthening the process and losing momentum.

Substantive content

The initial consensus-building stages of the dialogue tended to focus on less controversial elements of the WCD report (like core values and strategic priorities). However, enthusiasm and credibility will suffer unless the process eventually comes to grips with the more difficult and detailed issues that form the basis for implementable policies within countries.

Multilevel experience

Global level

The DD Forum has been unique in bringing together diverse groups and facilitating constructive engagement and learning from each other. The multistakeholder approach on dams has opened up discussions at many levels. Different viewpoints of multistakeholders on ground situations would have been of great interest and practical value to the parties concerned. Even though the issues are complex, a meaningful and result-oriented dialogue and goals need to be pursued.

- To maintain interest it is necessary to move beyond the core values and strategic priorities of the WCD and address more substantive, and even controversial, issues.
- The DDF included a wide range of disciplines and stakeholder groups. However, it was not possible to take advantage of the wide experience of the members in view of the time constraints as well as the problems encountered in servicing a large forum.
- There is a need for the dialogue to pursue different approaches for new dams as opposed to existing dams. This will promote, for example, emphasis on the application of regulatory instruments and options assessment for new dams, and social and environmental mitigation measures for existing dams.

Regional level

- There are built-in advantages and good potential for the development of a regional dialogue, as evidenced by the SADC experience. By holding regional meetings involving both governments and other stakeholders, the SADC had prepared the ground for addressing the problems of lengthy droughts and water sharing in a cooperative manner, within the national context and priorities of concerned countries.
- The proposal for the DDP to introduce dams and development issues within the regional body covering the Mekong River Basin warrants serious consideration, as it can promote and facilitate a dialogue between both upstream and downstream riparian users. Other regional-level possibilities under consideration include the La Plata River Basin in South America and a GWP South Asia network initiative.

National level

- The need to focus on national-level dialogue to achieve better and measurable development outcomes has emerged as an important step forward. Activities at national level were constrained due to the dearth of funds, lack of support for capacity building and non-participation of key stakeholders. Multistakeholder participation needs to begin at the early stages.
- Decision making on dams at the national level (including the DDP dialogue) needs to be closely coordinated, preferably by a key agency with an overarching responsibility in areas for such sectors as energy, water resources and river basin management. The credibility and effectiveness of this local focal point is an essential prerequisite for the success of such dialogues, as otherwise stakeholders can withdraw from the process.
- Scoping reports that make an assessment of the existing situation can provide the basis for future action, as evidenced by the experiences in Nepal and South Africa.
- There are great advantages for the national dialogue in working toward integration of dam policy within the national water-resources policy.

Dissemination and information exchange

- Information networking and dissemination of WCD material have taken place as planned. However, a centralized unit does not have the capacity to reach out to all potential beneficiaries. Assistance in capacity building in national-level agencies will ensure that relevant information will reach even ground-level stakeholders.
- The information and data collected from individuals and organizations need to be validated. There is a risk of politically sensitive data appearing in databases and websites sponsored by UNEP.
- A balanced approach is needed in respect of good and bad practice, as people learn as much from failures as from successes. Excessive and unstructured ad hoc information loses its effectiveness. Hence, information should be targeted to specific groups and classified accordingly (e.g. decision makers would prefer executive summaries without technical jargon, whereas experts and researchers would tend to look for more analytical approaches and detailed information in their relevant technical areas).

6.6.2 *Overall assessment and recommendations*

Assessment of DDP first phase

During its first phase of activity, the DDP achieved an overall rating of good, corresponding to the range 60–74%, or a numerical value of 3 on the UNEP scale of achievement (see Table 6.2). The rating in each category of the table is based on the survey results summarized in the previous section and Figure 6.6, as well as information from interviews and written documents. The final column of Table 6.2 indicates the correspondence between the survey questions and UNEP achievement categories.

DDP achievements in almost all the UNEP designated categories fall into the good range, except for three areas. The attainment of outputs and activities is rated 2, or very good. However, country ownership and cost-effectiveness both are rated 4, or satisfactory. Thus, the following recommendations reflect the need to strengthen in-country activities and reduce the fraction of staff costs in the total budget.

Table 6.2 *Rating of DDP activities by UNEP achievement categories*

	Achievement category	Rating	Survey questions
(a)	Achievement of objectives and planned results	3	(A) and (C)
(b)	Attainment of outputs and activities	2	(B)
(c)	Cost-effectiveness	4	(E)
(d)	Impact	3	(A), (G) and (H)
(e)	Sustainability	3	(F)
(f)	Stakeholder participation	3	(G)
(g)	Country ownership	4	(H)
(h)	Implementation approach	3	(D)
(i)	Financial planning	3	(E)
(j)	Replicability	3	(I)
(k)	Monitoring and evaluation	3	(J)
	All categories (overall average)	**3**	

The UNEP rating system used is as follows:
1 = excellent (90–100% achievement);
2 = very good (75–89%);
3 = good (60–74%);
4 = satisfactory (50–59%);
5 = unsatisfactory (less than 49%).

Recommendations

Question (A): What are the needs and priorities?
Recommendation 1: Dams and development issues will continue to have high priority in many countries, and efforts to address them must continue.

Dams have and will continue to have a major influence on development, increasing the need to make dams more sustainable. This applies equally to the management of existing dams, as well as to the planning, construction and operation of new dams. In particular, decisions regarding dams have to be made by using all available social, economic and environmental, as well as technical, information effectively, and with the involvement of all stakeholders (i.e. it is a multistakeholder process).

The DDP has sought to use the multistakeholder, multilevel approach to facilitate implementation of WCD findings regarding core values and strategic priorities. A major achievement has been the creation of an environment for constructive dialogue among stakeholders with widely different views, at various multilevel DDP gatherings. The success of the Steering Committee, the DDF and national processes provide a valuable example that may be replicated elsewhere in the water sector and in other controversial areas where the multistakeholder, multilevel process would be appropriate.

Nevertheless, the emphasis on engaging all stakeholders at the global level, in a non-confrontational manner, has been slow and costly, and has not moved beyond the stage of discussing relatively uncontroversial issues. Ultimately, the translation of a global consensus on broad aspects into practical policies, which address more controversial issues and influence decision making within countries, constitutes the crucial element of unfinished business required to maintain credibility and momentum.

Recommendation 2: The original DDP objectives need to be carefully reviewed, and fresh priorities determined to support future activities.

While its links with WCD will always be a source of strength, the time has come to move forward, beyond the comfortable umbrella of WCD core values and strategic priorities. Drawing confidence and strength from lessons learned during the first two to three years of operation of the DDP, existing priorities need to be reviewed and revised. While this evaluation report can suggest some general ideas and directions, the in-depth re-assessment of the four original objectives of the DDP, and their relative importance, is an important task for the Steering Committee and Secretariat, as a prerequisite for future DDP activities.

One fundamental new direction involves focusing country dialogues and making them more effective from the implementation viewpoint. Many of the more routine tasks, such as translation and dissemination of WCD materials and preparation of good practice examples, may be gradually phased out, farmed out to other institutions, or pursued as a lower priority.

Question (B): Who should do it?
Recommendation 3: A time-bound extension of the DDP is justified, to realize the benefits of the first phase.

This evaluation has determined that the DDP has made a promising start. Progress has been slow due to many reasons, including the fact that multistakeholder approach is unique and difficult. Nevertheless, the two to three year initial period has provided clear grounds to justify a continuation of the effort. One option would be to extend the DDP for a further two years, but with goals and approaches modified to reflect lessons learned so far. Another alternative might be to phase out the DDP and devolve the more important tasks to other agencies and institutions working on water issues.

The preponderance of evidence produced during this evaluation supports a time-bounded extension of the DDP, to realize the fruits of efforts made in the past two to three years. A two-year extension would appear to be a reasonable compromise between achieving longer-term goals and avoiding an open-ended commitment. At least the current level of donor funding is recommended to maintain the momentum, coupled with greater focus on high-priority activities, and corresponding streamlining of the Secretariat staff and functions.

A re-naming of such an extended activity as the 'Dams and Development Programme' would underline a greater focus on processes, policies and long-term goals (since 'Project' suggests a shorter-term, product-oriented task). Whatever the title, this activity would retain its status as a project within the UNEP definition.

Question (C): Where should the Secretariat be located?
Recommendation 4: The DDP Secretariat should continue to be located within UNEP.

The general consensus of stakeholder opinions and other evidence indicates that UNEP has played an indispensable and highly positive role in sponsoring the DDP. Its continued support of the DDP will do much to guarantee the success of future activities of the DDP.

Thus, UNEP is the clear choice to continue hosting the DDP, given the vital initial role played by UNEP in the WCD process, its past record of support for the DDP, its written commitment endorsing the continuation of the DDP and the existing location of the Secretariat in Nairobi. One compelling argument is the need to avoid another relocation, given the unanimous perception that the move of the Secretariat from Cape Town to Nairobi had already caused major delays and disruption.

Concern arose about potential delays that might occur if the DDP was subjected to excessive UNEP bureaucratic procedures. Any decision to relocate within UNEP should be an internal one, to be decided on the basis of where the DDP could derive the most synergistic benefits, while facilitating the mainstreaming of its work into UNEP programmes.

Question (D): How might work be better organized and carried out?
Recommendation 5: The Secretariat needs to become more focused, streamlined and cost-effective, in line with the revised objectives and priorities (see Recommendation 2). This would include the size and composition of staff and allocation of tasks among them.

Although the Steering Committee has indicated that the financial management has been good, almost two-thirds of the DDP budget is devoted to staff and administrative costs, which is rather high. In parallel with the greater focus on DDP tasks, the Secretariat needs to become more streamlined and cost-effective.

The DDP currently has five professional staff positions in Nairobi. Stakeholders feel that staff size and costs have increased since the Cape Town phase of operations, without a commensurate improvement in output. A significant improvement can be made to the composition of Secretariat staff and allocation of functions. The momentum of the DDP cannot be maintained unless the remaining challenges, including a noticeable lack of team spirit and uneven staff performance, are met soon. Assuming an extension of the DDP, the need simultaneously to place more emphasis on country processes, reduce staff costs and keep within budget limitations, will pose a major challenge. The staff composition in particular would need to reflect expertise in multistakeholder processes and multicultural sensitivities. Finally, the relatively small size of the Secretariat, to ensure the essential central coordination, coherence and continuity of activities, will put a high premium on high-quality performance, teamwork and burden sharing.

Outsourcing of selected activities needs to be explored. Reducing headquarters staff could be offset cost-effectively by expansion at the regional level – e.g. covering different regions with local consultants or dedicated staff within UNEP regional offices could lower salary costs, travel costs and overheads. Synergies and cost sharing with other departments within UNEP might be exploited better to reduce costs, particularly in areas such as information technology, accounting and administration. New technologies such as videoconferencing via the Internet could reduce travel costs and time.

Recommendation 6: Country (and regional) processes should be the main focus of future attention, while maintaining the already successful global dialogue at a lower level of intensity.

Dialogue and implementation at the regional and country levels is essential to move forward on the goals and objectives of the DDP.

Recommendation 7: DDP functions and resource allocation should reflect the emphasis on country and (regional) processes.

More resources and time need to be devoted to promote in-country (and regional) activities. Greater emphasis at the national level, and more effective follow-up, would help to move the multistakeholder process beyond the stage of discussing generic core values and strategic priorities, toward determining country-specific, action-oriented policy guidelines (starting from relevant WCD best practice guidelines) for action. The country processes should emphasize quality rather than quantity, relying on the examples of successful countries (like South Africa) to encourage replication elsewhere, to disarm suspicions in key countries (especially those with large dams) and to reach out to key countries which so far have not actively participated in the dams and development process.

Thus, the DDP Secretariat initially needs to focus on, and work more intensively with, a few key countries (spread across the different regions) that have the greatest prospects for early success in terms of influencing national policy. Better criteria and information (e.g. strong government commitment, highly credible focal point to energize the country process, or prevalence of serious dam issues), are required to identify such high-priority countries. The Secretariat needs to continue the emphasis on inclusiveness and participation of all stakeholders, to ensure ownership and eventual implementation of outcomes.

Regional dialogues offer great potential (as shown by SADC). They need to focus on specific issues such as riparian river basin development projects, or sharing of common experiences across countries, to energize in-country stakeholders who might otherwise feel isolated.

In general, global-level meetings could be fewer, but better prepared, focused and organized. Both the Forum and the Steering Committee have successfully provided a unique opportunity for divergent views to be presented constructively, and have also raised the profile of WCD findings in the international arena. However, past Forum meetings have tended to be too diffuse and have lacked follow-up (e.g. timely and short summaries of meeting results). Several sensible options to improve the governance, structure, content, frequency and timing of Forum meetings have been discussed at previous Steering Committee meetings, and should be reviewed prior to launching the next phase of DDP activities. The limited time of Steering Committee members could also be more effectively utilized with less frequent meetings, supported by a higher-quality, but reduced volume, of documents and information. In summary, the existing situation of holding one Forum meeting and two Steering Committee meetings per year should be maintained.

The narrowing of geographic focus on country processes needs to be accompanied by a broadening of the context in which dams are viewed. Linking the impacts of dams more broadly with planning for the water-resources sector and the macroeconomy (in relation to the social, economic and environmental dimensions of sustainable development), is especially important to convince decision makers, and helps to complement the wider view offered by the multistakeholder approach. A range of analytical tools, including environmental, social and poverty assessments, the AIM, multicriteria analysis, water-sector models and multisector macromodels could facilitate this process.

While constructively synthesizing the diverse views of members to guide both the Forum and the Secretariat successfully, the Steering Committee has sometimes gone beyond its originally envisaged 'advisory role.' The future relationship between the Steering Committee and the Secretariat needs to be well thought out in order to maintain the delicate balance between effective guidance and excessive micromanagement. The DDP Secretariat has a key role to play as catalyst, facilitator and advisor to country processes, as well as a clearing house for exchange of information across different countries. In particular, it would be in a good position to initiate a comparative study of different country processes, to learn from past experience (especially South Africa), and identify both generic and country-specific elements.

The DDP website has become the core of the information exchange activity, and needs to be maintained cost-effectively. The good (and bad) practice initiative has elicited mixed reactions, because it could provide useful information, but absorb significant resources. A time-bound continuation of this activity within the Secretariat may be the solution, followed by the devolution of the function to another institution.

Building capacity within countries to operationalize WCD findings is important. In this context, another DDP contribution that could accelerate the transition from discussions to policy implementation would be the provision of appropriate tools and methods for policy analysis to country teams. Relatively modest funding can go a long way to sustain country processes – especially in the early stages. Dissemination of WCD materials has also proved to be more effective at the country level. The DDP could also improve synergies with other water institutions (globally) and better integrate dam issues into broader water-resources policy (nationally).

6.6.3 *Response to evaluation recommendations*

The independent evaluation of the DDP Phase 1 described above was reviewed thoroughly by UNEP, the DDP Steering Committee, Forum and Secretariat (DDP/UNEP, 2004). Subsequently, all the major recommendations were implemented. Accordingly, the DDP Phase 2 programme was launched in February, 2005, as a two-year time-bound activity. The goal, objectives and work programme were streamlined and revised, based on the evaluation (DDP/UNEP, 2005).

Goal

To promote improved decision making, planning and management of dams and their alternatives building on WCD core values and strategic priorities and other relevant reference materials.

Objectives

- Support multistakeholder dialogues at country, regional and global levels on improving decision making on dams and their alternatives with the aim of engaging all stakeholders with emphasis on governments.
- Produce non-prescriptive tools, drawing on all relevant existing bodies of criteria and guidelines for planning and management of dams and their alternatives, which can help decision makers.

To support these main objectives, the DDP Phase 2 work programme seeks to:

- strengthen further interaction and networking among participants in the dams debate;
- disseminate further information on activities, processes and outcomes of national, regional and global dialogues on dams and development;
- disseminate further, tailored to a country and regional basis, the WCD report and the report of the Third WCD Forum, and make available other stakeholders' responses;
- facilitate further the flow of information and advice concerning initiatives relevant to dams and development in partnership with other appropriate organizations.

Specific work programme activities include: (a) promoting dialogue, (b) elaboration of practical tools, (c) networking and communication, (d) dissemination and (e) facilitating exchange of ideas on good practice.

Part III

National and macroeconomic applications

7

National economy-wide applications[1]

In this chapter, the sustainomics framework is used to study the powerful and wide-spread social and environmental impacts of economy-wide policies (see Section 3.7). Section 7.1 contains a brief review of the historical evolution of ideas linking economy-wide policies and the environment – starting with the seminal work of Malthus and Ricardo up to modern times. Economy-wide policies (both macroeconomic and sectoral) are often packaged within programmes of structural adjustment, stabilization and sectoral reform, aimed at promoting economic stability, efficiency and growth, and ultimately improving human welfare. Section 7.2 describes empirical evidence, beginning with a discussion of the environmental impacts of structural adjustment programmes since the 1980s, followed by some stylized results. It is the combination of growth and economic imperfections that lead to environmental damage and unsustainable outcomes. Section 7.3 sets out a basic framework for analysing environmental–macroeconomic links. Unforeseen economic imperfections can interact with growth to cause environmental and social harm. Second-best remedial measures could help to limit the damage. In some cases, the timing and sequencing of macroeconomic reform policies could be adjusted to limit environmental and social harm. The standard static IS-LM macroeconomic model may be extended to include environmental concerns. The role of green accounting is discussed. The Action Impact Matrix (AIM) is a key tool for prioritizing environmental–macroeconomic links. A 'policy-tunnelling' model shows how complementary policies that eliminate economic imperfections will permit continued growth while limiting environmental and social harm. A case study analysing options for making Brazilian long-run economic growth more sustainable is presented in Section 7.4. Both sectoral and macroeconomic models are used to examine the effects of growth-oriented strategies pursued by the government during the past decades, over a range of sustainable development issues such as poverty, employment, urban pollution and deforestation in the Amazon region. Finally, Section 7.5 sets out some concluding remarks, including directions for future work.

---

[1] The valuable contributions of W. Cruz, C. Ferraz, R. Serôa da Motta and C. Young to this chapter are gratefully acknowledged. Some parts of the chapter are based on material adapted from: Munasinghe (2002b), Munasinghe and Cruz (1994) and Munasinghe *et al.* (2006).

211

7.1 Historical evolution of ideas

This section describes selected macroeconomy–environment work, carried out mainly since the late 1980s, although some historical roots are discernible in several classical papers.

7.1.1 Tracing macroeconomy–environment linkages

Early work on such linkages pursued three interwoven lines of enquiry. First, economic activities require natural resources. The key role of land scarcities in limiting growth was shown by Malthus (1798), who stressed impoverishment due to agricultural constraints and exponential population growth. Ricardo (1817) explained how diminishing returns to land would check wealth and population growth. Hotelling (1931) further developed the theory of exhaustible resources (see Section 14.2.1).

Koopmans' (1973) classic paper optimizes a discounted infinite stream of consumption within a (Ramsey-type) growth model (see Section 2.3.2), by combining exhaustible natural capital in Hotelling's simple model with accumulating stocks of manufactured capital. The macroeconomic interest rate plays a significant role. Subsequent work (Withagen, 1990) explored many ramifications of this approach, leading to work by Hartwick (1990) and others (see following text). Stiglitz (1974) uses a model with capital, labour and natural resources as substitutes in production, to show that higher consumption levels are sustainable, provided increasing technological progress compensates for declining natural-resource stocks.

Daly and Cobb (1989) point out that getting macroeconomic policies right may ensure optimal resource allocation, but this work does not address scale issues as economies grow beyond the environmental carrying capacity. Solow (1993) defines net national product (NNP), adjusted to reflect both natural-resource depletion and changes in environmental quality, as a measure of maximum consumption that can be sustained forever. England (2000) identifies three conditions that would lead to a steady-state economy – scarcity of natural capital; complementarity (non-substitutability) between manufactured and natural capital in production; and constraints on technological progress that raises productivity of natural capital use. Recent work has focused on the interactions between sustainable development and long-term optimal growth (Markandya *et al.*, 2002; Munasinghe *et al.*, 2001).

The second historical approach draws on input–output (I–O) analysis developed during the 1930s. Leontief (1970) describes a seminal framework to analyse polluting outputs from productive sectors and the impact of policies to reduce such externalities in pollution-abatement sectors. Subsequent studies linked the I–O model with vintage models specifying labour demand and capital stock, and with endogenized consumer demand using linear expenditure systems. Advanced models made the technical I–O coefficients endogenous and dependent on prices. Computable general equilibrium (CGE) models used for macroeconomic–environmental analysis, as well as the integrated frameworks for environmental–economic accounting, use the I–O approach.

Third, environmental considerations have been incorporated into more conventional macroeconomic models, ranging from extensions of the Keynesian IS-LM type used in analyses of comparative statics, to sophisticated CGE models with environmental variables. Environmental considerations are increasingly examined in macroeconomic models, focusing on short-run Keynesian issues such as capacity utilization, unemployment and cyclical movements in the economy. Longer-run environmental–macroeconomic models, for both closed and open economies, are built around supply side issues such as capital accumulation, natural-resource depletion, long-run labour supply, discount rate and rate of technological progress.

7.1.2 Empirical surveys of macroeconomy–environment linkages

Grossman and Krueger (1995) question whether an inverted U-shaped 'environmental Kuznets curve' describes the empirical relationship between per capita income and several indicators of air and water pollution. Currently, there is agreement that environmental quality declines with increases in per capita income in the early stages of growth, but it is unclear whether continued growth reverses this trend, since the shape of the curve appears to vary widely by country and form of environmental degradation (De Bruyn and Heintz, 1999; *Ecological Economics*, 1998; *Environment and Development Economics*, 1997).

Opschoor and Jongma (1996) is a comprehensive review of environmental impacts of World Bank and International Monetary Fund structural adjustment and stabilization programmes in developing countries. They confirm the point, made by Munasinghe and Cruz (1994), that using complementary environmental policies to counteract adverse impacts of growth-oriented macroeconomic policies is a short-run remedy, but urge a more integrated approach in the long run. Panayotou and Hupe (1996) point out that using environmental and social policies to cushion the harmful impacts of structural adjustment is second-best, compared with full integration of these policies within the economic reforms. Partial reforms, or incomplete implementation of reforms, may do more harm than good if they are selectively applied without anticipating their social and environmental impacts. Kessler and Van Dorp (1998) draws attention to the unpredictable nature of impacts of structural adjustment programmes and the importance of remediation, focusing on key indicators relating to soils, water resources and forests.

7.1.3 Mathematical modelling

Useful qualitative insights about the environmental (and socioeconomic) consequences of macropolicy reforms may be gained with CGE models (Robinson, 1990). Early work by Jorgensen and Wilcoxon (1990) analysed the economic impact of environmental regulations on the US economy using a CGE approach that applies intertemporal analysis to a complex disaggregate model of long-term growth impacts, to estimate the share of abatement costs in total costs for industry and transport. Bergman (1990a) also used a CGE model to simulate the effects of environmental regulation and energy policy in Sweden. Here, the environmental market failure is corrected by creating a market for emission permits, which are included in the cost functions.

Chapter 9 contains a more detailed review of past CGE modelling work, as well as two case studies (O'Ryan, de Miguel and Miller, 2005; Persson and Munasinghe, 1995). Glomsrod, Monge and Vennemo (1999) use a CGE model to study the impacts of structural adjustment policies on deforestation in Nicaragua. Improving the fiscal balance by reducing public expenditure, or through sales tax reform, promotes economic growth and conserves forests. Some polices increase near-term deforestation, but ease pressure on forests in the longer term. Applying a CGE model to Brazil, Cattaneo (2005) concluded that agricultural growth in the Amazon increases deforestation, whereas technological improvements, for small farms outside the Amazon, raise incomes, improve income distribution and limit deforestation. Innovation in livestock in the Amazon also leads to higher agricultural income, but greater deforestation rates (see Section 7.4.5).

Chapter 8 reviews models that examine the sustainability of optimal growth, including a case study by Islam, Munasinghe and Clarke (2003). Holden, Taylor and Hampton (1999) simulate six types of village economies in Zambia to show that structural adjustment policies have significant adverse impacts on the environment. The removal of policy distortions may not lead to well functioning markets, due to high transactions costs and imperfect information in remote areas.

7.1.4 Trade and environment

Steininger (1999) provides a comprehensive review of trade–environment models, including Heckscher–Olin, statistical–econometric and applied general equilibrium models, which can address a variety of issues such as leakage, distribution, policy feedback effects, interlinkages between production and markets and specialization patterns. Batabyal (1994) traces impacts of domestic environmental policies on international trade. His theoretical study shows that a large developing country might be worse off by pursuing environmental policies unilaterally. Goldin and Roland-Host (1997) examine the converse question – how growth in international trade might affect the local environment in Morocco (see Section 8.6.3). In their CGE study, trade liberalization alone promotes export-led growth, but increases water stress. When complementary water price increases are simultaneously imposed with trade liberalization, the growth benefits are retained, while water stress improves.

Mani and Wheeler (1998) analyse data during 1960–1995 for a variety of industrial sectors and countries. They conclude that trade does not increase production of pollution-intensive goods, since production takes place primarily for domestic markets rather than exports.

7.1.5 Green national income accounting

We follow up the discussion in Section 3.7.5 with a brief mention of recent work. Hartwick (1990) derived net national product (NNP) as the current value Hamiltonian for an optimal growth problem, including conventional economic inputs and natural resources. To derive NNP, drawdown of natural-resource stocks should be netted out of gross national product (GNP), such as depreciation of economic capital. Repetto *et al.* (1989) show how Indonesia's conventionally measured economic output could keep rising, while its natural-resource base is being degraded, unless use of natural-resource stocks is netted out. Hultkrantz (1992) estimates monetary changes in timber stocks, non-marketed and non-timber products and depletion of other natural assets in Sweden.

The System of Environmental and Economic Accounting (SEEA) integrated environmental and resource accounting into the standard system of national accounts (SNA) (UN, 1993). Atkinson *et al.* (1997) describe methods of adjusting the SNA to account for environmental effects, including social accounting matrices. The concept of green national product (i.e. conventional GNP net of changes in environmental services and resources) is extended to develop the idea of 'genuine savings' (i.e. national savings net of environmental effects). Aronsson and Lofgren (1998) review developments, provide a theoretical framework summarizing the state of knowledge and set out areas of uncertainty and key questions for further research.

A revised version of the SEEA was issued in 2003, describing a satellite system of the SNA that combines economic and environmental data in a common framework and describes their interaction (UN, 2003). It also provides indicators and statistics to monitor these interactions, as well as a database for strategic planning and policy analysis to identify more sustainable development paths (UNCSD, 2005).

7.2 Empirical evidence

7.2.1 Environmental and social impacts of structural adjustment

During recent decades, structural adjustment programmes have emerged as a powerful form of macroeconomic intervention in the developing world (see Section 3.4.2). Many developing countries experienced economic hardship during the 'debt crisis' of the 1980s. Major oil price increases in 1974 and 1979 were a significant shock to oil-importing countries. Furthermore, restrictive monetary policies adopted by Western countries, to curtail their own inflation, raised real interest rates and made debt-service difficult for developing countries. Thus, developing countries faced balance-of-payment problems, making them even more reliant on foreign donors. Economic growth rates and unemployment worsened. The International Monetary Fund and the World Bank agreed to provide financial assistance to help countries service their debt, provided they adopted broad reforms called structural adjustment programmes (SAPs). These stringent economic and fiscal reform policies, which were designed to restore growth, also had adverse environmental and social impacts.

Stabilization policies sought to reduce pressure on foreign reserves by reducing domestic demand. Balance-of-payment problems were addressed by controlling inflation and reducing imports with contractionary fiscal policies and tight money supply. Simultaneously, currency devaluation aimed to improve the terms of trade and make exports more competitive. Adjustment policies focused on the supply side and addressed inefficiencies of the internal economic structure, including public sector reforms, to accelerate economic recovery and export growth. Parallel policies were adopted to improve the efficiency of resource allocation and competitiveness of markets at the sectoral level. Unfortunately, these reforms often had recessionary effects, resulting in loss of jobs and livelihoods, before the promised growth could materialize. Budget-cutting pressures also forced governments to abandon social 'safety-net' programmes, thereby causing further hardship to low-income groups.

Reform programmes have not always achieved their economic goals. Even where macro-economic gains have been realized through adjustment, environmental and social problems have worsened. Often, economic policies aimed at relieving economic problems under-mined the environmental resources and social fabric on which national long-term development will ultimately depend (Munasinghe and Cruz, 1994).

7.2.2 Some stylized results

Many case studies exist of environmental and social impacts of country-wide policies (Cruz, Munasinghe and Warford, 1997; *Environment and Development Economics*, 1999; Kessler and Van Dorp, 1998; Munasinghe, 1996a; Munasinghe and Cruz, 1994; Opschoor and Jongma, 1996; Panayotou and Hupe, 1996; Reed, 1996; Warford *et al.*, 1997; Young and Bishop, 1995). Nevertheless, generalizing about such impacts is difficult, since the links are complex and country-specific. Even the purely economic impacts of SAPs are difficult to trace (Tarp, 1993). However, in the following we seek to summarize some key lessons learned from recent studies.

Economy-wide policy reforms have major economic objectives. Their environmental and social consequences fall into three groups – beneficial, harmful and unknown. First are the so-called 'win–win' policies, which achieve simultaneous gains in the economic, social and environmental areas. Second, macroreforms may harm both the poor and the environment, unless they are complemented by further protective measures. The third group consists of impacts that are unpredictable because of the complex linkages involved and long-run-time perspective.

Beneficial impacts

Several studies indicate that liberalizing reforms (such as removing price distortions, promoting market incentives and encouraging trade) often contribute to both economic and sustainability gains. For example, reforms that improve the efficiency of industrial or energy-related activities could reduce waste, increase the efficiency of natural-resource use and limit environmental pollution. Similarly, improving land tenure rights and access to financial and social services will yield economic gains, promote better environmental stewardship and help the poor.

Analogously, shorter-run policy measures aimed at restoring macroeconomic stability will generally yield economic, social and environmental benefits. For example, price, wage and employment stability encourage firms and households to take a longer-term view, thereby encouraging environmentally sustainable activities. Lower inflation rates not only clarify price signals and enhance investment decisions, but also protect fixed-income earners and the poor.

Studies of macroeconomic policies in Zimbabwe and Mexico (Munasinghe and Cruz, 1994) and Thailand (Panayatou and Sussengkarn, 1991) illustrate win–win situations, with both economic and environmental gains. Birdsall and Wheeler (1992) argue that open trade policies in Latin America have promoted both economically productive and environmentally benign modern technologies. Other studies of environmental impacts of macroeconomic adjustment policies have been carried out for Sub-Saharan Africa (Stryker *et al.*, 1989); Thailand, Ivory Coast and Mexico (Reed, 1992); and the Philippines (Cruz and Repetto, 1992).

Country studies involving win–win outcomes of sectoral policy reforms cover energy and industry in Mexico (Munasinghe and Cruz, 1994) and Sri Lanka (Meier, Munasinghe and Siyambalapitiya, 1995); water and sanitation in Brazil, China and India (World Bank, 1992b, 1992c, 1993a); and land use in Tunisian rangelands (Munasinghe and Cruz, 1994), Zambian farms (World Bank, 1992d), Brazilian forests (Mahar, 1988; Schneider, 1993), Sudanese forests (Larson and Bromley, 1991) and Botswana pastures (Perrings, 1993). Stabilization policies to control inflation led to more sustainable logging in Costa Rica (Persson and Munasinghe, 1995) and sustainable farming in South America (Schneider, 1994; Southgate and Pearce, 1988).

Avoiding harmful impacts

Typical economy-wide reform programmes are implemented in stages, with the initial adjustment package targeting the most important macroeconomic issues. Often, some unaddressed distortions (policy, market or institutional imperfections) will combine with an adjustment programme to cause environmental or social harm (Abaza, 1995; Munasinghe and Cruz, 1994). Adverse social and environmental impacts may be avoided by implementing additional complementary measures that remove such distortions without necessarily reversing the original reforms. Some case studies are given in Section 8.6. Other brief examples are as follows.

Policy distortions

Promotional measures that increase profitability of exports might encourage excessive extraction of an underpriced natural resource (e.g. deforestation of open access areas due to subsidized timber stumpage fees). Similarly, trade liberalization could lead to more wasteful energy-intensive activities in nations with subsidized energy prices.

Market failures

Successful adjustment may be associated with severe environmental damage – e.g. if external environmental effects of growth (such as air or water pollution) are not adequately reflected in market prices. In Indonesia, liberalization and industrial promotion led to less pollution-intensive growth in the modern sector. However, the scale of expansion increased pollution externalities, requiring complementary pollution taxes and environmental regulations (Munasinghe and Cruz, 1994).

Institutional constraints

Unaddressed institutional problems (such as poor accountability of indebted state-owned enterprises, weak financial intermediation or inadequately defined property rights) undermine sustainable resource management and worsen equity. Thus, reform of regulations and institutions should not lag behind economic restructuring, as shown in the case of energy pricing and institutional reforms in Poland (Bates, Cofala and Toman, 1995). In Peru, economy-wide reforms could have potentially increased harvesting pressures on over-exploited fisheries, without complementary laws to protect various fishing grounds included within the adjustment programme (World Bank, 1993b). A study of privatization of property rights and community-based management of estuarine fisheries in India concluded that, even if users initially agree to cooperate and share rents from conservation, significant disincentives will soon emerge, due to lack of well defined property rights (Srinivasan, 2005). Therefore, a combination of state-based and community-based management systems will be required for effective resource management.

Short-term stabilization

Unless government budget-cuts to bring inflation under control are carefully targeted, they may disproportionately penalize critical expenditures on environmental protection or poverty safety nets (Cornia, Jolly and Stewart, 1992; ECLAC, 1989; Miranda and Muzondo, 1991). Other examples include increases in air pollution in Thailand and Mexico due to reduced infrastructure expenditures (Reed, 1992), adverse impacts on low-income groups in Africa (especially women and children) caused by lowered government spending in areas such as health (Nzomo, 1992), and underfunding of forest protection activities (World Bank, 1994b). Another adverse linkage is the possible short-term recessionary impact of adjustment on poverty and unemployment, whereby the migratory poor are forced to increase their pressures on fragile lands and 'open access' natural resources. The remedy would be to expand economic opportunities elsewhere.

Fiscal policy

Traditional fiscal policies do not favour environmental protection – they place the main tax burden on items such as income, profits and labour. Ecological tax reforms (ETRs) could address this problem by reducing tax rates on environmentally friendly activities and increasing tax rates on 'bads' such as resource depletion and pollution. While the former encourages value addition and emphasizes qualitative improvement rather than quantitative expansion (growth), the latter increases resource-use efficiency.

Longer-term and less predictable effects

Economy-wide policies may have unpredictable and counter-intuitive long-term effects on sustainability. Some of these effects may be traced through a general equilibrium analysis that captures both direct and indirect links. The Costa Rica CGE model includes indirect effects on deforestation, to show that economic and environmental impacts of wage restraints in structural adjustment are different from results of partial equilibrium studies (Persson and Munasinghe, 1995); see Chapter 9.

Adjustment often succeeds in generating new economic opportunities and livelihoods, thereby alleviating poverty and breaking the vicious cycle of environmental degradation and poverty (World Bank, 1992a). Higher incomes increase willingness-to-pay for better environmental protection. However, while such growth is important for poor nations, it may increase overall pressures on natural resources. Meanwhile, properly valuing resources, increasing efficiency and reducing waste will reshape the structure of growth and limit undesirable environmental impacts. The long-run economic and environmental consequences of adjustment programmes depend on capital and labour mobility. Environmental policies themselves could have impacts on income distribution and employment.

Inequitable access to land and rapid population growth exacerbate rural unemployment and income inequality, thereby forcing the poor to depend increasingly on marginal resources for their livelihood (Cruz and Gibbs, 1990; *Environment and Development Economics*, 2004; Feder *et al.*, 1988; Lele and Stone, 1989). The result is more pressure on fragile environments. A Philippines case study (Munasinghe and Cruz, 1994) evaluates the policy determinants of long-term changes in rural poverty and unemployment that have worsened lowland to upland migration and induced conversion of forest lands to unsustainable agriculture. Shifting cultivation and grazing could worsen land degradation, where capital and technical change are limited and population growth is rapid (Cleaver and Schreiber, 1991). Important long-term links between adjustment programmes, trade and agriculture have been analysed by Goldin and Winters (1992). A study of social security reforms in the USA postulates that, in the current social security system, investments in environmental stewardship may serve as an informal intergenerational contract (Farmer, 2005).

7.3 Framework for analysis

7.3.1 Linking micro- and macroeconomic views of environmental harm – magnitude and structure of growth

This section links micro- and macroeconomic analyses. Environmental damage due to the *magnitude of growth* could be reduced by policy measures that *restructure growth* – to make it less resource intensive and polluting (see Section 2.4). Munasinghe (1995a) analyses the interplay of price and income effects in an initially stagnant economy that has open access forests. He shows how economic reforms may combine with neglected economic distortions to cause environmental harm.

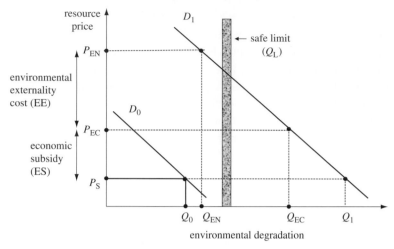

Figure 7.1. Using pricing policy to restructure growth and make development more sustainable. Source: Munasinghe (1995a).

The downward sloping curve D_0 in Figure 7.1, depicts demand for timber, which is assumed to depend on both price P and income Y (i.e. $D = D(P,Y)$). At the effective (subsidized) price P_S, representing the marginal cost of logging, the initial deforestation rate is given by Q_0. If Q_L is the safe limiting rate of deforestation beyond which serious ecological damage occurs, and $Q_0 < Q_L$, the situation may continue undetected and uncorrected.

Next, suppose economic reforms stimulate growth and shift the demand curve outward to D_1. This 'income effect' may result from increased domestic demand (e.g. construction timber) or higher timber exports (e.g. due to trade liberalization and devaluation). Now the deforestation rate could shift to $Q_1 > Q_L$ – causing serious environmental harm.

Clearly, the remedy is not to stop growth, but rather to introduce complementary measures that establish proper timber prices. First, property rights could be re-established in open access areas and 'efficient' stumpage fees imposed – to eliminate the economic subsidy (ES) and correctly reflect the opportunity cost of timber. The resulting efficient price (P_{EC}) would reduce the logging rate to Q_{EC}, which still exceeds Q_L. Second, an additional environmental externality cost (EE) may be charged to reflect loss of biodiversity or damage to watersheds, and thereby establish the full environmentally adjusted price (P_{EN}). The deforestation rate now falls to $Q_{EN} < Q_L$.

Exactly analogous reasoning would apply if we considered fuel prices and polluting emissions from transport or industry (see Chapter 11). In this case, P_S might be a subsidized diesel price, P_{EC} the equivalent trading opportunity cost, P_{EN} the full price including taxes to cover air pollution externality costs and Q_L the health-determined safety standard.

7.3.2 Modifying macropolicies to avoid environmental harm

In this section, we examine whether macroeconomic policies might be directly tailored to satisfy environmental considerations, without using additional complementary measures.

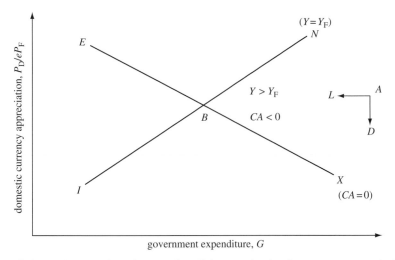

Figure 7.2. Timing and sequencing of economic policies to make development more sustainable. P_D = price of domestic goods; P_F = price of foreign goods; e = exchange rate; IN = internal balance equilibrium; EX = external balance equilibrium; Y = income; Y_F = full-employment income; CA = current account; AL = reduce government subsidies; AD = depreciate currency/liberalize trade.

Role of second-best policies

Maler and Munasinghe (1996) show theoretically that first-best macroeconomic policies that seek a Pareto optimum will not maximize welfare if an environmental externality exists (see Section 8.6). Here, second-best macropolicies ought to be pursued, to trade-off broad macroeconomic goals against environmental damage. Their model confirms both the empirical evidence and microeconomic analysis presented earlier, that environmental damage is indeed caused by the interaction of growth-inducing economy-wide policies with residual imperfections. Therefore, the first-best solution would be to correct the imperfections using complementary policies while pursuing the original macroeconomic reforms. However, if political or other constraints prevent or delay introduction of complementary measures, then second-best macroeconomic policies may be justified – especially in cases where environmental harm could be significant.

Second-best options also cover the dynamics of policy reform processes. For example, reforms might be gradually intensified (instead of being suddenly imposed), thereby allowing further time to phase out residual imperfections that degrade the environment.

Timing and sequencing of policy reforms

Could the timing and sequencing of economic reforms affect the extent of environmental damage? Some insights emerge from the literature on the timing and sequencing of adjustment measures to achieve economic goals (Edwards, 1992; Munasinghe, 1996b). In Figure 7.2, the *x*-axis indicates aggregate expenditure in a national economy (e.g. government budget, *G*) and the *y*-axis reflects the effects of domestic currency appreciation (e.g. ratio of domestic goods prices to foreign goods prices weighted by exchange rate, P_D/eP_E). The line *IN* represents the internal balance, or equilibrium combinations of *G* and P_D/eP_F, which enable policy makers to keep an economy producing at the full employment level Y_F. The line *EX* represents external balance, showing the equilibrium when the current account *CA* is zero (i.e. outgoing and incoming flows of foreign exchange are in balance).

Point *A* represents the initial state of the economy – below the line of internal balance *IN* and above the line of external balance *EX*. Typically, macropolicy makers would seek to move the economy toward equilibrium point *B* by reducing both the current account deficit (since *CA* < 0) and excess demand for goods and services (since *Y* > Y_F), to reduce inflationary pressures.

A downward movement *AD* is achieved by currency devaluation and removal of trade barriers, while a leftward shift *AL* occurs if government expenditures were reduced – e.g. eliminating subsidies on energy prices. Suppose that reforms affecting *AD* could be achieved first and *AL* somewhat later (e.g. because the latter was delayed by powerful transport or industrial lobbies insisting on cheap fuels). Then, economic liberalization represented by *AD* alone might lead to more foreign investment and growth of energy-intensive industries attracted by low energy prices. However, this apparent gain would also result in wasteful use of (subsidized) energy and more environmental pollution.

This simple analysis provides useful insights. However, good judgement is required to resist making major changes in economy-wide policies merely to achieve minor environmental (and social) gains. Once again, policy options that achieved 'win–win' gains would be the most desirable.

7.3.3 *Extending the conventional IS-LM macroeconomic analysis*

Next, we examine environmental concerns, based on the well-known IS-LM framework used in comparative static analysis of macroeconomic policies (Heyes, 2000). In Figure 7.3,

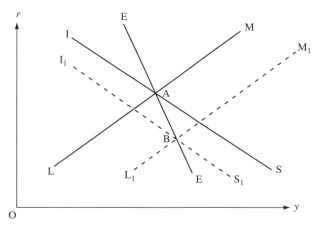

Figure 7.3. Extending conventional IS-LM analysis to include the environment.

the familiar IS-LM curves are plotted in (r, y) space, where r is the interest (discount) rate and y is aggregate demand.

The IS curve is derived from aggregate demand and supply identity, representing equilibrium in the goods market:

$$y = [c(y) + i(r) + g] = [c(y) + s(y) + t \cdot y],$$

or equivalently

$$[i + g] = [s + t],$$

where c is consumption, i is investment, g is government spending, s is saving and t is the tax rate. Simple calculus yields the basic IS curve:

$$\left[\frac{\mathrm{d}r}{\mathrm{d}y}\right]_{\mathrm{IS}} = \left[t + \frac{\mathrm{d}s}{\mathrm{d}y}\right] \Big/ \left[\frac{\mathrm{d}i}{\mathrm{d}y}\right],$$

which is downward sloping.

The LM curve is derived from the corresponding money market equilibrium:

$$M/p = L(r, y),$$

where M is (fixed) money supply, p is the price level and L is money demand. Simple differentiation yields the basic LM curve:

$$\left[\frac{\mathrm{d}r}{\mathrm{d}y}\right]_{\mathrm{LM}} = -\left[\frac{\mathrm{d}L}{\mathrm{d}y}\right] \Big/ \left[\frac{\mathrm{d}L}{\mathrm{d}r}\right],$$

which is upward sloping.

Environmental variables could be introduced into the familiar (r, y) space by examining the variation of environmental capital over time:

$$\left[\frac{\mathrm{d}(KE)}{\mathrm{d}t}\right] = [e(r) \cdot y + k \cdot KE],$$

where KE is the stock of environmental assets, t is time, e is the environmental intensity of economic activity (or pollutants emitted per unit of economic output) and k is the rate of environmental self-renewal in the natural state. In a steady-state economy, $\mathrm{d}(KE)/\mathrm{d}t$ is zero, and implicit differentiation yields

$$\left[\frac{\mathrm{d}r}{\mathrm{d}y}\right]_{\mathrm{EE}} = -\frac{[e]}{[y(\mathrm{d}e/\mathrm{d}r)]}.$$

Assume that environmental intensity increases with capital cost, i.e. $\mathrm{d}e/\mathrm{d}r > 0$. Therefore, $[\mathrm{d}r/\mathrm{d}y]_{\mathrm{EE}}$ is downward sloping. The EE curve is drawn steeper than the IS curve, assuming that e is relatively insensitive to r. Suppose that e is also a function of some regulatory framework parameter Z, which determines how effectively polluters are obliged to pay for environmental externalities. If $de/dZ < 0$, then EE would shift leftward as regulatory enforcement improves.

To demonstrate the pedagogic value of this approach, consider an economy initially at equilibrium, with the IS, LM and EE curves intersecting at point A. Expansionary monetary policies would shift the curve LM to L_1M_1. Restoring the tripartite equilibrium at point B would now require contractionary fiscal policies that yield the countervailing shift IS to I_1S_1. The EE curve is stable, assuming that it represents a longer-run equilibrium, compared with the short-run shifts in the IS-LM curves. Many similar policy exercises may be conducted, involving changes in various parameters and curves.

7.3.4 Macroeconomic performance measurement issues

To include sustainability concerns better in macroeconomic analyses, an improved system of national accounts (SNA) called the System of Environmental and Economic Accounting (SEEA) has been proposed by the United Nations (see Section 3.7.5), and new measures of environmental and social progress need to be developed, as suggested by the MDGs and CSD (see Chapter 1). Gross domestic product (GDP) is the common market-based measure which influences macroeconomic policy. Its shortcomings include neglect of income distributional concerns, non-market activities and environmental effects. Traditional SNA measures do not adequately reflect either the depletion of natural-resource stocks (like deforestation) or environmental damage (due to pollution) (USBEA, 1995).

7.3.5 Action Impact Matrix and tunnelling policies to restructure growth paths

The AIM described in Chapter 2 provides a systematic framework for prioritizing and addressing the most important environmental and social impacts of economy-wide policy reforms. The process includes: (1) AIM-based analysis to identify, prioritize and analyse the most serious economic–sustainability linkages; (2) specific *ex ante* complementary measures to limit environmental and social harm, before economy-wide reforms are implemented; (3) contingency plans and careful monitoring of sustainability issues, to deal with them *ex post*; and (4) reviewing the timing and sequencing of economy-wide policies and complementary measures, to minimize environmental and social damage.

Chapter 2 also set out a model for restructuring unsustainable growth patterns using a 'tunnelling' approach – whereby developing countries seeking sustainable development paths could learn from the experience of the industrialized countries and so avoid the same mistakes. Economic imperfections that make private decisions deviate from socially optimal ones, worsen environmental and social damage along some growth paths. Tunnelling through to avoid such harm is possible by: (1) adopting 'win–win' policies that provide simultaneous economic, environmental and social gains; (2) using complementary measures to address harmful impacts on sustainability; and (3) reshaping economy-wide policies in cases where environmental and social damage was severe.

7.3.6 Areas for further work

More country-specific case studies are needed to trace the social and environmental impacts of economy-wide policies – e.g. in areas like trade and privatization. Exploring the sustainability of long-run growth is important, especially in the context of worsening natural-resource scarcities, including global environmental degradation. Better practical models and analytical tools are required, based on approaches familiar to practicing macroeconomists (e.g. extended IS-LM framework).

Distributional, political economy and institutional issues also need to be addressed in future work. The cross-linkages between economic, environmental and social impacts of economy-wide policies need to be further explored. Better environmental and social indicators should be developed, including environmentally adjusted national accounts and improved techniques for valuing environmental impacts. Where economic valuation of environmental and social impacts is difficult, techniques such as multicriteria analysis can usefully supplement conventional cost–benefit analysis.

7.4 Case study of Brazil – making long-term development more sustainable

In the following sections we present a case study of Brazil to illustrate the generic arguments set out in Sections 7.1 to 7.3 and to show how sustainable development strategies could be devised on a country-specific basis, with due regard for local conditions, resource endowments and social needs.

7.4.1 Introduction

Generally, some past economy-wide reforms (including structural adjustment) have been implemented without adequate consideration of their environmental and social, as well as economic, impacts (see Section 7.2). Nevertheless, properly managed reforms could facilitate long-term growth while minimizing environmental harm. More broadly, non-growth scenarios (where poverty and stagnation inevitably lead to unsustainability) are less desirable than growth situations – especially where growth may be restructured more sustainably (see Section 2.5).

Hence, one promising approach toward making development more sustainable seems to be the successful implementation of sound economic policies aimed at the recovery or maintenance of growth, combined with the adoption of specific remedial environmental and social safeguard programmes. Appropriate sustainability indicators are a key prerequisite for this purpose. Most importantly, strategies to make development more sustainable must be country-specific.

Accordingly, the case study seeks to understand better the links between long-term growth and sustainable development in Brazil, by studying the extent to which growth-inducing economic policies are linked to environmental or social harm, the nature of the mechanisms underlying such interactions and the appropriate policy conclusions to be drawn.

7.4.2 *Economic growth and the challenges of social equity and environmental conservation*

The industrialization process and growth in income per capita achieved by Brazil since the 1960s has been accompanied by persistent social inequalities and increasing environmental degradation. Until the early 1980s, the Brazilian model of development was based on industrialization through import substitution. Protectionism, development of state companies and ambitious fiscal and credit incentives transformed the previous agrarian economy into a highly industrialized society within 30 years. During the most dynamic period, the 1970s, Brazil grew at an average annual rate of 8.7% and the urban population share increased from less than one-third to about three-quarters of the total population .

Nonetheless, this prosperity was not well distributed. About 40% of homes were below the poverty line at the end of the 1970s, and the Gini coefficient for income distribution was 0.60 in 1979, one of the highest in the world (Barros, Henriques and Mendonça, 2000). Low investments in primary and secondary education were key factors perpetuating income concentration. The lack of land-reform policies also led to highly concentrated land ownership. Further, instead of undertaking land reform, the government colonized the Amazon, which caused extensive deforestation.

The social inequalities were exacerbated by the oil and debt crises of the late 1970s that generated fiscal imbalances, slowed investment capacity and led to a long recession in the following decade. Rates of unemployment increased and inefficient industrial and agricultural structures were unable to sustain a dynamic growth process. Further, during the 1980s and early 1990s, high inflationary pressures combined with reduced growth opportunities to increase social conflict.

In the 1990s, several structural reforms were implemented. Market-oriented policies related to trade and capital liberalization, privatization and deregulation were introduced. As a result, during 1991–1997, foreign direct investment increased by US $14.7 billion and labour productivity in the manufacturing sector increased by 8.7% (Bonelli, 1998). In conjunction with previous policies, restrictive macroeconomic reforms were implemented during the 1990s. The most important was the Real Plan of 1994, which applied a successful monetary stabilization policy that reduced the monthly inflation rate from 80% to 1%. A positive outcome was an immediate income redistribution effect through the reduction of the inflationary tax. The Gini coefficient decreased from 0.58 in 1993 to 0.57 in 1995 (Rocha, 2000), but even this marginal redistribution soon faded due to more unemployment.

Other consequences of the Real Plan were massive unemployment, particularly in the industrial sector, and an overvalued exchange rate (resulting from increased external capital inflows to balance the huge current account deficit). High interest rates were partially successful in keeping the external balance under control until 1998, attracting short-term capital investment, but considerably worsening the fiscal balance. In early 1999, the lack of confidence in external stability led to a massive exchange-rate devaluation (which was allowed to float). Subsequently, Brazil has followed a stop-and-go pattern in terms of economic growth, with no sustained pattern of recovery in the 1990s – mainly due to the remaining problems of very high interest rates (which depressed productive investments) and substantial current account deficits (which left the exchange rate susceptible to wide oscillations).

Meanwhile, social and environmental policies remained less effective than desired. Although social care programmes for the poor in urban and rural areas have been continuously extended, they have not reduced poverty and inequality. The fraction of 10% richest households to the 40% poorer households is about 24 (below 10 in most countries). Similarly, small farms (with less than 10 ha) cover less than 3% of the total farming area, while the share of big farms (with more than 10 000 ha) is above 40%. Agrarian reform programmes have received a large share of the budget, and ambitious targets have been set. Nonetheless, rural poverty remains a serious problem, especially in the northeast of Brazil.

Furthermore, rural areas are suffering from serious environmental problems such as water pollution, soil degradation, deforestation and biodiversity loss. Urban regions also suffer from increasing environmental degradation through air and water pollution, lack of sewerage to poorer households and increasing solid-waste generation. Nevertheless, an opinion poll carried out in the late 1990s showed that only 47% of Brazilians agreed with the idea that the environment should take priority over economic growth, and the acceptance of lowered environmental quality in exchange for growth increased among the lower-income classes.

Thus, there are major challenges to resuming growth and strengthening the country's share in the global economy, while reducing social gaps and protecting the environment. This complex analysis was initiated with a preliminary AIM exercise (see Section 2.4.1). Based on the priorities that emerged, we will focus on three specific areas: (a) external trade, industrial growth and pollution; (b) consumption patterns, environment and income classes; and (c) deforestation in the Amazon.

The Brazilian economy has experienced successive policy changes to alleviate the pressure on the balance of payments caused by the external debt crisis. In the early 1980s, in order to improve the external account situation, export incentives were created. Indeed, the expansion of the export sector was a key element in the structural adjustment strategy supported by the IMF and the World Bank. This change in the orientation of the industrial policy, so far dedicated to import-substitution, has affected the Brazilian industrial structure. The export-oriented industries achieved a better performance relative to the traditional, domestic-market-oriented industries.

In the 1990s, imports expanded steadily due to sustained trade liberalization policies. This import expansion was boosted by the exchange-rate overvaluation after the 1994 Real Stabilization programme. As a result, there was a strong expansion in the use of imported inputs and a reduction in the use of domestic inputs.

During the same period, there is evidence that the pollution problem increased, although the index used is an estimate of potential rather than actual industrial pollution. Figure 7.4 shows that the industries with high pollution potential grew faster than the industry average. Thus, industrial growth since the 1980s has been diverted toward potentially polluting industries. The links between pollution potential and trade liberalization were studied by

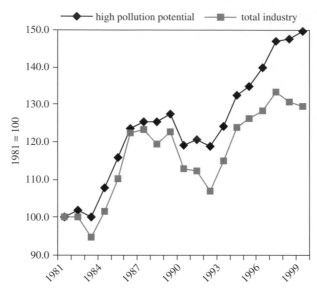

Figure 7.4. Evolution of the Brazilian industry according to its potential pollution. Source: IBGE/DPE/ Industry Department.

analysing the environmental profile of the Brazilian industrial sector using input–output (I–O) modelling and environmental indicators from a survey in the State of São Paulo. In order to capture all industrial pollution generated in industrial processing of manufactured goods, we need to include emission flows from input production to the assembly phase. Such an approach requires an I–O model relating changes in demand vectors to potential industrial pollution levels.

The exercise was carried out using the I–O matrices of the Brazilian Statistical Office (IBGE). Four different sets of emission coefficients were used. The first set (CEMA/IPEA) was estimated using pollution emission and abatement data for Brazilian industry in 1988 from the PRONACOP (Brazilian National Program of Pollution Control) project, adapted by Young (1997). The second set was the Industrial Pollution Projection System (IPPS), developed by the World Bank using data from US industry. The third group of coefficients refers to carbon dioxide emissions from fossil fuels consumption in Brazil during 1990– 1994, estimated by COPPE/UFRJ and adapted by Ferraz and Young (1999). Finally, the fourth set of emission coefficients (IPEA-IE/UFRJ) was calculated using emission data of industrial plants recorded in the inventory of the São Paulo State Environmental Protection Agency (CETESB) and value-added data from industrial surveys in 1996.

These various data sets incorporate important methodological differences, and all coefficients have shortcomings. The CEMA/IPEA coefficients were estimated using old data from emissions (1987). The IPPS data are based only on air pollutant emissions from fossil fuel consumption and assume that Brazilian industry has the same emissions profile as US industry in the late 1980s. The IPEA-IE/UFRJ coefficients are not derived from recorded

Table 7.1 *Pollution intensity per unit of output (kg/US $million)*

Parameter/year	Consumption	Investment	Exports	Total
CEMA/IPEA emission coefficients (kg/US $million), 1995				
BOD	1116	453	1370	861
Metals (water)	10	24	47	15
Particulates (air)	3398	8232	8549	4441
SO_2	3528	3356	6442	3298
NOx	1672	1574	3029	1603
HC	430	566	880	448
CO	10 899	31 445	55 460	17 855
IPPS coefficients (kg/US $million), 1996				
BOD	285	125	276	253
Total suspended solids	3507	8765	13202	5792
SO_2	1853	2735	3678	2263
NO_2	1127	1304	1562	1218
CO	1683	2347	3410	2037
VOC	825	781	1002	840
Fine particulates	261	717	584	391
Total particulates	501	839	907	619
Metals – land	129	306	453	206
IPEA-IE/UFRJ emission coefficients (kg/US $million) 1996				
Organic (water)	903	190	744	744
Inorganic (water)	6.6	7.2	11.5	7.4
Particulates (air)	2388	2794	3667	2634
SO_2	934	1151	939	976
CO_2 emissions (kg CO_2 per Brazilian Reais), 1994	0.635	0.281	0.303	0.326

emissions – instead they use official records of expected emissions (including abatement procedures), assuming that plants operate at the optimal output level. Nevertheless, the results of these I–O exercises showed a consistent result that production associated with industrial exports is more emissions-intensive than production-oriented toward domestic markets (Table 7.1). Thus, Brazilian industry is specialized in supplying potentially polluting goods to world markets. This result is compatible with the hypothesis that developing countries tend to welcome 'dirty' industries that are less competitive in developed countries because of tighter environmental controls.

Even if export-oriented production is more emissions-intensive for specific pollutants, some domestic-oriented production may also harm the environment. Depending on the methodology used, results may differ for specific parameters, which means that it is necessary to improve data gathering for a better understanding of environmental performance.

Table 7.2 *Difference between export and import emission intensities using IPPS coefficients (g/US $)*

Pollutant	1990	1991	1992	1993	1994	1995	1996
BOD	0.03	0.03	−0.01	0.08	0.06	0.14	0.08
TSS	11.73	11.83	9.37	10.29	8.72	7.31	8.23
SO_2	2.10	1.83	1.24	1.64	1.56	1.31	1.50
NO_2	0.65	0.58	0.33	0.51	0.55	0.42	0.47
CO	1.93	1.84	1.29	1.63	1.41	1.16	1.33
VOC	0.28	0.18	0.04	0.14	0.18	0.04	0.10
Particulates	0.50	0.48	0.37	0.47	0.42	0.42	0.42
Fine particulates	0.67	0.61	0.45	0.63	0.60	0.63	0.63

For two parameters, the output destined for domestic markets are more intensive in emissions (IPEA-IE/UFRJ data for organic and CO_2). Thus, there may be no 'natural' reason why inward-oriented industrial development would be better in environmental terms. In other words, there is also the need to improve environmental procedures within domestic-oriented firms. For example, promoting environmental certification (e.g. in public procurement procedures), and requiring firms to be in full accordance with environmental requirements (to get access to credit from the official development banks), are key steps toward a more sustainable industry.

Emissions 'savings' were a positive outcome of imports expansion caused by the trade liberalization process during the 1990s. Since they are produced abroad, imports 'displace' the associated emissions to the country of origin – i.e. if imports were produced domestically, emissions would have risen. Using the IPPS emission coefficients for each pollutant in the 1990–1996 period, there was an estimated average change in the associated level of (potential) emissions of 146% (i.e., the 'savings' of emissions because of industrial imports increased by 46%). There were differences in terms of pollutants.

However, emissions associated with imports would have been greater if rising industrial imports were not concentrated in relatively clean activities, particularly those that are technology-intensive (e.g. electronics). Table 7.2 shows that the emissions intensity of exports (mainly semi-manufactured and intermediate goods) is almost always greater than that of imports. However, the gap in emissions intensity between exports and imports reduced during 1990–1996. Overall, Brazil was a net 'exporter' of sustainability, since it traded through the export of industrial goods with higher pollution potential than those it imported.

One additional exercise estimated the direct costs of introducing environmental control strategies, combining the methodology proposed by Pasurka (1984), the costs for controlling water emissions (BOD and heavy metals) estimated by Mendes (1994) and aggregate price-elasticities of the exports quantum calculated by Cavalcanti, Ribeiro and Castro (1998). Even in the most pessimistic scenario, the estimated trade diversion caused by

Table 7.3 *Export losses caused by emission control costs*
(percentage of actual exports)

Optimistic scenario (elasticity = −0.34)

	1980–1984	1985–1989	1990–1994	1995–1996
Abatement of 50% of emissions				
Total	0.3%	0.4%	0.4%	0.4%
Latin America	0.4%	0.4%	0.4%	0.4%
NAFTA	0.5%	0.6%	0.6%	0.6%
European Union	0.2%	0.3%	0.3%	0.3%
Abatement of 100% of emissions				
Total	0.7%	0.8%	0.9%	0.9%
Latin America	0.7%	0.7%	0.8%	0.8%
NAFTA	1.1%	1.4%	1.6%	1.5%
European Union	0.5%	0.6%	0.8%	0.8%

These numbers roughly double for a pessimistic scenario
(elasticity = −0.78).

higher abatement costs was relatively low. Thus, the competitiveness of industrial exports would not be greatly affected if adequate environmental controls are introduced (Table 7.3). The highest risks of losing markets are in the footwear, non-ferrous metallurgic and other metallurgic industries. From a more dynamic perspective, the 1996 PAEP field survey of industrial firms in the State of São Paulo showed that firms with international links invest more in cleaner production than domestic firms. This finding is compatible with the hypothesis that trade and capital openness favour environmentally sound practices and products.

These results have key implications for policy making. First, the relatively high concentration of industrial exports in pollution-intensive activities makes them sensitive to environmental barriers to trade. If world trade is subject to stricter environmental criteria, Brazilian industrial exports may be at risk. There are two possible strategies to deal with this problem: (1) adopt an aggressive position against the proposed changes in trade regulations, maintaining the status quo of minimal environmental barriers in trade agreements and/or (2) enhance the environmental performance of local industries, either improving emission standards or changing the composition of industrial exports, becoming less dependent on exports associated with 'dirty' production chains.

The first option reflects a view that environmental restrictions in trade (and capital) flows will not be realized soon. However, if environmental controls are not standardized, and Brazil remains a Latin American leader in this area, Brazilian producers may not be able to compete with exports from neighbouring countries with fewer environmental controls. Thus, the second strategy may be better in dealing with the problem in the long term. There is a consistent trend in Brazilian policy making toward the adoption of economic instruments in environmental management, based on the user/polluter-pays principle. Some sectors may face relatively small short-term losses in their competitiveness (except for a few sectors that could receive special compensation during the transition to cleaner production). Many firms are already searching voluntarily for better environmental procedures.

This transition toward a more environmentally sound economy cannot however rely on a *laissez faire* mechanism based on the simple exposure of Brazilian firms to the market. One important step is the push for economic instruments for environmental management, allowing flexible but efficient measures to improve environmental standards. This must be combined with industrial policies aimed at spreading win–win environmental innovations. Some examples of these policies are the strengthening of firms to absorb and generate environmentally related technologies; investment in human capital; reduction in regional differences in environmental performance; incentives for environmental certification; and promotion of environmentally sound products and processes in order to create a domestic market for 'green' products.

7.4.3 Urban development, income and the environment

Growth, poverty and environmental issues

Urban pollution is a severe problem in many Brazilian cities, and the poor suffer most. Serôa da Motta and Rezende (1999) analysed 1980–1990 data linking child-death incidence with the six most common waterborne diseases (intestinal infections, cholera, typhoid fever, poliomyelitis, amoebic dysentery, schistosomiasis and shigellosis). Increasing the provision of public water supply by 1% to unserved homes (earning less than five minimum wages), keeping other sanitation services unchanged, would reduce the number of mortality cases of children under 14 years of age associated with waterborne diseases by 2.5% (462 lives). For a 1% increase in sewage collection and treatment, the equivalent reductions would be, respectively, 1.6% (298 lives) and 2.1% (395 lives). When all three services are jointly provided, the reduction levels would be 6.1% (1139 lives). The investment cost for each life saved related to public water supply is US $115 102, followed by sewage treatment and collection costs that are, respectively, US $175 207 and US $214 562 (Serôa da Motta *et al.*, 1994). When all three services, public water supply, sewage treatment and collection, are jointly expanded by 1%, the investment per life saved is US $164 385.

These costs provide one estimate of how much Brazilian society values one poor child's life. Assuming that sanitation facilities last over 50 years and that operation and maintenance costs are 10% of capital costs, the annualized value of the saved life for the joint alternative is around US $18 000 – over four times the Brazilian per capita income. These figures indicate that impacts of water pollution on human health are significant and that mitigation costs are very high.

Serôa da Motta and Fernandes Mendes (1996) determined health costs of air pollution by estimating mortality rates caused by respiratory diseases as a function of meteorological parameters (humidity and temperature), pollution concentration data (particulate and SO_2)

and socioeconomic data (medical care, education level, etc.) for the period 1980–1989. They show that a variation of 10 $\mu g/m^3$ of particulate matter changes the mortality rate by 1.62%. Using the estimated elasticity, the authors project that a 44% reduction in regional industrial emissions would lead to the level of 50 $\mu g/m^3$ (which reflects the legal primary ambient standard) and would reduce respiratory-related deaths by 6.4%. Based on foregone output due to illness and premature death, air pollution costs are estimated to be US $1.7–2.2 million.

The previously calculated pollution costs are due to increasing urbanization and consumption pattern changes, combined with a very unequal income distribution. Degradation can be highly concentrated in consumption patterns of high-income groups who exhibit high levels of ownership of durable goods, energy and water consumption, sewage and solid-waste generation. However, income constraints drastically reduce the poor's capacity for defensive expenditures against the effects of degradation (e.g. through better medical care and home environment). Thus, poor people may be bearing the burden of rich people's pollution.

Income distribution and pollution generation

Another aspect of income concentration is the unequal impacts of consumption. Recent surveys on household expenditures in Brazil have shown significant changes in consumption patterns in the period 1987–1996. While the population increased by 15% during this period, ownership levels of durable goods among households increased at higher levels. For all income groups, there was a large increase in the ownership of drier machines (173%), freezers (211%) and dishwashers (275%), and an even higher increase arising in the lower-income groups (IBGE, 1998). These trends led to a more intense consumption pattern based on industrial goods, and consequently a higher energy intensity.

The ratio of home energy consumption to GDP increased from 0.049 tonne/US $100 in 1987 to 0.060 tonne/US $100 in 1996 (BEN, 1997). Total residential per capita energy consumption in the period also increased from 0.192 tonne in 1987 to 0.206 tonne in 1996. Nevertheless, per capita residential energy for cooking decreased in the same period, from 0.110 to 0.078 tonne/inhabitant – mainly due to replacement of fuelwood by liquefied petroleum gas. Fossil fuel dominates in the transport sector, while more than 90% of Brazil's electricity consumption is based on hydro sources. Per capita energy consumption in transport increased from 1.131 tonne/inhabitant in 1987 to 1.348 tonne/inhabitant in 1996. While the energy intensity of agriculture was stable as a function of GDP during the period, the energy intensity of the industrial sector as a function of GDP rose from 0.304 tonne/US $1000 in 1987 to 0.359 tonne/US $1000 in 1997. The fossil-fuel share of energy consumption in Brazil increased by 38% during 1987–1997, mostly due to increases in transport and the substitution of fossil fuels for firewood in cooking. With the diminishing availability of hydro sources, the fossil-fuel share will tend to be higher in the future; 91% of urban households already receive treated water supply,[2] but less than 20% of sewage is treated (Serôa da Motta, 1996).

---

[2] Unpublished report by Pesquisa Nacional de Amostra Domiciliar (PNAD), IBGE, Rio de Janeiro, 1998.

Consumption patterns in Brazil are changing toward environmental-intensive goods and services that increase pressure on the environment. To analyse consumption patterns for urban-income groups in Brazil, we have estimated the household degradation level (E) for each income class estimated by the product of its propensity to degrade (Pmg) and average household income. In turn, Pmg is estimated as the propensity to consume weighted by the pollution intensity of each consumption item. Several scenarios involving progressive and regressive income transfers between income classes were analysed, in order to study corresponding changes in the degradation pressures due to differences in Pmg among income groups. The progressive scenario transfers US $10 billion from the richest classes – equivalent to 7% of their income or 3% of total urban income in Brazil in the year 1995. In the regressive scenario, the poorest classes were expected to lose about US $3.7 billion.

Due to data limitations, the analysis covers only two production sectors (industry and agriculture) and three direct services (transportation, water and sewage). The following key environmental linkages are considered: (1) industrial water pollution from organic and inorganic matter and air pollution from SO_2 and particulates; (2) agricultural pollution from fertilizer use; (3) household transportation pollution from atmospheric emissions of CO, HC and NOx; (4) household water consumption; and (5) household sewage discharge. The analysis covers urban areas in 1995 that represent more than 90% of national personal income. Industrial pollution is estimated based on I–O modelling of emission flows from the input production up to the assembling phase.

The results show that income distribution changes are not strongly linked to significant changes in degradation pressures. In most cases, the richest classes generate as much as 10 to 20 times the degradation of the lowest-income group. At the same time, there is a negative relationship between income and Pmg. The poor tend to degrade more per unit of consumption, mainly due to their high propensity to consume. An inverted U-shaped environmental Kuznets curve is not found for the degradation pressures exerted by different income groups.

In sum, variations in propensity to degrade were mainly explained by the greater concentration of income among the rich, and, when applicable, by variations in technological factors among income groups. Second, our estimates show that rich people tend to degrade more than their population share. Lastly, regressive transfers increase degradation and vice versa. In both cases, however, we found that industrial and transport sources show an inelastic relationship between income distribution and total degradation pressure, in which the transferred income share is bigger than the resultant change in share of degradation pressure.

High degradation pressure from rich people's consumption patterns shows another regressive aspect, and raises serious distributive issues: (1) while poor peoples' consumption is not the main source of harm, they bear more degradation impacts due to inadequate defensive expenditures and (2) as degradation pressure is mainly due to the consumption of the rich, avoiding stricter degradation controls that affect consumption decisions will subsidize rich people's consumption, at the expense of the poor. Yet, as degradation concentration ratios are lower than the respective income ratios, when degradation control becomes more stringent, poor people will tend to pay more for environmental control per unit of consumption if these costs are passed on through prices.

Table 7.4 *GDP growth and deforestation in the Brazilian Amazon*

State	GDP average growth rate (1985–1997)	Cumulated GDP growth rate (1985–1997)	Agricultural GDP average growth rate (1985–1997)	Cumulated Agricultural GDP growth rate (1985–1997)	Growth in deforested area (1978–1988) (%)	Growth in deforested area (1988–1998) (%)
Acre	4.86	58.31	0.31	3.71	256.0	65.3
Amapá	6.72	80.65	11.02	132.20	300.0	145.3
Amazonas	0.56	6.77	0.50	6.06	1058.8	46.5
Maranhão	1.05	12.56	0.94	11.24	42.1	10.8
Mato Grosso	2.91	34.96	2.68	32.13	257.5	84.3
Pará	2.68	32.17	5.14	61.65	133.2	43.2
Rondônia	4.01	48.11	4.57	54.85	614.3	77.6
Roraima	7.20	86.34	16.98	203.82	2600.0	114.5
Tocantins	2.53	30.41	0.22	2.65	575.0	22.2
Amazon region	3.61		4.71		146.1	45.9

Source: INPE (2000); Silva and Medina (1999).

If this regressive aspect is to be avoided, policy instruments need to include compensatory measures. Thus, environmental taxes may be useful since they reduce social control costs and generate revenue that can be recycled within the economy to compensate the poor (see Section 9.1).

7.4.4 Deforestation in the Amazon and production patterns

Growth and deforestation trends

The Brazilian Amazon comprises an area of almost 5 million km^2, of which about 70% is forest, including a major share of known global biodiversity. Deforestation has increased during the past 20 years. About 400 000 km^2 of tropical forest were cleared during 1978–1998 according to satellite data (INPE, 2000).

The Amazon also had substantial growth in income per capita. Economic growth was driven by colonization projects coupled with massive infrastructure investments and credit concessions; GDP grew by an average of 15% per year from 1970 to 1980, and the per capita income more than doubled. The economic boom was led by the industrial sector, with an average annual growth rate of 26%, spurred on by the Manaus Free Export Processing Zone. The share of industry in local production increased from 15% in 1970 to 40% in 1980 (Reis and Blanco, 1996).

During the 1980s and 1990s, there were substantial growth differences among states. In some states agriculture was the main driver of growth. Table 7.4 shows GDP growth for each

Table 7.5 *Land use in the Brazilian Amazon: 1985 and 1996 (km^2)*

Land use	1985	1996
Perennial crops	10 183.27	10 788.24
Annual crops	79 735.44	70 604.42
Planted forest	3031.78	5800.30
Planted pasture	298 423.46	477 273.20
Fallow land	43 517.64	29 030.27
Productive land not used	114 754.61	74 275.44
Total cleared area	1 378 194.56	1 524 032.00

Source: IBGE agriculture census 1985 and 1995 (includes Maranhão and Goiás).

state of the Legal Amazon from 1985 to 1997, including agricultural GDP growth as a comparator.

The most industrialized state, Amazonas, has a low average growth rate, whereas other states, such as Acre and Rondônia, which depend mostly on agriculture, cattle and extraction, had average growth rates exceeding 4%. The states with the highest growth rates, Roraima and Amapá, also had the highest agricultural GDP growth rates. They also had the highest growth rates of deforestation during 1985–1988, confirming that both cropping and cattle ranching cause deforestation. Between 1978–1988 and 1988–1998, the growth of deforestation in the Amazon region decreased. Nonetheless, the deforested area increased during the 1990s in Amapá, Mato Grosso and Roraima, while remaining stable in Acre and Rondônia.

Most of the deforested areas were converted to pasture land (Table 7.5). It is found that about 145 837 km^2 of land was cleared between 1985 and 1995/96 (close to the value of 174 292 km^2 obtained for the area deforested in from 1998 to 1988). The area of planted pasture increased from 298 423 km^2 in 1985 to 477 272 km^2 in 1996 – an increase of about 60% in 10 years. On the other hand, the area used for crops did not change much. Thus, these results indicate that the conversion of forest into planted pasture is still the main source of deforestation in the Brazilian Amazon. Logging is also an important source of deforestation. The volume of timber extraction increased from about 117 to 523 million m^3 from 1980 to 1995, although its rate of growth declined in the 1990s.

Poverty and income inequality

Despite the significant growth in GDP in many regions of the Amazon, inequality in income and land is strongly present. The Gini coefficient for land in the northern region of Brazil decreased from 0.86 in 1975 to 0.79 in 1985 (Schneider, 1995), but it is still relatively high. Additionally, land and environmental degradation and the lack of rural development have generated a massive migration to urban areas, creating additional problems. The rural share of population decreased from 44% in 1991 to 32% in 2000. The 5.9% annual growth in urban population in the Amazon was much higher than the Brazilian mean (2.7% per year). The fastest urbanization occurred in Amapá and Roraima – states which are both agriculture based. Rural-urban migration may be occurring due to unsustainable agriculture and poor living conditions in remote rural areas.

Social costs of deforestation

Deforestation and environmental degradation in the Amazon imposes social costs, both within and outside its borders. Locally, future growth prospects will be hampered. The conversion of forest into pasture land and crop area is almost irreversible since the soil nutrients are exhausted. Serôa da Motta and Ferraz (2000) show that logging (followed by land conversion to agriculture) does not reflect scarcity and depletion costs. The deforestation process harms other activities as well. In the absence of sustainable forestry practices, the possibilities of future income associated with the use of biodiversity, eco-tourism, carbon sequestration and other environmental services will decrease considerably with deforestation.

Biodiversity loss is a major result of deforestation. In 1997 there were 228 fauna species in danger of extinction in Brazil, of which about 90 were from the Amazon (IBAMA, 1997). The Amazon contains several unique ecosystems and species, having both existence and pharmaceutical values (see Chapter 3). Further, predatory logging practices can also cause extinction of valuable commercial tree species, such as mahogany. Martini, Rosa and Uhl (1994) show that of 305 commercially and ecologically valuable tree species, 45 are at risk. Deforestation also causes environmentally related social costs through CO_2 emissions. Reis and Andersen (2000) estimated average carbon emissions from the Legal Amazon of 168 million tonnes per year during 1970–1985 (or about 95 tonnes of carbon per hectare cleared).

Deforestation and logging are related to the increasing risk of fires in the region. With its humid microclimate, the tropical forest contributes to fire control. Both the selective logging and land-clearing processes greatly increase the probability of fire, particularly because logging opens up the forest canopy (up to 50%) – allowing the sun to dry out leaf litter and other combustible materials. Therefore, deforestation increases the potential for massive ecological and economic losses through accidental fires. Greater frequency and intensity of El Niño events will increase the risk of fires due to drying of forests (Nepstad *et al.*, 1999).

Economic incentives and deforestation in the Brazilian Amazon

Deforestation in the Brazilian Amazon is a complex phenomenon. The forest conversion process is undertaken by family farmers, large cattle-ranchers, frontier settlers, land speculators and logging companies. Moreover, the process is influenced by markets, as well as institutions and government policies. Therefore, modelling its dynamics is not an easy task.

We apply a simple model to annual panel-data for eight states in order to measure the causes of agricultural land clearing and cattle-head expansion in the Brazilian Amazon (Munasinghe *et al.*, 2006):

$$\ln y_{it} = \alpha + \beta \ln pa_{it} + \delta \ln pl_{it} + \gamma \ln w_{it} + \lambda \ln crd_{it}$$
$$+ \gamma \ln prd_{it} + \phi \ln nprd_{it} + \rho \ln dist_i + \zeta \ln sd_i + f_i + \varepsilon_{it}.$$

Table 7.6 *Determinants of cattle-head density in the Amazon, 1980–1995*

Independent variables	Alternative models		
	(1) Fixed effects	(2) Random effects	(3) GLS-AR
ln(price of cattle-head lagged)$_{it}$	−0.398 (0.095)[a]	−0.377 (0.106)[a]	−0.240 (0.092)[a]
ln(price of pastureland lagged)$_{it}$	−0.046 (0.076)	−0.080 (0.082)	−0.037 (0.058)
ln(cattle credit density lagged)$_{it}$	0.034 (0.024)	0.062 (0.026)[a]	0.060 (0.019)[a]
ln(paved road density lagged)$_{it}$	0.307 (0.063)[a]	0.261 (0.064)[a]	0.174 (0.058)[a]
ln(unpaved road density lagged)$_{it}$	0.104 (0.049)[a]	0.210 (0.051)[a]	0.404 (0.046)[a]
ln(distance to federal capital)$_i$		−0.799 (0.149)[a]	−0.676 (0.100)[a]
Constant	3.221 (0.454)[a]	9.168 (1.037)[a]	8.6558 (0.640)[a]
F-test all $f_i = 0$	30.26		
Breusch–Pagan LM test for $f_i = 0$		$\chi^2 (1) = 45.66$	
		Prob. $> \chi^2 = 0.0$	
Hausman test	$\chi^2(5) = 0$		
	Prob. $> \chi^2 = 1.0$		
N	128	128	128
R^2	0.58		
Log-likelihood			5.144

Dependent variable: ln(cattle-head density).
Standard errors are in parentheses.
[a] Variables significant at 5% level.
States included in the analysis are Acre, Amazonas, Maranhão, Mato Grosso, Pará, Rondônia and Roraima.

Here y_{it} is the fraction of cleared land in the agriculture estimation or the density of cattle-head in the pasture estimation; pa_{it} is the price of output (agriculture products for agriculture and the price of cattle-head for cut in the cattle equation); pl_{it} is the price of land (differentiated by crop land and pastureland according to the dependent variable); w_{it} is the rural wage rate; crd_{it} is the rural credit density (differentiated by agriculture and cattle raising credit for each equation, credit/state area); prd_{it} is the density of paved roads (paved roads/state area); $nprd_{it}$ is the density of unpaved roads (unpaved roads/ state area); $dist_i$ is the distance from the state capital to the federal capital; sd_i is the proportion of high quality soil; f_i is a specific effect for each state; and ε_{it} is the contemporaneous error term.

The conversion of forest into pastureland is still the main source of deforestation in the region, but this does not explain why cattle formation has been increasing. Results for both cattle-head density and cleared land fraction are summarized in Tables 7.6 and 7.7.

There are two types of factors driving the increasing cattle-head density. First, decreasing prices of land and cattle allowed farmers to increase their stock. The decreasing cattle price is more important than the change in the price of land. Second, government policies,

Table 7.7 *Determinants of cultivated area in the Amazon, 1980–1995*

Independent variables	Alternative specifications		
	(1) Fixed effects	(2) Random effects	(3) GLS AR
ln(price of agric. prod. lagged)	−0.007 (0.053)	0.250 (0.084)[a]	0.117 (0.057)[a]
ln(price of crop land lagged)	−0.046 (0.053)	−0.048 (0.087)	−0.129 (0.059)[a]
ln(rural wage lagged)	−0.198 (0.115)[b]	−0.302 (0.234)	−0.149 (0.115)
ln(agric. credit density lagged)	0.060 (0.0266)[a]	0.247 (0.039)[a]	0.148 (0.034)[a]
ln(paved road density lagged)	0.273 (0.068[a])	0.494 (0.056)[a]	0.425 (0.066)[a]
ln(unpaved road density lagged)	0.052 (0.046)	0.373 (0.047)[a]	0.216 (0.051)[a]
ln(distance to federal capital)		0.246 (0.114)[a]	−0.220 (0.137)
ln(fraction of high quality soil)		0.269 (0.035)[a]	0.390 (0.051)[a]
Constant	1.902 (0.331)[a]	2.568 (0.914)[a]	6.056 (0.954)[a]
F-test all $f_i = 0$	42.71		89.65
Breusch–Pagan LM test for $f_i = 0$		$\chi^2 (1) = 108.60$	
		Prob. $> \chi^2 = 0.0$	
Hausman test	$\chi^2 (6) = 19.86$		
	Prob. $> \chi^2 = 0.003$		
N	120	120	120
Log-likelihood R^2	0.34		2.69

Dependent variable: ln(proportion of crop area).

Standard errors are in parentheses.

[a] Variables significant at 5% level.

States included in the analysis are Acre, Amazonas, Maranhão, Mato Grosso, Pará, Rondônia and Roraima.

especially credit and road construction, promote cattle-head expansion. While paved roads increased access to markets and decreased transport costs, unpaved roads are also responsible for a substantial portion of cattle-head expansion – probably associated with smaller farmers' activities (Walker, Moran and Anselin, 2000).

The increase in crop area density (although causing less deforestation) is also important, since part of the land conversion process is due to nutrient mining. Farmers first convert forest into crop area and use the soil as much as they can. Then, when productivity has been reduced by nutrient mining, the area is converted to pasture.

Changes in the demand for agriculture-cleared areas seem to be more affected by economic variables. Output prices are found to be significant in two of our specifications. Surprisingly, land prices are not important in explaining agriculture land clearing (perhaps due to serial correlation).

Rural wages are significant in the fixed-effect model, showing that reduced real rural wages decrease the opportunity cost of going to the frontier, and, at the same time, reduce the costs of hiring temporary labour for land clearing. Analogous to cattle ranching, government agriculture credit is a significant factor in explaining agriculture land clearing.

Paved and unpaved roads also promote agriculture land clearing, for much the same reasons as cattle ranching. The results emphasize the importance of transport policy in managing future cattle ranching and crop area expansion. The Government *Avança Brasil* programme (Nepstad *et al.*, 2000) proposed to build a paved road network to foster growth and development in the Amazon, which may worsen deforestation and undermine prospects for sustainable and equitable growth.

7.4.5 Summary of main results and conclusions of Brazilian study

In recent years, a wide range of economy-wide policy reform programmes has been undertaken in Brazil. Although these policies are not directed explicitly toward addressing sustainability issues, they may, nonetheless, have significant environmental and social impacts. Even modest progress in recognizing such impacts of country-wide policies will help the design of economic programmes. At the same time, recognition of the underlying policy causes of environmental and social problems will help to make development more sustainable.

Industrial growth, external trade and pollution

The links between trade competitiveness and the environment are complex, with trade policies having both good and bad impacts. Brazilian industrial exports are more emission intensive than goods produced for domestic markets. This result is compatible with the hypothesis that developing countries tend to accommodate 'dirty' industries that are less competitive in industrial countries due to tighter environmental controls. However, this effect was offset by emissions 'savings' due to fast growth of imports in the 1990s. By importing goods, the emissions associated with production of those goods are avoided as they are produced abroad.

The direct costs of environmental control strategies are relatively low. The export loss due to higher production costs resulting from the control of water pollutants (BOD and heavy metals) would be 1–2% of the total value of Brazilian exports. The footwear, non-ferrous metallurgic and other metallurgic goods sectors face a higher risk of losing markets. Currently, highly polluting sectors risk future market losses in regions where consumers are becoming more environmentally conscious.

Export-oriented and/or foreign companies undertake environmental innovations more than inward-oriented and/or domestic firms, due to the higher environmental standards and pressures in international markets. This is compatible with the hypothesis that trade and capital openness encourages adoption of environmentally sound practices and products.

These results imply: (1) Brazilian industrial exports may be sensitive to environmental trade barriers and (2) stricter environmental regulation of trade may impose significant export losses. Strategies to deal with this problem include: (1) taking an aggressive stance against the changes in trade regulations to maintain the status quo of limited environmental barriers in trade agreements and/or (2) enhancing environmental performance of Brazilian industries, by either improving local emission standards or changing the composition of industrial exports through reduced dependence on exports associated with 'dirty' production chains.

The transition toward a more environmentally sound economy will depend on: (1) support for capacity building in environmentally related technologies; (2) better dissemination of new technology in the productive sector; (3) improvement of educational and technical skills of the labour force; (4) improvement in the quantity and quality of research centres, linking them to the productive sector interests; (5) specific programmes aimed at reducing regional differences in environmental performance; (6) incentives for certification programmes, including the process of public procurement; and (7) improvement of the domestic consumer's awareness and perception of the benefits of environmentally sound products and processes, creating a domestic market for 'green' products.

Urban development, income and the environment

In Brazil, there is no evidence of an inverse U-curve linking levels of degradation pressure and income groups, since per household degradation pressure generally falls with income. However, propensities to degrade from urban transportation show this inverse U-shape, due to the great reduction in emission levels of new cars usually owned by rich people. Rich people degrade more than their population share. Regressive income transfers (from poor to rich) increased degradation and vice versa.

High degradation pressure from rich peoples' consumption raises serious equity issues for environmental policy in Brazil: (1) while poor peoples' consumption is not the main source of degradation, they tend to bear more of the degradation impacts due to inadequate defensive expenditures and (2) as degradation pressure is mainly due to the consumption of the rich, avoiding stricter degradation controls that affect consumption decisions will subsidize rich people's consumption, at the expense of the poor. Yet, as degradation concentration ratios are lower than the respective income ratios, when degradation control becomes more stringent, poor people will tend to pay more for environmental control per unit of consumption if these costs are passed on through prices.

If this regressive aspect is to be avoided, policy instruments need to include compensatory measures. Thus, environmental taxes may be useful since they reduce social control costs and generate revenue that can be recycled within the economy to compensate the poor.

Deforestation in the Amazon and production patterns

Deforestation in the Brazilian Amazon is a complex phenomenon, involving farmers, large cattle-ranchers, frontier settlers, land speculators and logging companies. Cattle ranching is the main source of forest conversion. There are two types of factors driving the increasing cattle-head density. First, decreasing prices of land and cattle have allowed farmers to increase their stock. Second, the construction of roads has created access to markets and decreased transport costs.

Changes in the demand for agriculture-cleared areas are more affected by economic variables – e.g. output prices, rural wages and government agriculture credit. Increased labour mobility and decreased costs of transport through construction of new roads lead to more land clearing and timber logging. Paved and unpaved roads also promote agriculture land clearing, for much the same reasons as for cattle ranching. The results emphasize the importance of transport policy in managing future cattle ranching and crop area expansion. Construction of paved roads to foster growth and development in the Amazon may worsen deforestation and undermine prospects for sustainable and equitable growth.

8

Mathematical macromodel applications[1]

This chapter expands on the generic results of Chapter 7, by exploring two different theoretical approaches to making development more sustainable at the national macroeconomic level. In Section 8.1, we review the literature on the relationship between optimization and sustainability in growth models (see also Section 2.3). Section 8.2 describes the debate on the costs and benefits of economic growth, and outlines methods for making growth models more sustain-omics compatible. In Sections 8.3 and 8.4, such a mathematical model is developed to examine the conditions under which development paths focusing on optimal economic growth might also be made more sustainable. The model is numerically solved using stylized data and the results are analysed. The second case is developed, in Sections 8.5 and 8.6, around a theoretical model, which looks at the circumstances that may justify the use of second-best adjustments to macroeconomic policies, in order to counteract economic distortions that cause serious environmental harm. Three case studies of Botswana, Ghana and Morocco show how macroeconomic polices might harm the environment, and appropriate remedial measures are discussed.

8.1 Optimal growth models and sustainable development

The economic dimension of sustainable development (e.g. GNP growth) has long been pursued as a major objective. Traditional development based on growth theory has relied on the paradigm of economic efficiency and dynamic optimality. Growth models that optimize economic output are unable to guarantee sustainability (especially environmental and social). By contrast, assessing the economic, environmental and social sustainability of growth does not ensure that economic growth is maximized (Munasinghe, 1992a).

We explore optimality–sustainability issues by using a quantitative ecological growth model that assesses the long-run prospects for sustainable economic growth (Islam, 1998). The approach values all costs and benefits of growth (including environmental and social aspects) to the extent possible, and maximizes the resultant net benefits (i.e. benefits minus costs) using conventional cost–benefit analysis. Side constraints may be imposed, especially to ensure ecological sustainability. The results help to evaluate alternative growth strategies and explore policy options that can make optimal growth more sustainable.

[1] The valuable contributions of M. Clarke, S. K. N. Islam and K. G. Maler to this chapter are gratefully acknowledged. Some parts of the chapter are based on material adapted from Islam *et al.* (2003), Maler and Munasinghe (1996) and Munasinghe (1996a).

Next, we survey growth and sustainability issues. Then a quantitative model is developed to explore this nexus. The results show that concerns about the unsustainability of perpetual economic growth are justified.

8.2 Economic and non-economic costs and benefits of growth

The existing literature in this area has limitations. First, most studies are qualitative rather than quantitative. Few authors focus on costs and benefits within an ecological model (Islam, 1998). Second, the impacts on the three domains are generally not distinguished. Economic growth can affect the social or environmental domains in different ways. Sustainability depends on which type of costs and benefits are considered (Munasinghe, 1992a). Recent studies suggest that the costs of economic growth are higher than its benefits (Daly and Cobb, 1989; Diefenbacher, 1994; Islam, 1998; Rosenberg and Oegema, 1995), but others disagree (Beckerman, 1994; Gylfason, 1999). Although macroeconomic planning based on cost–benefit analysis has been proposed (Malinvaud, 1979), it has not been widely implemented (Islam 1998; Van den Bergh 1991, 1996). Thus, a practical growth model that included costs and benefits is needed.

8.2.1 Linking sustainability with costs and benefits of growth

Following the Second World War, economic growth was considered vital for improving both individual and collective welfare (Beckerman, 1974; Dodds, 1997; Eltis, 1966; Gyfason, 1999; Hufschmidt *et al.*, 1983; Manning and de Jonge, 1996; UN, 1992). The pursuit of higher incomes dominated environmental and social concerns. However, environmental and social harm can limit long-run growth (see Section 2.5.3). Munasinghe *et al.* (2001) provides a comprehensive review.

Some authors cite the environmental Kuznets curve (EKC). Growth induces pollution, but once society becomes richer additional resources would be expended to reduce pollution to acceptable levels; see Section 2.5.2 (Beckerman, 1992; Gylfason, 1999; World Bank, 1992b). Likewise, as resources become scarcer, market prices would increase to prevent natural-resource exhaustion by encouraging shifts to substitutes and through technical improvements that increase resource supply or reduce usage. In addition, previous predictions of resource exhaustion had proven incorrect.

The alternative view was that total costs of economic growth outweigh benefits, resulting in uneconomic growth (Daly, 2000) or impoverishing growth (Islam and Jolley, 1996). Some researchers reported that benefits of growth accrued to richer groups, whilst costs fell mainly on the poor (Adelman and Morris, 1973; Ahluwalia, 1975; Duloy, 1975; Fields, 1995; Munasinghe, 2002a). Thus, despite worldwide economic growth, over one billion people still live in absolute poverty (see Section 1.2). The EKC idea also has been challenged (Ayres 1996; Grossman, 1995).

A simple growth-maximizing model might value all costs and benefits (including environmental and social aspects) and optimize the resultant net benefits using conventional cost–benefit analysis (CBA), see Section 2.3.2. When environmental and social impacts cannot be monetarily valued, non-monetary indicators may be assessed using multicriteria analysis (Munasinghe, 1992a). Sustainability would be ensured by side constraints such as non-negative net environmental degradation and non-declining income, consumption or welfare. A key question is whether there is an absolute limit on economic growth imposed by ecological (and social) constraints (Islam, 1998).

8.2.2 Making macromodels more sustainomics compatible

Next, we outline how to integrate social and environmental considerations into macromodels. Such sustainomics-compatible models need to explore several interlinked aspects, including resource depletion, environmental degradation and sustainable economic growth, features of the sustainable growth process, efficiency and fairness in intertemporal allocation of natural resources, social discount rate, the relative importance of different variables affecting the growth rate of the economy, issues of savings, investment, technical progress and input substitutability in production.

These models could prove useful in formulating integrated economic, social and environmental strategies for countries. Specific policy issues that a sustainomics-compatible model can address include natural-resource management, expenditure for education, research and development, incentives for investment in physical capital relative to investment in natural-resource-intensive industries and pollution-control strategies. The model results could also generate future trajectories showing the growth path of key variables in the model, e.g. GDP, consumption, pollution, technical progress, capital and population. The model would compare optimal values over the past with actually observed values, and thus provide useful information about the operation, performance and evolution of the environmental–socioeconomic system.

A standard economic growth model may be made more sustainomics compatible by (a) capturing the underlying environment–economic interactions in the equations and (b) incorporating sustainability criteria in the objective function. We discuss below how these modifications are incorporated in both continuous- and discrete-growth models.

Theoretical (continuous) models include Hamiltonian-based models of social welfare that can be used to investigate the sustainomics approach. Here, social welfare is generally measured in terms of pure economic variables, such as income or consumption, with sustainable growth being ensured by non-declining consumption or capital over time. Islam and Craven (2001) develop mathematical models and computational methods relevant for sustainomics-compatible models, and show that this process requires substantial extensions to traditional models.

Applied large-scale discrete sustainomics-compatible models show the crucial relationships between capital accumulation, technical progress, the environment and economic growth. They can also capture continuous growth of the economy caused by increases in capital stock, population and technical progress, subject to constraints imposed by the accumulation of pollution and decline in the stock of natural resources.

Many solution algorithms are available to run these models; (see, e.g., Amman, Kendrick and Achath (1995), Barro and Sala-i-Martin (1995), Craven and Islam (2003), Fox, Sengupta and Thorbecke (1973), Schwartz (1996) and Sengupta and Fox (1969)). Specific computer programmes include GAMS (Brooke *et al.*, 1997), DUAL, MATHEMATICA (Amman, Kendrick and Rust, 1996), OCIM (Craven, 1995), RIOTS (Schwartz, Polak and Chen, 1997) and SCOM based on MATLAB (Craven and Islam, 2003).

8.3 An optimization model: Ecol-Opt-Growth-1

This section outlines a basic sustainomics-compatible model, and shows how it can be implemented and used for policy analysis and forecasting.

8.3.1 *Sustainomics-compatible optimal-growth model*

Optimal-growth models have been used widely to study issues in growth economics (Ayres, 1998; Faber and Proops, 1990; Perrings, 1987). These models have growth-directed objective functions and can be used to study the ecological sustainability of growth-optimization policies. Optimal-growth frameworks represent the mechanism and processes of economic growth in both descriptive and normative senses (Burmeister and Dobell, 1970). They can incorporate the qualitative and quantitative aspects of growth by including ecological and normative judgement factors in the model. Others (Snower, 1982) have also stressed the use of optimization models in environmental economic studies.

Ecol-Opt-Growth-1 (developed in Islam (1998, 2001a)) is a dynamic optimal-growth model with ecological constraints (Cesar, 1994; Faucheux *et al.*, 1996; Pearce and Turner, 1990). It is based on optimal planning theory and includes an optimal-growth program (Chakravarty, 1969; Heal, 1973). The descriptive part, constraints and data set of the Ecol-Opt-Growth-1 model draw heavily on a dynamic ecological–economic model developed by Van den Bergh (Van den Bergh, 1991, 1996; Van den Bergh and Nijkamp, 1994). At the same time, the descriptive part and constraints set of the Ecol-Opt-Growth-1 model extend the Van den Bergh model by adding 12 more equations, for economic ratios, damage indicators and costs and benefits of abatement and economic growth (see Appendix A, Section 8.7).

The model assumes that social welfare is a function of consumption and environmental quality. In the optimal-growth framework, the social planner maximizes intertemporal social utility by choosing optimal paths for consumption, investment and pollution-abatement variables. In the basic Ecol-Opt-Growth-1 model outlined below, the goal is to find optimal trajectories of the growth path for extraction, environmental quality and consumption in an economy that maximizes social utility subject to ecological–economic constraints. Resource use affects environmental quality, which in turn affects utility directly and also indirectly through its effect on production and resource regeneration.

This model establishes key links between social welfare, consumption, capital accumulation, technical progress, ecology and economic growth in a growth-maximizing framework. Growth is determined by (a) capital; (b) technical progress due to government expenditure for R&D, education, learning by doing and accumulation of knowledge in the private sector; (c) population; and (d) environmental quality, which is affected by pollution, government spending on environmental control and resource use.

8.3.2 Ecol-Opt-Growth-1 model

General conceptual version of the optimal ecological model, data,
boundary conditions and transversality

The model is summarized in Section 8.7 – see Islam (1998) for details. Most of the data for the model were obtained from Van den Bergh (1991), except for data related to the objective function and transversality conditions. In some model runs using different economic constraints, such as Cobb-Douglas objective and production functions, additional values of coefficients were specified. While the model data are illustrative, values of parameters and boundary conditions are realistic (Van den Bergh, 1991).

A pure time preference of 3% was used, in conformity with the mainstream view on intertemporal preferences of society (see Section 3.6). However, the total discount rate was 3% plus the economic growth rate, as the utility function incorporates log consumption as a variable. The model was also solved with a zero social discount rate, based on the argument that it ensures intergenerational equity and is consistent with social contracts of the individual–government relationship, and that society as a whole should have a higher savings rate than individuals because of the external benefits of public savings and the isolation paradox.

Key characteristics of the model are that (1) it is based on a holistic view of development with elements of social choice, ethics and political economy (Dopfer, 1979); (2) it is a multisectoral total ecosystem growth model; (3) it includes social and environmental constraints and feedbacks; (4) it represents an equilibrium ecosystem in the initial period, which can lead to disequilibrium depending on the growth process; (5) it analyses an idealized economic system rather than defending a specific growth theory (Burmeister and Dobell 1970); (6) it has key variables that are determined endogenously; and (7) it models issues of intertemporal equity through the social discount rate and values of variables and parameters.

Besides conventional utility functions, some new ones including net benefits of consumption are also specified in this model. The damage functions are based on Nordhaus (1994). The issues of social choice appear in the form of constant constraint optimization, and its components are: (1) objective function (social choices); (2) constraints (underlying the socioeconomic system); and (3) social time preference (intergenerational equity). Ethical views are captured by the discount rate, terminal conditions, sustainability indicators, cost–benefit equations and some parameter and data values. Environmental concerns are represented by constraints on resource exhaustion and resource extraction equations, while social concerns are included via objective functions, social constraints, sustainability indicators and cost–benefit constraints. A useful classification of variables might be as follows: (1) policy target variables (consumption, social and environmental quality, GDP); (2) policy tool variables (sector investments, pollution abatement, resource extraction, R&D expenditure, environmental regulations); and (3) all other variables.

First, we empirically study the sustainability of growth in an idealized system, and then we progressively modify different components to reflect real-world conditions. Growth impacts in the model include: standard of living (GDP, consumption), environmental benefits of lower pollution, lower rates of resource destruction and reduced total environmental damage. The costs include exhaustion of natural resources, over-utilization of non-renewable resources, pollution accumulation, total environment damage and increased abatement costs.

This model is more sustainomics compatible than conventional optimal growth models because (1) it represents environmental and economic systems better; (2) it focuses on specifying an ecological model within an optimal-growth framework; (3) it is solved for optimal trajectories over the planning period by the non-linear programming method, unlike other models that are solved for their steady-state values; and (4) it uses unique computer algorithms and data sets.

8.3.3 *Model specification and results of calculations*

Ecol-Opt-Growth-1 was solved for 11 sets of specifications. Each model spans eight periods, one period being equivalent to 10 years duration. The major differences in these models (see Table 8.1) are based on variations in their objective functions, production functions, time preference rate, etc. Model runs 1 to 9 are based on the optimal-growth model, while model runs 10 and 11 are forecasting models without an objective function. Only model runs 8, 9 and 11 did not have any feasible solutions.

Growth and ecological scenarios

The model results yield a set of ecosystem scenarios over the planning period that meet the static and dynamic efficiency conditions of resource allocation; see Tables 8.2 and 8.3 and Figures 8.1 to 8.5.

Table 8.1 *Different model specifications and runs*

Run	Model type	Objective function	Production function	Investment function/ Variable	Pure time pref. (%)
1	optimization	1(a)	2(a)	sectoral/aggregate	3
2	optimization	1(b)	2(a)	sectoral/aggregate	3
3	optimization	1(a)	2(b)	aggregate investment as a control variable	3
4	optimization	1(c)	2(a)	sectoral/aggregate	3
5	optimization	1(d)	2(a)	sectoral/aggregate	3
6	optimization	1(d)	2(b)	aggregate investment as a control variable	3
7	optimization	1(a)	2(a)	sectoral/aggregate	0
8	optimization with non-declining environmental quality	1(a)	2(a)	sectoral/aggregate	3
9	optimization with no abatement	1(a)	2(a)	sectoral/aggregate	3
10	forecasting	–	2(a)	sectoral/aggregate	–
11	forecasting without abatement		2(a)	sectoral/aggregate	–

Table 8.2 *Optimal values of policy variables and cost–benefit analysis*

		Period						
	Run	1	2	3	4	5	6	7
Rate of	1	0.649	0.715	0.774	0.797	0.823	0.823	0.829
pollution	2	0.649	0.748	0.816	0.846	0.858	0.859	0.86
abatement	3	0.649	0.645	0.646	0.64	0.64	0.633	0.633
	4	0.649	0.762	0.828	0.862	0.891	0.907	0.918
	5	0.649	0.653	0.666	0.669	0.676	0.678	0.677
	7	0.649	0.718	0.778	0.801	0.827	0.828	0.834
	10	0.649	0.73	0.812	0.848	0.882	0.9	0.911
Benefit of	1	21.5	23.76	29.59	43.575	48.015	64.558	82.282
abatement	2	3658	3102.2	8785.6	4115.5	14 486	29 509	20 870
	3	32.8	44.68	58.407	66.251	71.871	75.811	80.565
	4	−1151	−1214	−1280.05	−1349.7	−1423.12	−1500.5	−1582.07
	5	317.6	309	293.614	257.721	242.112	211.223	204.04
	7	1326	1506.9	2265.578	4154.411	5021.287	7625.489	11 458.57
	10	1394	4035	8161.57	30 173.21	69 035.39	60 324.68	150 265.9
Total cost of	1	4.934	6.713	9.369	12.008	13.466	15.086	17.603
abatement	2	7.371	10.407	18.842	15.490	22.346	28.468	25.551
	3	1.447	1.542	1.669	1.683	1.738	1.72	1.763
	4	7.434	11.96	25.298	42.468	63.264	80.012	87.366
	5	2.928	2.966	3.135	3.056	3.147	3.047	3.034
	7	5.079	6.907	9.875	12.691	14.324	15.749	18.659
	10	5.175	10.31	18.68	33.127	52.734	57.303	84.604
Total benefit of	1	4.948	1.117	−5.015	46.031	97.073	138.977	155.39
growth	2	39.135	−366.7	−149.168	14.418	170.252	199.656	186.072
	3	−66.66	−48.97	−31.243	−27.913	−30.199	−34.102	−37.65
	4	−1151	−1214	−1280.05	−1349.7	−1423.12	−1500.5	−1582.07
	5	−1151	−1214	−1280.05	−1349.7	−1423.12	7.893	0.774
	7	0.066	−4.01	−7.643	45.306	98.743	141.921	160.545
	10	−547.1	−579.5	−1279.94	−1349.59	−1423	−1500.38	−145.155
Total cost of	1	13.1	103.31	153.66	200.626	237.792	288.016	343.818
growth	2	53.2	146.28	203.458	195.77	263.286	350.748	386.457
	3	−109.6	−77.09	−44.441	−14.672	12.164	34.636	55.878
	4	54.17	155.93	232.766	306.705	376.925	434.472	475.71
	5	−39.1	34.8	80.239	108.55	134.705	151.519	170.38
	7	16	105.45	157.301	204.512	242.792	290.882	349.019
	10	17.8	143.25	220.103	291.848	362.528	396.639	472.346

Table 8.3 *Values of sustainability indicators*

	Run	Period 1	2	3	4	5	6	7
Environmental	1	0.258	0.241	0.232	0.226	0.219	0.213	0.209
quality	2	0.258	0.239	0.233	0.225	0.218	0.21	0.205
indicator	3	0.258	0.251	0.244	0.237	0.231	0.226	0.222
	4	0.258	0.239	0.233	0.225	0.217	0.209	0.204
	5	0.258	0.243	0.234	0.227	0.223	0.219	0.217
	7	0.258	0.241	0.232	0.226	0.219	0.213	0.209
	10	0.258	0.241	0.231	0.226	0.219	0.212	0.206
Ecological effect	1	0.017	0.034	0.043	0.036	0.033	0.029	0.031
indicator	2	0.015	0.056	0.048	0.04	0.02	0.02	0.028
	3	0.044	0.044	0.043	0.045	0.049	0.052	0.054
	4	0.015	0.057	0.049	0.042	0.04	0.036	0.032
	5	0.019	0.029	0.038	0.044	0.05	0.055	0.059
	7	0.017	0.035	0.043	0.036	0.033	0.029	0.03
	10	0.017	0.032	0.06	0.049	0.045	0.044	0.023
Indicator for	1	0.991	0.982	0.97	0.955	0.943	0.938	0.938
resource	2	0.991	0.97	0.942	0.905	0.894	0.891	0.878
supply	3	0.99	0.99	0.991	0.991	0.991	0.991	0.992
demand	4	0.991	0.97	0.939	0.888	0.812	0.705	0.57
	5	0.991	0.991	0.992	0.992	0.992	0.992	0.992
	7	0.991	0.982	0.968	0.953	0.94	0.933	0.933
	10	0.991	0.982	0.957	0.916	0.854	0.762	0.667
Unsustainability	1	0.066	0.144	0.19	0.168	0.161	0.146	0.159
indicator:	2	0.057	0.242	0.219	0.196	0.101	0.109	0.154
waste	3	0.174	0.175	0.178	0.193	0.214	0.231	0.247
	4	0.057	0.245	0.224	0.211	0.227	0.243	0.274
	5	0.076	0.122	0.162	0.196	0.225	0.252	0.272
	7	0.066	0.148	0.19	0.168	0.159	0.145	0.156
	10	0.065	0.134	0.273	0.239	0.244	0.274	0.166
Total damage	1	36.876	76.617	113.777	162.315	206.356	289.543	421.007
from	2	5384.2	24 200.7	44 451.4	44 858.95	88 333.23	243 839.9	426 256.5
pollution	3	1056.6	1911.9	3328.15	5432.663	8248.986	11 573.63	15 577.45
	4	5430.1	26421	57231.5	115 086.8	213 628.7	335 917.7	444 448.7
	5	2139	7360.3	15 004.7	23 248.11	33 020.71	41 555.4	51 643.17
	7	3709.9	15 348.1	30 610.8	52 792.07	84 040.18	144 603.2	273 324.9
	10	3778	22 056.9	55 248	105 752.2	193 808.3	252 066.1	429 809.7

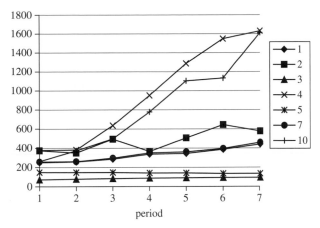

Figure 8.1. Socioeconomic variable: GDP.

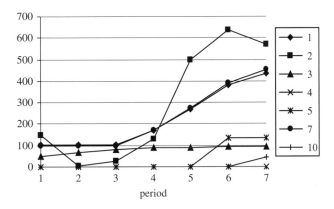

Figure 8.2. Socioeconomic variable: consumption.

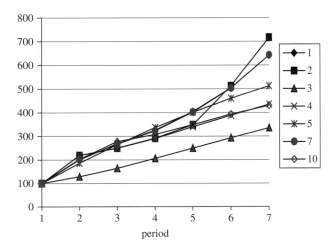

Figure 8.3. Socioeconomic variable: stock of pollution.

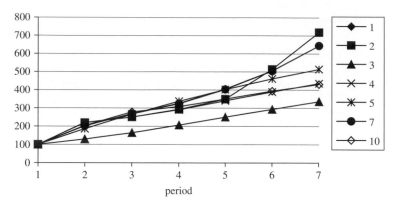

Figure 8.4. Ecological variable: stock of non-renewable resources.

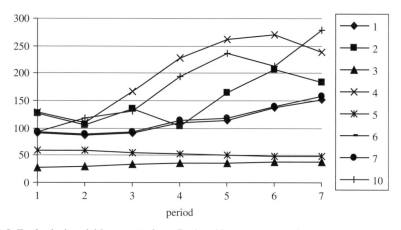

Figure 8.5. Ecological variables: waste from final and investment goods.

Model run 4 (output-maximization goal) has the greatest rise in per capita income over all periods. The second highest increase is in model run 10 (forecasting mode). Consumption results show a reverse pattern. Meanwhile, the savings level increases in model run 4. The zero discount rate causes initial consumption to be smaller, while the high initial saving and investment generate greater present and future GDP. More capital is available for future production, which lowers the rate of interest. The saving level varies from 0 to 60% in different model runs over the modelling period. The interest rate in model run 5 is lower over the entire time period than those under positive discount rate models.

Optimal values of output, consumption, per capita consumption and output, investment and other economic variables fluctuate widely among model runs. The model determines optimal investment rates in different sectors. Values of ecological variables vary widely among model runs. Growth generates ever-increasing amounts of pollution. Model results show the unsustainability implied by the infeasible model solutions. They show growing unsustainability in the economy, falling environmental quality, stronger ecological impacts, rising resource shortages and higher levels of both waste and total pollution damage, over the planning period. These sustainability implications are derived from an utilitarian approach based on the social rate of discount. Other sustainability criteria, such as biodiversity preservation and resource conservation, could have also been included. Model run 7 (with a zero discount rate) generates relatively average sustainability indicators, but other model runs yield more positive sustainability indicators (see Table 8.3). Thus, other variables, parameters or policies also affect sustainability, besides the rate of discount.

8.4 Ecol-Opt-Growth-1 model conclusions

The results of this model are similar to those of other models (Meadows *et al.*, 1972; Van den Bergh, 1991, 1996). A positive trend, or even a constant level of economic performance, cannot be sustained in the long run, due to declining environmental quality. More optimistic, but cautious, conclusions are also generated by other models (Faber and Proops, 1990). More definitive conclusions require further empirical study (Meadows *et al.* 1972; Nordhaus, 2000).

The major findings of this modelling study are that: (1) an ecologically sustainable economy cannot grow limitlessly; (2) economic growth is unstable and fluctuates; (3) optimal economic growth is fraught with difficulties such as infeasibility and non-sustainability. Thus, a long-run economic–ecological equilibrium does not appear to exist. Alternatively, optimal growth may not be durable. Further studies are needed to reconcile optimal and durable growth – see Section 2.3. In addition, (4) policy intervention is desirable to make development more sustainable, see Section 2.1.1 and (5) Ecol-Opt-Growth-1 does not show the key property, present in other multisector growth models, that investment in the relatively smaller (consumption goods) sector is initially lower relative to the bigger (capital goods) sector, but sectors grow uniformly after some period of time.

The empirical results support growing concerns that the costs of economic growth may outweigh its benefits, resulting in unsustainability. Environmental costs and benefits have more impact on sustainability, although socioeconomic costs and benefits are also important. Basically, it has been determined that, in a wide range of circumstances, long-term economic growth is unsustainable due to increasing environmental costs.

Nevertheless, the Ecol-Opt-Growth-1 model has many degrees of freedom and variables that can be explored by policy makers to make the development path more sustainable, as advocated by sustainomics. One example suggests that government-supported abatement programmes are needed to move toward sustainable development, since the model runs without abatement were infeasible. In most runs, the optimal rate of abatement increases over time. Therefore, pollution abatement is needed to improve ecosystem viability and make development more sustainable.

The modelling experiments therefore confirm the view that optimal economic growth is not necessarily sustainable (Islam and Craven, 2003; Munasinghe *et al.*, 2001). Further work is needed to seek specific conditions under which alternative growth paths are likely to be durable.

8.5 Macroeconomic policies, second-best theory and environmental harm

8.5.1 *Macroeconomic policies and general equilibrium theory*

Economy-wide policies (both macroeconomic and sectoral) often have much more powerful environmental and social effects than mere project-level investments (see Chapter 7). They need to be designed and implemented so that potential harm is anticipated and minimized, rather than reacting after the fact. Section 7.2.2 showed how imperfections (market, failures, policy distortions and institutional constraints) interact with economy-wide policies to cause environmental and social harm. Additional policies that complement (rather than hinder) macroeconomic policies may be used to correct such imperfections and avoid harmful impacts.

We extend this approach to study the effects of macroeconomic policy failures. The idea here is that macroeconomic policies themselves may have unintended side effects (both positive and negative) on the environment. There are few consistent theoretical models available that analyse whether macroeconomic policies might be directly adjusted to avoid environmental or social damage. Thus, we develop a basic analytical framework to trace the environmental impacts of macroeconomic policies, to identify where negative effects may occur and to design remedial measures. Illustrative case studies are presented from selected developing countries. Mathematical details are provided in Appendix B, Section 8.8.

8.5.2 *A simple case involving monetary policy and wage stickiness*

The first fundamental theorem of welfare economics states that, in an economy that is perfectly competitive and in which all goods and services are traded in markets, the resulting equilibrium is Pareto efficient – i.e. it is impossible to improve the welfare of anyone without impoverishing someone else. However, it is unclear if a competitive equilibrium exists, and whether the resulting income distribution among households is equitable. The second theorem of welfare economics addresses these two issues – if all goods and services are tradable, and if the economy is convex (production characterized by non-increasing returns to scale and to individual inputs, and consumption characterized by indifference curves, which are convex to the origin) and continuous (closed production possibility sets and ordinary consumer indifference curves), then any Pareto-efficient allocation of resources can be obtained as a competitive equilibrium after the initial endowments have been redistributed in a socially acceptable way.

These idealized theorems provide a starting point for discussing the consequences of macroeconomic policies. The economy described by the theorems is really a barter economy. In the real world, we assume that money is introduced to pay for all transactions (Arrow and Hahn, 1971; Patinkin, 1965). Furthermore, we assume that the money supply is controlled by the government. Still, the government has no role in carrying out macroeconomic policies. Because all the markets function perfectly, the only thing that the government should do is to keep the money supply constant. (Even if the money supply changes, that would not matter, because all transactions are in real terms.)

Let us now assume, however, that one central market does not operate smoothly enough – e.g. the labour market is characterized by sticky wages, due to union monopsonies or to insider–outsider relations or to any other realistic cause. The existence of sticky wages means that this single market in an otherwise perfect economy will not equilibrate automatically, and there may be unemployment or excess demand for labour with ensuing inflationary pressures. With sticky wages, macroeconomic policies now have a clear role. For example, if the initial situation is one with unemployment, an increase in money supply will tend to increase all monetary prices of goods and services outside the labour market, while nominal wages will remain unchanged – resulting in a fall in the real price of labour. If the increase in the money supply is adjusted until the real wage rate reaches the competitive equilibrium level, full employment will be restored. Conversely, decreasing the money supply will be the appropriate macroeconomic policy response if the economy is starting from a situation of excess demand for labour.

Thus, in this simple model, a government can use monetary policies to maintain full employment by increasing or decreasing the money supply. Furthermore, this managed full-employment equilibrium will correspond to a Pareto-efficient allocation. The monetary policy will be neutral vis-à-vis the allocation of resources (yielding the same outcome as in the case where the labour market equilibrates automatically).

Let us now introduce another distortion in the economy, which affects the use of environmental resources. Consider a traditional externality where the government may allow plants to emit pollutants into the air without simultaneously compensating the victims of the ensuing air pollution. Such externalities are basically due to the absence of well defined property rights (Coase, 1960). This situation may arise for several reasons. First, it could be due to the inherent difficulty or impossibility of defining individual property rights. For example, because clean air in a town is shared by all inhabitants living there, it is impossible to define individual rights to clean air (which is now a public good). Second, the government may be unable to define property rights (e.g. tribal lands). Now, there are (at least) two deviations from full optimality or first-best allocation of resources – labour-market failure and resource failure. This is the classic second-best situation. Should we try to manage the money supply so that full employment is restored, assuming that we can do nothing about the environmental resource failure? According to the theory of second best, it is not socially optimal to equilibrate the labour market given the failure to allocate the environmental resource efficiently (Lancaster and Lipsey, 1956). Thus, a macroeconomic environmental policy failure occurs when macroeconomic policies aimed at correcting one allocation failure (labour market, unrelated to the environment) results, at most, in a second-best allocation because of a deterioration of the environmental resource base.

8.5.3 Effects of taxes

Many macroeconomic policies can have environmental impacts, where the root of the problem is not directly connected to the environmental resource. When designing fiscal policies for macroeconomic stabilization, it is widely recognized that such policies carry deadweight burdens. An increase in taxes to reduce effective demand and generate government revenues generally creates distortions in the economy, especially in the case of taxes unrelated to real resource costs – such a tax increase cannot be implemented as a lump-sum tax. The conventional view is that the resulting deadweight burden is due mainly to distortions in the labour and capital markets. But taxes also affect the patterns of location and the structure of production, which in general also affect the environmental resource base. In this case, the root of the problem is that taxes have incentive effects, and an increase in taxes (to solve a macroeconomic problem) therefore has a deadweight burden that includes environmental deterioration. It is obvious that, in some cases, the deadweight burden will be negative. This would be the case when the environmental resources are underpriced and the tax increase takes the form of pricing these resources. Here there are three distortions: the general macroeconomic distortion, the distortion from tax increases and the lack of environmental pricing. With environmental taxes, the macroeconomic policy objectives can be achieved by taxes that improve the existing allocation of resources.

This situation has given rise to the idea of a green-tax reform. Taxes on conventional factors of production (labour and capital) and taxes on commodities are distortive, whereas taxes on underpriced environmental resources improve the efficiency of resource allocation as well as provide tax revenues. Thus, it is thought that such a tax reform should have a double dividend (see Chapter 9). The first dividend would be the improvement in the environment, and the second would be the reduction of deadweight burden from existing taxes. However, some argue that a green tax may increase the excess burden from existing taxes with more than the corresponding reduction achieved by lowering these taxes (Bouvenberg and De Mooij, 1994).

The same arguments obviously also apply to changes in expenditure patterns. Expenditures for ensuring increased effective demand will certainly have allocation effects. What are the effects of the increased government expenditures on environmental resource exploitation? They may be positive or negative, and it is necessary to take these effects into account when designing the fiscal and expenditure policies.

The solution to these problems is to try to reduce the market failure that gives rise to the environmental degradation and thereby to improve on the second-best solution (see the Botswana and Ghana case studies below).

Furthermore, because lump-sum taxes are not feasible, it follows that there will always be deadweight burdens. Ideally, the tax system should be designed to minimize the total deadweight burden (taking due account of distributional impacts). However, effects on the environment should then be included in measuring the deadweight burden. The mathematical model in Appendix B, Section 8.8, shows how this can be achieved in simple cases.

8.6 Developing country case studies

Three brief examples from Botswana, Ghana and Morocco illustrate how macroeconomic polices and local distortions may harm the environment.

8.6.1 *Botswana*

Unemo (1996) studies how changing world-market prices might affect a domestic environmental asset like grazing land in Botswana. The main export commodity is diamonds, and the world-market price of diamonds chiefly determines the terms of trade of Botswana. On the face of it, a change in diamond prices should have no impact on grazing behaviour. However, based on general equilibrium effects, a change in the price of diamonds may have such an effect. Unemo uses a computable general equilibrium model to study the impact of an exogeneous change in the world-market price for diamonds. From a policy perspective, we could look at changes in export subsidies that would result in effectively the same change in terms of trade.

A fall in diamond prices will increase overgrazing in Botswana and thus increase environmental costs. This is because a fall in terms of trade will reduce industrial profits and therefore the return on capital. Since capital is cheaper, investments in cattle will grow. Note that if there had been effective private property rights to land (or communal ownership with strict social control over the number of cattle that members of the community are allowed to graze) this would not be a problem. Each landowner would make a comparison of costs and benefits, taking into account the damage to grazing from increasing the herd. In fact, each cattle owner would bring as many cattle as possible to his grazing land up to the point where the selling price of the cattle would equal the marginal cost, including the environmental damage. Thus, he would balance the environmental damage with the increased profits from cattle herding. The change in terms of trade would not lead to macroeconomic policy failure.

In large parts of Botswana, however, the grazing areas are under open-access common property regimes. In this case, each cattle owner would bring as many cattle to the commons as is profitable to him. Because he does not consider the damage he is inflicting on others, he will continue to add cattle to the point where price equals average cost. The average cost curve is less steep than the marginal cost curve, and the result is therefore a bigger increase in the number of cattle brought to the grazing land than would take place with private property rights. Here we would have a macroeconomic policy failure. It is important to note that the lack of private property rights is basically responsible for this failure, rather than the original fall in diamond prices (or reduction in export subsidies).

8.6.2 *Ghana*

The role of institutional constraints in macroeconomic reforms is examined in (López, 1993). Here, trade liberalization reduces taxes on agricultural exports and leads to increased production incentives, while efforts to reduce the government wage bill increase unemployment. Thus, the adjustment process helps to stimulate production of export crops and combines with rapid population growth and lack of employment opportunities outside the rural sector to create increasing pressure on land resources, encroachment onto marginal lands and soil erosion. This effect on resource use is influenced by the allocation of property rights. Whether in relation to the security of land tenure of peasant farmers or to the right to extract timber of logging companies, uncertainty normally results in environmental degradation. In Ghana, as in many regions in Africa, agricultural lands are governed by traditional-land-use institutions, and farms are communally owned by the village or tribe. These common-property regimes may have been sufficient to ensure sustainable use of agricultural lands when populations were much smaller and fallow periods were long enough to allow land to regain fertility. However, such traditional arrangements have been overwhelmed by economy-wide forces, resulting in reduced fallowing, loss of soil fertility and environmental decline. The best remedy would be to revise the land-tenure regime to resist externally induced pressures.

This study analyses the effects of ongoing trade liberalization and public employment reduction on agricultural productivity and land use in the country's western region. A noteworthy outcome of the policy simulations is that the main source of supply response is the expansion of cultivated area rather than agricultural intensification. Biomass (proportion of land under forest cover) is an important factor of production, contributing 15–20% of the value of agricultural output. This compares with contributions from 'conventional' factor inputs: 26% for land cultivated, 25% for labour and 26% for capital. Because the share of agricultural output in GDP is about 50%, the contribution of biomass to national income is about 7.5%. Thus the stock of biomass is an important determinant, not only of agricultural production, but also of GDP.

A large proportion of the land is currently reserved exclusively for the use of villagers. The system is consistent with shifting cultivation because the individual has exclusive rights to the cultivated land, but, once the land is left fallow, it can be reallocated by village consensus. Under these conditions, biomass is already being overexploited. Fallow periods are too short, and the environmental resource stock is below socially optimum levels. The study finds that increasing agricultural prices or reducing wages causes an expansion in the cultivated area and raises output. For example, a 10% increase in land cultivated leads to a 2.7% increase in the direct output effect. However, such an increase in cultivated area leads to a reduction in fallowing, and total biomass declines 14.5%. This, in turn, leads to a 2.5% loss of sustainable agricultural productivity. Thus, the net effect of expanding the area cultivated (2.7% direct output effect less 2.5% biomass loss effect) is a mere 0.2% – many times smaller than the direct effect alone. In addition to policy changes, other factors contribute to expansion of cultivated area: large family size, availability of capital and the presence of migrant populations in the area.

The results suggest that, in general, economy-wide price and wage policy reforms that do not include changes in land management practices will have very limited impact on national income, once the existence of land quality effects is considered. For example, the effects of further reducing implicit taxation of agriculture are, in general, ambiguous, while the effects of import liberalization are perverse. However, reducing the fiscal deficit (through reducing public employment or wages) has unambiguously positive effects on agriculture and national income.

If agricultural price responsiveness relies less on land expansion and more on intensification, trade liberalization would be a better outcome. Without institutional reforms and with land still available for cultivation, the main supply response will continue to be based on agricultural expansion. Indeed, in the study area (the western part of Ghana), the economy-wide policy reforms lead to an expansion of cultivated area and thus a decline in fallowing. Environmental and socioeconomic data indicate that fallowing (measured as the ratio of forest biomass to cultivated land) contributes as much to agricultural production as other more conventional inputs, such as the area cultivated, labour or capital. Less fallowing reduces the positive effect of the reform on agricultural output. Thus, complementary institutional reforms will be needed to ensure that the current gains from adjustment reforms will be sustainable.

8.6.3 Morocco

The Morocco study focuses on how links between macroeconomic policies and existing water allocation system have led to sub-optimal and unsustainable patterns of water use (Goldin and Roland-Host, 1997). Specifically, low water charges (coupled with ineffective collection of these charges) have artificially promoted production of water-intensive crops such as sugar cane. Rural irrigation water accounts for 92% of the country's marketed water use. At the same time, irrigation charges cover less than 10% of the long-run marginal cost, and the corresponding figure for urban water tariffs is less than 50%. Thus, a water deficit is projected for Morocco by the year 2020, despite high water-sector investments.

Going beyond the traditional sectoral remedy of raising water tariffs, the study links sectoral policy reforms with ongoing macroeconomic adjustment policies (removal of nominal trade tariffs). As a consequence of the trade reforms, prices of sugar, cereals, oilseeds, meat and dairy products would decline to world levels from their current protected levels. Further, a simultaneous introduction of trade and water pricing reforms would imply increased input prices and reduced output prices. A computable general equilibrium model traces the impact of these reforms on output, consumption, imports, exports and the use of factors of production (including water) by the different sectors in the economy.

To separate out the effects of sectoral and macroeconomic reforms, the study considers three scenarios: trade reform only, water pricing reform only and a combination of the two. In the first scenario, the only policy change is a complete removal of nominal tariffs (which in 1985 averaged 21% for the whole economy and 32% for agriculture). In the second scenario, the sole change is that the price of rural irrigation water is doubled. In the final scenario, the two policy reforms are combined.

In the first scenario, liberalization of trade alone has positive effects – a small rise in real GDP, large gains in incomes and consumption as import barriers are reduced, more competitive exports, greater domestic purchasing power and more efficient resource allocation. However, two major drawbacks are that elimination of tariffs leads to budgetary deficits and domestic water use rises sharply due to growth – resulting in increased environmental pressures. In the second scenario, reforming water prices alone reduces water use by 34% in rural areas and by 29% for the whole economy. This static efficiency gain also causes real GDP to fall by about 0.65%, while incomes and real consumption of both rural and urban households decline by approximately 1%. In the final scenario, the growth in real GDP due to trade liberalization remains, but reforming water prices still induces substantial reductions in overall water use. Thus, the combination of trade reforms and improved water pricing provides both economic and environmental gains.

8.6.4 Concluding thoughts

The model confirms the empirically observed and intuitive conclusion that macroeconomic policies may combine with subsidiary imperfections to cause environmental harm. Many economic imperfections may remain unnoticed in a stagnant economy, if the resultant environmental damage is minor. However, once economic growth is induced by macroeconomic reforms, the environmental harm will rapidly worsen, and the underlying imperfections can no longer be ignored. The first-best remedy would be to eliminate the subsidiary imperfections without changing macroeconomic policies. If real-world constraints delay such corrective action, then a second-best situation arises. Then, there is justification for modifying, or fine-tuning, macroeconomic policies to reduce harm. Relevant policies could be progressively intensified over a period of time, as the subsidiary imperfections are gradually eliminated by other means. Because the impacts of macroeconomic policies on the environment work through complex and indirect mechanisms, a general equilibrium analysis will provide useful insights.

8.7 Appendix A: The Ecol-Opt-Growth-1 model

All symbols used in the following equations are explained in the following sections.
Objective function:

$$Obj = \sum_t (1 + \rho)^{-t} O(Pop(t), c(t), K(T)).$$

Definition of the per capita consumption:

$$c(t) \equiv C(t)/Pop(t).$$

Definition of GDP:

$$Y = Y(Q(t), I(t); t),$$

$$Y = Y_2(K(t), L(t), Trd(t), R_{\mathrm{sup}}(t), E(t), W_{Q,I}(t); t).$$

Output:

$$Q = Q(K_Q(t), E(t), R_s(t), T_{rd}(t)).$$

Capital accumulation in the final-goods sector:

$$K_Q'(t) = F_1(K_Q(t), I_Q(t); t).$$

Aggregation of sectoral capital:

$$K(t) = \sum_{j \in K} K_j(t).$$

Aggregation of sectoral investment:

$$I(t) = \sum_{j \in K} I_j(t).$$

Distribution of final goods:

$$C(t) + O_{rd}(t) = Q(t).$$

Final-goods-sector investment:

$$I_Q = I_Q(K_Q(t), K(t), I_Q(t); t).$$

Other sector investment:

$$I_i = I_i(K_Q(t), K_j(t), I_Q(t), I_j(t); t), \qquad j \in J.$$

Sectoral capital equations:

$$K_j'(t) = F_2(K_j(t), I_j(t), K_j(t); t), \qquad j \in J.$$

Technological growth rate equation:

$$T_{rd}'(t) = F_3(T_{rd}(t), e_e(t), O_{rd}(t), Q(t), I(t); t).$$

Population growth rate:

$$Pop'(t) = F_4(Pop(t), C(t); t).$$

Waste abatement:

$$R_{wa} = R_{wa}(K_{wa}(t), T_{rd}(t), W_{Q,I}(t); t).$$

Recycled resource rate:

$$R_{rec} = R_{rec}(T_{rd}(t), K_{rec}(t), W_{rec}(t); t).$$

Renewable resource extraction rate:

$$R_n = R_n(K_n(t), N(t), E(t); t).$$

Non-renewable resource extraction rate:

$$R_s = R_s(K_s(t), S(t); t).$$

Change in the stock of stored waste:

$$S'_{\text{wa}}(t) = F_5(S_{\text{wa}}(t), R_{\text{wa}}(t), W_{\text{rec}}(t), R_{\text{rec}}(t); t).$$

Change in the total supply of resources:

$$R'_{\text{sup}}(t) = F_6(R_{\text{sup}}(t), R_N(t), R_s(t), R_{\text{rec}}(t), T_{\text{rd}}(t), Q(t); t).$$

Gross waste from final-goods and investments sectors:

$$W_{Q,I} = W_{Q,I}(Q(t), I(t), T_{\text{rd}}(t); t).$$

Waste amenable for recycling:

$$W_{\text{rec}} = W_{\text{rec}}(Q(t), K_Q(t), K(t), R_{\text{wa}}(t); t).$$

Waste emitted:

$$W_{\text{em}} = W_{\text{em}}(W_{Q,I}(t), R_{\text{wa}}(t), W_{\text{rec}}(t), R_{\text{rec}}(t); t).$$

Required extraction rate of resources:

$$R_{\text{new}} = R_{\text{new}}(K_Q(t), E(t), T_{\text{rd}}(t), K_{\text{rec}}(t); t).$$

Ecological effect indicator:

$$E = E(N(t), B(t), P(t); t).$$

Change in stock of renewable resource:

$$N'(t) = F_7(N(t), E(t), R_N(t); t).$$

Pollution accumulation:

$$P'(t) = F_8(P(t), E(t), W_{\text{em}}(t); t).$$

Change in stock of slowly renewing resource:

$$B'(t) = F_9(B(t), E(t), I(t), K_Q(t), C(t), Pop(t), R_n(t), R_s(t), K(t), B(t); t).$$

Change in stock of non-renewable resources:

$$S'(t) = F_{10}(S(t), R_s(t); t).$$

Material balance condition:

$$G(N, E) = M(P, E).$$

Total damage:

$$\mathrm{d}m = \mathrm{d}m(Y(t), \theta_1(t), P(t); t).$$

Damage avoided by control:

$$\mathrm{d}v = \mathrm{d}v(Y(t), \theta_1(t), R_{\text{wa}}(t); t).$$

Abatement rate:

$$ar = ar(R_{\mathrm{wa}}(t), W_{\mathrm{Q,I}}(t); t).$$

Abatement cost:

$$ac = ac(Y(t), ar(t); t).$$

Savings rate:

$$s = s(I(t), Y(t); t).$$

Capital output ratio:

$$k = k(K(t), Y(t); t).$$

Capital labour ratio:

$$kp = kp(K(t), Pop(t); t).$$

8.7.1 Model notation

Stock variables

B = slowly renewable resource (soil, land, water)
K = total economic capital
K_{I} = investment-sector capital
K_{n} = renewable-resource-extraction capital
K_{Q} = productive sector
K_{rec} = recycling capital
K_{s} = non-renewable-resource-extraction capital
K_{wa} = waste-abatement/treatment capital
N = stock of renewable resources
P = stock of pollution in natural mediums or organisms
Pop = human population level
R_{sup} = total supply of natural-resource materials in inventory
S = stock of non-renewable resources
S_{wa} = stock of useless, stored waste
T_{rd} = progress indicator of environmental technology
Z = artificial variable (total 'real' output delayed)

Flow variables

C = consumption
e_{e} = ecological effect indicator for technical progress
E = indicator for overall environmental quality
I = total investment in replacement and new capital
$I_i(i \in K)$ = investment in sector i
K_{occ} = used economic capital
L_{D} = employment (jobs)

L_S = labour force
O_{rd} = social investment in research and development
Q = output of final-goods sector
R_{dem} = total productive and consumptive demand for resources
R_n = renewable resource extraction
R_s = non-renewable resource extraction
R_{wa} = abated/treated waste
U = long-term labour-market unbalance (unemployment)
W_{em} = emitted waste
$W_{Q,I}$ = gross waste from final- and investment-goods sectors
W_{rec} = waste amenable for recycling
W_{too} = indicator for unsustainability of waste emission

Functions

A = assimilation function
B = population growth rate
$b_i\ (i = 1,\ldots,5)$ = regeneration and damage functions of slowly renewable resources
c_Q = ratio of resource input to material output in final-goods sector
c_I = ratio of resource input to material output in investment-goods sector
$D_i(i \in K)$ = discarded capital
f_{rec} = part of waste amenable for recycling that is recycled
f_{wa} = part of production waste that is abated/treated
$F_i^{-1}(i = 1,\ldots,6)$ = determine for each sector used capital
F_I = unrestricted production function in investment-goods sector
F_N = unrestricted production function in renewable-resource-extraction sector
F_Q = unrestricted production function in final-goods sector
F_S = unrestricted production function in non-renewable-resource-extraction sector
G = regeneration function of renewable-resource capacity
H = environmental quality function
α = general investment effect parameter on technology
ε = effect of social R & D investment and part of production increase on technology
$dm(t)$ = total damage
$dv(t)$ = damage avoided by control
$ar(t)$ = abatement rate
$ac(t)$ = abatement cost
$s(t)$ = savings rate
$k(t)$ = capital output ratio
$kp(t)$ = capital labour ratio
$M(P, E)$ = waste assimilation
$G(N, E)$ = regeneration function

Table 8.4 shows the parameter values used in Ecol-Opt-Growth-1.

The boundary conditions on the state and control variables applied are shown in Table 8.5. The initial and the terminal values of the variables are also adopted from Van den Bergh (1991).

Table 8.4 *Values of parameters*

γ_1	0.1	δ_1	0.1
a	0.098	P_{crit}	450
a_B	500	N_{crit}	15 000
a_P	0.5	r	0.05
A_{Pop}	5	ρ	0.03
A_{rec}	0.8	s_1	0.5
A_{wa}	0.95	s_2	0.5
b_i	550	k_i	1
b_{crit}	100	p_N	1
B_{wa}	18	p_S	1
C_n	30 000	κ	100
C_{wa}	1.2	θ_2	2
d	1	θ_1	0.001 44
δ	0.025	b_1	0.0686
ε	0.096	b_2	2.887
E_{crit}	0.8	α_1	0.3
μ	0.1	β_1	0.5

Table 8.5 *Initial conditions*

$K_Q(0) = 43$	$K_i(0) = 3.6$	$K_{wa}(0) = 5$
$K_{rec}(0) = 5$	$K_N(0) = 30$	$K_S(0) = 30$
$Pop(0) = 100$	$T_{rd}(0) = 100$	$R_{sup}(0) = 300$
$N(0) = 100\ 00$	$S(0) = 3000$	$P(0) = 100$
$Z(0) = Q(0) + I(0)$		

8.8 Appendix B: Second-best nature of macroeconomic policies when environmental externalities are present

This simple model assumes that individuals value real balances for various reasons (mainly to reduce transaction costs) and that the demand for such balances is determined by prices, wealth and initial balance (Patinkin, 1965). Furthermore, it is a disequilibrium model with sticky wages. A typical consumer has the following utility function:

$$U = U\left(x, E, L^s, \frac{M}{p}\right), \tag{8.1}$$

where x is demand for the consumption goods, E is a vector of emissions of pollutants to the environment, L^s is the desired supply of labour, M is the demanded nominal money balance and p is the price for the consumption goods. Thus, $1/p$ is the price of money. The inclusion of money in the utility functions has been severely criticized (Arrow and Hahn, 1971).

The budget constraint for the representative consumer can be written as

$$px + M + T = wL^d + M_0, \tag{8.2}$$

where w is the wage rate, L^d is the demand for labour (which, in the case of wage stickiness, may be different from the desired supply) and T is the lump-sum tax paid by the consumer. With a fixed wage rate, the demand for labour, L^d, must be smaller or equal to the supply of labour, L^s.

Utility maximization subject to the budget and labour supply constraints yields the net demand functions for goods and money:

$$x = x^d(p, E, M_0, w),$$
$$M = M^d (p, E, M_0, w). \tag{8.3}$$

For the supply of goods and services, we assume that the production function has constant returns to scale and has the following form:

$$x = f(L^d, E). \tag{8.4}$$

Note that emission of pollutants is regarded as a factor of production. Let us assume that the government is internalizing the emissions by charging firms with q per tonne emitted. The profit is then given by

$$\pi = pf(L^d, E) - wL^d - qE. \tag{8.5}$$

Maximizing profits yields the following demand and supply functions:

$$x = x(p, w, q),$$
$$L^d = L^d (p, w, q),$$
$$E = E(p, w, q). \tag{8.6}$$

Let us now consider the public sector. The government is responsible for taxing individuals, controlling the money supply and controlling the emissions to the environment. The budget in the public sector is given by

$$T + M + qE = 0. \tag{8.7}$$

If the government has determined the marginal willingness-to-pay for environmental improvements and set the emissions charge equal to this marginal willingness-to-pay, then

$$q = -p\frac{\partial U/\partial E}{\partial U/\partial x} = \phi (p, E, M_0, w). \tag{8.8}$$

Here, ϕ gives the marginal willingness-to-pay for the public good as a function of the variables determining the budget constraint for the individual. By this assumption, we are assured that there will always be an optimal level of pollution.

Assume for the moment that wages are flexible so that the labour market clears. Then it follows from the model that money is neutral and a change in the money supply has no real consequences. Furthermore, the resulting allocation of resources is efficient. However, the point to be made has to do with sticky wages. Assume that the wage rate is exogenously given by

$$w = \bar{w}. \tag{8.9}$$

If $\bar{w}$ is high enough, the total demand for labour is less than the exogenously given supply L^s, and there is unemployment. Now there is room for government macroeconomic policies. An increase in the money supply now affects the real economy. The mechanism is the conventional one. After an increase in the money supply, each individual finds himself with real balances that are too high, which increases the net demand for goods and services. This increases the prices of goods and services in general and thereby reduces the real money balance held by individuals and increases the output and therefore the demand for labour. Thus, the real wage rate falls, and it is possible to reach full employment. However, in the process, the emissions have probably increased, and the environment has therefore probably deteriorated. This is as it should be, because the polluters are paying the marginal social cost of pollution. The gains from increasing the employment exceed the loss in environmental quality.

If the marginal social cost of pollution rises very sharply with increases in pollution, the end result comprises only marginal increases in emissions and the monetary expansion causes reallocations between different sectors so that less polluting sectors expand and more polluting sectors contract. In the end, full employment is generally reached.

Obviously, if the marginal willingness-to-pay for environmental quality is inelastic with respect to emissions, and if the emissions per tonne of output are very high, there may not exist a full employment equilibrium. However, we will disregard that possibility because plants always have ways of abating emissions other than reducing production.

In order to study this closer, let us depart from the assumption that the emission charge is optimal. On the contrary, assume that q is less than the marginal willingness-to-pay for pollution abatement. In such a situation, what is the effect of an increase in money supply? Differentiating the utility function yields the following:

$$
\begin{aligned}
dU &= U_x dx + U_E dE + U_L dL + U_M d(M/P) \\
&= p dx - q dE + w^s dL + Y d(M/P) \\
&= (\bar{w} - w^s) dL - (q - \bar{q}) dE + Y d(M/P).
\end{aligned}
\tag{8.10}
$$

The first parenthesis in the final line indicates that an increase in the demand for labour increases welfare as the fixed wage rate exceeds the reservation wage, w^s. The second parenthesis indicates, however, that the increase in pollution reduces well-being as the marginal willingness-to-pay exceeds the emission charge. If the emission charge were equal to the marginal willingness-to-pay, then it would obviously have been optimal to increase the money supply until the reservation wage rate equals the fixed wage rate. However, in the face of a less than optimal pollution charge, this is not optimal. In fact, equation (8.10) says that the increase in money supply should be smaller than what would correspond to full employment. Thus, if it is not possible to optimize the allocation rule regarding the environment, it is not optimal to try to achieve optimal macroeconomic policies.

9

Computable general equilibrium modelling applications[1]

In this chapter, two case studies demonstrate the use of computable general equilibrium (CGE) models to analyse economy-wide sustainable development issues and explore economic–social–environmental links. Sections 9.1 to 9.4 develop the ECOGEM model to assess economic, social and environmental policy linkages in Chile – focusing on urban air pollution, poverty, income distribution and employment. The model examines the potential for combining different policies to enhance positive cross-effects of environmental and social policies, or to mitigate the negative side-effects of any single policy. The results show that general equilibrium modelling is useful for holistically analysing the impacts of different economy-wide policies. Winners and losers may be identified with the potential magnitude of gains and losses, including indirect effects. In Sections 9.5 to 9.7, a static CGE model of Costa Rica is used to study the effects of macroeconomic policies on deforestation and to identify remedial policy options. The model confirms the results of partial equilibrium analyses: (1) establishing property rights tends to decrease deforestation, because such rights allow forest users to capture the future benefits of reduced logging damage today and (2) higher interest rates promote deforestation and vice versa. The CGE approach also clearly identifies the indirect effects (due to intersectoral links), which must be combined with the direct effects to determine the total impact. Finally, the model underlines the importance of pursuing sectoral reforms in the context of growth. A dynamic CGE model of Costa Rica gives essentially the same results as the static CGE model presented here.

9.1 Economy-wide cross-effects of social and environmental policies in Chile

Sustainomics encourages a wider view of human well-being that looks beyond traditional economic goals and pays more attention to social and environmental effects. Below, we analyse the links among social and environmental policies and their cross-effects as well as the impacts on key macroeconomic and sectoral variables, within a general equilibrium

---

[1] The valuable contributions of C. de Miguel, S. Miller, A. Persson and R. O'Ryan to this chapter are gratefully acknowledged. Some parts of the chapter are based on material adapted from Munasinghe (1996a), Munasinghe *et al.* (2006) and Persson and Munasinghe (1995).

macroeconomic modelling framework applied to Chile. This work extends recent research on the powerful and pervasive impacts of country-wide or economy-wide policies on environmental and social issues (Munasinghe, 2002b).

In Section 9.1, we summarize the CGE modelling framework that is used, and then we review the relevant literature. Section 9.2 describes the main economic, social and environmental issues and policies in Chile. The ECOGEM–Chile model is applied to simulate alternative environmental and social policies, and the results are discussed in Section 9.3. Finally, Section 9.4 summarizes the main conclusions.

9.1.1 CGE approach

General equilibrium models capture complex interlinkages among economic, social and environmental variables better than partial equilibrium methods. It is often difficult to integrate these three major domains (see Chapter 2). Given the complexity of direct and indirect links among economic, environmental and social variables, CGE models represent the economy of a country in a more realistic way by incorporating market mechanisms in resource allocation. They are useful in defining the main linkages and in evaluating quantitatively *ex ante* the effects of different economic, social or environmental policies, while capturing indirect side-effects. Our study focuses on changes in selected economic, environmental and social variables.

Figure 9.1 summarizes the relationships to be modelled by the CGE model, based on the circular flow of the economy. It includes the main agents (firms, households and government), flows of goods and services, payments to factors, international trade and relationships with the environment. Each agent is modelled according to certain behavioural assumptions,

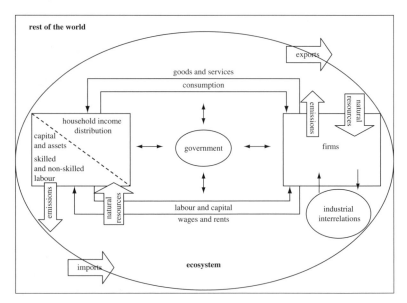

Figure 9.1. Circular flow in the economy. Source: Munasinghe *et al.* (2006).

including optimizing producers and consumers. Further, each market reflects economic reality, as a competitive or non-competitive market, or, in the case of the labour market, with or without full employment. These models reach equilibria according to Walras law, by equating demand and supply and thus determining prices and quantities. The productive sectors incorporate demands for intermediate inputs as well as capital and labour. However, they go beyond simple input–output models by allowing substitution among production inputs. This characteristic yields equilibria which capture transmission of effects through all relevant markets. Additionally, the government role is modelled via taxes, subsidies and transfers. Finally, the CGE model integrates the analysis of short- and long-run development strategies and growth paths, with the short-run view focusing on stabilization policies. Sectoral analysis is related to technological or investment processes.

Models for developing countries have become more practical by moving away from the original, strictly neoclassical, general equilibrium approach. Typical adaptations include departures from the Walrasian orthodoxy to account for structural rigidities such as fixed wages, absence of factor mobility (Taylor, 1990) and imperfect competition and increasing returns to scale in trade models.

9.1.2 Linkages with the environment

Chapter 7 reviewed the environmental and social impacts of economy-wide policies, some of which have emerged from CGE models applied to developing countries (De Miguel and Miller, 1998; Dessus and Bussolo, 1996; Munasinghe, 1996b; Munasinghe and Cruz, 1994; Persson and Munasinghe, 1995; Rodríguez, Abler and Shortle, 1997).

More generally, since the first environmental CGE models appeared (Dufournaud, Harrington and Rogers, 1988; Forsund and Strom, 1988), the recent literature includes: (1) models to evaluate the effects of trade policies or international trade agreements on the environment (Beghin *et al.*, 1996, 2002; Grossman and Krueger, 1993; Lucas, Wheeler and Hettige, 1992; Madrid-Aris, 1998; Yang, 2001) or diverse applications in the area of the Global Trade Analysis Program (Hertel, 1997); (2) models to evaluate climate change, focusing on the stabilization of CO_2, NOx and SOx emissions (Bergman, 1991; Edwards and Hutton, 2001; Jorgensen and Wilcoxon, 1993; Li and Rose, 1995; Rose and Abler, 1998); (3) models focused on energy issues, which evaluate the impacts of energy price changes on pollution or costs control (Pigott, Whalley and Wigle, 1992; Rose, Schluter and Wiese, 1995); (4) natural-resource allocation or management models, whose goal is usually the efficient interregional or intersectoral allocation of natural resources such as water among competing uses (Ianchovichina, Darwin and Shoemaker, 2001; Mukherjee, 1996; Robinson and Gelhar, 1995); and (5) models focused on evaluating economic impacts of specific environmental instruments or regulations, like the Clean Air Bill in the USA (Hazilla and Kopp, 1990; Jorgensen and Wilcoxon, 1990).

Finally, CGE models have focused recently on double dividend issues – i.e. the hypothesis that shifting from (distortionary) ordinary taxes to pollution taxes will improve both economic and environmental welfare (Auerbach, 1985; Repetto *et al.*, 1992). CGE models have been used to argue both in favour of and against the existence of a double dividend (see, e.g., Bento and Rajkumar (1998), Bovenberg and De Mooij (1994), Fullerton and Metcalf (1997), Jaeger (2001), Koskela, Schöb and Sinn (1999) and Parry and Bento (1999)). Van Heerden *et al.* (2006) shows a triple dividend (lower GHG emissions and poverty and higher GDP) when environmental taxes are recycled through reduced food prices in South Africa.

9.1.3 Applications in Chile

There are few applications of CGE models to Chile. Early attempts sought to analyse the economic effects of alternative tax policies and trade agreements between Chile and MERCOSUR, NAFTA, the European Union, the USA and Asia-Pacific (Coeymans and Larraín, 1994; Harrison, Rutherford and Tarr, 1997, 2002; Ruiz and Yarur, 1990). Bussolo, Mizala and Romaguera (1998) analysed the effects of trade agreements on the labour market, under competitive conditions and with some rigidities. Holland *et al.* (2002) studied the impacts of agricultural reforms consisting of price-band removal and elimination of tariffs on agricultural and food commodities in Chile, in relation to urban employment, rural–urban migration and welfare.

Environmental issues were addressed in the dynamic CGE model of Beghin *et al.* (1996) – based on the OECD TEQUILA model. This study analysed the impact of environmental policy, trade liberalization and trade agreements, using a multiregional model that included 26 regions and 72 productive sectors. It determined the emissions from productive activity at the national level, scaled for Santiago. The air concentration of particulates is estimated for Santiago by using a linear dispersion model for air pollutants. A dose–response function translates this concentration into indices of mortality and morbidity. The abatement of particulate matter, SO_2 and NO_2 will reduce mortality and morbidity significantly. Meanwhile, the entry of Chile into NAFTA would be beneficial for the environment, whereas the entry into MERCOSUR or a unilateral drop in tariffs will not. Taxing these pollutants leads to increased emissions and concentrations of substitutes which are also toxic, as well as bio-accumulative gases, thereby decreasing mortality and morbidity. Beghin and Dessus[2] (1999) applied a static version of the same model to assess the issue of double dividend, by substituting trade distortions for environmental taxes. O'Ryan, Miller and De Miguel (2003) applied an adaptation of the OECD model to evaluate policy options for reducing air pollution in Chile.

The preceding examples use CGE models to assess economic and environmental linkages. However, no one has evaluated the cross-links between the social and the environmental spheres of sustainable development. Section 9.3 addresses this issue.

9.2 Review of economic, social and environmental issues and policies

Since the mid 1980s and up to the end of the twentieth century, Chile was a role model for developing countries due to its rapid export-led growth. Further, there were major reductions

---

[2] Mimeograph by J. Beghin and S. Dessus (1999), 'The environmental double dividend with trade distortions. Analytical results and evidence from Chile'.

in poverty during that period, but the environment suffered severe harm. This section discusses the main economic, social and environmental issues and policies introduced to reduce such pressures after the mid 1990s

9.2.1 Economic issues and policies

During the 1980s, Chile engaged in trade liberalization and extensive privatization programmes, promoting exports and free markets as the main engines for growth. This trend continued in the 1990s, but less strongly. The government did not set prices, except for public transport, some public utilities and port charges. Tariffs applied to countries without free-trade agreements are uniform, and currently at 6%. Regulation of utilities, banking, security markets and pension funds was improved. At the same time, major efforts were made to maintain macroeconomic stability, improve infrastructure provision and focus resources to address social problems. Key reforms implemented include: privatization of public utilities; promotion of private investment in infrastructure, electricity, telecommunications and air transport; trade liberalization and trade agreement expansion; and educational reform. Legislation is now in place to privatize ports, water and sewage. In the future, a system of licenses is expected to replace direct privatization.

As a result, Chile's economic performance during the 1990s was the best of the twentieth century, growing at an impressive 8% per year between 1989 and 1998. The 1997/98 Asian Crisis caused a small recession in 1999. Despite adverse international events, the economic growth rate in 2000 remained at 4.5%, decreased to 3.4% in 2001, and rebounded to 5% by 2004. Chilean economic performance far exceeded that of other countries in the region (where growth rates are a poor 0 to 1%). Per capita GDP is around US $4.5 at current prices.

Key variables have been kept within acceptable limits. Since the beginning of the 1990s, the Central Bank has posted an inflation target for the year, resulting in a fall in inflation from 27% in 1990 to 2.8% in 2002. Tight government spending helped to achieve fiscal surpluses each year up to 1999. Fiscal expansion has been moderated and the deficit easily balanced. The current account was in deficit during most of the 1990s (currently under 1% of GDP), but has been easily financed by substantial foreign capital inflows. External debt composition changed from 30% private debt in 1990 to 85% in 2002, and comprises mainly medium- and long-term debt (83%). External debt (US $39 million) accounts for 58% of GDP. Gross internal investment has increased significantly in the period, reaching 27% of GDP in 1998, compared with the 16% average of the 1980s. However, internal savings did not grow much during the 1990s, and most of the increase in investment has been financed through foreign savings. After 1998, investment slowed to 23% of the GDP, with a parallel reduction in foreign savings.

Real wages increased in the 1990s at an average rate of 3.2%. Unemployment fell from an average of 18% in the 1980s to 6% in the 1990s. However, after 1999 unemployment rose to 10%, and, despite efforts by the government, this remains at 9%. Poverty declined sharply from 45% of total households in 1987 to 22% in 1998 and further to 20.6% in 2000. Income distribution is still a weak area. The minimum wage, although increasing at a higher real rate than wages, was only US $160 per month in 2002 (or about twice the value defined by the poverty line). The richest 20% of homes received more than 15.5 times the income of the poorest 20% in 2000; the Gini coefficient was close to 0.58. This situation has not changed since the 1960s.

Historically, Chile's growth has been based on renewable and non-renewable resources. Chile is the world's leading copper and iodine producer and is a growing source of gold, lithium and other non-metallic minerals. Copper is the main export product, equivalent to around 40% of its total exports – down from 80% in the 1980s, due to diversification of exports. Agricultural products, fish and fishmeal, forestry products and cellulose are other important export sectors that have grown rapidly since the mid 1990s. Imports are concentrated in capital goods and fuel/energy.

9.2.2 *Social issues and policies*

Since 1990, public expenditure on social issues has increased greatly in an attempt to reduce high levels of poverty. Following the basic principle of equal opportunities and an acceptable standard of living for the population, social policy since the mid 1990s has been geared to improving coverage in the health, education and housing sectors. In addition, efforts have been made to promote productive development in poor areas.

Three distinct periods can be identified in the evolution of social policies in Chile (Baytelman *et al.*, 1999; Schkolnik and Bonnefoy, 1994). During the first period (1950–1973), termed 'Universal Policies', there was a gradual growth in public social expenditure, coverage and number of beneficiaries. Programmes were designed to have universal coverage, and were basically aimed at health and nutrition, education, housing and sanitary infrastructure. However, these programmes were usually underfinanced and caused severe fiscal deficits.

The second period (1973–1989), called 'Assistance and Subsidies', was undertaken (by the military government) amidst intense economic and political reforms. Public-sector services were decentralized and the private sector was encouraged to deliver social services. Broad programmes were reduced and expenditure focused on specific objectives. The main goal was to eradicate extreme poverty and to provide mother–child care and basic services. Social expenditure was severely reduced. Nevertheless, there were significant improvements in human development indicators, such as child mortality, reduction of illiteracy and schooling, among others.

The third period, 'Integrating Policies', was begun by the democratic government in the 1990s. Spending on social goals increased greatly. Social policies are focused on improving the quality of services, and aim to develop skills in the low-income population. Social *investment* is preferred over assistance. This view reflects the new government goals of economic growth and macroeconomic stability *together* with equality and poverty reduction (and not just as a consequence of growth). Between 1990 and 1998, public social expenditure grew by 88% (66% in per capita terms), an annual growth rate of 8.2%. This increase was much higher than the regional average for Latin America (5.5%) (CEPAL, 1999, 2000). Thus,

Table 9.1 *Government social expenditures 1990–2002*

	1990	1992	1994	1996	1998	2000	2002
Social expenditures (% GDP)	**12.4**	**12.5**	**12.8**	**12.9**	**14.0**	**15.6**	**16.0**
Health	1.9	2.2	2.4	2.3	2.5	2.7	2.9
Housing	0.9	1.0	1.0	1.0	1.0	0.9	0.9
Social security	6.1	5.6	5.5	5.4	5.7	6.4	6.4
Education	2.4	2.6	2.7	3.0	3.5	3.9	4.3
Others[a]	1.1	1.1	1.2	1.2	1.4	1.6	1.6
Total expenditures	**20.2**	**20.3**	**19.9**	**19.6**	**21.3**	**22.4**	**22.9**
Share social/total (%)	61.4	61.7	64.2	66	65.9	69.5	69.9

[a] Includes monetary subsidies and social investment programmes for priority groups.
Source: DIPRES (2003).

social expenditure rose from 61% of total expenditure in 1990 to 70% in 2002 (Table 9.1), which was higher than the growth rate of GDP.

Intense health-sector reforms introduced in 1980 fostered the creation of a private health system, parallel to the public health service. Beginning in 1990, new criteria for health policies were defined, including care for the poorest groups and improvements in the quality of public health. Public investment and expenditure were increased substantially to achieve these goals, and new legislation was developed to coordinate the public and private systems. Despite these improvements, the public system is still weak. More focus is needed on vulnerable groups, especially the elderly. In order to achieve these goals, the government introduced a major public health reform plan (the AUGE) in 2002, which guarantees at least 80% financial coverage for 56 major diseases for the whole population. The plan is estimated to cost the government over US $200 million a year.

Chilean education was mainly public up to 1980. In the early 1980s publicly funded schools were decentralized and transferred to municipalities, and private schools were encouraged. The main goal of this reform was to promote competition among schools and increase the cost-effectiveness and quality of education. Reforms did increase access to both elementary and high schools, but did not improve the quality of education. Moreover, public expenditure on education was reduced during the 1980s, from 3.5% to 2.5% of GDP, affecting the poor in particular.

In 1990, specific education goals were introduced to: (1) improve the quality of education; (2) increase and provide more equal access to education; and (3) promote the participation of different sectors and institutions in education. These changes required a 136% increase in public expenditure for education from 1990 to 1998 (DIPRES, 2001). During 1990 to 1998, the average educational years for the over 15 group rose from 9 to 9.7 years. In terms of quality, tests have shown a systematic reduction in the gap between both subsidized schools and private schools, and between municipal schools and the rest.

Housing policy since the late 1970s was focused on the poor, and encouraged private agents to play an active role in design, localization and financing. The State's main role was to provide direct and indirect subsidies. In the early 1980s, there were two housing programmes – social housing and sanitation for houses and neighbourhoods. In both cases, homes were built by private construction firms. As this housing policy was under-financed, the housing deficit increased during the 1980s.

From 1990 to 1998 public expenditure on housing was around 1% of GDP. Housing policy in the 1990s was aimed at reducing the deficit substantially and encouraged the participation of beneficiary families, the private sector, NGOs and community social organizations. Consequently, there were large gains in housing in the 1990s compared with the previous decade, and 53.5% of benefits given out by social programmes were received by the poorest 40% of homes. Benefits received by the poorest quintile grew from 29.5% in 1996 to 32.1% in 1998. While housing quality also rose, there are still around half a million homes with some defect.

Finally, in the 1980s little attention was placed on improving productivity in poor areas. Promotion of production was focused on modern sectors of the economy, especially the export sector and bigger companies. At the end of the 1980s, direct support was given through subsidies for small and medium enterprises, but with little concern for low pro-ductivity, weak management and technological innovation and poor market access (MIDEPLAN, 1996).

In the 1990s, policies changed to support the main state goal of overcoming poverty. FOSIS (the Fund for Solidarity and Social Investment) was created in 1990 to finance productive development among the poor in weaker sectors. Emphasis on decentralization ensured that close to 50% of investment for 1998 was assigned to Regions. Slower economic growth during 1998 to 2001 forced the government to focus on unemployment; 96 000 new jobs were created up to May 2002 (MINTRAB, 2002), and hiring was subsidized to raise employment. Despite such improvements, the social security safety net is still weak. The gap between rich and poor is large in social areas such as education, health and housing, requiring targeted income transfers.

9.2.3 *Environmental issues and policies*

Chile developed a large number of environmental regulations and standards up to 1990, but they were diverse, dispersed among different sectors, fragmented and without coordination. Due to lack of overall coherence, many of the regulations were not applied. Nevertheless, environmental protection received strong support in the 1980 Constitution.

Due to poor environmental quality (particularly in Santiago), and the need to defend exports against accusations of ecological dumping, the democratic government of 1990 set up the Special Commission for (Santiago) Metropolitan Region Decontamination and the National Commission for the Environment (CONAMA). In 1994, the General Environmental Framework Law set the foundations for the National System for Environmental Management. Total environment expenditures by CONAMA, the Ministries of Economy and Mining and the Forestry National Corporation are now 50 times more than in 1990 (Brzovic, Miller and Lagos, 2002), having risen to over 2% of the public budget in 2000; see Table 9.2. Environmental

Table 9.2 *Environmental expenditures by objective 1999–2001*

All amounts are given in US $1000

Objectives according to CEPA,[a] 2000	1999	2000	2001[b]
Protection of air and clime	6337	13 440	6204
Management of liquid waste	12 960	17 428	3833
Management and protection of land, underground water and superficial waters	41 087	60 055	48 693
Noise pollution abatement	81	347	305
Waste management	45 568	43 754	5352
Protection of biodiversity	41 922	39 654	20 305
Other environmental protection activities (including management)	149 332	127 292	70 747
Total environmental expenditure	**297 286**	**301 970**	**155 439**

[a] Classification of Environmental Protection Activities and Expenditure.
[b] Preliminary commitments. Current values at the annual averaged observed dollar (Banco Central).
Source: based on FOCUS (2000).

authorities regulate and control some activities instead of intervening directly. Thus, environmental expenditures can be transferred to the private sector.

Despite this progress, policies and programmes for sustainable development still play a secondary role in Chile, resulting in many environmental problems: (1) air pollution, linked to urban areas, industrial activities (pulp and paper, fishmeal), mining and power generation (in specific areas, emissions of different pollutants exceed the national or international norms); (2) high levels of water pollution due to domestic and industrial effluents without treatment; this affects surface water, ground water and coastal seawater; (3) water scarcity at the regional level; (4) inadequate urban development management, high levels of pollution, lack of green or recreational areas, etc.; (5) poor solid-waste management and disposal, particularly hazardous wastes; (6) land degradation, due to poor agricultural and forestry techniques, urban growth and inadequate solid-waste management (this mainly affects agricultural land and river basins); (7) threats to native forests due to overexploitation (increase of forestry activity, coal making, wood collection) and absence of effective protection; and (8) hydro-biological resource overexploitation and biomass exhaustion.

The rapid and unmanaged urbanization due to economic growth has led to moderately severe air and water pollution in many cities. Preventive costs, health damages and productivity losses, particularly in Santiago, have been high. Air pollution in Santiago is the most obvious environmental problem in the country (see Figures 9.2 and 9.3 and Tables 9.3 and 9.4), while other cities are also becoming affected (Table 9.5). For Santiago, natural variables, demographic growth and both fixed and mobile air pollution sources are main causes. The total amount of vehicles in Chile has grown from 1.1 million in 1990 to over 2.1 million by 2000. However, important reductions in PM10 and PM2.5 (23.3% and 46%, respectively) have been achieved since 1989. These gains are due to the decontamination

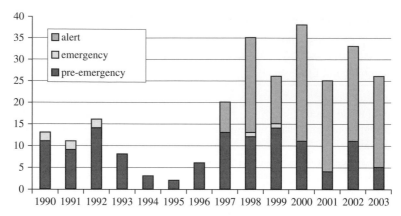

Figure 9.2. Number of events in the Santiago Metropolitan Region Air Monitoring System. The category 'alert' was established in 1997. Source: based on SESMA, www.sesma.cl.

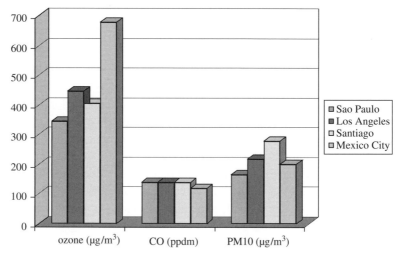

Figure 9.3. Comparison of maximum levels of pollution in selected cities (1995–1998). Source: Alliende (2002).

plan, the elimination of 3000 highly polluting buses, the use of natural gas in fixed sources and the introduction of catalytic converters in all new vehicles (50% of cars in Santiago had converters in 1999).

Transport contributes the most to air pollution, especially PM10 emissions, the most critical environmental problem in the city, where 25% are emitted directly and another 50% resuspended by vehicles on paved and non-paved roads. This sector is also responsible for 50% of PM2.5, 94% of carbon monoxide (CO), 83% of nitrogen oxides (NOx) and 42% of volatile organic compound (VOC) emissions. Private transport is generally more polluting than public transport in terms of concentration of pollutants per vehicle mile travelled (except for PM10). However, as air pollution in Santiago is subject to climate variables, and pollution strongly

Table 9.3 *Air pollution in Santiago (1995)*

Pollutant	CO (ppm)	Ozone (ppb)	PM10[a]	PM2.5[a]	SO$_2$[a]	NO$_2$[a]	TSP[a]
Max.	35.6	224	302	174	161	254	621
Min.	0.1	1	8	4	7	4	31
Average	2.04	13	87	42	17.8	64.8	186.3

[a] Data in μg/m^3.

Sources: Metropolitan Environmental and Health Service (SESMA) and National Statistics Institute (INE).

Table 9.4 *Air pollution in Santiago (2000)*

Pollutant	CO (ppm)	Ozone (ppb)	PM10[a]	PM10–2.5[a]	PM2.5[a]	SO$_2$[a]
Max.	19.3	162	230	105	153	135
Min.	0.1	1	5	1	4	1
Average	1.1	16	87	35.8	34.8	4.7

[a] Data in μg/m^3.

Source: SESMA, INE

Table 9.5 *Summary of air quality in Chile's major cities*

City	Region	Excedance of PM10 standard	Other pollutants with problems	Main emitting sources
Arica	I	yearly standard is exceeded	probably sulphates	no information
Iquique	I	daily standard exceeded eight times; yearly standard exceeded	no	fixed and mobile sources
Antofagasta	II	daily standard exceeded twice	particulates	no information
Calama	II	daily and yearly standards exceeded	SO$_2$	fixed sources
Valparaíso-Viña del mar	V	daily standard exceeded three times; yearly average very close to being exceeded	NO$_2$, SO$_2$, ozone	mobile sources
Santiago	metropolitan	daily standard exceeded 138 times; yearly average exceeded	PM2.5, ozone, CO	streets, vehicles, industry
Rancagua	VI	daily standard exceeded 11 times; yearly average exceeded	ozone	mobile sources
Concepción-Talcahuano	VIII	daily standard exceeded three times	SO$_2$	no information
Temuco	IX	daily standard exceeded nine times	no	fixed sources

Source: summarized from Universidad de Chile (2002).

varies among seasons, the annual average values may be less relevant. Other problem areas in Chile include poor air quality in Concepción-Talcahuano from the steel, petroleum, fishmeal, paper and pulp industries and high levels of ground-level ozone in Valparaíso-Viña del Mar. The Talcahuano environmental recovery plan is in operation, and air monitoring systems have been established in several cities with the goal of identifying saturated zones. Other significant sources of industrial pollution include fossil fuel use, the pulp and paper industry (sulphydric acid) and the fishmeal industry (sulphydric acid and trimethylamine).

Since the most significant effects on human health result from fine particles (PM2.5) in air pollution, the Santiago Metropolitan Region was declared saturated with PM10, CO_2, O_3 and latent of NOx in 1996. A compensation system for particulates from large fixed sources (up to $1000\,m^3/hr$) is in effect for air pollution. Sources emitting less than their goal may sell their emitting capacity. Even though the system has been in place for some years, few trades have occurred. Moreover, there is a general debate as to whether this instrument is appropriate in Chile. In addition, public transport providers must compete for some of the important roads in Santiago, and one key selection parameter is vehicular emission.

The rapidly growing domestic waste in Chile is unevenly distributed, with the Metropolitan Region generating 60% of waste while housing only 40% of the population. Water pollution and scarcity are also issues. Factors such as demographic growth, industrialization and concentration of urban areas have contributed to this decline. The problem is most serious in the north (fishing and mining), the metropolitan region of Santiago and central seaboard (sewage and industrial pollution) and coastal areas (Bay of Talcahuano – fisheries, petroleum, and pulp industries), while the south experiences the setback of periodic flooding.

The main water quality issue is microbiological contamination. While sanitation services function well, waste treatment facilities are inadequate. Rivers running through Santiago and surrounding (especially coastal) areas are badly affected by the dumping of untreated sewage. Water pollution due to agricultural runoff is a concern. The use of water for agricultural, forestry and aquacultural purposes, as well as the increase in human effluents into the lakes in southern Chile, have greatly increased nutrients, which promote a build-up of algae and a drop in biodiversity.

In conclusion, water and air pollution remain as important problems in Chile despite the increasing environmental expenditures, both public and private. The same is true for social issues. Environmental regulation has been hampered by concentration of policy in the centre, with little concern for regional development priorities. Remedies require both new policies to address environmental and social concerns, and improvement in the monitoring and enforcement of such measures.

9.3 Interactions between social, environmental and economic policies

Given the issues discussed in the preceding sections, are there major negative interactions or positive synergies between environmental, social and economic policies? This case study seeks to analyse the social effects of environmental policies and the environmental impact of social policies via economic forces.

We first simulate environmental policy (reduction by 10% of PM10, SO_2 and NO_2 emissions through emission taxes), to analyse their impacts on economic, environmental and social variables, and decide which measures are more effective. Next, we simulate the economic, social and environmental impacts of social policy (government income transfers to households). Finally we simulate both policies simultaneously (while maintaining the public savings constant) to identify synergies. We apply the ECOGEM–Chile model, a CGE model for Chile adapted from an OECD CGE model (Beghin *et al.*, 1996). This CGE model (Appendix A, Section 9.8), is a static multisector model with two kinds of labour, five quintiles of income, an external sector and specific productive factors. It is savings-driven, with energy-input substitution to reduce emissions, as emissions are related to the use of different inputs and not only to production levels. The main source of information is the 1996 Chilean social accounting matrix (SAM), based on the most recently available input/output matrix for 1996 (Banco Central de Chile, 2001). The study is denominated in billions of pesos at 1996 purchasing power.[3]

We assume zero capital mobility across sectors and adjustment within sectors in the short run. Long-term values are used for the income, substitution and other elasticities from the relevant international literature, giving more flexibility and realism to the adjustment process. However, investment and capital accumulation processes as a function of relative returns are not included due to the static nature of the model, and long-term elasticities will only minimize this flaw. With these parameters, the scenarios modelled here should account for medium-term effects. Although full employment is assumed, we also create a scenario that analyses the effects of high unemployment.

There are two types of emission coefficients: input-based and output coefficients; 13 different pollutants are identified. Toxic effluents are segregated by medium: air, water and soil (TOXAIR, TOXWAT, TOXSOIL). They contain mineral and industrial chemicals, fertilizers and pesticides, paints, etc. Bio-accumulative pollutants are also segregated by medium: air, water and soil (BIOAIR, BIOWAT, BIOSOIL). They contain metal elements such as aluminium, arsenic, copper, lead, mercury, zinc, etc., and they have a significant long-term risk to life. Other air pollutants include SO_2, NO_2, VOCs, CO and PM10. Other water pollutants include BOD (biological oxygen demand) and TSS (total suspended solids).

9.3.1 Environmental policies

We analyse the impacts of a 10% reduction in PM10 emissions by using emission taxes (the main target of the air pollution policy). This reduction level is easily achieved without high abatement costs, and is compatible with the current economic context of high unemployment. Furthermore, expected revenues associated with environmental taxes are similar to financial requirements for employment policy. We replicate the same exercise for NO_2 and SO_2 emissions, looking for efficiency gains, enhancing positive results and reducing

---

[3] Unpublished mimeograph by R. O'Ryan, C.J. De Miguel, S. Miller and C. Lagos (2001), 'A social accounting matrix for Chile 2001'.

Table 9.6 *Macroeconomic impacts of environmental taxation*

Taxation on	PM10	SO$_2$	NO$_2$
Real GDP	-0.2% [-0.1%]	-0.2%	-0.2%
Investment	0.8% [0.9%]	0.6%	0.7%
Consumption	-0.6% [-0.5%]	-0.5%	-0.6%
Exports	-1.1% [-1.0%]	-1.0%	-1.0%
Imports	-1.0% [-0.9%]	-0.9%	-0.9%

Results for PM10 with high unemployment are presented in square brackets.

Table 9.7 *Sectoral impact of environmental taxation*

	PM10	SO$_2$	NO$_2$
Construction	0.7% [0.8%]	0.6%	0.6%
Electricity	-0.1% [0.0%]	0.3%	0.3%
Renewable resources	-0.7% [-0.6%]	-0.6%	-0.6%
Wood products	-0.7% [-0.6%]	-0.6%	-0.6%
Gas	-0.8% [-0.7%]	-0.8%	-0.8%
Load and passenger transport	-2.2% [-2.1%]	-2.1%	-2.1%
Other transport	-2.3% [-2.1%]	-2.2%	-2.2%
Oil and gas extraction	-4.1% [-4.0%]	-4.3%	-4.3%
Coal	-5.2% [-5.0%]	1.1%	1.1%
Oil refinery	-9.7% [-9.6%]	-9.8%	-9.8%

Results for PM10 with high unemployment are presented in square brackets.

negative ones. Apart from causing acid rain, NO$_2$ and SO$_2$ are the main chemical components of PM2.5 – the fine fraction included in PM10 that causes most health problems. The higher public budget link is not offset by environmental tax revenues, leading to increased public savings. Thus, new taxes are imposed without any other taxation/subsidy compensation. Table 9.6 shows moderate impacts on all macrovariables despite the adjustment process that follows taxation. Real GDP and consumption are moderately reduced, as well as exports and imports, which are close to 1%.

Some significant sectoral impacts can be observed in Table 9.7. Emission taxes increase revenues, raising public savings by around 14%. Despite marginally reduced household and enterprise savings, global savings rise. Increases in savings raises investment, which is channelled to the economy mainly through the construction sector, raising sector output by 0.7%. The electricity sector also marginally benefits from these policies, since part of energy demand is substituted from oil and gas toward electricity (-0.1%–0.3%). Transport, oil and gas extraction and oil refining suffer the highest negative impact in these simulations, reducing their sectoral output by 2.1%–2.3%, 4.1%–4.3% and 9.7%–9.8%, respectively.

Table 9.8 *Environmental impact of environmental taxation*

	10% reduction of PM 10	10% reduction of SO$_2$	10% reduction of NO$_2$
TOXAIR	−0.6%	−0.6%	−0.6%
TOXWAT	−1%	−0.9%	−1%
TOXSOIL	−0.4%	−0.4%	−0.4%
BIOAIR	−1.4%	0%	0%
BIOWAT	0.2% [0.3%]	0.6%	0.6%
BIOSOIL	−0.4%	−0.4%	−0.4%
SO$_2$	−10.1%	−10%	−10.2%
NO$_2$	−10% [−9.9%]	−9.9%	−10%
CO	−9.5%	−3.5%	−3.5%
VOCs	−1.1% [−1%]	−1%	−1.1%
PART	−10%	−9.3%	−9.4%
BOD	−0.4%	−0.4%	−0.4%
TSS	−8.9% [−8.8%]	2.7%	2.7%

Results for PM10 simulation with high unemployment are presented in square brackets, when different.

Table 9.9 *Environmental impact of PM10 taxation*

	Total effect	Production effect	Demand effect
TOXAIR	−0.6%	−0.6%	−2.8%
TOXWAT	−1%	−0.8%	−6.3%
TOXSOIL	−0.4%	−0.4%	0%
BIOAIR	−1.4%	−1.5%	−0.1%
BIOWAT	0.2%	−2.2%	0.7%
BIOSOIL	−0.4%	−0.4%	0.1%
SO$_2$	−10.1%	−7.8%	−16.5%
NO$_2$	−10%	−7.7%	−16.5%
CO	−9.5%	−8.5%	−16.3%
VOCs	−1.1%	−1.3%	−0%
PART	−10%	−7.8%	−16.5%
BOD	−0.4%	−0.4%	−0%
TSS	−8.9%	−8.9%	−10.3%

From an environmental point of view, Tables 9.8 and 9.9 and Figure 9.4 show that almost all emissions can be reduced by taxing PM10 emissions, except for bio-accumulative effluents into water, which increase marginally due to improvements in the construction sector. Furthermore, NO$_2$ and SO$_2$ emissions fall by over 10% with PM10 taxes. The latter indicates strong links between different pollutants, especially among air pollutants. Taxing PM10 also shows greater positive environmental impacts than SO$_2$ or NO$_2$ taxation. The

Table 9.10 *Impacts on utility of taxation on PM10 emissions*

	PM10	PM10 + unemployment
1st quintile	− 0.6%	− 0.5%
2nd quintile	− 0.6%	− 0.5%
3rd quintile	− 0.5%	− 0.5%
4th quintile	− 0.5%	− 0.4%
5th quintile	− 0.2%	− 0.2%

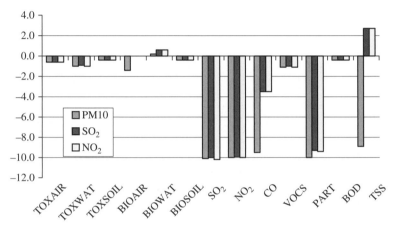

Figure 9.4. Environmental impact of environmental taxation Note that PM10 columns show the impacts on all pollutants when taxing PM10; the same applied for SO_2 and NO_2, respectively.

latter presents some increments on water effluents due to sectoral reaccommodation of production.

Vis-à-vis social effects, the simulations show a slight increase in employment (related to the slight decrease in wages), due to higher demand for labour in construction, offset by contractions in other sectors. A more positive effect on employment is seen when environmental taxes (on PM10) are applied in a high-unemployment scenario. There is also a moderate negative effect on household incomes, which are reduced by 0.6% for all quintiles (− 0.5% in the case of high unemployment). The effects for SO_2 and NO_2 taxes are similar. If another welfare measure is used (such as the utility function), this policy is slightly regressive, as part of the enterprise adjustment to the new environmental taxation involves wage reduction and consumer price increases, thereby affecting lower-income consumption relatively more (Table 9.10).

Finally, environmental policies have some negative social impacts, especially on welfare – partly because decreasing marginal utility of income is assumed. By contrast, all benefits from environmental gains (such as reduction in health costs, productivity gains, etc.) are not included. Thus, negative social and economic impacts are overemphasized.

We may conclude that: (1) taxing key pollutants can reduce global pollution more effectively than taxing other effluents – e.g. PM10 taxes yield superior environmental results with fewer macro, sectoral or social consequences; (2) there are strong links between different pollutants, and tax effects need to be carefully differentiated; and (3) macro-economic impacts are low and negative, but sectoral effects (positive and negative) can be strong. Therefore, policy and adjustment periods need to be flexible. Environmental tax revenues may be used to compensate the losers directly or to reduce/eliminate a distorting tax (achieving double dividends). Through careful targetting, taxing bads instead of goods could reduce pollution without economic and social losses. We may also conclude that (4), with high unemployment, the economy adjusts better to an environmental tax shock.

9.3.2 Social policies

The simulated social policy consists of an increase in transfers to households by 8.4%, which is equivalent to the cost of 100 000 new jobs created directly by the government, or an actual unemployment reduction from 10% to 8.2%. Public transfers would increase from 23% to 25% of government expenditure, with no offsetting revenue, thereby reducing government savings. The distribution of transfers is held constant at current levels: first quintile, 27.3%; second quintile, 26.6%; third quintile, 22.3%; fourth quintile, 17.9%; and the richest quintile, 5.9%.

The macroeffects are very minimal (Table 9.11); GDP is not affected. Investment falls by almost 1% due to the reduction of government savings (of more than 14%). However, consumption grows due to higher disposable incomes for almost all households. The construction sector is the most negatively affected, due to reduction in investment. The gas, hydraulic/water and load and passenger transport sectors benefit slightly from this social policy. Social impacts are positive, with real income for almost all quintiles increasing and the poorest improving the most. Impacts on utility are very similar. Finally, in terms of environmental effects, there are slight increases, mainly in air emissions. The demand effect is generally negative for environmental quality, whereas the production effect is positive (due to the construction slowdown). However, all impacts are small. This social policy has very low impacts on the environment, while the sign depends on the specific pollutant.

9.3.3 Joint policies: social and environmental

In the previous exercises, the environmental policy applied did not have major social impacts, and vice versa. Furthermore, a double dividend (social and environmental) did not exist. However, there seemed to be a trade-off among social and environmental policies/impacts. Therefore, we study joint social–environmental policies – taxes to reduce PM10 emissions by 10% and higher government transfers to homes using those tax revenues (thus keeping real government savings constant).

Macroimpacts are an average of the results of applying social and environmental policies independently (Table 9.12). The negative effect of environmental policy on consumption is

Table 9.11 *Impacts of a social policy consisting of an increment of transfers to households*

Macrovariables	real GDP	0.0%
	investment	− 0.8%
	consumption	0.4%
	exports	− 0.1%
	imports	− 0.1%
Sectoral production output	construction	− 0.7%
	electricity	0.1%
	renewable resources	0.0%
	wood products	0.0%
	gas	0.2%
	water	0.2%
	load and passenger transport	0.2%
	other transport	0.0%
	oil and gas extraction	0.0%
	oil refinery	0.1%
Households, real income	first quintile	3.2%
	second quintile	1.7%
	third quintile	1.0%
	fourth quintile	0.4%
	fifth quintile	0.0%
Environmental variables emissions	TOXAIR	− 0.1%
	TOXWAT	− 0.1%
	TOXSOIL	− 0.1%
	BIOAIR	− 0.1%
	BIOWAT	− 0.7%
	BIOSOIL	− 0.1%
	SO2	0.1%
	NO2	0.1%
	CO	0.1%
	VOC	0.0%
	PART	0.1%
	BOD	− 0.1%
	TSS	0.2%

Table 9.12 *Comparative macroeconomic impacts*

	PM10	Transfer	PM10+transfer
Real GDP	− 0.2%	0%	− 0.2%
Investment	0.8%	− 0.8%	− 0.1%
Consumption	− 0.6%	0.4%	− 0.2%
Exports	− 1.1%	− 0.1%	− 1.2%
Imports	− 1%	− 0.1%	− 1.1%

Table 9.13 *Comparative sectoral impacts*

	PM10	Transfer	PM10+transfer
Construction	0.7%	−0.7%	−0.1%
Electricity	−0.1%	0.1%	0%
Renewable resources	−0.7%	0%	−0.6%
Wood products	−0.7%	0%	−0.8%
Gas	−0.8%	0.2%	−0.5%
Water	−0.1%	0.2%	0.1%
Load and passenger transport	−2.2%	0.2%	−2%
Other transport	−2.3%	0%	−2.3%
Oil and gas extraction	−4.1%	0%	−4.1%
Oil refinery	−9.7%	0.1%	−9.6%

Table 9.14 *Comparative social impacts*

Real disposable income	PM10	Transfer	PM10+transfer
1st quintile	−0.6%	3.2%	2.6% (2.5%)
2nd quintile	−0.6%	1.7%	1.1% (1.1%)
3rd quintile	−0.6%	1%	0.4% (0.3%)
4th quintile	−0.6%	0.4%	−0.2% (−0.1%)
5th quintile	−0.6%	0%	−0.6% (−0.2%)

Utility levels are presented in brackets.

mitigated, while the negative investment effect due to the social policy is offset. Macrovariables suffer from a slightly negative impact.

At a sectoral level, the combined policies yield results that are the average of individual environmental and social policies (Table 9.13).

Social impacts are very positive (Table 9.14). Employment increases slightly and income distribution improves. There is a reduction in real income of the wealthier 40% of the population. In terms of utility, the results are quite similar. Environmental impacts of the joint policies are good (Table 9.15). Nine of the 13 types of emissions are lower than when applying the environmental policy only. In the other four cases, mitigation is close to the highest levels achieved by the separate policies.

In conclusion, it is better to combine environmental and social policies. Macro and sectoral impacts maintain their effects in the worst scenario, but both social and environmental variables improve even more. Nevertheless, the small cross-impacts of environmental/social policies indicate the value of separately identifying potential losers for later compensation or side policies.

Table 9.15 *Comparative environmental impacts*

	PM10	Transfer	PM10+transfer
TOXAIR	−0.6%	−0.1%	−0.8%
TOXWAT	−1%	−0.1%	−1.1%
TOXSOIL	−0.4%	−0.1%	−0.6%
BIOAIR	−1.4%	−0.1%	−1.5%
BIOWAT	0.2%	−0.7%	−0.4%
BIOSOIL	−0.4%	−0.1%	−0.6%
SO_2	−10.1%	0.1%	−10.1%
NO_2	−10%	0.1%	−9.9%
CO	−9.5%	0.1%	−9.5%
VOCs	−1.1%	0%	−1%
PART	−10%	0.1%	−10%
BOD	−0.4%	−0.1%	−0.6%
TSS	−8.9%	0.2%	−8.8%

9.4 Chile case study conclusions

During the 1990s, Chile sought to improve environmental and social standards. Further improvements will have increasing marginal costs. Therefore, innovative new approaches are required, including combining different policies so as to enhance synergies among them.

This case study presented an empirical application of the CGE model, ECOGEM–Chile, to assess economic, environmental and social linkages. Six different policies are simulated: three environmental policies that impose taxes on air emissions, aiming to reduce 10% of total PM10, SO_2 and NO_2 emissions, respectively; one social policy that increases government transfers to households; a joint social–environmental policy package, where the environmental tax on PM10 and the social transfer policy are combined (keeping public savings constant – i.e. environmental taxes finance social transfers); and PM10 taxation with high unemployment.

Taxing PM10 emission yields better environmental results than taxing SO_2 and NO_2, without substantial differences in the macro, sectoral or social results. With the PM10 environmental policy, the macroeconomic impacts are slightly negative, but sectoral effects (positive and negative) can be strong. Therefore, policy makers should consider a flexible policy with adjustment periods. Taxing environmental bads instead of goods yields good environmental results without economic and social losses. With high unemployment, an environmental tax shock is better absorbed by the economy, because firms have more freedom to adjust their production functions through the labour market. The impacts of social policy on environmental quality are very low, although the sign depends on the specific pollutant. Overall, the evidence suggests that environmental policies may have social impacts, but not vice versa.

Since cross-effects are relatively small, policy makers should focus on the specific policy under consideration. Nevertheless, social and environmental policy makers should coordinate among themselves, as it is possible to improve some results by combining both strategies, i.e. the mix of policies may improve overall results. Thus, compensating potential losers might increase their acceptance of environmental policies.

These results show that general equilibrium modelling is useful for systematically and holistically analysing different economy-wide policies and their impacts on the Chilean economy. Winners and losers may be identified, including the magnitudes of gains and losses. The results are not always straightforward, i.e. indirect effects are also relevant.

9.5 Economy-wide policies and deforestation in Costa Rica

This case study seeks to make development more sustainable in Costa Rica by studying links between deforestation and economy-wide policies.

9.5.1 Background

The economic analysis of environmental issues relies mainly on project-level studies, using cost–benefit analyses and environmental assessments. Chapter 7 showed how growth-oriented economic reform policies could interact with overlooked imperfections, such as market failures, policy distortions and institutional constraints, to cause environmental harm. General equilibrium analysis helps to trace the socioeconomic and environmental effects of economy-wide policy reforms.

When such comprehensive methods are not possible in developing countries, where data and skills are scarce, partial approaches that help to identify the most important impacts of economy-wide policies are frequently used. Because the full consequences of a policy are not traced, both quantitative and qualitative results of the partial equilibrium model may be wrong. For example, taxes that are not 'lump sum' may carry over from the sector for which they were intended into other sectors of the economy and affect consumption and production decisions there as well. In this context, the main purpose of this study is to investigate the effects of economy-wide policies in Costa Rica on forest areas and the environment (Persson, 1994). We also seek to determine whether new measures involving the allocation of property rights to these forests will yield different results when analysed using a general equilibrium model rather than a more conventional partial equilibrium approach.

In the remainder of this section, the main issues, analytical approach and results are summarized. The following section describes previous work on Costa Rica and the environmental priorities. The applicability of computable general equilibrium (CGE) models to such problems is discussed next, followed by further details of the model and data used here. Finally, the last two sections summarize the chief results and conclusions of the study. Appendix B (Section 9.9) provides model details.

Deforestation and soil erosion are major environmental problems in Costa Rica (see Table 9.16). The CGE model used here highlights economic activities that affect

Table 9.16 *Percentage of total land area in forests and agriculture*

	1963	1973	1986
Agriculture	30%	40%	57%
Forest	67%	57%	40%

Source: Solórzano *et al.* (1991).

deforestation. It goes beyond standard approaches in two key respects. First, it can simulate the effect of introducing property rights on forest resources, thus encouraging sustainable management of forests by private individuals who value future returns to forestry. Second, it includes markets for logs and cleared land: loggers deforest to sell timber to the forest industry and for exports, while squatters clear land for agricultural production and sale to the expanding agriculture sector.

A fairly standard CGE model is used. The tradable sectors – forestry, agriculture and industry – are price takers in the world market, while infrastructure and services produce non-traded output. To focus on the natural-resource sectors, the domestically mobile factors include, aside from capital and (skilled and unskilled) labour, cleared land and logs. The supplies of both labour and capital are exogenous. The demand for these factors arises from the producing sectors (agriculture, industry, etc.) and from deforestation by loggers and squatters. The supply of 'cleared' land is initially based on the total deforested land area. However, additional cleared land is made available from increased deforestation. This rate of land clearing depends on the definition of property rights as well as on taxes (or subsidies) that affect the forest and agricultural sectors. In addition, the expansion of squatting activities augments the cleared land factor. Agricultural production provides the demand for cleared land.

Poorly defined property rights in Costa Rican forests play an key role in deforestation. The model shows how correction of this market failure would reduce deforestation. If property rights are well defined and the interest rate is exogenous, the value that loggers assign to preserving the forests is crucial. In order to stop deforestation, the benefits from preserving the forests must be significantly higher than the value of the logs and the cleared land. Tax policies may generate unexpected side-effects, while substitution effects between inputs in the producing sectors may be important. Therefore, when impacts of macroeconomic policies are investigated, the general equilibrium approach generates results that are different from those derived from a partial equilibrium analysis.

9.5.2 *Status of forests in Costa Rica*

Deforestation in Costa Rica is proceeding at a rapid pace. MRN (1990) mentions the following economic and ecological benefits that Costa Rica may lose if deforestation continues: access to construction materials and other wood products, unchecked species of plants and animals that have possible and future uses for consumption and industrial production, recreation and eco-tourism, control of erosion and sedimentation and education and research possibilities. The greenhouse effect and concerns about the rich biological diversity in Costa Rica are important to the global community.

Deforestation and erosion are the main environmental problems in the country (Blomström and Lundahl, 1989; Foy and Daly, 1989). Most of the deforestation has occurred since 1950. If deforestation continues at the current rate, the commercial forests of Costa Rica will be exhausted within the next decade. The life zones with the highest rates of deforestation are the tropical wet forests, which are also ones in which biodiversity levels are highest (Solórzano *et al.*, 1991).

Deforestation takes place in several stages (Carriére, 1991; Keogh, 1984). First, a logging company involved in highgrading clears a vehicle tract to extract lumber. Then, the road is improved by the government due to pressures from lobbying groups, and this in turn enables local peasant families to clear and use the remaining forest for subsistence agriculture until the decreasing yields force them to sell or abandon the land (depending on whether it is titled or not). The land is still suitable for pasture and is therefore sold to cattle ranchers by urban-based real estate companies. After a few years, the land is almost completely degraded and unsuitable for any kind of economic use. The Costa Rican government is taking steps to preserve the forests. More than 13 000 square kilometers have been designated as national parks, although some deforestation was encouraged to diversify the country's production away from coffee and banana crops (Biesanz, Biesanz and Biesanz, 1987).

Deforestation in Costa Rica is caused by several factors, given in the following.

(1) The timber industry may be responsible for deforesting as much as 20 000 hectares annually. Logging requires a special government permit, but about half of the trees are cut illegally. Domestically cut logs are processed locally and are typically used in construction. Exports of wood and wood products are small and imports are negligible. The import tariff on logs is 5%. The efficiency in the forestry sector is low, and only a few species are commercially used. About 54% of the logs are processed, of which about half finally reach the market (MRN, 1990). The main part of the logs used in the timber industry are bought from sources other than the industry itself.

(2) Banana firms and other companies are expanding their plantations rapidly. The main products cultivated in Costa Rica are rice, coffee, fruits, sugar cane, beans, maize and sorghum (Hugo *et al.*, 1983). The Costa Rican tax structure for income and property taxes is regressive. Sales and other indirect taxes constituted 70% of total tax revenues in 1970. Although property taxes are low (in some cases about 1% of market value), tax evasion costs the country approximately 100 billion colones a year. One remedy may be to raise land prices by increasing land taxes, increase tax collection rates and prosecute tax evaders more effectively.

(3) Cattle ranchers have expanded their activities rapidly at the expense of forested areas in recent decades. However, this type of land conversion may be limited now because most of the land that can be sustainably used for pasture has already been cleared. In the 1950s and 1960s, there was a large increase in investment in cattle, encouraged by foreign aid and investment as well as government credit and provision of infrastructure. This increase of cattle ranching caused rapid

deforestation. The pasture trend peaked in the 1970s, but since then profits have decreased. Over 70% of the farmland is in pasture, while only 2.5% is in coffee and 1.1% is in bananas (Biesanz *et al.*, 1987).

(4) Squatting is taking place on both privately owned and government land. Some squatters produce agricultural outputs, but others sell the cleared land to cattle ranchers or other landowners. Buyers who buy 'in good faith' from squatters are not prosecuted. About twice as much is paid for cleared land as is paid for forests. By clearing the land, it is possible to get formal ownership of it (Blomström and Lundahl, 1989). Squatting by smallholders is a less significant part of the overall deforestation, although it may be locally important.

If ownership may be obtained with no costs other than those of clearing the land, the forests can be seen as a type of common property, while the cleared land is perceived as traditional private property. However, it is not the traditional case of undefined property rights and an open-access resource. We are here looking at insecure land tenure. This implies that there is no crowding effect on the stock of the resource, which is what occurs when each agent maximizes his own profit without taking into account the effect on the stock of the resource. There is a form of short-term property rights when deforestation occurs, but the property rights to the standing forests are not protected. The logger or squatter will continue to deforest only until the marginal cost of deforestation equals the marginal revenue, because of this structure of property rights. The social cost of deforestation will then be higher than the private cost since 'the world's' willingness-to-pay for the preservation of the Costa Rican forests will not be included in the private cost. Thus, deforestation would be driven by the difference in private and social objectives. For example, the loggers' main interest may be the profitability of the logging operation without much consideration about future, alternative uses of the land.

Deforestation may also be caused by high private discount rates that diminish the future value of forests. The impacts of tropical forests are often more significant in the long term than in the short term. However, the regenerative capacity of tropical forests is low, and the discounting of future environmental benefits often makes it more profitable to harvest forest resources as quickly as possible. Forest investments, such as replanting, take a long time to yield returns, and individuals therefore find little attraction in conservation and reforestation activities. In many developing countries, private market rates are very high and often exceed the rate that would be socially justifiable. Poor people often face even higher discount rates because of credit constraints. Finally, in addition to sectoral policies, economy-wide tax policies may also have a significant effect on deforestation rates.

9.6 Modelling approach

To summarize, the main reasons for deforestation and thereby erosion are as follows: (1) the price of land is too low because the full social opportunity value of rain forests is not included; (2) undefined property rights make the private cost of deforestation lower than the social cost; (3) discount rates may be too high, implying that future gains from forests are lower than the gains from deforestation today; and (4) impacts of economy-wide policies.

9.6.1 Relevant past research

CGE models have been applied before to environmental problems, mainly those involving air pollution and pollution taxes. Some relevant CGE models are briefly reviewed below.

Bergman's (1990a, 1990b) model is designed to simulate the effects of environmental regulation and energy policy on the Swedish economy. The environmental market failure is corrected by the creation of a market for emission permits. The cost of emission permits for carbon dioxide, sulphur and nitrogen is included in the cost functions. Jorgensen and Wilcoxon (1990) analyse the economic impact of environmental regulations in the USA by simulating long-term growth with and without environmental regulations. The abatement cost share in total costs is estimated for each industry, as are the share of investment in pollution control equipment and cost of pollution control devices in motor cars. The model is run with and without these costs to estimate economic impacts.

There are few examples of CGE models dealing with the impact on the economy of overexploitation of natural resources. Panayotou and Sussengkarn (1992) construct a model against the background of environmental problems in Thailand. The sources of the environmental issues are economic growth, exchange rate problems and government policies promoting deforestation. This implies that every unit of production in each sector generates a fixed amount of air pollution or deforestation. The environmental impacts are not part of the model per se, since the environmental degradation or improvement is not fed back into the model so as to affect future production and consumption decisions. The results include the findings that export taxes on rice and rubber increase investment in soil conservation, increase the use of agrochemicals and shift land from rubber to rice.

Little work has been done on modelling undefined property rights in a general equilibrium context, where the results may differ from those of a partial equilibrium model. Devarajan (1997) suggests that it may be useful to include a partial equilibrium model in the general equilibrium framework by first removing the first-order condition that labour is paid the value of its marginal product in some sectors and then replacing it with a condition that reflects the suboptimal behaviour of the sector. This helps to analyse the effects of policy interventions on deforestation. The model has to be dynamic to include both stock and flow effects of deforestation.

Unemo (1996) models the suboptimal use of land in Botswana that is caused by overgrazing of cattle due to undefined property rights to the land (see Section 8.6.1). In order to model property-rights-related behaviour in Costa Rican forests, we assume that the private cost of deforestation is lower than the social opportunity value of the forests when property rights are undefined. When property rights are defined, the social value of the rain forests is incorporated in the utility functions of the squatters and therefore in the private cost of deforestation. This facilitates analysis of the role of undefined property rights, following Chichilnisky (1993).

9.6.2 General features of the model

This open-economy CGE model is static, although it has certain implicit dynamic features because the discount rate is included in the future valuation of forested land. It differs from the standard approach of CGE modelling by including undefined property rights and modifying the functioning of markets for logs and cleared land. Land cleared by squatters is assumed to be sold to the agricultural sector.

The model has two types of sectors. The tradable producing sectors (*T* sectors – forest, agriculture and industry) are assumed to be price takers on the world market in the standard Heckscher–Ohlin fashion. The non-tradable producing sectors (*N* sectors) are infrastructure and services. Further, there are two sectors that clear land: loggers, who supply the forest industry and exports, and squatters, who sell land to the agriculture sector. The domestic intersectorally mobile production factors are unskilled labour (ULABOUR), skilled labour (SLABOUR) and capital (CAPITAL). Logs (LOGS) and cleared land (DLAND) are specific to the forest and agriculture sectors, but logs can be traded on the world market. No reafforestation is possible.

Key elements of the model are summarized below – mathematical details are given in Appendix B, Section 9.9 and Persson and Munasinghe (1995).

Factor market equilibrium and the stock of forested land

The supplies of both labour and capital are assumed to be exogenously given, and for factor markets to clear these supplies must equal the demands for labour and capital, respectively (see Figure 9.5). Demands arise from producing sectors and from squatters and loggers. The demand for each production factor (capital or labour) within the *T* and *N* sectors, as well as deforestation sectors, is given by the partial derivative of the cost function for the relevant sector with respect to the price of the same production factor. Both loggers and squatters generate demand for unskilled labour for deforestation, but only loggers generate demand for capital.

Costa Rica's total area is divided into cleared land and forested land. Cleared land is produced through deforestation, depending on the definition of property rights, taxes and subsidies on the factors of production, and profits in the forest and agriculture sectors. Logs are assumed to be tradable. Thus, the demand for forest land by the logging sector and the world market price determine the rate of deforestation. This demand is equal to the partial derivative of the logging cost function with respect to the user cost of logs plus the net export of logs.

The supply of cleared land includes the stock of cleared land plus deforestation by squatters. The demand for cleared land (for agriculture) is set equal to the partial derivative of the agriculture sector cost function with respect to the user cost of cleared land. A given user price is greater (smaller) than its supply price by a percentage tax (subsidy).

Technology, costs and producer behaviour

Production factors are aggregated into a composite factor input *Y*. Next, DLAND is combined with CAPITAL to yield an aggregate, *R*, which in turn is combined with LOGS

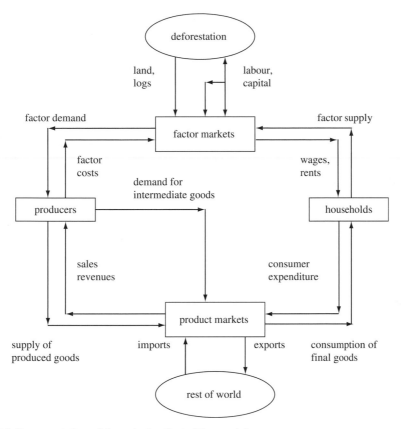

Figure 9.5. Representation of flows in the Costa Rica model.

to generate *M*. The latter is combined with SLABOUR to produce *V*, which is combined with ULABOUR to yield the composite *Y*. This aggregation uses a constant elasticity of substitution (CES) production function with constant returns to scale. Inputs and output are linked by a Leontief production function for each sector.

Because the technology exhibits constant returns to scale, the marginal cost and the average cost of production in a given sector can be expressed as a linear function of prices, relevant input–output coefficients and indirect tax rates. Producers are assumed to maximize profits. The producer output prices, P_i, in the tradables-producing sectors are equal to world market prices. Assuming perfect competition, this implies that pure profits are non-positive and output is non-negative (positive only if pure profits are zero). In the non-tradables-producing sectors, the sector-specific capital is endogenously adjusted so that price equals marginal cost.

Prices, domestic demand, foreign trade and market clearing

For goods produced in the tradables-producing sectors, the domestic producer price is equal to the world market price, and, in the non-tradables-producing sectors, the domestic user price is equal to the producer price times the tax rate. The intermediate demand for a good is given by the technology assumptions. Domestic final demand is given by a linear expenditure system, derived from the consumers' utility maximization. To equilibrate the market for a good, the net export for that good is defined as the difference between domestic supply and demand.

Deforestation sectors

Two sectors are responsible for deforestation. They interact with the rest of the economy through their demands for capital and labour by supplying forest products and clearing land for the rest of the economy and through changes in the relative prices of factor inputs and sectoral outputs.

The logging sector

The logging sector is assumed to have capital-intensive technology and to exhibit decreasing returns to scale – to reflect reductions in available forest area and illegal logging. The production of logs is assumed to depend only on labour and capital. A log-linear production function is used. Returns to the production factors fall with increased deforestation. Increased deforestation for logs is assumed not to affect the returns to deforestation for land, and vice versa. However, increased deforestation for logs lowers yields in the logging sector, and increased deforestation for land reduces returns in the squatting sector. With undefined property rights, loggers consider only the private cost of deforestation. When property rights are well defined, the opportunity value of saving the forests is included in the loggers' cost function.

Squatters

The forested land cleared by squatters is seen as a common property, although there is no crowding effect because the stock of forested land is not included in the squatters' production function. The base case assumes undefined property rights (Johansson and Löfgren, 1985). The squatters' production function for cleared land increases monotonically with labour inputs. Their total revenue from clearing the land is the price paid for cleared land. Part of the land cleared by squatters is sold to the agriculture sector. The rest is used for subsistence agriculture by the squatters. However, because both activities occur, the returns at the margin must be the same in each case. The squatters are assumed not to sell the timber or use it for other purposes, such as fuel.

The squatters' total private cost to clear the land depends only on the amount of labour needed in order to clear the land when property rights are undefined. This is the private cost, which does not include the future value of the forests and the cost of environmental damage. Therefore, the total social cost of deforestation is this private cost plus the future benefits from cleared forests that are foregone by clearing the land today. The future value of the forests is assumed to be greater than the value of the forests today. The analysis of the definition of property rights can then be accomplished through the simulation of two regimes. In the case of undefined property rights, the present-day squatters do not take the future value of the forests into account. When property rights are well defined, the squatters

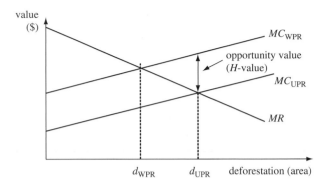

Figure 9.6. Definition of property rights.

own their land and take the future value of the forests into account. The owners of forested land (that is, the 'squatters aware of the future') decide whether to preserve the forests or clear the land.

When property rights are undefined, no market for the forests is available to squatters. A simple partial model of land clearing by squatters (in which each squatter receives an equal share of the private profits) is used to show that land will be cleared until marginal cost equals marginal revenue. This result corresponds to maximization of private profit, given insecure land tenure. When property rights are well defined, there is a market for the forests. The squatters take the future value of the forests into account, and they can choose to clear forested land or to preserve the forests. This is consistent with the condition for socially optimal forestry – that a tree should be harvested when the market value is equal to the shadow value (Hellsten, 1988). This result corresponds to the optimization of net social benefits.

The foregoing suggests that more land is cleared when property rights are undefined (point d_{UPR}) than when they are well defined (point d_{WPR}) – see Figure 9.6. This is because the squatters' marginal cost of deforestation is lower when property rights are undefined (curve MC_{UPR}) than when property rights are well defined (curve MC_{WPR}), and the cost includes the future value of the forests. MR is the marginal revenue curve.

When property rights are well defined, deforestation is increased by (1) a change of technology toward more efficient use of labour in the production of cleared land; (2) an increase of the time preference rate; and (3) an increase in the supply price of cleared land. Conversely, deforestation falls with rises in (1) future value of the forests and (2) price of labour. When property rights are undefined, the clearing of land is not affected by the future value of forests and the rate of time preference. The effects of other variables are the same as in the earlier case.

When property rights are well defined, the profit maximization condition for squatters includes the opportunity value of saving the forests for alternative uses or deforestation in a later time period. When property rights are undefined, this effect is absent, since future tenure is uncertain.

Macroeconomic closure and measures of welfare

The current account is assumed to be constant, and the surplus is defined as the sum of net exports. There are three welfare measures: disposable income (implicitly determined from the current account), green gross domestic product (GDP, determined as the sum of factor incomes plus a term that diminishes with increased deforestation to reflect the negative welfare effects) and utility (determined from the consumer utility function). Utility maximization results in a linear expenditure system for goods, based on a transformed Cobb–Douglas utility function.

9.6.3 Base case data, assumptions and limitations of the model

The data come from Solórzano *et al.* (1991), the national accounts (Banco Central de Costa Rica, 1990) and adjustments made by Raventós (1990). The input–output matrix was calculated from the disaggregated data used in Raventós (1990). Resource flows are shown in Figure 9.7.

The substitution elasticity between land and capital in the agriculture sector was set at 0.5. The substitution elasticity between the capital aggregate R and LOGS was assumed to be 0.8 in the forest sector, and the substitution elasticity between the aggregate M and SLABOUR was set at 0.8 in all producing sectors. Compared to other studies, such as Bergman (1990a, 1990b), these values appear reasonable. The remaining elasticities (involving land and logs in sectors that do not use those factors) were set to zero, which is consistent with a fixed coefficient (Leontief) technology. The parameters in the production functions for squatters and loggers are judgement-based estimates, assuming a labour-intensive technology for the squatters and a capital-intensive technology for the loggers.

There are some limitations. First, because of data adjustments, the results are more indicative than precise quantitative measures. Second, the static model provides comparative snapshots of the economy. Third, other linkages are not considered – e.g. migration, population growth, reafforestation, erosion and other external effects of deforestation.

Sector	Forest Agriculture Industry Service Infrastructure	Squatters Loggers	Net exports Domestic demand	Total demand
Forest Agriculture Industry Service Infrastructure	intermediate inputs	deforestation sectors	final demand	total production demand
Squatters	+lsq			deforestation demand
Loggers	+logf			
Labour	–lgl –lsq	+lsq +lgl		factor income
Capital	–lgk –lv	+lgk		
Land	+lv			
Indirect taxes	indirect taxes			government revenue
Total	output producing sectors	deforestation	total final demand	

Figure 9.7. Resource flows and data adjustments: lsq = labour input in squatting; logf = logging; lgl = labour input in logging; lgk = capital input in logging; lv = land value.

9.7 Main findings of the Costa Rica study

9.7.1 Numerical results

Some CGE results differ from what might be expected from the partial equilibrium frame-work discussed earlier due to substitution effects in producing sectors. Table 9.17 shows relative factor intensities in the base case (i.e. present state with undefined property rights). Property rights were defined and the opportunity value of forests (the *H*-value) was set 28% higher than the value derived from deforestation (Solórzano *et al.*, 1991). The discount rate was 10%. The results are shown in Table 9.18.

A comparison of the first and second columns shows that the definition of property rights results in a dramatic decrease in deforestation and an increase in the net import of logs (not shown). Activity in the forest sector increases greatly because logs can be

Table 9.17 *Initial capital intensities (percentages)*

Input	Forest	Agriculture	Industry
Land	0	14.81	0
Capital	31.93	14.68	11.73
Unskilled labour	25.63	19.41	8.25
Skilled labour	0.43	0.32	5.41

Table 9.18 *Effect of future valuation on production value (billion colones)*

		Property rights		
	Undefined	Defined (*H*-value)[a]		
Item	0.4792	0.2792		0.0792
Deforestation				
Logging	0.02	0	0.002	0.01
Squatting	0.02	0	0	0
Total	0.04	0	0.002	0.01
Production				
Forestry	0.552	0.713	0.711	0.691
Agriculture	13.984	13.876	13.876	13.879
Industry	18.477	18.416	18.417	18.424
Utility	0.232	0.232	0.232	0.232
Green GDP	31.962	31.972	31.971	31.971
Disposable income	37.681	37.679	37.679	37.679

[a] The *H*-value is the future value per unit of forest.

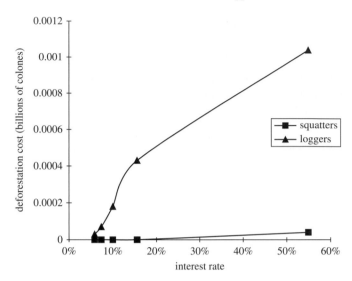

Figure 9.8. Effects of interest rates on the value of deforestation when property rights are well defined.

imported at a constant world market price. The increase in the price of capital is offset by decreases in the price for labour. Deforestation by squatters ceases, and activity in the agricultural sector declines slightly, because land (which is relatively less expensive than capital after the definition of property rights) and labour can be substituted for capital in the sector. The welfare measures remain constant because consumption of different goods is unchanged.

Sensitivity analysis (remaining columns in Table 9.18) shows that even a small opportunity value of forests reduces deforestation sharply. However, for deforestation to cease completely, a high value ($H = 0.4792$) is required. Both the opportunity value of forests and the interest rate are exogenous. Varying the interest rate while keeping the opportunity value fixed shows that high interest rates promote deforestation, and vice versa. The results of varying the interest rate may be deduced from Table 9.18 and Figure 9.8, because decreasing the interest rate is equivalent to increasing the opportunity value, and vice versa. Thus, while deforestation increases with interest rate, the relationship is not linear.

Next, the effects of taxes on logs, land, unskilled labour and capital were investigated, as summarized in Table 9.19. A 10% tax increase on logs generated predictable results, with no deforestation from loggers and no production in the forest sector. Resources were shifted to the agricultural sector, with an increase in deforestation for land and an increase in total deforestation. The increase in total deforestation can be explained by the lower price of unskilled labour, resulting from the discontinued production in the forest sector. The tax increase actually results in a higher level of utility, as well as an increase in green GDP.

Taxes and subsidies on land generate expected results, with changes in deforestation by squatters and roughly constant deforestation by loggers. Both the tax and the subsidy are

Table 9.19 *Effects of taxes and subsidies on product factors (billion colones)*

Item	Base case	Logs With tax	Logs With subsidy	Land With tax	Land With subsidy	Unskilled labour capital With tax	Unskilled labour capital With subsidy	Unskilled labour capital With tax	Unskilled labour capital With subsidy
Deforestation									
Logging	0.02	0	0.018	0.02	0.019	0.029	0.013	0.036	0.011
Squatting	0.02	0.044	0.004	0	0.255	0.21	0	0.02	0.02
Total	0.04	0.044	0.023	0.02	0.273	0.239	0.013	0.056	0.031
Production									
Forestry	0.552	0	1.562	0.672	0	0	0.689	0.515	0.574
Agriculture	13.984	14.204	13.748	13.877	15.122	14.922	13.877	13.987	13.983
Industry	18.477	19.248	17.017	18.430	17.656	17.946	18.424	18.487	18.471
Utility	0.232	0.243	0.214	0.231	0.226	0.229	0.232	0.232	0.233
Green GDP	31.962	32.017	31.848	31.960	31.757	31.797	31.965	31.943	31.958
Disposable income	37.681	37.748	37.561	37.678	37.592	37.62	37.679	37.680	37.682

Source: Authors' calculations.

distortionary and reduce utility as well as income and GDP. When land is taxed, land becomes relatively expensive compared to logs. Then resources are shifted from the agricultural sector to the forest sector, with a corresponding change in production. It is worth noting that the land subsidy dramatically increases deforestation for land, as empirically observed in Costa Rica earlier this century.

A 10% tax increase on unskilled labour adversely affects the forest sector and the industry sector, but logging continues and logs are exported. After the tax increase, the price of land is low relative to other production factors, and resources are shifted toward the agricultural sector. The price of unskilled labour in the deforestation sectors is actually reduced, because those sectors are considered to be 'informal' in the sense that their activities are, to a large extent, illegal and remain unaffected by government tax policies. Resources are shifted to the agricultural sector, with a large increase in land clearing by squatters as a result. These results also hold for the experiments with capital tax policies, although the magnitude of the changes is smaller.

Substitution effects are important when there are tax changes on goods produced in tradables sectors (Table 9.20). Tax changes on goods from the forest sector generate few economy-wide effects because this sector is small compared with the others. The industrial sector (which uses forest products relatively intensively as an intermediate input) gains from the tax reduction and grows, while the forest sector itself suffers. The effects are reversed for a doubling of the tax on forest products. Deforestation remains largely unaffected in both cases.

When the tax on agricultural products is reduced to half, the agricultural sector actually decreases, as does the forest sector. This is due to an elevated price of unskilled labour,

Table 9.20 *Effects of changes in taxes on final products (billion colones)*

| | | Sector (change relative to original tax rate) | | | | | |
| | | Forestry | | Agriculture | | Industry | |
Item	Base case	Half	Double	Half	Double	Half	Double
Deforestation							
Logging	0.02	0.02	0.02	0.02	0.02	0.02	0.02
Squatting	0.02	0.02	0.02	0.019	0.022	0.018	0.025
Total	0.04	0.04	0.04	0.039	0.042	0.038	0.045
Production							
Forestry	0.552	0.528	0.609	0.405	0.902	0.16	1.363
Agriculture	13.984	13.984	13.985	13.258	15.706	13.964	14.03
Industry	18.477	18.503	18.418	19.243	16.663	18.268	18.909
Utility	0.232	0.229	0.24	0.135	0.459	0.064	0.572
Green GDP	31.962	31.941	31.98	31.589	32.815	31.324	33.253
Disposable income	37.681	37.669	37.709	37.317	38.544	37.051	38.984

Source: Calculations from contributing authors.

which both sectors use relatively intensively. The industrial sector benefits because it uses agricultural products extensively as intermediate inputs, and capital becomes the least expensive production factor. Deforestation for logs remains constant, while deforestation for land is reduced. Utility, income and green GDP are reduced. A double tax on agricultural products generates the opposite effects. A tax on products from the industrial sector generates the same effects as a tax on agricultural products, although the magnitude is larger.

A dynamic version of this model, which captures the intertemporal optimization behaviour in the economy, is described in Persson (1994). This is a two-period model, which allows consumers and producers to consider the future effects of policy changes in their decisions in the first period. The opportunity value of forest conservation (the *H*-value) is endogenous and influenced by relative prices and the size of forests. Further, capital investments are endogenous, as is the domestic interest rate.

The qualitative dynamic model confirms the robustness of the results of the static model. Well defined property rights and lower taxes on capital reduce deforestation.

9.7.2 Conclusions

The results of the CGE study support the more conventional partial equilibrium approach that establishing property rights tends to decrease deforestation. The reason is that such rights allow forest users to capture the future benefits of reduced logging damage today. Initially, this potentially avoidable loss is presumed to be 28% of the value of the residual stand (Solórzano *et al.*, 1991). Using an interest rate of 10%, the deforestation is dramatically reduced to 5% of the base level as both loggers and squatters internalize deforestation losses and reduce the corresponding activities. Large reductions in deforestation occur even when the estimate of logging damage is substantially reduced. The CGE results concerning the effects of the discount-rate changes parallel the predictions of partial equilibrium models – higher interest rates promote deforestation, while lower interest rates contribute to conservation.

The CGE approach also clearly identifies the indirect effects arising from intersectoral linkages. This impact must be combined with the direct effects attributable to policies that are specific to the forest sector to determine the total impact. For example, partial equilibrium analysis predicts that stumpage price increases act directly to reduce logging, yet the model shows that, while deforestation from logging indeed declines, total deforestation nevertheless increases. This phenomenon arises from indirect linkages captured by the general equilibrium analysis. The contraction of the logging and forest industry sectors shifts resources toward agriculture, and, as agriculture expands, deforestation increases.

Because of intersectoral resource flows, the CGE captures indirect effects of economy-wide changes in wages that are different from partial equilibrium results. If wages of unskilled labour were increased (e.g. due to minimum wage legislation), the model predicts that deforestation could worsen instead of decline. Although logging declines due to increased direct costs of higher-wages, this is more than offset by the indirect effect of intersectoral flows because the industrial sector (where minimum-wage legislation is more binding) is much more adversely affected by the higher labour costs. Labour and capital thus tend to flow to agriculture, leading to the conversion of even more forest land for farming.

Both the preceding two examples underline the importance of pursuing sectoral reforms in the context of growth. Without alternative employment opportunities, reducing logging activities tends to direct labour and capital resources toward agriculture, industry and other sectors. Expansion of some of these sectors may lead to a second round of effects on forestry, which could ultimately result in more severe deforestation. A dynamic CGE model, in which the value of forest conservation, capital accumulation and the domestic interest rate are endogenized, gives essentially the same results as the static CGE model presented here.

9.8 Appendix A: ECOGEM–Chile CGE model summary

9.8.1 Characteristics of the model

The main indices used in the model equations are as follows:

i, j productive sectors or activities
l types of work or occupational categories
h household income groups (quintiles)
g public spending categories
f final demand spending categories
r trade partners
p different types of pollutants

Production

Production is modelled by the CES/CET nested functions (i.e. constant elasticity of sub-stitution – transformation). If constant returns to scale are assumed, each sector produces while minimizing costs:

$$\text{min } PKEL_i KEL_i + PABND_i ABND_i \text{ subject to } XP_i = \left[a_{kel,i} KEL_i^{\rho_i^p} + a_{abnd,i} ABND_i^{\rho_i^p} \right]^{1/\rho_i^p}.$$

Income distribution

Production-generated income is allocated in the form of wages, capital returns and taxes among the domestic economy, the government and the domestic and international financial institutions.

Consumption

Households distribute their income between saving and consumption through an ELES utility function (extended linear expenditure system). This function also incorporates the minimum subsistence consumption independently of the level of income:

$$\text{max } U = \sum_{i=1}^{n} \mu_i \ln(C_i - \theta_i) + \mu_s \ln\left(\frac{S}{cpi}\right)$$

subject to

$$\sum_{i=1}^{n} PC_i C_i + S = YD \quad \text{and} \quad \sum_{i=1}^{n} \mu_i + \mu_s = 1,$$

where U is the consumer utility; C_i is the consumption of good i; θ is the subsistence consumption; S is the saving; cpi is the price of savings; and μ is the consumption marginal propensity for each good and to save.

Other final demands

After defining the intermediate and household demands, the remaining final demands (investment, government spending and trade margin) are included as a fixed share of total final demand.

Public finances

The following types of taxes and transfers are defined: direct taxation on labour (differ-entiated by occupational category), taxes on firms and income (differentiated by quintile). We also define import tariffs and subsidies, export taxes and subsidies (by sector), a value added tax (VAT, for domestic and imported goods, by sector) and some specific taxes.

As a closure condition for public finances, the model allows two alternatives. First, government spending is defined as fixed and equal to the original level previous to any simulation, allowing it to adjust through some selected tax or government transfer. Alternatively, government spending is allowed to vary, while taxes and transfers are kept fixed.

Foreign sector

To incorporate the foreign sector, the Armington assumption is used to break down goods by place of origin, allowing imperfect substitution between domestic and imported goods and services. The domestic supply receives a similar treatment, modelled by a CET function to distinguish between domestic market and exports. For imports:

$$\min PD \cdot XD + PM \cdot XM \text{ subject to } XA = \left[a_d XD^\rho + a_m XM^\rho \right]^{1/l\rho},$$

where PD and PM are the prices of domestic and imported goods, and XD and XM are the respective amounts; XA stands for the good made up of both or the 'Armington good'. Parameter ρ is the substitution elasticity between both goods. For exports:

$$\max PD \cdot XD + PE \cdot ES \text{ subject to } XP = \left[\gamma_d XD + \gamma_e ES^{\hat{\lambda}} \right]^{1/l\lambda},$$

where PE is the price of the exported good and ES is the respective amount; XP is the sector's total production. Parameter λ is the substitution elasticity between both goods.

Factor market equilibrium conditions

To achieve labour market equilibrium, labour supply and demand are made equal for each occupational category, where supply is determined on the basis of real wages. As for the capital market, a single type of capital is assumed, which may or may not have sector mobility depending on the imposed elasticity.

Short-term or long-term elasticities could be chosen for the substitution between the factor nest and non-energy-producing inputs, as well as for the CES function between capital-energy and labour, between capital and energy, and for the various energy-producing sectors.

Closure conditions

The closure condition for the public sector has already been determined. Also, as is usual in such models, the value of the demand for private investment must equal the economy's net aggregate saving (from firms, households, government and net flows from abroad). The last closing rule refers to balance of payment equilibrium. This equation will be introduced into the model through Walras' Law.

9.8.2 Reduction of emissions in the model

Three options help to reduce polluting emissions: (1) reducing production of highly polluting sectors; (2) changing energy-producing inputs used in the productive process or in consumption (emissions could be reduced by allowing substitution toward less contaminating energy inputs); and (3) introducing 'end of pipe' technologies (e.g. filters, treatment plants, etc.).

Energy-producing inputs (i.e. coal, petrogas, electricity and gas) are associated with the emission of 13 types of pollutants (not all of them discharged by the energy-producing inputs) through emission factors. These emission factors link the use of each money unit spent in the input with the amount of emissions of each pollutant in physical units. The total volume of emissions in the economy for each type of pollutant is therefore determined by:

$$E_p = \sum_i v_i^p \cdot XP_i + \sum_i \pi_i^p \left(\sum_j XAp_{ij} + \sum_h XAc_{ih} + \sum_f XA \cdot FD_f^i \right)$$

that is, by the sum of all the emissions of the pollutant 'p' caused by all the productive sectors 'i,j' of the input–output matrix (74 sectors for Chile) generated in their productive processes per se, independently of the emissions associated with the use of polluting inputs, in addition to all the emissions derived from the use of polluting intermediate inputs in the productive processes of all the sectors, in their consumption by households 'h' and by other components of the final demand 'f'.

9.9. Appendix B: Costa Rica CGE model summary

9.9.1 Factor market equilibrium and the stock of forested land

$$K = \sum_{j \in T,N} \frac{\partial C_j}{\partial P_K^U} + k^{\log},$$

where P_K^U is the user price of capital and $k^{\log}$ is the capital used in deforestation by loggers, and

$$U = \sum_{j \in T,N} \frac{\partial C_j}{\partial P_U^U} + l^{sq} + l^{\log},$$

$$L = \sum_{j \in T,N} \frac{\partial C_j}{\partial P_L^U} + l^{sq} + l^{\log},$$

where P_U^U is the user price of unskilled labour, l^{sq} and $l^{\log}$ are the labour used in deforestation by squatters and loggers, respectively, and P_L^U is the user price of skilled labour. Further,

$$\alpha \, d^{\text{forest}} = \frac{\partial \, \text{forest}}{\partial P_F^U} - f^{\text{nexp}},$$

where d^{forest} is deforestation from the logging sector, P_F^U is the user price of logs, f^{nexp} is the net export of logs and α is a fixed coefficient reflecting the amount of timber extracted per unit of deforested land. Also,

$$\frac{\partial C_{\text{agric}}}{\partial P_{DL}^U} - DL^* - d^o = 0.$$

where DL^* is the stock of cleared land and d^o is squatter deforestation.

The user price, P_j^U, exceeds the supply price, P_j^S, by a percentage tax, T_j:

$$P_j^U = P_j^S(1 + T_j); \quad j = DLAND, LABOUR, CAPITAL$$
$$P_{\log}^U = P_{\log}^{WM}(1 + T_{\log}).$$

9.9.2 Technology, costs and producer behaviour

The gross output in sector j is given by

$$X_j = \min\left[\frac{Y_j}{A_j}, \frac{X_{ij}}{a_{ij}}\right] \quad i, j \in T, N,$$

where Y_j is a composite input of production factors in sector j, X_{ij} is the input of output from sector i in sector j, and A_j and a_{ij} are Leontief input–output coefficients.

The marginal and average cost in sector j is given by

$$C_j = P_{Yj} A_j + \sum_i P_i^D a_{ij} + t_j; \quad i, j \in T, N,$$

where P_{Yj} is the producer price of the composite input of production factors, P_i^D is the domestic price of sector i output, A_j is the use of production factors per sector j output, a_{ij} is the use of sector i input per sector j output and t_j is indirect tax per unit of sector j output. We have

$$P_i - C_i \leq 0; \quad i \in T,$$
$$(P_i - C_i) X_i = 0; \quad i \in T,$$
$$X_i = 0; \quad i \in T,$$
$$P_i = C_i; \quad i \in N.$$

9.9.3 Prices, domestic demand, foreign trade and market clearing

The domestic user price of goods produced in sector i, is given by

$$P_i^D = (1 + \sigma_i) P_i^W e = (1 + \sigma_i) P_i; \quad i \in T,$$
$$P_i^D = (1 + \sigma_i) P_i; \quad i \in N,$$

where P_i^W is the world market price of good i, P_i is the producer price of good i, e is the exchange rate and s_i is the ad valorem tax rate on good i. Further,

$$X_i = \sum_{j \in T,N} a_{ij} X_j + D_i + Z_i; \quad i \in T,$$
$$X_i = \sum_{j \in T,N} a_{ij} X_j + D_i; \quad i \in N,$$

where D is the domestic final demand and Z is the net export.

9.9.4 Deforestation sectors

Logging sector

$$d^{\text{forest}} = \left(k^{\log}\right)^{\alpha} \left(l^{\log}\right)^{\beta}, \qquad \alpha + \beta < 1.$$

Well defined property rights

$$\left(l^{\log}\right) = \left(\frac{P_{\text{U}}^{\text{U}} + \partial H(d)/\partial(l^{\log})}{\beta P_{\log}(k^{\log})^{\alpha}}\right)^{1/(\beta-1)},$$

$$\left(k^{\log}\right) = \left(\frac{P_{\text{U}}^{\text{U}} + \partial H(d)/\partial(l^{\log})}{\alpha P_{\log}(l^{\log})^{\beta}}\right)^{1/(\alpha-1)}.$$

Undefined property rights

$$\left(d^{\log}\right) = \left(\frac{P_{\text{K}}^{\text{U}}}{\alpha P_{\log}(l^{\log})^{\beta}}\right)^{\alpha/(\alpha-1)} \left(\frac{P_{\text{U}}^{\text{U}}}{\beta P_{\log}(k^{\log})^{\alpha}}\right)^{\beta/(\beta-1)}.$$

Squatters

$$d^{o} = d(l^{\text{sq}}) = l^{\text{sq}^{\gamma}}; \gamma < 1,$$

with

$$d(0) = 0,$$
$$d_{l}(l^{\text{sq}}) > 0,$$
$$d_{ll}(l^{\text{sq}}) < 0$$

and

$$\lim_{n \to \infty} d(l^{\text{sq}}) = B,$$

where n is the number of squatters, l^{sq} is the labour used in the clearing of the land and B is the total amount of land available for deforestation.

$$I^{\text{S}}(d^{o}) = P_{\text{DL}}^{\text{S}} d^{o},$$

where P_{DL}^{S} is the supply price of cleared land.

$$C^{s}(d^{o}) = P_{\text{L}}^{\text{sq}} d^{-1}(d^{o}),$$

where P_{L}^{sq} is the price of labour in squatting.

$$\frac{H(F)}{1+i} > 1.$$

Undefined property rights

$$d_i^o = \frac{1}{N} d(l^{\text{sq}}),$$

where N is the total number of squatters and their total cleared land is given by

$$d^o = \sum_{i=1}^{N} d_i^o,$$

$$g^s(d^o) = I^S(d^o) - C^S(d^o),$$

$$g_i^S(d^o) = \frac{1}{N} g^S(d^o),$$

$$l^{\text{sq}}(P_{\text{DL}}, P_{\text{U}}) = \left(\frac{P_{\text{U}}}{\gamma P_{\text{DL}}}\right)^{\frac{1}{\gamma-1}},$$

$$d^o = \left(\frac{P_{\text{U}}}{\gamma P_{\text{DL}}}\right)^{\frac{\gamma}{\gamma-1}}.$$

Well defined property rights

$$g^{\text{fs}}(d^o) = P_{\text{DL}}^S d^o - C^S(d^o) - \frac{H(d^o)}{1+i},$$

$$l^{\text{sq}} = \left(\frac{P_{\text{U}} + \dfrac{\partial(H(l^{\text{sq}^\gamma})/(1+i))}{\partial l^{\text{sq}}}}{\gamma P_{\text{DL}}}\right)^{\frac{1}{\gamma-1}},$$

$$d^o = \left(\frac{P_{\text{U}} + \dfrac{\partial(H(l^{\text{sq}^\gamma})/(1-i))}{\partial l^{\text{sq}}}}{\gamma P_{\text{DL}}}\right)^{\frac{\gamma}{\gamma-1}}.$$

Macroeconomic closure

$$\sum_{i \varepsilon T, N} P_i Z_i = S,$$

where S is the current account surplus.

$$\text{GNP} = P_K^U K + P_L^U L + P_U^U U + P_{DL}^U DL^* + \sum_{j \varepsilon T, N} \sigma_j X_j - \Delta(d^o + d^{\log}) H(1),$$

subject to

$$\max U = \prod_i D_i^{b_i}; \qquad \sum_i b_i = 1; \qquad i \in N, T,$$

$$I - \sum_i P_i^D D_i = 0.$$

Part IV
Sub-national sectoral and system applications

10

Energy-sector applications[1]

This chapter applies the sustainomics framework to the energy sector. Section 10.1 reviews energy-development issues and status. In Section 10.2, a comprehensive and integrated framework for sustainable energy development (SED) is developed, which identifies practical sustainable energy options by taking into account multiple actors, multiple criteria, multilevel decision making and many impediments and constraints. A case study of Sri Lanka is presented in Sections 10.3 and 10.4, which illustrates application of the SED approach to electricity planning and renewable energy. Both cost–benefit analysis (CBA) and multicriteria analysis (MCA) are used to show how environmental and social externalities may be incorporated into traditional least-cost power system planning. The study is relatively unique in focusing on assessing such concerns at the system level (including technology choices), instead of the more conventional project-level analysis. Sustainable energy policies for Sri Lanka are identified. Section 10.5 describes an SED application in South Africa, using MCA to assess the social, environmental and economic trade-offs arising from policy options relating to electricity supply and household energy use. Finally, Section 10.6 shows that decentralized energy may be more sustainable than centralized generation options for power system expansion in the UK.

10.1 Energy and sustainable development

10.1.1 General background

Sustainable energy development (SED) involves the harnessing of energy resources for human use in a manner that makes development more sustainable. Energy production and use have strong links with the economic, social and environmental dimensions of sustainable development. First, economic growth depends on energy services such as heating, refrigeration, cooking, lighting, communications, motive power and electricity. Over two billion people cannot access affordable energy services, impeding their opportunities for economic development and improved living standards.

---

1 The valuable contributions of P. Meier to this chapter are gratefully acknowledged. Some parts of the chapter are based on material adapted from: Meier and Munasinghe (1994), Munasinghe (1980b, 1990a, 1995b) and Munasinghe and Meier (1993, 2003a).

Second, energy is a basic social need that affects human well-being. Wide disparities in access to affordable commercial energy and energy services in both urban and rural areas threaten social stability. Access to decentralized small-scale energy technologies is an important element of successful poverty alleviation. Women and children, who are relatively more dependent on traditional fuels, suffer disproportionately.

Third, there are many environmental links (mainly negative), since energy production and use continue to be a primary source of local, transnational and global pollution. Specific impacts include: groundwater and air contamination; land degradation and changes in use; marine and coastal pollution; ecosystems destruction and loss of biodiversity; damage to health, structures and natural systems from SO_2 and NOx and ash particulates which degrade air quality; and, finally, greenhouse gas emissions which have harm the global environment (see Chapter 5).

Energy for sustainable development will require: the more efficient use of energy, especially at the point of end use in buildings, transportation and production processes; increased reliance on renewable energy sources; and accelerated development and deployment of new energy technologies. Some strategies and policies for globally achieving SED include: encouraging greater international cooperation in areas such as technology procurement, harmonization of environmental taxes and emissions trading, and energy efficiency standards for equipment and products; adopting policies and mechanisms to increase access to energy services through modern fuels and electricity; building capacity among all stakeholders to improve energy decisions; advancing innovation, with balanced emphasis on all steps of the innovation chain; encouraging competitiveness in energy markets to reduce total costs of energy services to end users; cost-based prices, including phasing out all forms of subsidies for fossil fuels and nuclear power and internalizing external environmental and health impacts; encouraging greater energy efficiency; and developing and/or diffusing new technologies to wider markets.

Recent trends

Economic growth prior to the 1970s was fuelled by increasing energy demand. After 1971, as a direct consequence of passing on the oil price increases to consumers, decoupling between economic growth and energy demand growth was achieved in industrialized countries (ICs). They were able to achieve better energy management by restructuring and through energy-efficient technologies. Such decoupling emerged only later in developing countries (DCs), because energy prices were initially subsidized and kept low for socio-political reasons. The current increase in oil prices will continue to curtail demand growth globally. As DCs are still in the early stages of development, and have higher growth rates, there is greater scope for making development more sustainable by delinking economic growth and energy consumption (Munasinghe, 1991).

World primary energy demand is projected to expand by more than one-half between 2005 and 2030, or 1.6% annually (IEA, 2005). Over two-thirds of this growth will come from DCs, where per capita use is low. At present, DCs comprise over three-quarters of the world's population, but utilize only one-quarter of the world's energy. Most of this population live in rural areas, have little or no access to commercial energy, and rely heavily on traditional biomass fuels such as wood, crop waste and animal dung. The OECD countries, in contrast, consume over one-half of the world's energy and nearly ten times more energy per person than DCs. Per capita use of primary energy in North America was 280 GJ in 2000, over eleven times the Sub-Saharan African value. In OECD Europe and OECD Pacific, per capita energy use was about 142 and 180 GJ, respectively (Goldemberg and Johansson, 2004).

Energy demand has been growing rapidly in DCs in recent decades, creating supply shortages. Making energy development more sustainable in the developing world will require reconciliation of economic growth (including increased use of energy) and poverty alleviation efforts, with responsible stewardship of the environment. This has to be done without overburdening already weak economies and without diverting funds from other key goals such as education and healthcare.

Energy–economy linkages

Modern economies cannot function without commercial energy. Figure 10.1 shows how energy consumption will continue to rise, with fossil fuels such as oil, natural gas and coal playing the dominant role.

The major increase will be in DCs, driven by economic expansion, urbanization, the increasing penetration of energy-using products, the transition from traditional energy sources to commercial sources and population growth.

The links between total energy use, electricity use and economic output are shown in Figure 10.2. One hopeful trend is that technological progress and efficiency improvements have reduced the energy intensity of economic production (i.e. lower requirements of energy per unit of economic output). Electricity will continue to play an increasingly important social role, as a safe, clean and convenient form of energy.

Oil markets

As world oil demand continues to grow, it is not surprising that prices are also rising steadily, in anticipation of tightening supplies. This will have serious implications for development,

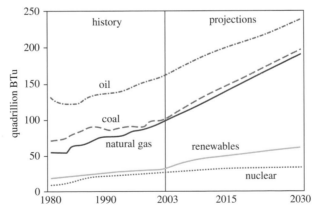

Figure 10.1. World marketed energy use by type (1980–2030). Sources: International Energy Annual, 2003; EIA (2006).

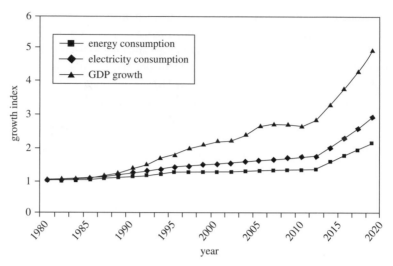

Figure 10.2. World energy and electricity use and GDP, 1980–2020. Source: Munasinghe (2004d).

especially for poorer oil-importing countries whose growth will suffer, and poor people who cannot afford expensive energy. Internationally, higher oil prices will help to equilibrate markets by curtailing demand growth and stimulating supply. However, the era of cheap and abundant oil appears to be coming to an end, barring an unforeseen (and highly unlikely) new development.

The status of oil supplies may be understood by examining the 'P50' reserves values, which is an important benchmark used by industry analysts to make assessments (Bentley, 2005). It designates the 50% probable industry estimate for the size of a field's reserves. P50 estimates correlate well with 'proved plus probable' reserves. P50 discovery data and geological estimates suggest that about two-thirds of the world's oil-producing countries are currently past their *resource-limited* peak of conventional oil production. According to Chevron, oil production has declined in 33 of the world's 48 largest oil-producing countries, including the USA, Iran, Libya, Indonesia, the UK and Norway. Others, such as Russia, China and Mexico, will soon go past peak. Figure 10.3 shows how the world has lived off past exploration success, with large finds being drawn down since about 1980 – the historical turning point when global production began to exceed new discoveries. The discovery peak was around 1960, while production may peak during 2005–2015 – based on a Hubbert's curve type of analysis, which assumes that the future production peak timing is related to the shape and peak of the past discovery curve.

10.1.2 Environmental and social issues

Oil- and coal-fired plants not only have national impacts, but also regional and global environmental and health effects. Electricity is an important form of energy, which has relatively few environmental and health consequences at the point of end use, but key

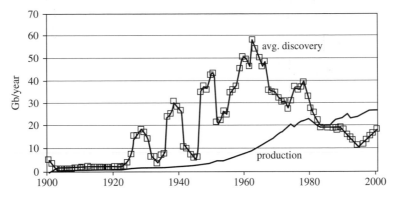

Figure 10.3. 'P50' discovery and production of oil and non-gas liquids during 1900–2000, in gigabarrels (Gb) per year. Source: IHS Energy. The discovered oil totals 2033 Gb; the produced oil is 46% of this (934 Gb).

environmental and social issues arise from power generation. Even sources like hydro, solar and wind power, geothermal energy and ocean energy, which are perceived to be 'clean', have some negative impacts on the surroundings.

National issues – conventional energy
Fossil-fired plants

Currently 65% of the world's commercial energy is produced from fossil fuels – oil (7.7%), coal (39.5%) and natural gas (18.2%) (EIA, 2005). In the case of oil- and coal-fired plants, major public health risks arise from emissions of sulphur dioxide, carbon monoxide, nitrogen oxides, hydrocarbons, polycyclic organic matter and additional pollutants from coal, such as fly ash, trace metals and radionuclides. Exposure to these pollutants leads to increased incidence of respiratory disease, toxicity and cancer. Disposal of solid waste leads to health risks associated with leaching and groundwater contamination. Natural gas-fired plants pose a public health risk from nitrogen oxides and particulate emissions, but are significantly less hazardous to health in comparison with oil- or coal-fired plants. Coal mining, transportation and washing also have substantial adverse impacts on environment.

Fuel oil emits 85–90% as much carbon dioxide as coal, and natural gas under 60% for the same thermal content. Without treatment or control, coal emits more particulate matter (PM), sulphur dioxide and nitrogen oxides than any other fuel. While PM emissions from oil and gas are negligible, coal emits almost 10% of its oil equivalent in weight as ash and other matter. Sulphur dioxide emissions depend on sulphur content of the fuels, while emissions of nitrogen oxides are not significantly different between fuels, with gas emitting only two-thirds that of coal.

Nuclear plants

Nuclear fission reactors currently produce over 15% of electricity worldwide and were intended to replace fossil-fuelled capacity in the medium-term (EIA, 2005). Safety concerns, driven by accidents at Three Mile Island and Chernobyl, have made nuclear energy politically and economically unattractive. However, in a few countries like France and Japan, nuclear reactors are used extensively. Though nuclear energy does not emit atmospheric pollutants like fossil-fuel technologies, the fission reaction generates long-lived, highly radioactive wastes whose ultimate disposal is extremely controversial. Nuclear power also causes groundwater contamination. It is more capital intensive than fossil-fuel power generation, and costs are controversial.

Occupational health risks, which may have intergenerational consequences, arise from exposure to radiation. Public health risks result from low-level radiation from power production and waste disposal. High exposure to radiation is possible in the event of major accidents, with potential long-term health implications. While actual public risk may be relatively small, public fears of risks from nuclear plants and waste disposal sites are extremely strong and cannot be dismissed (often based on risk-averse reactions to potentially catastrophic, though rare, accidents).

Hydroelectricity

Almost 7% of worldwide electricity is produced from large hydroelectric dams that utilize reservoirs or waterfalls – see Section 6.4 for details.

National issues – new and renewable energy

In 2002, biomass, wind and geothermal were the major contributors among new and renewable energy sources (excluding hydroelectricity). A six-fold increase is projected by 2030 (see Sections 15.4 and 10.2.3).

Small hydro

Mini- and microhydro plants are popular for providing local power supply and irrigation without the massive environmental and social impacts arising from large hydro schemes. Microhydro-projects are currently underway in many DCs, which have the advantage of providing electricity to rural areas beyond the central grid (Munasinghe, 1987).

Solar energy

Advances in solar thermal technologies and direct electricity generation by photovoltaics (PVs) have reduced costs significantly since the late 1990s.[2] While these techniques pose no significant occupational and health risks at the generation stage, some environmental impacts may arise from the loss of land use resulting from its high land intensity. Solar energy is constrained by its limited applicability.

Geothermal energy

Geothermal energy uses the Earth's heat to drive steam turbines. Cost-competitive exploitation of geothermal energy with current technology is largely limited to the volcanically active Pacific 'Ring of Fire' and the Mediterranean, where suitable steam reservoirs are

---

[2] Private communication: RE Focus (2005), 'Prospects for solar energy', pp. 25–9.

located within one mile of the surface. Geothermal steam carries with it a number of atmospheric pollutants, including carbon dioxide, mercury and radon. Currently, the toxins are commonly re-injected into the reservoir. With recent advances, hot dry rock technology will be competitive with conventional geothermal technology and fossil-fuelled plants.

Biomass power generation

A wide range of options exists for converting biomass into electric power. Dendro-thermal power plants use boilers to burn wood from fast-growing species (grown on dedicated plantations) to generate electricity through a conventional steam cycle. Most potential applications are for remote power supply in DCs. Concerns about the effects of dedicated fuelwood plantations on the local environment and competing land uses impose constraints on the widespread adoption of dendro-thermal power supply schemes. It is economical to use biomass for energy purposes only where it is available as a byproduct of other processes. Another source of biomass for power generation is municipal solid waste, whose use is limited both by public concern over emissions and the shortage of concentrated sources of solid waste. In tropical areas, the water content of solid wastes reduces its attractiveness as a fuel.

Wind power

Large grid-connected wind generators (75 kW–450 kW) in multiturbine 'wind farms' now supplement power grids in many countries. The total installed wind-power capacity was about 47 300 MW in 2004, with Germany, Spain and the USA accounting for 35%, 18% and 14%, respectively (MIT, 2005). However, wind energy provided only 0.3% of the total electricity supply. Research is underway on combined wind- and gas-turbine power supply schemes that would provide reliable power on demand, at minimal cost. Although wind generators do not produce air or water emissions, the larger turbines on the landscape are visually and aesthetically unappealing, emit acoustic noise, generate electromagnetic interference and present a hazard to birds.

Ocean energy

Pilot plant experience with ocean thermal energy conversion (OTEC) indicates that temperature differences of 20°C between surface waters and waters about 1000 m below are sufficient for economic power generation. There is a vast potential for this energy source in the tropical oceans. Due to high capital requirements and the unproven technology, no large commercial plants are functioning. Environmental concerns include effects on sea life and the atmospheric release of carbon dioxide stored in deep ocean waters. Conversion of wave energy into electricity is also in the R&D stage, although some commercial power plants (e.g. tidal power stations) are in operation. Impacts on marine organisms, shipping and fishing are potential concerns.

Transnational and global issues

Acid deposition is a serious transnational issue, resulting from oxides of sulphur and nitrogen emitted by fossil-fuel plants, falling to the ground as particulates and acid rain.

The transport of sulphur dioxide occurs over long distances (greater than 1000 km). Acid rain, caused by sulphur and nitrogen oxides, results in damage to vegetation and leads to acidification of streams and lakes, resulting in the destruction of aquatic ecosystems. They also cause corrosion, erosion and discoloration of buildings, monuments and bridges. Indirect effects on human health are caused by the concentration of heavy metals in acidified water and soil (USEPA, 2004).

Other important transnational issues include environmental and health impacts of radiation due to severe nuclear accidents (Chernobyl); oceanic and coastal pollution due to oil spills (*Amico Cadiz*, *Exxon Valdez* and the *Braer*); downstream siltation of river water in one nation, due to deforestation of water sheds and soil erosion in a neighbouring country; and changes in hydrological flow and water conditions caused by dams. Climate-change impacts due to greenhouse gas emissions are set out in Chapter 5.

10.1.3 Power-sector role and issues

Electricity is clean, versatile, easily accessible and simple to distribute. It is also essential to maintain a reasonable quality of life and for sustainable development. Thus, world electricity demand is increasing at over 1.5 times the growth rate of demand for primary energy. By 2040–2050, more than half the world's primary commercial energy sources would be utilized in electricity production.

Electricity in developing countries

Although electricity is essential to modern economies, over two billion people are without access to it. The industrialized countries contain about 15% of the world population, while consuming almost 60% of the globe's electricity. In DCs, per capita energy consumption is between one-third and one-fifteenth of industrialized countries (UN, 2006). While per capita energy and electricity consumption are generally correlated with per capita income (Figure 10.2), Europe and Japan are considerably less energy intensive than the USA. Meeting basic electricity needs (1 kWh per family per day) requires 60 GW more of generation, or less than 2% of currently installed global capacity. The cost of providing this additional power is about EUR 180 billion, or slightly over EUR 7 billion per year over 25 years (GENI, 2004). Worldwide electricity revenues were over EUR 800 billion in 2000. It is necessary also to supply population due to demographic growth of about 1.5% per year, or an additional one billion people up to 2030.

Electricity greatly enhances the quality of life in DCs, improving the health, education and productivity of the poor. Rural electrification (RE) also helps to retard migration from rural areas to cities and enhances opportunities for sustainable livelihoods. Electricity demand in DCs grew at 10% and 8% in the 1970s and 1980s, respectively, but declined to 6–7% in the 1990s and 2000s. World electricity consumption will double between 2003 and 2030, with non-OECD and OECD countries, respectively, accounting for 71% and 21% of this growth (EIA, 2006). The Asia Region (mainly China and India) dominates with almost two-thirds of the non-OECD total, and coal and hydro are the primary sources.

Power-sector problems

Electricity demand in many DCs has exceeded their power-generating capacities, resulting in frequent power shortages. Power cuts handicap productive activities and delay social development. On the output side, electricity shortages disrupt production. For example, power cuts in Sri Lanka during 1996 and 2001–2002 were estimated to have cost 1–2% of GDP (Munasinghe, 2003). Power shortages also restrict investment and employment – hindering production and requiring more costly investment for on-site electricity production or standby supplies (Munasinghe, 1990b).

Structural, institutional and financial problems further exacerbate electricity supply in DCs. Poor operating performances and maintenance of plants, high transmission and distribution system losses and high fuel consumption have resulted in unsustainable energy wastage and economic losses. The availability of generating capacity is below 60% for thermal plants in DCs, compared with over 80% in developed countries (World Bank, 1994a). Power plants in DCs consume 15–30% more fuel per unit of electricity than those in ICs (WRI, 1994).

Transmission and distribution system losses in DCs cost over $30 billion. Inadequate tariffs due to governmental policies and poor revenue collection due to inadequate metering, as well as poor accounting and billing, have led to large financial losses and difficulties in raising investment capital. While institution building has continued to progress, conflicts between governments' role as owner, and its role as operator of utilities, have affected sector performance. Opaque command and control management, poorly defined objectives, government interference in daily affairs and lack of financial autonomy have undermined institutional performance.

To meet growth in electricity demand, DCs will require several hundred billion US dollars per annum to finance future capital investments. Local capital is inadequate to meet these needs. Despite power-sector reform and privatization programmes encouraged by the donors, there is growing resistance in many DCs to selling off public assets in key sectors to private (mainly foreign) owners and skepticism about the 'benefits' claimed by privatization advocates. Furthermore, private investors are reluctant to re-enter DCs that continue to experience difficulties in servicing their foreign debt. Further, future power-sector expansion in DCs will have serious environmental impacts.

10.2 Framework for sustainable energy development

The sustainomics approach leads us to a comprehensive and integrated conceptual framework for energy-related decision making (Munasinghe, 1995b, 2002b). Najam and Cleveland (2003) identify three key energy–sustainable development links: (a) driving economic growth; (b) meeting basic human needs; and (c) stressing the environment – corresponding to the economic, social and environmental dimensions of the sustainable development triangle.

Power and energy planning must be part of, and closely integrated with, overall development planning and policy analysis to meet many specific, interrelated and frequently conflicting national objectives. Specific goals might include: (a) ensuring economic efficiency in the supply and use of all forms of energy, to maximize growth – other energy efficiency-related objectives are energy conservation and elimination of wasteful consumption, and saving scarce foreign exchange; (b) raising sufficient revenues from energy sales, to finance sector development; (c) addressing social concerns like basic energy needs of the poor, sustainable livelihoods and equity; (d) ensuring an adequate quality of energy supply; (e) diversifying supply, reducing dependence on foreign sources and meeting national security requirements; (f) contributing to development of special regions (particularly rural or remote areas) and priority sectors of the economy; (g) price stability; (h) preserving the environment, etc.

10.2.1 Integrated approach

Figure 10.4 summarizes a hierarchical decision making framework for sustainable energy development (SED) that takes into account multiple actors, multiple criteria, multilevel decision making and constraints. It may be implemented through a set of energy supply and demand management policy options.

The core of the SED framework is the multilevel analysis for integrated national energy planning (INEP) shown in the middle column (Munasinghe, 1980b, 1988). At the global level, there are exogenous constraints imposed on countries. The next hierarchical level focuses on links between the energy sector and the multisectoral national economy.

Energy planning requires analysis of the energy needs of user sectors (like industry and transport), the input needs of the energy sector and the impact on the economy of policies

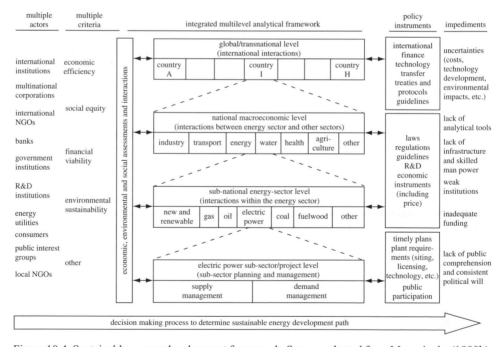

Figure 10.4. Sustainable energy development framework. Source: adapted from Munasinghe (1980b).

concerning energy prices and availability. The intermediate level of SED permits detailed analysis, with special emphasis on interactions among the different energy sub-sectors (like electricity and oil), substitution possibilities and resolution of any resulting policy conflicts. The lowest level focuses on individual energy sub-sectors, especially project planning and implementation. Social and environmental interactions (vertical bar) cut across all levels.

SED facilitates policy making and does not imply rigid centralized planning. Thus, such a process should result in the development of a flexible and constantly updated energy strategy designed to meet national sustainable development goals. This sustainable energy strategy may be implemented through energy supply and demand management options that make effective use of decentralized market forces and incentives. Figure 10.4 shows a variety of policy instruments for sound energy management. SED also considers the interests of multiple actors, ranging from international institutions to local energy users. The figure also indicates the most important impediments that limit effective policy formulation and implementation.

Sustainable energy options: 'win–win' outcomes versus trade-offs

Sustainable energy options that lead to improvements in economic, social and environmental are called 'win–win' options. Once 'win–win' cases are identified, trade-off situations may be addressed as set out in Section 3.5. Environmental and social impacts need to be valued in economic terms and introduced into conventional CBA. When such valuation is difficult, MCA may be used.

Better energy management could lead to improvements in economic efficiency (more net output produced with given resources), energy efficiency (higher value of net output per unit of energy used), energy conservation (reduced absolute amount of energy used), environmental protection (reduced energy-related environmental costs) and social benefits (more accessible energy). However, it may not always be possible to satisfy all the above goals simultaneously. The economic efficiency criterion, which maximizes the value of the net output from all scarce resources (including energy), effectively subsumes purely energy-oriented objectives such as energy efficiency and energy conservation.

Key sustainable energy options are discussed below.

10.2.2 Improving energy efficiency

Improving energy efficiency (by obtaining more light, heat and mobility from less energy) is usually a win–win option. It lowers investment and fuel costs, and increases business profits and consumer welfare, while reducing environmental harm and enhancing social benefits. However, the demand stimulated by subsequent reduction of energy costs, new uses of energy and population growth often expands energy use. During the past century, despite an over tenfold improvement in energy efficiency, world commercial energy use also increased tenfold.

The total final energy consumption per unit of GDP (TFC/GDP) in OECD countries fell 38% during 1973–1999. The IEA (2000a) projects TFC/GDP to decline over the next two decades by 1.0% a year in OECD countries, compared with the annual 1.2% decline registered between 1973 and 1999. Global TFC/GDP is projected to decrease by about

1.1% a year, compared with the annual rate of 0.9% during 1973–1999. The carbon intensity of world economic product dropped by more than 20% during 1970–1986, and 75% of this was achieved due to energy efficiency gains. In 1990, OECD countries were able to produce a unit of economic output using little more than half the energy required by non-OECD countries.

Energy efficiency may be improved via supply and end-use options.

Supply side improvements

Short-term supply efficiency enhancing technological options for the DC power sector include improving transmission and distribution losses and generation plant efficiencies. They yield net economic savings that are several times the corresponding costs incurred (Munasinghe, 1990b). Total energy losses in DC power systems are estimated to average in the 16 to 18% range. The average system losses in South Asia have been estimated at 17% and in East Asia at 13% (Munasinghe, 1991). Older power plants in many DCs consume 18 to 44% more fuel per kWh produced than those in OECD countries, and utilities suffer line losses that are two to four times higher (Levine *et al.*, 1991).

Gas-fired combined-cycle gas turbine (CCGT) plants offer high efficiency (up to 60%) combined with the low carbon content of natural gas, producing electricity with less than half the carbon emissions of coal-fired plants. Basic pulverized fuel (PF) coal technologies can achieve efficiencies of about 45–50%, and other advanced technologies are approaching commercial viability. Efficient transformer technology can generate major energy savings, typically 100–150 TWh/year of electricity in OECD countries (over 70 million tonnes of CO_2). Large-scale inexpensive electricity storage can lead to more efficient use and distribution of energy, can accelerate renewables use and it can lower liquid-vehicle-fuel use. Green house gas (GHG) emissions may be reduced with carbon-free technologies and CO_2 capture and sequestration. Overall, there is need for enhanced reliability, robustness and resilience of energy service networks, including system integration in energy supply, delivery and use.

Demand side improvements

Energy-efficient demand side management (DSM) programmes include the planning, implementing and monitoring activities of electric utilities, to encourage consumers to modify their level and pattern of electricity usage. These technologies could promote more efficient lighting, heating and cooling in the developing world. DSM will help to balance electricity supply and demand, stabilize prices, raise system reliability and security, rationalize investment in electricity supply infrastructure and reduce GHG emissions. Traditionally, DSM was used by electric utilities as a load and investment management tool, within a 'least-cost planning' framework. DSM is now finding new applications as a market-based service in liberalized energy markets (IEA, 2006). Since major demand growth in DCs will continue, and technologies and appliances are generally based on old designs, gains in overall electricity system efficiency are possible from DSM.

Policies to encourage cost-effective, energy-efficient technologies include (IEA, 2000b): (1) energy information, technical assistance and equipment labels; (2) regulations and

Table 10.1 *Key energy-efficient technologies and practices*

Building envelope	energy-efficient windows, insulation (walls, roof, floor), reduced air infiltration
Space conditioning	air conditioner efficiency measures (e.g. thermal insulation, improved heat exchangers, advanced refrigerants, more efficient motors), centrifugal compressors, efficient fans and pumps and variable air volume systems for large commercial buildings
Appliances	advanced compressors, evacuated panel insulation (refrigerators), higher spin speeds in washing machines/dryers
Cooking	improved efficiency biomass stoves, efficient gas stoves
Lighting	compact fluorescent lamps, improved phosphors, solid-state electronic ballast technology, advanced lighting control systems (including day lighting and occupancy sensors), task lighting
Motors	variable-speed drives, size optimization, improving power quality
Other	building energy management systems, passive solar use (building design), solar water heaters

standards for products and practices; (3) economic instruments, especially prices; (4) voluntary agreements (VAs) between industry and government; (5) energy research, development and dissemination (RD&D); and (6) public infrastructure planning and construction. Table 10.1 shows key DSM methods that reduce electricity use, local environmental and social impacts and GHG emissions. One major reason DCs hesitate to adopt these technologies is their fear of high costs. However, when all the system-wide costs are included, energy-efficient equipment often provides the same energy services at a lower installed capital cost than less efficient equipment (IEA, 2006). Unfortunately, potential buyers of new energy-efficient devices may still be unable to buy them because they do not have the necessary funds or access to credit facilities.

10.2.3 *Implementing environmentally and socially benign options*

As they expand energy supply to meet rapidly rising demand, DCs will look to industrialized nations to provide leadership in refining and testing new technologies before adopting them. In particular, renewable-energy sources and fuel switching are two important socially and environmentally benign technologies (Bryne, Toly and Glover, 2006).

Renewable-energy sources

Around 17% of the world's primary energy is supplied by renewable sources, including traditional biomass, large hydropower and 'new' renewables (small hydro, modern biomass, wind, solar, geothermal and biofuels). Traditional biomass, primarily for cooking and heating, represents about 9% and is growing slowly or even declining in some regions as biomass is used more efficiently or replaced by more modern energy forms. Large hydropower is about 6% and growing slowly, mainly in DCs. New renewables are 2% and growing very rapidly in ICs and in some DCs (REN21, 2005); see also Section 15.4.

Renewable energy has not made as much progress as expected in the past 20 years. In the OECD, the share of renewable energy in total primary energy has declined (Jefferson, 2005). The worldwide share of coal has increased since 2000, and that of large hydro and nuclear have decreased. In 2004, renewable power capacity (excluding large hydropower) totalled 160 GW worldwide, or about 4% of power-sector capacity. Small hydro and wind power accounted for two-thirds of this capacity; DCs had 70 GW. Renewable energy generated as much electricity as one-fifth of the world's nuclear power plants. During 2000–2004, electricity production from solar photovoltaic systems, as well as grid-connected wind turbines, has grown at about 30% per year, and geothermal and solar thermal heat production have grown about 10% per year (Goldemberg and Johansson, 2004). In developing countries, 16 million households use biogas for cooking and lighting, while over two million homes use solar PVs for lighting. The fastest growing energy technology in the world has been grid-connected solar PVs, with a total existing capacity increasing from 0.16 GW in 2000 to 1.8 GW by 2005 – a 60% average annual growth rate.

Between 2000 and 2004, renewable-energy technologies grew rapidly (annual average): wind power 28%; biodiesel 25%; solar hot water/heating 17%; off-grid solar PVs 17%; geothermal heat capacity 13%; and ethanol 11%. Other renewable-energy power-generation technologies, including biomass, geothermal and small hydro, are more mature and growing at more traditional rates of 2–4% per year. These growth rates compare with annual growth rates of fossil-fuel-based electric power capacity of 3–4%, a 2% annual growth rate for large hydropower, and a 1.6% annual growth rate for nuclear capacity during 2000–2002.

Large hydropower remains one of the lowest-cost energy technologies, although environmental constraints, resettlement impacts and the availability of sites have limited further growth (see Section 6.4). It supplied 16% of global electricity production in 2004, down from 19% a decade ago. Large hydro totalled about 720 GW worldwide in 2004 and has grown historically at slightly more than 2% per year (half that rate in developed countries). Small hydropower has developed worldwide for more than a century. Over half the world's small hydropower capacity exists in China – nearly 4 GW of capacity was added in 2004 alone.

Wind power has grown from a miniscule 1930 MW in 1990 to more than 47 317 MW in 2005. Especially noteworthy is the rapid growth of wind power in Denmark (35% per year since 1997), Spain (30% per year since 1997) and Germany (68% per year since 2000). Wind now generates more than 20% of Denmark's electricity. About 600 MW of offshore wind exists, all in Europe. Brown (2004) suggests that offshore wind alone might produce all of Europe's residential electricity. Nevertheless, it faces challenges for truly large-scale deployment. Public resistance in visible locations is growing, shifting the emphasis to over-the-horizon, off-shore wind platforms. The price of wind-generated electricity has declined sharply, from $0.46/kWh in 1980 to $0.03–$0.07/kWh in 2003 (Sawin, 2004). Brown (2003) notes that wind satisfies equally weighted economic, social and environmental criteria.

Biomass electricity and heat production is slowly expanding in Europe; e.g. in Sweden, biomass supplies more than 50% of district heating needs. Among DCs, small-scale power and heat production from agricultural waste is common, for example from rice or coconut husks. Sugar cane waste (bagasse) is used for power and heat production in countries with a large sugar industry. Modern biomass can be economically produced in rural areas, with minimal, or even positive, environmental impacts through perennial crops. Its production and use is helping to create international bio-energy markets, stimulated by policies to reduce carbon dioxide emissions.

Geothermal heating is used in 76 countries and geothermal electricity in 24 countries. Over 1 GW of geothermal power was added between 2000 and 2004. Geothermal direct-heat utilization capacity nearly doubled from 2000 to 2005, an increase of 13 GW. Iceland leads the world, supplying 85% of its total space-heating needs from geothermal.

Grid-connected solar PV installations are concentrated in three countries: Japan, Germany and the USA, with over 400 000 homes using rooftop solar PVs feeding power into the grid. This market grew by about 0.7 GW in 2004, from 1.1 GW to 1.8 GW cumulative installed capacity. Solar hot water/heating technologies are becoming widespread, with China accounting for 60% of total capacity worldwide (REN21, 2005). Despite steady declines in the cost per kWh of energy generated by PV cells, this alternative remains a costly solution by conventional standards. Moreover, the technology does not appear to have significant scale economies, partly because the efficiency of PVs cannot be improved by increasing the size of the device or its application. Solar PVs (and other small-scale electricity generation technologies) can overcome social barriers through a combination of clean energy, microfinance and community empowerment.

Biofuel production of 33 billion litres in 2004 compares with about 1200 billion litres annually of petrol production worldwide. Brazil has been the world's leading user of fuel ethanol for more than 25 years, producing about 15 billion litres in 2004, exporting a further 2.5 billion litres (more than half the global trade).

The future global share of renewables in energy use is projected to decline from 14% in 1997 to 12% in 2020. The world is expected to use 50% more hydroelectricity by 2020, mainly in DCs. The biggest increase in renewable-energy use is expected to come from wind and bioenergy, which are supported by policies and measures to curb GHGs and to diversify the energy mix. Despite this strong growth, the share of non-hydro renewable energy in the global energy mix will reach only 3% by 2020 because of the current low starting point of 2%. Future renewable-energy use in DCs (including hydro and 'non-commercial' combustible renewables and waste) will increase by 35% (IEA, 2006). Yet, their share of total DC energy demand will decline from 26% in 1997 to 18% in 2020. These baseline projections could change with the adoption of new policies.

In summary, non-conventional sources can help to meet energy needs in an efficient and cost-effective manner, particularly in DCs, where most of the growth in demand will occur. Hall *et al.* (2003) argue that subsidies and externalities have tilted the playing field toward hydrocarbons, which underlines the need for public-policy intervention that would encourage the research, development and adoption of renewable forms of energy, to make development more sustainable. Significant barriers will hamper renewable-energy development, unless action is taken by governments, the private sector and individual energy consumers to overcome risks, high costs, regulatory obstacles, limited availability of products, lack of public acceptance, information and technology gaps, lack of infrastructure and inadequate incentives.

Fuel switching

The substitution of primary energy sources in power generation is an important potential means of achieving dual benefits. In the case of substituting natural gas for coal or oil, the economic benefit comes from either import substitution for petroleum products or releasing these products for export. Further, natural gas firing typically achieves a 30–50% reduction in carbon emissions. Major reductions in polluting sulphate emissions can be achieved by substituting low sulphur coal or other fuels for low-grade coal. Investing in gas- and oil-fired power plants would also reduce carbon dioxide emissions, although this may increase dependence on expensive oil or gas imports.

Time lags are important. Historical experience suggests that, even with strong incentives, roughly 15 years are needed to switch from older production processes (e.g. in steel making) to newer ones, throughout a national industrial sector. Major fuel switches in energy systems have taken up to 20 years.

10.2.4 Institutional and regulatory reform

Over the twentieth century, many vertically integrated power companies, both state and privately owned, have emerged around the world. Michaels (2005) claims that such companies offer significant cost savings.

While the State-Owned Enterprise (SOE) model makes more sense for a smallish country with a weak private sector, it suffers from several shortcomings. Excessive government interference in organizational and operational matters has been a major problem in many parts of the developing world. This has adversely affected least-cost procurement and investment decisions, hampered attempts to raise prices to efficient levels, mandated low salaries and promoted excessive staffing. This in turn has resulted in inadequate management, the loss of experienced staff due to uncompetitive employment conditions and poor job satisfaction, weak planning and demand forecasting, inefficient operation and maintenance, high losses and poor financial monitoring, controls and revenue collection. Incentives for utility managers to pursue technical efficiency and financial discipline, to minimize consistently production costs and to provide reliable services are lacking in DCs. Lack of internal funding, together with poor planning, operation and maintenance practices has resulted in a widespread maintenance backlog and poor availability of generation capacity in DCs, thereby increasing the pressure for new generation. In some countries, state-owned power monopolies have grown to become a virtual mini-government, hardly accountable to anyone. There is little pressure to improve customer service or engage in technological innovation. With scant financial scrutiny, such SOEs tend to underperform. In many DCs, central governments do not have sufficient resources to invest adequately in infrastructure, resulting in chronic power shortages and poor service reliability (Sioshansi, 2006).

The natural monopoly characteristics of some power enterprise functions, and the necessity to manipulate these enterprises for general policy purposes, have been cited as reasons for maintaining large centralized public-sector organizations. Nevertheless, given the observed problems inherent in stimulating management of these enterprises to be cost conscious, innovative and responsive to consumer needs, there may be a need for more fundamental change. It could be worthwhile to trade off some of the perceived economies of scale in energy enterprises for other organizational structures, which provide greater built-in incentives for management efficiency and responsiveness to consumers.

Political decision makers, senior government officials and ministry-level staff should focus on critical macroeconomic and energy-sector strategy and policy. The senior management of a power company, appropriately guided and buffered by an independent board of directors, would then conduct their daily operations free from government interference to meet the overall national policy objectives and targets within regulatory guidelines. As far as possible, the utility management should be assured of continuity at the top, even in the face of political changes. While the enterprise enjoys wider autonomy, it would become more accountable in terms of performance measured against an agreed set of specific objectives and monitored indicators. Managerial training and education for staff are critical to ensure the success of such an approach.

There is considerable interest in the scope for more decentralization and greater private participation. DC power sector officials have been very active in studying such options, and some countries have already prepared the necessary legislative and institutional groundwork for this transition. In some countries, reform initiatives have begun, including divestiture of SOEs and encouragement of private power schemes.

Options for private and cooperative ownership of energy enterprises could include both local and foreign participation as well as joint ventures. As long as a given regulatory framework prevails, it can be argued that the form of ownership (private and public) would not by itself affect operating efficiency. A first step toward decentralization could be for government-owned power enterprises competitively to contract out activities or functions better handled by others, such as billing and collection process or routine maintenance. Among the advantages of such arrangements are lower costs and greater programming flexibility.

In the regulated monopoly model, the private sector owns and operates significant components of infrastructure, usually supervized by an independent regulator. This model offers a number of advantages relative to the centrally planned SOEs, such as the presence of an independent regulator, which should be competent, resourceful and vigilant. It offers the opportunity to capture the significant economies of scale of large vertically integrated monopolies while controlling their abusive tendencies. Another advantage is that the financial pressure exerted on privately owned monopolies is not as intense as it would be if they were private and non-regulated. Regulated monopolies are generally considered both low-risk and low-return. Although private investors finance projects and bear some risk, captive customers assume most of the risks through the regulatory review and approval process (Newberry, 2005).

There are also opportunities for spatial decentralization. For example, larger countries may have independent regional power grids. Power distribution companies could be separate by municipality, with perhaps limited overlap in fringe franchise areas, and have the right to purchase from various suppliers. If private participation were allowed, one advantage might be that at least the large power consumers could also be legitimate shareholders who would be concerned not only with service efficiency, but also with the financial viability of the company.

Power generation also has potential for efficiency improvements through divestiture. While the bulk power transmission and distribution functions might be regarded as having more natural monopoly common-carrier type characteristics, this is not so with generation. In fact, there is substantial scope for competition in power generation, with independent producers selling to a central grid (e.g. large industrial co-generation). Free-standing generation companies would put up all or part of the capital and be paid only out of revenues from power sold at guaranteed prices. This would reduce the emphasis on large, lumpy capital-intensive projects.

In theory, opening electricity markets could lead not only to lower prices in the short run, but also to innovations in technology and marketing plans with more substantial benefits. However, making electricity markets more competitive is complicated by an inability to approach the market ideal of perfect competition (see Box 2.3). For example, the local distribution of electricity is a monopoly because it would be wasteful for a second provider to install its own lines, poles and conduits over the existing grid. Until customers can economically produce electricity on their own premises using 'distributed-generation' technologies, local distribution and long-distance transmission will need to remain regulated monopolies.

The disastrous experience of California during the 1990s shows the pitfalls of energy reforms without adequate forethought (Brennan, 2001). In 1996, California loosened controls on its energy markets and increased competition. Deregulation involved partial divestiture of electricity generation stations by the utilities, who were still responsible for electricity distribution and were competing with independents in the retail market. A total of 40% of the installed generating capacity was sold to 'independent power producers'. By 2000, wholesale prices were fully deregulated, but retail prices were still regulated. After June 2000, bulk electricity prices skyrocketed, and reserves hit precariously low levels, resulting in blackouts. Incumbent utility companies incurred huge losses as they were forced to purchase wholesale power at high (unregulated) prices and sell at lower (regulated) retail prices. This allowed independent producers to manipulate prices by withholding electricity generation, arbitraging the price between internal generation and imported (interstate) power, thus causing artificial transmission constraints.

The incumbents (still subject to retail price caps) were faced with unabated end-user demand, while supply was restricted. Electricity and gas markets also interacted to produce erratic price movements that confused both energy producers and users. The dramatic collapse of Enron and the ensuing financial scandals were also closely linked to this process. Opponents of deregulation were quick to point out that the fully regulated system had worked perfectly well for 40 years, and that hasty deregulation created an opportunity for unscrupulous speculators to wreck a viable system. Pro-privatization advocates insist that the regulator overcontrolled and stifled the market. Beyond this debate, the California example (and others) show that DCs with fledgling market mechanisms and weak regulation must exercise caution before undertaking drastic sector reforms.

In a comprehensive recent review, Joskow (2006) states that 'the transition to competitive electricity markets has been a difficult process in the US'. He indicates that the results have been mixed, with no clear winner thus far between the half of the country, which is dominated by traditional regulated monopolies, and the other half, which is promoting privatization and competitive markets. To sum up, while the traditional model of large, monolithic, vertically integrated monopolies has major shortcomings, the transition to the other extreme of a fully privatised energy sector also poses significant risks (Griffin and Puller, 2005). Decision makers are searching for country-specific reform paths that strike the appropriate balance.

10.2.5 Sustainable energy pricing policy

This section briefly reviews how the principles of sustainomics may be used to frame a sustainable energy pricing policy. Further details are provided in Chapter 14, in the context of integrated energy pricing, and especially electricity pricing policy. Sustainable energy pricing policy as applied to the electricity sector needs to incorporate economic efficiency, as well as social equity and environmental considerations.

In the past, the electric-power pricing policy in most countries was determined mainly on the basis of financial or accounting criteria – e.g. raising sufficient sales revenues to meet operating expenses and debt service requirements, while providing a reasonable contribution toward capital needed for future power-system expansion. However, there has recently been increasing emphasis on the use of sustainable development principles to meet economic, social, environmental and other goals, described in Chapter 14, which are often conflicting.

The sustainomics-based approach leads to a tariff structure that is responsive to these multiple objectives. In the first stage, marginal supply costs are calculated to satisfy the economic (first-best) efficiency objective – using shadow priced future economic resource costs. The structuring of marginal costs permits an efficient and fair allocation of the tariff burden on consumers. In the second stage of developing sustainomics-based tariffs, deviations from strict marginal costs are permitted, to trade off among other important financial, social, political, environmental and economic (second-best) goals.

Past studies of the electric power sector in DCs indicate that electricity tariffs have not kept up with cost escalation (Besant-Jones *et al.*, 1990; Munasinghe, Gilling and Mason, 1988). Based on a survey of 60 DCs, electricity tariffs on average declined between 1979 and 1988 from 5.21 cents/kWh to 3.79 cents/kWh in 1986 US constant dollars. The operating ratio (defined as the ratio of operating costs before debt service, depreciation and other financing charges to operating revenue) for the almost 400 power utilities studied, deteriorated from 0.68

in the 1966 to 1973 period to 0.8 between 1980 and 1985 (Munasinghe, 1991). More recent information confirms these trends.

Advances in low-cost metering and switching equipment have made it possible to consider more sophisticated approaches to supply–demand balancing such as spot pricing and load control. In spite of the added costs of implementation, potential savings are large, to both power producers and users. Producers benefit by achieving some of their demand management objectives, such as peak shaving and load shifting. Consumers benefit by being able to select service levels according to their individual needs and by a reduction in total cost. Fernando, Kleindorfer and Munasinghe (1994) have shown that demand management through pricing and interruptible technologies (e.g. load switching) are especially important in DCs, where capital is scarce and shortage costs are higher. Environmental costs of energy reinforce this message even further.

10.2.6 SED options matrix and conclusions

Table 10.2 summarizes the impacts of selected options on the three elements of sustainable development. While efficient supply side options (e.g. reductions in T&D losses) have both economic and environmental gains from reduced capital investments and GHG emissions, they do not have obvious social benefits. Efficient end-use options, such as better fuelwood stoves, have benefits relating to all three elements. Although advanced technologies such as clean coal combustion technologies are essential for reducing air pollutants such as CO_2 and NOx, which cause respiratory diseases and reduce productivity, many poor countries cannot afford their high costs. Likewise, renewable-energy sources also provide environmental and social benefits by reducing dependence on fossil fuels, but may be more expensive than the latter. Pricing and privatization can have mixed effects, depending on circumstance.

SED identifies sustainable energy options, using a comprehensive and integrated framework for analysis, which takes into account multiple actors, multiple criteria, multilevel decision making and constraints. Various methods, including cost–benefit analysis (CBA) and multicriteria analysis (MCA), help to identify 'win–win' energy options that satisfy all

Table 10.2 *Matrix of selected sustainable energy development options*

	Impact		
Option	Economic	Environmental	Social
Supply efficiency	+	+	
End-use efficiency	+	+	+
Advance technologies	−	+	+
Renewables	−	+	+
Pricing policy	+	+	+/−
Privatization/decentralization	+	+/−	+/−

three elements of sustainable development (i.e. economic, environmental and social). Next, trade-offs can be made among other available sustainable energy options.

10.3 Applying SED to power planning in Sri Lanka

In this section, a practical case study of Sri Lanka is presented to show the application of the SED framework. Both CBA and MCA were used by Meier and Munasinghe (1994) to demonstrate how environmental and social externalities could be incorporated into conventional least-cost power system planning in a systematic and efficient manner. In the 1990s, Sri Lanka depended largely on hydropower for electricity generation. However, growing demand has forced planners to build large coal- or oil-fired stations, or hydro plants whose economic returns and environmental impacts are increasingly unfavourable. In addition, there are a wide range of other options (such as wind power, demand side management and system efficiency improvements), that complicate decision making – even in the absence of the environmental concerns. The study is quite unique in focusing on assessing environmental and social concerns at the system-level planning, as opposed to the more usual practice of doing so only at the project level, after strategic sectoral development decisions have already been made (see Chapter 15 for a sustainability analysis of energy projects).

10.3.1 Environmental issues

Sri Lanka is one of the more densely populated countries of the world, and land availability is an important issue. In general, hydro plants are in the wet zone areas where there is little vacant land nearby for resettled inhabitants to relocate, while land that is available at greater distances is unattractive to potential evacuees because of the unavailability of water. An effective way of comparing the potential land-related environmental impacts across projects is the area inundated, which varies between zero and 150 hectares kWh. The correlation between the installed capacity and the amount of land to be inundated is poor, because large projects do not necessarily imply worse environmental impacts, and vice versa.

The loss of Sri Lanka's natural forests due to agricultural land clearing, logging and fuelwood use since the 1960s is a major environmental concern. Because Sri Lanka is a small island (65 000 km^2), which has been isolated for relatively long periods, there are many endemic species. Among Asian countries, Sri Lanka has the highest level of biological diversity, which is under threat mainly due to loss of natural habitats. Although past power projects have contributed little to forest losses, future projects will be scrutinized carefully for their potential impact on what natural forest areas remain.

The air quality throughout Sri Lanka is fairly good, a reflection of the limited extent of industrialization, except in Colombo, and the natural ventilation provided by strong monsoon winds. However, rapid growth in vehicular traffic in Colombo during recent decades has led to a declining trend in air quality (see Chapter 11). It is fairly certain that, at present (2008), the power sector contributes only marginally to air pollution in Sri Lanka. However, this is expected to change significantly once the anticipated coal burning power plants are added to the system in around 2011. Acid rain (an increasingly important environmental issue in the Asia-Pacific region) is largely a long-range phenomenon, and its impact in Sri Lanka is as much a function of emission trends in India as in Sri Lanka itself.

Global warming and transnational acid rain are conceptually different from local environmental impacts, since, in the former case, the impacts will occur predominantly in other countries (see Chapter 5). Since the main national goal is to maximize welfare in Sri Lanka, decision makers would be unwilling to incur additional costs if the benefits of such actions accrue mainly to other nations. We assume that Sri Lanka will be reimbursed by the global community for incremental costs of GHG mitigation efforts.

As the generation mix shifts from hydro to fossil fuels, thermal power plant sites will be needed on the coast, with potential environmental risks to major economic activities such as foreign tourism and marine fisheries (which employ about 100 000 people, and is the largest source of animal protein for Sri Lanka). The main environmental issue is the discharge of heated effluents into coastal habitats that contain many temperature-sensitive ecosystems, including (1) coral reefs, sea grass beds, benthic communities and mangroves; (2) free floating zooplankton and phytoplankton communities; and (3) nursery grounds for fish and prawns.

10.3.2 Methodology

Power-sector strategies that have beneficial impacts on economic, social and environmental goals are the first priority, e.g. energy-efficiency measures that reduce costs and polluting emissions. However, most options involve trade-offs requiring MCA (see Section 3.5) – e.g. wind plants that provide substantial environmental benefits but are costly.

The overall methodology (Figure 10.5) involves: (1) defining the potential options; (2) selecting and defining attributes selected to reflect planning objectives; (3) economically valuing impacts (where possible) and including them in overall system costs; (4) quantifying remaining attributes (using non-economic measures) where economic valuation is difficult; (5) translating attribute value levels into value functions (known as 'scaling'); (6) displaying results in the trade-off space, to facilitate decision making; and (7) identifying key options for further study, by eliminating inferior ones. Here, we do not assign weights to attributes and aggregate the results to end up with a single overall ranking of options.

10.3.3 Application to the Sri Lanka power sector

Policy option definition

A variety of options were examined, including siting, pollution control mitigation and technology options, without making a priori judgements about their feasibility. The main policy options examined, beyond variations in the mix of hydro and thermal plants, included: (1) demand side management – e.g. compact fluorescent lighting; (2) renewable-energy options (using the illustrative technology of wind generation); (3) improvements in system efficiency (using more ambitious targets for transmission and distribution losses than the base

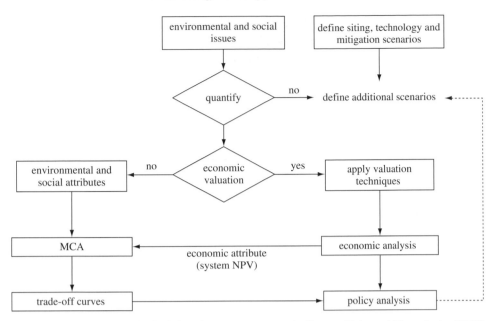

Figure 10.5. Methodology for the Sri Lanka power sector study. Source: Meier and Munasinghe (1994).

case assumption of 12% by 1997); (4) clean coal technology – e.g. pressurized fluidized bed combustion (PFBC) in a combined cycle mode; and (5) pollution control technology options – e.g. fuel switching and pollution control options like using imported low sulphur oil for diesels and fitting coal-power plants with flue gas desulphurization systems.

Attribute selection

The attributes selected reflected issues of national significance. They were limited in number, because the more attributes considered, the more complex the analysis, and the higher the probability that the results will be harder for decision makers to interpret.

Key environmental attributes were expressed as present discounted values. Carbon dioxide emissions were the proxy for potential impacts of climate change, assuming linearity of impacts – since Sri Lanka is a very small GHG contributor. Population-weighted increment in fine particulates and nitrogen oxides attributable to each source were used to capture health impacts. A simple Gaussian plume model was applied to all major sites, and incremental ambient concentrations for 1 km^2 cells were estimated inside a 20 km radius, and then multiplied by the population in each cell. Sulphur dioxide and nitrogen oxide emissions represented air pollution impacts like acid rain. A probabilistic index was derived for biodiversity impacts.

Employment creation was used as a typical social impact. It is a key goal of national policy, especially for youth. What is captured in this attribute is the separate, and purely political, objective of employment creation, and is to be distinguished from strictly economic benefits that would be captured by the use of shadow wage rates (that reflect high unemployment) in the construction cost estimates.

Attribute quantification

The biodiversity attribute illustrates the problems of quantification. Detailed site-specific information at power plant sites is unlikely to be available to planners. Thus, an index must be derived that gives decision makers information about the likelihood that the detailed environmental impact assessment will reveal the presence of an endemic species, harm high biodiversity ecosystems, or affect already vulnerable habitats. There are many practical problems in deriving such a probabilistic index. First, the value of the area lost is a function of the remaining habitat. For example, the loss of the last hectare of an ecosystem would be unacceptable, whereas the loss of one out of 1000 hectares would be tolerable. Second, ecosystems may require a minimum area for long-term survival, which implies that the value function would need to tend to infinity as it approaches that minimum value.

Some impacts resist direct quantification, even in terms of a probabilistic scale. For example, the quantification of potential damages to aquatic ecosystems from thermal discharges is difficult. Discharges into the well mixed surface layer would generally repel fish. On the other hand, discharges below the thermocline are beneficial, as the up-welling effect caused by plume buoyancy brings nutrients to surface. However, it is very difficult to assign numerical values to this general function. Instead, a rough calculation may be used to compare different sites by defining an acceptable environmental risk – e.g. a temperature increase less than 1 °C at the surface. The surface area over which this criterion is exceeded may be calculated for each cooling system design proposed.

10.3.4 Illustrative results and conclusions

After defining both options and attributes, the multidimensional trade-off space was derived. Using the ENVIROPLAN model, values for each environmental attribute and the system costs (i.e. average incremental cost over a 20-year planning horizon) were calculated for every option, with results displayed as a series of two-dimensional trade-off curves. Finally, the candidate plans for further study were derived by examining dominance relationships among all criteria simultaneously.

Figure 10.6 shows typical trade-off curves for biodiversity and health impacts. The 'best' solutions lie closest to the origin. The trade-off curve or set of 'non-inferior' solutions represents options that are superior, regardless of the weights assigned to the different objectives. For example, in Figure 10.6(b), the option 'iresid' (use of low sulphur imported fuel oil at diesel plants) is better on both the cost and the environmental objective than the use of flue gas desulphurization systems (option 'FGD').

Figure 10.6(a) shows a different trade-off curve between the biodiversity index and average incremental cost. Most of the options have an index value that falls in the range 50–100. The 'no hydro' option has a near-zero value, because the thermal projects that replace hydro plants in this option tend to lie at sites of poor biodiversity value (either close to load centres or on the coast). Wind plants would require rather large land area, but the vegetation of this land on the south coast has relatively low biodiversity value. Thus, the best

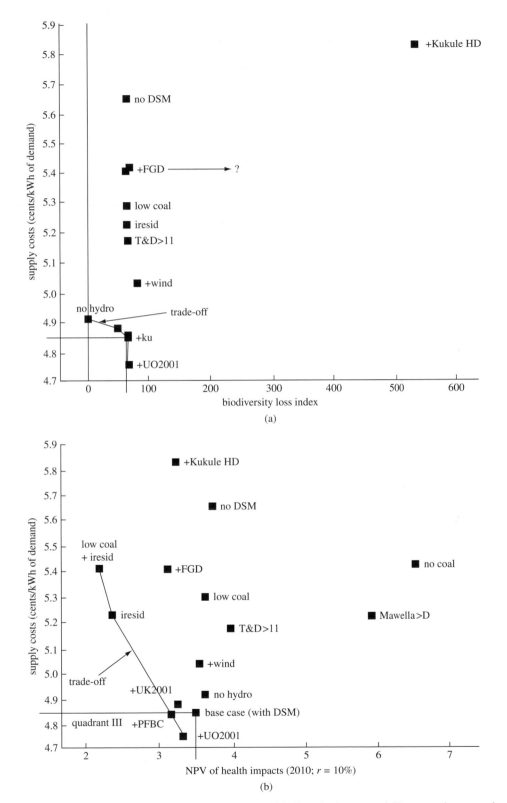

Figure 10.6. Trade-off between (a) economic cost and biodiversity impact and (b) economic cost and health impact. Source: Meier and Munasinghe (1994).

options (or non-inferior) curve includes the no hydro option, and run-of-river hydro options that require essentially zero inundation. Note that the extreme outlier at the top right hand corner is the Kukule hydro dam, which has a biodiversity loss index ($B = 530$) that is much larger than for other options ($B = 50$–70).

The case study yielded four useful conclusions, showing how MCA can assist decision makers, and five practical policy recommendations to help incorporate environmental issues into the system planning process.

First, impacts for which valuation techniques are quite straightforward and well established (like valuing opportunity costs of lost production from inundated land, or benefits of establishing fisheries in a reservoir), tend to be quite small in comparison to overall system costs. Their inclusion in the benefit–cost analysis does not materially change results.

Second, even where explicit valuation may be difficult (like health effects of air pollution), implicit valuation using trade-off curve analysis provides useful guidance to decision makers. For example, the study showed that the value of human life which justified flue gas desulphurization at coal power plants was about US $1.5 million. This is much greater than the cost of radically modernizing regional hospitals.

Third, certain options were clearly inferior (or superior) to all other options when one examines all impacts together. For example, the high dam version of the Kukule hydro project could be excluded from further consideration due to poor performance on all attribute scales (including economic cost). On the other hand, implementation of certain demand side management measures dominates all other options, because they yield gains in terms of both economic and environmental criteria.

Fourth, it is possible to derive attribute scales that can be useful proxies for impacts that may be difficult to value. For example, use of the population-weighted incremental ambient air pollution scale as a proxy for health impacts leads to some key conclusions that are independent of the specific economic value assigned to health effects. If the health effects of pollutants from fossil-fuel combustion (particularly fine particulates and nitrogen oxides) are to be reduced, then the most effective strategy for lowering the overall population dose is to install tighter pollution controls at oil-burning power plants located in or near urban areas, rather than installing FGD systems at the more remote coal-power sites.

Finally, specific recommendations on priority options for practical planning, include the need to: (1) examine systematically demand side management options, especially fluorescent lighting; (2) examine whether the present transmission and distribution loss reduction target of 12% ought to be further reduced; (3) examine the possibilities of PFBC technology for coal power; (4) replace some coal-fired power plants (on the south coast) by diesel units; and (5) re-examine cooling system options for coal plants.

10.4 Energy policy options

This section summarizes selected policy implications of the case study in Section 10.3 and subsequent studies of energy use in the Sri Lanka power sector (Munasinghe and Meier,

2003a, b). In particular, we seek to make power-sector development more sustainable by expanding on the recent debate on restructuring and reform of the sector to achieve the basic goal of an adequate and affordable electricity supply to consumers.

Sri Lanka will continue to pay the costs of the failures of decision making since the beginning of the twenty-first century. Most of the generating capacity added over the past decade has been based on auto-diesel, which is not only expensive, but also the most volatile in cost. Moreover, the environmental opposition to coal generation has been unjustified, e.g. the actual environmental impacts of diesel generation in densely populated urban areas is greater than those of modern coal-based plant. In 2005, about half of all generation was oil-based. While the private sector has captured a larger share of generation, the increased cost to users resulting from diesel far outweighs the benefits of private-sector competition in generation.

The new National Energy Policy recognizes that Sri Lanka is too dependent on oil-based generation. To diversify supply and lower cost, it is imperative to seek a more balanced generation mix by moving to coal. Over-reliance on diesel generation raises costs, under-mines trade competitiveness and imposes environmental costs. The first step in the right direction was taken in 2006, when construction began on a 300 MW coal plant at Norochalai (with subsequent planned expansion to 900 MW).

10.4.1 Environmental impacts

GHG mitigation

The first priority for GHG emission reduction in Sri Lanka is power-sector reform (which would reduce T&D losses) and the implementation of a comprehensive DSM lighting programme. Unlike in India, reform in Sri Lanka is win–win with respect to both net economic benefits and GHG emission reduction. Once reform has been implemented, use of residual oil for diesel-power generation is the next GHG mitigation option that would be the easiest to implement from an institutional and managerial standpoint. It will likely bring net economic benefits as well. However, the feasibility of this option depends on an expansion of Sri Lanka's domestic refinery capacity, which is still under study.

One promising least-cost option includes additional DSM and T&D loss reduction (beyond levels envisaged in the first stage of reform), plus an aggressive implementation of 45 MW of mini-hydro schemes. While these are 'win–win' (economic gains and reduced GHG emission), there are major financial and institutional barriers. Therefore, mini-hydro should continue to be supported by GEF and ESD (see Section 10.4.4).

Dendro-thermal power plants could reduce GHG emissions at a reasonable cost, subject to field verification of key issues about plantation management, land and labour availability and plant-gate cost. Therefore, a pilot project is recommended of at least a 1 MW power plant, with a fuelwood plantation of around 400 ha. Another option would be to study the costs of expanding the Norochalai coal power plant with a second 300 MW plant co-fired with fuelwood – a proven technology. If co-firing were too costly, the wood from the pilot plantation could still be sold in the Colombo fuelwood market, thus reducing project risks.

Sri Lanka has substantial wind power potential, but the costs are high. The maximum wind scenario examined here has a cost of avoided carbon of US $65/tonne. Even if capital costs were to fall to US $700–800/kW (currently over US $1000/kW), this would still be an expensive mitigation option – given the low plant factors achievable. The poor wind speeds and capacity factors achieved at the 3 MW pilot project on the south coast suggest the need for a more comprehensive wind resource assessment before committing to large-scale wind development.

The solar homes system (SHS) is justified by the importance that is attached to rural lighting (and the expense and difficulties of extending grid service to remote villages). However, SHS has a low priority as a GHG mitigation measure. Even under optimistic assumptions about market penetration, the GHG emissions reduced by the SHS programme are less than 1% of the value achieved through reforms.

Local environmental impacts

The review of local environmental impacts is deferred to the end of Chapter 11, after analysing sustainable transport options for Sri Lanka.

10.4.2 Hedging strategies

High sulphur fuel oil can be imported at relatively low cost from Middle Eastern refineries, and in the past this was often a cheaper fuel than coal. However, given the present rising trend in oil prices (see Section 10.1.1), and the impact of the 1970s oil shocks, the Government of Sri Lanka may be cautious about major commitments to large steam-cycle oil plant. While the historical dependence on hydro insulated the electric sector from the 1970s oil price shocks, the risks of overdependence on hydro were amply demonstrated during the 1996 and 2001 droughts, which caused reduced GDP growth by over 1%. Thermal generation reduces this hydro risk, but replaces it with a new dependence on oil.

One useful hedging strategy is dual-firing capability at the coal plant – with oil or wood co-firing. A key issue here is the amount of oil storage to be provided. The larger the volume of storage, the larger the capital costs, but the greater the ability to buy and store oil during periods of low oil prices and to avoid futures-market hedging.

10.4.3 Petroleum-sector issues

In 2003, Sri Lanka consumed about 3.4 million tonnes of oil products (Table 10.3). About half (mainly diesel) was imported, and the rest was produced at the Ceylon Petroleum Corporation's (CPC) refinery at Sapugaskanda (which imported 2 million tonnes of crude in 2003).

The recent introduction of competition in the petroleum sector, by selling one-third of CPC's monopoly share of the oil market to the Lanka Indian Oil Company (LIOC), was beneficial. However, as in the case of the power sector, the presumption that all can now be

Table 10.3 *Sri Lanka Petroleum product consumption, kilotonnes*

	2001	2002	2003
Petrol (90 octane)	244	277	328
Petrol (95 octane)	5	9	13
Auto-diesel	1675	1752	1652
Super-diesel	49	47	42
Kerosene	228	229	212
Furnace oil	811	780	715
Avtur	138	114[a]	139
Naphtha	14	56	102[b]
LPG	141	157	161
Total	3305	3423	3360

[a] Decline reflects the drop in tourist arrivals following the terrorist attacks at Colombo International Airport in 2001.
[b] Increase reflects commissioning of the CEB naphtha-fired CCCT in December 2002.
Source: Central Bank (1998, 2003).

left to the interplay of market forces carries long-term risks. The history of world oil markets since the 1960s illustrates the need to balance short-term market considerations with supply security, especially for transport (see Chapter 11).

The supply–demand balance for, and the relative prices of, various transport fuels depend on the availability of refined outputs. Thus, the future of the Sapugaskanda refinery in a privatized sector raises key issues. There is no requirement in the present agreement between the Government and LIOC that the latter should purchase some or all of its supply from the local refinery. If the restructuring of the sector evolves to include more players, the market share of Ceypetco (CPC) may drop below 30%, with the result that, unless the other players purchase a significant share of their requirement from Sapugaskanda, the refinery through-put will fall to levels at which it is no longer profitable. Sri Lanka will not wish to run an unprofitable refinery, and it is economically inefficient for the refinery to be protected by customs duties (which will simply raise the price to *all* consumers). However, if the refinery closes, then Sri Lanka will become entirely dependent on the international players dominating Asian markets. This was the situation faced by Sri Lanka in the 1950s, which led to nationalization of oil at that time.

Several options to address this problem may be considered. For example, if the Sapugaskanda refinery can match the landed cost of products as calculated by the new pricing formula (based on Platts), then the private-sector players could be required to purchase locally, in the broader national interest. In short, such issues need to be considered in a national sustainable energy planning process that balances the various long- and short-term interests, including the security of supply. All stakeholders, including private companies, should be consulted, but the final decision will remain the responsibility of the Government.

10.4.4 *Renewable energy for off-grid electrification*

As described in greater detail in Chapter 15, the Energy Services Delivery (ESD) project is one of the most successful renewable-energy programmes in the World Bank/GEF portfolio. ESD included the SHS and village hydro components, and a grid-based mini-hydro programme, which established a viable and sustainable private-sector business activity developing small hydro-projects.

Consumer surplus should be included in the economic benefits for off-grid electrification systems. This is supported by the empirical evidence – even poor households are willing to pay much more for higher quality electric lighting and TV viewing than alternative kerosene/battery cost.

While grid-based electrification is the long-term goal, access targets are often unrealistic, because grids are extended more for political objectives than for sound economic reasons. The result is high losses, poor grid service and unsustainable financial losses for the utility. In Asia, new models for rural electrification have the common theme of transparent subsidies and clear separation of O&M operations – the latter requires effective local institutional capacity.

10.4.5 *Key power-sector priorites*

Energy planning, particularly by the public sector, is often unfairly maligned, in the context of market liberalization and private-sector involvement. Yet Sri Lanka's experience suggests that energy planning can be effective for guiding change and mobilizing capital, provided it is coupled with the necessary political will.

The institutions established in the early 1980s (when President Jayewardene was also the Minister of Energy) were highly effective. One of the world's first integrated national energy plans was practically implemented. The Lanka Elecricity Company (LECO) was established with autonomous management, but under public ownership. LECO is a model for South Asia – e.g. reducing T&D losses from over 50% to less than 8% was a remarkable achievement under difficult circumstances, including years of civil strife, a poor tariff environment and disputes with CEB over large industrial customers. The keys to LECO's success were the commercialization of operations and the political will to enforce that mandate. In practice, this meant direct support from the President when political pressure was put on LECO to relax enforcement of those measures introduced to reduce commercial losses.

Planning by the main-sector institutions begun in the mid 1980s suffered due to lack of implementation. It is quite clear that the failure to ensure adequate capacity since the mid 1990s, and dependence of the CEB system on costly power generation (based on auto-diesel), was not a failure of planning, but a problem of political will to implement plans. Sri Lanka has not been well served by advice from those with a vested interest in privatization and private-sector generating plants. As in India, the view that the introduction of independent power producers would lead the way to reform was unsound (and, in the case of India, this was promoted in the early 1990s mainly by corrupt persons). While the scale of failures in Sri Lanka is much smaller than at Dabhol, the result is much the same – risk of power shortages, power generation plants using expensive fuel (auto-diesel) and located in environmentally harmful areas (like the barge-mounted plant in Colombo harbour) and vested interests (including donors promoting privatization) proposing unrealistic and unviable projects.

The problems of the power sector cannot be solved by restructuring alone, and competition in the marketplace will not necessarily ensure timely investments of new capacity. Examples include the California power crisis (see Section 10.2.4) and the inadequacy of the power transmission infrastructure in Europe, which caused widespread and costly blackouts in Italy in September, 2003. Because of long time lags, the relevant regulatory body must ensure a coherent investment planning process in the public interest, as recognized in the new Sri Lanka National Energy Strategy. A regularly updated long-term generation expansion plan for the electricity sector, and a parallel renewable-energy plan, is included. The Indian experience with the newly established electricity regulatory commissions shows that, despite their nominal independence and the unbundling of sector operations, political interference remains a problem. While sector reform and a predictable and stable tariff regime are necessary conditions for successful mobilization of private capital for major energy infrastructure projects, an important priority for energy-sector development is a sustainable settlement of the ethnic conflict.

10.5 Assessing the sustainability of energy policies in South Africa

This section illustrates the SED approach by summarizing a policy-relevant, sustainable development assessment of energy policy option in South Africa, carried out by Winkler (2006), using MCA.

10.5.1 Status of energy and electricity in South Africa

Making energy production and use more sustainable is a central challenge in South Africa's future development path. Growth rates for electricity consumption and economic output have been correlated. The electricity supply industry was originally driven by mining needs. The availability of cheap coal and electricity helped to establish manufacturing industries. The apartheid government made large investments to develop a synthetic oil industry and local nuclear capacity. The democratic government has shifted the focus from supply to demand – to improve household access to electricity and make energy services more affordable. Coal currently accounts for 75% of the primary energy supply (DME, 2003) and for over 90% of the total licensed capacity of over 43 000 MW (NER, 2002).

By 1948, the electricity industry was consolidated into a large and powerful, state-owned, vertically integrated monopoly (Eskom). Large power projects were initiated to meet demand up to 16% annually during 1972–1982 (Eberhard, 2003). Later, growth slowed, leaving a large excess capacity in the 1980s and 1990s, which helped to keep prices low. Power supply in South Africa was limited to established towns and areas of economic activity. In 1993, only 36% of the total population had access to grid electricity. The first phase of the National Electrification Programme (1994–1999) increased electrification to about 66% nationally – 46% in rural areas and 80% in urban areas (NER, 1999). Yet, one-third of the population still has no electricity, especially in rural areas.

Major changes are taking place at present in both the electricity industry (due to restructuring) and the petroleum sector (with the establishment of a Gas Regulator). The option of introducing LNG into South Africa is being examined (CEF, 2005). The amended Petroleum Products Act will alter licensing rules for petrol stations to give government more control, while the Petroleum Pipelines Bill is expected to establish pricing and access rules for oil and gas pipelines.

Energy-related environmental impacts are of increasing concern. Monitoring of emissions will soon be required through the National Air Quality Management Bill. Diversity of supply has been emphasized as South Africa intends to use every energy source optimally – coal, gas, oil, nuclear and renewable energy. The initial focus has been on importing natural gas from Mozambique and possibly Namibia, which could promote a major shift away from coal (DME, 2001; Marrs, 2000a, b). Renewable-energy sources are another option for increasing diversity, while focusing on sharing hydroelectricity from within the South African Power Pool (SAPP). Eskom has identified 9000 MW of potential regional imports (excluding Grand Inga in the Congo). The government target is that new renewable energy will contribute 10 000 GWh to energy supply by 2013 (approximately 4% of demand).

Good progress has been made in extending access to electricity, although affordability and productive use remain difficult issues. The main energy goals of the government include greater access to affordable energy services, improved energy governance, stimulating economic development, managing energy-related environmental impacts and securing supply through diversity (see Section 10.2 on SED goals).

10.5.2 Analysis and results

The SED indicators shown in Table 10.4 were selected to reflect South Africa's development objectives, to be consistent with energy policy goals and to mark progress toward sustainability. Table 10.5 summarizes the policy options that were assessed for their sustainability, and Table 10.6 shows the results for residential energy use.

Figure 10.7 ranks the different policies according to three sustainable development indicators – more affordable electricity (social); lower total power system costs (economic); and lower emissions (environmental). The higher the number, the more sustainable the policy. No clear winner emerges. If the priority were to reduce energy system costs, the importing of gas or hydroelectricity would be favoured, since the economic indicator is at the outer edge of the triangle, representing a more sustainable policy. Both imports reduce capital and overall system costs. The environmental priority of reducing emissions in South Africa would favour two domestic options, even though they show higher costs, i.e. renewables and the more costly nuclear pebble bed modular reactor (PBMR).

Table 10.4 *Indicators for sustainable energy development*

Indicator	Units
Economic	
Total cost of energy system	billion Rands
Marginal cost of electricity supply	cents/kWh
Diversity of electricity fuel mix – domestic sources, billion Rands	%
Environmental	
Local air pollutants in 2025	
sulphur dioxide	kilotonnes SO_2
nitrogen oxides	tonnes NOx
carbon monoxide	tonnes CO
Global greenhouse gases	megatonnes CO_2-equiv.
Social	
Fuel consumption in residential sector	petajoules
Cost of energy services to households	
shadow price of residential electricity	cents/kWh
shadow price of non-electric fuels	Rands/gigajoule
Monthly expenditure on electricity	Rands per household per month

Table 10.5 *Policy cases in residential energy and electricity supply sectors*

Short name	Key features
Households	
SWH	cleaner, more efficient water heating is provided through increased use of solar water heaters and geyser blankets; the costs of SWH decline over time, as new technology diffuses more widely in the South African market
CFL	more efficient lighting, using compact fluorescent lights (CFLs) spreads more widely, with a slight further reduction in costs beyond that achieved already
Eff house	the shell of the house is improved by insulation, prioritizing ceilings; since the technology has zero fuel costs, bounds are placed to ensure that no further building takes place
LPG switch	households switch from electric and other cooking devices to LPG stoves and rings
Combined elec	the combined effect of all the above policies
Electricity	
Renewable energy	share of renewable power rises to meet the target of 10 000 GWh by 2013; shares of solar thermal, wind, bagasse and small hydro rise over the base case; new technology costs fall as global production increases
PBMR	production of PBMR modules for domestic use increases capacity of nuclear up to 4480 MW by 2020; costs decline with national production and initial investments are written off

Table 10.5 (*cont.*)

Short name	Key features
Hydro	share of hydroelectricity imported from SADC region increases up to 15 GWh by 2010, from 9.2 GWh in 2001; as more hydro capacity is built in Southern Africa, the share increases
Gas	sufficient gas is imported to provide 1950 MW of combined cycle gas turbines, in units of 387 MW
Base w/out FBC	fluidized bed combustion using discarded coal, a low-cost resource, is part of the *base* case already; the implications of what would have happened without this resource are explored

The combined case scores poorly on costs, making emission reductions expensive. Diversity of supply is shown in Figure 10.7 only by the increased share of renewables. The renewables option still achieves a better mix among other fuels, but another indicator (e.g. reduction in coal use) would be needed to show that PBMR achieves the greatest diversity of supply in moving away from coal dependency. Both domestic options reduce local air pollutants and GHGs by similar percentages.

Figure 10.8 shows a more complex set of sustainable development indicator rankings for the same power supply policy options. Again no SED option is clearly superior, since the ranking of policies changes sharply depending on the indicator.

Figure 10.9 shows results for residential policies. Here a clearer picture emerges. Within the context of meeting the basic energy development objective, two residential policies show the greatest capability for making development more sustainable. The triangles for efficient houses and SWH/GB completely contain those for CFLs and LPG cooking. Efficient houses and SWH/GB make the greatest fuel savings and thus save the greatest energy costs for households. The policies reduce the electricity burden for households, particularly for poorer urban electrified ones. Increased affordability makes social disruption less likely. These two options also contribute the most to cleaner fuel use and improve environmental quality. Combining all policies seems to be a very sustainable option – as indicated by the largest triangle.

Comparing both residential and electricity policies against each dimension of sustainable development provides us with some idea of the synergies and trade-offs. There are clear win–win cases for residential policies. However, no single electricity supply option is preferable economically, socially and environmentally. One implication is that more trade-offs are required. Another is that short-term economic costs should not be the only factor in identifying durable long-term solutions.

The results identify home energy policies that have greater potential for making development more sustainable, including efficient houses and clean, efficient water heating. Renewable energy had multiple benefits among electricity supply options, but the trade-offs with the lower costs of imports require further consideration. Combining residential and

Table 10.6 *Overview of results for residential energy use*

Indicator	Year or unit	Base case	Efficient houses	CFLs	Water heating – SWH/GB	LPG for cooking	Residential policies combined
Social							
Fuel consumption in residential sector (petajoules)							
Electricity	2014	98.9	93.1	98.9	95.9	96.4	98.3
	2025	116.8	104.9	116.8	110.3	112.6	115.5
Liquid fuels	2014	51.9	43	51.9	51.9	41.3	51.9
	2025	58.9	39.3	58.9	58.9	36.1	58.9
Renewable energy	2014	1.7	7.9	1.7	1.7	9.5	1.7
	2025	3.5	16.7	3.5	3.5	20.1	3.5
Total fuel use	2014	201.1	195.3	201.1	201.5	195.2	200.5
	2025	213.5	202.3	213.5	214.4	202.1	212.3
Cost of energy services to households	cents/kWh	37.8	34.2	34.8	34.8	34.8	34.2
Cost of electricity in common units	Rand/gigajoule	105.1	95.1	96.7	96.7	96.7	95.1
Cost of energy services to households: shadow price of non-electric fuels, residential	Rand/gigajoule						
Coal for households		3.5	3.5	3.5	3.5	3.5	3.5
Biomass		30	30	30	30	30	30
LPG		149.4	149.4	149.4	149.4	149.4	149.4
Paraffin		96.9	96.9	96.9	96.9	96.9	96.9
Candle wax		70.3	70.3	70.3	70.3	70.3	70.3
Monthly electricity cost	Rands per household per month						
RHE		87	78	80	80	80	78
RLE		16	15	15	15	15	15

Table 10.6 (*cont.*)

Indicator	Year or unit	Base case	Efficient houses	CFLs	Water heating – SWH/GB	LPG for cooking	Residential policies combined
UHE		164	148	151	151	151	148
ULE		62	56	57	57	57	56
Environmental							
Local air pollutants (in 2025)							
Sulphur dioxide	kilotonnes SO_2	3571	3524	3568	3531	3559	3517
Non-methane volatile organic compounds	tonnes NMVOC	888 450	888 038	888 432	888 139	888 387	888 011
Nitrogen oxides	tonnes NOx	2 156 438	2 132 925	2 155 275	2 137 627	2 151 339	2 129 828
Carbon monoxide	tonnes CO	4 923 479	4 921 832	4 923 416	4 922 246	4 923 237	4 921 730
Global GHGs (in 2025)							
Carbon dioxide, total	kilotonnes CO_2	630 053	622 540	629 686	624 117	628 685	621 827
Methane	tonnes CH_4	50 325	50 234	50 323	50 261	50 380	50 301
Nitrous oxide	tonnes N_2O	8171	8065	8165	8082	8149	8052
Economic							
Total cumulative cost of energy system	billion Rands	6120	6119	6119	6115	6121	6115
Annualized investment in all residential technologies in 2025	billion Rands	29.78	30.23	29.58	29.71	30.65	29.75

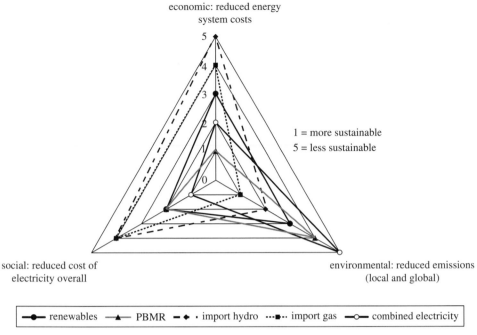

Figure 10.7. Electricity supply options ranked by three economic, social and environmental indicators.

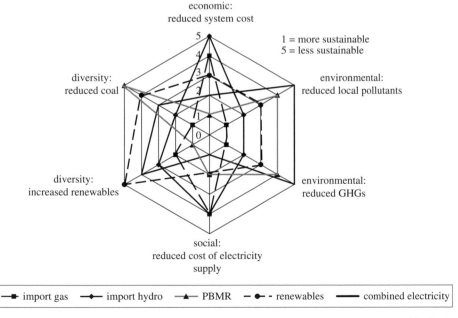

Figure 10.8. Electricity supply options ranked by six economic, social and environmental indicators.

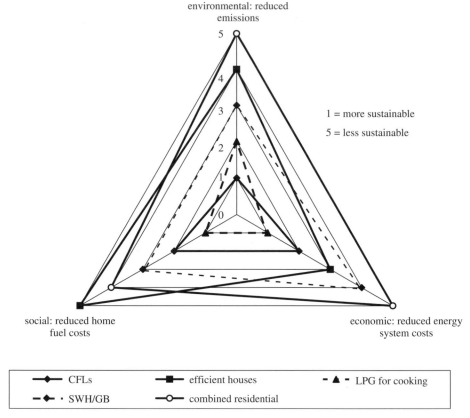

Figure 10.9. Residential energy options ranked by three economic, social and environmental indicators.

electricity policies would provide a mix that overall provides a durable balance of economic development, social sustainability and both local and global environmental benefits. The approach has been demonstrated for South Africa, but will resonate with other rapidly industrializing developing countries. Finally, the study confirms that national sustainable development is the appropriate starting point (conceptually and methodologically) to determine the energy and mitigation policies.

10.6 Making electricity development more sustainable in the UK

10.6.1 Background of the UK electricity system

Currently the UK's electricity supply is still highly centralized. Decentralized energy (DE) represents only 7.3% of total capacity and 7.2% of generation. Large-scale co-generation (>1 MWe) has the largest share of DE capacity (3.1 GWe), but other DE sources, such as on-site renewables, are growing rapidly (DUKES, 2006). In terms of fuel use, most generation in the UK is coal-fired (31.3%), with natural gas a close second (29.1%). However, gas is increasingly important, and declining North Sea gas reserves have raised concerns about energy security. Nuclear is another important energy source (18.2%). Other sources of energy for power come from oil (1.14%), hydro (0.42%), other renewables (2.99%) and other fuels (1.55%).

The WADE Economic Model

The WADE Economic Model calculates the economic and environmental impacts of supplying incremental electrical load growth with varying mixes of DE and central generation (CG). It uses detailed and comprehensive data about existing electricity generation facilities, as well as future fuel price trends and technology development. Starting with known generating capacity for year 0 and projections for capacity retirement and load growth, the model adds user-specified capacity to meet future growth and retirement over a 20-year period. It helps to make policy decisions by comparing concrete alternatives, using a sensitivity analysis of important variables such as fuel prices and demand growth, and allowing direct comparison between different power-system-expansion plans.

In this study, the model was used to analyse five cases for new capacity to meet incremental demand over 20 years, with the mix of future plant to be added ranging between two extremes, i.e. [0% DE, 100% CG] and [100% DE, 0% CG]. For each of the five scenarios, the results give the total capital costs (i.e. generation, transmission and distribution, T&D) over the 20-year period, as well as the retail costs (future costs adjusted or levelled to their present value), the annual CO_2 and other pollutant emissions from new and total generation and the fuel use (both absolute and by share of generation) in year 20. The model also gives results for intermediate years within the 20-year analysis period. These results relate directly to national policy goals, and are essential for sustainable development decision making.

10.6.2 UK energy scenarios

Two main illustrative scenarios are shown in Figure 10.10.

Baseline – central nuclear (100% CG)

The baseline scenario called 'central nuclear' assumes a 5% demand growth per year with 100% CG, and represents a likely future electricity system, based on the expected responses of the market and government to the existing issues. It assumes that new nuclear capacity will be built in the second decade of the analysis to replace existing plants, and assumes that nuclear will comprise 20% of the generation capacity at 2002. Until new nuclear plants become operational, it mainly uses gas combined-cycle gas turbines (CCGT) to meet demand, but also some coal-fired generation to limit the UK's reliance on gas imports. Renewable generation, mostly wind energy, is increased gradually.

Main alternative (100% DE/renewables)

DE/renewables is the main alternative. It had all the same inputs and assumptions as the central nuclear case, but a different generation mix: 75% of all new capacity was decentralized, while

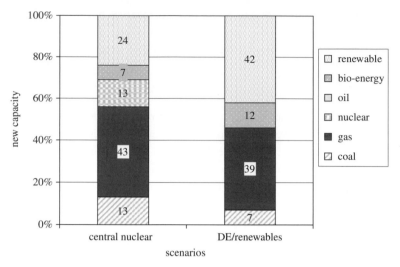

Figure 10.10. Baseline and main alternative scenarios.

25% consisted of renewables (centralized). No new nuclear capacity is built, while existing plants are retired at projected rates. There are no new centralized fossil-fired plants either, so that all new CG (25% of the total market) is renewable (mostly wind and bioenergy). The 75% market share of DE is mostly gas-fired combined heat and power (CHP), but shares of micro-CHP and on-site renewables will increase over the 20-year period.

10.6.3 Main results and conclusions

We analyse the model results within the sustainomics framework of making energy development more sustainable in the UK, using three typical indicators:

(1) economic – delivered energy costs;
(2) environmental – CO_2 emissions;
(3) socio-political – fuel used (representing dependence on foreign energy imports and reduced energy security).

Table 10.7 shows that the main alternative (with a more decentralized electricity supply system) results in lower delivered electricity cost (and lower capital costs), lower carbon emissions and less fuel use. Thus, it is clear that the decentralized scenario is the more sustainable option, as it is superior in all three dimensions of sustainable development – i.e. the triangle for 100% DE/renewables in Figure 10.11 is contained within the triangle of 100% CG, showing that the former is cheaper, less polluting and more energy secure.

The main reason for the cost savings is that the model assumes that DE requires less T&D capacity than CG, because it generates electricity much closer to the point of use. This assumption is valid, as most T&D capacity will require replacing within the next 10–20 years. The UK electricity demand is expected to grow in the commercial and residential

Table 10.7 *Main results*

	Scenarios		Saving	Percentage saving
	100% CG	100% DE/renewables		
Capital costs, generation and T&D	£70 billion	£51 billion	£19 billion	27
Delivered costs (£/kWh)	0.0683	0.0582	0.0101	15
CO_2 emissions (megatonnes/year)	36.75	33.92	2.83	7.7
Fuel use (petajoules/year)	2303	2163	140	6.1

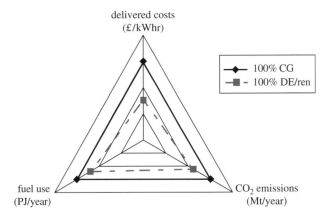

Figure10.11. Sustainability comparison of 100% CG and DE/renewables scenarios.

sectors, thus requiring additional T&D as well as generation capacity, with CG requirements being larger than DE. In addition, new CCGT power stations would most probably be built where new gas pipelines from the European continent come in, thus requiring new transmission lines to connect them to the grid.

Part of the savings made by the DE cases is also due to the higher operating efficiency of these technologies, particularly through co-generation and reduced transmission losses. Fuel use and CO_2 emissions are most strongly affected by this aspect. Note that the CG mix of the baseline scenario only introduces new nuclear generation from 2014, reflecting its long lead time. Consequently, the 100% CG scenario also includes a substantial amount of new gas-fired CCGT. This explains the savings in CO_2 emission and fuel use of the DE/renewables case, and shows that building any new gas-fired power stations that do not recover heat is clearly problematic in terms of Kyoto commitments and energy security.

Some sensitivity studies, assuming changes in some key assumptions, did not change the main conclusion of the study that DE options were more sustainable than CG options.

Fuel-price sensitivities

Sensitivity analysis of fuel prices, for which future trends are clearly uncertain, indicates that the effect of changes in fuel-price trends on the retail price is significant, and it affects DE/renewables more than CG, because retail prices are higher than wholesale prices. However, the results show that the benefits of DE/renewables are maintained at fuel-price rises of up to 10% per year.

Generation portfolios

When impacts of not building new nuclear or gas CCGT power stations were considered, carbon emission and fossil-fuel use increased, while costs remained largely unchanged. High reliance on gas imports from continental Europe confirmed that these were not attractive alternatives.

Demand growth

Reducing demand growth from 0.5% per year to 0% results in carbon emission savings comparable to a nuclear replacement programme (central nuclear scenario), and also reduces capital costs and fuel use by almost 20% and 10%, respectively. With zero demand growth, retail prices were slightly higher in the centralized case, because many costs are fixed, so that, with lower total generation, the unit price is higher. However, DE/renewables retail prices decreased with lower demand growth. Another more radical scenario (by Greenpeace) was also modelled, with a demand reduction of 0.5% per year through energy conservation, assuming rapid development of renewables and energy-efficiency measures surpassing government targets. The results were slightly better than for the 100% DE/renewables scenario.

11

Transport-sector applications[1]

This chapter continues our coverage of sustainomics applications to economic infrastructure sectors, focusing on transport (including fuel-pricing policy). Section 11.1 reviews generic priorities for sustainable transport, and discusses key issues worldwide, as well as economic, social and environmental linkages. Then we examine how transport policy could be made more sustainable in a typical developing country. In Section 11.2, health damage externalities due to transport-related air pollution in Sri Lanka are discussed, including a literature review, an estimation of damage costs from local air emissions using the benefit transfer method and finally an assessment of the specific health benefits of introducing unleaded petrol. Section 11.3 covers another classic externality – the effects of traffic congestion in the city of Colombo, including estimation of the cost of time wasted. Section 11.4 analyses several specific infrastructure projects and other measures for reducing congestion. The chapter concludes with Section 11.5, which provides an overview of sustainable transport policy options for Sri Lanka.

11.1 Generic priorities for sustainable transport

Sustainable transport is crucial for development as it provides access to jobs, health, education and other amenities, which determines the quality of life. Transport also provides physical access to resources and markets, which is essential for growth and poverty reduction. Poor transport policy could aggravate poverty, harm the environment, ignore the changing needs of users and overburden public finance. Several recent publications provide comprehensive expositions of sustainable transport and mobility, linked with the sustainomics framework and sustainable development triangle (SUMMA, 2003; World Bank, 1996c).

11.1.1 Key issues worldwide

Some actions to make transport infrastructure development more sustainable include (World Bank, 1996c): (1) *increasing access and affordability* by increasing access of rural poor to

---

[1] The valuable contributions of P. Meier to this chapter are gratefully acknowledged. Some parts of the chapter are based on material adapted from Munasinghe (1984b, 1990a) and Munasinghe and Meier (2003b).

markets and amenities, by expanding secondary and tertiary networks and improving public transport; (2) *providing adequate maintenance* in order to avoid increased costs of vehicle operation and higher long-run expenses borne by road agencies due to postponed repairs; (3) *responding to customer needs* in this era of rising incomes and rapidly changing markets, which generate demand for greater variety and higher quality services. (Priority should be given to greater safety, aesthetics and minimizing adverse health and environmental impacts.) (4) *Adjusting to global trade patterns* to move larger volumes of goods over longer distances, since bottlenecks in transport infrastructure hamper growth; and (5) *coping with rapid motorization* driven by rapidly expanding urban populations. In developing countries, ownership of vehicles is increasing at a faster rate than the amount of urban road space. Land-consuming urban structures have resulted in congested roads and slow-moving traffic, combined with a poorly maintained stock of vehicles causing immense pollution and long and costly journeys (especially for the poor).

11.1.2 Economic, environmental and social aspects

The application of the sustainomics framework (especially the sustainable development triangle) to the transport sector provides useful insights (Munasinghe, 1992a; SUMMA, 2003; World Bank, 1996c). Figure 11.1 summarizes the main elements of sustainable transport.

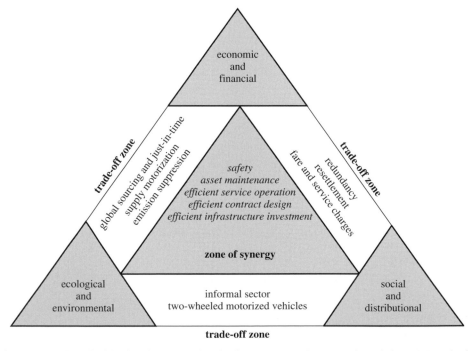

Figure 11.1. Sustainable development triangle for transport. Source: adapted from Munasinghe (1992a) and World Bank (1996c).

Economic and financial sustainability requires efficient use of resources and asset maintainance. Transport needs to be cost-effective and responsive to changing demands. Systematic economic appraisal of investments, appropriate price incentives and adequate financial and fiscal provisions for maintenance are essential. Suggestions for achieving economic sustainability include greater use of competitive market structures, higher efficiency in use, provision, financing and management of transport infrastructure and developing the strategic planning and system management capabilities to complement market forces.

Environmental and ecological sustainability requires that external effects of transport be considered when decisions are made. Cost-effective technology and strategic actions such as land-use planning, demand management and incentive to use public transport through pricing for congestion and pollution are needed. Ways of achieving environmental sustainability include addressing health impacts, integrating environmental elements into project appraisal and developing an environmentally sensitive strategic framework.

Social sustainability requires that the benefits of improved transport reach everyone. Greater attention should be paid to the role of the informal sector and non-motorized transport, the maintenance of rural transport facilities and the use of more labour-intensive techniques. We need to target the transport problems of the rural and urban poor, and protect them against adverse effects of changes in transport policies and programmes.

All three dimensions of sustainable transport need to be considered in decision making. The government should remain as the competitive provider and custodian of environmental and social interests, become more involved in setting efficient charges for the use of publicly owned infrastructure, protect the poor and facilitate greater community participation in decision making. Transport policy could take on a more market-based approach, with the private sector providing, operating and financing more transport services and some infrastructure.

11.2 Health-damage costs of air pollution in Sri Lanka

The impact of pollution on human health, especially of the poor, is important for social sustainability. This section analyses health damages due to transport-related air pollution in Sri Lanka. We review recent literature, estimate damage costs from local air emissions using the benefit transfer method and assess the health benefits of unleaded petrol.

11.2.1 Health effects

Chandrasiri and Jayasinghe (1998) provide health-damage valuation related expressly to vehicular emissions in Sri Lanka. Despite limitations, it is the only study based on clinical data. Since the late 1990s there has been a steady increase in hospital admissions and deaths related to respiratory disease that closely tracks the increase in vehicle emissions of particulate matter (Figure 11.2).

Figure 11.2 suggests that vehicle emissions increase faster than the hospital admissions/deaths, with a likely lag effect. Most physicians interviewed stated that respiratory diseases

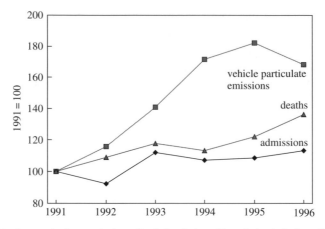

Figure 11.2. Vehicular particulate emissions (in Colombo) and hospital admissions/deaths (all Island) from respiratory diseases.

were related to vehicle emissions. This link was confirmed by a study of persons exposed to high emissions levels – trishaw drivers, traffic wardens and traffic police. While the emissions–illness causation is not proven, additional surveys of patients visiting doctors working in Colombo also provide more evidence.

Senanayake *et al*. (1999) analysed hospital admissions of children for asthma attacks, and found significant correlation between the highest daily rates of wheezing requiring immediate nebulization and the highest daily maximum one-hour averages of SO_2 and NOx (and similar correlation for the minimum rates). However, the link between asthma and air pollution is controversial – the UK Committee on the Medical Effects of Air Pollution (DoH, 1998) noted that the evidence does not support a causative role for outdoor air pollution, and opines that pollen and fungal spores are more likely to be influential. Indeed, in London, between 1976 and 1997, while asthma increased by 300%, emissions of air pollutants decreased by 180% (Glaister, Graham and Hoskins, 1999).

11.2.2 Valuation of local air emission damage

Ideally, environmental damage costs should be measured directly (Munasinghe, 1992a). In this study, the benefit-transfer method is used – the basis of which is the extrapolation to Sri Lanka of damage valuations estimated elsewhere. While country-specific damage valuations are preferable, such data do not exist for Sri Lanka. Provided the limitations are recognized, the method can provide useful indicative valuations of likely damage (Freeman, 2000). This approach has been used in a number of recent developing country studies (Abeygunawardena *et al*., 1999; Meier, 2004), in Sri Lanka – in a study of the impacts of the 1996 power shortage (LIFE 1998) – and in the Environmental Impact Assessment of the Colombo–Katunayake Expressway (RDA, 1997).

Table 11.1 *Damage estimates based on ADB benefit-transfer method and LIFE direct estimates*

Values given in US $/tonne

	ADB low	ADB high	LIFE[a]
Sri Lanka, 2000			
Particulates	258	478	483
SO_2	53	106	825
NOx	81	116	334
Sri Lanka, 2020			
Particulates	1623	2779	
SO_2	327	654	
NOx	506	697	

[a] Adjusted to 2000 using PPP.

Table 11.2 *University of Moratuwa damage valuations*

	SL Rs/litre[a]	SL Rs/vehicle-kilometre[b]
Car	0.57	0.06
Motorcycle	0.56	0.01
Three-wheeler	0.62	0.02
Van	0.65	0.07
Medium bus	0.71	0.14
Large bus	0.79	0.2
Medium lorry	0.71	0.14
Large lorry	0.79	0.23

[a] Kumarage (1999), Table B4-2.
[b] Based on average fuel efficiencies.

The method requires the following steps (Abeygunawardena *et al.*, 1999).

(1) Specify the base year unit damage values (as US $/tonne per 1000 persons). For this purpose ADB uses the study by Rowe *et al.* (1995) for New York State.
(2) Adjust price levels to the year 2000 using US GDP growth.
(3) Multiply the values by the ratio of per capita GDP. In 2000, the per capita GDP in Sri Lanka, adjusted for purchase power parity (PPP), was US $3900 (WRI, 1999), and that of the USA was US $34 000.
(4) Multiply the values by the estimated population resident within each radius.
(5) For future years, adjust by the estimated population and GDP growth in each radius.

Application of this approach yields the values shown in Table 11.1. Values derived by LIFE (1998) for impacts of power generation in Sri Lanka are shown in the third column.

Kumarage (1999) estimated damages in terms of SL Rs/litre for different vehicle types (Table 11.2). They show very little variation across vehicle types when expressed in

Table 11.3 *Marginal damage costs*

Values in US $/tonne

		Power plant (high stack) [1]	Large industry (medium stack) [2]	Small boilers and vehicular [3]	Ratio vehicle to power plant [4] = [3]/[1]
Mumbai	PM10	234	1077	7963	34
	SO$_2$	51	236	1747	34
	NOx	20	93	668	33
Shanghai	PM10	161	502	5828	36
	SO$_2$	36	112	1295	36
	NOx	11	33	385	35
Manila	PM10	345	1828	17 942	52
	SO$_2$	61	324	3183	52
	NOx	24	129	1265	52
Bangkok	PM10	828	2357	28 722	34
	SO$_2$	147	417	5087	34
	NOx	57	162	1971	34
Krakow	PM10	97	682	13 255	136
	SO$_2$	18	130	2522	140
	NOx	4	29	560	140
Santiago	PM10	692	4783	88 551	128
	SO$_2$	132	911	16 864	127
	NOx	35	240	4445	127

Source: Lvovsky *et al.* (2000), Table 1.5 (p. 16).

SL Rs/litre, but when converted to SL Rs/km travelled, the environmental damages show large variation, as expected.

Chandrasiri and Jayasinghe (1998) estimated the value of health damages attributable to particulates in Colombo at between SL Rs67–160 million/yr, based on limited data of highly exposed occupational groups (traffic wardens, trishaw drivers, traffic policemen). World Bank (2000) assessed health damages in Colombo due to PM10 at US $30 million, using average ambient concentrations of 40–50 μg/m^3.

The 'Six Cities Study'

Most health effect valuation studies in the USA and Europe relate to power-sector emissions (e.g. tall stacks in remote locations), which are difficult to use with the benefit-transfer method for vehicular emissions (at ground level in densely populated areas). One source of damage valuations is the 'Six Cities Study' (Lvovsky *et al.*, 2000), which enables the benefit-transfer method to be applied to the health effects of vehicular emissions. The study derives damage-cost estimates for vehicular emissions of PM10, SO$_2$ and NOx in six cities (Table 11.3). The

Table 11.4 *Unit health damages*

Values in US $/tonne per 1 000 000 population per US $1000 per capita income

One-tonne change in emission of	High stack (power plants)	Medium stack (large industry)	Low stack (boilers and vehicles)
PM10			
Range for six cities	20–54	63–348	736–6435
Average	42	214	3114
SO₂			
Range for six cities	3–8	10–56	121–1037
Average	6	33	487
NOx			
Range for six cities	1–3	3–13	29–236
Average	2	9	123

Source: Lvovsky *et al.* (2000), Table 6-3 (p. 65).

values for the four Asian cities are 30–50 times greater than for power-plant emissions from high stacks (and even greater in the case of Krakow and Santiago).

The marginal unit values shown in Table 11.4 provide useful guidance. Uncertainty is a major concern when determining the economically optimal level of renewable energy (Box 11.1).

If we apply the lowest values in Table 11.4 to Colombo (with a population of 4.9 million and GDP/capita of US $4933), then the values compute to US $17 790/tonne for PM10, US $2924/tonne for SO_2 and US $700/tonne for NOx, values, which is comparable to Manila. Table 11.5 summarizes all estimates, converted to Colombo for 2000.

Considering only PM10, SO_2 and NOx underestimates the total health damage. Glaister *et al.* (1999) estimated that the total damage cost for urban diesel emissions in the UK was 2.424p/km, of which 70% was due to to PM10 alone and 82% to the sum of PM10, SO_2 and NOx.

Lead

There are no systematic health damage studies of lead in Sri Lanka, except for Chandrasiri and Jayasinghe (1998). However, we may draw on a vast international literature on the subject (Lovei, 1998). In the USA, the benefit–cost ratio of eliminating lead in petrol was estimated to be over 10 (USEPA, 1985), and Schwartz (1994) estimated health benefits of US $18.9 billion per year for reducing the US populations' blood level by 1 µg/dlitre. Most governments in Asia have phased out leaded petrol.

Table 11.6 shows the results of a study of lead levels in blood in Sri Lanka, compared with data from other countries (Awegoda, Perera and Mathhes, 1994). Despite differences in age, sample year, etc., lead levels are high in the most exposed groups compared with the control population. The general levels appear to be less than half of those in other large Asian cities.

For Sri Lanka, we scale the estimate by ratio of population and ratio of PPP-adjusted GNP/capita. Then a reduction of lead concentration in blood of 1 µg/dlitre yields a benefit of

Box 11.1 The economically optimal level of renewable energy

Decisions about implementing renewable-energy targets are pending in several countries as mandated market-share mechanisms are being considered. The standard methodology to estimate the economically optimal quantity of renewable energy is to derive a supply curve for renewable energy and then to set the renewables target at the quantity at which the costs of the marginal plant are exactly equal to the avoided costs (including the avoided environmental damage costs).

In Figure 11.3, we assume that the cost of fossil-fuel generation (C), the externality value (V_{ENV}) and the supply curve (S) are all known. The optimal quantity of renewable energy is given by the intersection of the supply curve S with the avoided economic cost (including the value of the externality cost), i.e. by the point A. It follows that the economically optimal target is Q_N, which, if implemented by a system of tradable green certificates (TGCs), results in a TGC price equal to V_{ENV}.

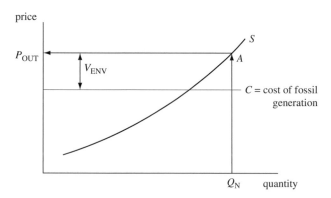

Figure 11.3. Optimizing the supply of renewable energy.

Clearly, if the actual damage cost were twice the assumed value of V_{ENV}, then a target set at Q_N would significantly underestimate the true economic optimum (and overestimate the optimum if the true damage cost were lower than the assumed value). This in turn has implications for the policy instrument used: if all quantities are known with certainty, then it matters little whether government sets a quantity target at Q_N or sets a price at P_{OUT}, since the result will be the same. But in the face of uncertainty, which may require a change in policy if new research findings reveal significantly higher (or lower) damage costs, adjusting a quantity target is likely to be much easier than adjusting a price (as vested interests defend the status quo); see Meier (2004).

SL Rs19 billion (for 2000), or about 1.5% of GDP. Given year 2000 petrol consumption of 277 million litres/yr, this translates to SL Rs68.7/litre of petrol. Even if this estimate were reduced by a factor of 10, the benefits of unleaded petrol would still correspond to around Rs7/litre – a substantial benefit.

Table 11.5 *Comparison of damage valuation estimates*

Values in US $/tonne

Basis	Source	Colombo, 2000
Particulates [a]		
Six Cities Study, low value of range	PM10	17 790
	as TSP	14 232
ADB benefit-transfer method	Table 11.1	258–478
RDA[b], CKE environmental assessment	see text	8500
LIFE	Table 11.1	483
University of Moratuwa		262
SO₂		
Six Cities Study, low value of range	see text	2924
ADB benefit-transfer method	Table 11.1	53–106
LIFE	Table 11.1	825
University of Moratuwa		447
NOx		
Six Cities Study, low value of range	see text	700
ADB benefit-transfer method	Table 11.1	506–697
LIFE	Table 11.1	334
University of Moratuwa		180

[a] The Six Cities Study gives PM10 health damage costs; the others are for total particulate matter. For ambient air quality, the Six Cities Study uses a PM10/TSP ratio of 0.55; however, emissions of PM10 are 0.8 of the TSP emission factor for diesel vehicles and 0.9 of the TSP emission factor for petrol vehicles. The share of PM10 in total TSP from typical power plant stacks is about 0.6.
[b] Road Development Authority.

Table 11.6 *Average lead levels in blood*

Sri Lanka (Colombo)	Mean (μg/dl)
School children (4–5 years)	5
Motorcycle riders	12
Street vendors	13
Three-wheeler drivers	15
Traffic police	53
Adult control group	9
Other locations	
Bangkok	40
Manila	20
Jakarta	15

Sources: International data from Lovei (1998);
Sri Lanka data from Awegoda *et al*. (1994).

11.3 Traffic congestion – economic and environmental sustainability

Traffic congestion, especially in the rapidly growing major cities of developing countries, is imposing increasing economic and environmental costs. Traditional methods of reducing congestion have failed, particularly on the supply side – e.g. road expansion only provides short-term relief and is limited by tight fiscal, physical and environmental constraints. However, demand side options like pricing offer better a long-term solution – e.g. the successful pricing scheme in Singapore, one of the few large Asian cities free of major road congestion (Jayaweera, 1999).

Most traffic entering Colombo uses seven main radial roads, which all connect to the central business district (CBD). These roads all exhibit very strong peak-hour traffic; Figure 11.4 shows typical inbound and outbound patterns for the A3 route. Congestion occurs when an additional vehicle entering a road segment causes the normal speed of other vehicles to decrease, thereby imposing costs not only on that additional vehicle, but also on all vehicles using that road segment (Jayaweera, 1999). Based on a definition of congestion as occurring whenever average speeds of 30 km/hr cannot be maintained, the Colombo Urban Transport Study (CUTS) estimates the costs of congestion at SL Rs11 billion/yr, which is equivalent to 1.5% of the 1996 GDP. This value is likely to rise in the absence of policy reforms. Already average speeds in the Greater Colombo Metropolitan Region (GCMR) have dropped to about 22 km/hr, and range from 10–15 km/hr in the centre to around 45 km/hr at the periphery of the GCMR.

Sharp reductions in road speed result in significant increases in air emissions, because fuel efficiency decreases non-linearly with speed (particularly for buses and trucks) – see the 2001 traffic data on the Colombo–Ratnapura road given in Figure 11.5.

Jayaweera (1999) estimated the optimal congestion toll in Colombo by setting it equal to the difference between marginal social cost and average private cost. We extend this microeconomic work to calculate aggregate economic effects and estimate related environmental benefits.

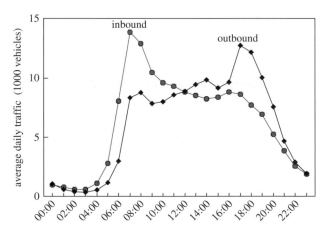

Figure 11.4. Hourly mean daily traffic for the A3 (Peliyagoda–Puttalam).

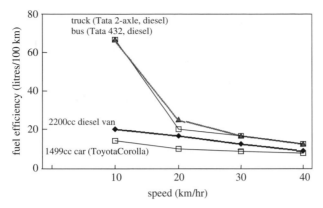

Figure 11.5. Fuel efficiency survey for typical vehicles.

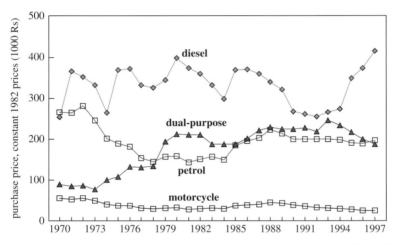

Figure 11.6. Vehicle prices, in constant 1982 rupees. Source: Sri Lanka customs. GDP deflator from Central Bank.

11.3.1 Price elasticities

In the following, we examine the influence of prices on decisions of road users (see also Chapter 14). The initial choice of vehicle (e.g. diesel or petrol) is likely to depend on purchase price and expected cost of operation (especially fuel price). Next, the pattern of vehicle use will depend mainly on fuel prices. Tax rates play as much a role in these decisions as world oil prices and CIF prices of automobiles. Customs and excise duties on vehicle imports show wide variations across different vehicle types, with complex and fast-changing exemptions and concessions (Chandrasiri, 1999).

Vehicles are not manufactured in Sri Lanka (although some are assembled), so the entire demand is met by imports, of which only 25% are new vehicles (Chandrasiri, 1999). The typical passenger car import is a 2–3-year-old, reconditioned Japanese vehicle. In Figure 11.6

Table 11.7 *Comparison of the diesel and petrol vehicle price for the Toyota model RAV4*

	Cost in rupees	
	Petrol	Diesel
Costs at purchase		
CIF	1 800 000	2 200 000
Import duty	267 000	534 000
Defence levy	108 489	217 000
Excise duty	254 400	508 800
GST	198 721	397 400
Stamp duty	21 380	42 800
Total tax	850 092	1 700 000
Total CIF + tax	2 649 992	3 900 000
Tax as percentage of total price	32%	44%
Registration	3500	6500
Diesel tax		10 000
Luxury tax[a]		50 000
Annual fuel cost		
km/yr	15 000	15 000
km/litre	10	10
litre/yr	1500	1500
Price/litre	50	21.50
Annual fuel cost	75 000	32 250

[a] Luxury tax falls by SL Rs10 000/yr, reaching zero in the sixth year.
Figures are tabulated for taxes and typical prices as of April, 2001.

we show the average nominal price, ex-customs, for four main types of passenger vehicle, expressed in constant 1982 rupees – most of the price variation reflects changes in taxation.

Table 11.7 shows a comparison of the taxes levied on diesel and petrol cars, using the same Toyota model differing only by type of engine (3-year-old reconditioned vehicles). The (absolute) tax on the diesel vehicle at the time of purchase is seen to be double that of the petrol-powered car, though as percentages of the initial cost the tax burden is comparable.

Asian price elasticities of aggregate transportation fuel demand are shown in Table 11.8. However, many of the Sri Lankan estimates are limited to the period 1970–1985, and do not properly capture the major changes in road transport consequent to liberalization of the economy in 1977.

There are some problems. For petrol-demand studies, defining the independent variable as consumption per vehicle fails to consider rapid changes in the vehicle mix – mainly the significant growth in motorcycles (whose fuel demand per vehicle is a small fraction of that of automobiles). For example, McRae (1994) did not cover motorcycles and

Table 11.8 *Estimates of own-price elasticities of demand for transport fuels in Asia*

	Year	Petrol	Diesel
Sri Lanka			
de Silva (1989)	1970–1985	−0.55	−1.21
Samaraweera (1989)	1970–1985	−0.387	−0.26
Ranasinghe (1989)	1970–1985	−0.508	−0.034
Meier *et al.* (1997)	1973–1991	−1.14 (long run)	
		−0.334 (short run)	
McRae (1994)	1973–1987	−0.337	
Jayaweera (1999)		−0.163 (long run)	−0.339 (long run)
		−0.115 (short run)	−0.154 (short run)
Other countries			
Philippines[a]	1973–1987	−0.391	
Thailand[a]	1973–1987	−0.304	
Malaysia[a]	1973–1987	−0.125	
S. Korea[a]	1973–1987	−0.496	
S. Korea[a]	1973–1997	−0.866 (long run)[b]	
		−0.385 (short run)[b]	
Indonesia[a]	1973–1987	−0.197	
India[a]	1973–1987	−0.321	
Taiwan[a]	1973–1987	+0.024	
Taiwan[c]	1954–1985	−1.362 (long run)	
		−0.245 (short run)	
Taiwan[d]	1973–1992	−0.519 (long run)[b]	
		−0.124 (short run)[b]	

Dependent variable is consumption per vehicle in all Sri Lanka studies.

[a] Source: McRae (1994).

[b] Demand for petrol and diesel are taken together (see discussion in the text).

[c] Source: Garbacz (1989).

[d] Source: Banaszak *et al.* (1999).

three-wheelers. Some studies add a variable for vehicles per capita, whose elasticity is almost always strongly negative – as vehicles per capita will reduce utilization (McRae, 1994). For Sri Lanka, only Meier, Munasinghe and Siyambalapitiya (1997) includes the fraction of motorcycles in the vehicle mix as a variable (with a corresponding elasticity of −0.17).

Among Asian studies, the most rigorously specified is that of Garbacz (1989) for Taiwan. However, even this study was unable to include vehicle price variables. Both Taiwan and Sri Lanka studies (Meier *et al.*, 1997) show similar results for both long- and short-run elasticities (Table 11.8), and agree with the average value of −1.05 for long-run elasticity across developing countries; see Dahl and Sterner (1991).

Since petrol and diesel are partial substitutes, their cross-price elasticities are important. Therefore, price and income elasticities must be estimated simultaneously, either by (1) combining petrol and diesel consumption and using a price variable that is the weighted diesel and petrol price or (2) simultaneously estimating the two equations. The former approach was taken by Banaszak, Chakravorty and Ljeung (1999) for Taiwan and S. Korea, and the latter by Chandrasiri (1999) for Sri Lanka.

However, the consensus view in the international literature favours the 'lagged endogenous model', which (for petrol demand) has the following functional form used by Meier *et al.* (1997) and Jayaweera (1999):

$$Q(g)_t = kQ(g)_{t-1}^{\lambda} Y_t^{\alpha} P(g)_t^{\beta} P(d)_t^{\mu} V_t^{\gamma}, \tag{11.1}$$

where

$Q(g)_t$ = petrol demand (sales/number of vehicles) at time t,
$P(g)_t$ = petrol price at time t,
$P(d)_t$ = diesel price at time t,
k = constant,
Y = per capita GDP (at constant prices),
V = vehicle mix variable (for example, fraction of motorcycles),
λ = lag coefficient,
α = income elasticity,
β = short-run own-price elasticity,
μ = cross-price elasticity for diesel,
γ = vehicle mix coefficient.

The long-run price elasticity may now be calculated; it is given by

$$\beta^* = \frac{\beta}{(1 - \lambda)}. \tag{11.2}$$

For the petrol equation, the relevant vehicle-mix variable is the fraction of motorcycles, while, for the diesel equation, the fraction of light diesel vehicles is the relevant variable. The results in Table 11.9 compare the OLS (ordinary least squares) and SURE (seemingly unrelated regression equations) estimates for the time series 1968–2000. In the SURE method, equations are estimated simultaneously to avoid problems when the error term across equations are correlated, which is the case in fuel-demand equations linked by cross-price elasticities (Lutkepohl, 1991).

The lag variables have the correct sign and magnitude, and the results of SURE and OLS are surprisingly close. The vehicle fleet variables (fractions of motorcycles in petrol and heavy vehicles in diesel) are significant and have the correct sign. The diesel own-price elasticity is not significant. Taking into account the wide variation in values reported in the literature, we summarize the elasticity values in Table 11.10.

A different approach (requiring more detailed data) is to derive vehicle-kilometre elasticities. They measure the change in vehicle-kilometres travelled in response to changes in total (private) vehicle operating costs (including fuel, lubricants and maintenance) by different vehicle class. The OLS results estimated in log-linear from 1988–2000 are shown in Table 11.11 and are used in the analysis of congestion tolls presented below.

Table 11.9 *Comparison of SURE and OLS estimates*

	Petrol		Diesel	
Variable	OLS	SURE	OLS	SURE
CNST	0.412	0.365	1.94	2.08
	(0.226)	(0.207)	(2)	(2.21)
Petrol price	**−0.151**	**−0.155**	0.045	0.039
	(1.82)	(1.9)	(0.833)	(0.74)
Diesel price	0.091	0.089	−0.07	−0.63
	(1.02)	(1.01)	(1.18)	(1.06)
Tax rates	−0.059	−0.054	**−0.144**	**−0.156**
	(0.317)	(0.3)	(1.96)	(2.17)
Lag effect	**0.704**	**0.693**	**0.765**	**0.758**
	(6.38)	(6.35)	(7.46)	(7.62)
Fraction of motorcycles	**−0.1**	**−0.099**		
	(2.18)	(2.18)		
Fraction of heavy-duty vehicles			**−0.151**	**−0.168**
			(1.37)	(1.54)
R^2	0.962	0.962	0.979	0.979

Statistically significant values are shown in bold; the t-value is given in parentheses.

Table 11.10 *Short- and long-run price elasticities*

		Petrol	Diesel
Own-price	short-run	**−0.16**	−0.07
	long-run	**−0.51**	**−0.29**
Cross-price		0.09	0.05

Statistically significant values given in bold.

Table 11.11 *Vehicle-kilometre elasticities*

Vehicle category	Elasticity
Car (diesel/petrol)	−0.349
Light truck (diesel)	−0.23
Medium truck (diesel)	−0.443
Heavy truck (diesel)	−0.26
Medium bus (diesel)	−0.15
Large bus (diesel)	−0.13
Motorcycle (petrol)	−0.462

Estimates by D. Jayaweera (personal communication).

Table 11.12 *Estimated price elasticities*

Public bus	-0.08
Private bus	-0.07
Rail	-0.04

Source: Dheerasinghe and Jayaweera (1997).

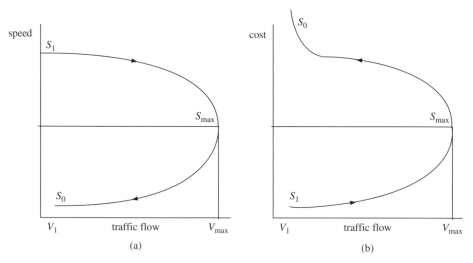

Figure 11.7. Speed and cost versus traffic.

Finally, Table 11.12 shows low own-price and negative cross-price elasticities of public transport, suggesting that the different modes are complements rather than substitutes (Dheerasinghe and Jayaweera, 1997). Rail usage increased significantly from 7% of person-kilometre to 9%, after the bus fare increases of 2000, although prior bus fare increases (in constant terms) in 1974, 1980 and 1987 had little effect.

11.3.2 Theoretical model

Figure 11.7 illustrates the fundamental relationship between speed, cost and traffic flow. In Figure 11.7(a), starting at low flows (V_1) and an empty road, the speed is given by S_1. Speeds decline as additional vehicles join the flow, reaching S_{max} at flow V_{max}. Beyond this point, additional vehicles result in a reduction in flow, reaching near-zero flow and speed (S_0).

Figure 11.7(b) shows the corresponding 'average private cost' curve faced by a motorist. The term 'average private cost' is used to stress the difference between private and social costs. As speeds decline, private costs to the motorist increase (because time per trip, and value of time per trip, rise, while fuel efficiency decreases). As more vehicles enter the road beyond V_{max}, costs continue to increase (tending to infinity with total gridlock). We

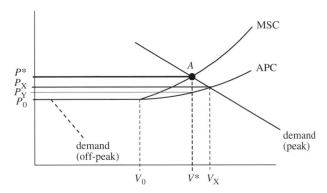

Figure 11.8. Optimal pricing and congestion.

may ignore the (upper) backward bending part of the curve, because optimal solutions always lie on the lower part.

Traffic congestion occurs because the marginal user considers only his or her private costs when making a decision regarding a particular trip at a particular time, ignoring any costs imposed on others. In Figure 11.8, up to some given traffic volume V_0 (i.e. the capacity of the road), the private cost is (roughly) constant, P_0.

As traffic increases beyond V_0, speeds fall and the individual's private costs increase – because covering a given distance requires more time and fuel efficiency is lower as speeds decrease (higher fuel costs). Therefore, beyond V_0, the private cost (APC) curve slopes upward, intersecting the demand curve at point A (V_X, P_X).

However, beyond V_0 the marginal user imposes these same externalities on the other road users as well, as the decrease in speed is experienced by all. The marginal social cost (MSC) curve therefore lies higher than the private cost (APC). Thus the societal optimal traffic volume is at V^*, P^* – where the (peak period) demand curve intersects MSC (rather than APC). Welfare theory argues for a 'Pigouvian' tax (see Section 3.2.2) on the use of congested roads in the amount $\Delta = P^* - P_Y$, at which point the private users' total cost (private cost plus tax) exactly equals the social cost (also equal to the marginal social benefit represented by the demand curve). The off-peak demand curve lies far to the left of the peak demand curve, and the optimal toll would be very small or zero (e.g. at night).

11.3.3 Estimating the value of time

Time savings provide the greatest economic benefits of reducing traffic congestion. People would pay more to avoid time delays, depending on their personal opportunity cost of time. Since detailed income data are unavailable for road users in Sri Lanka, average salary is used. Employers would place an opportunity cost on driver's time that is equal to gross salary. For bus riders (largely salaried), road congestion and longer commute times will reduce leisure time (or sleep). While there is no direct measure of the value of leisure time,

Table 11.13 *Average monthly income of drivers and passengers*

	SL Rs/month
Car passenger	21 000
Van passenger	16 500
Bus passenger	3800
Car driver	4700
Van driver	5040
Bus driver	10 080
Truck driver	11 280

Source: University of Moratuwa, Origin–Destination Survey, May, 1998.

Table 11.14 *Value of time*

	Value of time (SL Rs/hr)	Ratio to value for car passenger	Ratio based only on salary
Car passenger	26.5	1	1
Van passenger	21.4	0.81	0.79
Bus passenger	8.8	0.33	0.18
Car driver	16.8	0.63	0.22
Van driver	13	0.49	0.24
Bus driver	16.4	0.62	0.48
Truck driver	19.3	0.73	0.54

Source: Jayaweera (1999), Tables 5.8 and 5.2.

we may assume it would be related to income (Munasinghe, 1980c). Table 11.13 shows average monthly incomes of road users, as a guide to relative opportunity cost of time.

In the following, we use the value of car passenger time as the exogenous variable, and link other users, value by the proportions implied in Table 11.13. Escalating the passenger salary by 5% (real GDP growth rate in the reference case), the 2001 value is SL Rs24 310/ month, or SL Rs138/hr – (22 working days at 8 hr/day). The value of time is also related to trip purpose. The share of work commuting, education and business is 43%, 21% and 16% among the main peak period road users, respectively.

Jayaweera (1999) estimates lower values of time (Table 11.14). The value for car passengers is only SL Rs26.5/hr (SL Rs30/hr at 2000 prices). The greater value (SL Rs138/hr) may be justified for the expressway/A30 corridor, since the proportion of higher-valued business trips is likely to be more than for in-city average values. However, in Section 11.3.5, we use Jayaweera's figures for a more conservative estimate of benefits. The average value of time for goods vehicles was taken as SL Rs150/hr (plus driver's time as noted above), based on Jayaweera (1999).

Table 11.15 *Proposed tolls (daily equivalent)*

	Jayaweera	Colombo Council
Car	25	8
Light truck	20	8
Medium truck	20	8
Heavy truck	40	8
Medium bus	0	
Light bus	0	
Motorcycle	10	8

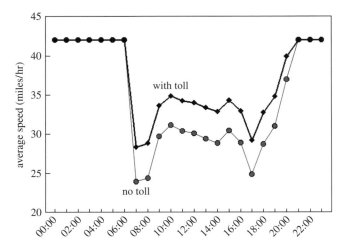

Figure 11.9. Average speed at various times of day (base-case tolls, A3).

11.3.4 Impact of a congestion toll

Table 11.15 shows Jayaweera's graduated toll proposal and the flat rate proposal of the Colombo Municipal Council. The former, which includes differences in externality costs by vehicle class, is used as our reference case. The response to a toll may not conform to estimates of past responses to changes in volatile organic compound (VOC) emissions.

Figure 11.9 shows the predicted changes in road speeds in response to a toll, based on the elasticities of Table 11.11. Meier and Munasinghe (2003) describe the detailed model used to relate vehicle speeds to traffic volume (which itself depends on the toll and price elasticity). The corresponding pattern of avoided trips is shown in Figure 11.10. A very minor correction is not shown in the figure – one additional bus trip for every 40 avoided motorcycle or car trips, which has little impact.

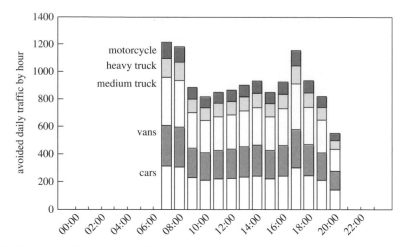

Figure 11.10. Impact of congestion toll on speed during the day (A3, outbound).

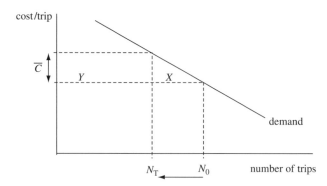

Figure 11.11. Welfare losses.

11.3.5 Economic analysis

The calculation of costs and benefits is straightforward, including welfare losses that depend upon behavioural responses to the toll. For passenger trips (cars, vans and motorcycles), the potential responses are: (1) make the trip at the usual hour and pay the toll; (2) forgo the trip; (3) take public transport (bus); and (4) avoid the toll by entering the city before 7 am and leaving after 8 pm (since toll stickers must be displayed for in-city driving, this response is unlikely and ignored in the model).

Figure 11.11 shows the loss of consumer surplus due to the reduction in number of trips induced by the toll. The loss of surplus is the area $Y+X$, where

$$X = \frac{\tau[N_0 - N_T]}{2},$$
$$Y = \tau N_T,$$

Table 11.16 *Physical impacts of the congestion charge*

	Toll = SL Rs75		Toll = SL Rs25	
	Low elasticity[a]	High elasticity[b]	Low elasticity	High elasticity
Car (%)	−10.1	−19.1	−3.9	−7.7
Light truck (%)	−7.9	−15	−3.1	−6.1
Medium truck (%)	−9.7	−18.3	−3.7	−7.2
Heavy truck (%)	−9.7	−18.3	−3.9	−7.6
Medium bus (%)	0.3	0.5	0.1	0.2
Large bus (%)	0.6	1	0.3	0.5
Motorcycle (%)	−14	−25.7	−5.6	−10.8
Total (%)	−5.7	−10.7	−2.2	−4.3
Environment (emission reductions)				
GHGs (lifetime) 1000 tonnes	17	33	6.4	12.8
Year 2010 reductions				
PM10 (tonnes)	1	2	0	1
SO$_2$ (tonnes)	7	13	3	5
NOx (tonnes)	39	75	15	29

[a] Low elasticity = values as in Table 11.11.
[b] High elasticity = 2 × vehicle operating cost values.

and where τ is the daily toll, and N_0 and N_T are the numbers of trips before and after the toll. Thus, Y is the toll revenue collected by the government and X is the deadweight loss. This is an approximation, since private travellers may experience further inconvenience and loss of utility when shifting to public transport.

Table 11.16 shows the physical environmental impacts as a function of the toll and elasticity. Based on historical VOC (low) elasticity, the total traffic reduction in response to a Rs25 daily toll will be only 2.2%, with 3.9% and 5.6% declines in car and motorcycle traffic, respectively. The decline in air emissions is also small. The reference case costs and benefits, under the Jayaweera toll, is shown in Table 11.17.

The big winners in Table 11.17 are (low-income) bus users – because of large numbers of passengers, aggregate time savings and economic benefits are greater. If deadweight losses (loss of surplus for those shifting to less convenient transport modes) are excluded, car passengers break even, because their time and fuel savings are about equal to toll payments. With deadweight losses, the net impact on car users is negative. For trucks, the net impact is always positive, so there is no basis for raising commodity prices. Figure 11.12 shows results as net present values over 20 years (10% discount rate). Thus, road pricing via a congestion toll has a major positive economic impact. Although environmental benefits amount to under 1% of economic benefits, the toll still yields a win–win outcome.

Table 11.17 *Impact of the Jayaweera toll in year 2010*

	Road users							Environment		
	Low income (bus)	Medium income (motorcycle)	High income (car)	Freight (truck)	Govt	Others	Total	Local	Global	Total
	[1]	[2]	[3]	[4]	[5]	[6]	[7]	[8]	[9]	[10]
Time savings	578	21	489	354			1442			1442
Tolls	0	−99	−1280	−593	1972		0			0
Petrol fuel tax		0	8		−8		0			0
Diesel fuel tax	5		1	2	−9		0			0
Diesel savings	87			47			134			134
Petrol savings		0	19				20			20
Deadweight losses	0	−7	−56	−27			−90			−90
Admin. costs					−30		−30			−30
Commissions					−197	197	−197			−197
Environment										
PM10							0	2		2
SO$_2$							0	2		2
NOx							0	3		3
GHG							0		1	1
Total	671	−85	−819	−217	1728	197	1278	7	1	1286

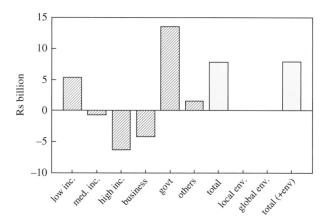

Figure 11.12. Congestion toll winners and losers (net present value over 20 years).

Figure 11.13 shows a sensitivity analysis of net economic benefits to the toll (for 2001), scaled by the passenger car charge. The optimum passenger car toll is about SL Rs35/day, which is higher than the value of SL Rs25 determined by Jayaweera based on microeconomic theory – because buses are exempted, so the toll for remaining vehicles has to

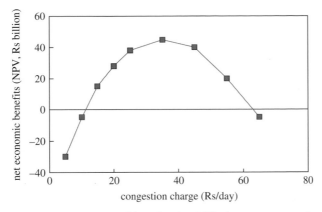

Figure 11.13. Net present value (NPV) of benefits (Rs billion) versus congestion charge (Rs/day/passenger car).

be increased to achieve same overall congestion benefit. Thus, results of this aggregate (macro) model are consistent with microeconomic theory.

11.4 Other options for reducing traffic congestion

Meier and Munasinghe (2003) examine several other options to reduce traffic congestion in the Colombo area: (a) a new expressway from the centre of Colombo to the Katunayake airport; (b) railway electrification; (c) reintroduction of school buses; and (d) dry container port, designed to reduce congestion in both the main northbound artery and Colombo Port. Each analysis uses the same methodology as described in Section 11.3.

11.4.1 Katunayake airport expressway

The present A3 road to the airport is the most heavily travelled in Sri Lanka, with average daily traffic (ADT) of 200 000 near Colombo (about 1% of all vehicle-kilometres in the country). A 25 km, four-lane, limited access expressway to link downtown Colombo with the Katunayake airport (the Colombo–Katunayake Expressway, or CKE) has been discussed for almost two decades. Due to delays and environmental objections (RDA, 1997; Sivagnasothy and McCauley, 2000), cost estimates have risen from SL Rs5 billion in 1995 to over Rs13 billion in 2000, when construction began. Meanwhile, the air pollution due to traffic congestion on the A3 road will continue to worsen. Insights derived from the analysis of the expressway project will help in studying other highway proposals, such as the Southern Highway (linking Colombo to Matara on the South Coast) and the Outer Circular Highway (Colombo orbital road, also connecting to the airport expressway).

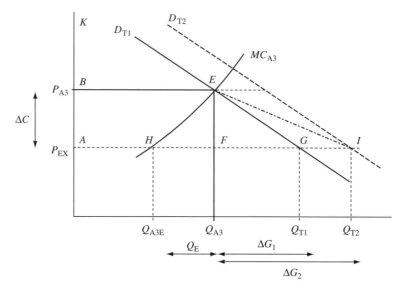

Figure 11.14. Estimating consumer surplus changes.

Theory

The economic benefits of the new road are calculated in our model, as the change in consumer surplus – for both new road users and old road users (who suffer less congestion). Consider the demand curve D_{T1} depicted in Figure 11.14. Before the project, users of the A3 experience costs of P_{A3} at traffic volume Q_{A3} (given by the intersection of the demand curve and the marginal cost curve MC_{A3}).

Once the project is built, some vehicles (Q_E) will elect to use the expressway, leaving Q_{A3E} on the original road. Road users will experience lower costs, P_{EX}, due to fuel and time savings $\Delta C = P_{A3} - P_{EX}$. However, at the new lower cost P_{EX}, the total travel demand increases from Q_{A3} to Q_{T1}, the difference ΔG_1 being the induced traffic (whose quantum is a function of the demand elasticity, i.e. of the slope of the line D_{T1}). The benefit is the change in consumer surplus, or increase from the original area *KBE* to *KBAHFGE* – assuming a linear demand curve. Thus:

$$\Delta B_1 = KBAHFGE - KBE = ABEF + EFG$$
$$= \Delta C \cdot Q_{A3} + 0.5\Delta C \cdot \Delta G_1. \tag{11.3}$$

There will also be an outward shift in the demand curve, shown in Figure 11.14 as D_{T2}. This intersects price P_{EX} at *I*, leading to an increase in traffic to Q_{T2} and a larger consumer surplus increase from *KBE* to *KBAHFGIE*:

$$\Delta B_2 = KBAHFGIE - KBE = ABEF + EFGI$$
$$= \Delta C \cdot Q_{A3} + 0.5\Delta C \cdot \Delta G_2. \tag{11.4}$$

Table 11.18 *Tolls proposed by Board of Investment (one-way toll)*

Vehicle type	SL Rs
Car	65
Van	95
Bus	140
Large bus	180
Delivery van	195
Truck	390
Container truck	650

However, at the higher level of traffic within the corridor, there will be increased congestion outside the corridor, particularly on the access roads to the expressway interchanges. This externality, say ΔC^*, would reduce the level of benefits. In this study we assume that this externality exactly offsets shifts in the demand curve induced by the expressway ($\Delta C^* = \Delta B_2 - \Delta B_1$), so that benefits are given by ΔB_1 (in Equation (11.4)).

Results

A large range of traffic forecasts exist (Kumarage *et al.*, 2000; University of Moratuwa, 2000). Typical 2025 estimates of daily vehicle-kilometres on the expressway range from 325 000 to 747 000, and on the A3 from 836 500 to 1 708 000, with toll revenues varying from Rs1.7 million/day to Rs4.1 million/day – based upon the toll structure shown in Table 11.18. Truck charges are high, but car tolls approximate potential time savings.

Table 11.19 shows values of environmental impacts. For air pollution, we use our estimates, since the CKE Environmental Impact Statement values are overstated. The 20-year net present value (NPV) of costs and benefits is shown in Table 11.20. Bus passengers are assumed to benefit only from time savings (since fuel savings would accrue to bus owners and offset tolls). Although motorcyclists would be banned from the expressway, they benefit from both time and fuel savings from the less congested A3. Time savings of bus, van and truck drivers accrue to the owners of these vehicles. Clearly, air emission benefits outweigh the non-air costs, and inclusion of the environmental benefits simply makes a good project better.

As expected, freight is the single largest beneficiary. Low-income road users (including bus passengers and pedestrians suffering fatalities and serious injuries) derive greater benefit than car passengers. Toll income (even at SL Rs50) would more than cover the operation and maintenance costs of the Road Development Authority (RDA), but still leave a significant funding gap for debt service.

11.4.2 Railway electrification

The government has been studying options for electrifying suburban rail in Colombo for several decades, including possible private-sector investment. The section of railway line

Table 11.19 *Valuation of local environmental impacts*

NPV (SL Rs million)

	Sigvagnasothy and McCauley (2000) (1991 prices)	CKE-EIS study (1995 prices)	Updated to 2000 for our study[a]
Conversion of agricultural land[b]	−42		−84
Noise and air pollution[c]	−41		−82
Noise pollution[d]		−29	−40
Air pollution		1377	see text
Reduced biodiversity and lagoon area		−83	−118
Water pollution and fishery losses	−8		−16
Reduction in road accidents[e]		112	159
Conversion of non-agric. lands	−660		−1331
Loss of structures	−598		−1206
Increased flooding		−70	−99

Negative numbers = costs; positive numbers = benefits.

[a] GDP deflator from Central Bank Annual Report.

[b] Opportunity costs of lost agricultural production.

[c] Estimated change in property values.

[d] Assuming a 10% loss of property value due to more noise.

[e] The CKE-EIS figures on an annual basis. These are converted to NPVs over 25 years at 12% discount rate.

proposed for electrification between Colombo Fort and Veyangoda is part of the main line. The benefits of railway electrification are as follows.

(1) Travel time savings to former diesel multiple unit (DMU) passengers, because electric multiple units (EMU) have higher travel speeds and greater operational frequency. The total time saving (DMU minus EMU passenger hours) is multiplied by the value of time taken as SL Rs10.83/hr (Kumarage, 1999). This value is assumed to increase in real terms with the increase in per capita income assumed for each scenario.

(2) Travel time savings to former bus passengers. Total time savings (bus minus EMU passenger hours) are multiplied by the same value of time.

(3) Vehicle operating cost savings from diversion of former bus passengers to EMU, because lower demand for passengers would lead to fewer buses on the congested road network. The operational economic cost of these buses is taken as SL Rs18.80/km, and each bus is assumed to carry 50 passengers (Ministry of Transport, 1999).

(4) Lower air emission damage from reduced use of buses.

(5) Reduced air pollution due to electrification. We assume that the incremental electricity required for EMU operation is based on oil or coal, and that roughly the same amount of fossil fuel would need to be used as is presently used by the DMU. The benefit arises because DMU emissions occur at trackside in densely populated areas, whereas power generation is at remote plants with tall stacks. Typical health damages for ground-level and high-stack emissions are in the ratio of 3114/42 for PM10, 487/6 for SO_2 and 123/2 for NOx (Lvovsky *et al.*, 2000). We apply these ratios to the emissions from 4.6 million litres of fuel used by DMU.

(6) Savings from accident costs due to reduced bus travel. Accident costs are SL Rs0.08/passenger-kilometre for road transport (Kumarage, 1999) and SL Rs0.04/passenger-kilometre for rail.

Table 11.20 *Airport expressway: distribution of costs and benefits*
NPV (Rs million) at 2000 price levels

		Road users							Environment		
	RDA[a]	Freight (truck)	Low income (bus)	Med. income (motorcycle)	High income (car)	Govt	CPC[b]	Total	Local	Global	Total
Tolls	2922	−2922			−841			−841			−841
Construction	−10 372							−10 372			−10 372
O&M costs	−1140							−1140			−1140
Time savings		14 505	4065	1371	3051			22 992			22 992
Diesel fuel tax						−419	419	0			0
Petrol fuel tax						−359	359	0			0
Diesel savings		1681					−1681	0			0
Petrol savings		−0		88	536		−624	0			0
Fuel imports							1472	1472			1472
Port distribution margins							55	55			55
Road accidents			115					115			115
Environment											
Non-air impacts									−357		−357
Air emissions											
PM10									147		147
SO_2									253		253
NOx									290		290
Carbon										574	574
Total	−8589	13 264	4180	1460	2746	−778	0	12 281	333	574	13 188

[a] Road Development Authority.
[b] Ceylon Petroleum Corporation.

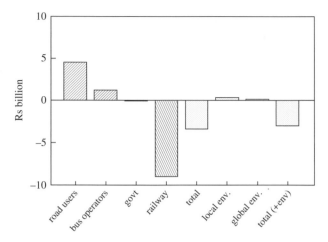

Figure 11.15. Winners and losers: railway electrification.

Railway electrification is found to be uneconomic (Figure 11.15), with an NPV of economic loss around SL Rs3 billion. While there are clear benefits to road congestion and reduced vehicle operating costs, these are insufficient to warrant the high capital costs of electrification. The environmental benefits are positive but small, and are insufficient to offset the large economic loss.

Using a 30-year time horizon appropriate for such projects, the switching values of discount rate (where NPV changes from negative to positive) are 4% and 3.5%, respectively, with and without environmental benefits. They are far below the opportunity cost of capital (6–10%).

Our analysis agrees with previous studies showing that electrification of the northern commuter line is uneconomic. We further show that environmental benefits are very small, and therefore that, electrification of railways is a very expensive method of reducing local air emissions.

11.4.3 Dry container port

The Colombo Port plays a economic key role, and the trans-shipment traffic is highly profitable. However, there are major harbour space constraints that prevent large-scale expansion. Thus, efficient operation of the port is vital. Colombo competes with Indian ports to become the regional hub for container operators and consortia. At the southernmost point of South Asia, Colombo has a unique geographical advantage for trans-shipment operations, which the government wishes to exploit.

Domestic containers spend too much time in the port, thereby occupying space that could be given to the more profitable trans-shipment traffic. This situation will worsen with the growth of domestic container traffic. To reduce dwell time and free up port capacity, a port inland clearance depot (PICD) has been proposed for all domestic containers.

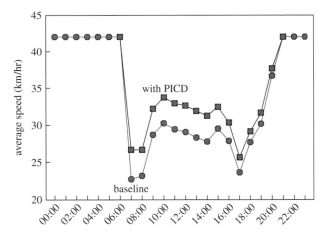

Figure 11.16. Impact of the PICD on speeds on the A3 (2001).

The problems of port congestion are aggravated by traffic problems in Colombo. As domestic container traffic has grown, more articulated lorries move containers to their private inland depots, many of which are located north of Colombo on the A3 radial road. This has significantly worsened congestion (see Figure 11.3). Heavy lorries (mainly container vehicles) account for 5% of vehicles, but 8% of road capacity.

While, a full cost–benefit analysis of port operations goes beyond the scope of this study, the benefits of the proposed PICD may be identified as: (1) increased throughput of transshipment container traffic; (2) deferral of the construction of a new port, or major new expansions to increase port capacity; and (3) cost savings to private operators due to reduction in dwell time in the port. The model presented earlier for evaluating congestion pricing is used to estimate benefits from reduced road congestion on the A3 (as container traffic is diverted to the railway) and the resulting environmental benefits (reduced emissions from container trucks and other road vehicles due to higher average speeds). Removal of this traffic from the A3 would improve average speeds by 3–4 km/hr during peak hours (see Figure 11.16).

Table 11.21 shows the distribution of costs and benefits. The analysis considers both the A3 and Kandy roads (the two radial roads with the heaviest container lorry traffic, having trip lengths of 12 km and 6 km from Colombo, respectively). It is assumed that the PICD would reduce heavy lorry traffic on the A3 by 75%, and on the Kandy Road by 50%. The residence time of rail shipment is conservatively assumed to be 50% that of road shipment. PICD costs incurred by the railways and port are recovered from container operators.

'Other efficiency savings' (minimum level of new benefits to container operators that make the project viable) are set so that the project economic rate of return (ERR) equals the opportunity cost of capital. Thus, net economic benefits are equal to the externality reductions to road users and the environment. The principal beneficiaries are bus passengers.

Table 11.21 *Costs and benefits of the PICD*

| | Road users | | | | | | | | Environment | | |
	Low income (bus)	Med. income (motorcycle)	High income (car)	Freight (truck)	COs[a]	Govt	SLR[b]+port	Total	Local	Global	Total
Time savings	5927	18	927	647	2639			10 157			10 157
Tolls	0	0	0	0		0		0			0
Petrol fuel tax	44	1	26			−27		0			0
Diesel fuel tax			4			−48		0			0
Diesel savings	765			273	63			1101			1101
Petrol savings		1	85					86			86
Deadweight losses	0	0	0	0				0			0
VOC savings					2957			2957			2957
Fees to SLR/ICD					−6579		6579	0			0
Other efficiency savings					919			919			919
Capital cost							−1712	−1712			−1712
O&M costs							−4866	−4866			−4866
Environment											
PM10								0	7		7
SO$_2$								0	11		11
NOx								0	13		13
GHG emissions								0		12	12
Total	6736	19	1042	920		0−75	0	8642	31	12	8685

[a] Container operators.
[b] Sri Lanka Railway.

Table 11.22 *Benefits and costs*

NPV in Rs million

	Road users	Students	Govt	Total	Local env.	Global env.	Total
VOC savings	736			736			736
Time savings	512	×		512			512
Fuel taxes	30		−30	0			0
Fees	×	×	×	0			0
Environment							
PM10				0	13		13
NOx				0	25		25
SO$_2$				0	24		24
GHG				0		33	33
Total	1277		−30	1247	61	33	1342

Positive value = benefit; negative value = cost; × = undetermined; fuel savings included in VOC savings.

11.4.4 Reintroducing school buses

Until the early 1980s, Colombo City had a reasonably well patronized school bus service operated by the state-owned Sri Lanka Transport Board. However, with cutbacks in state-owned bus operations, school bus services have been taken over by private vans that offer a charter service for a monthly fee. In 2001, only 50–60 school buses operated in Colombo, compared with 2167 vans (having increased from 1619 vans in 1996 at 5% per year). There are about 16 students per van.

These school vans have worsened congestion. Surveys indicate that about half the students travelling in vans would transfer to a dependable school bus service. A bus could carry 80 students – equivalent to five vans, with a saving of at least 50% in road space. A 1996 survey showed that the average cost of school van service was SL Rs570/month per student, only slightly lower than that charged by office vans (SL Rs650/month). Table 11.22 shows the NPV of benefits and costs of this policy option over 20 years. Environmental benefits are 7% of total economic benefits.

The distributional impacts are unclear. How the vehicle operating cost savings would be distributed among bus operators, students and government is difficult to say. Utility gains from time savings to students are another undetermined benefit. Even if new buses were purchased for SL Rs860 million (with zero scrap value for replaced vans), the net benefits would still be SL Rs482 million. Thus the reintroduction of school buses is self-evidently win–win, and is therefore strongly recommended.

11.5 Sustainable transport policy in Sri Lanka

11.5.1 Fuel and vehicle taxes

One major policy priority for making transport development more sustainable is the rationalization of fuel and vehicle taxes. A major issue is to reduce the gap between (low) diesel and (high) petrol taxes. Indeed, based on road damage externalities, the pollution tax on diesel should be greater than that on petrol. If fuel taxes are to be equalized on the basis of revenue neutrality, then, from an environmental perspective, there is a slight preference for an equalization based on carbon emissions (giving diesel a slightly higher tax rate than petrol on a Rs/litre basis).

The high tax on petrol may not serve the social objective of income redistribution. In fact, a major proportion of petrol taxes falls on the 700 000 motorcycle and three-wheeler owners, while private owners of petrol cars account for under 30% of vehicle-kilometres. The new petroleum pricing system introduced in 2002, which is better aligned to international oil price levels, is more efficient than the previous ad hoc system. However, the relative prices of diesel and petrol remain unsatisfactory, and do not reflect actual road damage and environmental externalities.

11.5.2 Reducing sulphur in auto-diesel

As in the case of leaded petrol, the actual sulphur content in diesel has been much lower than the 1.1% of the specification. Nevertheless, the benefits of reducing sulphur in diesel fuel are still high, as evidenced by the differential between international prices of gasoil having varying sulphur content. Given that modifying the kerosene unifiner for hydrotreating of gasoil is now a sunk cost, the refinery now produces large quantities of 0.1% sulphur gasoil, which can be blended with imports to almost any desired specification. There is little doubt that a 0.5% sulphur specification is cost-effective from a social standpoint, using highly conservative values for the health damage of SO_2. Using damage values in the 'Six Cities Study', even a reduction to 0.3% sulphur would be cost-effective.

11.5.3 LPG conversion of petrol cars

Although the growth rate of LPG conversion of petrol vehicles has slowed, 10% of the petrol-engine fleet runs on LPG, of which over 70% involve conversions to bottled gas. This conversion is driven entirely by distortions of fuel taxation policy. Most of them appear to be high-mileage vehicles (mainly taxis), where conversions have been highly profitable (in financial terms).

The main environmental benefit of LPG conversion is the avoided lead emissions from leaded petrol, which disappears with the introduction of unleaded petrol. Any remaining environmental benefits are dwarfed by the high economic costs of vehicle conversion and the higher economic costs of imported LPG and filling station costs. This is true even if the new 'tanktainer' concept were implemented. There is a major loss of government tax revenue from LPG conversion (given that petrol is more highly taxed). This is effectively a subsidy to taxi fleets (and their high-income passengers) and to businesses, for whom the conversion costs are justified by high mileage.

The obvious remedy would be to tax auto-LPG at filling stations at a rate commensurate with petrol, but this is likely to encourage use of bottled gas (unless the tax on bottled gas

Table 11.23 *Percentage of environmental benefit in total social benefit*

Option	Percentage
Congestion fee	1
School bus	5
Tax equalization	30
Unleaded petrol	120
Carbon tax (incremental)	40
Carbon tax (equalization)	31
Ban on 2-stroke motorcycles	135
CKE	3
PICD	0
Railway electrification	2
Sulphur 0.5%	116
Sulphur 0.25%	130
LPG (versus leaded petrol)	472
LPG (tanktainer)	148
LPG (versus unleaded petrol)	0

Where the figure exceeds 100%, it means that the option has a negative NPV before environmental impacts are included. Thus, with a ban on 2-stroke motorcycles, the value of (positive) environmental benefits is 135% of the (negative) non-environmental benefits (i.e. of the non-environmental costs).

was also raised, which will penalize homes). Efforts to ban bottled gas for auto use would also fail. The poor overwhelmingly still use fuelwood for cooking, and bottled gas is largely used by higher-income groups – the same groups who also use motorcycles and cars. Therefore, if a revenue neutral tax reform were undertaken (by equalizing tax on LPG and petrol), the distributional impacts would cancel out, with the remaining main benefit of Sri Lanka avoiding uneconomic use of LPG for transport.

11.5.4 Transportation infrastructure projects

Two of the transportation infrastructure projects (the airport expressway and the port inland clearance depot) are win–win, while railway electrification is uneconomic. Meanwhile, Table 11.23 shows that the proportions of environmental benefits of the expressway and the dry container port in the total benefit are quite small (3% and <1%, respectively) – including environmental benefits simply makes already good projects slightly better. The congestion mitigation options (school buses, congestion fee) are also win–win, though again the environmental benefits are modest.

The best options (having the highest NPV) are tax equalization, unleaded petrol and the CKE. However, in terms of environmental benefit achieved, by far the most attractive is the

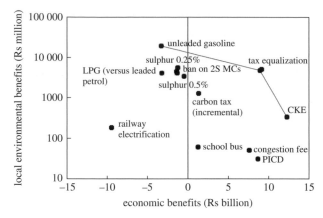

Figure 11.17. Trade-offs between economic and local environmental benefits (log scale for *y* axis). Note: 2S MCs = 2-stroke motorcycles.

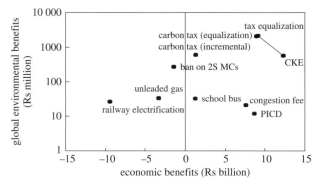

Figure 11.18. Trade-offs, economic versus global benefits (monetized at US $20/tonne carbon). Note: 2S MCs = 2-stroke motorcycles.

introduction of unleaded petrol. Figure 11.17 displays these results as a trade-off line defining the options in the non-inferior set – i.e. those that show the best set of options taking both objectives into account.

Figure 11.18 shows the corresponding figure for global benefits, based on a carbon price of US $20/tonne. Unleaded petrol drops out of the trade-off set, and again the CKE and tax equalization are the best options. Finally, Figure 11.19 shows the trade-offs between economic benefits and PM10. Banning the importation of 2-stroke motorcycles is most effective for reducing PM10, but at some economic cost.

11.5.5 Local environmental impacts

Based on other recent studies, the health-damage estimates given in earlier studies in Sri Lanka are an order of magnitude too low as regards vehicle emissions (or those arising from

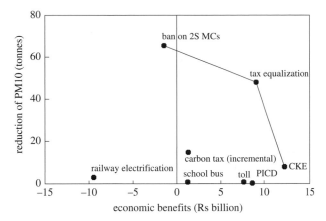

Figure 11.19. Trade-offs: economic benefits versus PM10 reduction. Note: 2S MCs = 2-stroke motorcycles.

self-generated electricity). While the benefit transfer method used here provides reasonable indicative estimates of health-damage costs, there is no substitute for local studies. The quality and consistency of urban monitoring data needs to be expanded to include rural sites. A rigorous damage cost study using Colombo medical and hospital data remains a high priority.

The air quality in Colombo has deteriorated since the beginning of the twenty-first century, and particularly in 2000/2001 the number of excedances (of both daily average and daily maximum) increased sharply. The most likely explanation is the start up of the 60 MW barge-mounted power plant located in Colombo harbour, rather than increasing traffic congestion during peak hours. Our calculations show that, per kilowatt-hour generated, the probable health damages from the barge-mounted plant are 20–40 times greater than those from the proposed Norochalai coal plant.

We may therefore conservatively conclude that: (1) health damages from the 60 MW barge-mounted plant are an order of magnitude greater than the emissions from a coal-based plant at Norochalai; (2) emissions from the barge-mounted plant add 25–50% to the auto-diesel emissions in the western province; (3) environmental objections to the coal plant at Norochalai are weak, given that probable health damages of oil plants are at least an order of magnitude greater; (4) reducing sulphur in diesel oil from the present 0.7% to 0.5% is 100–1000 times more cost-effective than installing fuel gas desulphurization (FGD) at the Norochalai coal plant.

All of the measures examined have net environmental benefits (when emissions are monetized), though some options involve trade-offs between emissions. Thus, a ban on imports of 2-stroke motorcycles would greatly reduce particulate emissions, while increasing NOx emissions; but since PM10 has far higher damage costs, there is still a net reduction in health damages. The railway electrification case shows that the traditional focus on emissions is misplaced. Since power for electrification would come from coal-power generation, sulphur emissions would increase (even if 0.6% low-sulphur coal is used), but the resulting health damages would decrease, because the location of the sulphur emissions changes from densely populated areas at more or less ground level (from DMUs) to tall stacks at remote locations (for the coal plant). Similarly, if the incremental electricity were generated from heavy fuel oil at a Colombo urban location (for example, at the location of the barge-mounted plant, or at Kelanitissa or Sapugaskanda), not only would sulphur emissions increase even more, but the damage costs would be equivalent.

12

Water-resource applications[1]

In this chapter, we examine how sustainomics principles may be applied to develop and manage water resources more sustainably. Section 12.1 describes the natural hydrological cycle and how interventions have affected it. Water and development linkages are examined in Section 12.2, including a review of the global status of water resources, water shortages and rising costs, poverty issues and sustainable livelihoods. In Section 12.3, a framework for sustainable water-resource management and policy (SWAMP) within a country is briefly outlined; this has many parallels with the sustainable energy development (SED) approach explained in Chapter 10. A rational and systematic integration of water-related social, economic, environmental and technical considerations is required within the broader framework of national sustainable development strategy. Sections 12.4 and 12.5 describe the practical application of SWAMP to a typical water-resources project involving groundwater for urban use in Manila, Philippines, including an analysis of the effects of harmful environmental externalities such as aquifer depletion, saltwater intrusion and land subsidence. Remedial policy measures are identified. Finally, Section 12.6 sets out the empirical example of a simple, low-cost, socially acceptable and environmentally desirable approach to purifying drinking water and reducing waterborne diseases that has yielded significant economic, social and environmental gains to poor villagers in Bangladesh. Another case study involving the evaluation of a classical rural water supply project in a poor African township is described in Chapter 15.

12.1 Hydrological cycle and human actions

The hydrological cycle is the driving force that determines how water is distributed throughout the natural landscape. The size, nature and location of sources play a key role in determining which resources can be exploited in an economically, socially, environmentally and technically sound manner. The interaction of water resources with activities in other sectors requires a systematic assessment of the hydrological cycle.

A better understanding of the hydrological cycle, and human modifications to it, helps in making rational trade-offs and water-allocation decisions among different users from

---

[1] Some parts of the chapter are based on material adapted from Munasinghe (1991, 1992b, 1994b).

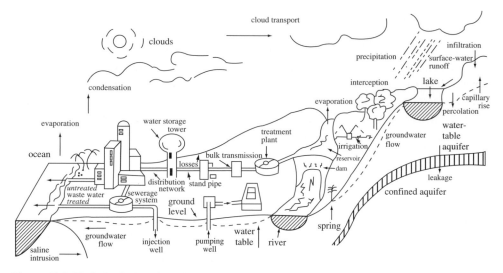

Figure 12.1. Hydrological cycle and typical human interventions.

various sources. Water is taken by consumers, and waste or surplus water is returned to the natural system. This can result in both upstream and downstream impacts, which could make hydrological conditions more or less sustainable. Thus, building a dam across a river will have a positive effect on the capacity of the river to supply peak daily, seasonal and annual water demands for users downstream. However, it may have a negative effect on the other uses, such as navigation, fish breeding or downstream irrigation. Downstream waste return may seriously pollute the waterway since the amount of flow let into the river from the dam is reduced compared with natural levels.

12.1.1 Basic hydrological cycle

Figure 12.1 shows the main elements of the hydrological cycle as a group of sub-cycles by which the water in nature circulates (between the air, vegetation, soil, rock, rivers, lakes and seas), and is transformed through the human management of these natural processes by means of hydraulic structures, storage and treatment facilities and conveyance systems.

Precipitation occurs where water vapour in the clouds condenses on suitable hygroscopic nuclei (or fine particles) in the air (Mason, 1975; Pettersen, 1964; Shaw, 1983). Many of the combustion products contain sulphurous and nitrous compounds resulting in the phenomenon of acid rain. Wind-blown clouds transport water vapour and nuclei. As moist air rises and cools, clouds form more frequently. Precipitation may fall directly on, or flow into, a water body such as a river, lake or ocean, from which evaporation will occur. It may also remain as snow or ice. It is estimated that 45 million km^3 of water per year evaporate from all oceans. Water vapour remains in atmospheric storage for about ten days before condensing back to the liquid state in clouds (Shaw, 1983).

Rain may: (1) evaporate back into the atmosphere; (2) be intercepted by vegetation; (3) infiltrate into the soil; or (4) run off into rivulets, streams, rivers, lakes and eventually, perhaps, into the oceans. Rain intercepted by vegetation will either evaporate or trickle slowly down to the ground. Precipitation infiltrates into the ground through the interconnecting air spaces between soil particles. When rain or snow-melt exceeds the absorptive capacity of the soil, surface runoff will occur. Infiltrated water will percolate down to the unweathered bedrock below the soil layer, or return to the surface by capillary action as water in the soil evaporates. Other water is taken up by plants and transpired through their leaves back into the air, as part of the evapotranspiration process from the soil. When an impermeable layer is encountered by percolating water, the rock or soil layer above may saturate and a water table will form, rising up toward the surface as more water percolates down. Some water may slowly leak to bedrock below the impermeable layer.

When a bedrock layer is porous and holds a lot of water, an aquifer is created, and this groundwater will flow downward along the hydraulic gradient of the water table. The volume and rate of flow will depend on the permeability of the rock or soil, which is determined by the size and connectivity of pore spaces. Where the water table intersects the land surface, water will flow back out on the surface to form springs, rivers or lakes. If water flows in a bedrock layer that dips below an impermeable confining layer, it can flow up to the surface under pressure through cracks (as artesian springs), or through boreholes drilled from the surface.

Surface runoff depends on the size, shape, slope and wetness of the land and the vegetation and surface material covering the land. It also depends on the precipitation and weather conditions. On steep converging hills with little vegetation, water will form fast-flowing streams and rivers that may cause surface erosion. On shallow undulating ground, water will form slow-moving rivers, ponds and lakes.

12.1.2 Human modifications and their impacts

Humans interfere in the hydrological cycle for two main purposes: (1) to provide a controlled water supply for domestic, industrial and agricultural uses and (2) to control the energy of water, thereby reducing soil erosion, preventing flooding, generating electric power, facilitating transport, etc.

There are many conflicting needs – for potable water, ecosystems and wildlife, recreation, transport, power generation, etc. Hydraulic engineers build large storage and transfer structures such as aqueducts, canals, bulk transmission pipelines, distribution networks and boreholes, through which water can flow by gravity or be pumped up to population centres from a distant source. Daily, seasonal and annual variations in the supply and demand for water determine storage facilities such as reservoirs that help to maintain long-term water-supply reliability.

Groundwater is extracted using pumping wells bored into water-bearing aquifers, or piped from remote springs. The management of groundwater is more difficult because aquifer characteristics are difficult to measure and may vary substantially over short distances. Surface and groundwater sources are referred to as 'blue' water, and tend to be heavily exploited already. Therefore, there is increasing interest in harnessing and managing relatively untapped 'green' water – rainwater that naturally infiltrates into the soil (Falkenmark and Rockstrom, 2006).

Water use from intakes can be conserved by reducing demand or reusing wastewater either through treatment or by substituting it for fresh water where quality is less important (e.g. for cooling). However, water can also be lost unproductively from the man-made water infrastructure by uncontrolled leakage out of pipes or reservoirs. Water may be purposely leaked back to protect the source, e.g. to keep aquifers from turning salty where saline intrusion occurs in coastal areas. This artificial recharge takes place through injection wells, which pump water into the ground, or by seepage from recharge basins.

The quality of natural water is not usually appropriate for drinking, and requires treatment. Runoff over the surface can pick up a range of harmful or distasteful materials including silt, agricultural and industrial chemicals, oil residues or human faecal waste. Pollutants may be discharged directly into unprotected sources by other users such as factories, power stations or sewerage works. Similar problems result from irrigation for agriculture. In addition to meeting crop-water demands, good irrigation practice provides for extra water to leach out any salts accumulated by agrochemical inputs. Drainage water containing the leachates will re-enter the hydrological cycle and may affect downstream water sources. Good environmental practice requires treating wastewater before dumping it into water sources or the ocean. Unfortunately, wastewater treatment remains the exception rather than the rule in many developing countries. This is especially true in cases where the incremental costs of exploiting new water sources appear to be less than the corresponding costs of treating and reusing wastewater (see Section 14.5).

Deforestation, urbanization and landscape modification can all change the pattern and timing of runoff and percolation in a way that alters the yield of water sources. Where evapotranspiration or the amount and type of condensation nuclei are also changed, micro-climatic modifications can reduce or acidify rainfall. Urbanization may reduce the permeability of the land surface, thereby increasing total and peak runoff and flow velocity (Hall, 1984; Lazaro, 1979). Urbanization could also lead to a net increase in groundwater recharge. An exception may be the case where irrigated agriculture is displaced by urbanization (Foster, 1988).

Human interference in the hydrological cycle reduces or increases net costs to each user. The costs that one user can impose on another, without payment of compensation, are termed externalities (see Section 3.2.2). What may have a positive cost impact (a net benefit) for one sector (e.g. the cheap and convenient disposal of industrial waste into a river that reduces the production costs), may have a negative impact for another sector (e.g. the cost of treating river water at a downstream intake to remove toxic chemicals before using it). Thus, the benefits (costs) arise from human interventions that raise (lower) the quality, quantity and reliability of water from a source. These short- and long-term impacts are included in sustainable water-resource management and policy (SWAMP).

12.2 Water and development

Historically, water has played a vital role in every facet of human activity. In recent times, water has emerged as a key natural resource for sustainable development. It is critical in a modern economy, through its widespread use in productive activities and its potential to improve living conditions.

Faced with a shortage of capital, as well as the need to improve the economic efficiency, social equity and environmental sustainability of projects, water decision making is becoming more demanding. Making development more sustainable requires rational and systematic integration of water-related concerns within the broader framework of national development strategy. Recent transnational and global concerns also suggest that water-resource analysis should have an even wider viewpoint. The SWAMP framework (see Section 12.3) includes a comprehensive framework that systematically takes into account multiple actors (ranging from multinational companies and international organizations to local citizens groups); multiple criteria (such as economic efficiency, poverty and equity, environmental protection, etc.); multiple levels of analysis (global, national, sectoral and sub-sectoral); multiple constraints (including inadequacy of institutions and human resources); and so on.

12.2.1 Status of water resources

From 1990 to 2000, the fraction of people with improved water supply rose from 79% (4.1 billion) to 82% (4.9 billion), while the proportion of world population with access to sanitation facilities increased from 55% (2.9 billion) to 60% (3.6 billion) (WHO/UNICEF, 2000). At the beginning of 2002, 1.1 and 2.6 billion people, respectively, were without access to improved water supply and sanitation (WHO/UNICEF, 2005). Most of them live in Asia and Africa – fewer than 50% of Asians have access to improved sanitation, and 40% of Africans lack improved water supply. In Sub-Saharan Africa, 300 million people lack access to improved water sources. South Asia has made excellent progress, but contamination of water sources poses new risks. In East Asia rapid urbanization is posing a challenge for the provision of water and other public utilities. Figure 12.2 shows access to improved water sources in the different regions and the predicted values for 2015 (World Bank, 2005a).

Rural services still lag far behind urban services. Although the greatest increase in population will be in urban areas, the worst levels of coverage are in rural areas (Figure 12.3). In Africa, Asia and Latin America, rural coverage for sanitation is less than one-half that of urban areas, with almost 2 and 1 billion people, respectively, without access to improved sanitation and water supply. Some 1.3 billion people in China and India lack adequate sanitation facilities (WHO/UNICEF, 2000).

Unlike urban and rural sanitation and rural water supply, the percentage coverage for urban water supply has decreased during the 1990s. The water supply and sanitation sector will face enormous challenges over the coming decades, as the urban populations of Africa,

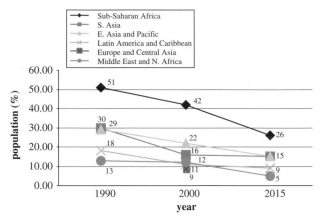

Figure 12.2. Population without access to improved water source (actual values 1990 and 2000; estimated values 2015).Source: World Bank (2003).

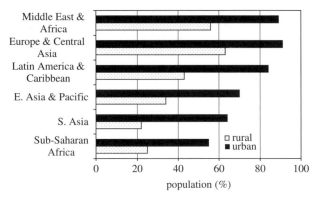

Figure 12.3. Population (%) with access to improved sanitation, 2002. Source: World Bank (2005a).

Asia, Latin America and the Caribbean are expected to increase dramatically. Meanwhile, rural areas also face the daunting task of meeting the existing large service gap (see Figure 12.3). Over the next 25 years, urban populations in Africa and Asia will double, and those in Latin America will rise by 50%.

Poor water supply and sanitation have a high health toll. Lack of drinking water and sanitation kills about 4500 children a day. Improving water and sanitation brings valuable benefits to both social and economic development. Meeting the MDG target of halving the proportion of people without sustainable access to safe drinking water and basic sanitation by 2015 would avert 470 000 deaths and result in an extra 320 million productive working days every year. Economic benefits range from US $3 to 34 for each dollar invested (WHO/ UNICEF, 2005). To achieve 2015 targets in Africa, Asia and Latin America, an additional 2.2 and 1.5 billion people, respectively, will need access to sanitation and water supply – i.e. requiring water supply services to 280 000 people and sanitation facilities to 384 000 people every day (WHO/UNICEF, 2000).

Over 90% of deaths from diarrhoeal diseases in the developing world occur in children under five years old. Improved drinking water and sanitation services and better hygiene behaviour, especially by mothers, is crucial in cutting child mortality. In Sub-Saharan Africa and South Asia, respectively, around 769 000 and 683 000 children under five years of age died annually from diarrhoeal diseases in 2000–2003. Contrastingly, in the developed regions, most mothers and babies benefit from safe drinking water, safe, private sanitation, adequate nutrition and other advantages. Of the 57 million children under five years old in the developed regions, about 700 succumbed annually to diarrhoeal disease (WHO/ UNICEF, 2005). Thus, a Sub-Saharan baby is almost 520 times more likely to die of diarrhoea than a baby born in Europe or North America.

Children, especially girls, mostly in Africa and Asia, are missing school because neither their homes nor their schools have adequate drinking water and sanitation facilities. In 2002, more than 500 million school-age children lived in families without access to improved sanitation, and 230 million were without an improved water supply. For girls, it is not only sickness that costs them their schooling, but also the burden of hauling water from distant sources – leaving them with neither the time nor the energy for schooling.

Every year, diarrhoeal diseases in the working-age population cost the economies of Eastern Asia more than 250 000 'disability-adjusted life years' (DALYs). Further, childhood diarrhoea in Sub-Saharan Africa costs 25 million DALYs. Globally, the WHO has estimated that productivity gains from diarrhoeal disease reductions by achieving the MDG drinking water and sanitation target will exceed US $700 million a year. Income earned by those saved from premature death attributable to diarrhoeal disease adds another US $3.6 billion a year. Fewer patients will need treatment, amounting to a saving of US $7.3 billion a year. Thus, meeting the MDG target would yield economic benefits close to US $12 billion a year. These benefits would justify the estimated US $11.3 billion a year investment to provide improved drinking water and sanitation services.

By far the biggest economic benefit comes from valuing the time saved when people currently with inadequate services gain access to nearby water and sanitation facilities. Assuming that the average one hour per day saved by each household member can be used to earn the minimum daily wage, the saved time is worth US $63 billion.

The elderly are more susceptible to, and more likely to die from, diseases related to water, sanitation and hygiene than other adults. More than one billion people will be 60 years old or older by 2025 (WHO/UNICEF, 2005). In industrialized nations, people aged 60 years and over are more likely to die from diarrhoea than the 0–5 year age group – unlike in developing countries.

12.2.2 Water shortages and rising supply costs

In the first quarter of this century, 2.7 billion people, or one-third of the world's population, will experience severe water scarcity (Munasinghe, 1992b). The bulk of this population will reside in the semi-arid regions of Asia and in Sub-Saharan Africa, where food production will be adversely affected due to overexploitation of groundwater.

Between 2000 and the year 2010, the population of developing countries is expected to grow by an amount greater than the total additional population served by the water and sanitation sector during the earlier decade. Thus, the level of investment in the water sector will need to increase if a sustained rise in coverage levels is to be achieved. As populations levels grow, already strained supply and treatment systems will need to be expanded and upgraded to cope with the increased demands. Additional sources of supply are available, or alternative technologies for the collection, treatment and disposal of wastewater can be applied, but at a higher economic, social and environmental cost.

Societies generally experience water shortages when annual renewable supplies fall below about 2000 m^3 per person. Water demands are outpacing supply in many developing countries and are also seriously affecting some industrialized nations (Munasinghe, 1992b). The situation in certain parts of Eastern Europe is precarious. The Aral Sea (one of the largest fresh-water bodies), had shrunk to 40% of its original area by 1990 due to poor irrigation efficiency. Preventing further ecological havoc will require authorities to take some prized farmland in Central Asia out of production (Perera, 1988). The Western USA (especially California) has experienced unprecedented shortages of fresh water for both urban and agricultural in recent decades. In 1991, rationing measures were imposed by many water suppliers in California for all users.

A survey of urban water-resource issues (Bhatia and Falkenmark, 1993) shows that many developing countries have not developed policy instruments (either regulations or economic incentives) for either encouraging conservation of water or including externalities. Thus, the opportunity costs of water use and environmental degradation are ignored. As a result, from an economic viewpoint excessive quantities of water are used and high levels of pollution are produced. Without a policy framework to take account of such externalities, human activities cause water quantity and quality problems, and are affected by them.

The quantity of water is as important as the quality in terms of its impact on human well-being (Munasinghe, 1992b). Furthermore, water quantity and quality are linked – because water scarcity leads to declining water quality and pollution, which has an adverse impact on the poor. In today's environment of growing water scarcity, more poor rural and urban consumers, rural producers and agricultural workers are coming to view entitlement to water as a more critical problem than access to food, primary healthcare and education. As water is withdrawn from agriculture, more attention must be paid to the management of irrigation systems, to water needs for domestic and health purposes, and to other consequences, such as the impact on the environment. Allocation cannot be accomplished solely through pricing mechanisms (see Chapter 14).

The increases in water-resource development costs will decrease the effectiveness of available investment capital in terms of population reached and service level achieved. The real costs of meeting rising demand for all water users at an environmentally acceptable quality level is dramatically increasing throughout the developing world (Falkenmark, Gamn and Cestti, 1990; Munasinghe, 1992b), due to: (a) the increase in long-run marginal costs of supply resulting from the added expenditure necessary to maintain supply and sanitation services at the existing quality level; (b) the incremental cost of upgrading and expanding

Table 12.1 *Costs of water supply 1990–2000 Given in US $ per person served*

Facility	Africa	Asia	Latin America and Caribbean
House connection	102	92	144
Stand post	31	64	41
Borehole	23	17	55
Dug well	21	22	45
Rainwater	49	34	36

Source: WHO/UNICEF (2000).

existing supply and sanitation systems and bringing additional systems online to meet greater demands; and (c) the higher per capita costs of supplying communities not yet covered – due to more complex technical, social and environmental factors affecting the exploitation of remaining water sources.

The most convenient and cost-effective sources have already been exploited, and what remains are the technically or environmentally more difficult (and hence more expensive) projects. The most dramatic examples of rising costs are in growing urban areas, where development of water resources cannot keep pace with the growth of demand (Munasinghe, 1992b). Increasing unit costs and scarcity of funds implies that more of the urban poor will have to depend on unreliable public supplies, or use polluted surface and groundwater sources. As a result, health problems and mortality rates will increase, since the poor will have to spend a higher portion of their income to obtain water for basic needs, or reduce their already meagre use of water. Estimates of typical income fractions spent on water for some countries are given in the following (see www.worldbank.org):

Latin America – Mexico 1.1% and Colombia 2.4%;
Europe – Albania 1.2% and Romania 4.9%;
S. Asia – India 0.8% and Nepal 1.2%;
Africa – Niger 0.8%.

Table 12.1 shows the rough estimates of construction costs of different types of water-supply facilities. Variations among regions are the result of differing water-resource endowment, unit costs for construction, levels of service offered, population density and access to water sources. The less conventional method of desalination costs about US $1/m^3 of salt water and US $0.6/m^3 of brackish water.

12.2.3 *Water and the poor*

Ensuring that poor communities have access to water resources helps to provide the basic needs of the poor in terms of safe and affordable drinking water and sanitation (see the MDGs in Chapter 1). Poor people depend upon water in several key ways (Munasinghe, 1992b, 1994b): as an input into production, to sustain livelihoods, for the maintenance of health and welfare, to ensure ecosystems integrity and through indirect paths.

Water as an input into production

In many poor communities, the economy depends on agricultural production, which is closely linked to water; 35% of the world population depends on agriculture, ranging from about 3% in Europe and America to 50–60% in Asia and 90% in Africa. Improved irrigation systems and access to land could greatly enhance sustainable livelihoods of the poor. Rain-fed agriculture presents an even bigger challenge. Rainwater harvesting, better access to groundwater and improved on-farm water management can bring about sustainable benefits. Integrated approaches to water management include better soil moisture management, selection of crop types and watershed and forest protection at the community level.

Water in the livelihoods of the poor

Livelihoods that depend crucially on water include fishing, tree and home garden cultivation, livestock, small-scale manufacturing, such as pottery, brick making and tanning, services such as laundering and others. Water is also vital for many types of manufacturing and other larger economic activities that provide employment for poor people – particularly in cities. Even where they are not the main livelihood activity, the poor often rely on such activities to supplement their incomes and overcome their lack of assets, such as land. Actions to sustain and expand these activities will often cost very little, and can have major benefits for the poor. A more effective approach to providing water services should recognize its significance for production as well as consumption by the poor.

Water for health and hygiene

The health and welfare of the poor, especially of vulnerable groups like children, the elderly and women, are closely linked to adequate, safe, affordable water services. The lack of clean water is one of the main reasons for ill health and premature death among the world's poorest communities. The toll taken by diarrhoea was highlighted in Section 12.2.1. Further, about 200 million people suffer from schistosomiasis, while millions have been blinded by trachoma, malaria, cholera and other diseases where poor water management is a major causal factor. Toxins like arsenic and fluoride in groundwater are another threat in South Asia and Africa. These problems have severe effects on nutrition, physical and mental development, costs of healthcare and loss of productive potential.

Role of ecosystems in supporting livelihoods of the poor

Water is critical for the viability of the *ecosystems* through which the poor gain access to natural resources that are the basis of many livelihoods. Even where water is not a direct input into production, other natural resources (such as forests, fish or pastures) depend on ecosystem services, which need water. While such resources may not be the main source of livelihoods, many poor people depend on them for fodder, fuelwood, supplementary foods (to augment food security) and other products that come from common property resources. Although rarely monetized, and often ignored, these goods are important for the rural poor in developing countries. Adequate and good quality water for human use reflect the condition of ecosystems through which it flows.

Indirect effects

Among the urban poor, high costs of water further undermine health and labour productivity, both directly through its impact on nutrition and indirectly through its impact on housing size and quality as well as residential density – especially in urban slums (see Chapter 16). Failure to account for the full range of benefits (economic, social and environmental) due to improvements in water supply may lead to underestimation of returns to investment.

12.2.4 Sustainable livelihoods and water

The sustainable livelihoods approach offers new insights into the dynamics of development and the diversity of circumstances of the poor. It improves our understanding of relationships among poor communities, their local environment and external socioeconomic, environmental and institutional forces. A livelihood comprises the capabilities, assets (including both material and social resources) and activities required for a means of living (Carney, 1998). A livelihood is sustainable when the individual can cope with, and recover from, stresses and shocks, while maintaining or enhancing capabilities and assets both now and in the future, whilst not undermining the natural-resources base.

The concept of sustainable livelihoods is critical to understanding the relationship between poverty and water security. Poverty is complex and multifaceted and reflects both the material and the non-material conditions of people's lives – it has social, economic and environmental dimensions (see Section 2.3.5). Any effective strategy to target the needs and potentials of the poor must reflect this multidimensional character of poverty. Water security suggests that people and communities have reliable and adequate access to water to meet their various needs, are able to take advantage of the many opportunities that water resources present, are protected from water-related hazards and have fair recourse when water conflicts arise.

It is predominantly the poor of the world who depend directly on natural resources, through cultivation, herding, collecting or hunting for their livelihoods. Therefore, for such livelihoods to be sustainable, the natural-resources base must be maintained (Rennie and Singh, 1996). The following points focus attention on the links between sustainable livelihoods, water and poverty. First, the conditions and composition of people's livelihoods change dynamically over time. Second, livelihoods are complex, since people are not solely farmers, labourers, factory workers or fisherfolk – 'rural families increasingly come to resemble miniature highly diversified conglomerates' (Cain and McNicoll, 1988). Third, livelihoods are influenced by a wide range of external forces that are beyond the control of the family – social, economic, environmental, political, legal and institutional factors both within and outside the local community. Fourth, people make conscious choices through deliberate strategies on the ways that they can best deploy whatever assets they possess to maximize the opportunities and minimize the risks they face.

For poor people, *vulnerability* is both a condition and a determinant of poverty, and refers to the ability of people to avoid, withstand or recover from the harmful impacts of disruptive factors that are beyond their immediate control. This includes both shocks (natural disasters, war or price changes) and trends (environmental degradation, decaying political systems or deteriorating terms of trade). In general, the more affluent a household and the more assets it possesses, the more *resilient* it is to disruption of its livelihoods from external shocks and trends (see Chapter 16).

12.3 Sustainable water-resources management and policy (SWAMP)

12.3.1 *Water resources and sustainable development*

Water resources and sustainable development interact in a circular manner. Different socio-economic development paths (driven by the forces of population, economy, technology and governance) will give rise to different patterns of anthropogenic water exploitation and use. The resultant changes in the hydrological cycle and water supply–demand balances will, in turn, impose stresses on the human socioeconomic and natural systems. Such impacts will ultimately have effects on socioeconomic development paths, thus completing the cycle. Different development paths will also have direct effects on the natural systems, in the form of non-water-related stresses, such as changes in land use leading to deforestation and land degradation.

Poverty has strong links with the quantity and quality of water available. Material- and water-intensive lifestyles and continued high levels of consumption supported by non-renewable resources, as well as rapid population growth, are inconsistent with sustainable water-resources development paths. Similarly, extreme socioeconomic inequality within communities and between nations (especially with respect to water resources) may undermine the social cohesion and sustainability. At the same time, socioeconomic and technology policy decisions made for water-related reasons have significant implications for water policy and environmental management. In addition, critical impact thresholds and vulnerability to water stress are directly connected to environmental, social and economic conditions and to institutional capacity.

Economic risks due to inadequate water quantity and quality

Shortages of water (caused by both inadequate quantity and quality) pose a significant potential threat to the future economic well-being of large numbers of human beings, especially the poorest. In its simplest form, the economic efficiency viewpoint will seek to maximize the net benefits (or outputs of goods and services) from the use of water resources, implying that the marginal product of water is equal to the marginal cost of production, and that scarce water is allocated to the most productive uses.

Social risks due to inadequate water quantity and quality

Water is a basic need for survival, and therefore scarcities and water stress will also undermine social welfare and equity. Many social values and institutions that have evolved over many years to share water are vulnerable, since they are already stressed due to rapid technological changes. Especially within developing countries, erosion of social capital is undermining the basic glue that binds communities together – e.g. the rules and arrangements that align individual behaviour with collective goals (Banuri *et al.*, 1994). Existing mechanisms and systems to deal with water-sharing issues (especially transnational and global problems) are fragile, and are unlikely to be able to cope with worsening water shortages – especially where water disputes among communities, user groups and nations are involved. Inequity will undermine social cohesion and exacerbate conflicts over scarce water resources. Furthermore, inequitable distribution of water is ethically unappealing, especially when the poor are the victims. Trondalen and Munasinghe (2005) explain the role of ethics in water-resource conflicts.

Both intra- and intergenerational equity are likely to worsen in the water sector. Existing evidence clearly demonstrates that poorer nations and disadvantaged groups within nations are especially vulnerable to water-related disasters such as droughts and floods (Banuri, 1998; Clarke and Munasinghe, 1995). Water scarcities are likely to worsen inequities due to the uneven distribution of the costs of damage, and such differential effects could occur both among and within countries. Climate change will worsen water problems, mainly in poor countries (IPCC, 2001b; Mirza and Ahmad, 2005). Future food security may be a major issue (see Section 1.2.3).

Environmental risks due to inadequate water quantity and quality

The environmental viewpoint draws attention to the fact that water scarcity and declining quality will significantly perturb critical global ecosystems (both terrestrial and marine). Environmental sustainability will depend on several factors, including: (a) water availability (e.g. magnitude and frequency of shocks such as floods and droughts); (b) system vulnerability (e.g. extent of impact damage); and (c) system resilience (i.e. ability to recover from impacts). More generally, changes in the global hydrological flows and balances will threaten the stability of a range of key, interlinked physical, ecological and socioeconomic systems and sub-systems (Watson *et al.*, 1996).

12.3.2 *National approach to SWAMP*

Given the key role of water resources and the substantial investments required to develop them, government involvement of some type becomes necessary. Thus, most countries pursue water-resources development programmes as part of their overall development efforts. Thus, water-resource problems need to be analysed within national sustainable development strategy.

Based on the foregoing, we develop a holistic framework for SWAMP based on the sustainomics approach. SWAMP seeks to analyse and address the full range of water-sector investment planning, pricing and management issues within an integrated framework, over a long period of time. In most developing countries, spending in the water sector constitutes 10% of all public-sector investments, or around 0.5% of total GDP. Yet, many face severe water problems and have relatively low water and sanitation coverage, particularly in rural areas. Thus, even small improvements in the efficiency of water-resource development and use would provide major benefits, especially when financial resources are scarce.

SWAMP includes planning, policy analysis and management. Water-resources planning, broadly interpreted, denotes a series of steps or procedures by which the many interactions involved in the production and use of water may be studied and understood within a systematic analytical framework. Planning techniques range from simple manual methods to sophisticated computer modelling. The complexity of water problems has forced increasing reliance on the latter approach. Water-resource policy analysis is the systematic investigation of the impact of specific water policies on socioeconomic and environmental systems. Water-resource management, which includes both supply and demand management, involves the use of selected policies and policy tools to achieve desirable patterns of water-supply consumption and to satisfy national objectives.

We note that the word planning, whether applied to the national economy or the water-supply sector in particular, need not imply some rigid framework along the lines of centralized and fully planned economies. Planning, whether by design or deliberate default, takes place in every economy, even in those where market forces are dominant. Therefore, it is important to stress that the SWAMP framework facilitates the coordination of water-resource planning, policy analysis and formulation, as well as policy implementation – carried out using market forces and decentralized mechanisms, especially pricing (see Chapter 14).

National objectives

SWAMP is an integral component of sustainable development strategy aimed at improving the quality of life of citizens. It begins from the major goals of national water-resources policy, including: (a) meeting the water needs of the economy to achieve growth and development targets; (b) choosing the mix of water sources to meet future water needs at lowest cost; (c) maximizing employment; (d) conserving water and eliminating wasteful use; (e) diversifying supply and reducing dependence on foreign sources; (e) meeting national security requirements; (f) supplying the basic water needs of the poor, many of whom are rural; (g) saving scarce foreign exchange; (h) identifying specific water policies to contribute to priority development of special regions (particularly rural or remote areas), and key sectors of the economy; (i) raising sufficient revenues from water sales to finance water sector development; (j) maintaining water price stability; and (k) protecting the environment.

Scope of SWAMP

Effective management of water to achieve desired national objectives must be accomplished through an integrated framework because of the many economic and environmental interactions between the water-resources sector and other elements of the economy. Such an approach will help decision makers in formulating policies, and in providing market signals and information to economic agents that encourage more efficient development and use of water resources. Figure 12.4 summarizes the SWAMP approach, including planning, policy analysis and management.

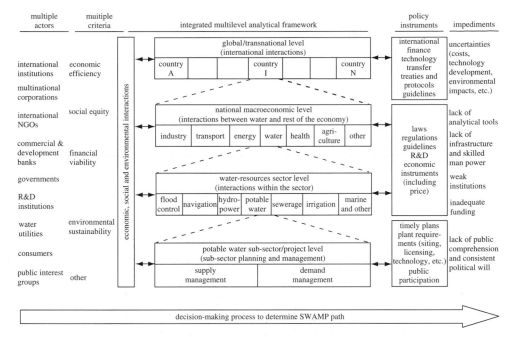

Figure 12.4. SWAMP: conceptual and analytical framework.

The first two columns of Figure 12.4 underline the complications facing decision makers in a modern economy due to multiple actors (with conflicting interests) and multiple criteria (or goals). However, the core of SWAMP is the integrated multilevel analytical framework shown in the centre. Although SWAMP is primarily country-focused, we begin by recognizing that many water-resource issues have global linkages. Individual countries are embedded in an international economic and environmental matrix. Thus, both the world economy (through trade and financial linkages) and the natural-resource base (through linkages via transitional water resources or global climate patterns) will impose an exogenous set of constraints and inputs on decision makers. The next hierarchical level in the figure treats the water sector as a part of the whole economy. Therefore, water-resource planning requires analysis of the links between the water sector and the rest of the economy. These links include the input requirements of the water sector (such as capital, labour, raw materials and environmental services), water-sector services and the impact on the economy of policies concerning water availability, prices and taxes, in relation to the national objectives.

Some of these links are at the macrolevel, such as foreign exchange needs for water-sector imports or investment requirements for water-supply facilities. Others concern specific user sectors. For example, policies targeting the agricultural sector, such as subsidies on farm inputs, guaranteed prices for farm products or access to credit, may have as profound an impact on the demand for water as policies directly affecting water pricing, allocation or supply management.

The next level of SWAMP treats the water-resources sector as a separate entity composed of sub-sectors such as potable water, sewerage, irrigation and drainage, hydropower, flood and drought control, navigation, recreation, fisheries and so on. This permits detailed analysis of the water sector with special emphasis on interactions among the different sub-sectors, possibilities for substitution and the resolution of any resulting policy conflicts. One example of such interactions would be the trade-offs involved in meeting the needs for irrigation, power production or navigation, from a single multipurpose reservoir. Furthermore, some of the water sub-sectors may interact directly with other major sectors, such as sewerage with the health sector, or hydropower with the energy sector. Intimate knowledge of the hydrological cycle and its sub-cycles are important at this level in determining resources use strategies and the nature of important environmental externalities.

The final and most disaggregated level pertains to planning within each of the water sub-sectors. Thus, for example, the potable water supply sub-sector must determine its own demand forecast and long-term investment programmes etc. It is at this lowest hierarchical level that most of the detailed formulation, planning and implementation of water-supply projects and schemes are carried out.

In practice, the various levels merge and overlap considerably in the formulation and implementation of integrated water-resource plans. Water–social–environment interactions (represented by the vertical bar) also cut across all levels and need to be incorporated into the analysis systematically (see also Chapters 3 and 4). Finally, spatial disaggregation may be required, especially in large and regionally diverse countries.

SWAMP facilitates policy making and does not imply rigid centralized planning. It yields a flexible, constantly updated sustainable water-resource strategy that meets national goals. This strategy (which includes the investment programme and pricing policy) may be implemented through water supply and demand measures that use decentralized market forces and incentives. Figure 12.4 shows a variety of policy tools for implementing sustainable water-resource management, and summarizes key impediments that limit policy implementation.

12.4 Management of groundwater depletion and saline intrusion in the Philippines

12.4.1 Overview of water-resource management

Metropolitan waterworks and sewerage system and groundwater use

Water supply and sanitation services in the Philippines have improved considerably since the 1970s. By the late 1980s, sector institutions were established and overall goals, strategies and development plans had been defined. By 1988, about 63% of the population had access to safe water, including 31% served by piped systems. Although absolute service levels are improving, the quality of service is often poor, with low water pressures throughout and rationed services in some areas (World Bank, 1986).

Sector financing

Sector development in metropolitan Manila was financed through funds self-generated by the Metropolitan Waterworks and Sewerage Systems (MWSS), government equity contributions and foreign or local loans. Government policy was to develop systems on the basis of a community's financial ability and willingness to pay for them. Thus, individual house connections were provided in the metropolitan and provincial urban areas, and some standpipe systems were provided on the basis of the willingness-to-pay. Wells with hand pumps were provided in rural areas. During 1984–1986, investment in the sector declined, and water and sanitation services remained poor. However, in 1987, the Government adopted a Water Supply and Sanitation Master Plan, which provided an integrated package of policies, programmes and projects to be implemented in two stages: from 1988 to 1993 and from 1994 to the year 2000.

Institutional arrangements

The National Water Resources Council (NWRC) is responsible for formulating water supply policies. The MWSS was established in 1972 to manage water supply and sewerage systems in or around metropolitan Manila. The MWSS Service Area (MSA) of about 150 000 ha includes Manila, four neighbouring cities and 32 municipalities. The Local Water Utilities Administration (LWUA) provides technical and financial assistance for water supply and sanitation development to about 730 provincial cities with populations above 20 000 and to rural communities. Both the MWSS and the LWUA are semi-autonomous corporations under the Department of Public Works and Highways (DPWH). The Health Department has a rural sanitation programme and monitors drinking water quality.

Groundwater use

Rapid growth of groundwater use in the Manila area since the 1970s has far exceeded the natural recharge, resulting in 'mining' of the aquifer. A devastating effect of this depletion is the encroachment of saline seawater into the coastal aquifer, the deterioration of water quality and major economic losses to users. Further costs are imposed on both the government and private individuals, due to surface subsidence arising from collapse of water-bearing geological strata below. This has serious impacts on infrastructure such as roads and the structural integrity of buildings and pipelines, while also exacerbating risks of flooding. Each groundwater user will continue to impose external diseconomies or costs on all other existing and further users (Munasinghe, 1984c). These environmental externalities would become more serious as the overpumping of aquifers is allowed to continue.

On the other hand, curtailing the use of groundwater for existing industrial users would have a negative impact on industrial production and employment. As part of its development planning, the largest users of groundwater in depleted zones have been identified by MWSS, and adequate transmission and distribution facilities are planned to provide them with piped water. If the problems of groundwater depletion persist, especially after adequate piped water is provided, it would be necessary to establish more rigorous controls on water use, and allow MWSS to charge for the use of groundwater, to reduce its excessive use and contribute to the financing of expanded water supply facilities in the MSA.

12.4.2 *Models and analysis*

This section calculates the long-run economic costs of groundwater use, over and above the cost of extraction, based on additional external costs imposed by existing users on all other potential present and future groundwater users. All costs and prices are in constant mid 1984 terms.

Groundwater-depletion model

All withdrawals in the Greater Manila Area (GMA) are assumed to be made from a common aquifer, whose physical details have been described in MWSS (1983a). For convenience, withdrawals from the aquifer are lumped together with no spatial disaggregation. A more sophisticated approach might involve analysis of a progressively advancing saline intrusion front and gradual salinization of wells in different zones, but the physical data available do not permit such discrimination.

On the basis of limited data and realistic assumptions, two scenarios shown in Figure 12.5 are compared, to estimate externality costs. The first, or depletion, case (curve *ABEFI*) is the base scenario applicable if present policies continued (MWSS, 1983a, b). The conservation scenario (curve *AJFH*) would be the result of a centrally managed groundwater extraction policy. Other scenarios are possible, but data constraints do not permit further fine-tuning.

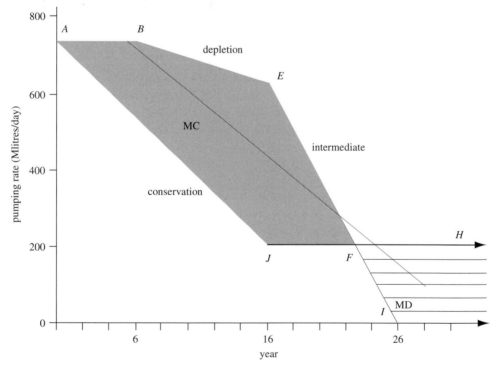

Figure 12.5. Alternative scenarios for groundwater use in Manila.

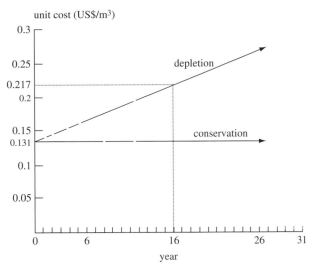

Figure 12.6. Long-run supply costs for the depletion and conservation scenarios.

Nevertheless, the contrast between the above two cases is sharp enough to draw some valuable policy conclusions.

In the depletion case, the withdrawal rate is 730 Mlitres/day in year 0 (1984) and remains constant until year 6 when the yield declines linearly to 620 Mlitres/day in year 16. Then a rapid decrease sets in with withdrawals dropping to zero by year 26, due to a progressive mining of water. As shown in the Appendix (Section 12.7) and Figure 12.6, the average costs of withdrawals will rise linearly from US $0.13/m^3 to US $0.22/m^3 from year 0 to 16, and finally to US $0.27/m^3 in year 26.

In contrast to the depletion case, we also explore a quasi-ideal conservation scenario in which groundwater use is controlled eventually to reach safe sustainable levels, where the sum of natural and artificial recharges equals the total withdrawals. Although the conservation case is hypothetical, it provides a useful practical benchmark for what might have been achieved with forethought and timely action initiated early enough. In this alternative, extraction rates are assumed to decline linearly from 730 to 200 Mlitres/day from year 0 to 16, which is the estimated safe sustainable yield for portable water, based on the physical model of the aquifer. Once equilibrium is reached, withdrawals can continue at this rate indefinitely without mining the aquifer. Pumping costs remain constant at US $0.13/m^3 throughout (see the Appendix, Section 12.7.)

Quantification of economic externality costs

The total volume of water to be supplied (from both the aquifer and the MWSS system) is the same in each scenario. Thus, consumption benefits derived by water users in both cases are identical, and only the costs are different. As shown in Figure 12.5, the total water supplied is indicated by the area under the curve *ABEFH*. To meet total demand, the MWSS system

Table 12.2 *Economic externality costs due to groundwater depletion*

(1) Depletion case	
Present discounted value of costs of supplying water[a]	406.87 (US $ million)
(2) Conservation Case	
Present discounted value of costs of supplying water[a]	377.56 (US $ million)
(3) Externality costs	
Difference in costs: (1) – (2)	29.31 (US $ million)
(4) QD	
Present discounted value of total groundwater withdrawals in the depletion case	2444 (million m^3)
(5) UEC	
Long-run economic externality costs due to depletion: (3) / (4)	0.012 (US $/m^3)

[a] See Table 12.3.

must supplement the groundwater supply with the amount MD (starting in year 23) in the depletion scenario and the amount MC (starting year 0) in the conservation case. The MWSS system draws water from sources other than the aquifer under consideration.

In Table 12.2, the costs of groundwater withdrawals in the depletion case are compared with the costs of pumping in the conservation case, including additional net costs to supplement the groundwater shortfall from MWSS piped supplies, based on the average incremental cost (AIC) of the MWSS supply (see Section 12.7). The present discounted value of the difference in costs between the two cases is assumed to be the long-run economic externality costs (ECs) incurred by following the depletion scenario, instead of the conservation case.

These additional ECs are incurred because of the consumption pattern followed in the depletion case. The present discounted value of total groundwater withdrawals in this case is also shown in Table 12.2. The unit externality cost, UEC = EC/QD, measures the long-run EC/m^3 of groundwater withdrawn, and also serves as a guideline for a user charge that might be imposed on the depleters, to compensate for the resulting loss of potential benefits (if the conservation scenario had been followed). Estimated UEC = US $0.012/m^3 of groundwater pumped. The average value of UEC may rise if estimated some years later. Higher UEC values over time (as the aquifer depletes) should be reflected in the policy measures discussed below.

Policy implications

While the physical model and groundwater extraction scenarios provide a benchmark value for the ECs of destroying the aquifer, very little further information is available about the consumption patterns and economic behaviour (especially water demand curves) of groundwater users. However, one may draw some policy conclusions, starting with a simplified static analysis. More dynamic aspects are introduced later, which do not change the logic of the following arguments.

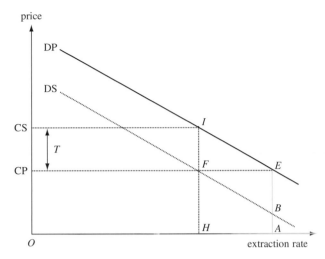

Figure 12.7. Groundwater extraction and user charges.

Figure 12.7 shows a normal downward sloping (private) demand curve for groundwater; DP represents the aggregate willingness-to-pay of groundwater users (i.e. use per year at various extraction costs), and the area under this demand curve measures benefits of water use, excluding ECs. Ideally, if there was full information about future aquifer destruction, and private well-owners had a good awareness of societal implications, the use of ground-water would be governed by a social demand curve, DS. This curve lies below DP because society has to incur an additional economic cost (like UEC) for every cubic metre of groundwater extracted under the depletion scenario. The divergence between DP and DS could arise because groundwater users are ignorant or unconcerned about externalities. Alternatively, those who deplete most heavily in the early years and enjoy low extraction costs may not be the same persons who face higher costs of pumping from a depleted aquifer in later years.

As mentioned earlier, the first best option for society would have been to restrict groundwater pumping and enforce the conservation scenario. This would result in cost savings of UEC = US $0.012/m^3 over the period of analysis. However, such an outcome is unlikely since policy options should have been introduced many years ago to achieve this result. Under present policies, the depletion scenario will occur, and in a typical year users will extract a volume *OA* at a cost CP (Figure 12.7). *BE* is the economic efficiency cost of each marginal unit of water used, because the extraction cost exceeds the use benefits to society. Ideally, if DS governed water use, the marginal consumption benefit FH would exactly equal CP. As a second best option, let us impose a user tax $T = UEC = IF = BE$. This would raise the private cost to: CS = CP + *T*. Then groundwater extraction would decline by *AH*, and marginal benefits and costs would be equalized, resulting in economically efficient water use.

If we introduce the time dimension, our analysis becomes somewhat more complicated. As shown in Figure 12.7, the reduced pumping *AH* will give rise to an intermediate groundwater extraction scenario, resulting in a different value of UEC. Nevertheless, the initial value of UEC is small relative to CP, and if the elasticity of demand is small (steeper slope for DP), this adjustment will be small. Finally, through an iterative process, it will be possible to arrive at a self-consistent set of values for CS, SP, UEC and the pumping rate. The efficient (second best) tax, *TE*, would be lower than the original UEC. More sophisticated dynamic analysis is possible, since the demand curve DP, the cost CP and tax *T* can all vary over time. Further, as the saline front gradually moves inland, greater spatial disaggregation also could be attempted if the data were available to determine extraction rates, costs and user charges by zone.

From the public finance viewpoint, a mean user charge of US $0.012/m^3 will yield present valued revenues of US $29.31 million, in the depletion scenario. If UEC increased over time, then revenues would rise. These resources could be used to develop alternative MWSS water resources to replace the failing aquifer.

12.4.3 Policy options

General rationale

Legally, all waters in the Philippines belong to the state, and the use of this water is a privilege granted to citizens by the government. From the socioeconomic viewpoint, the water resources of the Philippines are a public good, to be allocated and utilized for the optimal national benefit. The government is responsible for regulating water use, particularly where shortages exist or might occur in the future.

Groundwater use in the GMA has grown rapidly since the 1960s. As the extraction rate exceeds the natural recharge many times, continued overpumping will result in an economic loss to society due to rising pumping costs from the lower water table and due to the need to abandon wells as water quality steadily deteriorates with rising salination. Each current groundwater user imposes these external diseconomies on all other users. Thus, government must adopt rational policies for managing and controlling groundwater. A well designed package of groundwater user charges and associated water-resource management measures would help not only to restrict groundwater use in the GMA, but also to raise revenues and finance alternative sources of water supply in the future (especially by extending the MWSS pipeborne system) to supplement or replace (with artificial recharges) declining groundwater availability.

Precedents for groundwater management and existing measures

Groundwater laws exist in countries as diverse as the USA, Mexico and Mali. Within the Philippines, charges are levied for developing and exploiting other natural resources such as minerals, forest products and water for electricity generation. The imposition of charges for use of forest products such as timber and fuelwood is relevant, because, like groundwater, forests are renewable resources that can be damaged beyond the point of recovery through prolonged and uncontrolled overuse. However, there are problems in implementing such regulations.

In the specific area of groundwater, several water districts, such as Cebu and Batangas, have imposed user charges. Groundwater management measures relevant to the GMA are described in the Philippine Water Code (PWC) issued by the National Water Resources Council (NWRC), and the Republic Act No. 6234 of 19 June 1971, creating the MWSS. There are provisions for drilling and maintaining water wells, protection of water supply sources, filing fees, minimal user charges and limits on withdrawals rates in relation to the distance between wells. However, the penalties are both inadequate and not well enforced to combat the rapid depletion and salinization of groundwater resources in the GMA.

12.5 Policy implementation issues

In order to make water-resources development more sustainable, there is clearly a need for a new package of groundwater management and control measures that is consistent with and supplements the existing laws mentioned above. The new measures should include the definition of critical groundwater areas in the GMA, licensing of well drillers, requirements for drilling permits, specifications for construction, maintenance and sterilization of wells, metering and reporting requirements, user charges, limits on pumping, the return of cooling water to the aquifer and contamination controls. Coordinated use of all policy instruments is important to achieve the best results.

12.5.1 Drilling and licensing fees, controls and other regulations

New well-owners ought to be charged a fee for the right to drill and an annual licensing fee for well operation. In this way, all existing and new wells would be registered and their status verified at least once a year. The pumping permit should specify construction details, allowable volume and user fees, based on piezometric head and salt content of the water.

The government needs to adopt and impose a system for safe well abandonment. By filling the bore completely from bottom to top with impermeable material (cement or clay), the protection of the aquifer will be enhanced by eliminating new points of downward flow of saline water.

To discourage pumping in critical areas characterized by a low piezometric head and/or a high groundwater salt concentration, a surcharge (above the user charge) might be imposed on withdrawals over 'normal requirements' if alternative MWSS supply is available.

Rivers and stream channels pollute the aquifer by percolation from their beddings, which receive waste products from overland runoff, effluent discharge of industries, city dumps and sanitary landfills. While provisions for pollution control already exist at the national level, regulations more specific to the GMA should be specified and strictly enforced. The aquifer is seriously depleted and has a much lower capacity to assimilate potentially harmful waste.

12.5.2 Conservation, redistribution and recharge

In 1980–1981, groundwater contributed about 40% of the supplies for the GMA. MWSS (1983b) reported that groundwater extraction in 1982 of 740 Mlitres/day would be reduced to less than 615 Mlitres/day by the year 2000. Pumpage patterns would be redistributed away from the 'cones of depression' in Valenzuela and Makati. Groundwater pumpage in the GMA would continue to decline and stabilize at 200 Mlitres/day.

Existing depletion of groundwater storage extends over the entire GMA, with the piezometric surface for 1982 lying below sea level in all but the extreme northeastern portion (less than 10% of the area), and 40 to 140 m below sea level in many densely populated areas. Further, groundwater pumping from areas adjacent to GMA will further lower the GMA water table. Serious aquifer damage has been caused by saltwater intrusion laterally and downward along the coastal GMA, and there is upwelling from depths of 200 m or more in some areas.

In summary, the withdrawals of groundwater must be reduced and redistributed through the GMA as soon as practicable. Groundwater pumpage should be reduced in the highest priority depleted areas, by serving them from new surface water sources. Levying a surcharge on the normal groundwater user fee, for pumpage above a 'normal level of depletion', can provide a strong incentive to large volume users of water.

Aquifer recharge may be enhanced from fresh-water sources to the southeast, the highlands in the south, east and northeast and streams that cross the GMA during the rainy season. However, the relatively low permeability of the GMA aquifer system may hamper natural recharge. Artificial recharge via unused wells may be tried, utilizing cooling water from high-rise business and apartment buildings. The used cooling water should be chemically compatible with the aquifer. Along the coastal GMA, a fresh-water mound or ridge could be built to control the inland migration of saltwater. Finally, the water level and its quality in wells within the GMA need to be monitored, to determine progress.

12.5.3 Determining and enforcing user charges

A realistic pricing framework must include economic efficiency, social equity and environmental protection consideration (see Chapter 14). On sociopolitical grounds, one may distinguish between household users, who withdraw relatively small amounts of water for their basic needs, and industrial and commercial well-owners, who pump large volumes for profit-making productive activity. This discrimination would apply only to user charges, with well-owners subject to drilling and licensing fees.

Users near the brackish interface (see Figure 12.1) must not exceed the critical pumping rate, which causes a 'sucking upward' or upconing of saltwater and terminates the use of the well. The users close to the interface will face an additional externality cost. Excessive pumping by distant users will advance the saltwater front further inland, forcing the closer users to decrease their pumping and eventually abandon their wells. If information were available, spatial price discrimination or zoning (based on distance from the brackish interface) might be used. One could also argue for dynamic pricing over time.

Household users

Based on the sociopolitical goal of meeting basic water needs, two relief measures for home well-owners include exemption from: (a) the user charge up to 50 m^3/month household (based on basic needs allocation of 6 m^3 per capita/month, and assuming eight persons per average household), with the normal user charge being levied on all pumpage exceeding 50 m^3/month, and (b) the user charge for all consumption, provided the well diameter is below some critical size (say 13 mm). While both measures encourage conservation of groundwater, option (b) may be easier to implement, since it avoids metering, billing and collecting payments from a large number of small groundwater users.

Industrial and commercial users

Those users who would be using the water for profitable activities should be charged the full rate (US $0.012/m^3) on all withdrawals.

Other user charges

In critical zones, a surcharge should be imposed on the normal user charge that is high enough to encourage the well-owners to shift to MWSS supply. Additional charges may be imposed, based on the cost of disposal of groundwater that is pumped, including actual sewerage costs and other health or environmental costs associated with discharge.

To levy charges, there are three basic methods of determining the volume of water extracted from wells: (a) water meter; (b) electricity consumption; and (c) pump capacity. Of these methods, the direct reading of a water meter is the best suited to a water utility like MWSS, where the organization has trained manpower, local officers and procedures already in place. However, water meters can be tampered with to give erroneous readings, and therefore compliance should be ensured by imposing strong legal penalties. Also the decision to meter and the complexity of the installed device should be made after comparing whether the benefits of metering exceed the costs (Munasinghe, 1992b).

The second best method is based on power use, which requires skilled manpower, verified pump data and periodic readings from an electric meter. The records could be obtained from the power utility, or read directly by a water utility employee. Finally, using pump capacity to estimate water extracted entails practical problems. Technical data are needed to compute pumpage, requiring the cooperation of well-owners – the capacity of submerged pumps may be difficult to verify.

Each of these measures assumes that the MWSS can assemble a complete register of the characteristics and locations of all pumping installations, accessing the aquifer, as a basis for a universal levy of tariffs and enforce pumping controls.

12.5.4 Conclusions

This case study shows how the neglect of long-run externalities jeopardizes the availability and quality of groundwater resource and increases economic, environmental and social costs. When extraction rates exceed the combined natural and artificial recharge rates, the typical private groundwater users tend to be ignorant or unconcerned about the external diseconomies or costs they impose on all other existing and future users. In the GMA situation, not only aquifer depletion, but also its resulting side-effects of saline intrusion, worsens the long-term problem.

One key remedy is to introduce a system of user charges to make water-resources development more sustainable – by slowing down the groundwater extraction rate and safeguarding water for future use. User charges are determined based on the social demand curve for groundwater, which explicitly accounts for environmental–economic externality costs. A user tax equal to the long-run externality cost may be imposed per cubic metre of groundwater withdrawn, to equalize marginal groundwater extraction costs and marginal consumption benefits to society. A surcharge may be imposed on normal user charges in critical zones, based on more detailed spatial and temporal disaggregation that considers the advance of the saline front and the depletion of the aquifer.

It is the task of the government to regulate water use adequately, especially where shortages exist or are likely to occur in the future. Taxes based on user charges should be combined with various groundwater demand management and control measures, in order to cut down the groundwater use effectively. Sound policies for groundwater management would also raise revenues to develop other water sources, to supplement or replace declining groundwater availability.

12.6 Simple water filtration method for cholera prevention in Bangladesh

12.6.1 Problems of water contamination and disease

The scarcity of safe drinking water is a global problem that will worsen with population growth and environmental change (see Section 12.2). Cholera and other waterborne diarrhoeal diseases are major killers, especially of children in developing countries. About 5.5 million cases of cholera occur annually. In many countries, tube wells, which tap into groundwater, are expected to provide safe drinking water. However, they fail to protect against gastrointestinal diseases. Underground water systems are vulnerable to both microbiological and heavy metal contamination – e.g. arsenic contamination has been reported in countries such as Argentina, Chile, China, India, Mexico, Taiwan and Thailand. Up to half the wells drilled in the late 1960s to counter Bangladesh's severe surface-water pollution were found to be contaminated with arsenic in amounts that exceed 50 ppb, with higher concentrations in some areas.

A key aspect of the microbiology of drinking water is the viable but non-culturable (VBNC) phenomenon – i.e. the dormant state or survival strategy manifested by many waterborne pathogenic bacteria. In the VBNC state, bacteria remain viable and virulent, but do not grow on conventional bacteriological culture media. Thus, these bacteria will be left in the water if other detection methods are not used. Re-evaluation of disinfectant protocols to treat water (including those employing chlorine) is necessary, especially when the effectiveness of municipal filtration and water purification systems is low – such as during severe floods.

Field research carried out at the University of Maryland and at the International Centre for Diarrheal Disease Research, Bangladesh, found that simple filtration can be useful in reducing cholera and other enteric diseases (TWNSO, 2004). Intervention methods need to meet sustainable development criteria – low-cost, sociocultural acceptability and environmental soundness. They should also be readily accessible to the public in developing countries, especially after extreme weather conditions such as monsoons. Bottled water is too expensive an option for the poor who suffer from waterborne diseases.

Unlike many other illnesses, waterborne diseases cannot be readily eradicated because many pathogens occur naturally in water. However, intervention is possible by modifying social behaviour – changing the way water is used through general education, increased public awareness and better efforts to protect water from undesirable contamination. Chemical pollution also occurs in many developing countries, due to industrialization, lack of resources and poor management. In addition, the emergence of pathogens resistant to chemicals used in water treatment is a concern for those responsible for clean, safe drinking water supplies.

The infectious agent causing cholera is a bacterium called *Vibrio cholerae* (VC), which occurs naturally in the aquatic environment. If ingested, VC is likely to produce clinical cholera depending on the health of a given individual (Cash *et al*., 1974). Bangladesh faces two types of water-related problems – flooding during the monsoon and severe aridity in the dry season. During the summer, VC increases in cholera endemic areas (Sack *et al*. 2003). Flooding causes extreme conditions, where even basic needs are difficult to obtain. Boiling or chlorinating water (to purify it) becomes more difficult under such conditions.

Boiling water prior to drinking also helps to kill guinea worm larvae (which causes dracunculiasis) and Cyclops (a planktonic stage of the guinea worm) as well as other microorganisms. However, it is time consuming and may be expensive in countries like Bangladesh where fuelwood is scarce. In addition, boiling water is not the social norm in most rural villages of Bangladesh (and Africa; see WASH (1991)). Filtering water at the time of collection and before drinking has been successful in removing Cyclops. The Cyclops are removed using a nylon net, and filtration is now recommended as an effective method of preventing this life-threatening disease, at one time common in Africa (WASH, 1991).

In Bangladesh, a majority of villagers still depend on untreated surface water. Surface water from ponds and rivers is preferred as a source of drinking water – for reasons of taste, convenience and for the traditional belief that 'quality' water is 'natural' and not chemically treated. It has been shown that those who used VC-negative water for drinking but VC-positive water for cooking, bathing or washing had the same rate of infection as those using VC-positive water for drinking. This indicates the importance of using clean water for all home purposes, not only for drinking. Once a member of the family is contaminated, it is likely to spread among others via food or other methods of direct transmission.

During monsoon flooding, vast areas in Bangladesh are submerged, and only a few shallow hand-operated tube wells are available to the villagers. Many sanitary latrines also become flooded, causing a serious problem with hygiene, and posing a direct threat of contamination by enteric bacteria including VC. Previous studies indicate that, during late monsoons, phytoplankton blooms occur, followed by zooplankton blooms, to which vibrios are attached and multiply, increasing the number of VC in the natural water (Huq *et al*.,

1983; Colwell and Huq, 1994). When consumption of surface water is unavoidable, particularly during frequent flooding or other natural disasters, a simple but effective method for reducing the number of VC cells would be useful to curb cholera.

12.6.2 Field trial of simple sari filtration method

The field test used a simple, cheap and socially acceptable method that removes 99% of VC attached to the plankton, using four layers of sari cloth as the filter – thereby reducing the cases of cholera. Among potential filtration materials commonly found in homes, it was found that old sari cloth was better as a filter than new cloth, because the threads of an old sari were frayed, reducing the mesh size. Hence, four layers of old sari could yield a 30 μm mesh, which would filter over 99% of copepods carrying VC. Since cholera is dose-dependent, filtration is a practical method for reducing cholera in areas where people must depend on untreated water, as no other methods are available or affordable. This study targeted poor rural homes to reduce cholera by directly involving the local community. Mothers of households implemented the filtration system.

Three groups of 15 000 villagers participated in the trial. A first group used sari filters, a second group used nylon filters (as used to control guinea worm disease in Africa) and a third group served as a control, who continued their routine methods of water collection without filtering. The nylon and sari groups were educated on how to use their filters, while all three groups were informed about the importance of hygiene and personal health. Further, posters that described the process were shown, stressing the critical need to remove plankton from the water. Villagers were advised to use filtered water for all domestic purposes. Extensive pre- and post-study questionnaires were used to assess the knowledge gained by the participants concerning health value of filtration, as well as the willingness to participate in this programme.

12.6.3 Results

Four months after the trial began, it was found that 90% of the population accepted the sari filtration system in their daily lives. Cholera cases fell sharply in groups using the nylon and sari filtration systems. The latter group had about half the cholera cases suffered by the control group.

It was clear that sari filtration helped bring safer water into houses with few extra costs, resulting in major health benefits to people with few other alternatives. It satisfied the economic, social and environmental criteria indicated earlier – low-cost, sociocultural acceptability and environmental soundness, while being readily accessible to the public, especially after extreme weather conditions such as the monsoons. After the successful field trials, several villages have started using this method to filter water. Villagers must be properly informed through mass communication, so that more people use the sari filtration method.

12.6.4 Sustainable development assessment of sari-based filtration

The sustainomics-based SWAMP framework takes into account the economic, social and environmental aspects of sustainable development. Once 'win–win' options (that improve all three indices) are realized, policy makers are able to make trade-offs among other available options.

Conventional water-project evaluation uses cost–benefit analysis (CBA), where all impacts are valued in monetary terms. However, when environmental and social effects cannot be easily valued, multicriteria analysis (MCA) is attractive to decision makers who prefer to consider a range of feasible alternatives as opposed to one 'best' solution. MCA examines alternative ways of meeting multiple objectives assessed in differing units of measurement, since some impacts cannot be measured solely in monetary terms (see Chapter 3).

Figure 12.8 uses MCA to assess our simple sari-based water purification method within the SWAMP framework. Outward movements along the axes trace improvements in three indicators: economic efficiency (net monetary benefits), social equity (improved benefits for the poor) and environmental protection (reduced water pollution). Triangle *ABC* shows the existing situation. Waterborne diseases increase both morbidity and mortality rates, thereby causing economic harm (loss of earnings, medical costs, etc.). Social equity is also low because the poor are most affected, and overall environmental pollution is bad. Next, triangle *DEF* indicates a 'win–win' future option with the simplified sari filtration technique, in which all three indices improve. Economic losses fall due to better health. Social

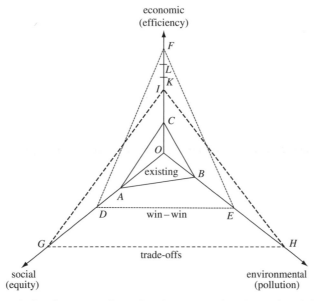

Figure 12.8. SD analysis of water quality using SWAMP and MCA. Adapted from Munasinghe (1992b, 2002a).

gains accrue to the rural poor, especially women and children. Environmental benefits arise from cleaner water.

After realizing such 'win–win' gains, the introduction of other options may require trade-offs. For example, triangle *GIH* suggests that more advanced water supply and purification methods (e.g. wells and surface-water sources with purification plants and pipe-borne supply, or nanotechnology-based techniques) may yield further environmental and social benefits, but with increased economic costs. After adopting the clearly desirable 'win–win' move from *ABC* to *DEF*, a policy maker may not wish to shift further from *DEF* to *GIH*, because it is difficult to know the relative weights to place on the three indices. However, one may narrow the options. Suppose a small economic cost, *FL*, yields full social gain *DG* (e.g. by targeting poor households), while a large cost, *LI*, is required to realize the environmental benefit *EH* (e.g. better water supply and sanitation). Here, the social gain may better justify the economic sacrifice. Further, if purely budgetary constraints limit cost increases to less than *FK*, then sufficient funds exist only to pay for the social benefits, and the environmental improvements will have to be deferred.

12.7 Appendix: Economic costs of producing water

Tables 12.3–12.6 provide production costs for (a) groundwater (depletion and conservation cases) and (b) MWSS public water supply. Unit economics costs of water produced are the average incremental cost (AIC) of supply (see Chapter 14).

$$\text{AIC} = \frac{\text{present value of incremental costs of producing water}}{\text{present value of volume of incremental water produced}}.$$

Table 12.3 *Groundwater withdrawals and supply costs*

	Depletion case							Conservation case				
				Production cost (US $1000/day)						Production cost (US $1000/day)		
Year	GW (MLD)	MWSS supply (MLD)	Unit prod. cost[a] (US $/m³)	GW[b]	MWSS	Total[c]	GW (MLD)	MWSS supply (MLD)	GW[b]	MWSS	Total[c]
1984	730	0	0.131	95.9	0	95.9	730	0	95.9	0	95.9
1985	730	0	0.137	100.1	0	100.1	697	33	91.6	7.6	99.2
1986	730	0	0.142	103.8	0	103.8	664	66	87.3	15.4	102.6
1987	730	0	0.148	107.9	0	107.9	631	99	82.9	23	105.9
1988	730	0	0.152	111.6	0	111.6	598	132	78.6	30.6	109.2
1989	730	0	0.159	115.8	0	115.8	565	165	74.3	38.3	112.6
1990	730	0	0.164	119.4	0	119.4	532	198	69.9	46	115.9
1991	719	0	0.169	121.7	0	121.7	499	220	65.6	51.1	116.6
1992	708	0	0.174	123.4	0	123.4	466	242	61.2	56.2	117.4
1993	697	0	0.18	125.4	0	125.4	433	264	56.9	61.3	118.2
1994	686	0	0.185	126.9	0	126.9	400	286	52.6	66.4	119
1995	675	0	0.191	128.7	0	128.7	367	308	48.2	71.5	119.7
1996	664	0	0.196	129.9	0	129.9	334	330	43.9	76.6	120.6
1997	653	0	0.201	131.5	0	131.5	301	352	39.6	81.7	121.3
1998	642	0	0.206	132.5	0	132.5	268	374	35.2	86.9	122.1
1999	631	0	0.212	133.9	0	133.9	235	396	30.9	91.9	122.8
2000	620	0	0.217	134.6	0	134.6	200	420	26.3	97.5	123.8
2001	558	0	0.223	124.4	0	124.4	200	358	26.3	83.1	109.4
2002	496	0	0.228	113	0	113	200	296	26.3	68.7	95
2003	434	0	0.234	101.4	0	101.4	200	234	26.3	54.4	80.6
2004	372	0	0.239	88.7	0	88.7	200	172	26.3	39.9	66.2
2005	310	0	0.244	75.7	0	75.7	200	110	26.3	25.6	51.9
2006	248	0	0.249	61.9	0	61.9	200	48	26.3	11.1	37.4
2007	186	14	0.255	46	3.3	49.3	200	0	26.3	0	26.3
2008	124	64	0.26	32.2	14.9	47.1	200	0	26.3	0	26.3
2009	62	138	0.266	16.5	32.1	48.6	200	0	26.3	0	26.3
2010 to infinity	0	200	0.271	0	46.4	46.4	200	0	26.3	0	26.3

[a] Unit cost of production is US $0.217/m³ for groundwater withdrawals (depletion case in year 2000), from Table 12.5.
[b] Unit cost of production is US $0.132/m³ for groundwater withdrawals (conservation case), from Table 12.4.
[c] Unit cost of production is US $0.23/m³ for MWSS supply, from Table 12.6.
Output is the same in both depletion and conservation cases.
GW = groundwater withdrawals.
MLD = megalitres per day.

Table 12.4 *Initial pumping costs and well output in 1984*

| Year | Costs (US $) | | Water produced ($m^3$) |
	Investment	Operating	
0	92 857	9400	179 050
1	0	9400	179 050
2	0	9400	179 050
3	5100	9400	179 050
4	0	9400	179 050
5	5100	9400	179 050
6	2607	9400	179 050
7	5100	9400	179 050
8	0	9400	179 050
9	16 900	9400	179 050
10	0	9400	179 050
11	7707	9400	179 050
12	0	9400	179 050
13	5100	9400	179 050
14	0	9400	179 050
15	5100	9400	179 050
16	2607	9400	179 050
17	5100	9400	179 050
18	11 800	9400	179 050
19	5100	9400	179 050
Present values in year 0 (discounted at 10%)	121 044	80 025	1 523 900

Unit cost = (121 044 + 80 025) / 1 523 900 = US $ 0.132/m^3

Based on exchange rate at 1 June 1984: US $1 = 14 Pesos.
Well characteristics in mid 1984: depth = 183 m; pumping rate = 0.454 m^3/min; efficiency = 0.6; capacity factor = 50%; life = 20 years.

Table 12.5 *Pumping costs and well output in 2000 (with depletion)*

Year	Costs (US $)		Water produced (m^3)
	Investment	Operating	
0	92 857	12 614	179 050
1	0	12 614	179 050
2	0	12 614	179 050
3	5100	12 614	179 050
4	0	12 614	179 050
5	5100	12 614	179 050
Present values in year 0 (discounted at 10%)	99 855	47 818	678 740

Unit cost = (99 855 + 47 818) / 678 740 = US $0.217/m^3

Based on exchange rate at 1 June 1984: US $1 = 14 Pesos.
Well characteristics in mid 2000 (projected figures): depth = 183 m;
pumping rate = 0.681 m^3/min; total dynamic head (TDH) = 116 m;
efficiency = 0.6; capacity factor = 50%; life = 6 years.

Table 12.6 *Average incremental cost (AIC) of MWSS water supply*
Present values of production costs and volumes discounted to
1984 at a rate of 10% per year, in constant mid 1984 prices

(1)	Capital costs (US $million)	632
(2)	Operating costs (US $million)	77
(3)	Value of power and energy sales (US $million)	59
(4)	Net present value of cost, (1)+(2)–(3) (US $million)	650
(5)	Water produced (million cubic metres)	2801
(6)	AIC of water produced (US $/m^3)	0.23

13

Ecological and agricultural system applications[1]

This chapter describes sustainomics applications to two main types of ecological systems – forests (natural ecosystems) and agriculture (managed ecosystems). Section 13.1 describes the underlying reasons for deforestation. It analyses the management of megadiverse natural ecosystems in rainforests, and then identifies generic policies that make forest use more sustainable. In Section 13.2, a case study of Madagascar seeks to understand better the specific impact of parks-management policies on tropical forests. The environmental, social and economic consequences of human actions are assessed, with specific focus on the economic valuation of environmental impacts. Various methods (e.g. opportunity cost, contingent valuation, travel cost) are used to value economically damage to forests and watersheds, timber and non-timber forest products, impacts on local inhabitants and bio-diversity and ecotourism benefits. Relevant policy implications are drawn. Sections 13.3 and 13.4 present a second case involving the vulnerability of managed ecosystems (agriculture) to climate change in Sri Lanka. A Ricardian agricultural production model estimates the past effects of natural variations in both temperature and precipitation. Then, several scenarios of future climate change are imposed to assess future agricultural production. The harmful impacts of rising temperatures dominate the beneficial effects of increased rainfall. Policy conclusions are drawn for sustainable agricultural policy in Sri Lanka.

13.1 Sustainable management of tropical forests

13.1.1 Deforestation issues

Tropical forests consist of dry and moist forests, each accounting for roughly half the total of about 3.1 billion hectares found worldwide. Tropical moist forest are further divided into rain forests and deciduous forests. Rain forests make up about two-thirds of all tropical moist forests and are the richest in terms of biomass and biological diversity. Deciduous forests generally lie on the outskirts of rain forests, and are characterized by more defined dry and wet periods. Although tropical dry forests are also subject to large-

[1] The valuable contributions of R. A. Kramer, J. McNeely, R. Mendelsohn, N. Seo and N. Sharma to this chapter are gratefully acknowledged. Some parts of the chapter are based on material adapted from Kramer, Sharma and Munasinghe (1995), Munasinghe (1993b), Munasinghe and McNeely (1995) and Seo, Mendelsohn and Munasinghe (2005).

scale destruction, the major emphasis by the global community has been on addressing the loss of tropical moist forests.

The term 'deforestation' is used in a rather broad context to imply the wasteful destruction of forest resources, especially primary forests. However, this is not always the case (Rowe *et al.*, 1992). 'Disturbance deforestation' refers to human activities that seriously alter the natural habitat of forest systems. 'Conversion deforestation' is the process of converting forest lands into alternative uses, such as agriculture and resettlement. Not all human activity results in complete destruction of forests. Certain human-induced disturbance or conversion deforestation practices leave the actual area under forest cover intact, although some of the forest-related services and functions may be significantly affected.

Well managed plantation forests that allow secondary forests to regenerate after each harvest, and sustainable agricultural practices that allow the land to be left in fallow for several seasons following a harvest, are considered to be less destructive uses of forest lands. Wasteful deforestation occurs when forests yielding high-valued goods and services are clear cut and replaced with land uses that yield lower returns. This latter type of deforestation is what poses a significant environmental problem and has local and national as well as global implications. Wasteful deforestation is, to a great extent, an irreversible process. Secondary forests regenerate quite rapidly if the land is left fallow after a season of cultivation or when deliberate reafforestation efforts are undertaken. However, biological diversity in natural tropical forests can take many decades to regenerate and may be lost permanently.

Deforestation in the tropics continues. While open access forests have suffered most, even parks and protected areas are threatened (Munasinghe and McNeely, 1995). Up to 1995, about 36% of the tropics was covered by natural forests (1715 million hectares). Tropical deforestation rates increased 8.5% from 2000 to 2005 when compared with the 1990s, while loss of primary forests may have expanded by 25% over the same period (FAO, 2005). Annual tropical deforestation rates increased from 0.57% in the 1990s (10.16 million hectares/yr) to 0.62% in 2000–2005 (10.4 million hectares/yr), while clearing of primary tropical forests rose from 0.66% in the 1990s to at least 0.81% in 2000–2005. Among primary forests, annual deforestation rose to 6.26 million hectares from 5.41 million hectares in the same period. Due to a significant increase in plantation forests, forest cover has been expanding in North America, Europe and China, whilst diminishing in the tropics. Industrial logging, agricultural conversion (commercial and subsistence) and forest fires (often set by people) cause the bulk of global deforestation today.

Brazil had the highest total annual forest loss of 2.8 million hectares between 1990 and 2005 (8.1% of total forest cover). Indonesia, Myanmar, the Democratic Republic of Congo and Zambia also suffered significant deforestation. Loss rates in countries with small areas of forest cover is much higher – e.g. 7.4% in Comoros and 5.2% in Burundi (FAO, 2005).

13.1.2 Forest benefits

Basic natural processes in tropical forests (such as soil formation, nutrient cycling and primary production) support key ecosystem functions (provisioning, regulation and cultural) on which sustainable development depends (see Chapter 4). Tropical forests provide many products and services that benefit people at local, national and global levels. Indigenous people and forest-based communities rely on forest resources for most of their consumption goods, such as food, shelter and even clothing. At the national level, forest resources are a source of foreign exchange and energy. Forest lands serve as 'new' land for expansion of food production and settlements. Forests also ensure a regular supply of fresh water, prevent flooding, protect crops from wind damage and also prevent soil erosion and siltation of river beds downstream. In all, about 2.5 billion people in the tropics rely either directly or indirectly on forest resources for consumption goods. Tropical forests stabilize the global climate, protect the diversity of biological species, support ecological systems and provide recreational benefits. People derive benefits from the amenity value of forests and the knowledge of their continued existence.

Forests have arguably played a bigger role in the development of human societies than any other resource, bar water and cultivable land. The forest products sector accounts for 1% of world GDP and 3% of international merchandise trade. The annual turnover of round-wood, sawnwood, panels, pulp and paper exceeds US $200 billion (FAO, 2005). In some countries they account for a higher fraction of GDP – about 5% in Malaysia, Liberia and Ivory Coast, and 4% in Cameroon and Tanzania. Sabah (Malaysia) generates about 70% of government revenue from forests. Yet, the potential rent from the forestry sector is under-estimated and goes uncaptured in most developing countries. The prime marketable products of most forests are timber, fuelwood, pulp and paper, providing 3.4 billion m^3 of timber-equivalent a year globally. After a 60% rise during 1960–1990, global wood use stabilized during the 1990s due to more efficient timber use and paper recycling.

There is no sharp divide in total wood consumption between poor and rich nations, largely because poor nations have a large demand for wood as fuel. The world's leading per capita consumers of timber (using more than three times the global average) include nations at all levels of economic development: Liberia, Zambia, Malaysia, Costa Rica, Sweden and the USA. Africa is the second largest per capita consumer of wood, after North America (FAO, 2005). The use of wood varies dramatically with levels of economic development. Worldwide, half the use is for fuel, but in developing countries this figure rises to 80%. For three billion people, wood is the main energy source for heating and cooking, making it a prime cause of African tropical forest loss. Many countries, particularly in South Asia, face a growing domestic shortage of fuelwood.

By far the most valuable economic product from tropical forests is wood, which accounts for about half of all forest-related revenue. The two main wood products are roundwood and fuelwood. Roundwood is wood in its natural state, which is then processed into sawnwood, pulp, panels, plywood and paper. Tropical hardwoods, the major industrial timber export trade of the tropics, accounts for just over 10% of the total international trade in timber (Munasinghe, 1992c). About 31% of the total volume of industrial timber produced in developing countries is exported as roundwood or wood products. Nevertheless, this constitutes only about 4% of the total tropical wood supply; 13% is consumed nationally as timber, and the rest is consumed in the form of fuelwood (Vanclay, 1993). Presently 33 tropical countries are net exporters of timber. However, that number will to drop to ten by 2010, as domestic demand in many countries catches up with the available supply.

Wood is used mainly as 'industrial roundwood' (building material, paper and packaging) in industrialized nations. Per capita use in the USA is 15 times the average value in developing countries. Over half the timber for industrial use goes to North America, Europe and Japan, a figure that rises to 70% for paper. Global paper use has grown sixfold since 1950, using one-fifth of all the wood harvested (FAO, 2005). Except for China and Brazil, most industrial roundwood production takes place in the developed world, which uses over twice as much as developing countries

Fuelwood is produced primarily to meet national needs. About 83% of all wood extracted from tropical forests is consumed as fuelwood. In Africa, over 90% of all wood supplies are used as a source of energy (Vanclay, 1993). Three billion people in developing countries rely on fuelwood as the primary source of energy, but only about 20% of total energy demand in developing countries is met by fuelwood. Along with increasing scarcity of wood, especially in severely denuded areas, the cost of fuelwood has risen sharply. Households (especially among the urban poor) may spend up to 20–30% of their income on fuelwood alone (Rowe *et al.*, 1992).

Forests are also the source of many non-wood products, including extractives, such as bark, dyes, fibres, gums, incense, latexes, oils, resins, shellac, tanning compounds and waxes; parts of plants and animals for medicinal, ceremonial or decorative purposes; and food such as bush meat, flowers, fruits, honey, nuts, leaves, seeds and spices. Most non-wood products are consumed locally. A study in the rainforests of southern Cameroon found more than 500 plant species and 280 animal species in use and often on sale in local markets (Van Dijk, 1999). Indeed sometimes the commercial value of non-wood products per hectare of land can exceed that of wood products. Rattan, latex, palm oil, cocoa, vanilla, nuts, spices, gum and ornamental plants are commodities for which expanding markets exist in developed countries. Several countries earn considerable revenue from exporting non-wood products. Sudan and Madagascar generate about US $60 million annually from gum and vanilla exports, respectively. Indonesia earned US $134 million in 1986 from non-wood exports. Many people living in or near tropical rain forests rely for half or more of their protein on wild animals caught in the forest. The subsistence meat harvest in the Brazilian Amazon is 160 000 tonnes/yr, equivalent to 20 million animals.

Because many non-timber forest products are used within the forests or are traded informally, their value to the economy is often underestimated by governments when considering the value of natural forests relative to other land uses. One exception were the 'extractive reserves' in the Brazilian Amazon in the late 1980s, dedicated to Brazil-nut harvesting, rubber tapping and other non-destructive uses of the forest. These non-timber resources can be overharvested, especially when local products gain access to large urban markets. The African bushmeat industry, which has become a global business, may exceed 1 million tonnes/yr. Such levels of exploitation are unsustainable and damage the forest ecology, since the same animals often disperse seeds.

The many ecosystem services generated by natural tropical forests are sufficient justification for protecting them. Tropical forests and soils store vast amounts of carbon due to high biomass density. Three times the amount of carbon found in the air is contained in tropical forests. Tropical deforestation contributes one-sixth of the total global carbon emission into the atmosphere, increasing climate risks (see Chapter 5).

Tropical forests cover 9% of the Earth's surface, but support about one-half the 1.4 million named species among the world biota (Schucking and Anderson, 1991). The species, genetic and ecosystems diversity found in the tropics are vital for maintaining the balance of natural ecosystems (see Section 13.1.3). Loss of genetic diversity can cause maladaptation to the changing environment, increase vulnerability to diseases and decrease benefits from ecosystem services (see Chapter 4).

Forests serve the important function of protecting watersheds and ensuring perennial supplies of fresh water. Erosion due to winds and surface runoff are mitigated by forests, reducing sedimentation and bed-loading of reservoirs and rivers downstream. Deforestation in the Himalayan foothills is linked with devastating floods in the Ganges and Brahmaputra river basins, resulting in crop damage, loss of animals, damage to human dwellings and infrastructure, displacement of people and spread of disease. Forests stabilize regional climate and hydrologic systems – e.g. in the Amazon it is estimated that about one-half the rainfall is the result of evapotranspiration (Rowe, *et al.*, 1992). Forests also help to improve air quality and to enrich soils through nitrogen fixation.

The recreational value of tropical forests has largely been latent. Eco-tourism is an emerging economic activity that could earn much foreign exchange for tropical countries. Local urban dwellers also derive recreational benefits from visiting tropical forest reserves. However, their willingness-to-pay for these services is generally lower. The mere existence of tropical forests yields benefits to people, most of whom may never intend to visit a forest reserve.

13.1.3 *Tropical forests and sustainable development*

The effects of deforestation on sustainable development can be extremely detrimental. Impacts of deforestation, such as repeated major floods in Bangladesh, Thailand and Madagascar, erosion of fertile soil and riverbed and reservoir siltation that impact on downstream hydroelectric projects, fisheries and other industries have severe impacts on development. Overall the estimated economic loss due to forest depletion is about 4–6% of GNP in the major timber exporting countries – the same order of magnitude as the gains from timber export (Rowe *et al.*, 1992).

Natural systems

Linkage of deforestation, greenhouse gases (GHGs) and climate change is also of critical importance. Currently, deforestation releases between 1 and 3 billion metric tonnes of carbon into the atmosphere. This is caused both by the absence of biomass to sequester carbon and the release of carbon during the burning of forests. Fossil fuel combustion, particularly from developed countries, accounts for the release of almost 6 billion metric tonnes of carbon into the atmosphere annually. Climate concerns are also mounting about GHG emissions due to the burning of tropical forests.

When forest resources come under extreme pressure from human activity, the result may be eventual desertification of the land. Loss of forest cover might cause changes in patterns rainfall and of vegetation. Less dense shrubs and bushes would replace the rich biomass, which required more moisture. If such human pressure continues, the surviving vegetation will disappear until the surface is denuded. Beyond a certain stage, the process of desertification would be difficult to reverse.

Loss of forest cover also affects the capacity to retain water, which enables watersheds to remain active, even during periods of drought. Denuded of tree cover, soils lose the capacity to retain water, and most rainfall disappears rapidly as surface runoff. Watershed destruction due to deforestation can be devastating, especially to rural poor communities that rely on natural sources, even for their basic requirements. The loss of forest cover also affects the hydrogeologic cycle.

Biodiversity

Tropical forests play a significant role in protecting biodiversity. The *Convention on Biological Diversity* (CBD, 1992) defines biological diversity as 'variability among living organisms'. There are three categories of biological diversity: species, genetic and ecosystem. The categories simply provide a convenient method to define different types of diversity and facilitate measurement, but are not mutually exclusive (Aylward and Barbier, 1993). The concept of 'biodiversity' is distinct from biological resources themselves. But the literature tends to consider efforts to conserve biodiversity and the conservation of biological resources, or natural habitats, as being one and the same objective.

While the total number of species in the world is estimated to range between 5 and 30 million, less than 5% of the biodiversity of rain forests is known to science. One study revealed that just 10 hectares of rain forest in Borneo contained some 700 tree species, the total amount of species found in North America (Botkin and Talbot, 1992). More typically, one hectare of South American tropical rain forest may contain 40 to 100 species; in Amazonian Peru these may be as many as 300 species. In contrast, a typical hectare of eastern North American forest contains 10 to 20 species, while boreal forests could have as few as one to five.

It is possible that 25% of all species may become extinct during the next 20 to 30 years. The extinction and evolution of species is an inevitable natural process. For example, 65 million years ago, the last mass extinction wiped out all dinosaurs, most marine invertebrates and marine plankton. Except during such periods, the rate of evolution has generally been slightly higher than the rate of species extinction, thus causing biological diversity to increase over time. However, the current rate of extinction may be 40 000 times higher than the natural rate of species evolution (Schucking and Anderson, 1991), mainly due to increased human activity. As many as 50 species may be driven to extinction each day.

The ecological view of sustainable development stresses the stability of bio-physical systems (see Chapters 2 and 4). Ecosystems are the key to ecologically sustainable development. First, it is essential to maintain the viability of ecological systems that support current production. Second, future needs are unpredictable, and potentially valuable species could be lost. Third, our understanding of ecosystems is insufficient to determine the impact of removing any component. In particular, the loss of a critical ecosystem or sub-system may have irreversible and catastrophic effects. Finally, variety is inherently more interesting and attractive.

Potential medicinal value is one aspect of biodiversity protection that is attractive to the private sector. Medicines from wild products are a growing industry, estimated at about US $40 billion/yr. Examples are as follows. (a) The US National Cancer Institute engaged in a five-year programme involving the screening of some 3000 plants active against cancer cells, of which around 70% are tropical plants (Munasinghe and McNeely, 1995). (b) One gene from a single Ethiopian barley plant now protects California's US $160 million annual barley crop from yellow dwarf virus. (c) In 1960, a child suffering from leukemia had only a 20% chance of survival; this has risen to 80% due to the availability of a drug containing active substances from the rosy periwinkle, a tropical-forest plant from Madagascar (Munasinghe, 1992c).

The millennium ecosystem assessment (MA) shows how ecological sustainability implies the preservation of biodiversity at a sustainable level (see Chapter 4). This approach involves local communities, scientists, indigenous peoples and many parts of government working together to ensure that biological resources – land, forests, oceans and so forth – are used in ways that are sustainable and contribute to both intra- and intergenerational equity. The sustainomics framework offers one practical method of incorporating concerns about ecological sustainability into sustainable development strategy (see Chapters 4 and 6).

Socio-cultural issues

Tropical forests play an important role in fulfilling the social dimension of development, in particular by serving the basic needs of numerous indigenous and tribal groups. There are some 300 million indigenous people around the world living in 70 countries inhabiting around 20% of the land mass. Along with increasing economic pressure, many indigenous groups have lost their traditional claims to forest lands and have been displaced by ranchers, loggers and settlers.

The objective is not to preserve these cultures and societies to meet some ideal standards of 'indigenousness'. Indeed as the world's finite resource base becomes increasing constrained due to rising demands of the growing population base, these indigenous communities are likely to encounter external economic, cultural and political pressures sooner or later. Indigenous communities often feel the external pressure when they come into contact with religious missionaries, mass media networks and market-oriented economic forces. Frequently these influences strain relationships between the older generation and younger members within the community. Older members strive to maintain traditional customs and rituals, while the youths are more open to external influences.

The policy analyst's challenge is to learn how to communicate with groups speaking different languages, holding different world views and cultural characteristics. By acknowledging the presence and importance of indigenous communities, policies must be designed and based on the notions of development that are important to each individual community, rather than subjecting them to pre-conceived notions of development. Doing so enables these communities to adapt to external environments gradually and in a non-threatening manner, whilst ensuring the continued maintenance of their cultural heritage. During the past 150 years, 87 indigenous groups have disappeared in Brazil alone. These are simply the cases that have been recorded; the actual number may be higher. Many more could suffer the same fate if proper measures are not adopted.

A fundamental difference between indigenous and non-indigenous people arises in their respective views of nature. Non-indigenous societies generally perceive human beings as an entity separate from nature. Hence the main focus is to establish the proper relationship of human beings with nature. The natural environment is perceived as an entity to be 'managed' or controlled to better serve human needs. Indigenous people generally believe that humans are an intrinsic part of nature. The relationship is one of coexistence with nature. The knowledge base contains both material and spiritual information.

Indigenous knowledge of the medicinal value of plant and animal species has been attractive to developed countries. About one-quarter of all western prescription drugs contain elements of rain-forest plants. Information from indigenous groups has contributed to the development of about three-quarters of these drugs. For instance, information on quinine and curare was provided by the Shuar of Ecuador and Peru. While the pharmaceutical industry based on rain-forest related drugs generates hundreds of millions of dollars in annual revenues, very few of these benefits are returned to the indigenous communities.

Policies that recognize and incorporate indigenous communities will most likely be successful if sufficient authority and power are delegated to the local level. Empowering these communities instills within them the direct responsibility for management and protection of the forest resources. Equally important is the need to educate local communities on the effects of forest destruction and the benefits from well managed forest resources. Once aware of such benefits, communities are more apt to adopt conservation methods and also ensure that such methods are adopted by other communities and groups.

In this respect, the biosphere-reserves concept is a promising approach, which places more emphasis on involving local communities in research, education and training programmes. Local people are integrated into the management system, and their indigenous knowledge of forests helps to design management practices. The reserves include use (or buffer) and non-use (or strict) zones.

This leads to the final objective of sociocultural development – the issue of equity. The typical scenario in many developing countries is rampant profiteering by logging firms and corrupt politicians at the expense of local communities that are deprived of even the most fundamental requirements such as food and shelter. Under proper forest policies, there should be a more equitable distribution of the benefits from harvesting forest resources. Local communities that suffer most of the externality effects are rightfully due a greater share of the revenue. Likewise, logging firms must bear the costs equivalent to the extent of damage caused by their activities. Holding logging firms more accountable for the cost of destructive forest uses will eventually result in their adopting less destructive measures and considering the efficiency and effectiveness of harvesting forest resources. It is then likely that the extent of forest destruction will decrease significantly.

13.1.4 Causes and symptoms of deforestation

Misdirected forest-management policies that address the symptoms rather than the causes usually fail (Vanclay, 1993). It is difficult to distinguish between causes and symptoms of deforestation, since some causes lie outside forest borders. For example, Gbetnkom (2005) showed how non-forest policies that increase prices of food crops, export crops and timber tend to accelerate forest clearing. In addition, forests were harmed by structural adjustment policies, the oil boom and currency devaluation, which improved consumer buying power and competitiveness of domestic crops. Impacts of economy-wide policies on forests are given in Sections 7.1 and 7.2, and case studies are provided in Sections 7.4.5 and 9.5.

Developing countries are driven to harvest forest resources and convert land into agricultural use to meet the growing demands of food and landless people. By 2025, the global population is expected to grow to 8 billion, and about 60% of this growth will be in developing countries. Tropical forests are seen as an invaluable source of new land and raw material. While low-lying forests are treated as potential agricultural lands, highland forests are used for extracting timber, fuelwood and other raw materials. With present yields, about 10 million hectares of forests will have to be cleared each year to provide the growing population with the current intake of nutrient content; 60% of all deforestation is due to expansion of agricultural settlements (World Bank, 1992a). The remainder is divided between other activities, such as logging, ranching and mining. However, in some regions, deforestation due to the expansion of small-holder agricultural settlements is modest in comparison with other activities. In the Amazon, deforestation is mainly due to conversion of land for livestock ranching. In Brazil alone, subsidized cattle ranching caused about 70% of deforestation – an area of 12 million hectares in 1980 (Rowe, *et al*., 1992). Similarly, in tropical East Asia, industrial logging constitutes the major form of deforestation.

Uncontrolled profiteering and corruption enable politicians, forestry officials, timber merchants and land owners to exploit forest resources. Developing countries are also largely preoccupied with rectifying urban and social problems that have a direct effect on human well-being, but often at the expense of environmental degradation, whose impacts are less clear. Thus, environmental issues have typically received relatively low priority. Lately, however, the consequences of ecological harm are receiving recognition, particularly due to efforts by non-governmental organizations (NGOs), which are holding governments accountable.

The mismanagement of forest resources is also due to the inefficiency of administrative and regulatory institutions. Forestry sectors are typically characterized by centralized administrative structures, where authority and power are concentrated at the top. Administrative staff at local levels do not have decision-making authority. Further, forestry institutions are understaffed and lack both training and equipment to implement proper management practices. Forestry officials must often rely on timber companies to provide transportation to logging sites within forests, thus limiting their ability to perform random inspections. Officials also lack incentives to perform diligently. Institutional reform measures and proper incentive structures need to be adopted to rectify some of these problems.

A clear manifestation of poor enforcement capacity within institutions is the irregularity or inability of forestry agencies to collect royalties, fees and reforestation taxes from logging firms. Typically, developing country governments collect less than 50% of due revenues from the forestry sector (Rowe *et al.*, 1992). Thus, private timber firms which capture a large percentage of the rent from timber harvesting are encouraged to exploit forest resources for private, short-term gains.

A related issue is the exclusion of local communities and indigenous people from the planning process for long-term management of forests. Traditional claims to forest lands held by these groups are often disregarded. Forest-management policies attempting to prevent entry to forest reserves and extraction of forest products have frequently failed. The main lesson has been that the participation and support of local communities is imperative for successful management of forest resources.

Market failures are another major threat to sustainable forest management (see Chapter 3) – e.g. the disparity in private and social cost of timber harvesting and other 'non-forest' related land uses. Timber prices are generally based on the stumpage value (or value of products derived from the timber less the processing costs). However, timber harvesting imposes large social costs in terms of opportunity costs from other forest-related good and services. The loss of economic, social and environmental benefits foregone must be included when determining the social cost of timber harvesting and the socially efficient level of harvesting. Other factors that cause market failures are the open access nature of forest resources, incomplete information and uncertainty of forest systems and imperfect competition.

Market failures are often complemented by policy failures that further aggravate deforestation. Over 80% of tropical forests are publicly owned. Hence government policies have a considerable effect on the management of forest resources and the distribution of benefits and costs from forest industries. Policies, such as encouraging timber harvesting by granting concessions and subsidies to logging companies, or providing infrastructure support to promote non-forest land uses, have a direct and negative impact on forests. Macroeconomic policies that distort prices of forest-related goods also increase deforestation (see Chapter 7). The joint effect of market and policy failures encourages private profit-driven firms to 'mine' forests for short-term gains rather than practice sustainable harvesting. The remedy often involves some form of public intervention by establishing regulations, providing economic (i.e. market-based) incentives, or making institutional changes that ensure sustainable management of forests. Logging firms must also be charged rent that more accurately reflects the opportunity cost of timber.

The foregoing shows the importance of valuing tropical forests for sustainable management (see Chapter 3). Estimating total economic value is complicated by the absence of markets for many forest-related products and services, difficulty in placing a monetary value on all resources, the lack of knowledge regarding the value and utility of some forest functions and difficulty in isolating the benefits of interrelated functions. Nevertheless, a combination of cost–benefit analysis and multicriteria analysis can help to provide policy analysts with better information upon which to base decisions involving alternative land uses. Conventional economic analysis can only account for the commercial value of forest resources. Disregarding the non-market value of forest resources (including amenity value) makes unsustainable land uses more attractive.

Correcting market and policy failures can be complicated and sometimes lie beyond the capabilities of sovereign governments. Internalizing the cost of wasteful deforestation can be undertaken to some extent by identifying benefits derived by local and national communities. However, there are also large global externalities from tropical forests that need to be valued and internalized at a global level.

Finally a nation's land-use policy is established to conform with political and social objectives and is not based solely on economic criteria. The institutional structure underlying land-use policy dictates the outcome of forest-management practices. When national land-use policy is based on legitimate political, social and economic concerns, the outcome is sustainable. However, if the policy is influenced by self-serving political motives and driven by corruption, reform is required.

13.2 Valuing forest ecosystems in Madagascar

This case study seeks to achieve a better understanding of the impact of national park's management on Madagascar's tropical forests. The socioeconomic and environmental consequences of human actions are assessed, with specific focus on economic valuation of environmental impacts, and relevant policy implications are drawn. A variety of techniques are used to value economically damage to forests and watersheds, timber and non-timber forest products, other impacts on local inhabitants, impacts on biodiversity and eco-tourism benefits (see Chapter 3).

13.2.1 Madagascar and the Mantadia National Park

Comprising 587 000 km^2, Madagascar is an island located 400 km off the southeast coast of Africa. With a 1990 per capita income of about $300, 80% of the 11 million inhabitants are rural and 85% work in agriculture. Only 14% of the 12 million hectares of forest in Madagascar are classified as non-degraded, high-density forest (World Bank, 1988). The island has a very high deforestation rate, losing an estimated 200 000 hectares/yr. At least 150 000 of Madagascar's 200 000 species are endemic – one of the highest rates in the world. Thus, Madagascar is a megadiversity site, and also a key tourist destination, focusing on beaches and nature parks. Nature tourism is among the fastest growing sub-sectors of the tourist industry, despite minimal promotion, high access costs and poor infrastructure. Of the 28 000 tourists who visited Madagascar in 1987, 8000 came specifically for nature tourism, compared with only 4000 in 1985 (World Bank, 1990).

Donor agencies and NGOs are providing funding to the Government of Madagascar (GOM) to establish a network of over 45 protected areas covering 1.4 million hectares as part of a National Environmental Action Plan (NEAP). The objectives of the protected area network include conserving the country's biodiversity and supporting a nature tourism industry. Funding projects for such activities have been justified assuming that increased tax revenues from nature tourism would cover operating costs (World Bank, 1990).

In 1988, the Madagascar Forests Management and Protection Project (FMPP) came into force. The project had three objectives: (1) to strengthen the forestry department; (2) to prevent further degradation of natural forests; and (3) to promote private-sector involvement in reforestation and wood processing. The project was budgeted at US $22 million over seven years. As a part of the natural forest protection objective, the Mantadia National Park was established near the popular Perinet Forest Reserve in the Andasibe region, east of Antananarivo, the nation's capital. It can be reached in about three hours from the capital by paved roads and is also accessible by rail. The park extends over an area of 9875 hectares of eastern rain forest. It varies in altitude from 850 to 1250 m, and is characterized by steep terrain and dense undergrowth. Many different species of trees and plants exist. The park contains up to eleven species of lemurs (prosimian primates endemic to Madagascar), four of which are endangered, two are rare and two vulnerable. Most importantly, the park is the habitat for the Indri, one of the largest known lemurs.

The Perinet Reserve's global reputation, easy accessibility and visitor facilities suggest large potential tourism benefits. In the following, we explore whether eco-tourism might help to alleviate poverty and provide jobs (economic view), without degrading the natural resources on which it is based (ecological view); see Grima *et al.* (2003).

13.2.2 *Methods of valuing biophysical resources*

In this section, the non-market costs and benefits (see Chapter 3) to local villagers and the international tourism benefits of establishing the Mantadia National Park are estimated. The creation of a national park generates many both indirect and direct costs and benefits. Costs arise from land acquisition (if the land had been previously privately owned), the hiring of park personnel and the development of roads, visitors' facilities and other infrastructure. Another key set of costs that are often ignored are the opportunity costs associated with the foregone uses of park land.

Benefits include both use values and non-use values. Most parks do not allow exploitation of forest resources; the primary uses are for tourism and research. Tourism can generate considerable revenues for the country from both entrance fees and travel services. National parks also generate many non-use benefits, among which existence value and option value are important (see Section 3.4). Other benefits may include reduced deforestation, watershed protection and climate regulation. This study focuses on some of the more important and difficult to measure economic impacts, namely the impact of the park on local villagers and the benefits of the new park to foreign tourists. Three main valuation methods are applied – opportunity cost, contingent valuation and travel cost. A brief description is provided in the following sections, and details of the underlying mathematical models are provided in the Appendix, Section 13.5.

Opportunity-cost method

This approach uses market values to determine the foregone economic benefits associated with alternative uses of resources. The creation of the park imposes a considerable economic burden on the local population. The opportunity cost is estimated from alternative uses of forest resources by people living near and in the park, based on recent land use and by projections of future land-use changes in the absence of a national park.

There are no human settlements within the Mantadia National Park boundaries, but several villages lie in close proximity, and these depend on the forests in and around the park for forest products and agriculture. The form of shifting cultivation used for agriculture production in eastern Madagascar is not only the key mechanism of deforestation, but also the only means of livelihood for many local inhabitants. Furthermore, the forest provides fuelwood, a wide range of fish and animals for food and many types of grass used for assorted purposes.

The opportunity costs associated with these economic activities were estimated using a survey of 372 households in ten villages within a 5 km radius around the park. The survey was administered by a local NGO, well versed in rural survey methods, and undertaken after a reconnaissance visit to the village, several focus group interviews, conversations with people who knew the area well and a pre-test covering 25 households. It was administered in Malagasy, the national language.

The questionnaire focused upon (1) establishing the extent of the dependence of the local villagers on forests nearby for obtaining a wide variety of forest products; (2) establishing how extensively the villagers used the forest for shifting cultivation; and (3) assessing local attitudes toward conservation of the forests. Questions on socioeconomic variables, land use, time allocation and household production activities were also posed. The final section used the contingent valuation method.

A separate questionnaire was administered to village leaders. It focused on issues pertaining to general agricultural patterns, markets and prices of goods sold, village history and migration patterns, forest-related cultural issues and details on shifting cultivation practices.

Contingent-valuation method

The contingent-valuation method (CVM) uses survey techniques to establish the value of goods and services that do not have market prices. Demand for non-market goods is established by first describing a simulated market to the respondents, and then asking them directly to reveal their preferences in terms of some common denominator.

In this study, the CVM was used in both village and tourist surveys. In the tourist survey, the CVM was used as an alternative method to the travel-cost method for estimating the total value of the park to the tourists. These questions were phrased in terms of how much more the foreign tourists would have been willing to pay for their trip, if the new park had been created for them to visit. These questions were also pre-tested and revised prior to the implementation of the tourist survey.

Travel-cost method

Travel-cost models use the amounts of time and money visitors spend travelling to a site as price proxies, as well as participation rates and visitor attributes, to estimate the recreational value of the site. Recreation in Madagascar's national parks contrasts sharply with the standard assumptions that the trip is a single-purpose, single-destination day-trip to a site that affords some particular recreational experience or typical quality which can be substituted for those available at similar sites. Instead, recreators in Madagascar can be divided into two groups consuming distinct goods: (1) local visitors who make day-trips to national parks to view the local natural environment; and (2) tourists from abroad who make lengthy trips to experience unusual natural settings and cultures. In what follows, we focus on the second aspect.

A novel international travel-cost method (Mercer and Kramer, 1992) assumes that individuals travel to a single country where they engage in a variety of activities. The model requires specific data on household distribution of time across activities over the modelling time horizon, and ideally it implies the collection of full-trip itinerary data as well as travel-cost information for foreign visitors. The itinerary data include the distribution of time between activities for each individual, the costs of pursuing such activities and the features of the various activities that lead to differences across individuals in their ability to undertake them.

Based on the theoretical model, questionnaires were prepared, translated into French and administered to visitors in the small Perinet Forest Reserve adjacent to the Mantadia National Park. They consisted of questions on the cost of the current trip to Madagascar, details of previous nature tourism trips, the method of selecting trip destinations, contingent valuation questions for the willingness-to-pay for visits to the Mantadia National Park and several sociodemographic and economic questions. In addition, a 'Madagascar Trip Diary' was developed which elicited detailed itinerary, cost, time and quality information for the current trip to Madagascar. The questionnaires were tested in the USA with a focus group of previous visitors to Madagascar, and in Madagascar the questionnaires were revised following pre-tests with a small sample of visitors to the Perinet Reserve and discussions with local Malagasy collaborators. Although the data set was inadequate for full implementation of the international travel-cost method, the estimates of mean willingness-to-pay to visit the new park derived from it provide useful insights.

13.2.3 Analysis and conclusions

Empirical results

The average household size in the surveyed villages was 4.6 persons. In 1988, average per capita income was US $190 in Madagascar, and the villages in the survey may well have incomes lower than the average. Several villages are very isolated, and many do not have access to medical facilities, running tap water, electricity and primary schooling. Approximately 95% of the households own land, and the average amount of land owned is 1.9 hectares per household (see Table 13.1). In the survey, 36% of the households own a

Table 13.1 *Land-use information for villagers*

Variable (per household)	Number of households	Range	Mean
Total quantity of farm land (ha)	311	0–9	1.89
Planned increase in cultivated land (ha)	256	0–10	1.7
Annual quantity of farmland planted with rice (ha)	289	0.04–5	1.04
Total annual rice yield (kg)	296	2–3600	487
Total annual quantity of rice marketed (kg)	249	0–990	41.8
Total annual value of rice yield (US $)	296	0.5–1101	128

Table 13.2 *Value of agricultural and forest products gathered by villagers*

Agricultural and forest products	Number of observations	Total annual value for all villages (US $)	Mean annual value per household (US $)
Rice	351	44 928	128
Fuelwood	316	13 289	38
Crayfish	19	220	12
Crab	110	402	3.7
Tenreck	21	125	6
Frog	11	71	6.5

watch, 33% own a radio and 97% have a kerosene lamp to light their huts; 80% of the households surveyed said that they would add to existing land for cultivation, and 99% of these acknowledged that they planned to cut forests to add to their land. The average household planned to cut 1.7 hectares of forested land in the coming year to undertake shifting cultivation.

The survey indicates that the average household produces 487 kg of rice per year (worth about US $128). Most households also engage in shifting cultivation. Fuelwood is the most important forest product collected (see Table 13.2). The average household collects about 5952 kg, or US $38 worth of firewood per year. The total value of firewood is $13 289 per year. The total value of other collected forest products was only US $818.

The contingent valuation study indicates the villagers' perceptions of the forest: 40% seemed to think that forests do not help soil protection, although 65% agreed that floods occur less frequently with forests; 91% of the respondents agreed that primary forests are 'more fun' than secondary forests, which suggests a recreational value of forests, but 77% did not think that preserving forests in order to preserve ancestral graves was very important. Finally, 68% of the respondents thought that it is advantageous to clear the forests as a form of pest management.

The responses to the contingent valuation study indicate that, on average, a compensation of 55 kg of rice per year will make the households as well off with the park as without the

Table 13.3 *Summary statistics for complete sample of tourists*

Variable	Range	Mean	Number of visitors
Income	US $3040–296 400	US $59 156	71
Education (years)	10–18	15	86
Age (years)	16–71	38.5	87
Number of days in Madagascar	3–100	27	83
Number of days in Perinet	1–8	2	80
Total cost of trip to Madagascar	US $335–6363	US $2874	78
Transport cost to Madagascar	US $352–5000	US $1388	47
Transport cost in Madagascar	US $8–2000	US $588	43

Table 13.4 *Summary statistics for tourists to Madagascar*

Country	Percentage of sample	Mean expenses (US $)	Mean number of days in Madagascar	Mean number of days in Perinet	Mean age (yr)	Mean time in education (yr)	Mean income (US $)
Great Britain	20.2	3332	18	1.6	45	15.8	36 891
Italy	21.4	2357	21.4	1.9	34	14.2	112 000
France	15.5	2481	36	1.9	34	15	63 197
Germany	11.9	3172	24.8	1.8	40	15	42 304
Switzerland	11.9	3200	37.6	2.3	36	15.6	51 243
USA	4.8	3097	18.5	2.75	49	16.5	53 515
Other	14.3	2726	26.6	2.91	40.8	14	33 997

park. Given the data on rice yields, this indicates that the average household is willing to accept approximately 1.5 months of their daily intake of rice to give up access to the forests. For all of the households covered by the survey, this implies a necessary one-time compensation of approximately US $52 000 at a discount rate of 10%, or $173 000 using a 3% discount rate.

In the tourist survey, income for the visitors ranged from US $3000 to US $300 000 with a mean of US $59 156 (see Table 13.3). The average tourist was 39 years old and had completed 15 years of education. Visitors came from 13 countries. Trips ranged from 3 to 100 days in length, with a mean of 27 days, and with 1–8 days spent at Perinet (mean of 2 days). Trip expenditures ranged from US $335 to US $6363, with an average cost of US $2874. The mean transport cost to reach Madagascar was US $1390, while travel costs within the island averaged almost US $590. A breakdown of tourist characteristics by country of origin showed considerable diversity (see Table 13.4).

Table 13.5 *Economic costs and benefits of establishing new national park*
(using different valuation methods)

	Annual mean value	Aggregate NPV (10% discount rate)
Welfare losses to local villagers (US $)		
Opportunity cost	91[a]	566 070
CVM	108[a]	673 078
Welfare gains to foreign tourists (US $)		
Travel cost 1 (random utility)	24[b]	936 000
Travel cost 2 (typical trip)	45[b]	1 750 000
CVM (use and non-use value)	65[b]	2 530 000

[a] per household.
[b] per trip.

Visitors indicated that their average willingness-to-pay to visit the new park would be US $118 if they saw twice as many lemurs as in Perinet, falling to US $75 if the same number of lemurs were seen. In 1990, there were about 3000 foreign visitors to Perinet. If the same number of people visited the new park, the total additional willingness-to-pay to see lemurs alone would be in the range US $292 500 to US $460 200 annually.

The overall economic valuation results for both local villagers and foreign tourists from the opportunity-cost, the two travel-cost methods and the CVM are summarized in Table 13.5.

Several conclusions can be drawn from this study. Non-market valuation techniques can provide useful information for economic evaluation of national parks that may be incorporated into CBA of projects, including conservation components, to determine their viability.

Improving the welfare of poor local communities, while protecting natural systems, permits developing countries to pursue all three dimensions of sustainable development goals. There is a need to identify policies that will make market forces work more effectively to improve natural-resource use by better aligning private and social costs and benefits. Measures must also address the issue of inequity of distribution – especially those arising from differences between those who bear the costs of environmental degradation and those who are the beneficiaries.

Policy implications and conclusions

Further research of this type would have implications for policy, investment decisions, resource mobilization and project design and management. The information can help governments decide how to (a) allocate scarce capital resources among competing land-use activities and (b) choose and implement investments for natural-resource conservation and development. Results can also be used in determining or influencing pricing, land use and incentive policies. At the local level, the findings can be used to determine compensation for local villagers for foregone access to forest areas designated as national parks. In addition, the research findings can show the value of a park as a global environmental asset to foreigners, thus influencing the external assistance for conservation programmes at the local level.

These findings also address future issues. Continuation of the status quo suggests that existing patterns of land use would perpetuate continuing degradation of the park (with potential loss of all forests within 30 to 40 years). On the other hand, a strict conservation regime for forest land would also deprive poor villagers of essential livelihoods. Reliance on willingness-to-pay is fundamental to the economic approach used in this study, but tends to overemphasize the importance of value ascribed to richer foreign visitors. If conflicting claims to park access were to be determined purely on this basis, residents (especially the poor local villagers) are likely to be excluded. Therefore, the sociocultural elements of the sustainomics approach (especially distributional equity) would need to be considered to protect the basic rights of local residents – perhaps in the form of a 'safe minimum' degree of access to park facilities, while sustainable tourism was pursued.

Aspects that merit more attention include greater emphasis on comprehensive valuation of natural habitats and their associated physical and biological systems. The value of environmental assets could then be used to improve and redesign development assistance policies and projects. Further research is needed to better understand the distribution of costs and benefits of exploiting or conserving natural habitats. The relationship between conservation of natural habitats and alternative strategies to manage these environmental assets (e.g. multiple use) need to be further investigated, and better use could be made of local people's knowledge of the optimal utilization of the natural habits. Recently, a policy of Secured Local Management of Natural Resources, known as the GELOSE Act, has created a framework for the transfer of rights from central government to local communities (Antona *et al.*, 2004).

13.3 Agriculture and climate change

13.3.1 Background

Climate change has become a major concern to human society because of its potentially deleterious impact worldwide (see Chapter 5). It poses especially significant threats to sustainable development in developing countries, which have fewer resources and are more vulnerable (Munasinghe, 2001a). More research is needed to identify specific areas of vulnerability. However, general considerations suggest that developing countries will be more vulnerable because: (a) they are already in hot climatic zones; (b) more of their citizens already lack sufficient food; (c) their economies rely more on climate-sensitive sectors like agriculture; and (d) a greater share of total population (in rural areas) depend on labour-intensive agriculture with fewer adaptation opportunities. These points are shown in Figures 13.1 and 13.2.

The Action Impact Matrix (AIM) approach was used to rank climate-change impacts and vulnerability of various sectors in Sri Lanka. The AIM workshop harmonized views among diverse participants (over 70 leading economists, ecologists, sociologists, climate specialists and other experts) – see Section 2.4.1. The results placed both traditional agriculture (rice

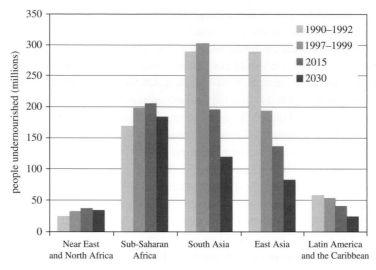

Figure 13.1. Estimated/projected undernourished population 1991–2030. Source: UNESCO (2001).

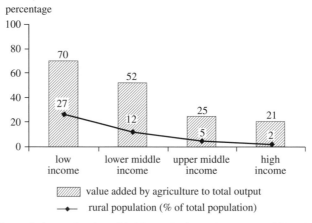

Figure 13.2. Rural population and value added by agriculture. Source: World Bank (2005a).

farming) and tree crops (plantations) among the most vulnerable areas (Munasinghe, Deraniyagala and Munasinghe, 2002). The urgent need for more detailed studies on climate-change impacts on agriculture was also highlighted.

Accordingly, the case study described in the following was undertaken to examine the effect of climate on agriculture in Sri Lanka. Two different sets of modelling assumptions and data are used to show how more disaggregate analysis helps to improve the policy conclusions. The study uses the Ricardian method (Mendelsohn, Nordhaus and Shaw, 1994) to look at how net revenue varies across climatic zones in Sri Lanka. Assuming that farmers adapt to where they live, the method captures adaptation implicitly by comparing net outcomes for farmers facing different climates. Instead of studying the yields of specific crops, the model examines how climate in different places affects the net revenue or value of farmland. By directly measuring net revenues, the Ricardian method includes the direct impacts of climate on yields of different crops as well as the indirect substitution of different inputs, introduction of different activities and other potential adaptations by farmers to different climates.

The Ricardian approach has been used primarily in the USA to predict the damages from climate change (Mendelsohn *et al.*, 1994; Mendelsohn and Neumann, 1999; Mendelsohn, Dinar and Sanghi, 2001). There have also been a number of studies in Brazil and India (Dinar *et al.*, 1998; Kumar and Parikh, 2001; Mendelsohn *et al.*, 2001), as well as one recent study of Canada (Reinsborough, 2003). These studies suggest that climate change would be slightly beneficial to US agriculture, whereas it is likely to be harmful to tropical and semi-tropical countries.

In addition to the Ricardian method, the 'agro-economic' model is also capable of measuring climate effects. This model uses a combination of controlled experiments on specific crops, agronomic modelling and economic modelling to predict climate impacts (Adams and McCarl 2001). The presumed changes in yields from the agronomic model are fed into an economic model, which determines crop choice, production and market prices. While this model contributed much to the scientific understanding of impacts, it is difficult to apply to developing countries. First, it has been criticized for underestimating adaptive responses to changing climate (Mendelsohn and Neumann, 1999). Second, there is insufficient data on agronomic responses in most developing countries. Finally, economic models of developing country agriculture are poorly calibrated.

13.3.2 Ricardian theoretical model

We assume that farmers maximize net revenues per hectare, NR:

$$\max \mathrm{NR} = P_i \cdot Q_i(R, E) - C_i(Q_i, R, E), \qquad (13.1)$$

where P_i and Q_i are, respectively, the price and quantity of good i; $C_i(\cdot)$ is the relevant cost function; R is a vector of inputs; and E reflects a vector of environmental characteristics of the farmer's land, including climate. Given that the farmer chooses inputs, R, to maximize NR, one can express the resulting outcome of NR in terms of E alone as follows:

$$\mathrm{NR} = f(E). \qquad (13.2)$$

The welfare value of a change in the environment from state A to state B is given by

$$W = \sum f(E_{iB}) \cdot L_i - \sum f(E_{iA}) \cdot L_i, \qquad (13.3)$$

where L_i is the amount of land of type i.

Cross-sectional observations across different climates can reveal the climate sensitivity of farms. The advantage of this empirical approach is that the method not only includes the direct effect of climate on productivity, but also the adaptation response by farmers to local climate.

Agronomic research and casual observation reveals that many crops have preferred temperature and precipitation zones. Temperatures and precipitation levels either below or above such optimal ranges reduce productivity. The evidence suggests that the relationship between net revenue and these climate variables should be hill-shaped. We attempt to capture this hill-shape using a quadratic functional form:

$$\text{NR}_i = a_0 + \sum (a_s T_s + b_s T_s^2 + c_s P_s + d_s P_s^2) + \sum f_c Z_c + e, \qquad (13.4)$$

where T_s and P_s represent normal temperature and precipitation variables in each season and Z_c represents relevant socioeconomic variables.

The original Ricardian studies used land value for the dependent variable. In many developing countries, however, land value is not available. Annual net revenue per hectare can be used instead, since land value is the present value of a future stream of net revenue (Dinar *et al.*, 1998). The use of annual net revenues, however, introduces a potential problem since the net revenue in any one year is influenced by the weather in that year.

The Ricardian method has been criticized on several counts. The original estimates did not include surface water or irrigation (Cline, 1996; Schlenker, Hanemann and Fisher, 2003). The method cannot measure the effect of variables that do not vary across space, such as CO_2. The method measures long-run adaptation, but not the speed of adaptation. The model assumes current technology, so that it does not take into account technology that may be available in the future. The model assumes no price effects (Darwin, 1999). If climate change alters supplies of individual crops, prices are likely to change. The measurements reflect current agricultural policies.

These problems are significant, but not fatal; for example, CO_2 effects can be included exogenously, as can new technology. Global prices are not expected to change dramatically as a result of climate change (Reilly *et al.*, 1996). Irrigation and surface water have been taken into account in more recent estimates and found not to influence climate sensitivity (Mendelsohn and Dinar, 2003). It is not clear what role current agricultural policies play in Ricardian measurements.

13.4 Climate impacts on agriculture in Sri Lanka

13.4.1 Sri Lanka overview

Sri Lanka is an island located under the Indian peninsula. It has an area of 66 000 km², stretching over 433 km from north to south (latitude 5°55 N to 9°51 N) and 244 km east to west at its widest point (longitude 79°41 E to 81°53 E). The country consists of nine provinces and 25 districts. Colombo, the capital, has the highest monthly income, whereas the Eastern province (Baticaloa, Trincomalee, Ampara) and Northern province (Jaffna,

Kilinochchi, Mannar, Vavuniya, Mullaitivu) have the lowest income, levels. The Western province (Gampaha, Colombo, Kalutara) and Southern province (Galle, Matara) show high population density and low altitude, whereas the Northern and Eastern provinces have low population density. The Central province has the highest elevation in the nation.

Sri Lanka is a tropical country with distinct dry and wet seasons. The climate is characterized by two monsoons. The 'Yala' season, during the southwest monsoon, lasts from May to August, bringing rain to the south and west-coast regions as well as to the central highlands. The dry season in these regions is from December to March. The second wet season arrives with the northeast monsoon, which blows from October to January (called the Maha season), bringing rain to the north and east of the island. The dry season in the northeast is from May to September. There is also an inter-monsoonal period in October and November when rain and thunderstorms can occur in many parts of the island.

The nation is commonly categorized into dry and wet zones depending on annual rainfall. Wet zones are divided into maritime and hill-country wet zones, based on the altitude. Table 13.6 shows climatic zones and districts. The south, southwest and central highlands are much wetter than the north and north central regions. Colombo and the low-lying coastal regions have an average temperature of 27 °C. The temperature falls rapidly with increasing altitude. At Kandy (altitude of 500 m) the average temperature is 20 °C and at Nuwara Eliya (1889 m) it drops to 16 °C. We use 'normal temperature' and 'normal rainfall' to be the 30-year average temperature and rainfall.

Sri Lanka's main agricultural outputs are paddy rice, commercial tree crops and highland crops. Rice is grown all around the country and contributed about 3.0% to GDP in 2005 (Central Bank, 2005). Production costs vary, depending on the methods of paddy rice production (i.e. irrigation-rainfed or irrigated). Three commercial tree crops (coconut, rubber and tea) are grown on the west coast and hill areas. Tree crops comprise a significant portion of national exports, and are taken care of by the Ministry of Plantation Industries. They contributed 1.2% (tea), 1.1% (coconut) and 0.4% (rubber) to GDP in 2005 (Central Bank, 2005). In 2005, agricultural exports totalled US $1153.8 million, of which tea exports were US $810 million, rubber exports were US $47 million and coconut exports were US $113 million.

Table 13.6 *Climatic zones and districts in Sri Lanka*

Climatic zone	Sub-zone	Districts
Wet zone	maritime	Colombo, Gampaha, Kalutara, Galle, Matara
	hill country	Kandy, Nuwara Eliya, Ratnapura, Kegalle
Dry zone[a]		Matale, Hambantota, Jaffna, Mannar, Vavuniya, Mullaitivu, Batticaloa, Trincomalee Ampara, Kurunegala, Puttalam, Anuradhapura, Polonnaruwa, Badulla, Moneragala

[a] Some parts of Matale, Badulla and Kurunegala districts are in the intermediate zone.
Source: Sri Lanka Census, 1980, 2001.

These three commercial crops represented 84% of the total agricultural exports. The 2005 GDP in market prices was SL Rs2366 billion (US $23.5 billion), and agriculture accounted for 17.2% (SL Rs178 billion) of this total (Central Bank, 2005).

13.4.2 Analysis and results 1 – preliminary 1995 data set

The first modelling exercise uses preliminary agricultural data from 1995 to estimate the model, and combines it with broad global-level climate-change forecasts to predict future agricultural impacts.

Regression estimates 1

The Ricardian model regresses net revenue on climate and other explanatory variables (see equation (13.4)). Net revenue for each district was constructed from the data recorded by the government. Net revenue per unit area equals total net revenue of the district per hectare of cropland. For rice production, net revenues were constructed from the national statistics data book (Department of Census and Statistics, 1997). We use the average of irrigated and dryland farming for the cost of production of paddy crops.

The Plantation Sector Statistical Pocket Book (Ministry of Plantation Industries, 2001) was used to construct net revenues of commercial crops. Area data of districts were multiplied by average productivity to obtain the total production of each crop. Table 13.7 shows the total net revenues of districts for paddy crops, coconut, rubber and tea. The five districts in the Northern province and the two districts in the Eastern province have the lowest revenues, whereas the western and southern districts, along with the hill region, show higher revenues. The main area for paddy production lies in the northeast of the country. Tea and rubber are cultivated mostly in the west and central areas of the country, while coconut is harvested largely on the western coast.

Our dependent variable is defined as follows:

$$\text{net revenue per unit area} = \frac{\text{total net revenue of the district}}{\text{area of cropland in hectares of the district}}$$

Four months are selected as explanatory variables to represent Sri Lanka's climate. November and January represent the Maha monsoon period. May represents the Yala monsoon period. September is included to see the effects of the period between the two monsoons.

We present two regressions in Table 13.8. Our first regression, the full model, includes climate variables of the four months and is specified as a quadratic equation. Three control variables are included, i.e. irrigated land, population density and altitude. All three have been shown to be important in earlier studies. The regression shows a high degree of fit, with an adjusted R^2 of 0.84. The climate variables are all significant at the 5% level. The control variables are not significant.

We also present a simpler model. In the previous model, the temperature coefficients were highly correlated and the quadratic specification seemed to make the situation worse.

Table 13.7 *Total net revenues of districts in 1995 values given in million Sri Lankan rupees*

Province	District	Paddy	Coconut	Rubber	Tea	Total
Western	Gampaha	194	2415	164	–	2775
	Colombo	67	388	339	4	800
	Kalutara	375	541	1386	242	2546
Central	Matale	530	506	84	296	1417
	Kandy	339	356	68	1651	2415
	Nuwara	103	44	2	3562	3712
Sabaragamuwa	Kegalle	485	914	1538	385	3323
	Ratnapura	489	714	1007	1844	4055
Southern	Galle	82	548	375	1361	2368
	Matara	363	689	178	1310	2541
	Hambantota	1076	987	0.7	19	2083
Uva	Badula	623	51	11	2100	2786
	Monaragala	357	272	51	8	689
Eastern	Baticaloa	436	174	–	–	611
	Trincomale	464	76	–	–	541
	Ampara	2497	165	–	–	2662
Northcentral	Anuradhapu	1638	244	–	–	1882
	Polonnaruw	3116	127	–	–	3244
Northwestern	Puttalam	333	2205	–	–	2539
	Kurunegala	2721	6808	106	3	9639
Northern	Mannar	68	50	–	–	118
	Vavuniya	214	18	–	–	232
	Kilinochchi	336	–	–	–	336
	Jaffna	95	427	–	–	522
	Mullaittivu	182	93	–	–	276
Total		17 192	18 823	5316	12 792	54 124

Total = total net revenue from four crops production in all districts.

Consequently, the confidence intervals resulting from the full model were quite large. By simplifying the model, we estimate fewer coefficients, but the coefficients are more independent of each other. The resulting national impact estimates are more precise.

The simplified model includes just three months of rainfall (in January, September and November) and one month of temperature (in May). They are all specified in a linear form (i.e. without the temperature-squared terms in equation (13.4)). The model includes two important control variables: irrigated land and altitude. It yields an adjusted R^2 of 0.59, which is significantly lower than that of the full model, but better T-statistics for coefficient estimates. The temperature coefficient implies that net revenue will decrease by –4105 per degree of warming. Summing the coefficients on the rain variables implies that rain is in general beneficial, although increased rain in November is harmful.

Table 13.8 *Climate regressions*

Variables	Full model			Simple model		
	Estimates	Standard error	T value	Estimates	Standard error	T value
Jan. temp.	347 785	153 092	2.27[a]			
(Jan. temp.)^2	−5999	2794	−2.15[a]			
May temp.	443 965	185 709	2.39[a]	−4105	1173	−3.5[a]
(May temp.)^2	−7760	3202	−2.42[a]			
Nov. temp.	−745 121	330 648	−2.25[a]			
(Nov. temp.)^2	12 901	5907	2.18[a]			
May rainfall	−190	81	−2.33[a]			
Sept. rainfall	227	93	2.43[a]	93	28	3.27[a]
Jan. rainfall				103	49	2.11[a]
Nov. rainfall				−141	68	−2.05[a]
Irrigated land	−0.08	0.06	−1.42	−0.154 94	0.099 68	−1.55
Pop. density	−3.31	2.62	−1.27			
Elevation	−13.16	11.13	−1.18	−27.301 2	8.980 63	−3.04[a]

[a] Estimate is significant at 5%.

Rainfall is measured in millimetres; temperature is measured in degrees Celsius; area is measured in hectares; elevation is measured in metres.

Full model: number of observations = 25; $R^2 = 0.91$; adjusted $R^2 = 0.84$.

Simple model: number of observations = 25; $R^2 = 0.69$; adjusted $R^2 = 0.59$.

Future climate impacts 1

In this section, we use AOGCM climate predictions for Sri Lanka, by 2100. The five AOGCMs are CGCM (Boer, Flato and Ramsden, 2000), CSIRO (Gordon and O'Farrell, 1997), CCSR (Emori *et al.*, 1999), HAD3 (Gordon *et al.*, 2000) and PCM (Washington *et al.*, 2000). The five climate models predict a wide range of outcomes – see Table 13.9.

Table 13.10 describes the national-level impact estimates for all the climate models. In all five models, the changes in rainfall are beneficial to the nation. The benefit ranges from 11% to 122% of the current net revenue of the crops included in this model. In all five models, the impacts of temperature change are predicted to be harmful to the nation. The loss is −18% to −50% of the current agricultural productivity.

The combined effect of temperature change and rainfall change varies. The CSIRO and PCM models predict a loss from climate change. Both models predict an increase in November rains that offset precipitation increases in the other months. The remaining three models predict welfare gains as precipitation benefits outweigh temperature losses. These three models predict that precipitation will rise in the beneficial months of January

Table 13.9 *AOGCM climate-change predictions*

	Jan. rainfall (mm)	Sept. rainfall (mm)	Nov. rainfall (mm)	May temp. (°C)
Current value	8.71	17.91	29.74	27.18
Value in 2100				
CCSR	5.14	37.36	17.01	29.83
CGCM	7.32	38.32	14.05	31.2
CSIRO	10.85	23.58	31.75	30.14
HAD3	2.36	40.88	22.32	30.59
PCM	31.27	24.92	44.21	28.76
Percentage change of rainfall				absolute change
CCSR	−40	108	−42	2.65
CGCM	−15	113	−52	4.02
CSIRO	24	31	6	2.96
HAD3	−72	128	−24	3.41
PCM	259	39	48	1.58

Table 13.10 *National-level impacts*

Scenarios	Temp. effect	Rain effect	Temp. + rain effect
			−11.0 (−20%)
CSIRO	−19.9 (−35%)	8.9 (+14%)	(−23, 1)
			−4.3 (−7%)
PCM	−10.6 (−18%)	6.2 (+11%)	(−34, 25)
			35.2 (+64%)
CCSR	−17.8 (−31%)	53.1 (+98%)	(−7, 77)
			39.3 (+72%)
CGCM	−27.0 (−50%)	66.4 (+122%)	(−13, 91)
			16.9 (+29%)
HAD3	−22.9 (−40%)	39.9 (+72%)	(−19, 53)

The absolute numbers are in billion Sri Lankan Rupees. The percentage numbers show the fractions of aggregate net revenue of the crops included in this analysis.

and September. However, these models also predict decreased rainfall in November – the one month when rainfall is harmful.

Table 13.10 also shows the uncertainty associated with the national-level impact predictions. In the right-hand column, the numbers in parentheses below the impact estimates are 95% confidence intervals of net benefits. The net climate-change impacts predicted are uncertain in that all the intervals include zero. They are not statistically different from zero. These results reveal a limitation of the Ricardian method when applied to small countries.

Table 13.11 *District-level impacts*

Values given in thousands of Sri Lankan Rupees

District	HAD3		CSIRO	
	Impact	Change (%)	Impact	Change (%)
Gampaha	19	61	−7	−22
Colombo	35	98	−3	−8
Kalutara	38	92	−1	−2
Matale	0	−1	−7	−20
Kandy	14	44	−5	−17
Nuwara	23	59	−3	−9
Kegalle	43	121	−2	−5
Ratnapura	33	85	−2	−6
Galle	30	73	−3	−6
Matara	17	52	−5	−15
Hambantota	−3	−11	−10	−44
Badulla	−4	−13	−6	−18
Moneragala	−1	−2	−11	−25
Baticaloa	−13	−54	−8	−35
Trincomalee	−3	−20	−9	−54
Ampara	−14	−74	−7	−39
Anuradhapura	−3	−15	−10	−46
Polonnaruwa	−5	−28	−8	−48
Puttalam	2	7	−10	−46
Kurunegala	6	27	−10	−45
Mannar	−6	−35	−12	−72
Vavuniya	1	4	−10	−51
Kilinochchi	−1	−17	−11	−202
Jaffna	−1	−12	−11	−121
Mullaitt	1	9	−10	−62

There may not be enough variation in the climate over a small region to estimate reliable impacts for non-marginal climate changes.

Table 13.11 summarizes how the impacts vary across districts for two of the AOGCM models, CSIRO and HAD3. The changes in net revenue due to climate change are shown for each district using the simple model. In the HAD3 scenario, the central highland and west-coast areas are expected to gain from climate change, while the northern and eastern dry lands will lose. In the CSIRO scenario, all districts are expected to lose due to the future climate. However, the impacts in the central highlands are small compared with those in the northern and eastern provinces. The damages in these regions amount to more than 50% of the current net revenue. Based on both scenarios, we may expect a likely future shift in Sri Lankan agricultural output, from the north and east to the central highlands.

13.4.3 Analysis and results 2 – updated 2003 data set

The same basic model is re-estimated below, with the following changes:

(a) revised agricultural data for 2003 are used;

(b) separate modelling runs are made for paddy and plantation crops;

(c) impacts on future agricultural output are forecast using disaggregate, district-specific climate predictions for Sri Lanka, based on a down-scaled version of the global Hadley climate-change model projections; and

(d) a range of climate forecasts are considered based on the IPCC A1F1 and B1 scenarios (see Box 1.2).

Regression estimates 2

The model was re-estimated, with one major change. The paddy is grown under climatic conditions different than for plantation crops, separate models were estimated to capture changes in the net revenue of paddy and plantation crops due to climatic changes. Further, in many districts paddy is not dependent only on rainfall – e.g. there are many irrigation systems which provided water for 71% of the total extent of paddy cultivation in 2002/2003. When there is good rainfall in the Maha season (September to February) in Kurunegala, A'Pura and Polonnaruwa districts, farmers save more water in small tanks and reservoirs to use in the Yala season, which is a dry period. Thus, paddy cultivation in the Yala season, is less dependent on rainfall during that season. Similarly, even with a low rainfall in Polonnaruwa and Anuradhapura districts, some farmers cultivate both seasons using water diverted from the Mahaweli river.

The data set was slightly adjusted by omitting one district (Nuwara Eliya) out of the original 25. This was due to unreliable data from Nuwara Eliya district, which has the lowest temperature in the country. As a result, the accuracy of the overall results increased significantly (better F-statistics and adjusted R^2).

Estimation of net revenue

The extent of cultivation, cost of production and harvest and producer prices of paddy are available from the Department of Census and Statistics and the Department of Agriculture. The paddy cultivation area in each year depends on rainfall and water available in irrigation systems, especially the area cultivated in Yala season in districts in the dry zone.

The district-wise production of plantation crops (i.e. tea, rubber and coconut) is not available. Net revenues of plantation crops in each district were estimated using data on extent and productivity rates of plantation companies in each district provided by the Ministry of Plantation Industries and the Agrarian Data Bank of HARTI.

Meteorological data in 2003

District-level rainfall and temperature data are available from the Department of Meteorology (DOM). The rainfall data are available for every district, but temperature data for four districts were estimated using the adjoining districts, in consultation with the officers of the DOM.

Table 13.12 *Climate regressions – paddy*

Independent variables	Coefficient	Standard error	T value
Rainfall, June	−146.84	35.4	−4.15[a]
(Rainfall, June)^2	0.26	0.08	3.10[a]
Temp., July	3451.57	1359.6	2.54[b]
(Temp., July)^2	−81.83	46.02	−1.78[c]
Extent major irrigation	0.22	0.07	2.97[a]
Elevation	−18.71	6.5	−2.88[a]

[a] Significant at 1% level.
[b] Significant at 5% level.
[c] Significant at 10% level.
Dependent variable = net revenue of paddy (Rs/ha).
F-statistic = 88.4, adjusted R^2 = 0.96, R^2 = 0.97, number of observations = 24.
Estimate is significant at 5%. Rainfall is measured in millimetres; temperature is
measured in degrees Celsius; area is measured in hectares; elevation measured in metres.

Monthly rainfall by district varies during the year. However, rainfall in January is statistically correlated at the 1% level with that of February, November and December because these months fall within the northeast monsoon. Rainfall in April is statistically correlated at the 1% level with the rainfall in March, May, June, July and September. Thus, monthly rainfall was selected to avoid collinearity problems in the regression analysis.

According to Table 13.12, the net revenue of paddy cultivation is strongly explained by climatic variables (rainfall and temperature), the land extent under major irrigation schemes and the elevation of the area. The model is specified as a quadratic equation. Both the rainfall variables (rainfall in June and square of rainfall in June) are statistically significant at the 1% level. The temperature in July and square of temperature in July are statistically significant at the 5% and 10% levels, respectively. The other two control variables (extent under the major irrigation and the elevation) are both significant at the 1% level.

There is a slight correlation between temperature and the elevation, but when the elevation was added into the model, the adjusted R^2 and the F-statistics increased and the overall standard error of the model declined. Moreover, the elevation is statistically significant at the 5% level.

According to the above analysis, the net revenue of plantation crops per hectare is explained by the rainfall in November and temperature in May and its square value. This model is also a quadratic one, and all the climatic variables are statistically significant at the 5% level. The elevation of the cultivation area is not statistically significant in this model.

Future climate impacts 2

Basnayake (2004) developed rainfall and temperature scenarios for 2025 and 2050 in Sri Lanka, using two global emission scenarios – the IPCC SRES A1F1 and B1 scenarios

Table 13.13 *Climate regression – plantation crops*

Independent variables	Coefficient	Standard error	T value
Rainfall, Nov.	32.48	12.3	2.63[a]
Temp., May	−3314	1525	−2.17[a]
(Temp., May)^2	137.96	53.3	2.59[a]

[a] Significant at 5% level.
Dependent variable = net revenue of plantation crops (Rs/ha).
F-statistic = 89.1, R^2 = 0.93, adjusted R^2 = 0.92, number of observations = 24.

Table 13.14 *National-level impact on agriculture revenue in 2050*

A1F1 scenario based projection

Crop	Temperature effect	Rainfall effect	Combined effects
Paddy	−3.5%	−7.8%	−11.4%
Plantation crops	+1.5%	+2%	+3.5%

Table 13.15 *Impact on the national economy in 2050*[a]

Crop	Change (% total GDP in 2050)	Change (% agriculture GDP in 2050)
Paddy	−0.36	−2.46
Plantation crops	+0.1	+0.7
Paddy + plantation crops	−0.26	−1.76

[a] Assuming the same economic structure in 2050.

(Munasinghe and Swart, 2005). The first one assumes lower global economic growth and less emissions, and the second has higher emissions with rapid economic growth. These two scenarios provide a range of climate-change predictions to test our results for Sri Lanka. Spatially interpolated baseline climatologies and downscaled future-climate-change patterns of the Hadley Centre Global Circulation Model (HadGCM) are input to the SimCLIM model to generate future climate scenarios of temperature and rainfall over Sri Lanka on a 500 m resolution grid (Basnayake, 2004). In the study, we use the A1F1 scenario as our baseline because (1) the likelihood of achieving the B1 scenario is small, given current trends in global emissions, (2) predicted climate differences in Sri Lanka between the A1F1 and B1 scenarios by 2050 are relatively small and (3) for policy purposes, it is more useful to examine the scenario with higher risks.

Table 13.14 shows that paddy revenues decrease by 11.4% with projected changes in rainfall and temperature in 2050 – this negative impact is mainly due to the change in rainfall (7.8%). In contrast, there is an overall gain of 3.5% in plantation revenues. Table 13.15

shows that the overall impacts on agricultural production and GDP in 2050 are negative: −1.76% for agriculture and −0.26% for GDP, assuming no change in economic structure. However, if the share of agriculture in GDP follows past trends and declines, then the impact on GDP in 2050 would be less.

13.4.4 Conclusions

This study describes a Ricardian analysis of agriculture in Sri Lanka, with different data sets and climate projections. It yields effects of temperature and precipitation on different crops grown in different geographical areas. It is seen that 31% of the labour force (Central Bank, 2005) is engaged in agriculture, while plantation crops earn a large amount of foreign exchange (15.3% of total exports in 2005). Therefore, any impact due to climate change on paddy and plantation crops will affect the economy seriously. One major policy conclusion is unchanged under a variety of assumptions and scenarios – agricultural production will shift from the dry to the wet zone. Spatially more disaggregate agricultural analysis for different crops, and detailed climate projections, yield results which are more accurate and useful for policy making. Therefore, future research must fine-tune analysis to determine long-run climate-adaptation strategy in Sri Lanka.

According to analysis 1, warming is generally expected to be harmful to Sri Lanka, but increases in rainfall will be beneficial. Applying the estimated regression results to five climate scenarios yields a range of effects, ranging from a loss of 20% to a gain of 72%. The scenarios with losses had harmful temperature impacts, which more than offset precipitation benefits. The scenarios with gains had beneficial rainfall changes, which dominated harmful temperature effects. In the beneficial scenarios, there were large increases of precipitation in beneficial months and decreases of precipitation in harmful months (November).

The second regression analysis of agriculture and climate change based on the Ricardian model separately measured the impact of changes of temperature and rainfall on the revenue of paddy and plantation crops. This spatial disaggregation is helpful, since paddy and plantation crops are concentrated in different geographical areas, in which the predicted rainfall and temperature vary significantly. Based on the likely A1F1 (IPCC-SRES) scenario, both temperature and rainfall changes in 2050 will affect paddy revenues negatively (decrease of 11.4%). The paddy plant needs a considerable amount of water in its growing period (2–2.5 months) and then needs a warm climate during the ripening and cropping period (1 month). Since paddy cultivation in Sri Lanka is heavily concentrated in the dry zone, low rainfall and increased temperature in those districts decrease the yield significantly.

Meanwhile, increased rainfall and temperature will affect plantation crops positively in 2050, yielding a modest gain in total revenue of 3.5%. Climate projections indicate that rainfall will increase in many districts where tea and rubber crops are grown. Tea is grown in the hill country, where the average present temperature is relatively cool (around 25 °C). Thus, according to the regression results, a temperature increase of 1 to 1.5 °C will not be harmful to the crop. Furthermore, around 70% of the coconut lands are located either in the wet zone or the intermediate zone, where projected rainfall is in favour of plantation crops.

Table 13.16 *Change in net income: Ricardian results*

Country	Temperature rise (°C) with 7% precipitation rise	Net income change (%)	Source
Sri Lanka	2	−27	basic model – analysis 1[a]
Sri Lanka	3.5	−46	basic model – analysis 1[a]
Sri Lanka: paddy	2	−10	improved agricultural data – analysis 2[a]
Sri Lanka: tree crops	2	+39	improved agricultural data – analysis 2[a]
Sri Lanka: paddy[b]		−11.4	improved agricultural and climate data – analysis 2[a]
Sri Lanka: tree crops[b]		+3.5	improved agricultural and climate data – analysis 2[a]
USA	2	−3 to +3	Mendelsohn, *et al.* (1994)
India	2	−3 to −6	Sanghi, Mendelsohn and Dinar (1998)
India	3.5	−3 to −8	Sanghi *et al.* (1998)
India	2	−7 to −9	Kumar and Parikh (1998)
India	3.5	−20 to −26	Kumar and Parikh (1998)
Brazil	2	−5 to −11	Sanghi (1998)
Brazil	3.5	−7 to −14	Sanghi (1998)

[a] Source is this study.
[b] Temperature = +1.1–1.2 °C; rainfall = +70–520 mm.

Table 13.16 compares our results with other Ricardian analyses, using a uniform scenario with a 2 °C warming and a 7% increase in precipitation. We find that the Sri Lankan simple model using Analysis 1 predicts national impacts of −27% (loss) of agricultural output. A 3.5 °C uniform increase yields impacts of −46%. The Sri Lankan impacts are more severe than those found in other countries. This is surprising, especially given the close proximity of India. Clearly, more analysis of both Sri Lanka and other countries is warranted. Note that the AOGCM-based Sri Lankan results show a much wider range of variability because they test a much larger range of climate scenarios.

Regression analysis 2 is based on the model estimated with spatially disaggregated climate scenarios, especially prepared for the variations in different climate zones in Sri Lanka. If we use more disaggregate and better agricultural data with the former climate-change predictions (+2 °C temperature rise and +7% increase in rainfall), the net revenue of paddy will decrease by 10%, but plantation crops net revenue will increase by 39%. Finally, if we apply the downscaled climate projections specific to Sri Lanka, the results are more pessimistic – paddy outputs decline by 11.4%, while the offsetting increase in plantation crop revenues is only 3.5%. Overall impacts on agricultural output and GDP in 2050 are negative: −1.76% for agriculture and −0.26% for GDP, assuming no major changes in economic structure by 2050.

It is also helpful to compare these results with agronomic studies carried out in South and South East Asia. An examination of the literature shows that there is a wide range of predicted effects across crops and countries (Chang, Mendelsohn and Shaw, 2003; Sanderson, 2002; Watson, Zinyowera and Moss, 1998). In general, agronomic studies predict that warming will be harmful to production, but these studies do not include farmer adaptation or carbon fertilization effects. Including these factors, warming is likely to reduce production by about 4% (Mathews *et al.*, 1997) in the region. However, agronomic studies definitely find effects in specific crops as large as those listed in this study. The study also demonstrates that the impacts will vary by district. Northern and eastern districts, which are currently marginal from a climate perspective, are particularly vulnerable to future warming.

This study re-confirms that tropical developing countries are sensitive to the predicted climate changes over the next century. Depending on the climate scenario, the crop and the geographic features of the cultivation area, the damages could be substantial. However, not every scenario is harmful to the country. Some of the climate scenarios that predict an improvement in rainfall patterns for Sri Lanka may be beneficial. Furthermore, the estimates in this study do not include the beneficial effects of carbon fertilization, which could offset many of the damages expected from the climate alone. For example, in the specific context of Sri Lanka, De Costa *et al.* (2003) have shown that carbon fertilization could significantly increase rice yields. Further, since there is a large variation of this effect among different types of rice, selection of types of rice that have a better yield response (to changes in temperature, precipitation and atmospheric CO_2 concentration) may reduce Sri Lanka's vulnerability to climate change. There is still much to be learned about climate sensitivity, especially in the tropical regions of the world.

13.5 Appendix: Models used for tropical forest valuation

13.5.1 *Household production model for impacts on villagers*

Household production models have been used to study a number of issues pertaining to farm households, including labour supply, transportation, intrahousehold decision making, etc. (Gronau, 1977). The same framework can be used to study the impact of the establishment of a national park on Malagasy villagers, based on demand for forest and agricultural products and their land-use practices (Shyamsundar, 1993).

Households are assumed to consume vectors of market goods X_m, subsistence goods X_a and minor forest products X_f. Two of these, X_a and X_f, are both produced and consumed by the household. Furthermore, households obtain utility from the consumption of leisure X_l.

The household utility function is given by

$$U = U(X_m, X_a, X_f, X_l). \tag{13.5}$$

The household uses the surplus from agricultural production and minor forest products to buy market goods and faces the following income constraint:

$$p_m X_m = p_a(A - X_a) + p_f(F - X_f) - Wl_h - p_k k + I - \alpha c T_p^a, \tag{13.6}$$

where

X_m	= a vector of market goods purchased by the household,
A	= a vector of quantities of the different agricultural goods produced by the household,
F	= a vector of quantities of forest products harvested or processed by the household,
p_m	= a vector of prices of market goods,
p_a	= a vector of prices of agricultural goods,
p_f	= a vector of prices of forest products,
l_h	= hired labour used in the production of agricultural goods,
k	= a vector of capital goods used in the production of agricultural output,
W	= the market wage,
p_k	= a vector of prices of capital goods,
I	= other income available to the household,
$\alpha c T_p^a$	= costs of clearing primary forests for swidden agriculture.

Thus, the right-hand side of equation (13.6) represents household net surplus, available after consuming a portion of its produce and purchasing the inputs used in home production. This income is used to purchase a vector of market goods, X_m, at market prices, p_m. The household also faces land, labour, agricultural and forest production constraints.

The establishment of the Mantadia National Park will result in a change in the total area the household has access to, both for agriculture and forest products. Initially, i.e. without the park, the average household is assumed to have access to T hectares of land. With the establishment of the park, the household retains access to only T' hectares of land ($T' \leq T$). This land is under primary (T_p) and secondary (T_s) forest cover:

$$T - T' = \ddot{A}T = \ddot{A}T_p + \ddot{A}T_s. \tag{13.7}$$

The loss in accessible land has a direct impact on household production, income and consumption. The change in production and consumption behaviour in turn affects household welfare. The welfare loss can be estimated *indirectly* by the opportunity cost borne by the household due to the establishment of the park. As long as the household is using optimal quantities of land for production, a fall in land availability yields a decline in household profits as a result of the change in access to land.

An alternative method for establishing the welfare loss to the household is based on the household expenditure function. The expenditure function is used in standard welfare economics to link income and utility through the indirect utility function (minimum expenditure required to obtain a given level of utility). The contingent valuation method can be used to estimate changes in the expenditure function through direct questions.

13.5.2 Travel-cost model of impacts on tourism

When environmental conservation projects increase nature tourism, economic valuation techniques can be used to measure the associated benefits. Despite the fact that international nature travel has become 'big business' (Laarman and Durst, 1987), only a few attempts have been made to estimate the economic value of tourism to national parks in developing countries. Most have focused on the value to domestic tourists. Below, we examine the potential benefits which accrue to international nature tourists from creating the Mantadia National Park.

The decision by foreigners to pursue nature tourism in Madagascar is more complex than the models presented in many recreation demand studies. Foreign visitors fly great distances and utilize various modes of travel to visit numerous sites and enjoy many different activities in Madagascar. Few plan trips solely to visit a particular national park in Madagascar. Generally, they decide to visit Madagascar to view nature, and then choose an itinerary that includes several parks, cultural sites, etc.

Assume that households (or individuals) travel to a single country (like Madagascar) and engage in a variety of activities – enjoying the flora, fauna, scenery, etc., in various areas. Households considering international nature tourism attempt to maximize utility as a function of recreation service flows (Z_R) and non-recreation service flows (Z_{NR}):

$$U = U(Z_R, Z_{NR}). \tag{13.8}$$

Non-recreation service flows are produced by combining the composite market commodity (X_{NR}) with time (T_{NR}). Recreation service flows are produced by combining market travel services (XT_i) and time to travel to country i (T_i) with nature tourism trip experiences in country i (V_i). Therefore, the household production functions for Z_R and Z_{NR} are given by

$$Z_R = Z_R(V_1, \ldots, V_i, T_1, \ldots, T_i, XT_1, \ldots, XT_i), \tag{13.9}$$

$$Z_{NR} = Z_{NR}(X_{NR}, T_{NR}). \tag{13.10}$$

Non-homogeneous nature tourism trip experiences in country i (V_i) are produced by choosing a bundle of j activities (A^j_i) and utilizing in-country market services (Xt^j_i) and time (t^j_i) to travel to the activity areas. The A^j_i may be a single destination within the country or groups of destinations. Activities in Madagascar, for example, might include travelling to the proposed Mantadia National Park to view the Indiri lemurs and to a specific beach to swim and sunbathe, or to a group of parks and a group of beaches. Therefore, the production function for V_i is expressed as follows:

$$V_i = V_i(A^1_i, \ldots, A^j_i, t^1_i, \ldots, t^j_i, Xt^1_i, \ldots, Xt^j_i), \tag{13.11}$$

where

A_i^j = activity j in country i and is a function of the site's environmental services (s_i^j), market
goods (Xr_i^j) and onsite time (tr_i^j),

t_i^j = travel time to location of A_i^j,

Xt_i^j = market goods used to travel to location of A_i^j.

The household's problem is to maximize its utility (equation (13.8)) by choosing nature tourism trips (V_i) and market goods (X_{NR}) subject to production constraints (equations (13.9) – (13.11)) and a full income constraint. This decision problem is examined using two empirical models: (1) a typical trip model and (2) a random utility model.

14

Resource-pricing-policy applications[1]

This chapter concludes our focus on sub-national applications of sustainomics, by examining sustainable pricing of natural resources such as energy and water within a national economy. Both renewable and non-renewable resources are analysed. A practical and effective sustainable pricing policy (SPP) framework that meets national goals is developed and applied to energy, based on the sustainable energy development approach set out in Chapter 10. Price is most effective as a long-run policy tool, with two-edged implications for sustainable development. Prices are developed in two stages. Sections 14.1 to 14.3 use economic principles to determine strictly efficient prices based on marginal costs, which will lead to economically optimal production and consumption of energy. Environmental issues are included by valuing relevant impacts and externalities (see Chapter 3), and then incorporating the results in the economic analysis. Next, Section 14.4 shows how such efficient prices may be further adjusted to derive more sustainable and practical tariff structures that meet social goals such as affordability and basic needs of the poor, other objectives, such as regional or political considerations, and practical metering and billing constraints. Finally, in Section 14.5, we show how the SPP framework may be used for pricing of other natural resources such as water, and we discuss water-specific issues.

14.1 Sustainable pricing policy (SPP)

An SPP framework (responsive to economic, environmental and social aspects) is explained using the example of energy. The principles of sustainable energy development (SED) and energy pricing, introduced in Chapter 10, are developed further to integrate and rationalize the complex (and often inconsistent) web of pricing policies adopted in various energy sub-sectors such as electric power, petroleum, natural gas, coal and traditional fuels. Non-conventional sources may also be fitted into this framework.

---

[1] The valuable contributions of C. Fernando, P. Kleindorfer and J. J. Warford to this chapter are gratefully acknowledged. Some parts of the chapter are based on material adapted from Fernando *et al.* (1994), Munasinghe (1980a, 1984d, 1990b, 1992b) and Munasinghe and Warford (1982).

14.1.1 Background

Within the SED framework (see Chapter 10), the advantages of an integrated and sustainable pricing policy are evident – due to rapidly rising energy costs, changes in relative fuel prices, emerging new technologies and substitution possibilities (Munasinghe, 1990a).

The principles of SPP are clarified by focusing on sustainable energy pricing in developing countries, where, generally, higher levels of market distortion, shortages of foreign exchange and development resources, more poor households whose basic needs must be met, greater reliance on traditional fuels and inadequate energy data add to already complicated problems of energy planning. Major investment issues that strongly influence pricing policy are discussed. In particular, the SED approach relies on analysis at three hierarchical levels in relation to fundamental national objectives: (1) links between the energy sector and other sectors (e.g. industry); (2) interactions between different sub-sectors (such as power, coal and oil) within the energy sector; and (3) activities within each energy sub-sector.

14.1.2 Scope and objectives of sustainable pricing policy

Pricing is only one of the policy tools available for sustainable energy supply–demand planning and management – others include physical controls, technical methods (including research and development) and education and propaganda (see Section 10.2). As these tools are interrelated, their use should be well coordinated. Physical controls are more effective in the short-run when there are unforeseen shortages of energy. All methods of physically limiting consumption are included in this category, such as load shedding in the electricity sub-sector and rationing the supply of petrol. Technical means on the supply side include the least-cost or cheapest means of producing a given form of energy, the best mix of fuels and research and development of substitute fuels such as wood-alcohol for petrol; on the demand side, they include introducing higher efficiency energy conservation devices, such as better stoves for fuelwood. Education and propaganda on the supply side include making energy developers aware of external diseconomies such as pollution and encouraging them to be supportive of reforestation schemes to preserve the environment; on the demand side, they include public education for energy conservation.

Pricing is a key long-run policy tool, with two-edged implications for sustainable development. For example, raising (subsidized) energy prices to reflect the true resource costs of supply (including externalities) will enhance the economic efficiency of resource allocation and improve management and conservation of energy-related natural assets. However, higher prices may also worsen social equity by making basic energy needs less affordable to the poor and reserving scarce energy for the rich.

Sustainable pricing and investment decisions should be closely related. However, energy supply systems (e.g. electricity generation, transmission and distribution; oil and gas wells and pipelines; coal mines; forests) usually require large capital investments with long lead times and lifetimes. Therefore, once the investment decision is made, usually on the basis of the conventional least-cost method of meeting demand by sub-sector (including interfuel substitution possibilities), there is a lock-in effect with respect to supply. Thus prices should be related to the long-run planning horizon. On the demand side also, energy-conservation devices (e.g. motor cars, gas stoves and electric appliances) are expensive relative to average income levels and have long lifetimes, thus limiting consumer short-run ability to respond to changes in relative fuel prices.

The objectives of sustainable energy pricing are closely related to SED goals (see Chapter 10), but they are more specific. First, the economic growth objective requires that pricing policy should promote economically efficient allocation of resources, both within the energy sector and between it and the rest of the economy. In general terms, this implies that future energy use would be at optimal levels, with the price (or the user willingness-to-pay) for the marginal unit of energy used reflecting the incremental resource cost of supply to the national economy. Relative fuel prices should also shift consumption toward the optimal or least-cost mix of energy sources required to meet future demand. Distortion and constraints in the economy require the use of shadow prices and economic second-best adjustments, as described in the following (see also Chapter 3).

Second, the social objective recognizes every citizen's basic right to be supplied with certain minimum energy needs. Given the existence of significant numbers of poor consumers, and also wide disparities of income, this implies subsidized prices, at least for low-income consumers.

Third, government would be concerned with financial goals relating to the viability and autonomy of the energy sector. This would require pricing policies that permit energy institutions (typically, government-owned) to earn a fair rate of return on assets and to self-finance an acceptable part of investments needed to develop future energy resources.

Fourth, environmental protection is an important goal of pricing policy. For example, energy conservation reduces waste, deforestation, pollution and dependence on foreign sources (e.g. oil imports).

Fifth, there are other specific objectives, such as promoting regional development (e.g. rural electrification) or specific sectors (e.g. export-oriented industries), as well as socio-political (e.g. national security) and legal (e.g. international agreements) constraints.

In summary, therefore, price is most effective as a long-run policy tool. From the viewpoint of economic efficiency, the price indicates willingness-to-pay and the use-value of energy; to the user, it signals the present and future opportunity costs of supply of various energy sources.

Governments play a major role in the pricing of commercial energy resources, but often neglect issues relating to traditional forms of energy. They exercise direct influence, usually through the ownership of energy sources or price controls. Indirect influences occur through means such as taxes, import duties, subsidies, market quotas, taxes on energy-using equipment and government-guided investments in energy resources.

In many countries, electric utilities are government-owned, although privatization is increasing. In oil and gas production, refining and distribution, as well as in coal mining, both public and private organizations operate, often side by side. However, irrespective of the form of ownership, all governments exercise some form of wholesale or retail price control, usually at several levels (including production, refining, transport or transmission, etc.). Income and excise taxes are also levied from both public and private energy-sector companies.

Generally, certain fuels in specific uses tend to be subsidized, although leakages and abuses of subsidies by non-targeted consumer groups also occur. Thus, kerosene for lighting and cooking, rural electricity for lighting and agricultural pumping and diesel fuel for transport commonly qualify for subsidies. Cross-subsidies exist between different fuels, user groups and geographic regions. Thus, high-priced petrol may finance kerosene subsidies, industrial electricity users may subsidize household consumers, and a uniform national pricing policy usually implies subsidization of energy users in remote areas by those living in cities. One key issue with subsidies is that energy producers may not be able to raise sufficient revenues to finance investment to meet expanding demand, or even to maintain existing facilities, and thus shortages eventually result. Furthermore, cross-subsidies give users the wrong price signals, with consequent misallocation of investments.

Import and export duties, excise taxes and sales taxes are levied, often by several levels of government from federal to municipal, at various stages in the production, processing, distribution and retailing chain. In many cases, the combined levies are several hundred per cent of the original product price for some items and negative (or close to zero) for others. Several less obvious methods, such as property taxes, water rights and user charges and franchise fees are also used to influence energy use. Energy prices are also affected by a wide range of royalty charges, profit-sharing schemes and exploration agreements made between governments and multinational companies, to develop oil and gas resources.

Other policy instruments are often used to reinforce pricing policies, such as quotas on imported or scarce forms of energy. Conservation regulations may affect depletion rates for oil and gas, while availability of hydropower from multipurpose dams may be subordinate to the use of water for irrigation or river navigation. Other policies, such as tax relief, import subsidies, export bonuses, government loans or grants, high taxes on large automobiles, etc., are also used to control energy use.

Traditional fuels have been relatively neglected because these forms of energy are not usually traded in markets. However, less direct methods may be used, such as displacement of fuelwood for cooking by subsidized kerosene and LPG, increasing the supply of fuelwood by reforestation programmes and effective distribution of charcoal, enforcing stiffer penalties for illegal felling of trees and proper watershed management.

14.1.3 Analytical framework

Two-stage approach

Because the objectives mentioned in the preceding section are often not mutually consistent, a realistic integrated energy-pricing structure must be flexible enough to permit trade-offs among them. Thus, energy-pricing policy must be carried out in two stages. In the first stage, prices that strictly meet the economic efficiency objective are determined, based on a consistent and rigorous framework. The second stage consists of adjusting these efficient prices to meet all other objectives. The adjustment procedure is more ad hoc, and is determined by the relative importance attached to the different goals. Next, we review shadow pricing (see Chapter 3 for details) and develop the economic framework for efficient pricing of energy. The second-stage adjustments for non-economic factors are discussed later in this section.

Economically efficient prices using marginal opportunity cost

Shadow-pricing theory has been applied mainly for cost–benefit analysis of projects (Munasinghe, 1979b; Squire and van der Tak, 1975). However, since energy-investment decisions are closely linked to energy prices, for consistency in both cases, the same shadow prices should be used. The latter represent the economic opportunity costs of scarce resources, better than market prices (or private financial costs) – see Box 2.3 and Section 3.2.

Lack of data, time and skills (particularly in developing nations) will generally preclude the use of a full economy-wide model (see Chapters 7 to 9) for energy analysis. This holistic, or general equilibrium, analysis is conceptually important. For example, the efficient shadow price of a given resource may be represented by the change in value of aggregate national consumption output, due to a small change in the availability of that resource. However, in practice a partial equilibrium approach is used, where key linkages and resources flows between the energy sector and the rest of the economy, as well as inter-actions among different energy sub-sectors, are selectively identified and analysed using appropriate shadow prices, such as the opportunity cost of capital, shadow-wage rate and marginal costs of different fuels (Munasinghe, 1979a). Useful results may be obtained from relatively simple models.

To clarify the basic concepts involved in optimal energy pricing, we first analyse a simple model. Next, more complex features are examined, including short-run versus long-run dynamic considerations, capital indivisibilities, joint output cost allocation, quality of supply and price feedback effects on demand. Efficient energy prices are determined in two steps (see Appendix A, Section 14.6, for details). First, the marginal opportunity cost (MOC) or shadow price of supply is estimated. Second, this value is further adjusted to compensate for demand-side effects arising from distortions in the prices of other goods, including energy substitutes. From a practical viewpoint, it is easier to estimate optimal prices starting with the MOC, because supply costs are better known (from technoeconomic data), whereas information on the demand curve is relatively poor.

Suppose that the MOC of supply in a given energy sub-sector is the curve MOC(Q) shown in Figure 14.1. For a typical non-traded energy resource like electricity, the MOC that is generally upward sloping is calculated by first shadow pricing the inputs to the power sector and then estimating both the level and structure of marginal supply costs (MSCs) based on a long-run system expansion programme – in this particular sector, the MSC is represented by the long-run marginal cost, LRMC (Munasinghe, 1979a; Munasinghe and Warford, 1982). For tradable items like crude oil, and for fuels that are substitutes for tradables at the margin,

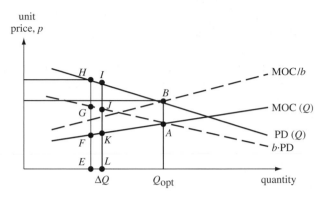

Figure 14.1. Efficient pricing with shadow prices.

the MOC is given by the international or border price of the tradable (i.e. CIF price of imports or FOB price for exports, with adjustments for internal transport and handling costs) – the use of these border prices does not require the assumption of free trade, but does imply that the numeraire for shadow pricing is uncommitted foreign exchange (see Chapter 3).

For most developing countries, such import or export MOC curves will generally be flat or perfectly elastic. Other fuels, such as coal and natural gas, could treated either way, depending on whether they are tradables or non-traded. A non-traded item is generally characterized by a domestic supply price that lies above the FOB price of exports but below the CIF price of import. The MOC of non-renewable, non-traded energy sources will generally include a 'user cost' or economic rent component, in addition to the marginal production cost. For traditional fuels, where there is no established market, the MOC may be valued indirectly by the savings on alternative fuels, such as kerosene, the opportunity costs of labour for gathering firewood and/or the external costs of deforestation and erosion.

For a non-traded energy type, the MOC is the opportunity cost of inputs used to produce it plus relevant user costs. For a tradable fuel or a substitute, the MOC is the marginal foreign exchange cost of imports or marginal export earnings foregone. In each case, the MOC measures the shadow-priced economic value of alternative output foregone due to more energy use. Next, we examine demand-side effects, especially second-best corrections that capture interactions between various energy sub-sectors.

Demand-side considerations

In Figure 14.1, the market-priced demand curve for energy (e.g. oil) is given by the curve PD (Q), which is the consumer's willingness-to-pay (see Appendix B, Section 14.7, for details). Consider a small increment of consumption ΔQ (i.e. the area between the demand curve and the x-axis) and the corresponding supply cost (i.e. the area between the supply curve and the x-axis). Since the MOC is shadow-priced, PD must also be transformed into a shadow-priced curve to make the comparison valid. This is achieved by asking what is the shadow-priced marginal cost of resources used up elsewhere in the economy if the market priced amount ($p\Delta Q$) is devoted to alternative consumption (and/or investment).

Suppose that the shadow cost of this alternative pattern of expenditure is $b(p\Delta Q)$, where b is a conversion factor (see Appendix A, Section 14.6, and Chapter 3). Then the transformed PD curve, which represents the shadow costs of alternative consumption foregone, is given by PD(Q) – we assumed that $b < 1$ in Figure 14.1. Thus, at price p, incremental benefits *EGJL* exceed incremental costs *EFKL*. The optimal consumption level is Q_{opt}, where the MOC and $b \cdot$ PD curves cross, or equivalently where a new pseudo-supply curve MOC/b and the market demand curve PD intersect. The optimal or efficient selling price to be charged to consumers (because they react along the market demand curve PD, rather than the shadow-priced curve $b \cdot$ PD) will be $p_{\mathrm{e}} = \mathrm{MOC}/b$ at the actual market clearing point B. At this level of consumption, the shadow costs and benefits of marginal consumption are equal, i.e. MOC $= b \cdot$ PD. Since b depends on user-specific consumption patterns, different values of the efficient price p_{e} may be derived for various user categories, all based on the same value of the MOC – as shown by the practical examples below.

First, suppose that all the expenditure ($p \cdot \Delta Q$) could have purchased a fully substitute fuel. Then the conversion factor b is the relative distortion or ratio of the shadow price to market price of this other fuel (see Chapter 3). Thus, $p_{\mathrm{e}} = \mathrm{MOC}/b$ represents a specific second-best adjustment to the MOC of the first fuel, to compensate for the distortion in the price of the substitute fuel. For example, $\mathrm{MOC}_{\mathrm{EL}}$ could represent the long-run marginal cost of rural electricity (for lighting) and the substitute fuel could be imported kerosene. Suppose that the (subsidized) domestic market price of kerosene is set at one-half its import (border) price for sociopolitical reason. Then $b = 2$, and the efficient selling price of electricity $p_{\mathrm{e}} = \mathrm{MOC}_{\mathrm{EL}}/2$. A more refined analysis would have to include additional aspects, such as partial substitution, the differences in quality between the two fuels and capital costs of conversion equipment (light bulbs and kerosene lamps). It would be misleading, however, to then attempt to justify the subsidized kerosene price on the basis of comparison with the newly calculated low price of electricity, p_{e}. The integrated pricing framework avoids such circular reasoning, which might occur when pricing policies in different energy sub-sectors are uncoordinated. All energy subsidies must be carefully targeted to avoid leakages and abuses.

Next, consider a less specific case in which the amount ($p \cdot \Delta Q$) is used to buy an average basket of goods. If the consumer is residential, b would be the consumption conversion factor, or the shadow-to-market-price ratio of the household market basket (see the Appendix to Chapter 3, Section 3.8). In the general case of an unspecified user, or if detailed information on consumer categories was unavailable, b would be the standard conversion factor (SCF) – the ratio of the official exchange rate (OER) to the shadow exchange rate (SER). The SCF converts domestic prices into border shadow prices. Assume $b = \mathrm{SCF}$ represents a global second-best correction for the divergence between market and shadow prices, averaged over the economy. For example, suppose the border price of imported diesel is 4 pesos per litre (i.e. US $0.20, converted at the OER of 20 pesos per US $). Let the appropriate SER that reflects the average level of import duties and export subsidies be 25 pesos per US $. Therefore SCF $=$ OER/SER $= 0.8$, and the appropriate strictly efficient selling price of diesel is given by $p_{\mathrm{e}} = 4/0.8 = 5$ pesos per litre.

14.2 Extensions of the basic model

The analysis so far has been static, but practical energy-pricing policy needs to be implemented under dynamic conditions.

14.2.1 Dynamic effects – resource depletion

Often the availability of a given energy source, interfuel substitution possibilities and so on vary over time, leading to disequilibrium in fuel markets and divergence of the short-run price from the long-run optimal price. This aspect is illustrated below, using an example that shows how the optimal depletion rate and time path for the MOC of a domestic non-renewable resource will be affected by varying demand – due to tradability, extent of reserves, and substitution possibilities.

In Figure 14.2, the international energy price that acts as the benchmark rises steadily in real terms, along the path BE. Suppose that the present-day marginal supply cost (MSC) (including extraction costs plus appropriate transport and environmental costs, etc.) of a domestic energy source such as coal lies below the thermal equivalency price of an internationally traded fuel (e.g. oil), as indicated by points *A* and *B*. Thermal equivalents are defined as the quantities of two substitutable fuels that provide the same useful energy output in a given use (i.e. including the efficiency of conversion). We note that the choice between the energy forms would also depend on the quality of final heat output, capital and handling costs of conversion, and so on, but to simplify the analysis here we compare the fuels only on the basis of unit price.

Let us initially examine two polar extremes based on simple arguments. First, suppose the reserves are very large and that the use of this fuel at the margin will not affect exports or substitute for imported fuels. Then the long-run MOC of the domestic-energy source would be based on the marginal supply cost, along the path *AC*, which is upward sloping to allow

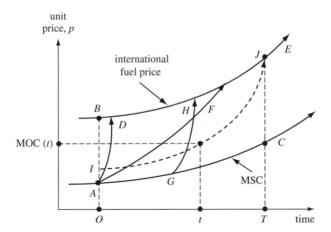

Figure 14.2. Dynamic price paths for domestic exhaustible energy.

for increases in real factor costs or extraction costs. On the other hand, suppose there is an export market for local-energy resource, or substitutability for imported fuels. If reserves are small, or output capacity is limited, the marginal use of the resource will reduce export earnings or increase the imported fuel bill in the short run. Then, the MOC would follow the path *AD* and rise quickly toward parity with the world energy price.

The actual situation is likely to fall between these two extremes, thus yielding alternative prices such as *AFE* or *AGHE*. Here, the initial use of the resource has no marginal impact on exports or import substitution, but there is gradual depletion of finite domestic reserves over time, and eventual transition to higher-priced fuel in the future. The rate of depletion of a given volume of domestic-energy reserves will be greater and the time to depletion will be shorter if its price is maintained low (path *AGHE*) rather than when the price rises steadily (path *AFE*). The macroeconomic consequences of path *AGHE* are also more undesirable because of the sudden price increase at the point of transition, when the local resource is exhausted. In practice, the price path may well be determined by non-economic factors. For example, the price of newly found gas or coal may be kept low for some time to capture the domestic market and displace imported liquid fuels (which are subsidized for political reasons). Generally, the desire to keep energy prices low today must be balanced against the need to avoid a larger future price shock.

The preceding discussion is more useful for oil-importing or energy-deficit developing countries. For major oil exporters, the ability to influence world market prices and determine the rate of resource depletion provides greater flexibility. Large foreign exchange surpluses and limited capacity to absorb investment will decrease the attractiveness of marginal export earnings and help to conserve oil resources. There is also greater ability to subsidize domestic oil use to meet basic needs and to accelerate economic development by increasing investment and expanding non-oil output.

More rigorous dynamic models, which maximize the net economic benefits of energy consumption over a long period, have been developed to determine the optimal price path and depletion rate. However, such models depend on factors such as the social discount rate, size of reserves, growth of demand and the cost and time lag needed to develop a backstop technology (which could replace the world energy price as the upper bound on price). Uncertainties in future supply and demand – such as the possibility of discovering new energy resources or technologies – add to the complexities of dynamic analysis. Hotelling's (1931) classical formula indicates that the rate of increase in optimal rent (or difference between price and marginal extraction cost) for the resource should equal the rate of return on capital (r). In our shadow-pricing framework, r would be the social discount rate or 'accounting rate of interest' (ARI).

The foregoing implies that the optimal path of the MOC would be *IJE* in Figure 14.2, defined at any time t by

$$\mathrm{MOC}(t) = \mathrm{MSC}(t) + JL/(1 + r)^{T-t},$$

where *JL* is the rent at the time of depletion *T*. Thus, the MOC consists of the MSC (the current marginal costs of extraction, transport, environmental degradation, etc.), plus the

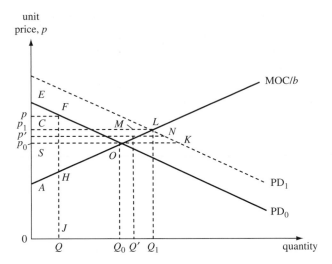

Figure 14.3. Dynamic effects due to demand curve shifts.

discounted 'user cost' or foregone surplus benefits of future consumption (*JL*). As *T* approaches infinity, *IJ* would tend toward *AC*, which is the infinite-reserves case, while, as *T* falls to zero, *IJ* would approximate *AD* more closely, corresponding to the case of very small reserves and rapid transition to the expensive fuel.

14.2.2 *Dynamic effects – shifting demand*

Figure 14.3 shows that in year 0, supply and demand are equal at the correct market clearing price p_0 and quantity Q_0, where supply and demand curves (MC and PD_0) intersect (at *O*). Due to demand growth, the demand curve shifts to PD_1 in year 1 (see Appendix B, Section 14.7). If the price p_0 continued to prevail in year 1, excess demand equal to *GK* will occur. Ideally, the supply should be increased to Q_1, and the new optimal market clearing price established at p_1 (point *L*). However, information about the demand curve PD_1 may be incomplete, making it difficult to locate *L*. Fortunately the MOC curve may determined more accurately using known production functions or international prices. Therefore, as a first step, the supply may be increased to an immediate level *Q'*, at the price *p'*. Observation of the excess demand *MN* indicates that both the supply level and price should be further increased. Conversely, if we overshoot *L* and end up in a situation of excess supply, then it may be necessary to wait until the growth of demand catches up with the oversupply. In this interactive manner, it is possible to move along the MOC curve toward the optimal point *L*. As we approach it, the optimum may also shift with demand growth, and therefore we may never hit this moving target. However, a policy that pegs the price to the MOC of supply, and expands output until the market clears, is still a good basic guideline.

Next, we examine the practical complications raised by price feedback effects. Typically, a long-range demand forecast is made assuming some future-price forecast, a least-cost investment programme is determined to meet this demand, and optimal prices are computed. However, if the estimated future optimal price that is to be imposed on consumers is different from the original price forecast, then the first-round price estimates must be fed back into the model to revise the demand forecast and repeat the calculation. In theory, this iterative process could be repeated until future demand, prices and MOC estimates become mutually self-consistent. In practice, data uncertainties may make only one such iteration worthwhile. The behaviour of demand is then observed over some time period, and the first round prices are revised to move closer to the optimum, which may itself have shifted as described earlier.

14.2.3 *Capital indivisibilities*

When the MOC is based on marginal production costs, the effect of capital indivisibilities or lumpiness of investments causes difficulties. Energy investments are large and long-lived, due to economies of scale. We illustrate this issue by applying the MOC approach to the electricity sector – based on the long-run marginal costs (LRMCs) of power supply.

Marginal cost pricing theory dates back to the groundbreaking efforts of Dupuit (1844) and Hotelling (1938). Ruggles (1949a, b) provides a useful review of the early literature. Theoretical developments, especially for application in the electric-power sector, received strong impetus from the 1950s onwards (Boiteux, 1949; Munasinghe, 1990b; Munasinghe and Warford, 1982; Steiner, 1957; Turvey, 1968). Recent work focused on spot pricing, uncertainty and costs of power shortages, etc.

As shown in Figure 14.4, suppose that in year 0 the maximum supply capacity is QM_1, while the optimal price and output combination (p_0, Q_0) prevails, corresponding to demand curve D_0 and the short-run marginal cost (SRMC) curve (e.g. variable, operating and maintenance costs).

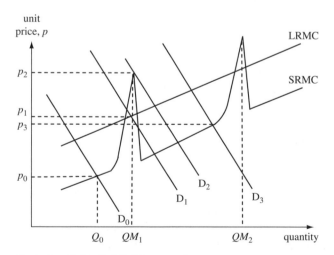

Figure 14.4. The effect of capital indivisibilities on price.

As demand grows from D_0 to D_1 over time, and the limit of existing capacity is reached, the price must be increased to p_1 to clear the market – that is 'price rationing' occurs. When the demand curve has shifted to D_2 and the price is p_2, capacity is increased to QM_2. However, as soon as the capacity increment is completed and becomes a sunk cost, price should fall to the old trend of SRMC – for example, p_3 is the optimal price corresponding to demand D_3. Generally, the large price fluctuations during such a process will be disruptive and unacceptable to consumers. This practical problem may be avoided by adopting an LRMC approach, which provides the required price stability while retaining the principle of matching willingness-to-pay and incremental supply costs. Essentially, the future capital costs of a single project or an investment programme are distributed over the stream of output expected during the plant lifetime. For example, capital costs could be annualized at the social discount rate and divided by the annual output, or an average incremental cost approach could be used (Munasinghe, 1979a). This average investment cost per unit of incremental output is added to the variable cost (SRMC) to yield LRMC, as shown in Figure 14.4. If continued demand growth is expected, initial consumer willingness-to-pay a price equal to the annual equivalent LRMC is assumed to imply willingness to do so over the lifetime of the asset.

Sometimes, deviations from the LRMC may lead to efficiency gains. If substantial excess supply capacity exists, it may be appropriate to set the price temporarily equal to SRMC (including both variable and user costs) for specific consumers (see Section 14.2.5). However, SRMC-priced supplies must be decreased as LRMC-priced demand grows, and the temporary use of low-priced supplies should not be allowed to become a permanent burden, e.g. an interruptible load in electric-power systems.

14.2.4 Peak-load pricing and structuring

Another method of allocating capacity costs, known as peak-load pricing, is relevant for electricity (and natural gas). The basic peak-load pricing model shown in Figure 14.5 has two demand curves: D_{pk} is the peak demand during the x working hours of the day, when electric loads are large, and D_{op} shows the off-peak demand during the remaining $(24-x)$ hours when loads are light. The simplified marginal cost curve shows a single type of plant with the fuel, operating and maintenance costs given by the constant a, and the marginal capacity cost given by the constant b. The figure shows how pressure on capacity arises due to peak demand D_{pk}, while the off-peak demand D_{op} does not infringe on the capacity limit QM. The optimal-pricing rule now has two parts linked to two distinct rating periods (i.e. according to the time of day) – see Appendix A, Section 14.6: peak-period price $p_{pk} = a + b$; off-peak-period price $p_{op} = a$.

The logic of this simple result is that peak-period users (who are the cause of capacity additions) should bear full responsibility for the capacity costs as well as fuel, operating and maintenance costs, while off-peak consumers pay only the later costs. Peak-load-pricing can also be applied in different seasons of the year. More sophisticated peak-load-pricing models indicate that, in an optimally planned system, marginal capacity cost should be allocated in

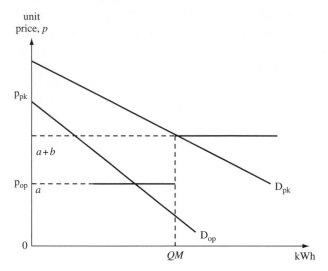

Figure 14.5. Peak-load pricing model.

proportion to marginal shortage costs during two or more different rating periods. If the peak period is too narrowly defined, peak-load pricing may shift the peak to another rating period.

Related problems of allocating joint costs also arise in other energy sub-sectors – e.g. in allocating capacity costs of natural gas, or refinery costs among different oil products. The former may be treated like the electricity case. For oil products, the tradable light refinery cuts (like kerosene, petrol and diesel) have benchmark world prices. Other items, such as heavy residual oils, may have to be treated like non-tradables. Further, associated gas that is flared at the refinery is often assumed to have a low MOC, although subsequent storage and handling for use as LPG will add to the costs. A more complicated approach would be to use a refinery programming model to solve the dual problem and determine the shadow prices of distillates.

A more general aspect of the capacity constraint, which encompasses peak-load pricing, is that energy prices have to be structured. For example, the MOC shown in Figure 14.1 may vary by the type of consumer, geographical location, time and level of consumption, voltage level (for electricity) and so on. These values of the MOC then have to be modified to reflect demand-side considerations (as discussed earlier). Therefore, the economically efficient prices in a given energy sub-sector may exhibit considerable structuring.

14.2.5 Shortage costs and capacity constraints

The interrelated issues of supply and demand uncertainty, safety margins and shortage costs also raise complications. We first illustrate this issue for electricity, and then generalize the results for other sub-sectors. The least-cost system expansion plan to meet an electricity demand forecast is generally determined assuming some (arbitrary) target level of system reliability – loss-of-load probability (LOLP), frequency and duration (F&D) of outages, reserve margin, etc. Therefore, marginal costs depend on the target reliability level. However, economic theory shows that reliability should also be treated as a variable to be optimized, and both price and capacity (or equivalently, reliability) levels should be optimized jointly. The optimal price is the marginal cost price described earlier, while the optimal reliability level is achieved when the marginal cost of capacity additions (to improve reliability) is equal to the expected value of cost savings to users due to power shortages averted by those capacity increments. Such ideas lead to a more general model of system expansion planning and pricing, as shown below (Munasinghe, 1979b, 1980a, 1990b).

Consider a simple expression for the net benefits (NB) of electricity consumption, which is to be maximized:

$$\mathrm{NB}(D, R) = \mathrm{TB}(D) - \mathrm{SC}(D, R) - \mathrm{OC}(D, R),$$

where TB = total benefits of consumption if there were no outages; SC = supply costs (i.e. system costs); OC = outage costs (i.e. costs to consumers of supply shortages); D = demand; R = reliability.

In the traditional approach based on least-cost system expansion planning, both D and R are exogenously fixed, and therefore NB is maximized when SC is minimized. However, if R is treated as a variable,

$$\frac{\mathrm{d(NB)}}{\mathrm{d}R} = -\frac{\partial(\mathrm{SC} + \mathrm{OC})}{\partial R} + \frac{\partial(\mathrm{TB} - \mathrm{SC} - \mathrm{OC})}{\partial D} \cdot \frac{\partial D}{\partial R} = 0$$

is the necessary first-order maximization condition.

Assuming $\partial D/\partial R- = 0$, we have $\partial(\mathrm{SC})/\partial R = -\partial(\mathrm{OC})/\partial R$. Therefore, as described earlier, reliability should be increased by adding to capacity until the above condition is satisfied, at which point both reliability and capacity are optimal (assuming that the price is also set optimally at marginal cost). An alternative way of expressing this result is that, since TB is independent of R, NB is maximized when the total costs, TC = (SC + OC), are minimized. The above criterion effectively subsumes the traditional system planning rule of minimizing only the system costs. The emphasis on outage costs requires greater effort to measure these costs (Munasinghe, 1979b, 1980b; Munasinghe and Gellerson 1979).

This approach may be generalized for application in other energy sub-sectors. Thus, while measures of reliability as sophisticated as LOLP etc. do not exist outside the power sub-sector, the concept of minimizing total costs to society is still relevant. For example, in oil and gas investment planning, the cost of shortages due to petrol queues, lack of furnace oil, or gas for domestic and industrial use may be traded off against the supply costs of increased storage capacity and greater delivery capability incurred by augmenting surface transport or pipeline systems. The latter case could justify raising fuel prices, vehicle licensing fees, road user and parking charges, etc., in urban areas, relative to rural ones. Clearly, such considerations would modify the marginal costs of energy supply and optimal pricing policies.

Let us reconsider the choice between short- and long-run marginal costs (SRMC and LRMC) for optimal price. The SRMC is the cost of meeting additional electricity consumption (including shortage costs) with capacity fixed. The LRMC is the cost of providing a sustained increase in consumption when optimal capacity adjustments are possible. If the system is optimally planned and operated (i.e. capacity and reliability are optimal), SRMC = LRMC. However, if the system plan is suboptimal, significant deviations between the SRMC and LRMC will have to be resolved. For example, if demand is overestimated, significant excess capacity may be built. Thus, marginal capacity costs may fall in the short run, justifying a reduction of demand charges below LRMC. However, as peak demand grows and the system approaches optimality again, the capacity charges should rise smoothly toward LRMC. This transition could become undesirably abrupt if the initial reduction in demand charges were too large and demand growth were overstimulated.

Finally, if there are substantial outage costs outside the peak period, then the optimal marginal capacity costs may be allocated among the different rating periods in proportion to the corresponding marginal outage costs. Capacity costs could also be allocated to ratings periods in inverse proportion to LOLP, but this is an approximation because aggregates reliability indices like LOLP are poor proxies for prorating outage costs.

Real-time pricing (RTP), which provides users with frequent price signals (e.g. varying hourly), has been tested for over a decade (Barbose, Goldman and Neenan, 2004). The economic efficiency of RTP and how well it reconciles SRMC and LRMC is the subject of debate (Borenstein, 2005).

14.2.6 Environmental considerations

Finally, externalities (especially environmental ones) have to be included as far as possible in determining efficient energy prices (see Chapter 3). For example, if the building of a new hydroelectric dam results in the flooding of land that had recreational or agricultural value, or if urban transportation growth leads to congestion and air pollution, these costs should be reflected in the MOC. While such externality costs may often be difficult to quantify, they may already be included (at least partially) on the supply side. Examples include measures taken to avoid environmental degradation, such as the cost of pollution-control equipment at an oil refinery or coal-fired electricity plant, or the cost of landscaping strip-mined land.

Estimation of environmental costs is most problematic in the case of non-commercial or traditional energy sources, such as woodfuel, where MOCs could be based (when appropriate) on the externality costs of deforestation, erosion, loss of watershed and so on. Other measures of the economic value of traditional fuel include the opportunity cost of labour to collect woodfuel, or the cost savings from displaced substitute fuels such as kerosene and LPG.

Environmental costs may be incorporated into sustainable energy pricing policy to make energy development less resource intensive and polluting (see Section 7.3.1). Figure 14.6 shows the interplay of price and income effects in an initially stagnant economy with low fuel prices, to clarify how subsequent growth could combine with neglected economic

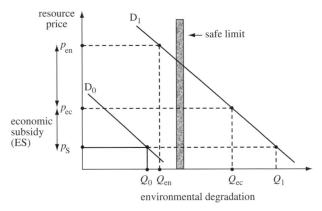

Figure 14.6. Incorporating environmental concerns to make energy prices more sustainable Source: Munasinghe (1995b).

distortions to cause environmental harm. The downward sloping curve D_0 depicts demand for liquid fuel, which depends on both price p and income Y (i.e. $D = D(p, Y)$). At the price p_S, representing the marginal cost of imported fuel, the initial air pollution level is Q_0. Suppose Q_L is the safe limiting rate for urban air pollution, beyond which serious health damage occurs. If $Q_0 < Q_L$, the air pollution level is acceptable. Next, suppose economic reforms stimulate growth and shift the fuel demand curve outward to D_1 – e.g. more road transport. Now the air pollution index could shift to $Q_1 > Q_L$, posing major risks to human health.

Clearly, the remedy is not to stop growth, but rather to introduce complementary measures that establish appropriate energy prices. First, fuel prices may be increased to more efficient levels by eliminating economic subsidies (ESs) – e.g. to reflect correctly the opportunity cost of time wasted due to road congestion. The resulting efficient price (p_{ec}) would reduce the air pollution level to Q_{ec}, which still exceeds Q_L. Second, an additional environmental externality cost (EE) may be charged, to reflect health costs (lung diseases, lead poisoning, etc.), and thereby establish the environmentally adjusted price (p_{en}). The air pollution index now falls to $Q_{en} < Q_L$, which is a sustainable fuel price, since the health-determined safety standard Q_L is no longer exceeded.

14.3 Calculating economically efficient prices based on strict LRMC

In this first stage calculation, strict LRMC (and the optimal investment programme) are estimated using shadow prices (instead of market prices), which correct for distortions in the economy.

14.3.1 Estimating strict LRMC

Strict LRMC is defined as the incremental cost of optimal adjustments in the system expansion plan and system operations attributable to a small, sustained increment of demand. LRMC must be structured within a disaggregated framework, including differentiation of marginal costs by time of day, voltage level, geographic area, season of the year and so on. The degree of structuring and sophistication of the calculation depends on data constraints and the desired results, given the practical problems of computing and applying a complex tariff; e.g., in theory, the LRMC may be estimated for each individual user at each moment of time. The method of calculating strict LRMC is summarized below (see the detailed theory and case studies in Munasinghe (1990b) and Munasinghe and Warford (1982).

Cost categories and rating periods

The three broad categories of marginal costs are: (a) capacity costs; (b) energy costs; and (c) consumer costs. Electricity is generated by power plants and fed successively into the extra-high- and high-voltage (EHV and HV) transmission systems, the medium- and low-voltage (MV and LV) distribution systems, before reaching the end user. Marginal capacity costs include the investment costs of generation, transmission and distribution facilities associated with supplying additional kilowatts. Marginal energy costs are the fuel and operating costs of providing additional kilowatt-hours. Marginal customer costs are the incremental costs directly attributable to users, such as costs of hook-up, metering and billing. Operation and maintenance (O&M) costs, and administrative and general (A&G) costs must also be allocated to these basic cost categories. Finally, these elements must be structured by time of use, etc.

The first step in structuring is the selection of appropriate rating periods. System-load duration curves and generation schedules should be examined to determine periods during which demand presses on capacity and supply costs are highest. These critical periods may be due to daily demand variations (e.g. evening lighting load) or seasonal variations in both demand (e.g. summer air conditioning load) and supply (e.g. dry season for hydro systems). We begin with a simple all-thermal system that does not exhibit marked seasonability of demand, choosing only two rating periods by time of day, i.e. peak and off-peak. Seasonal variations in LRMC and the analysis of hydroelectric systems are discussed later.

14.3.2 Marginal capacity costs

The typical power system load during 24 hours may be divided into two pricing (or rating) periods: peak and off-peak. As demand rises over time, the peak load also grows. In Figure 14.7, the resulting forecast of peak demand is given by curve D, starting from the initial value *MW*. The LRMC of capacity is the ratio $\Delta C/\Delta D$, where ΔC is the change in system capacity costs associated with a sustained increment ΔD in the long-run peak demand (as shown by the dashed curve in Figure 14.7). The increment of demand ΔD is marginal both in time, and in terms of *MW*. In theory, ΔD can be either positive or negative, and generally the ratio $\Delta C/\Delta D$ will vary with the sign as well as the magnitude of ΔD. If many such values of $\Delta C/\Delta D$ are computed, it is possible to average them to obtain the LRMC.

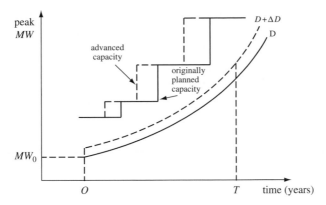

Figure 14.7. Forecast of peak power demand and incremental demand.

In an optimally planned system, new load would normally be met by advancing future plant or inserting new units, such as gas turbines or peaking hydro; see Figure 14.7. Using a generation planning model, it is easy to determine the change in capacity costs ΔC by simulating the expansion path and system operation, with and without the demand increment ΔD. This process may also be generalized to derive a more complex tariff structure with many rating periods. The method simulates the optimal system planning process, using the dynamic LRMC concept.

When constraints due to time, data and resources preclude this ideal approach, more approximate methods may be used. Several practical methods of estimating LRMC are provided in Munasinghe (1979a, 1990b). Simple considerations based on more static interpretation of the LRMC often yield good results. Suppose that gas turbines are used for peaking. Then the LRMC of generating capacity ($\text{LRMC}_{\text{Gen. Cap.}}$) may be approximated by the cost per kilowatt installed, annuitized over the expected lifetime. This figure must be adjusted for the reserve margin (RM %) and losses due to station use (L_{su} %). Thus a typical expression would be:

$$\text{LRMC}_{\text{Gen. Cap.}} = (\text{annuitized cost kW})(1 + \text{RM}\%)/(1 - L_{\text{su}}\%).$$

In our model, all capacity costs are charged to peak-period users. Thus, if capacity costs of base-load generating units are included, it is important to net out potential fuel savings due to displacement of less efficient plant by these base load units (see Appendix A, Section 14.6). It would be incorrect to charge peak consumers the high-capacity costs of base load units (such as nuclear), e.g. encouraging them to install their own captive gas turbine plant.

Next we examine transmission and distribution (T&D) investment costs (except customer costs), which are allocated to incremental capacity, because the designs of these facilities are determined principally by the peak kilowatts that they carry rather than the kilowatt-hours. However, particularly at the distribution level, the size of a given feeder may depend on local

peak demand, which may not occur within the system peak period, and this could complicate the problem of allocating distribution capacity costs among the various rating periods
(Boiteux and Stasi, 1964). Structuring by voltage level is introduced at this stage, in three
supply categories: high, medium and low (HV, MV, LV). Since consumers are charged only
upstream costs, capacity costs at each voltage level must be identified.

The simplest approach is to use the average incremental cost (AIC) method to estimate the
LRMC of T&D. Suppose that in year i, ΔMW_i and I_i are the increase in demand served
(relatively to the previous year) and the investment cost, respectively. Then, the AIC of
capacity is given by

$$\text{AIC} = \left[\sum_{0}^{T} I_i/(1+r)^i \right] \Bigg/ \left[\sum_{L}^{T+L} \Delta MW_i/(1+r)^i \right],$$

where r is the discount rate (e.g. the opportunity cost of capital), T is the planning horizon
(e.g. 10 years) and L is the average time delay between the investment and commissioning
dates for new facilities.

We note that, in the AIC method, the actual additional increments of demand are
considered as they occur, rather than the hypothetical fixed demand increment ΔD used
(more rigorously) in calculating generation LRMC. However, because there is no problem
of plant mix with T&D investments, AIC and the hypothetical increment method will yield
similar results, while AIC is also usually much easier to calculate using readily available
planning data. Furthermore, AIC is the unit cost which equates the present discounted value
of power output (denominator) and its supply costs (numerator). Thus, it is the monetary
value of ΔMW_i that is effectively discounted, rather than the physical units.

An alternative method of determining marginal T&D costs at various voltage levels is to
use historical data to fit regression equations such as

$$(\text{transmission costs}) = a + b(\text{peak demand}).$$

However, there is no guarantee that such a past relationship would hold true in the future as
the system expands.

Let $\Delta \text{LRMC}_{\text{HV}}$ be the AIC of EHV and HV transmission, annuitized over the life of the
plant (e.g. 30 years) to yield marginal costs. Then, the total LRMC of capacity during the
peak period, at the HV level, would be given by

$$\text{LRMC}_{\text{HV Cap.}} = \text{LRMC}_{\text{Gen.Cap.}}/(1 - L_{\text{HV}}\%) + \Delta \text{LRMC}_{\text{HV}},$$

where $L_{\text{HV}} \%$ is the percentage of incoming peak power that is lost in the EHV and HV
network. This procedure may be repeated at the MV and LV levels. The LRMC of T&D
calculated in this way is based on actual growth of future demand, and averaged over many
consumers. However, facilities associated with given generating sites or loads should be
specifically allocated to those uses rather than averaged out, e.g. transmission spur line, or
distribution line to a given customer.

14.3.3 Marginal energy costs and treatment of losses

The system lambda concept is useful to calculate marginal energy costs. The LRMC of peak-period energy will be the running costs of machines used last in the merit order, to supply the incremental peak kilowatt-hour (ΔD). In our model, this would be the fuel and operating costs of gas turbines, adjusted by relevant peak loss factors at each voltage level. Similarly, the LRMC of off-peak energy would be the running costs of least-efficient base-load or cycling plants used during this period. Exceptions occur when the marginal plant used during the rating period was not necessarily the least-efficient machine that could have been used. For example, less-efficient plants which have long start-up times, and are required in the next rating period, may be operated earlier in the loading order than more efficient plant. This would correspond to minimization of operating costs over several rating periods rather than on an hourly basis. Again, since the heat rate of the plants could vary with output level, the simple linear relationship usually assumed between generation costs and kilowatt-hours may need to be replaced by a more realistic non-linear model. Loss factors for adjusting off-peak costs will be smaller than those for the peak period when current flows are greatest (Munasinghe, 1979a).

The treatment of losses raises several important issues. While total normal technical losses vary from system to system, if these are much greater than about 15% of gross generation, then loss reduction should have a high priority. When engineering losses in excess of acceptable levels are routinely passed onto the customer, it acts as a disincentive to efficiency improvements. Losses due to theft and unpaid bills are also often loaded onto paying customers. Here again, the issue is whether these non-technical losses could be reduced by appropriate measures, or if incremental consumption always has an avoidable component of such losses associated with it. Theft in US systems is about 2% of gross generation, but norms in developing countries may have to be set higher (Munasinghe and Warford, 1982). LRMC analysis at generation, transmission and distribution levels helps establish whether marginal costs are large because of overinvestment, high losses, or both.

14.3.4 Consumer costs

It is difficult to allocate part of the distribution system investment costs to customer costs, on the basis of a skeleton system required to serve a hypothetical minimum load. Similarly, attempts have been made to fit past data with equations such as

$$(\text{distribution costs}) = a + b \cdot (\text{peak demand}) + c \cdot (\text{number of customers}).$$

Such regression analyses are also problematic because peak demand and number of customers are usually highly correlated. Therefore, general distribution network costs may be considered as capacity costs, while customer costs are defined as those which can be readily allocated to users. Initial customer costs include items such as service drop lines, meters and labour for installation. They may be charged to the user as a lump sum or distributed payments over time.

Recurrent customer costs that occur due to meter reading, billing, administrative and other expenses, could be imposed as a monthly flat charge, in addition to kilowatt and kilowatt-hour charges. Allocation of incremental (non-fuel operation, maintenance and administrative costs among the categories of capacity, energy and customer costs, varies from system to system, but these costs are usually small.

14.3.5 Analysis of hydroelectric generation

Several specific issues arise in the analysis of hydro systems, when seasonal variations in LRMC are important (Munasinghe 1990b; Turvey and Anderson, 1977). In an all-hydro system, the LRMC of generating capacity would be based on the cost of increasing peaking capability (i.e. additional turbines, penstocks, expansion of powerhouse, etc.), while incremental energy costs would be the costs of expanding reservoir storage. When there is spilling of water (e.g. wet season), incremental energy costs would be small (e.g. O&M costs only), and when demand does not press on capacity, incremental capacity costs may be ignored. However, if the system is likely to be energy-constrained, and all-incremental capacity is needed primarily to generate more energy because the energy shortage consistently precedes the capacity constraint, then the distinction between peak and off-peak costs, and between capacity and energy costs, tends to blur. In an extreme case, because hydro-energy consumed during any period (except when spilling) leads to a drawdown of the reservoir, it may be sufficient only to levy a simple kilowatt-hour charge at all times, e.g. by applying the AIC method to total system costs.

In a mixed hydrothermal system, a general guideline is that if hydro displaces thermal plant during a rating period, then the running cost of the latter is the relevant incremental energy cost. If pumped storage is used, the marginal energy costs or value of water used would be the cost of pumping net of losses. Also, if the pattern of operation is likely to change rapidly in the future (e.g. shift from gas turbines to peaking hydro as the marginal peaking plant, or vice versa), then the value of the LRMC would have to be calculated as a weighted average, with the weights depending on the share of future generation by the different types of plant used.

14.4 Adjusting efficient prices to meet other objectives

14.4.1 Deviations from strict LRMC

The strict LRMC calculation completes the first stage of tariff setting. In the second stage, a practical sustainable pricing structure that meets economic second-best, sociopolitical, financial, environmental and other constraints must be derived by modifying the strict LRMC. This adjustment process will result in deviations in both the magnitude and structure of strict LRMC. The tariff structure at this stage may be differentiated by the type of user or by income level. Practical considerations, such as the difficulties of metering and billing, will also affect the final tariff.

Constraints that cause the final tariffs to deviate from strict LRMC fall into two categories (Munasinghe and Warford, 1978). The first group of constraints include second-best considerations and subsidized (or lifeline) tariffs for low-income consumers, which may be analysed within an economic framework. The second group consists of all other issues, such as financial viability, sociopolitical constraints and environmental impacts, which cannot be monetized, as well as problems of metering and billing, where strict economic analysis is difficult to apply. These two groups of constraints may be linked, e.g. subsidized tariffs can have simultaneous economic welfare, financial and sociopolitical implications.

Second-best considerations

A 'second-best' departure from strict marginal cost pricing may be needed when prices elsewhere in the economy do not reflect marginal costs (especially for electricity substitutes and compliments). More generally, price distortions affecting inputs into the production of electric power and outputs of other sectors which are electricity intensive (e.g. aluminium) should also be considered. The former type of distortion may be dealt with by direct shadow pricing of inputs, as discussed earlier, but the latter case requires more detailed analysis of the market for the output. As an example of price distortion for an energy substitute, consider the subsidies for imported generators and/or diesel fuel, which exist in some countries. This may encourage private users to set up their own captive plant, even though it is not the least-cost way of meeting the demand (for the whole economy). The best solution may be for the government to revoke such subsidies or restrict imports of private generating plant. However, if transportation policy dictates the need to maintain subsidies for diesel fuel, or if strong pressure groups make such changes politically unfeasible, the low cost of (subsidized) private generation may require the setting of an optimal grid-supplied electricity price which is below strict LRMC. The extent of the deviation from strict LRMC is determined by the magnitude of the subsidy and substitutability of the alternative energy source (Munasinghe and Warford, 1982).

A related question concerns the availability of subsidized kerosene, which is aimed mainly at providing basic energy needs for low-income consumers at prices they can afford. The subsidy may also prevent low-income users (especially in developing countries) from shifting to use of non-commercial fuels for heat, e.g. wood, the overuse of which leads to deforestation and environmental harm. If we assume the kerosene subsidy as given, then the price of electricity must be reduced (to compete for lighting). Meanwhile, undesirable leakages may occur if cheap kerosene is not targeted to the poor, e.g. it is often mixed with more expensive petrol or diesel and used by wealthy car owners or industrialists.

14.4.2 Social considerations – subsidized prices and lifeline rates

In addition to the second-best economic arguments, sociopolitical or equity arguments are made in favour of 'lifeline' rates to meet basic energy needs, especially where costs of electricity use are high relative to income. The ability of power suppliers to act as discriminating monopolists permits systematic practical adjustments to make energy prices more sustainable, within the analytical framework described in the following.

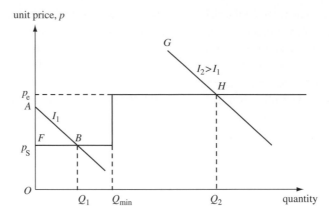

Figure 14.8. Basis for the social or lifeline tariff.

The subsidized 'social' block, or 'lifeline' rate, for low-income consumers has an important socioeconomic rationale, based on the equity argument. We clarify this point with the aid of Figure 14.8, which shows that respective demand curves AB and GH for low- (I_1) and average- (I_2) income domestic users, the social tariff p_S over the minimum consumption block O to Q_{min} and the marginal cost-based price level p_e. If the actual tariff $p = p_e$, then the average household will be consuming at the 'optimal' level Q_2, but the poor household will not be able to afford the service.

If increased benefits accruing to the poor have a high social weight or value, the consumer surplus portion ABF should be multiplied by the appropriate social weight (greater than unity) – see Appendix A, Section 14.6. Then, although point A lies below p_e (in market prices), the weighted distance OA may be more than the marginal supply cost. The increasing block tariff shown in Figure 14.8, consisting of the lifeline rate p_S, followed by the full tariff p_e, helps to capture this 'weighted' consumer surplus of the poor user. It does not affect the optimum consumption pattern of the average consumer, if we ignore the income effect due to reduced expenditure of the average consumer for the first block of consumption, i.e. up to Q_{min}. In practice, the magnitude Q_{min} should be based on acceptable criteria for identifying 'low-income' groups, and reasonable estimates of their minimum consumption levels (e.g. sufficient to supply basic requirements for lighting, heating, appliances).

In rich countries, where the average home uses around 1000 kWh/month, the minimum consumption level may be several hundred kWh/month, while in developing countries, where average electricity use is much lower, Q_{min} is typically around 50 kWh/month. For p_S, a simple model yields

$$p_S = \text{strict LRMC} \times (\text{poor person's income/critical income}),$$

where the critical income describes a nationally established poverty line (Munasinghe and Warford, 1978). The utility revenue constraints and the ability to pay of the poor consumer would also be considered in determining p_S and Q_{min}. This approach may be reinforced by an appropriate connections policy (e.g. subsidized house connections). The rights of poor and disadvantaged customers may also be protected through legislation, to protect against unfair termination of service.

14.4.3 Financial viability

The most common financial constraints relate to revenue requirements of the sector, and are embodied in criteria such as some target financial rate of return on assets, or an acceptable rate of contribution toward the future investment programme. In principle, for state-owned power utilities, the most efficient solution would be to set price equal to marginal cost and rely on government subsidies (or taxes) to meet the utility financial needs. In practice, some measure of financial autonomy and self-sufficiency is an important goal for the sector. Because of the premium that is placed on public funds, a pricing policy that fails to achieve minimum financial targets for continued operation of the power sector would rarely be acceptable. However, marginal cost pricing more typically results in financial surpluses well in excess of traditional revenue targets, which may lead to consumer resistance. Therefore, revenue changes have to be achieved by adjusting strict marginal-cost-based tariffs.

A widely used criterion of financial viability is an acceptable rate of return on assets – net operating income after taxes given as a fraction of net fixed assets in operation plus adequate working capital (in some cases). In the case of US private utilities, regulatory authorities have traditionally imposed a fair rate of return as an upper limit on earnings and, therefore, on average price per unit sold (Garfield and Lovejoy, 1964). Where utilities are government owned, as in many developing countries, the target rate of return is usually considered a minimum requirement to help resist sociopolitical pressures that tend to keep prices low. If the asset base is defined in revalued terms, then this requirement is more consistent with the forward looking approach of the LRMC. Another future-oriented financial criterion, useful for a rapidly expanding system, requires the utility to make a reasonable contribution to its future investment programme from its own revenues. This self-financing ratio is often expressed by the amount of internally generated funds available after operating costs and debt service, as a fraction of capital expenditures.

The application of the financial criteria may raise serious conceptual and practical problems. Thus, if a rate of return test is to be used, then the question of asset revaluation arises. The use of historical costs for working assets, typically original cost less depreciation, would tend to understate their value when capacity costs are rising rapidly. If assets are to be revalued, the costs of either (a) exactly reproducing the power system at today prices or (b) replacing it with an equivalent system at today prices might be used after netting out depreciation to allow for the loss of value due to obsolescence of existing equipment. Difficulties of interpretation will occur in the practical application of either approach.

Whichever combination of criteria are used, it is important to include the initial tariffs based on strict LRMC in the utility financial forecast. Then, these first-round tariffs may be adjusted through an iterative process until the chosen parameters of financial viability fall within the acceptable range. Although this process is usually quite ad hoc, some practical guidelines may be effectively used for reconciling strict LRMC and the revenue require-ment. The relative adjustments to strict LRMC between major consumer categories (such as residential and industrial), as well as among the different rating periods (such as peak and off-peak) within a given consumer category, will determine the share of the revenue burden to be borne by each user group in a given rating period.

A simple and equitable method of adjustment is to retain the relative structure of LRMC and vary the average rate level by equiproportional changes. In general, this procedure will not be economically efficient.

The 'inverse elasticity' pricing formula allocates the price burden among various con-sumer categories, so that greater divergence from the marginal opportunity-cost-based price occurs for consumer groups with the lowest price elasticity of demand, and vice versa. This will result in the smallest deviation from 'optimal' levels of use derived from strictly efficient prices (Baumol and Bradford, 1970). A simple version is given by

$$(1 - \text{LRMC}_1/p_1)/(1 - \text{LRMC}_2/p_2) = (1/e_1 + 1/e_{12})/(1/e_2 + 1/e_{21}),$$

where LRMC_i and p_i are the respective strict LRMC and price of good i; while $e_i = (\partial Q_i/\partial p_i)/(Q_i/p_i)$ and $e_{ij} = (\partial Q_i/\partial p_j)/(Q_i/p_j)$ are the own- and cross-price elasticities of demand (Q) with respect to price (p).

The two goods 1 and 2 may be interpreted as either the electricity consumption of two different consumer groups in the same rating period or the consumption of the same consumer groups in two distinct rating periods. In practice, a larger number of consumer types and rating periods must be considered, and application of the rule will be limited by lack of data on price elasticities. This technique may appear to penalize some customers more than others, thus violating the fairness objective.

Adjustments involving lump-sum payments and rebates or changes in user and connec-tion charges are also consistent with economic efficiency, if electricity usage is relatively unaffected by these procedures, i.e. use depends mainly on the variable charges. Another related approach that reduces revenues is to charge strict LRMC only for marginal use and reduce the price for initial consumption blocks. Such subsidies on customer charges, or on the initial block, also meet lifeline-rate needs for poor consumers, but tend to complicate the price structure.

In practice, an eclectic approach involving a combination of all these methods is most likely to be successful.

14.4.4 Environmental and other considerations

Energy conservation is an environment-related goal that is also used to deviate from strictly efficient prices, but it may run counter to subsidy arguments. One solution is to encourage energy efficiency in productive sectors (via higher prices) and target energy subsidies to meet the basic needs of the poor. In other cases, conservation and subsidized energy prices are consistent. For example, cheap kerosene in rural areas might reduce high fuelwood consumption and prevent deforestation and erosion.

The decision to electrify a remote rural area, which may also entail subsidized tariffs to poor homes, could be made on completely non-economic grounds, e.g. to maintain a viable regional industrial or agricultural base, stemming rural to urban migration, or alleviating local political discontent. However, the indirect economic benefits of such a policy may be greater that the direct efficiency costs of diverging from strict LRMC – especially in the developing world, where energy is costly relative to incomes and the administrative or fiscal machinery to redistribute incomes or achieve other development goals is ineffective.

In practice, price increases need to be gradual, in view of the costs which may be imposed on those who have already incurred expenditures on electrical equipment and made other decisions, while expecting little or no changes in traditional power-pricing policies. The efficiency costs of 'gradualism' can be seen as an implicit shadow value placed upon the social benefits that result from this policy. Another macroeconomic-type argument that power-price increases may be inflationary is rarely valid, since costs of electricity use are usually a small fraction of home expenses and of industrial production costs. Low electricity prices cause more serious issues by overstimulating demand and limiting supply investments.

Metering, billing and customer comprehension

Tariff structures must be simplified, due to practical problems and costs of metering and billing, and to make it comprehensible to users – who are expected to adjust their consumption according to the price signal. Thus, user classes, rating periods, voltage levels, etc, need to be limited.

Metering sophistication depends on the practical problems of installation and maintenance and on the net benefit of metering based on a CBA that compares the lower supply costs of reduced use with the cost of metering plus the decrease in net consumption benefits. Thus for very poor consumers paying a subsidized rate, a simple current-limiting device may suffice, because the cost of even simple kilowatt-hour metering may exceed its net benefit. In general, various forms of peak-load pricing (i.e. maximum demand or time-of-day metering) would be more applicable to large MV and HV industrial and commercial consumers (Munasinghe, 1990b). Most LV consumption, especially for households, is metered only on a kilowatt-hour basis, with the price per kilowatt-hour based on a combined energy and 'rolled in' capacity charge (e.g. using coincidence and load factors). More sophisticated meters (such as time-of-day meters with synchronous clocks) may be affected by power outages. At the other end of the scale, current-limiting devices are easier to tamper with.

The concept of homeostatic utility control is growing, using advanced solid-state technology (including use of microprocessors) to implement sophisticated metering, automatic meter reading, load management techniques and pricing structures (MIT, 1979). In contrast, some developing countries may lack technically skilled labour for installation and maintenance of sophisticated meters, or even reliable meter readers. Therefore, choice of appropriate metering is usually very country-specific, and is likely to involve many practical considerations.

Gas offers the potential to apply quite sophisticated pricing approaches, including different charges for various consumption blocks with conventional metering. However, for liquid fuels like kerosene, subsidized or discriminatory pricing would usually require schemes involving rationing and coupons, and could lead to leakage and abuses.

14.5 Sustainable pricing of water resources

The integrated framework for sustainable energy pricing set out above may be adapted *mutatis mutandis* to price water resources (Munasinghe, 1992b). Water supply systems (for irrigation, potable water, etc.) may be analysed in the same way as electric power systems. Below, we explain aspects of SPP specific to water resources; see also Chapter 12.

14.5.1 Joint-cost allocation

A typical multipurpose reservoir could yield benefits in terms of potable water, irrigation, hydropower, navigation, flood control, fishing, etc. While total project costs are most useful for the overall investment decision, the exact allocation of such joint costs are important for cost recovery and efficient pricing of water to various uses (Munasinghe, 1992b). Thus, if a dam provides urban water supply, the share of costs allocated to potable water will determine the price of water to consumers.

There is no theoretically rigorous method of allocating joint costs, to meet various requirements such as economic efficiency, social equity, etc. One approach may be to simulate how incremental project costs might vary for a small change in one output (e.g. providing more potable water by raising the dam height). However, this method may also change the outputs and benefits of other project goals (e.g. flood control). The allocation of such truly joint costs gives rise to major problems.

A more equitable method is the allocation of total costs to different uses in proportion to the benefits accruing to those uses. However, this approach is difficult to apply, especially when the benefit measurement is not consistent or accurate across different outputs and uses.

A related and more practical method is the separable costs and remaining benefits (SCRB) technique, which offers a good compromise between economic efficiency, social equity and ease of application – in the spirit of the sustainomics approach and sustainable resource pricing. This method is shown in Table 14.1 for the simple case of a dam with two typical purposes (hydropower and drinking water). The procedure can be generalized easily to cases involving more outputs or purposes. The first step identifies a set of single-purpose alternative schemes that will provide the same benefits as the multipurpose project. In our example, the two alternatives might be an equivalent thermal power plant and the pumping of the same volume of water from an underground aquifer, with cost adjustments for transport of the electricity and water, to the point of delivery. The costs of the single-purpose alternatives (2) are compared with the benefits corresponding to each purpose (3), and the smaller of these quantities (4) is selected. The procedure eliminates the risk of

Table 14.1 *Separable costs and remaining benefits (SCRB) technique for joint-cost allocation: a simple two-purpose example*

Item	Potable water	Hydropower	Total
	Project purpose		
(1) Total multipurpose project costs			i
(2) Alternative single-purpose project cost	a	b	
(3) Benefits of multipurpose projects	c	d	
(4) Smaller of item (2) or (3)	c	b	
(5) Separable costs	e	f	$(e+f)$
(6) Remaining benefits (item (4) – item (5))	$g=(c-e)$	$h=(b-f)$	$(g+h)$
(7) Remaining benefits fraction	$[g/(g+h)]$	$[h/(g+h)]$	1.0
(8) Residual joint cost (item (1) – item (5))			$k=[i-(e+f)]$
(9) Allocation of residual joint cost	$gk/(g+h)$	$hk/(g+h)$	$[i-(e+f)]$
(10) Total allocated cost (item (5)+ item (9))	$e+[gk/(g+h)]$	$f+[hk/(g+h)]$	i

having to rely on unrealistic and expensive alternative projects. Item (5) shows the separable costs, defined as those directly attributable to a specific purpose (e.g. transmission pipes that carry the potable water away from the dam), plus the portion of the joint costs (e.g. the dam) that is traceable to the inclusion of a specific purpose within the project. The remaining benefits (6) are defined as the difference between items (4) and (5). The residual joint costs (8) are the difference between the total project costs (1) and the separable costs (5). These residual joint costs are allocated to the different purposes (9) in direct proportion to the remaining benefits fraction (7). Finally, the sum of separable and allocated joint costs yields the total allocated costs (10).

The above process is unlikely to provide a rigorous apportionment of project costs. However, such allocated costs are usually only a small fraction of total costs of a given water supply system. Thus, inaccuracies in the joint-cost allocation exercise will not significantly affect the overall economic and financial analysis of the water system.

14.5.2 Environmental impacts

Environmental changes due to water-related activities can have considerable economic and social impacts (see Chapter 12). These effects need to be included in the long-term calculation of costs to give a realistic estimate of the true costs of supplying water. Those responsible for negative externalities should bear the burden of the costs passed on to others (see Chapter 3). Prices based on the LRMC provide a vehicle for implementing this concept. For example, if a new storage dam results in the flooding of land having ecological, recreational or agricultural value, then these costs should be reflected in the LRMC. Similarly, if water is extracted from an underground aquifer, externality costs might include damages to buildings or infrastructure due to land subsidence, depletion costs and groundwater pollution, which impose further costs on future users of water, e.g. due to saline water intrusion (see Section 12.4).

While some pollution and depletion costs may be difficult to quantify, they are already being passed on to consumers in many countries. Environmental costs are also included in the mitigation or preventive aspects of water-resource projects, and may constitute 5% of investment costs. Section 12.4 sets out a case study involving groundwater depletion.

14.5.3 *Marginal costs of water supply and prices*

Based on the framework of Sections 14.1 to 14.3, the total cost of using a water resource is the sum of three components: (1) the conventional cost of extraction, treatment, storage, bulk transmission, distribution and disposal; (2) the depletion cost due to higher expenses borne by future users of the same source; and (3) the additional cost due to environmental harm, or cost of mitigating such impacts. There may be overlap among these categories, depending on their interpretation.

Next, we estimate the LRMC of water using the AIC method (see Section 14.3). In a water system, water is produced at the headworks, and then conveyed to users via pipelines or channels. For example, in the case of piped water systems, water is transported through trunk mains, to primary and secondary distribution systems, and finally to the consumer.

First, without differentiating between peak and off-peak periods, we define the AIC (i.e. the LRMC) of water produced at the headworks as follows:

$$
AIC_{HP} = \frac{\displaystyle\sum_{t=0}^{T}(I_{Ht} + R_{Ht})/(1+r)^t}{\displaystyle\sum_{t=L}^{T+L}Q_{Ht}/(1+r)^t},
$$

where, I_{Ht}, R_{Ht} and Q_{Ht} are the respective investment, incremental operating and maintenance (O&M) cost and incremental water produced at the headworks in year t and r is the discount rate (e.g. opportunity cost of capital). AIC is the unit cost, which equates the present discounted value of water output to supply costs, and it is the monetary value of Q that is effectively discounted rather than the physical quantity.

The AIC of water delivered from the headworks to the trunk mains is given by

$$
AIC_{HS} = \frac{AIC_{HP}}{1 - LF_H},
$$

where $LF_H = L_H/Q_1$ is the fraction of water lost at the headworks.

The AIC of the trunk main system is given by

$$
AIC_M = \frac{\displaystyle\sum_{t=0}^{T}(I_{Mt} + R_{Mt})/(1+r)^t}{\displaystyle\sum_{t=L}^{T+L}Q_{Mt}/(1+r)^t},
$$

Table 14.2 *Average incremental costs of existing and future water-supply projects for some developing countries; 1988 prices*

Country: city	Present project	AIC (US $/m³)	Future project	AIC (US $/m³)
Algeria: Algiers	groundwater	0.23	surface water (raw)	0.5
Bangladesh: Dhaka	groundwater	0.08	surface water	0.3
China: Shenyang	groundwater	0.04	surface water	0.11
China: Yingkuo	groundwater	0.07	reservoir intakes	0.3
India: Hyderabad	reservoir (phase 2)	0.17	reservoir (phase 3)	0.62
India: Bangalore	pumped (river)	0.1	pumped (river)	0.22
Jordan: Amman	groundwater	0.41	surface – piped	1.33
Mexico: Mexico City	groundwater	0.54	pumped (river)	0.82
Peru: Lima	surface	0.25	interbasin transfer	0.54

Source: Munasinghe (1992b).

where I_{Mt} and R_{Mt} are the respective investment and incremental operating and maintenance (O&M) costs in the trunk mains system and Q_{Mt} is the incremental water flowing through the trunk mains system in year t.

Finally, the AIC of water delivered out of the trunk main system is given by

$$AIC_{MS} = \frac{AIC_{HS} + AIC_M}{1 - LF_M},$$

where $LF_M = L_M/Q_1$ is the fraction of water lost in the trunk main system.

Corresponding expressions may be derived for the AIC of water delivery at all successive levels – i.e. primary and secondary distribution.

Accurate estimation of the AIC for water is important for decision making, because the costs of supplying water are rising, while prices have failed to keep up. Between 1966 and 1981, the AIC of water (at 1988 prices) per cubic metre of water was US $0.49, whereas the average water tariff was US $0.26. Since unaccounted for water (or losses) are around 35% for all the projects, the effective price per cubic metre produced was US $0.17 or only one-third of the AIC. During the period 1987–1990, the AIC was US $0.55 (1988 prices), while the average price was US $0.32 per cubic metre, not including unaccounted for water (Munasinghe, 1992b). The AIC is not only greater than tariffs, but also rising due to more difficult water supply conditions in many developing countries (Table 14.2). Often, the AIC of urban water supplies are commonly two to three times greater than the cost of existing water-supply schemes (Munasinghe, 1992b).

14.5.4 Sewerage charges and pollution externalities

Wastewater costs are generated by higher levels of water supplied to growing populations. Such costs vary widely, and are borne by consumers themselves or by the wider community or public authority. They must be included in the water tariff or charged separately – e.g. a sewer fee based on water use. Costs may be incurred for sanitation and treatment facilities, or as environmental costs due to wastewater impacts, such as drinking-water pollution, reservoir eutrophication, loss of work though illness, or reduced property values. Generally, as service levels increase, unit costs of handling wastewater decrease – as long as environmental impacts are limited to their community of origin. However, as environmental impacts of higher service levels extend beyond community boundaries (due to sewerage outflow), unit costs of collection and treatment may rise exponentially with water use.

The foregoing underlines the importance of integrating the incremental costs of sanitation into pricing policy. Effective sanitation is always more costly than the water supply from which it is generated. At a low service level (20 litres per capita per day (lcd) – handpump and pit-latrine), the ratio is around 1.3 to 1 and is often absorbed by the users as a self-help input or through cost-recovery. As the service level rises to 700 lcd, this ratio becomes 15 to 1.

To prevent environmental externalities, the cost of sanitation services should be factored into water-supply tariffs. The AIC of dealing with wastewater can be calculated based on the cost of conducting sewerage from the consumer, through the collection system to the treatment plant, and back into water courses. The basic AIC at each level of the sewerage system must be adjusted, because leakages of outside effluents into the sewerage collection network actually increases the flow volume. The AIC of sewerage and water supply are added to obtain a combined charge.

Two issues arise. First, for the combined water and sewerage charge, it is conceptually difficult to separate the benefit derived by users from each service, or to measure their willingness-to-pay for water and sewerage separately, since they do not usually consider them to be two distinct decisions. This issue is more important for investment analysis than for pricing policy. Consumers use water to the point where benefits per marginal unit of water used equal costs of supply and disposal.

Second, the external aesthetic and health benefits enjoyed by the community at large, due to sewerage services, are obvious. There are also indirect external health benefits to the community due to water supply. While users should pay the marginal cost of sewerage disposal wherever possible, there is therefore an economic case for offering a sewerage subsidy to poor consumers who cannot afford to pay for such services. Further, the 'polluter pays' principle requires that costs arising from pollution of surface or groundwater resources by wastewater or sewerage sludge should be included in the sewerage charges (see Section 12.4).

14.6 Appendix A: Optimal energy pricing

14.6.1 *Socially optimal prices*

We derive a general expression for the socially optimal price of a given energy type A (based on shadow prices) and apply it to three cases: (a) perfectly competitive economy (classic result); (b) efficient prices, including economic second-best and environmental considerations; and (c) social subsidized prices or lifeline rates for poor consumers.

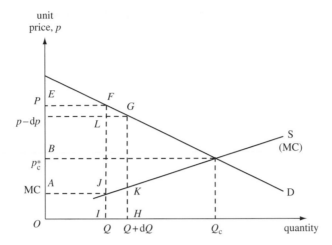

Figure 14.9. Supply and demand in energy sub-sector A.

Figure 14.9 shows the supply and demand for energy type A, where S is the supply curve or marginal cost of supply (MC) in domestic market prices and D is the demand curve for a specific user. We define a_p as the energy conversion factor (ACF), which transforms MC into the corresponding real economic resource cost; i.e. with correct shadow pricing, the marginal opportunity cost is $MOC = (a_p \cdot MC)$. Next, we assign a social weight W_c to each marginal unit of use (valued in market prices) for a given individual. Typically, the poorer the user, the higher will be the social weight, to reflect social emphasis on poverty alleviation. Third, if the individual's consumption of goods and services other than energy type A (valued in market prices) rises by one unit, then the shadow-priced marginal cost of economic resources used (or shadow cost) is given by b_c.

Starting from the initial price and consumption (p, Q), consider the welfare impact of a small price reduction (dp) and the resultant increase in demand (dQ). Consumer spending on energy falls by $(p\ dQ)$ (i.e. area *IFGH*), but income rises by the amount $pQ - (p - dp) \cdot (Q + dQ)$. If none of the latter is saved, this person's consumption of other goods and services will increase by $(Q\ dp - p\ dQ)$, also valued in market prices (i.e. area *BEFG* minus area *IFGH*). Therefore, total consumption (energy A plus other goods) will increase by the net amount $(Q\ dp)$ in market prices. This is the increase in consumer surplus, whose shadow value is $W_c(Q\ dp)$.

Next, consider the resource cost of these changes. The shadow cost of increasing the supply of energy type is given by $(a_p \cdot MC\ dQ)$, i.e. a_p times area *IJKH*, while the resources used up to provide all other goods consumed is $b_c(Q\ dp - p\ dQ)$. Finally, we ignore the income change of the energy producer by assuming that it is the government.

The total increase in net social benefit of the energy price change is given by

$$d(NB) = W_c(p\ dQ) - a_p(MC\ dQ) + (W_c - b_c)(Q\ dp - p\ dQ).$$

Thus, $d(NB)/dp = Q[(W_c - b_c) + nb_c - na_p(MC/p)]$, where $n = (p\ dQ)/(Q\ dp)$ is the elasticity of demand (magnitude).

The first-order condition for maximizing the net social benefits is given by $d(NB)/dp = 0$. This yields the optimal price level:

$$p^* = a_p \cdot MC/[b_c + (W_c - b_c)/n]. \tag{14.1}$$

Case 1

Perfect competition; market prices and shadow prices are equal; income transfer effects are ignored (no social weighting).

In this case, $a_p = W_c = b_c = 1$, and equation (14.1) reduces to: $p^* = MC$.

This is the basic marginal cost pricing result. Net benefits are maximum, with price equal to marginal cost at the market clearing point (p_c, Q_c).

Case 2

Income transfer effects ignored because the marginal social benefit is equal to the marginal cost of consumption. In this case, $W_c = b_c$, and equation (14.1) becomes

$$p_e^* = (a_p \cdot MC)/b_c = MOC/b_c. \tag{14.2}$$

The optimal price p_e^* ensures efficient allocation of resources, but neglects income distributional considerations. The MOC may be evaluated directly (e.g. border price for a tradable fuel or, for a non-tradable like electricity, by applying shadow prices to the least cost mix of inputs used in production). However, the parameter b_c depends crucially on the user. For average consumers, b_c is the consumption conversion factor (CCF), based on the resource cost or shadow value of one (market-priced) unit of the household marginal consumption basket. If CCF < 1, then p_e^* > MOC. If user consumption patterns are not known, b_c could be defined broadly as the standard conversion factor (SCF) – for all energy users.

Equation (14.2) may be used to correct the economic second-best consideration arising from energy substitution possibilities. Suppose all expenses now spent on energy type A are used to purchase alternative energy type B, which is subsidized (e.g. electricity replaced by kerosene for lighting). In this case, b_c is the ratio of the MOC of energy type B to its market price, $b_c = MOC_{ae}/p_{ae}$.

Thus, $p_e^* = MOC(p_{ae}/MOC_{ae})$. Since the alternative energy B is priced below its border marginal cost ($b_c > 1$), $p_e^* <$ MOC also. Therefore, the subsidy on substitute energy B prices will yield an optimal price for energy A that is below its shadow cost.

Case 3: General subsidized price

Equation (14.1) is the optimal energy A price including equity concerns.

Consider a group of very poor consumers for whom we may assume that $W_c \gg b_c(n-1)$. Then, equation (14.1) may be written as $p_s \approx n \cdot MOC/W_c$. We may simplify further by assuming that $n = 1$. Thus, $p_s = MOC/W_c$.

Suppose that the net income or consumption of these poor consumers (c) is one-third the critical income or consumption level ($\bar{c}$) – e.g. a poverty line. Then a simple expression for the social weight is $W_c = \bar{c}/c = 3$. Therefore, $p_s = MOC/3$, which is the 'lifeline' rate, or subsidized tariff, appropriate to this group of low-income consumers.

14.6.2 Dynamic version of marginal cost pricing rule

We show that setting price equal to marginal cost over a period of time will maximize the net social benefits of energy use (Munasinghe, 1981). The model also yields the peak/off-peak two-part pricing structure.

We seek a set of price (and output) levels over a given period of time that will maximize the present value of net benefits or welfare given by the area under the demand curve minus the area under the supply curve. The net benefits of consumption at any given time t are represented by the following expression:

$$\text{NB} = \int_0^Q p(q, t)\mathrm{d}q - c(q, Kt) - i(t),$$

where p is consumer willingness-to-pay or the price curve, q is the energy output per unit time, c is the energy production cost function, K is capital stock or available capacity and i is the investment rate.

The welfare maximum is derived from the optimal control problem:

$$\text{Max} \int_0^T \text{NB} \exp(-rt)\mathrm{d}t$$

subject to

$$K(t) \geq q(t) \geq 0; \qquad I(t) \geq i(t) \geq 0; \qquad i(t) = K(t) + \delta K(t),$$

where r is the discount rate, I is the upper limit on investment rate, δ is the rate of capital depreciation and T is the time horizon.

We define the Hamiltonian:

$$H = \text{NB} + \lambda(i - \delta K)$$

and the corresponding Lagrangian function

$$L = H + m_1(K - q) + m_2 q + m_3(I - i) + m_4 i.$$

By Pontryagin's maximum principle, the solution to the optimal control problem must also maximize the Lagrangian function at each instant of time over the time horizon under consideration, thus giving rise to the following set of conditions (Takayama, 1985):

$$(\partial L/\partial q) = 0; (\partial L/\partial i) = 0; \qquad (\partial \lambda/\partial t) = r - (\partial L/\partial K).$$

The first condition yields the optimal price:

$$p^*(t) = (\partial c/\partial q) - m_1 + m_2.$$

We may interpret the above using the following complementary conditions:

$$m_1(K - q) = 0; \qquad m_2 q = 0; \qquad m_1 \geq 0, \ m_2 \geq 0.$$

Case 1: Peak period, capacity constrained, $K(t) = q(t) > 0$.

In this case, $m_2 = 0$ and $p^*_1 = (\partial c/\partial q) + m_1$.

During the peak period, the optimal price is the marginal operating cost $\partial c/\partial q$ (with capacity fixed) plus the marginal cost of new capacity (m_1).

Case 2: Off-peak period, no capacity constraint, $K(t) > q(t) > 0$

In this case, $m_1 = m_2 = 0$ and $p^*_2 = (\partial c/\partial q)$ – only the MOCs enter into the optimal price.

These basic marginal cost pricing conditions hold for a dynamic price path over a given time period, just like in the static case (see Section 14.1.3).

14.6.3 Allocating capacity and energy cost to peak and off-peak users

We show how an LRMC analysis based on the optimal system expansion plan yields the following idealized conclusions:

(1) peak users should pay the peak LRMC of capacity as well as energy;
(2) off-peak users should pay only the off-peak LRMC of energy; and
(3) LRMC of peak capacity = LRMC of base load capacity − net fuel savings due to this baseload plant.

Figure 14.10 shows the annual LDC for an all-thermal generation system with only two types of plant, whose linearized cost characteristics are given in the Table 14.3. A more realistic generalized system model would have to consider a number of complicating factors, such as a larger number of rating periods and plant types, non-coincidence of the rating

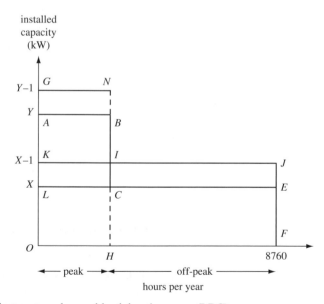

Figure 14.10. Plant costs and annual load duration curve (LDC).

Table 14.3 *Types of generation plant and costs*

Plant type	Capacity cost per kW installed (annuitized)	Operating costs per hour
(1) Peaking (e.g. gas turbines, GTs)	a	e
(2) Baseload (e.g. steam)	b	f

periods with the economic crossover points between different plant types, economies of scale and variable heat rates for various plants, hydroelectric plant, losses, reserve margins, stochasticity of supply and demand, etc. The key difference in this general case is that a small fraction of capacity costs could be allocated to consumers outside the peak period.

As per Table 14.3, the total costs of 1 kW used over h hours per year are given by (1) $a + eh$ for gas turbines (GTs) and (2) $b + fh$ for baseload plant. Let H be the number of hours of operation which denote the crossover point for which GT and baseload plant total costs are equal. Then, $a + eH = b + fH$, which yields $H = (b - a)/(e - f)$.

The most economic use of plant can be determined by examining the LDC, Figure 14.10, *OABCEF*. For planned base load operation (i.e. more than H hours per year), X kW of base load plant are used; and for planned peak operation (i.e. fewer than H hours per year), $(Y - X)$ kW of GTs are used. The total annual costs of meeting demand is are given by

$$C_0 = X(b + fT) + (Y - X)(a + eH).$$

Case 1: Only peak-period demand increases by 1 kW (area *AGNB*)

The optimal system planning response is to increase GT by 1 kW. Total annual costs are given by

$$C_1 = X(b + fT) + (Y + 1 - X)(a + eH),$$

and the cost rises by $C_1 - C_0 = a + eH$. Since this cost increase is caused by the 1 kW rise in incremental demand in the peak period, peak users must pay this cost: capacity charge $= a/$ kw/yr and energy charge $= ek$Wh. The peak-period users' payment $= a + eH =$ increase in system costs.

Case 2: Only off-peak demand increases by 1 kW (area *CIJE*).

The optimal system planning response is to add 1 kW more of baseload plant. But now there is 1 kW less of GT required than before. The total annual costs are given by

$$C_2 = (X + 1)(b + fT) + \{Y - (X + 1)\}(a + eH).$$

Then the increase in cost is given by

$$C_2 - C_0 = (b + fT) - (a + eH) = (b - a) + (f - e)H + f(T - H).$$

Substituting for H yields

$$C_2 - C_0 = (b - a) + (f - e)(b - a)/(e - f) + f(T - H) = f(T - H).$$

Thus, the increase in system cost incurred due to the 1 kW increase in marginal off-peak demand equals the energy cost of operating the baseload plant during this period. Therefore, off-peak users must pay only this energy charge, f/kWh. No capacity costs are charged to off-peak users, since their payment $f(T - H)$ exactly equals the increased system cost. We note that the baseload capacity cost, b, is exactly offset by the total cost saving due to GT, which is no longer required (i.e. capacity cost a plus net fuel cost saving $(e - f)H$ inside area *LKIC*) in Figure 14.10. In other words,

$$\text{peak capacity cost} = \text{baseload capacity cost} - \text{net fuel savings}$$

or

$$a = b - (e - f)H.$$

Case 3: Both peak and off-peak demand increase by 1 kW

This case is a linear combination of Cases 1 and 2. User charges are given by

$$\text{peak capacity charge} = a/\text{kW/yr},$$

$$\text{peak energy charge} = e/\text{kWh},$$

$$\text{off-peak energy charge} = f/\text{kWh}.$$

Again

$$\text{total payment by all users} = b + fT = \text{rise in system cost.}$$

These results may be generalized to include more plant types and rating periods.

14.7 Appendix B: Demand analysis and forecasting

14.7.1 Introduction

Using electricity as an example, we examine the key reasons for making accurate demand projections. First, the timely and reliable anticipation of energy needs is vital for the whole economy. Second, the expansion of power systems requires many years to plan and implement. Third, system investments are very capital-intensive. If forecasts are too low, shortages may retard development, while the costs of shortages to users are many times the costs of producing the unsupplied energy. However, if forecasts are too high, large amounts of capital with high opportunity costs might be uselessly tied up for long periods. Such costly errors may be avoided by undertaking relatively inexpensive demand studies.

The commonly used unit of energy in power system studies is the kilowatt-hour (kWh). The rate of energy per unit time is called power (or capacity), and is measured in kilowatts (kW). Therefore, energy in kilowatt-hours is the product of power in kilowatts and time in hours. The load factor (LF) is the ratio of average to maximum (or peak) kilowatts over a given interval of time. It is important because the size (and cost) of power-system components are determined mainly by their capability to handle peak power flows. Since practically all customers require their maximum kilowatts only during a short peak period during the day, the LF is also a measure of the intensity of capacity use. A load forecast may be made either in terms of the peak power, or the total energy consumed during a given period (e.g. one year). In general, the kilowatt peaks of different customers will not occur simultaneously. The diversity factor for a group of consumers is a measure of the divergence of spreading over time of the individual peak loads, and permits the computation of the combined peak load for the group in terms of the disaggregate peak values.

The total kilowatts and kilowatt-hours generated at the source will be greater than the corresponding values consumed because of system losses. Generation losses are mainly for station use, i.e. for driving auxiliary equipment at power plants. Transmission and distribution network losses are resistive losses, including transformer losses. Theft is another type of loss.

Load forecasts are made for various time periods. Very short-term demand projections are made on a daily or weekly basis to optimize system operation or schedule hydro units. Short-run forecasts ranging between one and three years are used in hydro reservoir management, distribution system planning, etc. The time horizon for medium-term demand projections is about four to eight years, which is sufficient to plan for major transmission and generation projects. Long-range demand projections (usually several decades) are most important in long-run system expansion planning, and are relevant for the sustainomics framework.

Several methods are used for this purpose, including time trend analysis, econometric multiple-correlation techniques and field surveys.

14.7.2 Time trend analysis and extrapolation

Trend analysis is a commonly used approach when relevant historical data on electricity use are available. Past growth trends are extrapolated, assuming that there will be little change in the growth pattern of the determinants of demand such as incomes, prices, consumer tastes, etc. These trends are usually estimated by a least-squares fit of past consumption data against time or by some similar statistical methodology. Depending on the availability of data, they may be estimated either on a global basis for a given area or broken down by user sector (e.g. domestic, industrial, etc.). Ad hoc adjustments may be made to account for known major changes in future demands. For example, the expected demands of large new industrial plants may be identified. This combination of overall trend projection, together with survey-research type-specific adjustments, is frequently used.

The advantages of this approach are its simplicity and modest demands on data and analytical skills. Forecasts use available data. The disadvantage is that no attempt is made to explain why certain usage trends were established in the past. The underlying assumption is that the factors that drove consumption changes in the past will continue unchanged in the future. This is a rather limiting assumption, especially in a world in which relative energy prices are changing rapidly.

14.7.3 Econometric multiple regression

Econometric forecasting methods are more sophisticated, and potentially more accurate. Past electricity demand is first correlated with other variables, such as prices and incomes, and then future demands are related to the predicted growth of these other variables. However, these methods are frequently nothing more than a special form of trend analysis if the projections of the determinants are themselves based on historical trends. Furthermore, it is often difficult to obtain the required time series needed to produce statistically significant results. Data series are often short, incomplete and subject to changes in definition over time. Besides which, statistical significance requires long time-series data, during which the underlying structure of the economy may have changed. Hence, the results may not be accurate, even though they are statistically significant.

A key advantage of econometric studies is that they can take a number of important, demand-determining variables, such as price and income, explicitly into account. A specific type of forecasting approach called 'end-use analysis' is used, especially for household consumption, based on the numbers and types of electricity-using devices.

Residential demand models are usually based on consumer theory in economics (Nicholson, 1978). The direct utility function of a consumer, which indicates the intrinsic value derived from consumption of various goods, may be written as follows

$$U = U(Q_1, Q_2, ..., Q_n; Z),$$

where Q_i represents the level of consumption of good i in a given time period (e.g. one year) and Z is a vector representing consumer tastes and other factors. The budget constraint is given by

$$I \geq \sum_{i=1}^{n} p_i Q_i;$$

$p_1, p_2, ..., p_n$ are the prices of these n goods (including electricity) and I is the consumer income. Maximizing consumer utility U subject to the budget constraint yields the set of Marshallian demand functions for each of the goods consumed by the household:

$$Q_i = Q_i(P_1, P_2, ..., P_n; I; Z) \text{ for } i = 1, ..., n.$$

For electricity, the above demand function may be simplified:

$$Q_e = Q_e(p_e, p_k, p; I; Z),$$

where subscript e denotes electricity, subscript k indicates the substitute form of energy kerosene (e.g. for lighting) and p is an average price index representing all other goods.

If demand is homogenous of degree 1 in the money variables (i.e. prices and income), we may write

$$Q_e = Q_e(p_e/p, p_k/p; I/p; Z).$$

Thus, starting from consumer preference theory, we may derive a demand function for electricity that depends on its own price, the prices of substitutes and income, all in real terms. The effects of other factors (Z) may also be explicitly considered. Effects of supply quality on demand are discussed in Munasinghe (1990b) for electricity, Munasinghe (1992b) for water and Munasinghe and Corbo (1978) for telecommunications.

The final specification of such an expression could vary widely (Munasinghe, 1992b; Pindyck, 1979; Taylor, 1976). For example, Q_e could be household consumption or per capita consumption; the demand function could be linear, or linear in the logarithms of the variables, or in the transcendental logarithmic form, and could include lagged variables; and Z could include supply side-constraints such as access to supply and so on.

Analogously, the industrial demand for energy may be derived from production function theory in economics. For example, consider the annual output of a particular firm of industry:

$$X = F(K, L, M, Q_1, ..., Q_n; S),$$

where K, L and M are inputs of capital, labour and other non-energy materials, respectively; Q_i is the input of energy type i; and S is a set of parameters representing other factors, such as technology changes, etc.

To avoid the problem of different types of capita, labour, etc., it is necessary to assume weak separability of the inputs K, L, M and $E_i = (Q_1, Q_2, ..., Q_n)$, so that each may be represented as an aggregate, with a distinct, composite price index, i.e. p_K, p_L and p_M. Further, in order to determine the minimum-cost mix of capital, labour, materials and energy, we assume that individual energy inputs like oil and electricity are subject to homotheticity. First, the mix of fuels that make up the energy input are optimized, and, in a second step, the optimal amounts of capital, labour, other material inputs and energy are chosen.

Production theory seeks to minimize costs of producing some quantity of output X, given exogenous prices of inputs (Shepard, 1953). As in the household case, the solution yields an electricity demand function, normalized with respect to non-energy input prices (P_K) as numeraire:

$$Q_e = Q_e(p_1/p_K, p_M/p_K, p_L/p_K, ..., p_n/p_K; X/p_K; S).$$

Thus, the demand for electricity at time t is a function of its own price, the prices of energy substitutes and non-energy inputs, output level and other factors S. Many different variables and specifications may be chosen.

Similar demand functions could be developed for other end-use sectors (like agriculture and commerce), estimated with econometric techniques, and used to make future demand forecasts.

There are several problems with this approach. First, the mechanistic extrapolation of econometric equations into the future often fails to capture structural shifts in demand. Second, it is difficult to separate out short- and long-run effects. Third, data may be unavailable, especially in developing countries. Fourth, estimation procedures that focus on energy prices as demand determinants may not adequately account for the costs, availability, life expectancies and replaceability of energy-using equipment. Fifth, time-series energy prices could be erratic. Sixth, energy may rationed physically (rather than through price), and service quality could vary. Finally, demand elasticities might change significantly over time.

14.7.4 Field surveys

Given the limitations of the other forecasting methodologies, surveys potentially provide a direct and reliable tool of demand analysis and forecasting. In essence, surveys consist of a list of more or less sophisticated questions that are put to existing and potential electricity users in order to measure and record their present consumption and future consumption plants. Energy surveys could also be usefully combined with other types of survey, such as general population censuses, income studies, etc.

Major problems with surveys are: (a) large time requirement; (b) high cost; (c) need for skilled interviewers; (d) user inability or unwillingness to provide the requested information; (e) user deliberately or unwittingly giving inaccurate answers; (f) future energy use plans may be vague.

14.7.5 Practical application

In summary, there is no single universally superior approach to load forecasting. More sophisticated techniques might obscure weak data and methodological assumptions. Thus, simpler methods may be more useful when information is unreliable. Often, the sum of many disaggregate demand forecasts may be compared to an independently made global forecast for the same area. Survey approaches are most effective to forecast the demand of large users. The determinants of demand for diverse users have to be carefully selected because they vary. The level of disaggregation will depend both on the data and the ultimate purpose of the projection. Demand forecasting is dynamic, and requires frequent iteration in light of better data and techniques of analysis. Building a reliable data bank is invaluable in this process of constant revision.

An experienced forecaster will be able to make appropriate adjustments, based on judgement, about constraints and complicating factors that cannot be incorporated mechanistically into a numerical forecasting. Load promotion, consumer education and the attitudes of community leaders can also significantly affect demand growth.

The demand forecast for a given consumer group will depend on the number of connections the average electricity use per connection and user characteristics. Thus, the evolution of each of these variables needs to be analysed. Connection policy is another key factor. If income levels are low, high connection charges could act as a significant barrier and negate the favourable effects of low electricity prices. Finally, a distinction should be made between the underlying or potential demand and the consumption level that is actually achievable. Practical limitations may prevent the realization of overambitious demand forecasts. Institutional constraints that suppress demand, such as power cuts or non-connection of consumers and the presence of captive generation, will create a gap between the potential and achievable (or realistic) demand.

Part V
Project and local applications

15

Project applications[1]

Applications of the sustainomics approach at the project level are illustrated in this chapter. In Sections 15.1 and 15.2, the sustainable energy development framework applied at the sector level (Chapter 10) is extended and used to evaluate small hydroelectric power projects in Sri Lanka. Multicriteria analysis is used to assess social, economic and environmental indicators. Section 15.3 highlights the use of different policy tools (including the interplay of shadow and market prices) – to influence human behaviour relating to new and renewable energy use in a typical developing country. Practical investment and pricing policies are formulated to make energy development decisions more sustainable, in the case of solar photovoltaic energy projects for agricultural pumping. In Section 15.4, rural electrification projects in Sri Lanka are analysed, focusing on new and renewable energy technologies. Rural energy priorities (solar homes and village hydro) in Sri Lanka are compared with renewable energy projects in the Philippines and Vietnam. Section 15.5 presents a case study involving the analysis of a project that supplies water to a poor African village, by drilling wells and boreholes. The focus is on quantitative economic cost–benefit analysis, using both border and domestic shadow prices to determine water-investment decisions and pricing policy.

15.1 Small hydro-projects and sustainable energy development in Sri Lanka

Energy is a key resource which affects the economic, environmental and social dimensions of sustainable development (see Chapter 10). Further, hydroelectricity is a key renewable source of energy that contributes toward sustainable energy development (UNEP, 2000). Accordingly, this case study illustrates the application of sustainomics principles (e.g. using multicriteria analysis) to assess the economic, social and environmental impacts of hydro-power projects in Sri Lanka.

The case study is presented in three parts. Section 15.1.1 describes the power sector in Sri Lanka and the transition from a predominately hydro to a mixed hydrothermal system.

---

[1] The valuable contributions of R. Morimoto and P. Meier to this chapter are gratefully acknowledged. Some parts of the chapter are based on material adapted from Morimoto and Munasinghe (2005), Munasinghe (1977, 1983) and Munasinghe and Meier (2003b).

Section 15.1.2 sets out the methodology. The results are analysed in Section 15.2, and are followed by some key conclusions.

15.1.1 Brief review of the Sri Lanka power sector

Growth rates of GDP and electricity demand in Sri Lanka are well correlated – see Figure 15.1 (CEB, 1999, 2003). The Pearson correlation is 72% (1% significance level). Electricity use fell sharply in 1996 and 2001, due to serious droughts and hydro shortages, which also lowered GDP growth (−1.5% in 2001).

The demand for electricity in Sri Lanka is increasing very rapidly. In 2003, the maximum electricity demand was 1422 MW, and this is expected to double every ten years (CEB, 2003). Currently, Sri Lanka depends largely on hydropower for power generation (Figure 15.2). In 1998, over 60% of energy demand (3351 GWh) was met by hydropower, about 30% (1599 GWh) by thermal power, and less than 5% (159 GWh) through self-generation (CEB, 1999). However, hydrogeneration share has fallen since then. In 2002, hydropower met only about 39% of the demand, whereas the thermal share had increased to 60%, while self-generation had declined to 1%. By 2003, over 1200 MW of major hydro had been developed, to provide about 3858 GWh of energy in an average year (CEB, 2003). The CEB will install a 300 MW coal plant by 2011, as well as more oil-fired plant. Thus, Sri Lanka is now in a transitional period, moving from a predominantly hydropower system to a mixed hydrothermal power system, using imported oil and coal.

In 2003, the electrification rate in Sri Lanka was 66%, and the majority of the rural population did not have access to electricity (Department of Census and Statistics, 2003). The target electrification rate of the government for 2006 was 77% (CEB, 2003). About 400 000 homes without access to electricity use automobile batteries to power lamps, radios and TVs. Others use kerosene for lighting and firewood for cooking.

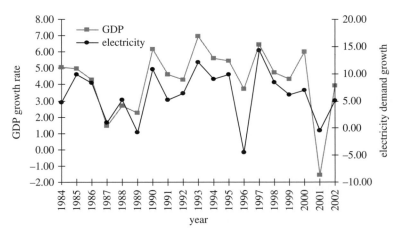

Figure 15.1. GDP and electricity demand growth rates in Sri Lanka. Source: Central Bank (1998, 2003), CEB (1999, 2003).

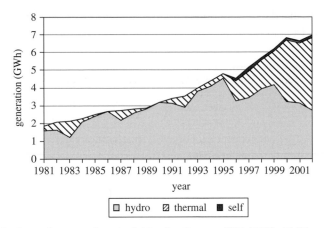

Figure 15.2. Hydrothermal energy share in Sri Lanka. Source: CEB (1999, 2003).

Renewable energy sources will provide only a fraction of Sri Lanka's power needs in the coming years. However, mini-hydro, solar, wind and biomass (including dendro-thermal) are drawing more attention, since they could play a key role in sustainable energy development (see Section 15.7).

15.1.2 Methodology

Multicriteria analysis (MCA) is used in order to examine the impacts of hydroelectric projects and make development more sustainable in this study. MCA is a powerful tool to quantify and display the trade-offs that must be made between conflicting objectives that are difficult to compare directly (see Section 3.5). The MCA approach provides decision makers with useful additional information to supplement the economic data from cost–benefit analysis (CBA). Three main sustainable development issues considered comprise the economic costs of power generation, ecological costs of biodiversity loss and social costs of resettlement.

The main objective is to generate additional kilowatt-hours of electricity to meet the growing power demand in Sri Lanka. We compare the sustainable development impacts of power projects on the basis of the economic, social and environmental costs of generating one unit of electricity from various hydro sites, assuming that the same benefit from each additional kilowatt-hour. With MCA, social and environmental impacts are measured in non-economic units, instead of monetarily valuing and incorporating them within the single-valued CBA framework.

Economic indicator – power-generation costs

The usual economic indicator in project evaluation is the maximization of net present value (NPV). However, in this study, minimizing average generation costs per unit of generation will be used as the main economic comparator instead of NPV – assuming that the total benefit per unit generated is the same for all projects under comparison (see Section 3.2.1).

If we wish to rank two projects according to the net benefit per unit of electricity generated, then project 1 will be better than project 2 if

$$NB_1/Q_1 > NB_2/Q_2, \qquad (15.1)$$

where $NB_i = (B_i - C_i) =$ net benefit; $Q_i =$ quantity of electricity generated; $B_i =$ total benefit; and $C_i =$ total economic cost, of project i.

Then, the following assumption may be made:

$$B_1/Q_1 = B_2/Q_2. \qquad (15.2)$$

This is a reasonable approximation, since one unit of electricity will produce the same total benefit within the electricity grid, irrespective of the source of generation (if transmission costs to connect generators to the grid are equal). Thus, equation (15.1) can be expressed as follows:

$$(C_1/Q_1) > (C_2/Q_2). \qquad (15.3)$$

We may interpret equation (15.3) to mean that the project with the lower cost per unit of electricity generated is preferred. Cost C_i is estimated as the present discounted value of project costs (10% discount rate), annuitized over the project lifetime, while Q_i would be the average expected generation per year. In this illustrative case study, we have focused on energy generated by assuming equal plant factors and we have ignored capacity considerations. Hence, average generation costs per year are used as the economic indicator of sustainable energy development.

Environmental indicator – biodiversity index

In electric-power-plant evaluation, detailed site-specific environmental data are unlikely to be available at the long-range system planning stage. Thus, the quantification of biodiversity impacts that is possible at this level of aggregation is a probabilistic estimate that gives decision makers advance warning about the likelihood that a more detailed environmental impact assessment will reveal adverse effects on an endemic species, significant ecosystems impacts, or degradation of a habitat already in a marginal condition (see Chapter 4). Although endemicity and biodiversity are not necessarily correlated, endemic species in Sri Lanka are most likely to be encountered in areas of high biodiversity.

A biodiversity index must reflect several key characteristics. First is the nature of the impacted system itself. In Table 15.1, the main agroecological zones encountered in Sri Lanka are ranked and assigned a value (w_j) that captures the relative biodiversity value of different habitats. The scale is a strict ratio scale (i.e. zero indicates a zero amount of the characteristic involved, and a value of 0.1 implies ten times the value assigned to a value of 0.01). The second element concerns the *relative* valuation, because the *value* of the area lost

Table 15.1 *Biodiversity index values of Sri Lankan agroecological zones*

Rank	Ecosystem	Relative biodiversity value
1	lowland wet evergreen forest	0.98
2	lowland moist evergreen forest	0.98
3	lower montane forest	0.9
4	upper montane forest	0.9
5	riverrine forest	0.75
6	dry mixed evergreen forest	0.5
7	villus	0.4
8	mangroves	0.4
9	thorn forest	0.3
10	grasslands	0.3
11	rubber lands	0.2
12	home gardens	0.2
13	salt marshes	0.1
14	sand dunes	0.1
15	coconut lands	0.01

Adapted from Meier and Munasinghe (1994).

is a function of the proportion of the habitat that is lost. For example, the loss of the *last* hectare of an ecosystem would be unacceptable, and hence assigned a very large value (even if it had a low biodiversity, such as a sand dune), whereas the loss of 1 hectare out of 10 000 would be much less valuable.

The total biodiversity index value associated with site i is defined as follows:

$$E_i = \sum_j w_j A_{ij}, \tag{15.4}$$

where A_{ij} denotes the number of hectares containing an ecosystem of type j at site i and w_j is the relative biodiversity value of type j (as defined in Table 15.1).

Since E_i may be correlated with reservoir size (i.e. inundated land area and energy storage capacity), two further scaled indices are defined:

$$F_i = E_i / \left(\sum_j A_{ij} \right) = E_i / (\text{total land area affected at site } i) \tag{15.5}$$

and

$$G_i = E_i / (\text{hydroelectric energy generated per year at site } i). \tag{15.6}$$

Thus, F_i is the average biodiversity index value per hectare of affected land and G_i is the average biodiversity index value per unit of energy produced per year. These formulae are applied to each hydro site to determine the biodiversity index value and are used as the environmental indicator of sustainable energy development.

Social indicator – resettlement

Although dam sites are usually in less densely populated rural areas, resettlement is still a serious problem. In general, people are relocated from the wet to the dry zone in Sri Lanka (where soils are less rich), and therefore the same level of agricultural productivity cannot be maintained.

In the wet zone, multiple crops including paddy, tobacco, coconuts, mangos, onions and chilies can be grown. However, these crops cannot be cultivated as successfully in the dry zone, due to limited water and poor soil quality. Living standards often become worse and problems (like malnutrition) could occur. Moreover, other social issues, such as erosion of community cohesion and psychological distress due to change in the living environment, might arise. Hence, minimizing the number of people resettled due to dam construction is an important social objective. Thus, the number of resettled people per year per unit of energy produced is used as the social indicator of sustainable energy development.

15.2 Main findings of small hydro study

15.2.1 Analysis of results

Table 15.2 lists the 22 hydro-projects in Sri Lanka used in this study (CEB, 1987, 1988). The size of the hydro-projects varies from 10.9 to 512 GWh/yr. All three variables used (i.e. generation costs, biodiversity index and number of resettled people) are given per unit of electricity produced, which scales by project size and makes them comparable.

In Figure 15.3, the values of each criterion are provided for all 22 projects. Clearly, on a per kilowatt-hour per year basis, the project AGRA003 has the highest biodiversity index, HEEN009 has the highest number of resettled people and MAHA096 has the highest average generation cost. Table 15.2 shows that small hydro-projects tend to have high unit generation costs, while larger projects appear to have more resettlement. The impact on biodiversity provides a more mixed picture. More generally, ranking projects according to each criterion separately on the basis of Figure 15.3 does not provide a clear basis for making decisions.

Small hydro-projects (say up to 10 MW) can become more favourable economically if present technology trends continue to reduce average generation costs. Larger hydro-projects would gain more favour if the scale of resettlement is controlled and reduced. In order to reduce the impacts of hydropower development on biodiversity, careful considerations and studies would be needed for the location of dam sites. Some important comparisons may be made using Figure 15.3. For example, KALU075 is a relatively large project, where costs are low, whereas MAHA096 is a smaller scheme with much higher costs with respect to all three sustainability indices. Further, a project like KELA071 fully dominates GING053, since the former is superior in terms of all three indicators. Similar comparisons may be made between other projects. There is a little correlation between quantity of

Table 15.2 *Description of the hydropower projects in Sri Lanka*

Project number	Project name	River basins	Electricity generated (GWh/yr)
1	AGRA003	Agra Oya	28
2	DIYA008	Diyawini Oya	10.9
3	GING052	Ging Ganga	159
4	GING053	Ging Ganga	210
5	GING074	Ging Ganga	209
6	HEEN009	Heen Ganga	19.9
7	KALU075	Kalu Ganga	149
8	KELA071	Kelani Ganga	114
9	KOTM033	Kotmale Oya	390
10[a]	KUKU022	Kukule Ganga	512
11	LOGG011	Loggal Oya	22
12	MAGA029	Magal Oya	77.8
13	MAGU043	Maguru Oya	161
14	MAHA096	Maha Oya	33.5
15	MAHO007	Maha Oya	50
16	MAHW235	Mahaweli Ganga	83.4
17	MAHW287	Mahaweli Ganga	42.2
18	NALA004	Nalanda Reservoir	17.9
19	SITA014	Sitawaka Ganga	123
20	SUDU009	Sudu Ganga	79
21	SUDU017	Sudu Ganga	113
22	UMAO008	Uma Oya	143

[a] Since KUKU022 is a multipurpose project, some non-power benefits may be excluded.
Source: CEB (1987, 1988).

electricity generated, average generation cost, the number of resettled people and the biodiversity index.

Figure 15.4 shows sustainable development indicators for these hydro sites in three dimensions, with the axes representing economic ecological and social objectives, respectively. The distance from the origin to each coordinate point is critical. Generally, the closer to the origin, the better the project is in terms of achieving the three objectives. As explained in Chapter 3 (see Figure 3.6), projects that are superior to others on the basis of all three indicators will define a non-inferior (or trade-off) surface.

In the case of Figure 15.4, hydro-projects on such a surface will dominate all others lying outside and more distant from the origin, whereas the opposite is true for Figure 3.6 (since the directions of the axes are reversed). Next, choosing among the projects on the trade-off surface will need further definition of relative weights to be assigned to the respective objectives. This kind of three-dimensional figure gives a visually clearer view of hydro-projects in terms of the three sustainable development indicators than a simpler two-dimensional figure, such as

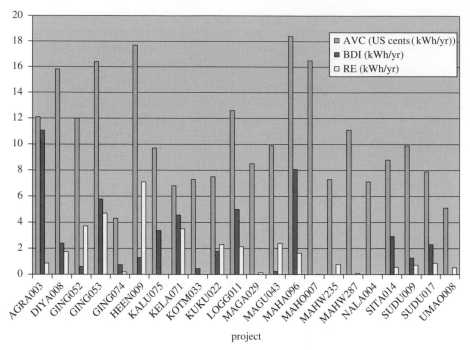

Figure 15.3. Average generation costs (AVC), biodiversity index (BDI) and number of resettled people (RE) by hydro-project. All indices are per kilowatt-hour per year. Generation costs are calculated using a 10% discount rate. Numbers of people resettled and the BDI are scaled for convenience (by the multipliers 10^{-5} and 10^{-9}, respectively). Source: CEB (1987, 1988); Meier and Munasinghe (1994).

Figure 15.3. Hence, it provides policy makers with a better idea about which project is more favourable from a sustainable energy development perspective.

For illustrative purposes, we arbitrarily give all three objectives an equal weight, assuming that all of them are equally important for sustainable energy development. Then, each project may be ranked by its absolute distance from the origin, given by

$$\text{distance} = [(x\text{-coordinate})^2 + (y\text{-coordinate})^2 + (z\text{-coordinate})^2]^{1/2}.$$

For example, rank 1 is given to the one closest to the origin, rank 2 is the second closest, etc. This ranking makes visual comparison of projects easier, although a different weighting scheme could change the rankings.

From this overall sustainable energy development perspective, the most favourable project is GING074 (rank 1), whereas the least favourable is MAHA096 (rank 22) – see Table 15.3 (final column). Table 15.3 also shows a more complete set of rankings, where the three objectives are considered two at a time. For economic–ecological, economic–social, and ecological–social indices, GING074 has rankings of 1, 2 and 7, respectively. This indicates that it is also quite a balanced project from a sustainomics viewpoint. Thus, this

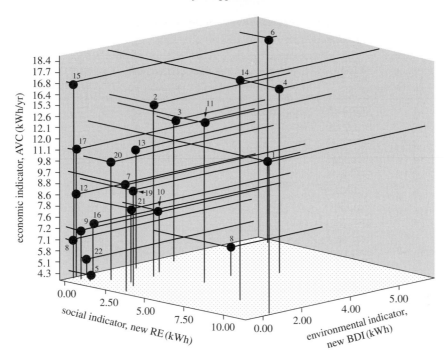

Figure 15.4. Three-dimensional graphical analysis of impact on sustainable development.

approach seems to provide more intuitively appealing and robust results when policy makers wish to make their decisions.

15.2.2 Conclusions

Sri Lanka has moved in recent decades from a predominantly hydroelectric system to a mixed hydrothermal system. Renewable sources of energy are a key factor in successfully achieving the transition to sustainable energy development. MCA has been used to assess the impact of hydro-projects on sustainable energy development.

The strength of this type of analysis is in helping policy makers to compare project alternatives more easily and effectively. The simple graphical presentations more clearly identify the sustainable development characteristics of each scheme. MCA supplements the more conventional CBA, based on economic analysis alone. Since each project has different features, assessing them by looking at only one aspect (e.g. generation costs, effects on biodiversity or impacts on resettlement) could be misleading. Together, with more detailed analyses for each hydro-project, this type of graphical MCA could be a useful tool for project assessments.

There are several possible improvements that could be made in the MCA approach used here. First, for simplicity each major objective is represented by only one key variable. In reality, there may be more than one variable that describes the economic, social and environmental aspects of sustainable development. Further analysis that includes other

Table 15.3 *Rankings of projects based on any two objectives and overall (arbitrary equal weighting of indicators)*

Project Number	Project name	Economic–ecological	Economic–social	Ecological–social	Overall '3D MCA' (Figure 15.4)
1	AGRA003	13	22	22	19
2	DIYA008	18	17	14	17
3	GING052	19	13	16	15
4	GING053	21	20	20	20
5	GING074	1	2	7	1
6	HEEN009	22	19	19	21
7	KALU075	7	14	13	13
8	KELA071	15	15	18	9
9	KOTM033	4	5	5	4
10	KUKU022	12	7	14	6
11	LOGG011	16	17	17	16
12	MAGA029	5	6	4	8
13	MAGU043	4	8	10	12
14	MAHA096	20	21	21	22
15	MAHO007	17	16	2	18
16	MAHW235	6	4	8	5
17	MAHW287	10	11	3	14
18	NALA004	2	3	1	3
19	SITA014	8	12	12	10
20	SUDU009	10	10	9	11
21	SUDU017	8	9	11	7
22	UMAO008	2	1	6	2

variables may provide new insights. Second, a possible extension of this study is to analyse other renewable sources of energy. Third, the choice of discount rates could affect the calculations and rankings relating to the economic variable. Fourth, exclusionary screening techniques (i.e. eliminating dominated projects like GING053, and focusing only on non-dominated ones) may provide a clearer picture. Finally, better three-dimensional graphic techniques may yield a clearer representation (Tufte, 1992).

15.3 New and renewable energy projects: case study of solar photovoltaics

Modern societies require increasing amounts of energy for domestic, industrial, commercial, agricultural and transport uses. Arrayed against these energy needs are short-term, depletable fossil-fuel supplies (oil, coal and natural gas), as well as the longer-run, renewable energy sources, like hydro, solar, geothermal, wind, tidal and biomass.

Commercial forms of energy, such as electricity, oil, coal and gas, have dominated the world energy scene. However, rising oil prices and environmental problems (including climate change) associated with fossil-fuel use have increased the attractiveness of renewable-energy sources. The potential for biomass-based energy is indicated by the fact that the total world use of energy in the early 1990s was less than one-fifth of the annual photosynthetic conversion of sunlight via biomass.

In 2003, renewables accounted for 13% of the 10 579 megatonne of world total primary energy supply (TPES) – see also Section 10.2.3. Combustible renewables and waste (97% biomass) represented about 80% of total renewables and 16% of hydro. Total renewables supply grew annually at 2.3% during 1971–2003 – marginally higher than the annual growth in TPES. However, 'new' renewables like geothermal, solar, wind, etc., had a much higher annual growth of 8%. Starting from a low base in 1971, wind experienced the highest annual growth rate (49%), followed by solar (29%) (IEA, 2005). Asia, Africa and Latin America are the main renewables users, with most of the use occurring in homes for cooking and heating. OECD accounted for 47% and 67%, respectively, of the use of hydro and other (or 'new') renewables (solar, wind) in 2003.

A consistent methodology based on sustainomics principles is outlined below, to make small or decentralized energy projects development more sustainable, by analysing and correcting for distortions in financial prices. The latter would lead to economically ineffi- cient allocation of resources as well as environmental and social harm. The principles underlying this framework are also applicable to other large-scale public investment projects in the energy sector, but here the analysis has been adapted to meet the special difficulties that arise in the evaluation and implementation of the new and renewable technologies. Section 15.3.1 outlines the methodology, including economic criteria for accepting a new technology (based on shadow prices and the national viewpoint), the financial requirements for successful implementation (based on market prices and the private viewpoint) and policy implications of this analysis. Finally, a case study involving solar photovoltaic water pumping (for irrigation) is presented, to show how economic and financial analyses could interact to make national energy policy more sustainable.

15.3.1 Economic and financial methodology

This approach focuses on the sector-project level of the sustainable energy development framework (see Figure 10.4). The basic steps for making and implementing an investment decision involving rural energy sources, as well as the underlying economic and financial criteria are shown in Figure 15.5. Consider a decentralized rural energy source, which we identify as technology R. First, it is important to establish the existence of a demand or market for energy services of the type to be provided by technology R. For example, the use of kerosene for lighting in rural areas indicates that there is a potential market for an alternative energy source, such as local small-scale hydro plants or diesel generators, to provide the same service.

The second step involves choice of the least-cost technology based on the national view- point. Shadow prices (or economic opportunity costs) are used to determine whether techno- logy R is cheaper than alternative means of providing the same energy services (see Chapter 3). If technology R is not least-cost, it is rejected and we proceed no further with the analysis.

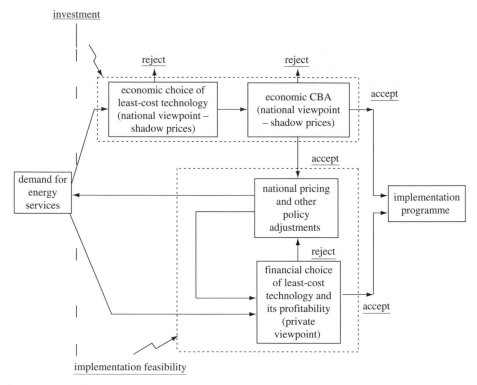

Figure 15.5. Principal steps in economic and financial analysis for investment decision and implementation.

If technology R is accepted on a least-cost basis, an economic CBA is required to confirm the investment decision. The benefits derived by using technology R are compared with the project costs, once again using shadow prices. Environmental impacts and other external-ities, which may be valued in economic terms, are included in the analysis (see Chapter 3). If costs exceed benefits, the project is rejected and goes no further. If net benefits (i.e. benefits minus costs) are positive, then technology R is acceptable from the national viewpoint and the decision to invest is economically justified.

The next stage in the analysis tests the feasibility of project implementation. If the project is to be financed and built by the government (e.g. small-sale hydro plant to provide rural electricity), then the pricing of the output is a key issue. Basically, it should be verified that the demand for the energy service would still exist at the market or financial price to be charged to the user. As described in Chapter 14, this price should generally reflect the marginal economic opportunity cost (or long-run marginal cost) of supply, to meet the economic efficiency objective. The energy-pricing policy would also be modified by sector financial viability considerations, social-subsidized or lifeline pricing needs of poor consumers and other constraints and national goals.

The analysis of financial feasibility is more complicated in the case of a project involving a decentralized technology such as solar photovoltaic (PV) powered electric pumps for farm use,

which is essentially purchased or paid for by private individuals who are the ultimate beneficiaries. In Figure 15.5, two financial tests seek to verify from a private individual's viewpoint,
using market prices, whether technology R is (i) cheaper than any alternative method of meeting
the same need and (ii) profitable, i.e. whether the benefits derived from using technology R
outweigh the costs. In an ideal distortion-free economy, market prices and shadow prices are
identical, and the economic and financial tests of the project would yield the same answer (see
Box 2.3 and Chapter 3). In practice, market prices diverge significantly from shadow prices, and
therefore both economic and financial calculations have to be carried out separately.

If technology R is financially least-cost and profitable, it is clear that rational private
individuals would adopt the technology. Thus the government and private investment decisions coincide, and the project implementation programme can begin. If an economically
justifiable project fails one or both of the financial tests, then the government must seek to
adjust market prices or other policies to make the new technology more financially attractive to
private individuals. For example, a competing technology may be financially cheaper because
the market price of fuel is subsidized. The required policy change then might be to remove the
fuel subsidy, thus making the alternative technology more expensive, or to ban the latter
altogether through legislation. The rationale underlying the policy changes is that the government should manipulate the market environment to make technology R financially attractive.
Thus market prices would be brought more in line with shadow prices by eliminating taxes and
subsidies, and legislative and physical controls would also be brought into play, as appropriate.
Such policy changes will not affect shadow prices significantly, so economic acceptability of
the project from the national perspective would be unchanged. When the project passes both
the economic and financial tests, the implementation programme may begin.

15.3.2 PV energy for agricultural pumping

The economic evaluation of a decentralized new energy technology such as the PV irrigation
pumping system discussed in the following, and the decision to implement this technology,
illustrates the close interaction between the economic and financial analyses in policy
making. The example and numbers selected are purely illustrative, and do not necessarily
prove the superiority of one technology. The economic analysis is based on the cost–benefit
criteria and efficiency shadow pricing (see Chapter 3).

We assume that the agricultural area under consideration is so remote that electrification
via the main power grid would be too costly. The main competitor of PV systems in this case
is the diesel pump. To compare these two discrete alternatives, we look only at a single
representative farm, and we analyse both economic and financial data.

Consider a typical 1 hectare farm that requires about $20\,\text{m}^3/\text{day}$ of water, with a head
of 5 m. Since the benefits are identical in both cases, we first determine the least-cost
alternative by comparing diesel and PV system costs. The basic data for a simplified
hypothetical example are shown in Table 15.4. In actual practice, a range of parameters
(e.g. different farm sizes, insolation rates, cropping patterns, system costs, etc.) may have to
be considered.

Table 15.4 *Basic data for solar PV and diesel pumping systems*

	Solar PV		Diesel	
	Market prices (DRs)	Shadow prices (BRs)[a]	Market prices (DRs)	Shadow prices (BRs)[a]
Initial cost	66 000	60 000	28 800	36 000[c]
Annual maintenance costs	1100	1000[b]	1500	1050[d]
Annual fuel costs	–	–	840[e]	1200
Lifetime[h] (yr)	10	10	5	5
Discount rate (%)	15[f]	10[g]	15[f]	10[g]
Annual inflation rate (%)	10	–	10	–

[a] All foreign costs converted into border rupees (BRs) at official exchange rate of US $1 = Rs 20.
[b] All foreign exchange costs with 10% import duty.
[c] Import subsidy of 20% on diesel pumps provided to farmers.
[d] Conversion factor = 0.7 based on spare parts and labour.
[e] Subsidy of 33% provided on diesel fuel imported at US $3/1itre, and international fuel price assumed to rise at 3% per annum in real terms.
[f] Bank borrowing rate for farm loans.
[g] Opportunity cost of capital used as proxy for the accounting rate of interest (ARI).
[h] Solar PV is assumed to be inherently more longer lived.

15.3.3 Investment decision

We compare the present value of costs (PVC) of the two alternatives over a ten-year period, in economic efficiency shadow prices. The monetary unit (numeraire) is the border rupee (BRs), equivalent to US $0.05.

$$\text{Solar:} \quad \text{PVC}_{SE} = 60\,000 + \sum_{t=0}^{9} 1000/(1.1)^t$$

$$= \text{BRs } 66\,760.$$

$$\text{Diesel:} \quad \text{PVC}_{DE} = 36\,000 + 36\,000/(1.1)^5 + \sum_{t=0}^{9}[1050/(1.1)^t$$

$$+ 1200(1.03/1.1)^t]$$

$$= \text{BRs } 74\,540.$$

For diesel, the real fuel price increase of 3% per annum will partly offset the effect of discounting at the opportunity cost of capital of 10%. The above results show that the solar PV system is the least-cost alternative.

Next, assume that, due to the increased irrigation, the shadow-priced value of farm annual output of grain increases from BRs 10 000 to BRs 20 500/hectare, based on the export price of grain. This increase in output value is net of any changes in costs of other inputs such as

Table 15.5 *Economic and financial tests for investment decision*

All amounts are in present value terms

Item	A National viewpoint: shadow prices (BRs)	B Private view-point (initial) market prices before policy changes (DRs)	C Private viewpoint (interim): market prices after first policy change (DRs)	D Private viewpoint (final): market prices after second policy change (DRs)
Solar PV costs	$PVC_{SE} = 66\ 760$	$PVC_{SF} = 75\ 080$	$PVC_{SF} = 75\ 080$	$PVC_{SF} = 75\ 080$
Diesel costs	$PVC_{DE} = 74\ 540$	$PVC_{DF} = 71\ 110$	$PVC_{DF} = 85\ 070$	$PVC_{DE} = 86\ 070$
Irrigation benefits	$PVB_F = 78\ 000$	$PVC_E = 70\ 970$	$PVB_F = 73\ 670$	$PVB_F = 73\ 670$

fertilizer and labour. Then the present value of benefits (PVB) for the ten-year period is given by

$$PVB_E = \sum_{t=0}^{9} (20\ 500 - 10\ 000)/(1.1)^t$$
$$= \text{BRs } 70\ 970.$$

Since $NPV = PVB_E - PVC_{SE} = BRs\ 4210$, there is a positive net benefit to the country by installing solar PV pumps in farms (see column A of Table 15.5). Thus, from a national viewpoint, the government is justified in taking a policy decision to encourage use of solar PV systems by farmers.

Box 15.1 Conclusion

Condition (columns A to D, Table 15.5)	Consequences
A: Shadow-priced values	
$PVC_{SE} < PVC_{DE}$	Solar PV is the economically preferred least-cost technology
$PVB_E > PVC_{SE}$	Investment in solar PV is economically justified
B: Market-priced values before policy changes	
$PVC_{SF} > PVC_{DF}$	Financially, farmers will prefer diesel to solar PV pumps
C: Market-priced values after first policy changes	
$PVC_{SF} < PVC_{DF}$	Financially, farmers will prefer solar PV to diesel pumps
$PVB_F < PVC_{SF}$	Farmers will find solar PV pumps financially unprofitable
D: Market-priced values after second policy changes	
$PVC_{SF} < PVC_{DF}$	Financially, farmers will prefer solar PV to diesel pumps
$PVB_F > PVC_{SF}$	Farmers will find solar PV pumps financially profitable

15.3.4 Implementing the investment policy

Irrespective of government decisions, farmers will make their irrigation pumping decisions on the basis of private financial costs and benefits. Therefore, we analyse the present value of costs of solar and diesel systems in financial terms, using market prices (domestic rupees, DRs).

$$\text{Solar:}\quad \text{PVC}_{\text{SF}} = 66\,000 + \sum_{t=0}^{9} 1100(1.10/1.15)^t = \text{DRs } 75\,080.$$

$$\text{Diesel:}\quad \text{PVC}_{\text{DF}} = 28\,800 + 28\,800(1.10/1.15)^5 + \sum_{t=0}^{9} [1500(1.10/1.15)^t$$
$$+ 840(1.03 \times 1.10/1.15)^t]$$
$$= \text{DRs } 72\,110.$$

Since $\text{PVC}_{\text{SF}} > \text{PVC}_{\text{DF}}$, the average farmer would prefer to buy a diesel pump rather than a solar PV system. Because the market price signals are distorted, the private individual's decision does not coincide with the national policy decision based on shadow prices (column B of Table 15.5). Therefore, the government must adjust the market prices, or adopt other policies that will make the solar PV option attractive to farmers.

First, authorities could remove the 10% import duty on solar PV systems. Then $\text{PVC}_{\text{SF}} = \text{DRs } 68\,250$, and solar PV pumps become the least-cost alternative both financially and economically. However, this measure may also require reduction of import duties on many similar PV and electric components, which the government is unwilling to consider.

A second policy option is to raise diesel fuel prices until PVC_{DF} exceeds PVC_{SF} – but this may be blocked by a strong anti-inflation lobby on the grounds that it would raise transport costs too much. A third choice might be for the government to legislate that farmers could no longer buy diesel pumps. This non-price policy option is cumbersome and has its own implementation problems. A fourth possibility is for the government to provide low-interest agricultural loans or credits to buy solar pumps.

Finally, the government could remove the import subsidy on diesel motors. This increases PVC_{DF} to DRs 85 070, which exceeds PVC_{SF}. Then, farmers will voluntarily prefer solar PV pumps to diesel pumps. We assume that this policy option is selected (column C of Table 15.5).

It is still necessary to consider the financial benefits aspect. The irrigation programme increases the market value of farm output from DRs 8 500 to DRs 17 425, based on the guaranteed government purchase price for grain (which is 85% of the export or world market price). The present value of financial benefits for ten years of output is given by

$$\text{PVB}_{\text{F}} = \sum_{t=0}^{9} (17\,425 - 8500) \times (1.10/1.05)^t$$
$$= \text{DRs } 73\,670.$$

Since PVB_{F} is less than the value $\text{PVC}_{\text{SF}} = \text{DRs } 75\,080$, the average farmer will be financially worse off if he adopts the (least-cost) solar PV technology. Then, the government must make a further change in policy. For example, it could raise the domestic grain price to 90% of the world price. This policy change raises the value of financial benefits, and since $PVB_F = DRs\ 78\,000 > PVC_{SF}$, the farmer will find solar PV powered pump sets financially profitable to install (column D of Table 15.5).

This case study shows that demand management via implementation of a given investment decision (based on shadow prices) could help to make renewable energy development more sustainable. However, it would require a related series of wide-ranging policy decisions by the government.

15.4 Sustainable rural electrification based on renewable energy

This section discusses rural electrification (RE) projects based on renewable energy. Due to the high costs involved, we focus on the sustainability of economic and financial aspects. RE is important for poverty reduction. As in most developing countries, poverty is largely a rural phenomenon in Sri Lanka – a 1996 survey concluded that 88% of the poor live in rural areas, compared to 8% in urban areas and 4% in estate areas (Nexant, 2004). At the end of 2002, only 63% of homes in Sri Lanka had power, with electrification rates ranging from 87% in the Colombo district to 32% in Moneragala. Electricity access and poverty are highly correlated (see Figure 15.6). The higher the poverty rate, the lower the electrification rate. The data shown do not include unsettled districts in the northern and eastern areas, where poverty rates are substantially higher and electrification rates are lower.

Off-grid schemes account for a small but growing fraction of household electrifications. In 2003, about 28 000 homes had PV solar home systems and 3000 homes were supplied by village-scale hydro systems. These off-grid options are two key components of the Energy Services Delivery (ESD) programme (the other components included a 3 MW wind demonstration programme and grid-connected small hydro), discussed in the following. We begin with a discussion of the key issue of how the benefits of rural electrification are to be quantified.

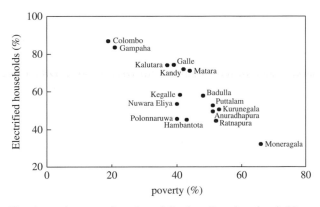

Figure 15.6. Electrification and poverty for selected districts. Based on data in Nexant (2004) and from Sri Lanka Central Bank.

15.4.1 *Measuring economic benefits of rural electrification*

There are two basic methods for estimating economic RE benefits (Munasinghe, 1987). The first is to set benefits equal to the avoided costs of the various means, presently used to supply energy, which would be replaced by the mini-hydro scheme – including kerosene, diesel generation for battery charging and productive uses, candles and dry cells. This 'avoided cost' method is easily applied because the data can be provided from surveying existing households and the calculations are straightforward. However, the method generally underestimates the actual benefits.

First, the quality of energy supply from electricity is far superior to that from most alternative devices. For example, the illumination from a compact fluorescent lamp (CFL) is much higher than that provided by candles or kerosene lamps. Individuals are prepared to pay more for high-quality service because they value a given number of lumens from electric light bulbs much more than the equivalent number of lumens from candles and kerosene. In other words, the benefits are greater than those that may be inferred from replacement costs alone.

Electric lighting also avoids many other harmful side-effects (such as smoke and odour, risk of fire and injury). In Sri Lanka, 50% of burn injuries are attributable to accidents involving kerosene lanterns and candles. Similar problems are reported in other countries (Foster and Tre, 2000; Reyes, 2001). This is an important area for further research, because burn injuries and child deaths have high social costs, whose avoidance should be counted as one of the benefits of rural electrification in general (and solar PV systems in particular). Such direct costs may be easier to ascertain than those related to local air pollution.

Second, as shown in Figure 15.7, the demand curve (which shows the quantity demanded as a function of price) for electricity services is downward sloping, while the total benefits of

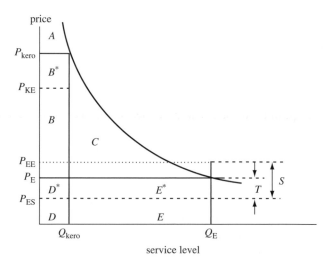

Figure 15.7. Demand curve for electricity services and reconciliation of economic and financial flows.

electricity consumption are given by the area under that curve (see Section 3.3.2). It is well established that individuals are prepared to pay very high prices for the first few kilowatt-hours of electricity (or lumens), sufficient for one or two CFLs. They are also prepared to pay high prices for enough electricity to power a TV. But the amount they are prepared to pay for subsequent CFLs will be less than the first CFL (which replaced candles or kerosene).

An alternative approach to calculating benefits requires estimation of such a demand curve. This is generally more difficult, because there the data may not be available to determine the shape of the curve accurately. Despite the additional uncertainty, this method of estimating the demand curve and formalization of willingness-to-pay is generally accepted as a better measure of the benefits of electrification. In Figure 15.7, the demand curve is shown typically concave (with respect to the origin). This shape frequently emerges where more than two points on the curve can be plotted. A concave shape also follows from the (convenient) assumption of constant elasticity (often made in econometric models).

Before electrification, these services are usually provided by a mix of kerosene (for lighting) and batteries (for TVs and radios). For simplicity, assume that the only service provided is lighting from kerosene lamps. Then the quantity of services consumed is Q_{kero}, at the market price p_{kero}. Thus, the total lighting cost to the household is ($Q_{kero} \times p_{kero}$), equal to the area $(B + B^* + D + D^*]$. The total willingness-to-pay for the service at level Q_{kero} is the total area under the demand curve up to that level of consumption, or area $(A + B + B^* + D + D^*]$. This is the total benefit to the consumer. Therefore, the net benefit (benefit minus cost), also called the consumer surplus, is given by area A. After electrification, the level of service (for lighting – the number of lumen-hours) typically rises sharply. Thus, consumption increases from Q_{kero} to Q_E, but the price paid for electrified service also falls from P_{kero} to P_E. Now household expenditure for electricity is given by ($p_E \times Q_E$), equal to area $(D + D^* + E + E^*)$.

At this level of consumption, the total benefit is the new area under the demand curve up to Q_E, $(A + B + B^* + C + D + D^* + E + E^*)$. Then the net benefit, or consumer surplus (after subtracting costs), is given by $(A + B + B^* + C)$. Thus, the net economic benefit (with versus without electrification) is the increase in consumer surplus, which is the area $(B + B^* + C)$.

Areas $(B + B^*)$, $(D + D^*)$ and $(E + E^*)$ are readily calculated from data on consumption with and without electrification, the household budget for kerosene (and battery charging) and the tariff of electrified service. But area C is more difficult to estimate, since it requires knowledge of the shape of the demand curve. A linear demand curve is the most convenient and frequently used one (ECA and Vernstrom, 2003).

Unfortunately such an assumption may lead to an overestimation of area C (and net benefits of electrification), since empirically the demand curve is more likely to have a concave shape. Given some functional form for such a demand curve, area C is readily calculated as the definite integral. Consumer surplus calculations use financial costs (since these are the costs actually seen by the user). However, financial and economic costs need careful estimation and reconciliation, because often the quantities both with and without electrification are subject to taxes and subsidies. Figure 15.7 shows a typical situation where the price of kerosene includes taxes (i.e. market price p_{kero} exceeds economic price p_{KE}) and

Table 15.6 *Reconciliation of economic and financial flows*

	Kerosene	Electrification	Difference
Consumer surplus	A	$A + B^* + B + C$	$B + B^* + C$
Taxes and duties (VAT)	B^*	$D^* + E^*$	$D^* + E^* - B^*$
Subsidy		$-SQ_E$	$-SQ_E$
Economic cost	$B + D^* + D$	$D + E + SQ_E$	$E + SQ_E - B - D^*$
Total benefit to consumer (= area under demand curve)	$A + B^* + B + D^* + D$	$A + B + B^* + C + D^* D + E^* + E$	$C + E^* + E$

where electrification involves both taxes (like VAT on construction costs) and subsidies (provided by government).

Suppose the electrification subsidy is Rs S/kWh. Then we may write $p_{ES} = p_{EE} - S$, where p_{EE} and p_{ES} are the economic and subsidized prices, respectively. Thus, the total amount of the subsidy is the area SQ_E. Suppose that this subsidized price is also taxed at the rate Rs T/kWh. Then, the market price to the consumer increases to $p_E = p_{ES} + T$ (the amount of taxes collected being the area $D^* + E^*$). In Figure 15.7, the subsidy exceeds the tax – which is the case for microhydro systems in Sri Lanka, where the proposed subsidy far exceeds the amount of VAT and profits tax on construction. For kerosene, the total (financial) cost to the user is given by $(B^* + B + D^* + D)$. Of this total, area B^* represents taxes.

Table 15.6 reconciles various economic and financial quantities. For example, without electrification, the economic benefit is $(A + B^*)$, but area B^* is captured by government as tax, rather than benefiting the consumer.

15.4.2 Solar homes programme in Sri Lanka

Solar home systems (SHSs) are designed to provide the most high-valued, initial tranche of electricity consumption, in rural areas in Sri Lanka, that are unlikely to be grid-connected soon. Nevertheless, according to Shell Solar, the leading supplier of SHSs, 10 000 of 17 000 systems sold to date have been to households where the grid was extended after the SHS had been installed. Indeed, there are also reports of households *already* connected to the grid buying an SHS. Evidently the erratic nature of rural supply (due to power cuts) and CEB's high consumer tariff are powerful incentives for SHS purchases. The ESD project, supported by the World Bank and GEF, has helped finance SHSs.

The solar industry was at a nascent stage when the ESD project became effective, with only three small operators (Solar Power and Light, Sarvodaya and RESCO) selling 20–30 systems per month in 1998. The ESD project has catalysed the market for SHSs. By 2002, sales had reached 850 systems per month, achieved by four companies (Shell Solar, Access Solar, SELCO and Alpha Thermal); 21 000 systems were installed, and 2003 sales exceeded 10 000 systems.

The very success of the ESD project in stimulating a successful private-sector involvement poses difficulties for economic analysis, because much of the data on actual system costs and margins are confidential. In addition, tax concessions vary by company. However, both strong consumer and vendor interest in this market are testimony to the economic benefits of SHSs (given the demonstrated willingness-to-pay for lighting and TV service at a cost well above the cost of kerosene and battery charging) and to the financial benefits (given the financial success of the vendors).

Several surveys provide information on monthly expenditures of households that purchased SHSs (see Table 15.7). Although the results show considerable variation, the data do indicate a substantial willingness-to-pay for the safety, convenience and superior light quality from an SHS.

Before SHSs, monthly average energy expenses totalled Rs 582 (Rs 340 for kerosene, Rs 92 for dry cells and Rs 152 for battery charging). However, there was little correlation between energy expenses and disposable income. Monthly energy expenses increased sharply upon purchase of the SHS (see Figure 15.8). Households did recognize that these higher costs would be limited to the debt-repayment period, and that thereafter their energy expenditures would decrease sharply. The average monthly energy expenditure of SHS

Table 15.7 *Survey results before and after SHS purchase*

	Masse (2001)	IRG (2002)	AC Nielsen (2003)
Monthly kerosene expenses (Rs)	231	340	312
Total monthly energy expenses before SHS	321	582	495
Average monthly energy expenses after SHS	–	1450	1286
Sample size	–	100	250

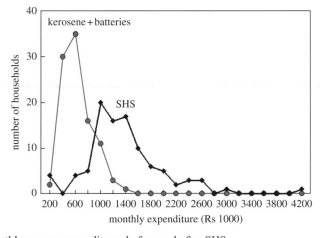

Figure 15.8. Monthly energy expenditures before and after SHS.

households was Rs 1450. There was little correlation between income and the size of the SHS purchased.

If one calculates the benefits on the basis of avoided costs, the economic returns of an SHS are negative. The AC Nielsen survey (AC Nielsen, 2003) shows: (1) mean monthly expenditure on kerosene and battery charging before the SHS is Rs 495/month; (2) four-year loan at 24% interest, with 25% down-payment; (3) 12% discount rate; (4) VAT on SHS is 11% of retail price; (5) kerosene tax limited to National Security Levy (Rs1.23/litre); and (6) SHS retail price is Rs 46 000 (45 watts-peak (WP) system). Table 15.8 shows a 7.7% internal economic rate of return (IERR), less than the opportunity cost of capital (OCC = 12%), while the financial rate of return to homes is negative. This result is consistent with other estimates, where avoided costs are used to measure benefits. For example, Meier (2003) found that the IERR of a 40 WP SHS in the Philippines was 11.7% (below the OCC = 15%).

Table 15.9 reconciles economic and financial flows among stakeholders. Because the financial interest rate is 24%, whereas the discount rate is 12%, the difference appears as a residual benefit to financial institutions (FIs). GEF is a source of funds, and thus shows up as a financier, while the government is a net beneficiary, since the VAT levied on the SHS (paid by the dealers) significantly exceeds any VAT on kerosene lamps and battery charging and the National Security Levy on kerosene.

The apparent negative financial return to homes reflects the highly negative cash flows in early years, when the loan is paid off (see Figure 15.9).

Therefore, the returns must be higher than those assessed purely on the basis of the replacement costs – since consumers are in fact willing to pay the higher outlays for SHS. Using the approach outlined earlier, we may derive the demand curve for lighting shown in Figure 15.10, for a homeowner purchasing a 45 WP system.

The corresponding distribution of costs and benefits is summarized in Figure 15.11, based on the consumer surplus calculations shown in Table 15.10. The IERR is a robust 31%, which increases to 42.6% when the GEF contribution is added as an environmental benefit. A 75 WP system generates about 315 Wh/day, or 115 kWh/yr, whose NPV over 15 years is 700 kWh. The NPV of the financial costs of the PV system is Rs 63 054. Hence, the implied willingness-to-pay for the first 115 kWh/yr provided by SHS (for lighting and TV viewing) is 63 054/700 = Rs 90/kWh (about US $1/kWh).

To conclude, it seems reasonable to claim that SHS represents a viable approach to off-grid electrification, and that subsidies from GEF are cost-effective for levering economic benefits not otherwise achievable because of financing problems. Moreover, the demonstrated willingness-to-pay for SHS (above replacement costs) shows the value of estimating consumer surplus, rather than using replacement costs, which underestimate benefits.

15.4.3 *Village hydro*

Small microhydro systems were a second successful part of the ESD project in Sri Lanka. They are under 50 kW and implemented by village cooperatives. AC Nielsen (2003) surveyed 100 village hydro system (VHS) beneficiaries and 30 of the VHSs implemented

Table 15.8 *Economic and financial returns based on avoided costs*

	NPV	1	2	3	4	5	6	7	8
Costs of PV system									
Down payment (Rs)	10 268	11 500							
GEF to consumer (Rs)	0	0							
Govt. grant (to consumer) (Rs)	0	0							
Loan principal (Rs)	30 804	34 500							
Financial cost (Rs)	**41071**	**46000**							
Finance (Rs)	38 217		16 905	14 835	12 765	10 695			
Loan repayments (Rs)	−38 217		−16 905	−14 835	−12 765	−10 695			
Less VAT & duties (Rs)	−4107	−4600							
Less income tax on margin (Rs)	−5252	−5882							
Less transfers (Rs)	−4877	−5462							
Economic capital cost (Rs)	**26 835**	**30 055**	**0**	**0**	**0**	**0**	**0**		
O&M costs									
Bulbs (Rs)	3539		582	582	582	582	582	582	582
Controller (Rs)	2465						3104		
Battery (Rs)	8566				4753			4753	
Financial cost to consumer (Rs)	14 570		582	582	5335	582	3686	5335	582
Less VAT (Rs)	−1457		−58	−58	−534	−58	−369	−534	−58
Economic O&M costs (Rs)	**13 113**	**0**	**524**	**524**	**4802**	**524**	**3317**	**4802**	**524**
Total economic costs (Rs)	**39 948**	**30 055**	**524**	**524**	**4802**	**524**	**3317**	**4802**	**524**
Benefits at avoided costs									
Kerosene consumption (l)	1314		216	216	216	216	216	216	216
Kerosene (Rs)	32118		5282	5282	5282	5282	5282	5282	5282

Table 15.8 (*cont.*)

	NPV	1	2	3	4	5	6	7	8
Battery & charging (Rs)	4006		659	659	659	659	659	659	659
Dry cell (Rs)	0	0	0	0	0	0	0	0	0
Hurricane lamp (Rs)	0	0			0			0	
Petromax lamp (Rs)	0	0			0	0			
Wick, gauzes (Rs)	0		0	0	0	0	0	0	0
Total, financial (Rs)	37 437	0	5940	5940	5940	5940	5940	5940	5940
Kerosene duties (Rs)	−1616		−266	−266	−266	−266	−266	−266	−266
VAT (Rs)	0								
Avoided costs (Rs)	35 822	0	5675	5675	5675	5675	5675	5675	5675
Net economic flows (Rs)	−4126	−30 055	5151	5151	873	5151	2357	873	5151
ERR		7.7%							
Net financial impact on consumers									
PV system (Rs)	63 054	11 500	17 487	15 417	18 100	11 277	3686	5335	582
Replacement (Rs)	36 124	0	5940	5940	5940	5940	5940	5940	5940
Net flow (Rs)	−26 930	−11 500	−11 547	−9477	−12 160	−5337	2254	605	5358
FRR		−4.5%							

ERR = economic rate of return; FRR = financial rate of return.

Table 15.9 *Reconciliation of economic and financial flows (as NPV)*

	Consumer	Dealers	Govt	FIs	GEF	Total
Benefits	37 437		−1616			35 822
Purchase price	−41 071	41 071				0
Loan	30 804			−30 804		0
GEF grant		6 790			−6790	0
Govt grant						0
VAT (on equipment)		−4107	4107			0
Income tax (dealers)		−5252	5252			0
Income tax (FIs)			2595	−2595		0
Economic cost		−26 835				−26 835
Consumer finance	−38 217			38 217		0
O&M costs	−14 570		1457			−13 113
Total	−25 617	11 667	11 795	4819	−6790	−4126

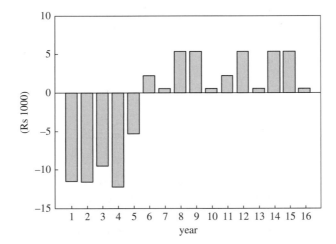

Figure 15.9. Cash flows to homeowners, in Rs/yr.

under ESD. Unfortunately, inadequate data from the village cooperatives make it difficult to determine precisely some key parameters, such as actual monthly and annual capacity factors. At the time of appraisal, the IERR was estimated at 12%, which has the appearance of being contrived for the sake of meeting the OCC = 12% hurdle rate. However, evaluation of systems actually implemented reveals lower costs, and thus greater economic benefits than expected. For example, while the estimated cost is US $2023/kW, the completed projects reported by the survey show an average capital cost of US $1892/kW.

Figure 15.12 shows how unit capital cost varies against installed capacity, and confirms the strong presence of scale economies. Further, there is a large 'sweat equity' component

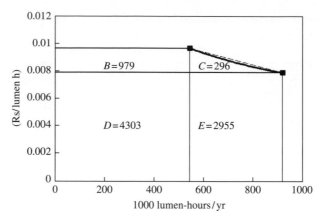

Figure 15.10. Demand curve for lighting (based on 45 WP PV system).

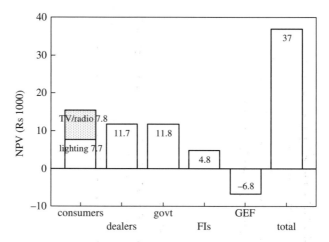

Figure 15.11. Distribution of costs and benefits.

based on voluntary labour. Using an average income of Rs 300/day, the survey report estimates the 'minimum opportunity cost of voluntary service rendered by the average VHS user at Rs 9000 (30 man-days)'. The beneficiary survey reveals that 20–30 days is the most frequent contribution of voluntary service.

Table 15.11 shows sweat equity costs, using the opportunity cost of contributed time (based on home income). Taking the cash equity fraction at 15%, and conservatively assuming that 25% of project cost are imports, then economic capital costs (including sweat equity) are US $2060/kW, and financial capital costs are US $2225/kW (excluding sweat equity).

Records of kilowatt-hours actually produced are sparse. Indeed, actual readings were available for only seven systems (column [3] of Table 15.12). The period of operation could

Table 15.10 *IERR with consumer surplus benefits (15 year life of SHS)*

	NPV	1	2	3	4	5	6	7	8
Lighting costs, PV system									
[1] Allocated costs	70%								
[2] PV costs, financial (Rs)	44 138	8050	12 241	10 792	12 670	7894	2580	3735	407
[3] PV costs, levelized (Rs)	44 138	6329	6329	6329	6329	6329	6329	6329	6329
[4] PV lighting (lumen)	5 593 422	0	919 800	919 800	919 800	919 800	919 800	919 800	919 800
[5] P_{PV} (Rs/lumen h)	0.0079								
[6] Area ($D + E$) (Rs/yr)	7258								
Lighting costs, kerosene									
[7] Fuel cost (Rs)		0	5282	5282	5282	5282	5282	5282	5282
[8] Wick lamp (Rs)		0	0	0	0	0	0	0	0
[9] Petromax lamp (Rs)		0	0	0	0	0	0	0	0
[10] Wick, gauzes (Rs)		0	0	0	0	0	0	0	0
[11] Total costs (Rs)	32 118	0	5282	5282	5282	5282	5282	5282	5282
[12] Kerosene lighting (lumen)	3 315 928		545 282	545 282	545 282	545 282	545 282	545 282	545 282
[13] P_{kero} (Rs/litre)	0.0097								
[14] Area ($B + D$) (Rs/yr)	5282								
Radio/TV: PV system									
[15] Allocated costs	30%								
[16] PV costs, financial (Rs)	18 916	3450	5246	4625	5430	3383	1106	1601	175
[17] PV costs, levelized (Rs)	18 916	2712	2712	2712	2712	2712	2712	2712	2712
[18] PV non-lighting (VL-h)	11 098		1825	1825	1825	1825	1825	1825	1825
[19] P_{PV} (Rs/TV-h)	1.7								
[20] Area ($D + E$) (Rs/yr)	3111								
Radio/TV: battery									
[21] Total costs (Rs)	4006	0	659	659	659	659	659	659	659
[22] PV non-lighting (VL-h)	1665		274	274	274	274	274	274	274
[23] $P_{battery}$ (Rs/TV-h)	2.4								
[24] Area ($B + D$) (Rs/yr)	659								

Table 15.10 (*cont.*)

	NPV	1	2	3	4	5	6	7	8
Net economic flows									
Lighting (see chart)									
[25] Total benefits ($B + C + D + E$) (Rs/yr)	51 887	0	8532	8532	8532	8532	8532	8532	8532
[26] Total costs ($D + E$) (Rs/yr)	44 138	6329	6329	6329	6329	6329	6329	6329	6329
[27] Net consumer benefits, lighting (Rs/yr)	7749	−6329	2203	2203	2203	2203	2203	2203	2203
TV/radio									
[28] Total benefits ($B + C + D + E$) (Rs/yr)	26 708		4392	4392	4392	4392	4392	4392	4392
[29] Total costs ($D + E$) (Rs/yr)	18 916	3450	5246	4625	5430	3383	1106	1601	175
[30] Net consumer benefits, TV/radio (Rs/yr)	7792	−3450	−854	−233	−1038	1009	3286	2792	4217
Total consumer surplus (Rs/yr)	**15541**	**−9779**	**1349**	**1970**	**1165**	**3212**	**5490**	**4995**	**6421**
[31] ERR		30.7%							
[32] Total financial costs (Rs/yr)	−63 054	−11 500	−17 487	−15 417	−18 100	−11 277	−3686	−5335	−582
[33] Total consumer surplus benefits (Rs/yr)	78 595	0	12 924	12 924	12 924	12 924	12 924	12 924	12 924
[34] Net financial flows (Rs/yr)	15 541	−11 500	−4563	−2493	−5176	1647	9238	7589	12 342
[35] ERR		21.1%							
[36] Economic cost adjustment (Rs/yr)	−0	−30 055	4413	4413	4413	4413	4413	4413	4413
[37] Adjusted net financial flow (Rs/yr)	15 541	−41 555	−150	1920	−763	6060	13 651	12 002	16 755
[38] ERR		16.8%							
[39] Less net govt subsidies (Rs/yr)	11 795	13 211							
[40] Less GEF subsidies (Rs/yr)	−6790	−7605							
[41] Plus FI surplus (Rs/yr)	4819	5397							
[42] Plus dealer surplus (Rs/yr)	11 667	13 067							
[43] Net economic flows (Rs/yr)	37 032	−17 485	−150	1920	−763	6060	13 651	12 002	16 755
[44] ERR		31.0%							
[45] With GEF as economic benefit (Rs/yr)	43 822	−9881	−150	1920	−763	6060	13 651	12 002	16 755
[46] ERR		42.6%							

Without the 'economic cost adjustment' of rows [36]–[38], the economic flows have more than one turning point (since subsidies and adjustments occur in year 1). Then IERR is indeterminate. NPV calculations are unaffected. The adjustment for taking the GEF contribution as a benefit in year 1 assumes that it is equal to global environmental benefits.

Areas *B*, *C*, *D* and *E* refer to Figure 15.10.

Table 15.11 *Estimates of sweat equity*

System	Sweat equity	Cash equity	Total village equity	Project cost	Sweat equity (%)	Cash equity (%)	Adjusted cash equity (%)
	[1]	[2]	[3]	[4]	[5]=[1]/[4]	[6]=[2]/[4]	[7]=[2]/([4]−[1])
Handunella	0	125	125	1325	0	9	9
Aluthgama	561	102	603	1307	43	8	14
Diyapoda	280	134	414	1152	24	12	15
Manamperigama	168	24	912	800	21	3	4
Dumbara	1527	470	1997	3700	41	13	22
Average					26	9	13

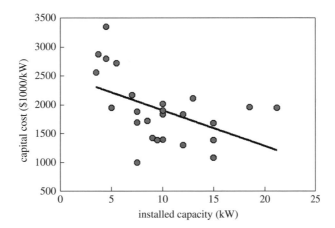

Figure 15.12. Capital cost versus installed capacity.

be inferred from knowledge of commissioning dates to derive average annual kilowatt-hours, and hence estimate the average capacity factor, with the results as shown in column [5]. Overall, it seems reasonable to infer that the achieved capacity factors are in the range of 80–95%.

These capacity factors are much higher than the 50% estimated at appraisal. However, they are consistent with the design philosophy, which matches system size to dry season flows. Clearly, if a village hydro system were only operated at a 50% capacity factor, then diesel backup would be needed to supply year-round power.

Although VHSs were built in small watersheds and generally well above gauging stations, none maintained records of gauged flows at the intake. Therefore, the likely monthly variation in flows can only be inferred from precipitation records that are generally available. Figure 15.13 shows the monthly variation in rainfall at the Ingoya Estate, on which the design flow for the Handunella–Atulauda VHS is based.

If one matches the design flow to January/February conditions, high annual capacity factors are achievable. However, on a daily load curve basis, it seems unlikely that this

Table 15.12 *Capacity factor estimates*

	Estimated annual kWh survey	Estimated capacity factor survey	Actual meter reading (Spring 2003)	Months	Estimated capacity factor (meter reading)
	[1]	[2]	[3]	[4]	[5]
Maddabaddara	35 040	0.889			
Kandaloya	74 256	0.848	352 716	56	0.863
Handunella	113 568	0.997	321 776	34	1.012
Gedarawat	76 752	0.73			
Golahinna	162 060	1			
Kaduoya	109 200	0.831	327 600	37	0.809
Kawudubukka	131 400	1			
Veediyawa	51 480	0.131	179 406	24	0.232
Samanala	148 512	0.997			
Ihalagonna	60 840	0.926	91 260	18	0.926
Glime	33 670	0.769	73 002	21	0.976
Hathkella	87 360	0.997			
Hinguralakande	65 700	1			
Gamperigama	4269	0.139	2490	7	0.139
Dumbara-Manana	24 768	0.133			
Wewagama	32 850	1			
Ritigala Ella	131 400	1			

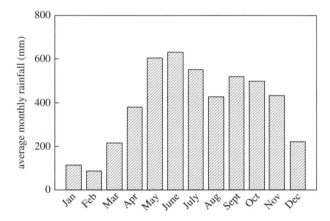

Figure 15.13. Monthly rainfall patterns for Ingoya Estate.

continuously available power is actually consumed, given the probable end uses of lighting and TV.

The VHS beneficiaries have average monthly costs (on kerosene, batteries and dry cells) of Rs 322/month. Taking this as the benefits (plus the GEF grant), and using the actually

Table 15.13 *Achieved IERR*

	NPV	[0]	[1]	[2]	[3]	[4]	[5]	[6]
Capital cost = US $2050/kW								
Kilowatts = 15.0								
GEF grant ($US)	4783		6000					
Capital costs ($US)	−27 455	−30 750						
O&M costs 0.8% ($US)	−1702		−6255	−255	−255	−255	−255	−255
Total costs ($US)	−24 374	−30 750	5745	−255	−255	−255	−255	−255
Capacity factor = 0.8								
Benefit/kWh = 5.7 US cents/kWh								
Benefits (MWh)			105	105	105	105	105	105
($US)	39 960		5992	5992	5992	5992	5992	5992
Total flows ($US)	15 586	−30 750	11737	5737	5737	5737	5737	5737
IERR	21.8%							

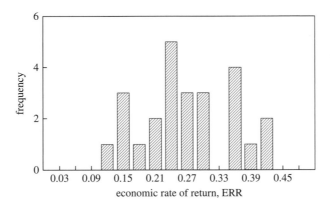

Figure 15.14. IERRs for surveyed VHS.

achieved capital cost of US $2050/kW, the IERR is 21.8% for the same VHS (15 kW, 150 households) used at appraisal. Without the GEF grant benefit, the IERR is 17.9%. Whether or not high levels of electricity are actually used does not affect this result, since benefits are taken as pre-electrification energy expenses. If smaller amounts of electricity were used, then the average benefit US $0.057/kWh would be that much greater. Based on the survey results, we may estimate the IERRs achieved for individual VHS systems as shown in Figure 15.14.

These estimates of IERR (based on replacement costs) significantly underestimate actual economic returns, because willingness-to-pay for the first tranche of electricity use is much greater than replacement costs. In Section 15.4.2, we showed that this first tranche (115 kWh/yr) may be valued at US $1/kWh (VHS and SHS customers have similar income

Table 15.14 *Benefits based on consumer surplus*

	NPV	[0]	[1]	[2]	[3]	[4]	[5]	[6]
Capital cost = US $2050/kW								
Kilowatts = 15.0								
GEF grant ($ US)	4783		6000					
Capital costs ($ US)	−27 455		−30 750					
Lost earnings (sweat equity) ($ US)	−690	−773						
O&M costs 0.8% ($ US)	−1702		−255	−255	−255	−255	−255	−255
Total costs ($ US)	−25 065	−31 523	5745	−255	−255	−255	−255	−255
Capacity factor = 0.8								
Benefit/kWh = 20.2 US cents/kWh								
Benefits (MWh)			30	30	30	30	30	30
($ US)	115 043		17 250	17 250	17 250	17 250	17 250	17 250
Total flows ($ US)	89 978	−31 523	22 995	16 995	16 995	16 995	16 995	16 995
Estimate of benefits based on willingness-to-pay TP								
Consumption = 6h/day								
Number of households (HH) = 150								
90 W/HH								
Wh/day/HH	3601		540	540	540	540	540	540
kWh/yr/HH	1314		197	197	197	197	197	197
First tranche 1 US $/kWh								
115 kWh	767		115	115	115	115	115	115
US $/yr/HH	767		115	115	115	115	115	115
Second tranche kWh	548		82.1	82.1	82.1	82.1	82.1	82.1
0 US $/kWh								
US $/yr/HH	0		0	0	0	0	0	0
Total WTP US $/yr/HH	767		115	115	115	115	115	115
US $/yr	115 043		17 250	17 250	17 250	17 250	17 250	17 250

levels). Assuming further that actual use is limited to evening TV viewing and lighting, and that each household has 100 W of installed devices that run for 6 h/day on average, then total annual consumption is given by $6 \times 100 \times 0.9 \times 365/1000 = 197$ kWh/yr, implying a second tranche of 82 kWh/yr. Then, even the willingness-to-pay is zero for this second tranche, and the computed IERR is 61%, as shown by the calculations of Table 15.14 (54% without the GEF grant).

Table 15.15 shows the distribution of costs and benefits. The bulk of the economic benefit accrues to the consumer, with some portion accruing to village cooperatives – though, in

Table 15.15 *Distribution of costs (−) and benefits (+) in US dollars*

Item	Consumers	Govt	VHS	GEF	Total	Global environment	Total (including environment)
Electricity	115 043				115 043		115 043
Environmental					0	4783	4783
Fees	−39 974		39 974		0		0
Lost earnings	−690				−690		−690
Grants			0	−4783	0		−4783
Capital costs			−27 455		−27 455		−27 455
O&M costs			−1702		−1702		−1702
NSL, kerosene	2216	−2216			0		0
Taxes and duties on capital cost		2344	−2344		0		0
Total	76 594	128	8 472		85 195		89 978

practice, some of this surplus is likely to be passed back to the consumer beneficiaries (because of non-payment of dues, refunds of cash surpluses, etc). The GEF grant is shown as a subsidy, assumed to be equal to the global environmental benefit. For government, the loss of National Security Levy (on kerosene) is roughly offset by taxes and duties on capital costs.

Box 15.2 shows contrasting results from the Philippines, where diesel plant is cheaper than small hydro. Further, IERR calculations may be uncertain, and are better viewed as probability distributions, rather than single deterministic numbers. In Box 15.3, Monte Carlo simulations are applied to estimate the likely probability distributions of *ex-ante* rates of return on projects in Vietnam.

In summary, the achieved economic benefits are substantially greater than those estimated at appraisal. First, capacity factors are significantly greater, as a consequence of the design approach followed by consulting firms and developers – where systems are sized on the basis of the available average dry season flow. Second, actual capital costs are slightly lower than estimated. Finally, expenses for kerosene and battery prior to electric service have increased significantly since 1996, due to real income gains. Thus the willingness-to-pay for electric service is higher. Thus, from an economic viewpoint, village hydro systems bring large benefits and should continue to be promoted for off-grid electrification in areas where the grid access is not possible in the short to medium term.

15.5 Evaluating a typical water supply project in a poor African village

In this section, a simple rural water supply project in a poor African village is analysed (Munasinghe, 1977, 1992b). The focus is on the quantitative study of economic aspects, using CBA (see Chapter 3). Our procedure includes the demand forecast, the least-cost investment programme, the IERR, the incremental cost of supply and price. The emphasis is

Box 15.2 Philippines – analysis of isolated mini-grids

Hydro is not always as economic as in Sri Lanka for isolated mini-grids. In the Philippines, diesel plants were least-cost when compared with small hydro alternatives. Table B15.1 summarizes some key results of feasibility studies for six communities on two islands, where grid extension was not economic.

Table B15.1 *Comparison of diesel and small hydro costs in the Philippines*

	First-year number connected homes	First-year installed capacity (kW)	IERR, diesel (%)	Levelized costs (US cents/kWh)	
				diesel	hydro
Roxas	1441	625	**32.6**	15	26
El Nido	479	250	11.2	19.1	54
SanVicente	413	185	**19.7**	18.1	39
Taytay	1216	575	**25.6**	16.1	
Palawan	3549	1625	**28.2**	15.3	
Jose Abas Santos	796	310	8.9	21.6	
Malita	1778	685	**25.1**	16.3	23
Davao	2575	990	**20.6**	17.6	41

Boldface = economically viable (IERR > 15% hurdle rate).

The average willingness-to-pay in the Philippines was estimated for a typical household consumption tranche of 300 kWh/yr at US $0.3/kWh. Figure B15.1 shows the demand curve for the Philippines, derived from empirically established marginal willingness-to-pay for different types of systems.

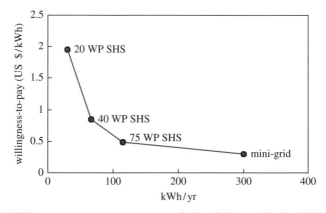

Figure B15.1. Willingness-to-pay versus annual electricity use in the Philippines.

The highest willingness-to-pay is for the first tranche of about 30 kWh/month, as is typically provided by 20 WP solar home systems, but thereafter the willingness-to-pay falls sharply to a typical US $0.15/kWh tariff charged in a Philippines mini-grid – which is a level confirmed by the observed willingness-to-pay for TV viewing of non-electrified households (by battery charging).

Box 15.3 Vietnam: probability distribution of the rate of return

Simple calculations of an economic rate of return may suffice for an *ex-post* analysis to evaluate whether a project has met its original objectives. However, for an *ex-ante* analysis during project appraisal (when data are less certain, and there may be a number of project alternatives), more sophisticated approaches are required. One common technique is Monte Carlo simulation, where each key input assumption is specified as a probability distribution (rather than one 'best' value). The IERR calculation is then repeated a large number of times (typically 1000 to 10 000), drawing at each calculation some sample value for each of the input assumptions. In this way a probability distribution of IERR is generated.

Figure B15.2 exemplifies the approach, based on the analysis of small hydro-projects in Vietnam to serve isolated communes not presently connected to the grid. Probability distributions for each alternative (hydro, grid extension and diesel plants) are shown – each of which is subject to its own set of uncertainties. This allows not only an assessment of the expected value of IERR, but also the trade-off with risk, which we can express as the probability that the hurdle rate is not achieved (i.e. area under the curve to the left of the 10% hurdle rate).

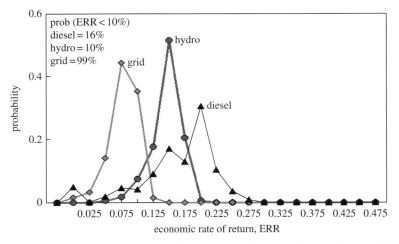

Figure B15.2. Probability distribution of the economic rate of return for small hydro-projects in Vietnam.

The comparison of expected returns and risks for four communes is shown in Tables B15.2 and B15.3. The clearly expected value alone does not tell the full story. For example, in the case of Phu Nam and Giap Trung, all three alternatives have comparable expected values, but hydro has significantly lower risk, and so the hydro option would be preferred. In the case of Bat Mot, diesel has both the highest expected return (and lowest risk). For Giap Trung, grid extension is indicated (since neither hydro nor diesel has a clear advantage), though the diesel option has the highest risk.

Table B15.2 *Internal economic rate of return (IERR)*

	Bat Mot	Giap Trung	Thong Thu	Phu Nam
Hydro (%)	11.9	13.4	14.3	15.0
Grid extension (%)	12.1	**14.7**	7.3	14.4
Diesel (%)	**16.1**	12.8	**18.4**	**15.7**

Table B15.3 *Risk of IERR < hurdle rate of 10%*

	Bat Mot	Giap Trung	Thong Thu	Phu Nam
Hydro (%)	27	**4**	**11**	**14**
Grid extension (%)	20	8	98	20
Diesel (%)	**18**	26	18	28

This example shows not only that a probability distribution of IERR is better than a single point (deterministic) estimate, but also that trade-offs between expected return and risk are often required.

on how demand, costs and revenue data may be used for effective decision making. The evaluation also takes environmental and social considerations into account, but in a qualitative manner.

15.5.1 Water-demand forecast

The demand forecast for the township area encompassed by the project is shown in Table 15.16 (see Section 14.7 for details about demand projections). In the second and third columns, total population and total demand give an indication of overall system size. The incremental demand refers to water which must be supplied via new investments, inclusive of sources required to replace existing ones that are expected to go out of service in the future. Thus, the increase in total demand from year 1 to year 2 is only 413 m³/day (i.e. 4548–4135 m³/day), but the total incremental demand met (from new investments) is 700 m³/day, because of existing sources that have to be replaced. By year 11, the total demand and total incremental demand met are identical (8763 m³/day), since all existing sources would have gone out of service. Incremental demand is the key variable for this calculation – domestic consumers are the most important, followed by government and, finally, industrial users.

The percentage of water unaccounted for (or fraction of water produced which is not used) decreases steadily due to improvements to the system, better billing, etc. Total incremental supply is equal to the sum of total demand and unaccounted for water. We note that incremental demand (and supply) begin in year 2, only after corresponding investments which had started in year 0 (Table 15.17) have become operational. The 20-year time

Table 15.16 *Demand forecast*

Year	Total population (1000)	Total demand (m³/day)	Incremental demand met by new sources (m³/day)				Water unaccounted for (%)	Total incremental supply (m³/day)
			Household	Government	Industrial	Total		
0 (now)	121.5	3717	0	0	0	0	20	0
1	125.7	4135	0	0	0	0	20	0
2	130.1	4548	420	210	70	700	20	875
3	134.6	4983	900	450	150	1500	20	1875
4	139.4	5416	1356	678	226	2260	20	2825
5	144.2	5904	1860	930	310	3100	20	3875
6	149	6350	2328	1164	388	3880	19	4790
7	153.9	6796	2760	1380	460	4600	19	5679
8	158.9	7250	3030	1515	505	5050	19	6235
9	164.2	7647	3476	1737	579	5793	19	7152
10	169.7	8134	4035	2017	672	6724	18	8200
11	175.3	8763	5258	2629	876	8763	18	10 687
12	180.9	9328	5597	2798	933	9328	18	11 376
13	187	9892	5935	2968	989	9892	18	12 063
14	193.1	10 600	6360	3180	1060	10 600	18	12 927
15	199.6	11 300	6780	3390	1130	11 300	18	13 780
16	207	12 000	7200	3600	1200	12 000	18	14 634
17	no additional demand		6667	3333	1111	11 111	18	13 550
18	is considered beyond		6173	3086	1029	10 288	18	12 546
19	this period since it		5716	2858	952	9526	18	11 617
20	will not be serviced by		5292	2646	882	8820	18	10 756
	sources included in this analysis							

horizon is sufficient to ensure that due to the cumulative effects of discounting, events occurring beyond this period have negligible impact on the results. In fact, by year 16 all facilities are operating at full capacity. Thereafter, no new sources are considered, and the incremental demand met by existing sources declines steadily due to wear and tear.

15.5.2 Least-cost investment programme

For illustrative purposes, we assume that the two best feasible alternative system expansion programmes or sequences for meeting the demand, are:

(1) a reservoir followed by a series of boreholes; or
(2) a borehole followed by a reservoir and more boreholes.

Table 15.17 *Supply costs for alternative 1*

	Investment costs (10^3L)[a]			O & M costs (10^3L)[a]								Total costs (10^3L)
		Local construction[c]		Direct imports[b]	Local investment goods[d]		Electricity[e]		Local labour[f]			
Year	Direct imports[b]	DP	BP		DP	BP	DP	BP	DP	BP		BP
0	300	200	170	0	0		0		0			470
1	200	133	113.1	0	0		0		0			313.1
2				6	3	2.7	2	1.6	10	8.5		18.8
3				14	7	6.3	4	3.2	25	21.5		45
4				20	10	9	6	4.8	35	29.8		63.6
5				32	20	18	14	11.2	60	51		112.2
6				44	32	28.8	28	22.4	90	76.5		171.7
7				56	48	43.2	42	33.6	110	93.5		226.3
8	30	20	17	60	56	50.4	50	40	150	127.5		324.9
9	75	25	21.3	88	85	76.5	81	64.8	195	165.8		491.4
10				92	96	86.4	95	76	250	212.5		466.9
11	120	40	34	97	106	95.4	106	84.8	275	233.8		665
12				103	114	102.6	114	91.2	300	255		551.8
13	150	50	42.5	110	125	112.5	125	100	315	267.8		782.8
14				115	136	122.4	136	108.8	340	289		635.2
15				119	145	130.5	145	116	360	306		671.5
16				110	134	120.6	134	107.2	335	284.8		622.6
17	30	20	17	102	124	111.6	124	99.2	316	268.6		581.4
18				94	113	101.7	113	90.4	280	238		524.1
19				87	105	94.5	105	84	260	221		486.5
20				80	97	87.3	97	77.6	240	204		448.9

DP = domestic price; BP = border price.

[a] All costs in real 1990 local currency units (L); official exchange rate US $1 = L1.

[b] Net of duties and taxes, already in border prices.

[c] Construction conversion factor = 0.85 for general inputs from the local construction sector (including labour).

[d] Investment conversion factor = 0.9 for aggregate of locally purchased investment items.

[e] Electricity conversion factor = 0.8 for electricity input; ideally, the border price should reflect the long-run marginal cost of supply of electricity.

[f] Labour conversion factor or shadow wage rate (SWR) = 0.85. This is a weighted average of unskilled SWR = 0.55 and skilled SWR = 0.95.

There are ample supplies of both groundwater and surface water available, so that cost complications due to depletion effects (e.g. lowering of the water table and increased pumping costs) do not arise – externalities due to groundwater depletion are described in Chapter 12.

We wish to identify the least-cost alternative (i.e. the one with the lowest present value of costs) – see Section 3.2.1. In this study (and most cases) there could be more than two alternatives. However, we compare only two different expansion options to illustrate the methodology. The same principles may be used to compare more than two alternatives.

The typical cost breakdown associated with the first alternative is given in Table 15.17. The second alternative (not shown here) has a somewhat different profile of costs. Certain costs that are common to both alternatives (e.g. distribution, operation and maintenance and connection costs) may be netted out without affecting the results of the least-cost analysis. However, these costs have been included in the tables because they will be required for the rate of return and marginal cost estimation to follow. The shadow-pricing procedure described in Chapter 3 is used. All costs are in local currency units (L), in real 1990 prices. The reference official exchange rate is US $1 = L1. The two columns in Table 15.17 marked 'Direct imports' are net of duties and taxes and are converted directly into border prices (using the official exchange rate). Local construction sector inputs are converted from domestic to border prices using the construction conversion factor of 0.85. Similarly, an investment conversion factor of 0.9 applies to locally purchased goods used in operation and maintenance.

Domestic-priced electricity inputs are converted to border prices using the electricity conversion factor of 0.8. Thus, border-priced electricity is adjusted to reflect the long-run marginal cost (LRMC) of power supply (see Chapter 14). Finally, a shadow wage rate (SWR) or labour conversion factor of 0.85 is used to border price local labour inputs. This aggregate SWR is a weighted average of 75% skilled labour (with SSWR = 0.95) and 25% unskilled labour (USWR = 0.55). Finally, all columns involving direct imports and border-priced costs are added together in the final column to yield the total costs of alternative 1 in border prices. Exactly the same procedure is followed to analyse the costs of the second alternative.

The present values of cost streams for both alternatives are given in Table 15.18, for several different discount rates. Clearly, alternative 1 is better than alternative 2 for discount rates ranging from 0 to over 20% (i.e. alternative 1 has a lower present value of costs). The opportunity cost of capital for this specific example falls in the range 10% to 12%. Therefore, the first investment programme, which begins with the construction of the surface-water reservoir, is chosen as the least-cost alternative.

15.5.3 Costs, benefits and IERR

Ideally, incremental water-use benefits should be estimated in terms of consumer willingness-to-pay (i.e. area under the demand curve – see Section 3.3.2). However, since no demand curve is available for this simple example, incremental benefits are estimated in terms of incremental revenues from users. Thus, these benefits are only a minimum measure, because consumer surplus is ignored. Further, there may be other social and environmental

Table 15.18 *Comparison of water-system expansion alternatives*

Discount rate (%)	Present value of total costs (10^3L)		
	Alternative 1	Alternative 2	Difference
0	8721	9134	413
5	4971	5267	296
10	3134	3321	187
20	1639	1649	10
30	1129	1018	−111

Equalizing discount rate = 20.5% and opportunity cost of capital = 10% to 12%.

externalities that are difficult to value economically and are therefore excluded from this cost–benefit calculation (see Section 3.3.5).

The incremental revenue (benefit) stream is calculated using the incremental water demand met (see Table 15.16). The incremental consumption benefits begin in year 2 (i.e. after two years of initial investment). The incremental water used by households (in m^3) is multiplied by the average household tariff of L0.32/m^3 to obtain the corresponding benefits (in domestic prices). This domestic-priced benefit is converted to border prices using the consumption conversion factor of 0.8 (see Section 3.8). Similarly, the government and industrial water-use benefits (in domestic prices) are calculated after multiplying the physical water consumption by the average government and industrial user tariff of L0.28/m^3. These benefits are converted to border prices using the standard conversion factor of 0.85 (since there is no specific conversion factor for government and industry). The household, government and industrial benefits are added to yield total border-priced project benefits.

The internal economic rate of return (IERR) for the project is the value which equalizes the present discounted value of the economic cost and benefit streams. In this example, this value falls between 13% and 14%. Since the opportunity cost of capital (OCC) lies in the range 10 to 12% (as indicated earlier), we see that IERR > OCC. This implies that the net present value of benefits (NPV) is positive, which provides the green light to go ahead with this investment plan (see Section 3.2.1).

15.5.4 *Average incremental cost of supply and pricing policy*

The LRMC of water is important for efficient resource allocation in the sector (see Section 14.3). Since the investments are lumpy, the average incremental cost (AIC) may be used to estimate the LRMC.

Thus, we may write: LRMC = AIC = PVC(OCC) / PVD(OCC), where PVC(OCC) = present value of costs discounted at OCC and PVD(OCC) = present value of incremental demand discounted at OCC.

The values of AIC range from L0.210 to L0.222/m^3 of water in border prices, for discount rates of 10 to 12%. As shown in Chapter 3, dividing this AIC value by the standard conversion factor (SCF = 0.85), for governmental and industrial consumers, yields the benchmark LRMC range of AIC$_{GI}$ = L0.248 to 0.261/m^3 (in domestic prices), which may be compared with the existing average tariff level. Similarly, using the consumption conversion factor (CCF = 0.8) for household consumers, their LRMC (in domestic prices) is given by AIC$_H$ = L0.263 to L0.278/m^3.

The prevailing average tariff levels for government/industrial and household consumers are p_{GI} = L0.28 and p_{H} = 0.32/m^3 of water, respectively, both of which are slightly higher than the corresponding benchmark values AIC$_H$ and AIC$_{GI}$, calculated above.

Economic efficiency and financial viability are among the major objectives of resource pricing policy (see Section 14.2.1). The foregoing calculations indicate that existing water prices are close to levels that will meet the economic efficiency objective. Financial viability will also be ensured, because actual tariff levels are a little greater than the AIC, so that incremental revenues exceed investment costs over the time horizon considered. If financial, sociopolitical and other constraints permit it, we might be justified in urging a small decrease in overall tariff levels, based solely on economic efficiency considerations. However, detailed recommendations on both the level and structure of tariffs ought to be made only after a thorough pricing study (see Chapter 14).

16

Local applications – hazards, disasters and urban growth[1]

In this chapter, we use the sustainomics framework to analyse more localized events like hazards and disasters, as well as to assess the sustainability of growth in densely populated urban areas. Section 16.1 describes how the harmful impacts of hazards on both socio-economic and ecological systems are often exacerbated by heightened vulnerability and prior damage inflicted by unsustainable human activities. A practical framework is presented for mainstreaming sustainable hazard reduction and management (SHARM) into national development – including the stages of relief, rehabilitation and reduction (planning, preparedness and prevention). Two-way linkages between hazards and sustainable development are analysed. In Section 16.2, the SHARM approach is used to assess the impacts of the biggest single disaster in modern history – the 2004 Asian Tsunami, which resulted in over 250 000 deaths in five countries (India, Indonesia, Maldives, Sri Lanka and Thailand). Effects on the macroeconomy, vulnerable sectors, employment and livelihoods, poverty, women and children and the environment are analysed, and appropriate policy responses are identified. A comparison of the impacts of the 2004 Asian Tsunami on Sri Lanka, and of Hurricane Katrina on New Orleans in 2005, raises important questions about the role of social capital in coping with disasters. Section 16.3 describes generic issues concerning the sustainability of long-term growth in Asian cities, arising mainly from growth and pollution affecting air, water and land. Policy options to address these problems are discussed – especially in the rapidly expanding mega-cities. In Section 16.4, we study the vulnerability of urban development to environmental damage and hazards (like floods, landslides and earthquakes) and we present a case study of Rio de Janeiro. Finally, Section 16.5 provides two examples of how urban development is becoming more sustainable in developed nations – in Canada and the European Union.

16.1 Sustainable hazard reduction and disaster management (SHARM)

This section describes a framework, based on sustainomics principles, to explore the links between hazards and sustainable development. The approach helps disaster experts,

---

[1] The valuable contribution of C. Clarke to this chapter is gratefully acknowledged. Some parts of the chapter are based on material adapted from MIND (2005), Munasinghe, (1997) and Munasinghe and Clarke (1995).

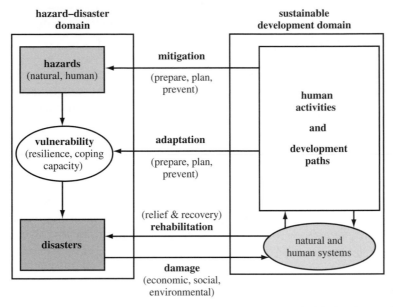

Figure 16.1. Circular relationship between the hazard–disaster and sustainable development domains and the role (SHARM).

development specialists and decision makers to identify measures to reduce hazard vulnerability and potential losses – by making development more sustainable (MDMS).

16.1.1 Hazards, vulnerability and disasters

Since the dawn of civilization, human society, the natural environment, hazards and disasters have been closely interlinked. Both hazards and the increasing environmental degradation continue to threaten development. Humankind's relationship with nature has gone through several stages, starting with symbiosis with nature in primitive times, through a period of increasing mastery over nature since the industrial age, when vulnerability to natural hazards was reduced. However, the rapid material-intensive growth patterns of the twentieth century have increased some hazard risks and made many groups (especially the poor) more vulnerable to disasters.

Hazards are extreme events (both natural and anthropogenic) that threaten sustainable development (see Figure 16.1 and Box 16.1). When hazards strike vulnerable populations (especially the poor and disadvantaged), the consequences are often disastrous. The left-hand side of Figure 16.1 (the hazard–disaster domain) shows that hazards are potentially risky events that result in disasters when vulnerability is high. Once the disaster has struck, there will be significant damage to human and natural systems in the sustainable development domain, and rehabilitation efforts are needed to recover. The harm to human and natural systems will further affect future development efforts. At the same time, many

---

Box 16.1 Hazards, disasters, vulnerability and SHARM – definitions

Hazard

An extreme event that can cause significant potential damage or loss. Natural hazards are linked to nature (e.g. earthquakes, floods, storms, tsunamis, etc.). Human-induced disasters are usually of industrial origin (e.g. oil spill, chemical or nuclear accident, etc.). Hazard risk rises when either or both the magnitude and probability of occurrence of a hazard increases.

Vulnerability

The degree to which socioeconomic and ecological systems are sensitive to and unable to cope with hazards. A system will suffer greater damage or loss if it is more vulnerable, less resilient and lacks adaptive capacity.

Disaster

A hazard that causes significant damage or loss to a vulnerable community or locality, resulting in deaths, property losses, environmental harm and disruption of normal functions.

SHARM

A practical framework that can reduce harm by integrating hazard-reduction measures into sustainable development strategy. Specific actions seek to strengthen resilience, reduce vulnerability to hazards (*ex-ante*) manage disasters more effectively (*ex-post*) and generally make development more sustainable.

(non-disaster-related) human activities are already affecting human and natural systems. Finally, alternative human development paths could increase (or decrease) both the vulnerability to, and likelihood of, future hazards.

Sustainable hazard reduction and disaster management (SHARM) seeks to reduce the harm from disasters by integrating hazard reduction and disaster-management measures into sustainable development strategy. As shown in Figure 16.1, the goal is to identify actions that will make development more sustainable by recovering faster from disasters (*ex-post*), reducing vulnerability to hazards (*ex-ante*), and wherever possible mitigating future hazards (*ex-ante* reduction of hazard likelihood) – through planning, preparedness and prevention. This process parallels the climate-change adaptation and mitigation response measures described in Chapter 5 (see Figure 5.1). Indeed, the SHARM approach may be extended to meet the long-term challenges of climate-related extreme events.

Types of natural disasters

'Natural disasters' arise from two broad categories of physical hazards – hydrometeorological (floods, droughts and storms) and geophysical (earthquakes, volcanic eruptions and related tsunamis). They have different human and economic impacts, and distinct patterns and forms of vulnerability, due to varying frequencies of occurrence and predictability.

Hydrometeorological hazards, associated with climatic variability, tend to be recurrent, thereby allowing adaptation in economic and social activity, e.g. the distinctive crops and cropping patterns in flood-or drought-prone areas of Bangladesh. Climatic and hydrological records allow formal assignment of risk in investment and production decisions, e.g. adopting decision rules for water use that reflect extreme rainfall variability, or building storm-resistant infrastructure.

Costly failures of prediction include the repeated hurricane-related damage to donor-funded but inadequately protected port facilities and roads in the Caribbean island of Dominica, beginning with Hurricane David in 1979 up to Hurricane Lenny in 1999, where repair and retrofitting have absorbed a high proportion of public investment. The suffering and wider economic disruption caused by poor management of southern African hydroelectric systems affected by extremely low rainfall (Kariba in 1991–1992) or very high rainfall (Caboro Baso in 1999–2000) have highlighted the need for improved science-based decision making. The potential effects of climate change are now recognized as introducing an additional source of uncertainty into the very data that underpin risk-sensitive decisions (see Chapter 5).

Geophysical hazards are mostly low-probability or seemingly random events (location-specific annual risks of under 1 in 100 or less). Over 80% of the major volcanic eruptions in the twentieth century – from Mont Pelé in 1902, which killed almost everyone in Martinique's capital, St Pierre, to Montserrat, ongoing since 1995 and forcing 90% of the island's population to relocate – had no precedent in historical time. Yet, in highly exposed areas, they can cause enormous loss of life, physical damage and disruption to public infrastructure and private assets. As economies grow and mega-cities emerge, more people and expanding investments across the globe are at risk from earthquakes, as demonstrated by recent disasters in Marmara, Turkey and Kobe, Japan. The Tsunami of 2004 showed that coastal locations, which have a high share of human urban activity, are vulnerable to tsunamis unleashed by seismic and volcanic activity (see Section 16.2).

The *geo-extent* or localization of the hazard is another purely physical determinant of relative economic vulnerability. A micro-island economy such as Montserrat (area 102 km^2; pre-eruption population 10 000) can be overwhelmed by an event like the Rabaul eruption of 1994, which might be less significant in Papua New Guinea (700 islands; area 463 000 km^2; population 4.2 million). Dominica (area 751 km^2; population 75 000) suffered many severe short-run shocks from cyclones. The latter are frequent, but scarcely disrupt the national economy in the Philippines (7200 islands; area 298 000 km^2; population 76 million).

Impacts

Since the late 1980s, natural hazards, such as earthquakes, volcanic eruptions, landslides, floods, tropical storms, drought, locust invasions and other natural calamities have killed three million people, inflicted injury, disease, homelessness and misery on one billion others, and caused billions of dollars of material damage. In the early 1990s, annual global economic costs of disasters averaged almost US $500 billion/yr (IFRC, 1996) and doubled from 1995 to 2000 (Munich Re, 1996).

All these events reconfirm a relatively clear picture of disaster impacts – the human suffering, the people affected and the financial cost continue to rise precipitously. From the 1950s to the 1990s, the reported global cost of 'natural' disasters increased 15-fold. In 1995, the year of the Kobe earthquake, disaster-related losses of US $178 billion were equivalent to 0.7% of global GDP. For an affected country, the costs can be beyond the domestic revenue raising and commercial borrowing capacity of government: for example, after Hurricane Mitch in 1998, in Honduras, with a GNP of $850 per capita, the government faced reconstruction costs equivalent to $1250 per capita. Recent extreme events include the 9.0 Richter scale earthquake, which unleashed the 2004 Tsunami with over 250 000 deaths, and the scale 5 Hurricane Katrina in the USA, with losses put at around US $200 billion. In October 2005, the South Asian Earthquake centred on Kashmir killed tens of thousands and made over three million homeless. Meanwhile, poor harvests and pests threaten famine in the Sahel and East Africa.

A major global meeting, the 1994 United Nations World Conference on Natural Disaster Reduction, in Yokohama, Japan, highlighted hazard reduction (Clarke and Munasinghe, 1995). Recently, the follow-up 2005 UN World Conference on Disaster Reduction, in Kyoto, Japan, focused on the 2004 Asian Tsunami.

The developing countries, where two-thirds of the world's population lives, suffer the most debilitating consequences due to natural disasters – 90% of all natural disasters and 95% of total disaster-related deaths occur in the developing countries. Furthermore, the risk of loss of life per million population due to disasters is 12-fold greater in the developing world than in the USA. The per capita losses in GNP in developing countries are estimated to be 20 times greater than in industrial countries. Since the 1960s, global economic losses have increased at least five-fold. Losses in the industrial countries are also rising. For example, in the highly insured USA, insurance payouts from natural disasters during 1990–1994 were more than quadruple those accumulated for all of the 1980s, which themselves were quadruple those of the previous decade. Losses are growing largely due to increasing concentration of population and investments in vulnerable locations and to inadequate investment in measures to reduce risk (UNCRD, 1994).

From an economic perspective, a disaster is a *shock* that results in a combination of *losses* in the human, social and physical capital stock and a *reduction* in economic activity such as income generation, investment, production, consumption and employment. The poor are likely to be worst affected, with major distributional implications. There may also be severe financial effects on the revenue and expenditure of public and private bodies. Disaster experts commonly distinguish *direct* impacts, including physical damage (capital stock) and losses in output such as crops destroyed and reduced fish catch, from *indirect* impacts, including most changes in the 'flows' of economic activity.

Vulnerability to hazards is determined by a complex, dynamic set of factors, such as economic structure, stage of development, prevailing economic conditions and the policy environment. Vulnerability can change quickly in countries experiencing rapid growth or socioeconomic decline. Appropriate investments in disaster mitigation and favourable developments in the structure of the economy can reduce economic vulnerability to natural hazards. Increasing sensitivity, such as that of southern Africa, reflects a complex mix of factors, including climatic variability (encompassing both droughts and floods), as well as the HIV/AIDS pandemic and a deteriorating policy environment.

Most extreme events that trigger disasters are beyond human control, although some human activities increase hazard risk. For example, unsafe practices may increase the likelihood of industrial hazards (like Bhopal or an oil spill), and environmental degradation (such as soil erosion or climate change) may worsen prospects for natural hazards. More importantly, vulnerability to hazards is often the result of human behaviour. Such actions include large-scale urbanization, population exposure to hazards, natural-resource degradation, poverty, population pressure and certain patterns of consumption, production and development. Lack of an early-warning system in South East Asia (unlike the well monitored Pacific region), coupled with exposed (and often illegal) settlements in coastal areas, worsened the impact of the 2004 Tsunami. Similarly, earthquakes occur naturally, but the amount of damage they cause is largely a function of development activities. Uncontrolled growth of cities and expansion of slums into marginal areas, poor design and building techniques and lack of enforcement of land-use regulations are some development decisions that result in significant losses when an earthquake strikes.

Poverty issues

Economic impacts of disasters vary by country income. The least-developed countries are the most vulnerable – suffering the greatest direct losses relative to a country's wealth. Poor groups in these nations may become even more vulnerable as socioeconomic changes force them to seek livelihoods in more hazard-prone places. However, economic losses may appear to be low, because a higher proportion of direct and indirect losses are less likely to be recorded, due to poor data.

Middle-income economies are more integrated – sectorally and geographically. Hence, an impact on one area generates negative impacts on the entire economy-wide system. The government of a middle-income country is likely to meet a larger share of the costs of relief and rehabilitation, as more international assistance flow toward least-developed countries. Although financial costs of capital losses are massive in developed countries, the economic impacts of disasters are proportionately less because of better mitigation and preparedness, and greater access to financial and insurance resources. More private-sector assets are likely to be well insured against disaster, and the loss shared with both local and global insurers and reinsurers.

Environmental vulnerability and poverty are mutually reinforcing: 80%, 60% and 50% of the poor in Latin America, Asia and Africa, respectively, live on marginal lands that are unproductive and highly vulnerable to environmental degradation and hazards. Developing countries, which must place high priority on food production and industrial activity, have fewer resources left to reduce hazard risk. Even in industrial countries, rising economic losses suggest that mitigation efforts are not keeping pace with the factors that are increasing vulnerability.

Many developing countries are also experiencing rapid population growth, with increasing concentration of population and investments in vulnerable locations. These trends increase pressures on natural resources and the environment and raise the consequent risks associated with human activity. In rural areas, rangelands are heavily overgrazed and forestlands are severely degraded by overexploitation and neglect. Acute shortages of firewood have accelerated deforestation, which, together with destruction of the vegetative cover on natural pastures, has increased the threat of floods and the deterioration and desertification of previously fertile land.

Rapid urbanization, and the growing scale of urban-industrial activity, is exacerbating environmental stresses in developing-country cities and increasing the vulnerability of urban dwellers to hazards – see Section 16.3 (Kreimer and Munasinghe, 1991). Accelerated changes in demographic and economic trends have disturbed the balance between ecosystems – see Chapter 4 (MA, 2005a). There is growing evidence of causal links between environmental degradation and vulnerability to hazards. Harming the environment (e.g. deforestation) can also worsen impacts of natural hazards. There is a rising correlation between the frequency and severity of extreme events and growing local and global environmental degradation – see Chapter 5 (IPCC, 2001b, 2007b). Environmental degradation intensifies disasters, thereby increasing the risk from secondary disasters: storms are followed by floods and landslides, floods by drought, and drought by pest epidemics and famines. Ecological harm due to extreme weather events has escalated, increasing faster than population growth.

As greater vulnerability is linked with poverty, sustainable development oriented toward poverty alleviation will diminish the effect of hazards. Difference in losses between developing and industrial nations support this view. Nevertheless, although evidence indicates that development helps to diminish the effects of hazards (at least in the aggregate), patterns of unsustainable development – such as greater use of resources, urbanization and use of environmentally harmful technologies – have increased vulnerability. Thus, more emphasis is needed on SHARM as a key element of national sustainable development strategy.

16.1.2 *Framework for mainstreaming SHARM*

Hazards and sustainable development

As indicated above, both natural and anthropogenic disasters destroy human effort and investments, thereby placing new demands on society for reconstruction and rehabilitation. Extreme events can have profound, negative impacts on long-term development, causing distress and increasing dependency. For many years, the response to hazards and environmental threats was reactive and characterized by increased defensive activities. More recently, our attitude toward such risks has evolved to include the more proactive design of projects and policies, that seek to anticipate hazards and limit damage. This approach also makes development more sustainable.

The basic SHARM framework has three key phases – *reduction, relief and recovery* (the three Rs). First, *reduction* focuses on *ex-ante* planning, prevention and preparedness (the three Ps), which lower the probability and severity of a hazard taking place and limit disaster damage by reducing vulnerability. Second, *relief* efforts seek to alleviate human suffering immediately the disaster has occurred. It is the short-term component of disaster management programmes, and usually lasts some days or weeks. Third, *recovery* refers to the short- to medium-term response of disaster management programmes, involving rehabilitation of human lives and reconstruction of damaged buildings and infrastructure, which could last a few months or years.

Section 16.2 assesses the 2004 Asian Tsunami relief and (ongoing) recovery activities *ex-ante*, and provides suggestions to improve future reduction and prevention strategy *ex-post*, based on lessons learned.

Analytical framework

National decision makers pay more attention to conventional development strategies that seek to achieve objectives such as economic growth, poverty alleviation, food security, human health and employment. Figure 16.2 shows that sustainable development (SD) is considered a special (and rather obscure) aspect of conventional development. In turn, the environment is one component of sustainable development, and finally natural hazards are themselves seen as a minor element of the environment. The double arrow in the figure shows the two-way links between hazards and sustainable development. It is an essential step, in the practical implementation of SHARM within a country, to show the explicit linkages between hazard risks and conventional development activities, to identify priority issues and to determine appropriate policy remedies and responses in the development domain.

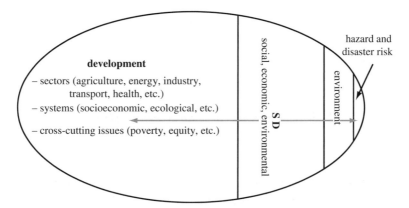

Figure 16.2. Hazards–sustainable development nexus: decision makers see hazards as a minor element of national development strategy.

Sustainable hazard-reduction and disaster-management measures ultimately must be implemented by nations, and will receive more favourable attention from both national decisions makers and the international development community if we can show their relevance for sustainable development. Thus, we start from the basic premise that the most effective way of protecting humans from hazards is to mainstream appropriate measures and policies into development activities. More specifically, SHARM seeks to integrate protective measures into sustainable development strategy at the national and local levels and implement them on a more disaggregate basis through local communities and individuals. Thus, SHARM builds on the basic elements of sustainomics, including the principle of making development more sustainable, the sustainable development triangle, transcending boundaries and full-cycle application of analytical tools (especially the Action Impact Matrix – see Section 2.4.1).

16.1.3 Two-way linkages between hazards and sustainable development

Economic, social and environmental aspects

As shown in Figure 16.1, hazards and sustainable development are linked in circular fashion – hazards have significant impacts on sustainable development through vulnerabilities, and, in turn, the sustainability of development paths can alter hazard risks and vulnerability. Hazards threaten prospects for sustainable development in all three dimensions. Economic, social and environmental capital is damaged by disasters, causing major losses of benefits flowing from those assets. Such losses depend on the resilience and vulnerability of socio-economic and environmental systems.

Some economic development paths can worsen vulnerability. Thus, growing interconnectedness has exacerbated hazard risks. The number of people indirectly harmed by disasters worldwide is typically 1000 times the number of people killed (Munasinghe and Clarke, 1995). For instance, losses could be propagated via capital markets, through capital flight, depreciation of domestic currency, greater indebtedness, etc. Developing economies are especially sensitive to vagaries of international capital flows, which makes them more vulnerable to disasters. Key needs for economic growth include investment, effective governance and social stability – unfortunately, disasters lead to exactly the opposite conditions. Loss of man-made and natural capital causes sudden disinvestment, post-disaster relief increases both the financial and administrative burden on government, and, finally, disasters are socially destabilizing.

The social dimension of sustainable development also has a two-way link with hazards. Hazard risk and vulnerability depend on social behaviour. Conversely, disasters undermine sustainable development by eroding social capital and further increasing vulnerability. Thus, the resilience of socioeconomic systems may be increased through prevention and adaptation in anticipation of a perceived hazard risk, and more generally by making development more sustainable. The critical role of social capital in coping with disasters is explored in Section 16.2 (see Section 16.2.5).

As the impacts of natural disasters fall disproportionately on the poor, the social view stresses the participation of at-risk communities in devising and implementing effective strategies to reduce vulnerability. Communities must directly identify site-specific solutions and assess the efficacy of proposed measures. The implementation of SHARM is best performed jointly by local communities, the government and industry. Better public awareness is essential. There is a need to understand people's perception of risk, develop better channels of communication and popular consultation and to rely on local resources. Often, major changes due to urbanization have undermined the traditional support system for coping with crises. Decentralized decision making and subsidiarity are important to strengthen the implementation of SHARM, particularly given the need for rapid and localized responses to sudden catastrophes. For example, informal networks among slum-dwellers in Turkish cities provided support for communities during crises (Parker, Kreimer and Munasinghe, 1995).

Hazards also interact both ways with the environmental dimension of sustainable development. Hazards, risk and vulnerability depend on how development activities affect nature. In turn, disasters can harm the environment and hamper sustainable development. Environmental sustainability emphasizes preserving the resilience and dynamic ability of biophysical systems to adapt to external shocks and disasters. While most hazards are beyond human control, recent changes in demographic and economic trends are harming ecosystems (see Chapter 4) and increasing vulnerability to hazards.

Vulnerability and poverty are mutually reinforcing. Developing countries face the most severe impacts of natural disasters. The analysis of vulnerability must include poverty, sociopolitical marginalization, lack of social safety nets and other social, political and economic indicators that cause people to act in ways which exposes them to higher risk. Often, proximity to extreme events combines with low socioeconomic status to yield deadly results. By the year 2025, 80% of the world's population will reside in developing countries, and up to 60% of these people are highly vulnerable to extreme events (Munasinghe and Clarke, 1995).

Some policy implications

Economies need to incorporate disaster risk into decisions on investments (e.g. infrastructure and house construction to withstand extreme events) and share risks and costs through insurance. To formulate effective policies, externalities have to be included in cost–benefit analysis. When valuation is difficult, multicriteria analysis will reduce risk and costs.

Widespread dissemination of accurate and vital information to people at risk is essential. Improved warning and mitigation have greatly reduced lives lost in technologically advanced nations. This underscores the need for developing countries to increase their own capabilities in this area.

Yet, any measures are effective only when associated with appropriate regulatory structures. For developing countries, key features of broad-scope insurance programmes should include providing all natural-hazard insurance, government reinsurance to ensure stability of insurance markets and subsidized or low-cost insurance to the poor. Thus, insurance can be used to promote mitigative actions and limit vulnerability. Other market-based control mechanisms (pricing and taxation) may be used to reinforce such behaviour. Improved institutional arrangements, such as better urban management, are also critical. The focus must be on providing more comprehensive environmental protection within basic services.

National capacity to respond to and face such unpredictable events depends on the ability to measure, appraise and evaluate possible losses. While cost–benefit analysis is useful, issues such as moral hazard problems, role of expectations and undervaluation of benefits (due to uncertainty, inadequate data or lack of accounting framework), must be recognized. When the risk is of a more global/widespread nature, and mitigation costs are large, fewer incentives exist for an individual country, especially a poor one. Cooperative efforts between countries will realize greater benefits.

Finally, a comprehensive approach based on SHARM involves several elements: reduction, relief and recovery. Usually, the *ex-post* focus is on relief and recovery, but the greatest potential for improvement is through hazard reduction, involving planning, preparedness and prevention. Even in the recovery phase, good mitigation principles need to be exercised instead of mere rebuilding. For example, the World Bank (2004) estimated that US $3.15 billion spent on flood control in China over the final four decades of the twentieth century prevented losses of US $12 billion.

Communities at risk must participate in devising and implementing effective strategies to reduce vulnerability, identifying site-specific solutions and assessing the efficacy of proposed measures. Implementation of SHARM is best performed jointly by local communities, the government and industry. Thus, there is a need to identify and understand people's perception of risk, develop better channels of communication and popular consultation and rely on local resources and traditional support systems. Lastly, lessons learned from one phase of SHARM may be extended and applied to other phases, different countries and future hazards.

16.2 The 2004 Asian Tsunami – a preliminary assessment

This case study uses the SHARM framework to review and assess the consequences of the Asian Tsunami of 2004 for five affected countries (India, Indonesia, Maldives, Sri Lanka and Thailand), in order to identify lessons learned and reduce the potential impacts of future hazards (MIND, 2005). It seeks to better understand the impacts of the 2004 Tsunami, promote sustainable development that is more resilient to the impacts of disasters and guide future decisions about *ex-ante* policies for hazard reduction through better prevention and management. More generally, we explore practical links between hazards and sustainable development based on recent experience, and attempt to enhance the dialogue between disaster experts, development specialists and decision makers, on reducing potential losses and long-term vulnerability of sustainable development.

A more systematic method of mainstreaming SHARM measures into national sustainable development strategy would have been to use the Action Impact Matrix (AIM) – see Section 2.4.1. Furthermore, post-Tsunami recovery activities should be subjected to full sustainable development assessment (SDA) – Chapters 3 and 4. However, such a detailed analysis was

Table 16.1 *Tsunami impacts: economic, social and environmental*

	Social			Economic			Environmental		
	Number of deaths (% pop.)	Pop. displaced ('000)	Rise in poverty ('000)	Loss (US 10^6) [% of GDP]	Loss of employment ('000)	GDP growth (before [after])	Coral reefs	Mangroves	Land salinity
Sri Lanka	35 000 (0.2)	517	287	1500 [5.2]	400	5.5 [5.2]	low	medium	high
Indonesia	16 400 (0.07)	704	1035	5000 [2.3]	600	5.2 [5.5]	low	low	high
Thailand	8000 (0.01)	60	24	235 [0.8]	100	6.6 [5.6]	low	medium	high
India	16 000 (0.001)	650	644	1070 [0.3]	2700	6 [6.8]	low	low	high
Maldives	<100 (0.02)	13	39	470 [53.1]	25	5 [1.0]	low	medium	high

Source: MIND (2005).

beyond the scope of this preliminary assessment. Table 16.1 shows a snapshot of the main economic, social and environmental impacts, by country. Below, we review a full range of impacts across countries, by sector and topic: (1) macroeconomy and the insurance market; (2) sectors – fisheries, tourism, agriculture, SME and other sectors; (3) employment; (4) poverty and inequality; (5) women, children, different ethnic groups and psychosocial effects; (6) environment; (7) summary and policy implications.

16.2.1 Macroeconomic impacts and the insurance market

There are many key macroeconomic impacts, mainly due to the heavy damage to vital productive sectors, i.e. agriculture, fishing, tourism and small enterprises. The magnitude of these impacts depends on the capability to absorb shocks and the level of dependency of economies on the affected sectors. Generally, countries with diversified economic structures are more resilient than those with only a few dominant sectors. National governments and regional administrations also faced significant financial and administrative difficulties after the disaster, as they had to divert resources from other productive sectors into unbudgeted relief and rehabilitation activities. The effect is more severe when there is a larger coastal population. There are many economic activities based on ocean resources and infrastructure, such as roads, bridges, electricity, water, etc., in the densely populated coastal areas that were affected by the Tsunami.

Although government and private-sector investments on reconstruction will partly offset negative impacts on economic growth, the increased growth from reconstruction will not really contribute to new development, since all these new investments simply fill the pit created by the disaster.

In Sri Lanka, the Tsunami severely harmed outputs amounting to US $1.5 billion in fisheries, agriculture, tourism and small enterprises. While there were many impacts on local economies, livelihoods and lifestyles of people in affected areas, the effect on economic growth was not large, as the share of the affected sectors in GDP is small. Thailand was able to maintain over 4% growth rate in 2005. According to the previous predictions made by ADB and IMF, the growth would have been 5.5%. The present slow down of the economy is not only due to the Tsunami damage, but also to the rising global crude oil prices, drought, avian influenza, temporary closure of petroleum, petrochemical and steel plants for future capacity expansion and unrest in three southern provinces.

The expected impact of the Tsunami on growth of GDP in Indonesia is not significant (only a 0.25% reduction), though the impact on the affected provinces was very significant, amounting to almost US $5 billion. The Tsunami had no impact on the overall Indian GDP, which was about 7% in 2005. However, economic activities, such as fisheries, agriculture and microenterprises, along the coastline in four states and the Andaman and Nicobar islands were devastated, with damage over US $1 billion. Unlike the other countries, the Tsunami impact on Maldives was nationwide and hit key sectors such as tourism and fisheries. The short- to long-term impact on the overall economy will mainly depend on recovery rates in these two sectors. Since tourism accounts for 33% of GDP, overall growth and other macroeconomic indicators have been severely affected by the Tsunami.

Government expenditure and revenue

Governments played a bigger role in activities ranging from relief distribution to restoration of assets and livelihoods, because the rate of insurance penetration is very low and the poor were the major victims of the disaster. Donors, the private sector and civil society generously provided funds. A total of US $10.5 billion was pledged to Indonesia, Maldives, Sri Lanka and India by November 2005. Unlike in previous disasters, the ratio of commitment to pledges was high and was 75% by November 2005. Thailand and India declined any debt relief or relief aid and only accepted concessional loans for infrastructure restoration.

Since key economic sectors such as tourism, fishing and agriculture were affected, tax and other income from these sectors for national and regional governments will decrease. All the affected countries, except the Maldives, have well diversified economies. Thus, the decreased government income could be made up to some extent from other productive sectors.

Inflation

Increased money supply, due to donor funding for reconstruction, and the large number of foreign and local workers in the affected areas push prices up locally and nationally. In addition, rising oil prices also contributed to inflation in the affected countries. However, central banks managed the inflation to some extent by sterilizing the money supply.

Foreign exchange reserves and external debt

Due to the high oil price increases starting in early 2005, imports rose in the first half of the year, but there was no major impact on merchandise exports from the Tsunami. Together, the materials imported for Tsunami reconstruction and decreased tourism revenues caused a current account deficit in 2005. However, Tsunami recovery grants, loans and debt-relief facilities offered by donor agencies and individual countries and private transfers offset the current account deficit. Thus, foreign exchange reserves in these countries were unaffected, except the Maldives.

Affected countries were offered a moratorium – mainly a deferral of debt on the foreign debt from the Paris Club of creditor nations. However, donors refused to write off debts. The IMF, ADB, EU and World Bank gave a number of loans to supplement the large grants. Thailand and India have high external resources and did not request debt relief. Thailand declined financial assistance for recovery.

Labour market

The Tsunami disaster destroyed many livelihoods of people in affected countries. Employment was mainly affected by decreased tourism, loss of fishing vessels and gear and destruction of small enterprises and farmland. Early reconstruction and rehabilitation of infrastructure generated employment opportunities in the construction sector.

Insurance market

Due to low insurance rates, insured losses were modest relative to the scale of the disaster. In January 2005, Swiss Re estimated insured losses from the disaster at around US \$5 billion. More recent insured loss estimates range from US \$2.5 to US \$4 billion, while total economic losses are US \$13–14 billion. Better risk transfer among vulnerable communities is important to lessen the impacts of future disaster.

16.2.2 Impacts on sectors

Fisheries and agriculture in coastal areas were severely damaged by Tsunami waves, and damage varies greatly between localities. The worst-hit sectors were fisheries and aquaculture. The agricultural sector has been affected by losses to human capital, crops (especially rice stocks), productive lands (due to salinity) and livestock. Tourism was also severely impacted in countries such as the Maldives.

Fisheries and aquaculture

The Tsunami has led to a loss of livelihood for millions of small-scale coastal fishermen, with high losses of fishery fleets and industrial infrastructure. Loss of coastal aquaculture installations (ponds, hatcheries, equipment and infrastructure) has badly affected coastal populations and ecosystems. A sharp decrease in fish population and destruction of coral reefs occurred. Fish consumption fell because of unfounded fears that it is dangerous to eat seafood from the Tsunami zone.

Agriculture and livestock

Rice is the main staple in the affected countries. The main season paddy crop was planted before the Tsunami struck, causing scarcity of future food supplies. Farm animals have been killed, and food and tree crops were washed away or died due to saltwater. There has been a severe loss of productive lands due to erosion, scouring, deposition and salinity. Deterioration in food and livelihood security would have been serious if agriculture and fishing had not been restarted rapidly. There was a major lack of managerial capacity to cope with agricultural activities, planning and implementing rehabilitation projects. Many buildings that housed animals were destroyed. The main losses were poultry, pigs, goats, sheep and, to a lesser extent, cattle and buffalo.

Tourism

Severe damage was caused to many hotels and resorts along the coastline, in addition to damages to souvenir shops, vehicles, etc. Job losses in tourist-related services have been very high, including those working in internet cafés and diving shops, those driving taxis and selling souvenirs. Tourist arrivals and revenues fell sharply following the disaster. The effects were very severe in the Maldives, where tourism dominates.

Other small enterprises

Private enterprises along the coast (mainly of tourist-related business such as hotels, restaurants, shops and small stores) have been badly affected.

Infrastructure

Education. The Tsunami damaged many schools, vocational/industrial training centres and universities, including equipment, machinery, tools, furniture, books, and other library resources, and consumable teaching learning material, such as chemicals, chalk and white-board pens.

Health. Damage to the health system consisted of the loss of services, human resources and health-related infrastructure such as hospitals, drug stores, cold rooms, preventive healthcare offices, health staff facilities, district health offices, vehicles (ambulances, lorries, vans, double cabs, motorbikes) and medical equipment (in hospitals, stores and clinics).

Housing. Many homes were destroyed and had to be rebuilt urgently.

Power. Power-sector impacts were marginal, with damage mainly confined to medium- and low-voltage distribution lines and transformers located in coastal areas. Other infrastructure (such as grid-substations, major transmission lines and power plants) were not directly damaged.

Water supply and sanitation. Many wells were damaged, chiefly by salt water intrusion. Physical damage to existing water-supply schemes was restricted to distribution networks along the shoreline. Harm to individual home latrines contaminated much of the water supply.

Transportation. Bridges and culverts were displaced and embankments eroded by advancing and retreating waves. The main damage occurred to roads that were already greatly deteriorated due to lack of maintenance.

Table 16.2 *Estimated employment losses in the region*

India	Indonesia	Maldives	Sri Lanka	Thailand
650 000	600 000	25 000	275 000	100 000

Source: UN Needs Assessment Survey, 2005.

16.2.3 Impacts on employment and livelihoods

The loss of life and damage to property by the 2004 Tsunami was the highest recorded in contemporary history. To compound the tragedy, the survivors lost all access to employment and livelihoods (see Table 16.2). The livelihoods of the poor were hardest hit. Directly, or indirectly, nearly 645 000 households were affected, including fishermen, employees in the tourist trade, farmers, landless and casual labourers, small businesses and microenterprises and other categories of workers in the informal sector.

Other than the direct loss of employment, destruction of resources that sustained livelihood of the people, such as agricultural lands and wetlands, have deprived the informal sector of gainful self-employment.

Fisheries

Although the contribution of fisheries to the GDP of affected countries was marginal, the sector provides significant employment opportunities, in both direct fishing and linkage activities. While the proximity of fishery settlements to the coast was the main reason for large-scale losses, the poverty prevalent in the sector made it more vulnerable. In Tamil Nadu, Banda Aceh and Northern Sumatra and Sri Lanka, respectively, 300 000, 100 000 and 100 000 fisheries-related jobs were affected. On the Andaman coast of Thailand, about 490 fishing villages were devastated.

Tourism

The greatest loss of tourism was felt in the Maldives and Phuket in Thailand. Tourism is the largest industry in the Maldives, accounting for 33% of GDP and more than 60% of foreign exchange receipts, and employing both locals and expatriate workers. The experience in Maldives and Phuket clearly showed the risk of overdependence on a single economic activity. Diversified economic activities would offer alternative job opportunities and absorb the shock of a disaster. When the multiplier effects of tourism are considered, this industry accounted for more than 25 000 jobs. Aceh and Northern Sumatra are not major tourism destinations and, as a result, the direct impact on tourism was marginal. In Sri Lanka, although the tourism sector accounts for about 2% of GDP, it generates direct employment for about 50 000 and indirect employment for 65 000 more. About 27 000 people working in tourist and tourist-related services lost their jobs. In Thailand an estimated 100 000 people in the tourism sector lost their jobs, and half a million jobs were at risk unless tourism picked up fast.

Agriculture

Loss of standing crops and death or injury to livestock in coastal areas had a major impact on the livelihoods of the poor. Salinity effects were severe in some areas. Current estimates in Banda Aceh indicate that over 600 000 persons (about 25% of the total working population) have lost their livelihoods. In the Maldives, the agriculture sector accounted for a small percentage of GDP. In Sri Lanka productivity in coastal lands was already low. Although considerable damage was experienced in the north and east, impacts on immediate agricultural output was marginal. However, the long-term impacts of soil salinity on agriculture productivity is yet to be assessed. In Thailand, crop losses occurred in six affected provinces.

Microenterprises and the informal sector

The informal sector includes wage labourers and seasonal and subsistence workers. It is most vulnerable to disasters, due to the socioeconomic structure of affected areas. The Tsunami exposed the absence of organized schemes and safety nets to protect this sector. Damages were primarily due to loss of employment opportunities and, consequently, wages. Skilled artisans lost their tools and equipment. Many individuals along the coast involved in trade, industry and microenterprises across a broad socioeconomic spectrum suffered losses to livelihoods. All these vulnerable groups required support to get their livelihoods back on track.

Recovery efforts

Given the magnitude of the disaster, and the limited capacity of affected countries to cope with such disasters, the recovery effort in respect of livelihood rehabilitation can be termed moderately successful. The response of the international community, donors, governments, the private sector and, above all, civil society was overwhelming. Cultural traits and extended family systems stood in good stead at the time of disaster. In all countries, civil society bore the initial burden of relief, long before government could get organized to take over the recovery task.

Recovery was faster in the informal sector and fisheries, and slower in tourism and agriculture. Rehabilitation programmes require skills at all levels, including managerial and middle-grade levels. Strategic approaches, such as achieving stable employment and livelihoods through developing local economies, has not been developed except in India. One key issue that inhibited recovery was the inadequate institutional mechanisms for restoring jobs and livelihoods lost.

Governments have concentrated on improving institutional structures, and disaster management mechanisms have been strengthened by giving wide administrative powers to implementers. 'Incident Command Systems' have been introduced by the Government of India, and six regional resource centres have been created, with a headquarters support centre to coordinate their efforts. In Thailand, recovery programmes were brought under the Ministry of Social Development and Human Security, which coordinates activities with relevant institutions. In Sri Lanka, recovery and rehabilitation falls under the Prime Minister's office, while a separate Ministry has been created for disaster management.

Table 16.3 *Poverty indicators and poverty impacts of the Tsunami*

Country	Base year	Total pop. ('000)	Number of poor ('000)	National HCR (%)	Additional number of poor ('000)	New national HCR (%)
Indonesia	2002	212 000	38 584	18.2	1035	18.7
India	1999	1 001 000	261 261	26.1	644	26.2
Sri Lanka	1995	17 280	4355	25.2	287	26.6
Maldives	2004	300	66	22	39	35
Thailand	2002	63 430	6216	9.8	24	9.8

Figures are based on the national poverty lines and ADB staff estimates.

The importance of skills training has been acknowledged by all countries. Some countries have embarked on training of higher-level managers as well. 'Cash for work' programmes proved to be a successful strategy to provide much needed funds to vulnerable persons such as women and children. Such programmes offered cash to meet immediate needs, since the benefits of other rehabilitating programmes took too long to percolate down to the poor. UNDP has encouraged these programmes. Sri Lanka has given high priority to self-employment programmes. Employment via construction activity was followed by all countries. However, only a few large-scale construction activities were undertaken during the first six months to accommodate displaced workers. Microcredit and other financial services were helpful to small-scale entrepreneurs in returning to normality. India, Sri Lanka and Thailand promoted microcredit as a recovery strategy.

16.2.4 Impacts on poverty and inequality

The poverty impact of the Tsunami is most damaging. Tsunami impacts have been less severe at national levels, but more severe at local and community levels along the coast. It has not only added over two million to the number of poor, but also dragged millions of already poor into deeper poverty. Table 16.3 summarizes the immediate poverty impact. The highest impact is in Indonesia, followed by India and Sri Lanka. The highest head count ratio (HCR) is in the Maldives.

Recovery scenarios

A future-scenarios analysis (see Table 16.4) suggests that, if recovery is slow, more than one million will stay poor, even by 2008 (Hagiwara and Sugiyarto, 2005). The recovery speed and its poverty impact depend on the extent of damage, sectors affected, government response, political stability and macroeconomic management. *Fast recovery* assumed that the process in Thailand is one year, India and Sri Lanka two years and Indonesia three years. Similarly, for the *slow scenario* three years were needed in Thailand, four years in India and Sri Lanka and five years in Indonesia. The Maldives would follow Sri Lanka and India (ADB, 2005a).

Table 16.4 *Recovery scenarios*

Country	Fast-recovery scenario	Slow-recovery scenario
	Number of poor	
Indonesia	345 000	621 000
India	0	322 000
Sri Lanka	0	144 000
Maldives	0	20 000
Thailand	0	8000
Total	345 000	1 115 000

There is no simple universal blueprint for implementing a poverty-reduction strategy, since it depends on national economic, socio-political, structural, and cultural aspects. A concerted effort among the various sectors is required to ensure the success of poverty reduction efforts.

Recovery and reconstruction

In aiming for the fast-recovery option, the concept of *recovery plus* should be the target, where poverty reduction goes beyond what existed prior to the Tsunami. Medium- and long-term rehabilitation and reconstruction efforts offer a chance to overcome previous weaknesses and create better livelihoods. New investments in the affected areas should aim not only to offset the initial damages to infrastructure, but also to use new methods in building better and improved communities. The focus should be on incorporating the Millennium Development Goals of poverty reduction in reconstruction plans, including (a) clean water, (b) sanitation, (c) education and (d) 'safety nets' for vulnerable groups.

The principle of *subsidiarity* needs to be included in the planning process, with the central government setting standards, policies and principles, while implementation starts from the lowest competent level of government and civil society. Coordination at central, district and local levels is essential. In addition, for efficient implementation there must be a concerted effort in *capacity building* in governance at all levels.

Priority should be given to the concept of making development more sustainable, where emphasis is laid not only on economic, but also on social and environmental dimensions of sustainable development. The recovery effort has now moved to the medium- and long-term phase of reconstruction – e.g. shifting emphasis from cash for work programmes (which alone will not restore sustainable livelihoods) to restoring local economies. However, economic recovery will take much longer in some places. Meanwhile, it is vital to build social capital in the affected regions and other disaster-prone areas through consultation and empowerment of stakeholders. In the long run, social capital will be a key factor in building resilience and reducing vulnerability to hazards (see Section 16.2.5).

Political impediments to recovery exist in Indonesia and Sri Lanka, where rebel groups control parts of Tsunami-affected areas. Progress in Indonesia was initially slow because of the time it took to establish the Rehabilitation and Reconstruction Agency, which will play a central role in managing recovery programmes. Now that the agency is in place, and a peace agreement has been reached between the Government and separatist rebels in Aceh, the reconstruction process is expected to accelerate. A holistic approach to reconstruction in Aceh and Nias Islands is still needed, with a comprehensive strategy that takes all aspects of life into account.

The main focus of poverty reduction must be homes for the displaced and income generation by kick-starting the economy to create jobs.

16.2.5 Role of social capital: comparing impacts of the Asian Tsunami on Sri Lanka and Hurricane Katrina on New Orleans[2]

The 2004 Asian Tsunami and Hurricane Katrina struck within nine months of each other. Despite many differences, which make comparisons difficult, the two disasters provide useful insights.

The Asian Tsunami

The 2004 Asian Tsunami, triggered by a Richter scale 9 magnitude earthquake off the coast of Indonesia, was the most devastating disaster in modern history, killing over 250 000 people in South and East Asia. A comprehensive review and comparison of impacts on five affected countries (India, Indonesia, Maldives, Sri Lanka and Thailand) is provided in MIND (2005).

We focus on Sri Lanka, which was the most heavily affected in relative terms. Within a few hours on 26 December 2004, without prior warning (because early warning systems did not exist), about 35 000 Sri Lankans were killed (i.e. one in every 570 persons), and over half a million were displaced (i.e. one in every 40 persons). By any standards, this was a catastrophic blow to a small developing country of around 20 million people, with a per capita income of barely US $1000/yr.

In the immediate aftermath (and for several weeks afterwards), the government was overwhelmed. There were dire predictions of civil breakdown and spread of epidemics among the homeless, in a country already undergoing serious internal conflict. However, civil society rallied on an unprecedented scale. Within hours of the Tsunami, local groups were combing the coastal areas for survivors, refugee camps were established in neighbourhood homes, schools and places of worship (Buddhist, Hindu, Islamic and Christian), while private relief supplies began to pour into affected areas from other parts of the nation. Food, water and shelter were provided to survivors, and tens of thousands of decomposing corpses were safely disposed of before they became a health hazard. Incidents of looting and predatory behaviour were minimal. Even the ongoing ethnic conflict subsided as combatants (temporarily) set aside their differences to face the common disaster – many instances of

---

[2] Taken from Munasinghe (2007b).

cooperation were recorded to provide immediate relief to Tsunami victims, but only in the initial weeks.

One example of civil society initiative was the People's Consultative Meeting organized just ten days after the disaster by the Munasinghe Institute of Development (MIND) and other Civil Society organizations (ISEE, 2005), to share ideas and promote networking to cover all aspects of the post-Tsunami situation – relief (short-term), recovery (medium-term), and reduction (long-term prevention). The meeting was attended by over 100 leaders from government, political parties, universities, business, industry, international agencies, media, NGOs and CSOs.

This multistakeholder forum achieved all its main objectives. Participants were able to exchange the latest information and take stock of the rapidly evolving situation. Important gaps and needs were identified, while potential duplication was avoided in the immediate relief activities. Partnerships and alliance building were facilitated, and many participants developed ideas for joint follow-up activities. Useful ideas for the next phase of recovery were identified, while special attention was also paid to future disaster reduction through preparedness, planning and prevention. A comprehensive action plan was submitted to government authorities on behalf of civil society, and a full report was sent to the Second UN World Conference on Disasters held in Kobe several weeks later (January 2005).

In summary, civil society in Sri Lanka proved remarkably resilient and helped to hold the country together, especially during the first few weeks – apparently, the social capital embedded within traditional communities in affected areas and throughout the nation played a crucial role. After several weeks, government relief efforts and assistance pouring in from abroad took on the major burden of relief and recovery, although civil society continued to play a significant role.

The Asian Tsunami also showed some interesting economic–social–environmental linkages. Economic infrastructure was inadequate, including the flimsy homes of the coastal poor, which were swept away. There was no Tsunami early-warning system (since such phenomena are virtually unknown in the Indian Ocean), which would have saved many lives.

Among the social aspects was the ad hoc observation that the poor were relatively more resilient than the wealthy. This phenomenon was also noted in the case of earthquakes in Turkey (Munasinghe and Clarke, 1995). When extreme disasters strike, everyone is severely affected. However, the poor are better able to fall back on traditional, informal mutual-help networks, whereas the rich, who are more dependent on mechanical devices, abundant electricity, water, food and the services of domestic aides, simply cannot cope with their absence. Lack of traditional knowledge also played a part. Unlike Pacific Islanders, who have learned to seek higher ground when the sea recedes from the shoreline, many curious Sri Lankans walked into the shallows as the ocean withdrew and became the first victims of the resurging tidal waves.

On the environmental side, there was surprisingly little loss of wildlife in game parks extending into coastal areas of Sri Lanka – apparently, the subsonic vibrations which preceded the Tsunami provided an early warning to wild animals. There are also some sketchy reports that areas where coral reefs and mangroves had suffered prior damage tended to be more vulnerable to the waves.

Hurricane Katrina

The story of New Orleans after Hurricane Katrina struck (in late August 2005) was somewhat different. Levees protecting New Orleans from Lake Pontchartrain were breached by the surge, flooding roughly 80% of the city. Damage from Katrina to the Gulf Coast was estimated to be as high as US $100 billion, making it the costliest hurricane in US history. The storm killed at least 1836 people. About 1.3 million lived in the New Orleans metropolitan area, with almost half a million people in the city of New Orleans itself. Of the 245 large cities in the USA (those with populations of 100 000 or more), New Orleans was the sixth poorest (28% of the city's residents were living in poverty before the hurricane) (Sherman and Shapiro, 2005).

While the geographic scale of the disaster was much smaller than the Asian Tsunami, the impact on society was even more unprecedented. Unlike the Tsunami, which struck in the pre-dawn period and wreaked damage within a few hours, Hurricane Katrina built up over a week (23–29 August), and there should have been sufficient time to prepare – given the advanced early-warning systems and technological and economic resources available. Nevertheless, a city of about half a million within a country of 300 million (with a 2006 per capita income of US $44,000/yr, and one of the richest and most powerful in the world), suffered a major social breakdown. As the nation and world watched in amazement and horror, lawlessness, looting and crime gradually engulfed the survivors. The forces of government authority, including the police, were overwhelmed due to lack of numbers and the breakdown of transport and communications. Many storm-battered citizens had to defend their lives and property unaided. Both violent, armed robbery of valuable items and simple looting of essential supplies prevailed.

Subsequent relief and recovery efforts have sought to remedy the early problems in New Orleans. There were severe criticisms of government delays in responding to the plight of the poor (especially to the flooding), and about general public policy issues involving emergency management, environmental policy, poverty and unemployment. While sophisticated technical and administrative systems are being put into place to prevent a recurrence, the vulnerability of the social structure raises more serious long-term questions about social capital (or its apparent absence during an emergency).

Some research questions

These preliminary observations have been made in the spirit of learning valuable lessons that might help us deal better with future disasters, rather than of emphasizing failures or assigning blame. Most other studies have focused on economic and environmental factors, whereas this commentary argues that social capital also plays a key role and needs to be studied more intensively. The SHARM framework, which seeks to make development more sustainable through balanced treatment of social, economic and environmental dimensions, provides a useful analytical framework and starting point (Munasinghe, 2007a).

Accordingly, the following questions need to be examined more closely by the research community.

(1) Can we identify some of the underlying reasons for perceived behavioural differences – e.g. economic, social and environmental variables, scale and relative intensity of disaster, community or country size, etc.?

(2) Does the concept of 'social capital' help to explain the differences?

(3) Are different types of social capital effective for disaster emergencies and for long-term sustainable development, and what are the possible linkages?

(4) What are the roles of the various types of capital (social, economic and environmental) and their interactions in emergency situations?

(5) Is it possible to build communities that are more resilient to future disasters (including climate change and associated extreme events) by making development more sustainable?

(6) Are there specific actions and policies that government, civil society and the private sector could take, especially from the social perspective?

16.2.6 Impacts on women and children, and psychosocial impacts

Disasters are very discriminatory. Factors that were present before the disaster (like poor social conditions) will exacerbate impacts on the poor. Especially vulnerable populations include (1) children that are orphaned and need the care of adults and (2) widows that need to care single-handedly for children with no prior experience in the labour force and in an environment where communal networks have been lost.

Four times as many women as men were killed in the Tsunami-affected areas of Indonesia, Sri Lanka and India. Many women died because they stayed behind to look for their children and other relatives. Often, they were unable to swim or climb trees. Children represent almost 49% of the overall population in the hardest-hit countries, and thus account for a large share of casualties. After the disaster, women and children continued to be vulnerable because of their lower socioeconomic standing and limited access to resources. They lack influence due to disempowerment and inequality, and less decision-making power and control over their lives. The death or injury of a male breadwinner forces them to accept dual roles – the family income earner, as well as the main caregiver for children, the elderly and the sick. At the same time, the lack of skills and work experience puts women at special risk of other kinds of exploitation.

Since women traditionally take care of the sick, their burden increased due to the high number injured or sick after the Tsunami. In addition, as women usually have the responsibility to fetch water, they would need to increase the amount of time dedicated to collect both drinking water and fresh water for agriculture crops. Post-Tsunami, both women and men are taking on new roles and responsibilities to adapt to their new conditions, and ensure their own and their families' survival. Measures to save lives and secure livelihoods will be more effective when gender issues are properly understood and addressed. International experience shows that protection of women and children is inadequate during disaster conditions. Thus, the care of children, women and other vulnerable people in the camps should be an urgent priority.

Loss of social capital

In addition to the loss of housing, most refugees are not with people of their own communities. They have lost large numbers of family members, friends and, in many cases, entire neighbourhoods. The sense of community and mutual self-help built up over generations has thus ceased to exist, at least for the time being. This further impacts on livelihoods, and certainly means a poorer quality of life for many. It also adds to the loss of confidence that many refugees are experiencing. Yet, there is a sense of mutual purpose and solidarity building amongst people from different areas who are working and living together. Reports also suggest that people are choosing representatives to meet immediate needs, even where their traditional or administrative leaders have died or are missing.

Trauma

Social fragmentation and trauma at the family and community level will remain a major problem for many years. Millions of people are suffering from psychological problems such as post-traumatic stress. It is difficult for many individuals to think about the future and to comprehend how their lives have changed. The effects of large numbers of missing or dead on household and community decision making processes and work force are huge. This situation is a major challenge to identifying and implementing appropriate interventions at household and community levels.

There are many effects of trauma. At worst, individuals are incapacitated and need medical treatment. For many, lives and livelihoods continue, but will be adversely affected. These people need counselling and public support. In addition, they need information about what has actually happened to them. People are still very confused, providing many opportunities for rumours and additional fear and panic. Trained mental health professionals are needed to assist traumatized victims, in addition to broad counselling – through schools, community organizations and existing village structures. While being sensitive to different effects of trauma, it is important also to make use of the different social roles and support networks available to women, men and children, which provide a variety of coping mechanisms to deal with traumatic events.

16.2.7 Impact on the environment and ecosystems

The Tsunami disaster has caused major damage to important coastal environments, such as wetlands, which support inland and marine fisheries, agriculture and other sources of food and income for local populations.

Immediate damage was variable. In some areas, salt, sediment and debris deposits and the uprooting of trees and bushes, etc., have profoundly damaged the continental side of coastal ecosystems. The salt and biochemical balances of lagoons have been completely altered. Flora and wildlife were particularly affected, and it will take years to recover their pre-disaster capacity. Coastal aquatic ecosystems have also suffered to some extent. Sandy-mud ecosystems and estuaries were less damaged. Coral reefs have been seriously harmed in some areas (particularly the very superficial ones), while they have been unaffected elsewhere. There are reports of reefs covered with sand (e.g. India).

Seawater intrusion on agricultural lands (especially areas covered with stagnant seawater) resulted in deep salinization of soils which will become unfit for any kind of vegetation and rice cultivation. Salinization and deposits may also change vegetation and character of important wetlands. Fresh water in storage tanks and wells used for domestic supply and agriculture have been contaminated by seawater and debris, and groundwater supply important to coastal communities is contaminated by brine from evaporating seawaters. In areas where coastal fish or shrimp ponds have been destroyed, the coastline and water flows toward the sea have changed. Where sand dunes and their vegetation cover have been washed away, the change in the landscape will require radical changes in land use for an unspecified amount of time.

Many mangroves and coastal forests helped to save lives by reducing the impact of waves. In the process, they suffered extensive destruction, with ensuing loss of livelihoods (given the key role played by mangroves in sustaining local fisheries). There has been a major loss of water resources surrounding the affected coastal areas. In many cases the domestic water supply (wells) has been contaminated by salt water, dead bodies and pollutants from the disruption of chemical containers or other infrastructure. Many of the lagoon systems (physical linkage to the sea and chemical water balance) have been disturbed or destroyed.

The global assessment of the long-term consequences of this damage to ecosystems is yet to be carried out. The most likely assumption is that, except in some hardly hit superficial reefs, the long-term damage to the environment will be limited. In the medium-term, however, resources (eggs, larvae, juveniles, adults) have been washed ashore and recruitment shortage is likely, possibly for a year or so. On the other hand, the de facto closure of fisheries may lead to a (short-lived) stock recovery in areas that were strongly overexploited in the past.

16.2.8 Summary of main findings

Impacts by country

The most vulnerable groups, pre-Tsunami (poor fishing communities, single-headed households, illegal migrant workers and others), who were already depending on fragile and marginal livelihoods and enjoying a substandard status in society, are likely to be made more vulnerable and pushed further into poverty if appropriate support is not provided to them. The destruction caused by the Tsunami appears to be localized and varies from total to almost invisible destruction. Areas that were worst affected include: (1) crowded human settlements near the shoreline (tourist facilities and fishing communities) that experienced a boom and poorly planned development in recent years; (2) settlements at low elevations (flat lands a few metres above sea level) in exposed wide bays (to the west and south west) without coral reef barriers, but with sea beds presenting steep slopes and no natural protective barriers such as islands; and (3) areas that were totally unprepared, with no past records of similar disasters (including typhoon and hurricane sea surges), and no early-warning systems or structures to mitigate potential damages.

Chief recommendations

The medium- and long-term rehabilitation and reconstruction efforts offer an opportunity not only for restoring livelihoods and rehabilitating ecosystems to the pre-Tsunami situation, but also for creating conditions to overcome previous weaknesses. Recovery and rehabilitation should aim for 'recovery plus', which means development that goes beyond pre-Tsunami conditions. New investments in affected areas should aim both to offset the initial damages and use new technologies in rebuilding better and improved communities.

Actions taken should have a clear indication of measurable outcomes with an emphasis on *accountability* and *transparency*. Effective communication is a core element of any intervention, and such actions will support coordinated partnership among governments, civil society, international agencies and bilateral donors. Institutional mechanisms and procedures need to cope with future hazards and disasters at all level, with appropriate legal and administrative powers.

Though the Tsunami affected similar economic sectors in different countries, the *indirect* impacts on the five economies have varied. This has necessitated the adjustment of work plans in unaffected sectors and geographical regions (through transfer of funds and modification of planned activities), to share the burden.

This principle of *subsidiarity* should be used wherever applicable. It implies that reconstruction and recovery activities should be designed, implemented and monitored at the lowest competent level of government, private-sector and civil society. The central government plays the lead role, setting standards, policies and principles.

Priority should be given to the concept of sustainable development where balanced emphasis is laid on economic, social and environmental dimensions. Consultation and empowerment of affected communities and stakeholders are essential aspects of building social capital, which would facilitate the restoration of local economies, in addition to the more traditional approach of rebuilding economic and natural capital.

16.3 Sustainability of long-term growth in Asian cities

Asia is emerging as a dynamic force within the globalizing world economy. The region has experienced high levels of growth in recent decades (especially East Asia), and many believe that Asia will become an even more dominant influence in the twenty-first century. From 1965–1990, per capita GDP grew at an average annual rate of 6.7% in East Asia, 3.8% in Southeast Asia and 1.7% in South Asia (ADB, 1997). The aggregate regional growth rate reached 6.6% in 2005, and exceeded 7% in 2006 (ADB, 2006). Despite recent financial setbacks, it is expected that the basic conditions which sustain long-term growth remain unchanged. To fully realize their future potential, Asian countries must aim to maintain rapid growth rates for several more decades. East and

Southeast Asian nations need to sustain the momentum that they have already built up, while South Asia must continue with its recent economic resurgence. If decision makers in Asia wish to continue current development trends over the next few decades, the groundwork must be laid now. In particular, the broad issues and constraints to development that the region will face need to be clearly identified, and appropriate strategies formulated to respond to these challenges – especially the problems of making rapid urban growth more sustainable.

While there are many constraints to sustained growth, environmental issues have emerged as a serious long-term threat – especially in economies with high rates of growth. Further, the combination of uncontrolled growth and environmental degradation will increase urban vulnerability to hazards (see Section 5.1). Thus, we seek to review how growth-inducing economic policies and growth itself may cause environmental or social harm, analyse mechanisms underlying such links and draw appropriate policy conclusions for cities in Asia (see Chapter 7).

16.3.1 Review of urban growth in Asia

Overall development

Asia has experienced significant development, especially in the past few decades. Japan is the most striking example, where sustained growth rates, which approached 10% annually following the post-war decades, tapered off in the 1970s and 1980s, to settle down eventually to about 2% in recent years – a value more consistent with growth rates in other mature market economies. Other Asian countries have exhibited explosive growth in the past three decades, particularly China, South Korea and India (ADB, 2005b). Several key characteristics for this success have been identified, including open trade and targeted export promotion, business-led development, increased agricultural productivity through modernization, high domestic savings rates, accelerated human resource development, export competitiveness, internal demand and development of flexible market-based institutions (ADB, 2005b).

At the same time, regional decision makers need to recognize that social and environmental factors are just as important as economic growth for sustainable urban development. Generally, the quality of life in Asia has improved greatly, although deep pockets of poverty still persist. On average, almost all conventional indicators, such as life expectancy, infant mortality, literacy, nutrition levels and access to basic services, have improved. Unfortunately, Asia's environment has undergone significant degradation, particularly during periods of high economic growth. Pollution in urban areas and degradation of natural resources continue at an alarming rate, further undermining environmental sustainability (see Chapters 2 and 3). Meanwhile, the erosion of social capital (driven by increased migration from rural areas, poverty, unemployment, breakdown of traditional values, etc.) is reducing the quality of urban living due to increasing levels of alienation, social exclusion, tension and violence (see Chapters 2 and 4).

Overall vulnerability to hazards and disasters is increased by such unsustainable urban growth.

16.3.2 Urbanization

The urban population in developing countries has increased from 100 million in 1920 to 1.7 billion in 1990, and is projected to reach 4 billion by the year 2030 (Worldwatch, 2003); 2.2 billion persons will be added from 2000 to 2030 (World Bank, 2005a). By the year 2000, eight of the top ten mega-cities were in developing countries, and 45% of poor households in Asia were located in urban areas. Projections for Asia are high – 40 million new urban residents per year, reaching an urbanization rate of 53% by the year 2025, starting from 30% in 1995 (Worldwatch, 2003). This increasing urbanization has been possible due to the rapid growth in food production in past decades. However, this trend may become more constrained by diminishing growth of food (due to pressures on land use), water scarcities, weaker response to fertilizers and unsustainable utilization of marine sources.

In the developed world, many large cities seem to be moving away from sustainable patterns. For example, industrialized nations have invested in transit systems, but still show continuing increase in private car usage, including gas-guzzling SUVs. Unfortunately, cities in developing countries seem to have adopted some of the worst features of their industrialized world counterparts – for instance, present rates of car ownership in many Asian cities resemble those in the developed world of the 1960s, further exacerbated by a large number of lower-income car owners operating old and inefficient vehicles. Furthermore, the urban population in Asia is concentrated in single metropolitan cities rather than dispersed among many large cities or towns. Several Asian cities have more than 10 million people. Industrial, educational, cultural and political activities are concentrated in a few cities, leading to further in-migration, congestion and declining quality of urban life (in terms of the social, economic and environmental dimensions).

Nevertheless, there is an excellent opportunity to reverse this trend in Asia, by learning the lessons of experience to forge a new strategic synthesis of transportation and land-use policies – see Chapter 11 for a discussion on sustainable transport. Urban development could be made more sustainable if cities conserve energy, minimize pollution, discourage wasteful forms of transportation, reduce water pollution and limit water use, promote biomass fuels, conserve environmental resources, encourage business to adopt ecologically friendly technology, maintain an ecologically sustainable workplace and develop eco-friendly products.

16.3.3 Environmental issues

Air pollution, water quality and land degradation issues are worsening rapidly in cities of the developing world, including Asian urban areas.

Table 16.5 *Status of pollutants in mega-cities, 1992*

City	Sulphur dioxide	Suspended particulate matter	Lead	Carbon monoxide	Nitrogen dioxide	Ozone
Bangkok	low	serious	moderate	low	low	low
Beijing	serious	serious	low	–	low	moderate
Bombay	low	serious	low	low	low	–
Buenos Aires	–	moderate	low	serious	–	–
Cairo	–	serious	serious	moderate	–	–
Calcutta	low	serious	low	–	low	–
Delhi	low	serious	low	low	low	–
Jakarta	low	serious	moderate	moderate	low	moderate
Karachi	low	serious	serious	–	–	low
London	low	low	low	moderate	low	low
Los Angeles	low	–	low	moderate	moderate	serious
Manila	low	serious	moderate	–	–	–
Mexico City	serious	serious	moderate	serious	moderate	serious
Moscow	–	moderate	low	moderate	moderate	–
New York	low	low	low	moderate	low	moderate
Rio de Janeiro	moderate	moderate	low	low	–	–
Sao Paulo	low	moderate	low	moderate	moderate	serious
Seoul	serious	serious	low	low	low	low
Shanghai	moderate	serious	–	–	–	–
Tokyo	low	low	–	low	low	serious

'–' means no data are available or there are insufficient data for assessment.
Serious: WHO guidelines exceeded by more than a factor of two.
Moderate: moderate to heavy pollution; WHO guidelines exceeded by up to a factor of two (short-term guidelines exceeded on a regular basis at certain times).
Low: WHO guidelines normally met (short-term guidelines exceeded occasionally).
Source: Serageldin *et al.* (1995).

Air

In 1988, more than 600 million people lived in urban areas in which sulphur dioxide levels exceeded WHO guidelines, while 1.25 billion people were living in cities where suspended particulate matter levels were unacceptable by WHO standards. Levels of sulphur oxides, photochemical oxidants, sulphate and nitrate oxides and airborne toxic substances such as lead are high. A joint study by WHO and UNEP covering 20 of the world's mega-cities reveals that each of these mega-cities had at least one major pollutant exceeding WHO guidelines (see Table 16.5). Evidence suggests that the combined effects of these pollutants may be far more serious than the adverse effects of one pollutant alone.

Air-lead levels in urban areas of developing countries of 1.5 to 3 $\mu g/m^3$ are not uncommon. It has cost children in Bangkok an average of four IQ points, and, even before clinical symptoms appear, it diminishes the victims' neurological capacities, powers of concentration and prospects of mastering advanced skills. Mandatory use of only unleaded petrol has helped reduce the problem. The hidden costs annually to urban dwellers from both dust and lead pollution in Bangkok, Jakarta and Kuala Lumpur combined are US $5 billion (10% of city incomes) – see Box 16.2.

Severe environmental damage may be reduced by increasing peoples' reliance on public transport, for example 90% of commuters in Tokyo use railways and only 1% use automobiles. Policies such as the area-controlled traffic system in Bangkok, the area-restriction system in Tokyo and the area-license system in Singapore have also helped to control damage. Eighty cities (many of them in Asia) are participating in a coordinated global effort to improve and share information on air-quality monitoring under the WHO/Global Environmental Monitoring System (GEMS) Urban Air Quality Monitoring Project.

More generally, national and local governments can use a range of policy tools to improve air quality rapidly. While some of these tools have been adopted, others are still being developed. Ambient air-quality standards, emissions standards, permits, licenses and land-use control are examples of regulatory policy tools, while economic instruments include charges, fees, tradable permits and subsidies (see Box 16.3).

Water

Worldwide, per capita water use has increased 30-fold in the past three centuries (see Chapter 12). Water withdrawals have recently been increasing, while water quality has been declining. In fact, the problems of water quantity and quality are closely intertwined. With the growth of the population and the urbanization of developing nations, demand by domestic and especially industrial users has risen rapidly. Thus, the costs of water supply are also expected to rise very sharply as new and more expensive sources of water need to be tapped.

Water-resource-management practices in developing country cities have three main shortcomings: (1) fragmented management that leads to environmental degradation, poor water quality, human suffering and wasteful investment; (2) overcentralization of water service delivery and absence of incentives, giving rise to a vicious cycle of unreliable service, low willingness-to-pay and deteriorating capacity to provide services; and (3) underpricing of water and absence of cost recovery, leading to excessive and wasteful water use and misallocation of resources. Some innovative practices have emerged in Asian cities – e.g. Manila has a water rate, sewer rate and environmental rate in a single bill, while Dhaka and Jakarta have private user fees for groundwater extraction.

Table 16.6 shows the water situation in eight mega-cities in Asia. The evolution of these cities has not been based on methodical planning of water demand and supply – responses are basically crisis-oriented. There was major water pollution in seven cities, problems of competing uses and severe groundwater depletion in six, inadequate cost recovery and intermittent water supply in five, major flooding problems in four, water losses greater than 50% in three, sewage coverage less than 15% in three, and interbasin water transfers planned

---

Box 16.2 Pricing urban pollution[3]

What does unsafe drinking water cost?

In Jakarta, the cost is about US $300 million a year in impaired health. In Bangkok, 6% of annual deaths are now caused by dysentery, enteric fever, encephalitis, polio, typhus and acute diarrhoea.

What is the price of dust and lead pollution?

The price amounts to an average of nearly 10% of annual city incomes of Bangkok, Kuala Lumpur and Jakarta.

What can be saved by cutting the level of particulates, dust and soot in urban air?

In 18 Central and Eastern European cities, 18 000 fewer premature deaths annually and US $1.2 billion a year in working time gained would come from achieving EU air pollution standards.

How many lives will cleaner air save?

In Cairo, with the highest levels of such emissions among the world's 20 largest cities, an annual total of 4000 to 16 000 lives now lost to pollution from industry, power plants, motor vehicles, trash burning, construction and natural sand and dust would be saved.

How much does traffic congestion cost?

In Bangkok, over US $400 million a year could be saved if peak-hour traffic moved 10% faster.

Where can pollution be cut and savings gained?

In energy production and use, efficiency gains of 20% in electricity production and use could have saved Asians about US $90 billion in the year 2000, in terms of new capital investment.

---

in three. These results indicate the need for a comprehensive water-resource-management system, improved use management and the recognition that water is a scarce resource.

Some key problems of water-resource management identified for Asian cities include: groundwater overexploitation, poor water metering, low tariff levels, intermittent water

---

[3] Taken from World Bank (1996c).

Box 16.3 Tools to reduce urban air pollution

Stationary sources

To prevent emissions at source

(1) Ambient air-quality standards, emission standards; (2) emission phase-out, restricted use of certain types of energy sources; (3) development of overall clean production approach in housing and industry, by improving environmental management tools and clean technology; (4) economic incentives (tradable permits, taxes); (5) education and training.

To treat emissions

(1) Emission standards; (2) economic incentives.

Transport

To reduce use of motor vehicles

(1) More public transport systems; (2) land-use planning; (3) car-sharing/pooling; (4) public information; (5) economic incentives (taxes, fees, tolls, pricing of transport and energy).

To improve traffic conditions

(1) Planning and traffic management programmes (control of on-street parking, control of traffic lights); (2) land-use and town planning; (3) public information.

To improve vehicle performance

(1) Vehicle exhaust and gas regulations; (2) vehicle technology (electric and light cars, etc.); (3) fuel selection (reformulated fuels, alternative fuels, indigenous resources); (4) vehicle inspection and maintenance; (5) training; (6) public information.

---

supply, inadequate city planning and pollution control, overlapping jurisdictions of water-resource-management agencies, inadequate sewerage coverage, non-payment of water bills by government agencies and increasing unavailability of new water sources.

Land

The problem of dealing with greater volumes of waste materials is particularly acute in Asian cities, especially where these issues have not been addressed through improvements

Table 16.6 *Comparative review of water-resources management in Asian mega-cities*

Indicator	Bangkok	Beijing	Delhi	Dhaka	Jakarta	Karachi	Manila	Seoul
Population (millions)	6	11	10	5	8.8	10	9	11
Population growth (%)	2.5	3	4	5.1	2.4	4.5	2.8	2
Urban poor (%)	20	–	47	40	15	40	35	0
Water service coverage (%)	75	95	69	65	44	83	70	100
Sewerage coverage (%)	10	–	37	28	6	42	12	90
Water supply service (%)	24	24	7	6	19	4	16	24
Connections (millions)	1.0	0.2	1.1	0.1	0.3	0.6	0.7	1.8
Public taps (thousands)	0	–	14	1.3	2	21	1.7	0
Water losses (%)	30	7	40	50	52	–	58	38
Metered (%)	100	99	53	68	100	–	100	100
Domestic water use (litres/ person/day)	240	190	225	120	157	124	116	198
Water tariff structure	block	flat	various	various	block	land tax	block	block
Staff/1000 connections	5.5	17	8.9	21.3	8.7	11.7	9	1.9
Groundwater depletion	SR	SR	SF	SF	SR	–	SF	–
Major flooding	SF	–	–	SR	SF	SF	–	–
Water pollution	SR	SF	SF	SF	SR	SF	SF	–
Competing uses	SF	SF	SF	–	SF	SF	SF	–

SF: significant; SR: serious.

Figures are indicative. Operating ratio is annual operating and maintenance cost divided by annual billing. Net figures exclude costs of depreciation, interest charges or amortization.

Source: Serageldin (1995).

in waste-management technologies (Munasinghe, 1994b). Development of controls over solid-waste disposal and their implementation have been given low priority by many governments, often because of a failure to appreciate the harm that inadequate management may cause to human health and the environment.

Each year, reported human fatalities include millions of children and adults who have died from diseases caused by improper disposal of human and solid waste. In developing countries, less than 20% of solid wastes are treated (processed), and only a small fraction of treated waste meets acceptable standards. Typically, in Bangkok, Jakarta and Manila, municipal solid-waste generation is close to 1 kg per capita per day. In 2000, over 2 billion people lacked basic sanitation, and about half the urban population in developing countries did not have adequate waste disposal.

Municipal solid waste (MSW) normally contains paper, plastics, glass, metals, various other household items, street sweepings and general refuse from commercial and institutional establishments. In some countries, sludge from sewage and water treatment plants are sometimes co-disposed with MSW. Hazardous waste (HW), including heavy metals, dioxins and polycyclic aromatic hydrocarbons, is defined as chemical and other industrial wastes that can cause significant hazards to human health and the environment when improperly managed. The major characteristics of HW include acute or chronic toxicity to humans, ignitability, reactivity, infectiousness and potential ecological damage. Clinical and medical waste (CW) includes wastes generated by hospital and other healthcare services. It includes pharmaceutical, pathological and infectious wastes, needles, syringes, scalpels, chemical (aerosols/disinfectants) and low-level radioactive wastes (X-rays, radiation vials).

Inappropriate waste-management practices have significant financial and economic costs. The income and productivity lost due to those who become sick or die early is large. Healthcare costs represent a major economic burden. The large bill for remedial actions is a budgetary burden to a country trying comprehensively to address a clean-up of both municipal and industrial wastes. There are risks to the well-being of future generations as they are forced to pay increased remedial costs, suffer health impacts, or have their options for use of environmental resources significantly limited. These risks also have ethical implications.

16.3.4 Implications for Asian researchers

The foregoing discussion suggests that large payoffs may be realized (in terms of sustained growth) with a targeted programme of policy-oriented research to solve Asian urban problems. Such an approach would also reduce the vulnerability of urban areas (especially mega-cities) to hazards and disasters, in line with the SHARM framework (see Section 16.1).

Asian researchers and policy makers need to work together to formulate practical strategies for sustainable development, facilitate networking among research and policy institutions, help identify relevant research agendas and initiate and support high-quality, strategic research in these areas. Key steps include: (1) identifying and prioritizing the most important (urban-related) development issues – the AIM method would be most effective; (2) determining critical gaps in knowledge, research needs, research capacity and points of entry; and (3) developing an 'Action Plan' to initiate activities in these key areas. It is prudent to use existing research institutions and capacity more effectively, before creating new formal research organizations.

16.4 Urban vulnerability, natural hazards and environmental degradation

16.4.1 General policy issues and options

We seek to understand better the vulnerability of major metropolitan areas to hazards, and reverse the failure of conventional development programmes and policy during the past decades, which caused massive urbanization in disaster-prone areas – especially in developing countries. Unless major changes in development policies are undertaken, risks will increase for people already suffering from social, economic and environmental degradation in urban areas. City development can be made more sustainable by improving government policies and redirecting incentives to make better use of market forces. To meet the challenge, significant changes must take place in institutional organizations, and more creative methods must be used to deal with the new technological landscape.

The previous sections of this chapter have highlighted two themes: (a) the two-way relationship between environmental degradation and urban disaster vulnerability and (b) use of sustainable development criteria for public and private sector actions that will help to implement SHARM.

Traditionally, approaches to urban development need to be updated. The complexity of physical and social mechanisms linking environmental degradation and natural hazards indicates that the goals of reducing vulnerability and enhancing resilience require fundamental shifts, not only in public policy concerning disasters, but also in scientific and technical innovation and dissemination. Analytical tools and programmes in developing countries have focused on traditional economic criteria that do not necessarily address these complex issues or improve hazard preparedness. Developed nations are increasingly recognizing hazard and risk assessment as an important element of a balanced and comprehensive strategy to mitigate the impact of natural disasters. The implementation of this strategy must involves an approach like SHARM, which maintains the balance among disaster relief, rehabilitation and long-run reduction.

Policy makers are concerned about the rising social, ecological and economic costs of urban growth. SHARM shows that integration of risk concerns within the sustainable development process opens up a much wider array of policy alternatives, to address social, economic and environmental issues. For example, cost-effective approaches to hazard reduction include better land use to reduce disaster impacts, using past experiences to identify vulnerabilities, and using knowledge and technical judgement when siting and designing new buildings. Reducing urban vulnerability requires a consultative process to define the role of both public and private sectors, and the level of risk a society is willing to take. The economic choice among different alternatives should be based on efficient use of existing resources based on the social perception of risk.

More emphasis is needed on ensuring more effective participation of all stakeholders in assessing risk. The AIM methodology (see Section 2.4.1) is a proven tool to help achieve this goal. Capacity to assess risks requires an administrative structure, a climate conducive to mitigation investment and access to new scientific and technical knowledge for evaluation, monitoring and warning. Social capital underlying civil society and the private sector can play a key role in complementing government efforts (see Section 16.2.5). Policy makers need to determine hazard reduction goals in relation to sustainable development and make choices among instruments and approaches. Moreover, effective cooperation among central and local governments and the international community on hazard-reduction issues requires better sharing of experiences among countries and regions exposed to similar kind of hazards and the competent functioning of local agencies. It is essential to enhance the sharing of data and experiences within and across countries and regions to: (1) improve assessment capacity; (2) encourage the adaptation of research results to different contexts; and (3) strengthen existing human resources, experience and facilities for the implementation of prevention and mitigation programmes.

Building national and local capacities for hazard prevention and mitigation can be enhanced by: (1) diffusing information among governmental decision makers as to the merits and cost-effectiveness of hazard-reduction programmes; (2) identifying alternative options for better allocation of resources; (3) training in disaster-mitigation techniques to facilitate the understanding of interactions between natural hazards and human activities; and (4) developing and using methodologies like SHARM to assist national and local organizations in assessing risks.

Past experiences help to identify vulnerabilities, highlight areas for policy action and make development more sustainable in the future. Long-run benefits of hazard reduction depend on a better understanding of basic causes of urban vulnerability, the potential costs of hazards and disasters and the techniques available to reduce their effects.

Identifying the responsibilities of governments at multiple levels, and using the principle of subsidiarity to assign responsibilities, are of prime importance. It will help formulate policy that not only responds to public interests, but also makes cities function more sustainably. Innovations in social organization and financing, as well as diffusion of technology, are indispensable for mobilizing private initiative, resources and cooperation among countries (particularly technology transfer from industrialized countries). Socio-economic or political factors, which hamper developing country efforts to implement measures, may be overcome if explicitly defined when feasible strategies are considered at the outset. For example, technical collaboration through cooperative ventures is a useful option that could stimulate research and influence strategic choices. Successful attempts to reduce hazard-related losses are also linked to effective legislation and enforcement. However, regulatory controls are not always cost-effective, and higher environmental standards in developing countries need to be linked with private-sector innovation and initiative in the pursuit of environmental quality and hazard reduction.

16.4.2 Rio de Janeiro case study – the 1988 Flood Reconstruction and Prevention Project

The 1988 Rio Flood Reconstruction and Prevention Project sought to make development more sustainable by reducing disaster vulnerability and promoting long-term multisectoral development (World Bank, 1988). It was a precursor of the SHARM approach, and pioneered a new type of reconstruction project that also included a hazard-reduction component to reduce future vulnerabilities, and met cross-sectoral needs by improving urban environmental management. Until then, disaster-related funding by development organizations focused mainly on relief and reconstruction – especially short-term relief and recovery. The Rio project was a significant step toward integrating efforts for long-term prevention and mitigation of hazards and environmental degradation into urban development strategy. It also made development more sustainable by supporting long-term social and environmental policies that strengthened local managerial and planning capabilities – something that was not possible previously through short-term recovery projects.

In February 1988, unusually heavy rains fell in the metropolitan region of Rio de Janeiro, Brazil's second most important economic centre and second largest city. In some areas, the equivalent of three months' annual rainfall fell in less than 24 hours. By early March, the resulting floods and landslides had left about 300 dead, 750 injured and almost 19 000 homeless, and had extensively damaged physical infrastructure (roads, bridges, canals, drainage networks, dikes, water and sewerage networks, electric power networks, factories and commercial establishments). The physical losses severely disrupted Rio's economic activity (particularly in the north) and left the predominantly low-income population with limited access to schools, health facilities and basic sanitation. This was the heaviest recorded rainfall since 1966, the time of the last flood and landslide disaster in the metropolitan region.

The severity of disaster is attributable to the region's vulnerability to natural hazards (Munasinghe, Menezes and Preece, 1991). Environmental degradation (due to unplanned expansion of human settlements, faulty construction, congested drainage, and poor maintenance) contributed to the catastrophic outcome. The poor of Rio de Janeiro live in high-risk areas, e.g. steeply sloping hillsides, landfills and floodplains. They became both the perpetrators and the victims of environmental degradation. Poverty, social exclusion and poor environmental management continue to place the city's population at risk from future hazards.

In 1989, the population of the metropolitan region was about 10.2 million, with roughly one-sixth of the region's families living in poverty (on less than three minimum salaries a month). Low-income human settlements had spread rapidly in unsafe areas. Unplanned squatter settlements (*favelas*) had developed along the narrow coastal strip and across the coastal mountain range. Located on steep hillsides, they often perched precariously above the city or lived in lowlands along riverbanks in the flood-prone Baixada Fluminense area, north of the city.

Increasing urban poverty has placed heavy demands on national and local institutions and infrastructure, and basic needs for housing and services have not been met. Local institutions for urban environmental planning are weak and uncoordinated. Planning, programming and budgeting are inadequate, with poor information systems and technical staff. Investment decisions are often politically guided, leading to inefficient resource allocation and poorly targeted spending.

On much of the city's periphery, especially in *favelas*, the supply of services has been affected by social exclusion and lack of empowerment, flawed infrastructure planning, inadequate investment in infrastructure, several years of neglect in management and poor or non-existent maintenance of facilities. Drainage networks are severely blocked by silt and uncollected solid wastes, and they overflow, depositing garbage and raw sewage on precariously constructed squatter settlements. Poorly disposed solid wastes and uncollected garbage (5400 tonnes/day), became raw material for landslides, burying homes and sweeping away hillside squatter settlements. To compound the problem, most municipal refuse goes to open dumps, which are often occupied by squatters who have no formal access to land. These landfills are hazardous sites for construction because the soil is unstable, and susceptible to runoff and erosion. Uncontrolled wastewater ends up in nearby drains or streets, further degrading the land. Landslides and flooding are common because these environmentally sensitive areas are highly susceptible to rain washout.

Poor environmental management and disaster planning

Urban environment degradation is caused by institutional inaction, lack of empowerment of the poor and political conflict, coupled with physical damage to health facilities and sanitation networks during the floods. This sharply increased the risk of epidemics. Floodwaters contaminated with garbage and human wastes led to widespread outbreaks of leptospirosis, hepatitis, typhoid fever and other gastrointestinal diseases.

Floods and landslides cost an estimated US $935 million: $400 million in direct costs (physical damage) and $535 million in indirect costs ($435 million in lost production, $50 million in lost revenues from tourism and $50 million for the clean-up operation immediately after the disaster). Poor policy analysis and programme development, inefficient targeting of resources, ineffective implementation, weak and unenforced laws and institutional friction have accentuated conflicts among institutions and between government and users. Policy makers focused on short-term approaches to resource allocation. Projects were unsustainable because they competed for scarce resources for operations and maintenance.

Rescue and salvage equipment were inadequate and were located far from emergency sites. Gaps in emergency response and preparedness plans compounded flood damages. The emergency response was poorly planned, with people and materials converging on the area and creating confusion. Much effort was wasted, and urgent tasks were not addressed.

After the disaster, state and municipal governments slowly initiated short-term relief activities – roads were reopened, emergency services were restored and the homeless were temporarily housed in public buildings. The government also began to consider the longer, more arduous and costly tasks of rehabilitating affected areas and restoring economic activity and physical infrastructure. The disaster stimulated local government to undertake preventive measures to mitigate the effects of minor periodic floods and to improve capacity to cope with the major floods that occur every 20 years or so. By April 1988, the state governor had created an Executive Group for Reconstruction and Emergency Works to oversee and coordinate short-term disaster relief and medium- and long-term reconstruction and prevention activities. The municipality of Rio also created a special unit to coordinate activities.

Response

The World Bank responded early to strengthen the flow of technical assistance to improve long-run policy development in urban planning and initiate a US $394 million flood reconstruction project, to which the Bank contributed $175 million. The project was designed to: (1) provide a quick response to immediate needs; (2) restore assets and productivity to pre-flood levels; and (3) reduce the vulnerability of Rio to floods. The project's main goal was to strengthen the city's institutional and financial ability to manage urban development and environmental planning, through fundamental reforms that: (1) improved institutional capability to respond to emergencies and hazards; (2) rebuilt and rehabilitated infrastructure; (3) implemented physical and institutional preventive measures to reduce damage from future floods; (4) helped the Rio de Janeiro state and municipal governments to develop flood prevention and mitigation programmes; and (5) improved management policies of the municipality of Rio and increased the ability to mobilize financial resources for routine maintenance and environmental protection.

From the early stages of implementation, the project confronted institutional weakness, because responsibilities for execution were distributed among many uncoordinated agencies. Political rivalry between the municipal, state and federal governments greatly increased project risk. Numerous managerial changes in the Caixa Economic Federal (CEF), Brazil's financial intermediary and cofinancier of the project, contributed to an 18-month delay in the project.

After a slow start, most infrastructure work in Rio was substantially completed. Roads and bridges were repaired, and the massive dredging of rivers and drainage canals choked with debris and silt deposits begun. Stabilization of steep hillsides and slopes was completed. Repairs of sewerage systems were designed to permit improved collection of sewage that currently drained into open waterways. Institutional problems delayed the implementation of a metropolitan regional programme for improving the collection and disposal of solid waste, but some progress was made. The project's serviced-sites component provided emergency recovery assistance in high-risk areas. Families were provided with unrestricted title to the land on 11 000 minimally serviced lots. Housing sites were provided for about 5000 families who either lost their homes or needed to be resettled. Most relocation from housing along the rivers was done under state auspices. Within the city, about 5700 refugee families who lost their dwellings were moved to lower risk areas.

The state of Rio de Janeiro was given technical assistance focusing on developing hazard-reduction methods and reversing environmental degradation. An integrated system was developed that improves communication technology, land transport and equipment needed for effective emergency responses. The municipal civil defence plan covered hazards like floods, landslides, fires in high-rise buildings and toxic-waste spills. The Rio municipality was given technical assistance in: (1) handling and disposal of solid waste; (2) safe self-help techniques for low-cost housing construction; (3) protecting forests; (4) inspection and control of illegal mineral exploration; and (5) improving the fiscal administration.

Summary and conclusions

In the short and medium term, the project focused on key areas, including: (1) housing and sanitation; (2) landslide control; (3) environmental planning and management of spatial development; and (4) urban-waste collection and disposal. In the long run, the project promoted reform in urban environmental policies by: (1) formulating a preparedness plan for the greater metropolitan region; (2) preparing a medium- and long-term reforestation plan; (3) analysing land-use practices and land tenure issues; and (4) implementing a programme in environmental education.

The Rio Flood Reconstruction and Prevention Project is a unique example of an effort to reduce hazard-related losses. Unlike previous disaster projects, which focused on short-term relief, this project laid emphasis on making development more sustainable through long-run disaster prevention. It relied on a comprehensive technical assistance programme that foreshadowed the SHARM approach of integrating economic, social and environmental rehabilitation efforts into sustainable development, and reducing vulnerability to future hazards.

16.5 Making urban development more sustainable in North America and Europe

This section examines two promising examples showing how urban development has been made more sustainable in developed countries.

16.5.1 Canada – Greater Vancouver Regional District

The Greater Vancouver Regional District (GVRD) focuses on how to contribute to the long-term economic prosperity, social well-being and ecological health of Greater Vancouver (GVRD, 2003b). The city has seen an increase in population of 2.9% from 2002 to 2005, along with an increase in labour force of 4.6% and an increase in number of jobs of 7.1%, resulting in a drop in unemployment by 26.5%. Since around 2003, sustainability practices have been incorporated into activities, such as in waste management, land acquisition and usage, greenways, housing, transportation, corporate practices and learning and exchanging knowledge.

Common design elements within these capital projects include: recycling or reusing excavated soils and construction debris; reducing water use through efficient landscaping and low-flow fixtures; using environmentally friendly construction products; using natural lighting and ventilation design features; consulting with the public on how best to mitigate the impact on surrounding areas during construction; conducting environmental and noise monitoring and mitigating programmes; holding plant salvage events; protecting existing trees, and replanting and replacing trees.

Waste disposal

Water. The existing Little Mountain Reservoir was replaced due to its structural and seismic deficiencies and operational limitations. A modern replacement was built on the same site, which contains 25% more water and is designed to survive earthquakes. Sustainability innovations include a state-of-the-art earthquake-resistant design; optimizing water-storage capacity and cost without encroaching on park areas; implementing a partnering strategy with all stakeholders; providing alternative facilities for the daily tai chi practitioners who were using the reservoir rooftop for their daily exercise; and providing a wheelchair-accessible construction viewing platform.

Solid waste.   The 5600 m^2 transfer station receives solid waste from neighbouring municipalities for reloading into transport trailers to be disposed at the landfill. The location enables residents and haulers to drop off residential and commercial wastes, reducing fossil-fuel use and exhaust emissions. Sustainability benefits of the construction include a 40% water-use reduction, 40% reuse/recycling of materials, 26% increase in energy efficiency, 80% local manufacture of materials, 96% of the construction debris diverted from disposal and diversion of storm water to reduce the discharge of suspended solids. Green transportation methods are being encouraged – bicycle storage and change rooms are provided, public transit is nearby and the facility has an onsite charging station for electric vehicles. The facility was fully enclosed with a concrete pit for unloading and storage, including a built-in odour-neutralizing spray system.

The GVRD Waste-to-Energy Facility absorbs more than 20% of the waste disposed in the region and supplies the total energy needs of a nearby paper recycling facility, while generaing 120 000 MWh of electricity per year. The generator creates enough power for 15 000 homes, with little or no impact on the environment, generates revenue and reduces air emissions by supplying energy that might otherwise have been created by burning fossil fuels.

Sewer overflows.   Sanitary sewer overflows result from excessive inflow and infiltration of water into sanitary sewers during major storms. The new system automatically diverts overflows to a concrete storage tank, and returns the stored flow to the wastewater conveyance system. Sustainability innovations incorporated into the facility include: using gravity for most operations, saving pumping energy; a vacuum flushing system that uses a small amount of retained wastewater to avoid pumping in fresh water for tank cleaning and flushing; and automated controls to monitor the process, thus reducing the need for operators to travel to the site.

Water supply.   Water is filtered through twin tunnels located in bedrock. Sustainable innovations incorporated include on-site concrete batch plants and gravel resource extraction to reduce the need to drive concrete and gravel trucks through adjacent communities, protecting wildlife habitats and large trees, enhancing terrestrial habitat by using green-roof technology designs, use of low-energy ultraviolet light disinfection for primary disinfection of water and building 42 km of heating and cooling coils in the ground under the treated water storage area.

Ecological conservation

The GVRD developed 'Ecological Conservancy Areas', to maintain and protect the ecological integrity and biodiversity value of the lands, and be used as ecological benchmarks for environmental research and monitoring climate change. The GVDR is restoring the habitat of Stoney Creek to allow fish to return to their spawning grounds by constructing baffles that allow fish to pass through impassable creek culverts located under the highway and reach their traditional spawning grounds. Stumps and woody debris were used for bank stabilization, followed by the planting of native shrubs and trees to improve fish habitat. After a 50-year absence, salmon are now returning to the upper reaches of Stoney Creek to spawn. A regional greenway network incorporates utility functions with recreation, habitat protection and the vehicle-free movement of people. For example, installation of sewer pipes was combined with some of the area's natural open spaces.

Affordable housing

In Greater Vancouver, finding affordable rental and purchased housing is a significant challenge. In 2005, almost 21% of Greater Vancouver residents spent more than 30% on shelter – well above the national average of 16%. Between 2002 and 2005, the Greater Vancouver Housing Corporation (GVHC) increased social housing units from 3397 to 3559 units. Rising costs and declining federal grants forced the GVHC to reduce funding for 'rent-geared-to-income' units, from 40% to 30% of the housing stock.

Transportation

A portion of the gas tax was provided to the GVRD for development of Greater Vancouver Transportation Authority (GVTA) public transportation. Introduction of the U-Pass saw a marked increase in the number of public transit trips, along with a decrease in trips made by automobile. Transportation-cost savings to students were over Can $3 million per month. Greenhouse gas (GHG) emission savings are over 16 000 tonnes/year. Not having to provide additional parking spaces generated a cost savings of over Can $20 million.

Corporate sustainability

The successes are due to effective leadership, thoughtful goal-setting, teamwork and innovative technologies in re-examining operations with a sustainability perspective.

Integrated asset management.   Maintaining assets and planning for their disposal and replacement, and the acquisition of additional assets needed to support growth, is complex. Understanding what is expected of an asset management system, communicating plans within the organization and determining how to store and distribute information throughout the organization is essential. Successful integrated asset management programmes have reduced operating and capital costs of utilities by up to 40%.

Occupational health and safety.   Fewer GVRD workers are being affected by injury and illness, and the severity of those incidents is also decreasing. Staff participate in extensive training, and are committed to safe work practices.

Community involvement.   The GVRD ensures community involvement and mutual support. Employees are encouraged to participate in community events and charitable fundraising. Many charity events are organized, such as golf tournaments, karaoke contests, blood-donation campaigns, etc.

16.5.2 European Union urban strategy

Four out of five European citizens live in urban areas, and their quality of life is directly influenced by the state of the urban environment. The environmental challenges facing cities have significant consequences for human health, the quality of life of urban citizens and the economic performance of the cities themselves. The 6th Environment Action Programme called for the development of a Thematic Strategy on the Urban Environment, which seeks to provide a better quality of life through an integrated approach concentrating on urban areas (CEC, 2004). It will contribute to a higher quality of life and social well-being for citizens by providing an environment where the level of pollution does not give rise to harmful effects on human health and the environment, and by encouraging more sustainable urban development. There are four priority themes: urban management, sustainable transport, construction and urban design.

Sustainable urban transport plans

Urban transport has a direct impact on air pollution, noise, congestion and CO_2 emissions, and it is fundamental to citizens and business. Sustainable transport planning requires long-term vision to plan financial requirements for infrastructure and vehicles, to design incentive schemes that promote high-quality public transport, safe cycling and walking and to coordinate with land-use planning at the appropriate administrative levels. Transport planning will take account of safety and security, access to goods and services, air pollution, noise, GHG emissions and energy consumption, land use, cover passenger and freight transportation and all modes of transport. Solutions need to be tailor-made, based on wide consultation of the public and other stakeholders – see Chapter 11.

EU wide exchange of best practices and information exchange

Improving local authorities' access to existing solutions is important to allow them to learn from each other and develop solutions adapted to their specific situation. The information has to be well structured, easily available and supported by the right experts. An internet portal for local authorities would provide links to all information of relevance and improve the flow of information.

Training

An integrated approach to management, involving cross-sector cooperation and training on specific environmental legislation, effective public participation and encouraging changes in citizens' behaviour is essential.

Further research

Further research is recommended on innovative urban management, rehabilitation of the man-made environment, including the cultural heritage, environmental risk, energy efficiency, clean vehicles and alternative fuels, mobility, safety and security.

Synergies with other policies

Climate change.   Urban areas have an important role to play in both adapting to climate change and mitigating GHG emissions. Cities are vulnerable to the consequences of climate change, such as flooding, heat waves and more frequent and severe water shortages. Integrated urban management plans should incorporate measures to limit environmental risk. Wider implementation of sustainable urban transport plans will help reduce GHG emissions at the local level – measures include promotion of low-CO_2-emitting and energy-efficient vehicles. Sustainable construction improves energy efficiency, also decreasing CO_2 emissions. Raising awareness, setting and enforcing standards and adopting best practices for buildings can be promoted through green public procurement. Energy efficiency and use of renewable energy among local and regional actors is promoted.

Nature and biodiversity.   Sustainable urban design (appropriate land-use planning) will help reduce urban sprawl and the loss of natural habitats and biodiversity. Integrated management of the urban environment should foster sustainable land-use policies that avoid urban sprawl and reduce soil-sealing, include promotion of urban biodiversity, and raise awareness for urban citizens.

Environment and quality of life.   Sustainable urban transport plans will help reduce air pollution and noise, and encourage cycling and walking, thus improving health and reducing obesity. Sustainable construction methods will help promote comfort, safety, accessibility and reduce health impacts from indoor and outdoor air pollution. Some action suggested by the European Commission to contribute to the improvement of the urban environment include new vehicle standards, taxes in environmentally sensitive areas and designation of low-emission zones with restrictions for polluting transport. The role of private vehicles in cities and means to improve the quality of public transport are being investigated. Noise maps are required by EU law to reduce noise in major urban areas.

Sustainable use of natural resources.   The thematic strategy on the sustainable use of natural resources seeks to use natural resources in an efficient way, thereby reducing environmental impacts. Avoiding urban sprawl through high-density and mixed-use settlement patterns offers environmental advantages regarding land use, transport and heating, which reduces resource use per capita. The proposed directive under the thematic strategy on the Prevention and Recycling of Waste requires Member States to draw up waste-prevention programmes.

References

Abaza, H. (1995). 'UNEP/World Bank workshop on the environmental impacts of structural adjustment programmes – New York, 20–21 March 1995', *Ecological Economics*, **14** (1), 1–5.

Abed G. and Davoodi, H. (2000). *Corruption, Structural Reforms, and Economic Performance in the Transition Economies*', IMF Working Paper 00/132, 2000.

Abeygunawardena, P., Lohani, B. N., Bromley, D. W. and Barba, R. C. V. (1999). 'Yunan Dachaoshan Power Transmission Project', in *Environment and Economics in Project Preparation: Ten Asian Cases*, (Manila: Asian Development Bank).

AC Nielsen (2003). *Statistical Baseline Survey of Renewable Energy Projects*, AC Nielsen, Colombo.

Acemoglu, D., Johnson, S. and Robinson J. A. (2001). 'The colonial origins of comparative development: an empirical investigation', *American Economic Review*, **91** (Dec.), 1369–401.

Adams, R. and McCarl, B. (2001). 'Agriculture: agronomic-economic analysis', in Mendelsohn, R. (ed.), *Global Warming and the American Economy: A Regional Assessment of Climate Change* (Cheltenham: Edward Elgar), pp. 18–31.

ADB (1996). *Economic Evaluation of Environmental Impacts* (Manila: Asian Development Bank).

ADB (1997). *Asian Development Outlook 1997* (Manila: Asian Development Bank).

ADB (2005a). *Asian Development Outlook 2005: Promoting Competition for Long-Term Development* (Manila: Asian Development Bank).

ADB (2005b). 'Growth and trade horizons for Asia', *Asian Development Review*, **22** (2).

Adelman, I. and Morris, T. (1973). *Economic Growth and Economic Equity in Developing Countries* (Stanford: Stanford University Press).

Adger, W. N. (1999). 'Social vulnerability to climate change and extremes in coastal Vietnam', *World Development*, **27** (2), 1–21.

Adriaanse, A. (1993). *Environmental Policy Performance Indicators* (Den Haag: Sdu Uitgeverij).

Ahluwalia, M. S. (1975). 'Income inequality: some dimensions of the problem', in Chenery, H., Ahluwalia, M., Beu, C., Duloy, J. and Jolly, R. (eds.), *Redistribution with Growth* (London: Oxford University Press).

Ahmad, Q. K. (ed.) (2005). *Emerging Global Economic Order and the Developing Countries* (Dhaka: Dhaka University Press).

Alcorn, J. B. and Toledo, V. M. (1995). 'The role of tenurial shells in ecological sustainability: property rights and natural resource management in Mexico', in

Hanna, S. and Munasinghe, M. (eds.) *Property Rights and the Environment* (Stockholm and Washington, D.C.: Beijer Institute and the World Bank).

Alfsen, K. H. and Saebo H. V. (1993). 'Environmental quality indicators: background, principles and examples from Norway', *Environmental and Resource Economics*, **3** (Oct.), 415–35.

Alkire, S. (2002). 'Dimensions of human development', *World Development*, **30** (2), 181–205.

Alliende, F. (2002). *Estudio de Caso Completo Basado en el Plan de Descontaminación de la Región Metropolitana*, Taller Instrumentos de Mercado y Fuentes de Financiamiento para el Desarrollo Sostenible, División de Desarrollo Sostenible y Asentamientos Humanos, CEPAL, Santiago de Chile, 24 October, 2002.

Amman, H., Kendrick, D. and Achath, S. (1995). 'Solving stochastic optimization models with learning and rational expectations', *Economics Letters*, **48**, 9–13.

Amman, H., Kendrick, D. and Rust, J. (1996). *Handbook of Computational Economics* (Amsterdam: Elsevier).

Andersen, E. (1993). *Values in Ethics and Economics* (Cambridge, MA: Harvard University Press).

Andersen, P. (1983). 'On rent of fishing grounds: a translation of Jens Warming's 1911 article, with an introduction', *History of Political Economy*, **15**, 391–6.

Anderson, J. and Quiggin, J. (1990). *Risk and Project Appraisal*. Paper presented at the 2nd World Bank Development Economics Conference, Washington, D.C.

Antona, M., Bi Nabe, E. M., Salles, J-M., Péchard, G., Aubert, S. and Ratsimbarison, R. (2004). 'Rights transfer in Madagascar biodiversity policies', *Envrionment and Development Economics*, **9**, 825–47.

Armitage, D. R. (2003). 'Traditional agroecological knowledge, adaptive management and the socio-politics of conservation in Central Sulawesi, Indonesia', *Environmental Conservation*, **30**, 79–90.

Aronsson, T. and Lofgren, K. G. (1998). 'Green accounting: what do we know and what do we need to know?', in Tietenberg, T. and Folmer, H. (eds.), *International Yearbook of Environmental and Resource Economics 1998/99* (Cheltenham: Edward Elgar), chap. 6.

Arrow, K. J. and Hahn, F. (1971). *General Competitive Analysis* (San Francisco, CA: Holden-Day).

Arrow, K. J., Bolin, B., Costanza, R. *et al.* (1995a). 'Economic growth, carrying capacity and the environment', *Science*, **268**, 520–1.

Arrow, K. J., Cline, W., Maler, K. G., Munasinghe, M. and Stiglitz, J. (1995b). 'Intertemporal equity, discounting, and economic efficiency', in Munasinghe, M. (ed.), *Global Climate Change: Economic and Policy Issues* (Washington, D.C.: World Bank).

Arrow, K. J., Dasgupta, P., Jorgensen, D. W. *et al.* (1996). *Symposium on the Environment and Sustainable Development* (Tokyo: Research Centre on Global Warming, Japan Development Bank).

Assefa, G. (2005). 'On sustainability assessment of technical systems'. Unpublished Ph.D. Thesis, Royal Institute of Technology, Stockholm, Sweden.

Atkinson, G., Dubourg R., Hamilton, K., Munasinghe, M., Pearce, D. W. and Young, C. (1997). *Measuring Sustainable Development: Macroeconomics and the Environment* (Cheltenham: Edward Elgar).

Auerbach, A. (1985). 'The theory of excess burden and optimal taxation', in A. J. Auerbach and M. Feldstein (eds.), *Handbook of Public Economics, Vol. I* (Amsterdam: North Holland).

Awegoda, C. M., Perera, M. S. and Mathhes, D. T. (1994). '*An assessment of blood lead levels of the population exposed to vehicle emissions*' (Colombo: Sri Lanka Academy of Science), Abstracts, E2.

Ayensu, E., Claasen, D. R., Collins, M., *et al.* (2000). 'International ecosystem assessment', *Science*, **286**, 685–6.

Aylward, B. and Barbier, E. B. (1993). 'Valuing environmental functions in developing countries', *Biodiversity and Conservation*, **1** (1), 34–50.

Ayres, R. U. (1996). 'Limits to growth paradigm', *Ecological Economics*, **19**, 117–34.

Ayres, R. U. (1998). *Turning Point* (London: Earthscan Publications).

Azar, C., Homberg, J. and Lindgren, K. (1996). 'Socio-ecological indicators for sustainability', *Ecological Economics*, **18** (Aug.), 89–112.

Baer, P. and Templet, P. (2001). 'GLEAM: a simple model for the analysis of equity in policies to regulate greenhouse gas emissions through tradable permits', in Munasinghe, M., Sunkel, O. and de Miguel, C. (eds.), *The Sustainability of Long-Term Growth* (Cheltenham: Edward Elgar).

Baillie, J. E. M., Bennun, L. A., Hilton-Taylor, C., Brooks, T. M. and Stuart, S. N. (eds.) (2004). *IUCN Red List of Threatened Species: A Global Species Assessment* (Geneva: IUCN).

Banaszak, S., Chakravorty, U. and Ljeung, P. (1999). 'Demand for ground transportation fuel and pricing policy in Asian Tigers: a comparative study of Korea and Taiwan', *Energy Journal*, **20** (2), 145–65.

Banco Central de Chile (2001). *Matriz de Insumo-Producto de la Economía Chilena 1996* (Santiago: Banco Central de Chile).

Banco Central de Costa Rica (1990). *Cuentas Nacionales de Costa Rica, 1980–1989* (San José: Banco Central de Costa Rica).

Banuri, T. (1998). 'Human and environmental security', *Policy Matters*, **3**, 196–205.

Banuri, T. and Spanger-Siegfried, E. (2002). 'Equity and the clean development mechanism: equity, additionality, supplementarity', in Pinguelli-Rosa, L. and Munasinghe, M. (eds.), *Ethics, Equity and International Negotiations on Climate Change* (Cheltenham: Edward Elgar), pp.102–36.

Banuri, T., Hyden, G., Juma, C. and Rivera, M. (1994). *Sustainable Human Development: From Concept To Operation: A Guide For The Practitioner* (New York: UNDP).

Barbose, G., Goldman, C. and Neenan, B. (2004). *A Survey of Utility Experience with Real Time Pricing*, Paper LBNL-54238, Lawrence Berkeley National Laboratory, http://repositories.cdlib.org/lbnl/LBNL-54238.

Barrett, C. B., Brandon K., Gibson C. and Gjertsen H. (2001). 'Conserving tropical biodiversity amid weak instiutions', *BioScience*, **51**, 497–502.

Barro, R. J. and Sala-i-Martin, X. (1995). *Economic Growth* (Boston, MA: McGraw-Hill).

Barros, R. P., Henriques, R. and Mendonça, R. (2000). 'A Estabilidade Inaceitável: Desigualdade e Pobreza no Brasil', in Henriques, R. (ed.), *Desigualdade e Pobreza no Brasil* (Rio de Janeiro: IPEA).

Barrow, C. J. (2000). *Social Impact Assessment: An Introduction* (London: Arnold).

Bartelmus, P., Stahmer, C. and van Tongeren, J. (1989). 'Integrating environmental and economic accounts', Paper presented at the *Twenty-First General Conference of the International Association for Research in Income and Wealth*, West Germany, 20–25 August.

Bartelmus, P., Stahmer, C. and van Tongeren, J. (1991). 'Integrated environmental and economic accounting: framework for a SNA satellite system', *Review of Income and Wealth*, **37** (2), 111–48.

Basnayake, B. R. S. B. (2004). *Development of Rainfall and Temperature Scenarios for Sri Lanka*, Report published by the Climate Change Secretariat, Ministry of Environment and Natural Resources, Colombo.

Batabyal, A. A. (1994). 'An open economy model of the effects of unilateral environmental policy by a large developing country', *Ecological Economics*, **10** (3), 221–32.

Batabyal, A. A., Beladi, H. and Lee, D. M. (2001). 'Dynamic environmental policy in developing countries in the presence of a balance of trade deficit and a tariff', in Munasinghe, M., Sunkel, O. and de Miguel, C. (eds.), *The Sustainability of Long Term Growth* (London: Edward Elgar).

Bates, R., Cofala, J. and Toman, M. (1995). *Alternative Policies for the Control of Air Pollution in Poland*, Environment Paper 7, World Bank, Washington D.C.

Bator, F. M. (1957). 'The simple analytics of welfare maximization', *American Economic Review*, **47**, 22–59.

Baumol, W. J. and Bradford, D. F. (1970). 'Optimal departures from marginal cost pricing', *American Economic Review*, **60** (3), 265–83.

Baumol, W. J. and Oates, W. E. (1988). *The Theory of Environmental Policy* (Cambridge: Cambridge University Press).

Baytelman, Y., Cowan, K., De Gregorio, J. and González, P. (1999). 'Política Económica-Social y Bienestar: El Caso de Chile', Documento preparado para proyecto de UNICEF.

BC Hydro (1995). *Electricity Plan*, BC Hydro Report, Vancouver, British Columbia.

Becker, C. D. and Ghimire, K. (2003). 'Synergy between traditional ecological knowledge and conservation science supports forest preservation in Ecuador', *Conservation Ecology*, **8** (1), 1; http://www.consecol.org/vol8/iss1/art1.

Beckerman, W. (1974). *In Defence of Economic Growth* (London: Jonathan Cape).

Beckerman, W. (1992). 'Global trade offs in linking development and the environment', *World Development*, **20** (4), 481–96.

Beckerman, W. (1994). 'Sustainable development: is it a useful concept?', *Environmental Values*, **3** (3), 191–204.

Beghin, J., Bowland, B., Dessus, S., Roland-Holst, D. and Van der Mensbrugghe, D. (2002). 'Trade integration, environmental degradation and public health in Chile: assessing the linkages', *Environment and Development Economics*, **7** (2), 241–67.

Beghin, J., Dessus S., Roland-Holst, D. and Van der Mensbrugghe, D. (1996). *General Equilibrium Modelling of Trade and the Environment*, Technical Paper no. 116, OECD Development Center, Paris.

BEN (1997). *Brazilian Energy Balance*, Report, Ministry of Mining and Energy, Brazil.

Bennet, R. (2000). 'Risky business', *Science News*, **158**, (Sept.), 190–1.

Bentley, R. W. (2005). 'Global oil and gas depletion', *IAEE Newsletter*, 2nd quarter, 6–14.

Bento, A. M. and Rajkumar, A. S. (1998). *Rethinking the Nature of the Double Dividend Debate*, First World Congress of Environmental and Resource Economists, Venice, Italy, 25–27 June, 1998.

Bergman, L. (1990a). 'Energy and environmental constraints on growth: a CGE modeling approach', *Journal of Policy Modeling*, **12** (4), 671–91.

Bergman, L. (1990b). *General Equilibrium Effects of Environmental Policy: A CGE-Modeling Approach*, Research Paper 6415, Economic Research Institute, Stockholm.

Bergman, L. (1991). 'General equilibrium effect of environmental policy: a CGE modeling approach', *Environmental and Resource Economics*, **1**, 43–61.

Bergstrom, S. (1993). 'Value standards in sub-sustainable development: on limits of ecological economics', *Ecological Economics*, **7** (Feb.), 1–18.

Berkes, F. (1995). 'Indigenous knowledge and resource management systems: a Native Canadian case study from James Bay', in Hanna, S. and Munasinghe, M. (eds.), *Property Rights in a Social and Ecological Context* (Stockholm and Washington, D.C.: Beijer Institute and the World Bank).

Berkes, F. (1999). *Sacred Ecology: Traditional Ecological Knowledge and Management Systems*, (London: Taylor & Francis).

Berkes, F. and Folke, C. (eds.) (1998). *Linking Social and Ecological Systems: Management Practices and Social Mechanisms for Building Resilience* (Cambridge: Cambridge University Press).

Berkes, F. and Folke, C. (2002). 'Back to the future: ecosystem dynamics and local knowledge', in Gunderson, L. H. and Holling, C. S. (eds.), *Panarchy: Understanding Transformations in Human and Natural Systems* (Washington, D.C.: Island Press), pp. 121–46.

Berkes, F., Colding, J. and Folke, C. (2000). 'Rediscovery of traditional ecological knowledge as adaptive management', *Ecological Applications*, **10**, 1251–62.

Berkes, F., Colding, J. and Folke, C. (2003). *Navigating Social–Ecological Systems: Building Resilience for Complexity and Change* (Cambridge: Cambridge University Press).

Besant-Jones, J. E., Cordukes, P. and Mason, M. *et al.* (1990). *Review of Electricity Tariffs in Developing Countries During the 1980s*, IEN Series Paper no. 32 (Washington, D.C.: The World Bank).

Bhatia, R. and Falkenmark, M. (1993). *Water Resources Policies and the Urban Poor: Innovative Approaches and Policy Imperatives* (Washington, D.C.: World Bank).

Biesanz, R., Biesanz, K. and Biesanz, M. (1987). *The Costa Ricans* (New York: Prentice-Hall, Inc.).

Binswanger, H. (1989). *Brazilian Policies that Encourage Deforestation in the Amazon*, Environment Working Paper 16, Environment Department, World Bank, Washington, D.C.

Birdsall, N. and Wheeler, D. (1992). 'Trade policy and industrial pollution in Latin America: where are the pollution havens?', in Low, P. (ed.), *International Trade and the Environment*, World Bank Discussion Paper 159 (Washington, D.C.: World Bank).

Blomström, M. and Lundahl, M. (1989). *Costa Rica en Landstudie* (Stockholm: Institute of Latin American Studies).

Boer, G., Flato, G. and Ramsden, D. (2000). 'A transient climate change simulation with greenhouse gas and aerosol forcing: projected climate for the 21st century', *Climate Dynamics*, **16**, 427–50.

Bohle, H. G., Downing, T. E. and Watts, M. J. (1994). 'Climate change and social vulnerability: toward a sociology and geography of food insecurity', *Global Environmental Change*, **4** (1), 37–48.

Boiteux, M. (1949). 'La Tarification des Demandes en Pointe', *Revue Generale de l'Electricite*, **58**, 321–40.

Boiteux, M. and Stasi, P. (1964). 'The determination of costs of expansion of an interconnected system of production and distribution of electricity', in Nelson, J. (ed.), *Marginal Cost Pricing in Practice* (Englewood Cliffs, NJ: Prentice-Hall).

Bonelli, R. (1998). *A Note On Foreign Direct Investment (FDI) and Industrial Competitiveness in Brazil*, IPEA Working Paper 584, Rio de Janeiro, Brazil.

Bongaarts, J. (1994). 'Population policy options in the developing world', *Science*, **263**, 771–6.

Borenstein, S. (2005). 'Time varying retail electricity prices: theory and practice', in Griffin, J. M. and Puller, S. L. (eds.), *Electricity Deregulation: Choices and Challenges* (Chicago, IL: Chicago University Press).

Botkin, D. B. and Talbot, L. M. (1992). 'Biological diversity and forests', in Sharma, N. P. (ed.), *Managing the World's Forests: Looking For Balance Between Conservation and Development* (Dubuque, IO: Kendall/Hunt), pp. 47–74.

Boulanger, P-M., and Brechet, T. (2002). *Improving Scientific Tools for Sustainable Development Decision Making* (Brussels: Directorate General Research, European Commission).

Boulding, K. (1966). 'The economics of the coming spaceship earth', in Jarrett, H. (ed.), *Environmental Quality in a Growing Economy*, (Baltimore, MD: Johns Hopkins University Press).

Bovenberg, L. and De Mooij, R. (1994). 'Evironmental levies and distortionary taxation', *American Economic Review*, **84**, 1085–9.

Braden, J. B. and. Kolstad, C. D. (eds.) (1991). *Measuring The Demand For Environmental Quality* (New York: Elsevier Science Publishing Co. Inc.).

Brennan, T. (2001). 'Drawing lessons from the California power crisis', *Resources*, **144** (Summer issue), 8–12.

Bromley, D. W. (1989). *Economic Interests and Institutions* (Oxford: Blackwell).

Bromley, D. W. (1991). *Environment and Economy: Property Rights and Public Policy* (Oxford: Oxford University Press).

Brooke, A., Kendrick, D., Meeraus, A. and Raman, R. (1997). *GAMS: A User's Guide*, GAMS homepage, http://www.gams.com.

Brown, L. (2003). *Plan B: Rescuing a Planet Under Stress and a Civilization in Trouble* (New York: W. W. Norton and Company).

Brown, L. (2004). *Europe Leading World into Age of Wind Energy*, www.earth-policy.org/Updates/Update37.htm.

Brown, P. G. (1998). 'Towards an economics of stewardship: the case of climate', *Ecological Economics*, **26**, 11–21.

Bruce, J. P., Lee, H. and Haites, E. F. (eds.) (1996). *Climate Change 1995: Economic and Social Dimensions of Climate Change* (Cambridge: Cambridge University Press).

Bryne, J., Toly, N. and Glover, L. (2006). *Transforming Power: Energy, Environment and Society in Conflict* (New York: Transaction Publishers).

Brzovic, F., Miller, S. and Lagos, C. (2002). *Gasto, Inversión y Financiamiento para el Desarrollo Sostenible en Chile*, Serie Medio Ambiente y Desarrollo no. 57, División de Desarrollo Sostenible y Asentamientos Humanos, CEPAL.

Burmeister, E. and Dobell, A. (1970). *Mathematical Theories of Economic Growth* (London: Macmillan).

Burmeister, E. and Dobell, R. (1971). *Mathematical Theories of Economic Growth* (New York: Macmillan).

Burton, I. (1997). 'Vulnerability and adaptive response in the context of climate and climate change', *Climatic Change*, **36** (1–2), 185–96.

Bussolo, M., Mizala, A. and Romaguera, P. (1998). *Beyond Heckscher–Ohlin: Trade and Labour Market, Interactions in a Case Study for Chile*, Working Papers Series Fedesarrollo no. 9, Eundación para In Educación Superior y el Desarrolo, Santiago, Chile.

Cain, M. and McNicoll, G. (1988). 'Population growth and agrarian outcomes', in Lee, R. D., Arthur, W. B., Kelley, A. C., Rodgers, G. and Srinivasan, T. N. (eds.), *Population, Food and Rural Development* (Oxford: Clarendon Press).

Capistrano, D. and Kiker, C. F. (1990). *Global Economic Influences on Tropical Closed Broad-Leaved Forest Depletion, 1967–1985* (Gainesville, FL: University of Florida).

Carney, D. (ed.) (1998). *Sustainable Rural Livelihoods*, UK Government Report, Department for International Development, London.

Carpenter, S. R. and Gunderson, L. H. (2001). 'Coping with collapse: ecological and social dynamics in ecosystem management', *Bioscience*, **51** (6), 451–7.

Carriére, J. (1991). 'The political economy of land degradation in Costa Rica', *International Journal of Political Economy*, **21** (1), 10–31.

Cash, R. A., Music, S. I., Libonati, J. P., Craig, J. P., Pierce, N. F. and Hornick, R. B. (1974). 'Response of man to infection with Vibrio cholerae, II: protection from illness afforded by previous disease and vaccine', *Journal of Infections Diseases*, **130** (4), 325–33.

Caspary, G. and O'Connor, D. (2002). *Au-delà de Johannesburg: politiques economiques et financières pour un développement respectueux du climat,* Cahier de politique économique no.21, Centre de developpement de l'OECD, Paris.

Cattaneo A. (2005). 'Inter-regional innovation in Brazilian agriculture and deforestation in the Amazon: income and environment in the balance', *Environment and Development Economics*, **10** (4), 485–511.

Cavalcanti, M. A. F. H., Ribeiro, F. J. and Castro, A. S. (1998). 'Desempenho Recente e Perspectivas das Exportações Brasileiras', *Revista Brasileira de Comércio Exterior*, **57**, 39–46.

CBD (1992). *Convention on Biological Diversity*, Text and Annexes (Geneva: The Interim Secretariat for the CBD, Executive Centre).

CEB (1987). *Masterplan for Electricity Supply in Sri Lanka*, Vol. 1 (Colombo: Ceylon Electricity Board).

CEB (1988). *Masterplan for Electricity Supply in Sri Lanka*, Vol. 2 (Colombo: Ceylon Electricity Board).

CEB (1992). *Wind Energy Resources Assessment for the Southern Lowlands of Sri Lanka* (Colombo: Ceylon Electricity Board).

CEB (1999). *Long Term Generation Expansion Plan 1999–2013* (Colombo: Ceylon Electricity Board).

CEB (2003). *Long Term Generation Expansion Plan 2003–2017* (Colombo: Ceylon Electricity Board).

CEC (2004).*Towards a Thematic Strategy on the Urban Environment*, Communication from the Commission to the Council, the European Parliament, the European Economic and Social Committee and the Committee of the Regions, COM2004(60), http://europa.eu. int/eur-lex/lex/LexUriServ/site/en/com/2004/com2004_0060en01.pdf.

CEF (2005). Central Energy Fund, iGas website, http://www.cef.org.za/group/iGas/index. htm, 14 September 2005.

Central Bank (1998). *Annual Report* (Colombo: Central Bank of Sri Lanka).

Central Bank (2003). *Annual Report* (Colombo: Central Bank of Sri Lanka).

Central Bank (2005). *Annual Report* (Colombo: Central Bank of Sri Lanka).

CEPAL (1999). *Panorama Social 1998 de América Latina* (Santiago: United Nations).

CEPAL (2000). *Panorama Social 1999/2000 de América Latina* (Santiago: United Nations).

Cesar, H. S. (1994). *Control and Game Models of the Greenhouse Effect*, (Heidelberg: Springer Verlag).

CGSDI (2006). Consultative Group on Sustainable Development Indicators, Winnipeg, Canada; http://www.iisd.org/cgsdi/members.asp and http://esl.jrc.it/envind/dashbrds.htm.

Chakravarty, S. (1969). *Capital and Development Planning* (Cambridge, MA: MIT Press).

Chambers, R. (1989). 'Vulnerability, coping and policy', *IDS Bulletin*, **20**, (2), 1–7.

Chandrasiri, S. (1999). *Controlling Automotive Air Pollution: The Case of Colombo City*, Research Report Series, Economy and Environment Programme for Southeast Asia.

Chandrasiri, S. and Jayasinghe, S. (1998). *Health Effects of Vehicular Emissions in Colombo*, UC-ISS Project Working Paper Series, 9805, University of Colombo.

Chang, C. C., Mendelsohn, R. and Shaw, D. (eds.) (2003). *Global Warming and the Asian Pacific* (Cheltenham: Edward Elgar).

Chenery, H. and Srinivasan, T. N. (eds.) (1988–1989), *Handbook of Development Economics*, Vols. i and ii (Amsterdam: North-Holland).

Chichilnisky, G. (1993). 'North–south trade and the dynamics of renewable resources', *Structural Change and Economic Dynamics*, **4** (2), 219–48.

Chichilnisky, G. and Heal, G. (eds.) (2000). *Environmental Markets: Equity and Efficiency* (New York: Columbia University Press).

Chopra, K. (2001). *Social Capital and Sustainable Development: The Role of Formal and Informal Institutions in a Developing Country*, (Delhi: Institute of Economic Growth).

Choucri, N. (2003). *Mapping Sustainability*, Global System for Sustainable Development (GSSD) (Cambridge MA: Massachusetts Institute of Technology); http://gssd.mit.edu/.

CIDIE (1992). *Workshop on Environmental and Natural Resources Accounting*, United Nations Environment Programme, Nairobi, Kenya.

Cialdini, R. B. (2001). *Influence: Science and Practice*, 4th edn, (London: Allyn and Bacon).

Cicin-Sain, B. and Knecht, R. W. (1995), 'Analysis of Earth summit prescriptions on incorporating traditional knowledge in natural resource management', in Hanna, S. and Munasinghe, M. (eds.), *Property Rights and the Environment* (Stockholm and Washington, D.C.: Beijer Institute and the World Bank).

Ciriacy-Wantrup, S. V. (1952). *Resource Conservation: Economics and Politics* (Berkeley, CA: University of California Press).

Clarke, C. and Munasinghe, M. (1995). 'Economic aspects of disasters and sustainable development', in Munasinghe, M. and Clarke, C. (eds.), *Disaster Prevention for Sustainable Development: Economic and Policy Issues* (Washington, D.C.: World Bank and IN, and Geneva: IDNDR and United Nations).

Cleaver, K. and Schreiber, G. (1991). *The Population, Environment, and Agriculture Nexus in Sub-Saharan Africa*, Africa Region Technical Paper, World Bank, Washington, D.C.

Cline, W. (1996). 'The impact of global warming on agriculture: comment', *The American Economic Review*, **86** (5), 1309–11.

Coase, R. H. (1960). 'The problem of social cost', *Journal of Law and Economics*, **3** (Oct.), 1–44.

Cochrane, P. (2006). 'Exploring cultural capital and its importance in sustainable development', *Ecological Economics*, **57**, 318–30.

Cocklin, C. R. (1989). 'Methodological problems in evaluating sustainability', *Environmental Conservation*, **16**, 343–51.

Coeymans, J. E. and Larraín, F. (1994). 'Efectos de un Acuerdo de Libre Comercio entre Chile y Estados Unido: Un Enfoque de Equilibrio General', *Cuadernos de Economía*, **31** (94), 357–99.

Colding, J. and Folke, C. (1997). 'The relations among threatened species, their protection, and taboos', *Conservation Ecology*, (**1**), (1), 6; available from http:// www.consecol. org/vol1/iss1/art6.

Cole, M. A. (1999). 'Examining the environmental case against free trade', *Journal of World Trade*, **33** (5), 183–96.

Cole, M. A., Rayner, A. J. and Bates, J. M. (1997). *Environmental quality and economic growth*, University of Nottingham, Department of Economics Discussion Paper no. 96/ 20, pp. 1–33.

Coleman, J. (1990). *Foundations of Social Theory*, (Cambridge, MA: Harvard University Press).

Colwell, R. and Huq, A. (1994). 'Vibrios in the environment: viable but non-culturable Vibrio cholerae', in Wachsmuth, I. K., Blake, P. A. and Oslvik, O. (eds.), *Vibrio cholerae and Cholera: Molecular to Global Perspectives* (Washington, D.C.: ASM), pp. 117–33.

Commonwealth of Australia (1999). *Global Trade Reform – Maintaining Momentum* (Canberra: Ministry of Foreign Affairs and Trade).

Corfee-Morlot, J., Berg, M. and Caspary, G. (2002). *Exploring Linkages Between Natural Resource Management and Climate Adaptation Strategies* (Paris: Environment Directorate, OECD).

Cornia, G. A., Jolly, R. and Stewart, F. (1992). *Adjustment with a Human Face,* Vol.1, *Protecting the Vulnerable and Promoting Growth* (Oxford: Clarendon Press).

Costanza, R. (2000). 'Ecological sustainability, indicators and climate change', in Munasinghe, M. and Swart, R. (eds.), *Climate Change and its Linkages with Development, Equity and Sustainability* (Geneva: IPCC).

Costanza, R., Cumberland, J., Daly, H., Goodland, R. and Norgaard, R. (1997). *An Introduction to Ecological Economics* (Boca Raton FL: St. Lucia's Press).

Craven, B. and Islam, S. M. N. (2003). 'On multiobjective dynamic optimization: issues in growth, social welfare, and sustainability', *Journal of Multicriteria Decision Analysis*, **12**, 273–84.

Craven, B. (1995). *Control and Optimisation* (London: Chapman and Hall).

Cropper, M. L. and Oates, W. E. (1992). 'Environmental economics: a survey', *Journal of Economic Literature*, **30**, 675–740.

Cruz, W. and Gibbs, C. (1990). 'Resource policy reform in the context of population pressure, and deforestation in the Philippines', *American Journal of Agricultural Economics*, **72** (5).

Cruz, W. and Repetto, R. (1992). *The Environmental Effects of Stabilization and Structural Adjustment Programs: The Philippines Case* (Washington, D.C.: World Resources Institute).

Cruz, W., Munasinghe, M. and Warford, J. (1997). *The Greening of Economic Policy Reform. Vol. I (Principles) and Vol. II (Case Studies)* (Washington, D.C.: World Bank).

Dabla-Norris, E. and Freeman, S. (1999). *The Enforcement of Property Rights and Underdevelopment*, IMF Working Paper 99/127.

Dahl, C. and Sterner, J. (1991). 'Analyzing gasoline demand elasticities: a survey', *Energy Economics*, **3** (13), 203–10.

Daly, H. (2000). *Ecological Economics and the Ecology of Economics* (Cheltenham: Edward Elgar).

Daly, H. (2001). 'Globalization versus internationalization: some implications', in Munasinghe, M., Sunkel, O. and de Miguel, C. (eds.), *The Sustainability of Long Term Growth* (London: Edward Elgar).

Daly, H. E. and Cobb, Jr, J. B. (1989). *For the Common Good: Redirecting the Economy Toward Community, the Environment, and a Sustainable Future* (Boston, MA: Beacon Press).

Daniels, P. L. (2005). 'Economic systems and Buddhist world view: the 21st century nexus', *Journal of Socio-economics*, **34**, 245–68.

Darwin, R. (1999). 'The impact of global warming on agriculture: a Ricardian analysis: comment', *The American Economic Review*, **89** (4), 1049–52.

Dasgupta, P. (1993). *An Inquiry Into Well-Being and Destitution* (Oxford: Clarendon Press).

Dasgupta, P. S. (1995). 'Population, poverty, and the local environment', *Scientific American*, **272** (2), 40–6.

Dasgupta, P. and Maler, K. G. (1997). 'The resource basis of production and consumption: an economic analysis', in Dasgupta, P. and Maler, K. G. (eds.), *The Environment and Emerging Development Issues,* Vol. 1 (Oxford: Clarendon Press).

Davis, A. and Wagner, J. R. (2003). 'Who knows? On the importance of identifying experts when researching local ecological knowledge', *Human Ecology*, **31**, 463–89.

Davis, M. (2001). *Late Victorian Holocausts: El Nino Famines and the Making of the Third World* (New York: Verso).

DDP/UNEP (2004). *Proceedings of the Third Dams and Development Forum – June 2004* (Nairobi: Dams and Development Project, United Nations Environment Programme).

DDP/UNEP (2005). *DDP Phase 2 Goals and Work Programme, Information Sheet no. 1* (Nairobi: Dams and Development Project, United Nations Environment Programme).

De Bruyn, S. and Heintz, R. J. (1999). 'The environmental Kuznets curve hypothesis', in Van den Bergh, J. C. J. M. (ed.), *Handbook of Environmental and Resource Economics* (Cheltenham: Edward Elgar), Chap. 46.

De Costa, W. A. J. M., Weerakoon, W. M. W., Herath H. M. L. K. and Abeywardena, R. M. I. (2003). 'Response of growth and yield of rice (oryza sativa) to elevated atmospheric carbon dioxide in the subhumid zone of Sri Lanka', *Journal of Agronomy and Crop Science*, **189**, 1–13.

De Miguel, C. and Miller, S. (1998). *Macroeconomía, Medio Ambiente, y Modelos de Equilibrio General*, Documento de Trabajo, Programa de Desarrollo Sustentable, Centro de Análisis de Políticas Públicas, Universidad de Chile, Santiago.

De Silva, A.P.D.S. (1989). 'Impact of energy price changes on transport', in Wijeratne, E. N. (ed.), *Energy Pricing Options in Sri Lanka* (New York: International Labor Organization).

De Soto, H. (1993). 'The missing ingredient', *The Economist*, **328** (7828), 8–12.

De Vries, B. and Goudsblom, J. (eds.) (2002). *Mappae Mundi* (Amsterdam: Amsterdam University Press).

Department of Census and Statistics (1997). *Statistical Abstract of the Democratic Socialist Republic of Sri-Lanka*, Ministry of Interior, Sri Lanka.

Department of Census and Statistics (2003). *Poverty Indicators – Household Income and Expenditure Survey 2002*, Ministry of Interior, Sri Lanka.

Dessus, S. and Bussolo, M. (1998). 'Is there a trade-off between trade liberalization and pollution abatement: a computable general equilibrium assessment applied to Costa Rica, *Journal of Policy Modelling*, **20** (1), 11–31.

Devarajan, S. (1997). 'Can computable general equilibrium models shed light on the environmental problems of developing countries?', in Dasgupta, P. and Maler, K. (eds.), *The Environment and Emerging Development Issues*, vol. 1 (Oxford: Clarendon Press).

Devkota, M. P. (2005). Biology of mistletoes and their status in Nepal Himalaya, *Himalayan Journal of Sciences*, **3** (5), 85–8.

DFID, EC, UNDP and World Bank (2002). *Linking Poverty Reduction and Environmental Management*, Combined Report, Department for International Development, UK, Directorate General for Development, European Commission, United Nations Development Programme and The World Bank, Washington, D.C.

Dheerasinghe, K. G. D. D. and Jayaweera, D. S. (1997). *Economic, Social and Environmental Demands on Transport: Past Performance and Emerging Challenges*, Sri Lanka Transport Sector Study, vol. II, South Asia I Infrastructure Division, World Bank Report 16269-CE, Washington, D.C.

Diamond, J. (1997). *Guns, Germs and Steel: The Fates of Human Societies* (New York: W. W. Norton).

Diefenbacher, H. (1994). 'The index of sustainable economic welfare', in Cobb, J. and Cobb, C. (eds.), *The Green National Product* (Lanham, MD: University Press of America).

Dietz, T., Ostrom, E. and Stern, P. C. (2003). 'The struggle to govern the commons', *Science*, **302**, 1907–12.

Dinar, A., Mendelsohn, R., Evenson, R., Parikh, J., Sanghi, A., Kumar, K., McKinsey, J. and Lonergan, S. (eds.) (1998). *Measuring the Impact of Climate Change on Indian Agriculture*, World Bank Technical Paper no. 402, Washington, D.C.

DIPRES (2001). *Estadísticas de las Finanzas Públicas 1991–2000*, Series Estadísticas, Dirección de Presupuestos, Ministerio de Hacienda, Gobierno de Chile.

DIPRES (2003). *Estadísticas de las Finanzas Públicas 1987–2002*, Series Estadísticas, National Budget Office, Ministry of Finance, Chile.

DME (2001). *South Africa National Energy Balance 1999*, Microsoft Excel Spreadsheet, Department of Minerals and Energy, Pretoria, South Africa.

DME (2003). *South Africa National Energy Balance 2001*, Department of Minerals and Energy, Pretoria, South Africa.

Dodds, S. (1977). 'Economic growth and human well-being', in Diesendorf, M. and Hamilton, C. (eds.), *Human Ecology and Human Economy* (Sydney: Allen and Unwin).

DoH (1998) *Quantification of the Effects of Air Pollution on Health in the UK*, UK Committee on the Medical Effects of Air Pollution, Department of Health.

Dopfer, K. (1979). *The New Political Economy of Development: Integrated Theory and Asian Experience* (London: The Macmillan Press Ltd).

Dreze, J. and Sen, A. (1990). *Hunger and Public Action* (Oxford: Clarendon Press).

Du Toit, J. T., Walker, B. H. and Campbell, B. M. (2004). 'Conserving tropical nature: current challenges for ecologists', *Trends in Ecology and Evolution*, **19**, 12–17.

Dufournaud, M., Harrington, J. and Rogers, P. (1988). 'Leontief's environmental repercussions and the economic structure revisited: a general equilibrium formulation', *Geographical Analysis*, **20** (4), 318–27.

DUKES (2006). *The Digest of UK Energy Statistics* (London: BERR).

Duloy, J. (1975). 'Sectorial, regional and project analysis', in Chenery, H. and Srinivasan, T. N. (eds.) (1988–1989). *Handbook of Development Economics*, Vols. i and ii (Amsterdam: North-Holland).

Dupuit, J. (1844). 'De la mesure de l'utilité des travaux public', reprinted (1952) in English translation as 'On the measurement of the utility of Public Works', in Peacock, A. T., Lutz, F. A., Turvey, R. and Henderson, E. (eds.), *International Economic Papers, No. 2* (London: Macmillan).

Durayappah A. K. (1998). 'Poverty and environmental degradation: a review and analysis of the nexus', *World Development*, **26** (12), 2169–79.

Easterbrook, G. (1995). *A Moment on the Earth: The Coming Age of Environmental Optimism* (New York: Viking).

Eberhard, A. (2003). *The Political, Economic, Institutional and Legal Dimensions of Electricity Supply Industry Reform in South Africa*, Political Economy of Power Market Reform Conference, 19–20 February 2003, Stanford University, CA.

ECA and Vernstrom, R. (2003). *EVN Bulk Power, Distribution Margin, Retail Consumer Tariff Design and Development of an Independent Creditors' Model*, Interim Report to EVN, Hanoi.

ECLAC (1989). *Crisis External Debt, Macroeconomic Policies, and their Relation to the Environment in Latin America and the Caribbean*, paper prepared for the meeting of high-level government experts on Regional Co-operation in Environmental Matters in Latin America and the Caribbean, United Nations Environmental Programme, Brazil.

Ecological Economics (1998). *Special Issue on the Environmental Kuznets Curve, Ecological Economics*, **25** (May).

Ecological Economics (2000). *Special Issue on the Human Actor in Ecological-Economic Models, Ecological Economics*, **35**, (3).

Ecological Economics (2006). *Special Issue on Environmental Benefits Transfer, Ecological Economics*, **60** (2).

Ecology and Society (2006). *Special Issue on Resilience in Social-Ecological Systems, Ecology and Society*, **11**, (1); http://www.ecologyandsociety.org/ vol11/iss1/.

Edwards, S. (1992). *Structural Adjustment and Stabilization: Issues on Sequencing and Speed*, EDI Working Papers, Economic Development Institute, World Bank, Washington D.C.

Edwards, T. H. and Hutton, J. P. (2001). 'Allocation of carbon permits within a country: a general equilibrium analysis of the United Kingdom', *Energy Economics*, **23** (4), 371–86.

Eggertsson, T. (1990). *Economics Behaviour and Institutions* (Cambridge: Cambridge University Press).

Ehrenfeld, D. (2003). 'Globalization: effects on biodiversity, environment, and society', *Conservation and Society (New Delhi)*, **1** (1), 99–111.

EIA (2005). *International Energy Outlook 2005*, Report DOE/EIA-0484(2005), Energy Information Administration, Department of Energy, USA.

EIA (2006). *International Energy Outlook 2006*, Report DOE/EIA-0484 (2006), Energy Information Administration, Department of Energy, USA.

Ekins, P., Folke, C. and de Groot, R. (2003). 'Identifying critical natural capital', *Ecological Economics*, **44** (2–3), 159–65.

Electrowatt (1996). *Thermal Options Study* (Zurich: Electrowatt Engineering).

Eltis, W. (1966). *Economic Growth* (London: Hutchinson and Co.).

Emori, S., Nozawa, T., Abe-Ouchi, A., Namaguti, A. and Kimoto, M. (1999). 'Coupled ocean-atmospheric model experiments of future climate change with an explicit representation of sulfate aerosol scattering', *Journal of the Meteorological Society of Japan*, **77**, 1299–1307.

Energy Conservation Fund (1996). *Sri Lanka Energy Balance* (Colombo: Energy Conservation Fund).

England, R. W. (2000). 'Natural capital and the theory of economic growth', *Ecological Economics*, **34** (3), 425–31.

Environment and Development Economics (1997). *Special Issue on the Environmental Kuznets Curve, Environment and Development Economics*, **2** (4).

Environment and Development Economics (1998). *Policy Forum*, **3** (4).

Environment and Development Economics (1999). *Special Issue on Structural Adjustment and the Environment, Environment and Development Economics*, **4** (1).

Environment and Development Economics (2004). *Special Issue on Poverty and Forest Degradation, Environment and Development Economics*, **9** (2).

Environment and Development Economics (2006). *Special Section on the Dynamics of Coupled Human and Natural Systems, Environment and Development Economics*, **11** (1).

Estrada-Oyuela, R. A. (2002). 'Equity and climate change', in Pinguelli-Rosa, L. and Munasinghe, M. (eds.), *Ethics, Equity and International Negotiations on Climate Change* (Cheltenham: Edward Elgar Publishing), pp.36–46.

Esty, D. C. (2004). 'Environmental protection in the information age', *New York University Law Review*, **79**, 115.

Eurostat (2006). *European Union Sustainable Development Indicators*, Brussels, Belgium; http://epp.eurostat.cec.eu.int.

Faber, M. and Proops, J. L. R. (1990). *Evolution, Time, Production and the Environment*, (Heidelberg: Springer-Verlag).

Fabricius, C. and Koch, E. (2004). *Rights, Resources and Rural Development: Community-Based Natural Resource Management in Southern Africa*. (London: Earthscan).

Falkenmark, M. and Rockstrom, J. (2006). 'Green water breaking new ground', *Water Front*, (1), 10–11; http://www.siwi.org/documents/Resources/Water_Front/WF-1-2006.pdf.

Falkenmark, M., Gamn, M. and Cestti, R. (1990). *Water Resources: A Call for New Ways of Thinking*, Draft Paper, INUWS, World Bank, Washington, D.C.

FAO (2005) *State of the World's Forests 2005*, (Rome: Food And Agriculture Organization).

Farmer, C. M. (2005). Environmental consequences of social security reform: a second best threat to public conservation, *Ecological Economics*, **53** (2), 191–210.

Faucheux, S., Pearce, D. and Proops, J. (eds.) (1996). *Models of Sustainable Development* (Cheltenham: Edward Elgar).

Feder, G., Ochan, T., Chalamwong, Y. and Hongladarom. C. (1988). *Land Policies and Farm Productivity in Thailand* (Baltimore, MD: Johns Hopkins University Press).

Fernando, C. and Munasinghe, M. (1998). 'A real options framework to assess environmental policy, programs and strategy for GHG mitigation', Working Paper, World Bank, Washington DC.

Fernando, C., Kleindorfer, and Munasinghe, M. (1994). 'Integrated resource planning with environmental costs in developing countries', *The Energy Journal*, **15** (3), 93–121.

Fernando, S. (1998). 'An assessment of the small hydro potential in Sri Lanka', Intermediate Technology Development Group, Colombo, Sri Lanka.

Ferraz, C. and Young, C. E. F. (1999). *Trade Liberalization and Industrial Pollution in Brazil* (Santiago: ECLAC).

Fields, G. (1995). 'Income distribution in developing economies: conceptual, data, and policy issues in broad-based growth', in Quibira, M. and Dowling, M. (eds.), *Current Issues in Economic Development* (Hong Kong: Oxford University Press).

Fischer, S. and Thomas, V. (1990). 'Policies for economic development', *American Journal of Agricultural Economics*, **72** (3), 809–14.

Fisher I. (1906). *The Nature of Capital and Income* (New York: Augustus M. Kelly).

Fitzpatrick, T. (2000). *Horizontal Management & Trends in Governance and Accountability, Service and Innovation Sector* (Ottawa: Canadian Centre for Management Development).

FOCUS (2000), *Presupuesto Nacional Ambiental 1999–2000*, Estudios y Consultarías, Comisión Nacional de Medio Ambiente, Santiago, Chile.

Focus the Nation (2007). http://www.focusthenation.org/index.html.

Folke, C. and Berkes, F. (1995). 'Mechanisms that link property right to ecological systems', in Hanna, S. and Munasinghe M. (eds.), *Property Rights and the Environment* (Stockholm and Washington, D.C.: Beijer Institute and the World Bank).

Folke, C. and Gunderson, L (2006). 'Facing global change through social-ecological research', *Ecology and Society*, **11** (2); http://www.ecologyandsociety.org.

Forsund, F. and Strom, S. (1988). *Environmental Economics and Management: Pollution and Natural Resources*, (New York: Croom Helm Press).

Foster, S. S. D. (1988). 'Impacts of urbanization on groundwater', *UNESCO-IHP Proc. Intl. Symp. Urban Water 88*, Duisberg, Germany.

Foster, V. and Tre, J-P. (2000). 'Measuring the impact of energy interventions on the poor – an illustration from Guatemala', *World Bank–UK Government Conference, Infrastructure for Development: Private Solutions and the Poor*, May 31–June 2, London; http://www.ppiaf.org/conference/section1-paper4.pdf.

Fox, K., Sengupta J. and Thorbecke, E. (1973). *Theory of Quantitative Economic Policy* (Amsterdam: North Holland).

Foy, G. and Daly, H. (1989). *Allocation, Distribution, and Scale as Determinants of Environmental Degradation: Case Studies of Haiti, El Salvador, and Costa Rica*, Environment Working Paper 19, Environment Department, World Bank, Washington, D.C.

Frankel, J. and Romer, D. (1999). 'Does trade cause growth?', *American Economic Review*, **89** (June), 379–99.

Freeman, A. M. (1993). *The Measurement of Environmental and Resource Values: Theory and Methods*. (Washington, D.C.: Resources For the Future).

Freeman, A.M. (2000). *Valuation of Environmental Health Damages in Developing Countries: Some Observations*, EEPSEA Special Paper, Biannual Workshop of the Economy and Environment Programme of Southeast Asia, Bangkok.

French, H. (2000). *Vanishing Borders: Protecting the Planet in the Age of Globalization* (Washington D.C.: Worldwatch).

Friedman, J. W. (1986). *Game Theory with Applications to Economics* (Oxford: Oxford University Press).

FT (2006a). *Financial Times*, 29 October.

FT (2006b). *Financial Times*, 3 December.

Fullerton, D. and Metcalf, G. E. (1997). *Environmental Taxes and the Double-Dividend Hypothesis: Did You Really Expect Something for Nothing?*', NBER Working Paper 6199, National Bureau of Economic Research, Cambridge, MA.

Gadgil M., Rao, P. R. S., Utkarsh, G., Pramod, P. and Chatre, A. (2000). 'New meanings for old knowledge: the people's biodiversity registers programme', *Ecological Applications*, **10**, 1307–17.

Gadgil, M. and Rao, P. R. S. (1995). 'Designing incentives to conserve India's biodiversity', in Hanna, S. and Munasinghe, M. (eds.), *Property Rights in a Social and Ecological Context* (Stockholm and Washington, D.C.: Beijer Institute and the World Bank), pp. 53–62.

Gallopin, G. C. (1997). 'Commentary on Gordon Baskerville's perspective', *Conservation Ecology* [online], **1**, (1), 12, http://www.consecol.org/vol1/iss1/art12/.

Garbacz, C. (1989). 'Gasoline, diesel and motorfuel demand in Taiwan', *Energy Journal*, **10** (2), 153.

Garfield, P. J. and Lovejoy, W. F. (1964). *Public Utility Economics* (Englewood Cliffs, NJ: Prentice-Hall).

Gbetnkom, D. (2005). 'Deforestation in Cameroon: immediate causes and consequences', *Environment and Development Economics*, **10** (4), 557–72.

GENI (2004). Global Energy Network Institute; http://www.geni.org/globalenergy/policy/renewableenergy/index.html.

Georgescu-Roegen, N. (1971). *The Entropy Law and the Economic Process* (Cambridge, MA: Harvard University Press).

Ghimire, S. K., McKey, D., Thomas, Y. A. (2004). 'Heterogeneity in ethnoecological knowledge and management of medicinal plants in the Himalayas of Nepal: implications for conservation', *Ecology and Society*, **9** (3), 6; http://www.ecologyandsociety.org/vol9/iss3/art6.

Gilbert, A. and Feenstra, J. (1994). 'Sustainability indicators for the Dutch environmental policy theme 'diffusion' cadmium accumulation in soil', *Ecological Economics*, **9**, 253–65.

Gintis, H. (2000). 'Beyond homo economicus: evidence from experimental economics', *Ecological Economics*, **35** (3), 311–23.

Githinji, M. and Perrings, C. (1992). *Social and Ecological Sustainability in the use of Biotic Resources in Sub-Saharan Africa: Rural Institutions and Decision Making in Kenya and Botswana*, Mimeo., Beijer Institute and University of California, Riverside, CA.

Glaister, S., Graham, D. J. and Hoskins, E. (1999). *Transport and Health in London*, Report for the NHS Executive, London, UK.

Glomsrod, S., Monge, M. D. and Vennemo, H. (1999). 'Structural adjustment and deforestation in Nicaragua', *Environment and Development Economics*, **4** (1), 19–43.

Goldin, I. and Roland-Host, D. (1997). 'Economic policies for sustainable resource use in Morocco', in Cruz, W., Munasinghe, M. and Warford, J. (eds.), *The Greening of Economic Policy Reform, Vol. II: Case Studies* (Washington, D.C.: World Bank), chap. 3.

Goldin, I. and Winters, A. (1992). *Open Economies: Structural Adjustment and Agriculture*, (Cambridge: Cambridge University Press).

Gordon, C., Senior, C., Banks, H., Gregory, I., Johns, T., Mitchell, J. and Wood, R. (2000). 'The simulation of SST, sea ice extents, and ocean heat transports in a version of the Hadley Centre coupled model without flux adjustments', *Climate Dynamics*, **16**, 147–68.

Gordon, H. and O'Farrell, S. (1997). 'Transient climate change in the CSIRO coupled model with dynamic sea ice', *Monthly Weather Research*, **125**, 875–907.

Gordon, H. S. (1954). 'The economic theory of a common-property resource fishery', *Journal of Political Economy*, **62**, 124–42.

GOSL (2002). *Regaining Sri Lanka: Vision and Strategy for Accelerated Development* (Colombo: Government of Sri Lanka Press).

Gottret, M. A. V. N. and White, D. (2001). 'Assessing the impact of integrated natural resource management: challenges and experiences', *Conservation Ecology*, **5** (2), 17.

Gowdy, J. and Erikson, J. (2005). 'Ecological economics at a cross roads', *Ecological Economics*, **53** (1), 17–20.

Gray, A. (1991). 'The impact of biodiversity conservation on indigenous peoples', in Shiva, V. (ed.), *Biodiversity: Social and Ecological Perspectives* (London: Zed Books).

Green, T. L. (2001). *Mining and Sustainability: The Case of the Tulsequah Chief Mine* (Victoria, BC: Environmental Mining Council).

Gren, I. M. and Brännlund, R. (1995). 'Enforcement of regional environmental regulations: nitrogen fertilizers in Sweden', in Hanna, S. and Munasinghe, M. (eds.), *Property Rights in a Social and Ecological Context* (Stockholm and Washington, D.C.: Beijer Institute and the World Bank), pp. 41–9.

Griffin, J. M. and Puller, S. L. (eds.) (2005). *Electricity Deregulation: Choices and Challenges* (Chicago, IL: Chicago University Press).

Grima, A. P. L., Horton, S. and Kant, S. (2003). 'Introduction to natural capital, poverty and development', *Environment, Development and Sustainability*, (**5**), 297–314.

Gronau, R. (1977). 'Leisure, home production, and work – the theory of the allocation of time revisited', *Journal of Public Economics* **85** (6), 1099–1123.

Grootaert, C. (1998). *Social Capital: The Missing Link*, Social Capital Initiative Working Paper no. 3, World Bank, Washington, D.C.

Grossman, G. (1995). 'Pollution and growth – what do we know?', in Goldin, L. and Winters, L. (eds.), *The Economies of Sustainable Development* (Cambridge: Cambridge University Press).

Grossman, G. and Krueger, A. (1993). 'Environmental impacts of a North American free trade agreement', in Garber, P. (ed.), *The MexicoCUS Free Trade Agreement* (Cambridge, MA: The MIT Press).

Grossman, G. M. and Krueger. A. B. (1995). 'Economic growth and the environment', *Quarterly Journal of Economics*, **110** (2), 353–77.

Gunderson, L. and Holling, C. S. (2001). *Panarchy: Understanding Transformations in Human and Natural Systems*. (New York: Island Press).

Gupta S., Davoodi, H. and Alonso-Terme, R. (1998). '*Does Corruption Affect Income Inequality and Poverty?*, Working Paper 98/76, IMF, Washington, D.C.

Gupta, S., Davoodi, H. and Tinogson, I. (2000). *Corruption and the Provision of Health Care and Education Services*, Working Paper 00/116, IMF, Washington, D.C.

Gupta, S., Mello, L. and Saran, R. (2000). *Corruption and Military Spending*, Working Paper 00/23, 2000, IMF, Washington, D.C.

GVRD (2003a). *Taking Care of Our Region, Everyday* (Vancouver: Greater Vancouver Regional District).

GVRD (2003b). *2003 Annual Report, Livable Region Strategic Plan* (Vancouver: Greater Vancouver Regional District).

Gylfason, T. (1999). *Principles of Economic Growth*, (Oxford: Oxford University Press).

Hagiwara, A.T. and Sugiyarto, G. (2005). *Poverty Impact of the Tsunami: An Initial Assessment and Scenario Analysis*, Report, Asian Development Bank.

Hall, C. (ed.) (1995). *Maximum Power: The Ideas and Applications of H. T. Odum*, (Niwot, CO: Colorado University Press).

Hall, C., Tharakan, P., Hallock, J., Cleveland, C. and Jefferson, M. (2003). 'Hydrocarbons and the evolution of human culture', *Nature*, **426**, 318–22.

Hall, D. L. (1989). 'On seeking a change of environment in nature', in Calicott, J. B. and Ames, R. T. (eds.), *Asian Traditions of Thought: Essays in Environmental Philosophy* (Albany, NY: State University of New York Press).

Hall, M. J. (1984). *Urban Hydrology*, (London: Elsevier Applied Sciences Publishers Ltd.).

Hammer, M. (1995). 'Integrating ecological and socioeconomic feedbacks for sustainable fisheries', in Hanna, S. and Munasinghe, M. (eds.), *Property Rights in a Social and Ecological Context* (Stockholm and Washington, D.C.: Beijer Institute and the World Bank).

Hanna, S. (1992). 'Lessons from ocean governance from history, ecology and economics', in Cicin-Sain, B. C. J. N. and Cicin-Sain, D. W. (eds.) *Ocean Governance: A New Vision* (Newark, NJ: University of Delaware, Center for the Study of Marine Policy, Graduate College of Marine Studies).

Hanna, S. (1995). 'Efficiencies of user participation in natural resource management', in Hanna, S. and Munasinghe, M. (eds.), *Property Rights and the Environment* (Stockholm and Washington, D.C.: Beijer Institute and the World Bank).

Hanna, S. and Munasinghe, M. (eds.) (1995a). *Property Rights and the Environment* (Stockholm and Washington, D.C.: Beijer Institute and the World Bank).

Hanna, S. and Munasinghe, M. (eds.) (1995b). *Property Rights in a Social and Ecological Context* (Stockholm and Washington, D.C.: Beijer Institute and the World Bank).

Hanna, S. and Munasinghe, M. (1995c). 'An introduction to property rights and the environment', in Hanna, S. and Munasinghe, M. (eds.), *Property Rights and the Environment* (Stockholm and Washington, D.C.: Beijer Institute and the World Bank).

Hanna, S., Folke, C. and Maler, K. G. (eds.) (1996). *Rights to Nature* (Washington, D.C., and Stockholm: Island Press and Beijer International Institute of Ecological Economics).

Hansen, A.C. (2001). 'Estimating non-renewable resource capital consumption', in M. Munasinghe, O. Sunkel and C. de Miguel (eds.), *The Sustainability of Long Term Growth* (London: Edward Elgar).

Hansen, A. C. (2006). 'Do declining discount rates lead to time inconsistent economic advice?', *Ecological Economics*, **60**, (1), 138–44.

Haque, N. and Sahay, R. (1996). '*Do Government Wage Cuts Close Budget Deficits? Costs of Corruption?*, IMF Staff Papers, IMF, Washington, D.C.

Harberger, A. C. (1976). *Project Evaluation: Collected Papers* (Chicago, IL: University of Chicago Press).

Hargrove, E. C. (1989). 'Foreword', in Calicott, J. B. and Ames, R. T. (eds.), *Nature in Asian Traditions of Thought: Essays in Environmental Philosophy*, (Albany, NY: State University of New York Press).

Hardin, G. (1968). 'The Tragedy of the Commons', *Science*, **162**, 1243–8.

Harrison, G. W., Rutherford, T. F. and Tarr, D. G. (1997). 'Opciones de política comercial para Chile: una evaluación cuantitativa', *Cuadernos de Economía*, **34** (Aug.), 101–37.

Harrison, G. W., Rutherford, T. F. and Tarr, D. G. (2002). 'Trade policy options for Chile: the importance of market access', *World Bank Economic Review*, **16** (1), 49–79.

Hartwick, J. M. (1990). 'Natural resources, national accounting and economic depreciation', *Journal of Public Economics*, **43**, 291–304.

Hassan, M. H. A. (2005). 'Small things, big changes', *Third World Academy of Sciences Newsletter*, **17** (3).

Hazilla M. and Kopp, R. (1990). 'Social cost of environmental quality regulations: a general equilibrium analysis', *Journal of Policy Modeling*, **98** (4), 853–73.

Heal, G. (1973). *The Theory of Economic Planning* (Amsterdam: North Holland Publishing Co.).

Hellsten, M. (1988). 'Socially optimal forestry', *Journal of Environmental Economics and Management*, **15**, 387–94.

Hertel, T. W. (ed.) (1997). *Global Trade Analysis: Modeling and Applications* (Cambridge: Cambridge University Press).

Heyes, A. (2000). 'A proposal for the greening of textbook macroeconomics: IS-LM-EE', *Ecological Economics*, **32** (1), 1–8.

Hicks, J. (1946). *Value and Capital*, 2nd edn (Oxford: Oxford University Press).

Hindriks, J., Keen, M. and Muthoo, A. (1999). 'Corruption, extortion, and evasion', *Journal of Public Economics*, **74**, 395–430.

Hinterberger, F. and Luks, F. (2001). 'Dematerialization, competitiveness and employment in a globalized economy', in Munasinghe, M., Sunkel, O. and de Miguel, C. (eds.), *The Sustainability of Long Term Growth* (London: Edward Elgar).

Holden, S. T., Taylor, J. E. and Hampton, S. (1999). 'Structural adjustment and market imperfections: a stylized village economy-wide model with non-separable farm households', *Environment and Development Economics*, **4** (1), 69–87.

Holland, D., Figueroa E., Alvarez, R. and Gilbert, J. (2002). *Imperfect Labor Mobility, Urban Unemployment and Agricultural Trade Reforms in Chile* International Conference on General Equilibrium Models for the Chilean Economy, Central Bank of Chile Santiago, 4–5 April, 2002.

Holling, C. S. (1973). 'Resilience and stability of ecological systems', *Annual Review of Ecology and Systematics*, **4**, 1–23.

Holling, C. S. (1986). 'The resilience of terrestrial ecosystems: local surprises and global change', in Clark, W. C. and Munn, R. E. (eds.), *Sustainable Development of the Biosphere* (Cambridge: Cambridge University Press), pp. 292–317.

Holling, C. S. (2004). 'From complex regions to complex worlds', *Ecology and Society*, **9**, (1), 11; http://www.ecologyandsociety.org/vol9/iss1/art11.

Holling, C. S. and Walker, B. (2003). 'Resilience defined', in *Online Encyclopedia of Ecological Economics* (International Society for Ecological Economics); http://www.ecoeco.org/education_encyclopedia.php

Holmberg, J. and Karlsson, S. (1992). 'On designing socio-ecological indicators', in Svedin, U. and Aniansson, B. (eds.) *Society and Environment: A Swedish Research Perspective*, (Boston, MA: Kluwer Academic).

Holtz-Eakin, D. and Selden, T. M. (1995). '*Stoking the Fires? CO$_2$ Emissions and Economic Growth*, National Bureau of Economic Research, Working Paper Series 4248, pp. 1–38.

Hotelling, H. (1931). 'The economics of exhaustible resources', *Journal of Political Economy*, **39** (2), 137–75.

Hotelling, H. (1938). 'The general welfare in relation to problems of taxation and of railway and utility rates', *Econometrica*, **6**:(3), 242–69.

Hufschmidt, M. M., James, D. E., Meister, A. D., Bower, B. J. and Dixon, J. A. (1983). *Environment, Natural Systems and Development* (Baltimore, MD: John Hopkins University Press).

Hugo, V., González, B., Jiménez, R. and Vargas, T. (1983). *Problemas Económicos en la Década de los 80* (San José: Agencia para el Desarrollo International).

Hultkrantz, L. (1992). 'National account of timber and forest environmental resources in Sweden', *Environmental and Resource Economics*, **2** (3), 283–305.

Huq, A., Small, E. B., West, P. A., Huq, M. I., Rahman, R. and Colwell, R. R. (1983). 'Ecological relationships between Vibrio cholerae and planktonic crustacean copepods', *Applied Environmental Microbiology*, **45** (1), 275–83.

Hyde, W. F., Newman, D. and Sedjo, R. A. (1991). *Forest Economics and Policy Analysis: An Overview*, World Bank Discussion Paper no.134, Washington, D.C.

IAIA (2003). *Social Impact Assessment: International Principles*, Special Publication Series no. 2, (Fargo, ND: International Association for Impact Assessment).

Ianchovichina, E., Darwin, R. and Shoemaker, R. (2001). 'Resource use and technological progress in agriculture: a dynamic general equilibrium analysis', *Ecological Economics*, **38**, 275–91.

IBAMA (1997). *Portaria de Biodiversidade no. 62*, Report, Brazilian Institute for the Environment.

IBGE (1998). *Anuário Estatístico do Brasil* (Rio de Janeiro: Brazilian Institute of Geography and Statistics).

IEA (2000a). *World Energy Outlook* 2000 (Paris: IEA).

IEA (2000b). *Energy Labels and Standards* (Paris: OECD/IEA).

IEA (2005). *World Energy Outlook 2005* (Paris: International Energy Agency).

IEA (2006). *Technology Agreements – Demand Side Management*; http://www.iea.org/textbase/techno/iaresults.asp?Ia=Demand-Side%20Management.

IFRC (1996). *World Disasters Report 1996*, International Federation of Red Cross and Red Crescent Societies (Oxford: Oxford University Press).

IISD (2006). *Compendium of Sustainable Development Indicators* (Winnipeg: International Institute for Sustainable Development). http://www.iisd.org/measure/compendium/.

IMF (2002).'Globalization: threat or opportunity?' http://www.imf.org/external/np/exr/ib/2000/041200.htm.

INPE (2000). *Relatório Anual de Desflorestamento na Amazônia* (São Paulo: São José dos Campos).

IPCC (1997). *Climate Change and Integrated Assessment Models (IAMs)* (Geneva: IPCC).

IPCC (1999). *Special Report on Technology Transfer*, IPCC draft report, Geneva.

IPCC (2000). *Special Report on Emission Scenarios (SRES)* (Geneva: IPCC).

IPCC (2001a). *Climate Change 2001: The Scientific Basis*, Third Assessment Report (Cambridge: Cambridge University Press).

IPCC (2001b). *Climate Change 2001: Impacts, Adaptation and Vulnerability*, Third Assessment Report (Cambridge: Cambridge University Press).

IPCC (2001c). *Climate Change 2001: Mitigation*, Third Assessment Report (Cambridge: Cambridge University Press).

IPCC (2001d). *Climate Change 2001: Synthesis Report*, Third Assessment Report (Cambridge: Cambridge University Press).

IPCC (2007a) *Climate Change 2007: The Physical Science Basis*, Fourth Assessment Report, Cambridge University Press, London, UK.

IPCC (2007b). *Climate Change 2007: Impacts, Adaptation and Vulnerability*, Fourth Assessment Report, Cambridge University Press, London, UK.

IPCC (2007c). *Climate Change 2007: Mitigation of Climate Change*, Fourth Assessment Report, Cambridge University Press, London, UK.

IPCC (2007d). *Climate Change 2007: Synthesis Report*, Fourth Assessment Report, Cambridge University Press, London, UK.

IRG (2002). *Impacts Assessment and Lessons Learned* (Washington, D.C.: International Resources Group).

ISEE (2005).*The Importance of Social Capital: Comparing the Impacts of the 2004 Asian Tsunami on Sri Lanka, and Hurricane Katrina 2005 on New Orleans*, ISEE Report.

Islam, S. (1998). *Mathematical Economics of Multi-Level Optimisation: Theory and Application*, Physica series: Contributions to Economics (Heidelberg: Springer Verlag).

Islam, S. (2001a). 'Ecology and optimal economic growth: an optimal ecological economic growth model and its sustainability implications', in Munasinghe, M., Sunkel, O. and de Miguel, C. (eds.), *The Sustainability of Long Term Growth* (London: Edward Elgar), pp. 227–73.

Islam, S. (2001b). *Optimal Growth Economics* (Amsterdam: North Holland).

Islam, S. and Craven, B. (2001). 'Computing optimal control on MATLAB the SCOM package and economic growth models', in Rubinov, A. and Glaver, B. (eds.), *Optimisation and Related Topics* (Amsterdam: Kluwer Academic Publishers).

Islam, S. and Craven, B. (2003). 'Measuring sustainable growth and welfare: computational models and methods', in Fetherston, J. and Batten, J. (eds.), *Governance and Social Responsibility* (Amsterdam: Elsevier–North Holland).

Islam, S. and Jolley, A. (1996). 'Sustainable development in Asia', *Natural Resources Forum*, **20** (4), 263–79.

Islam, S., Munasinghe, M. and Clarke, M. (2003). 'Making long-term economic growth more sustainable: evaluating the costs and benefits', *Ecological Economics*, **47** (2–3), 149–66.

Jaeger, W. K. (2001). 'Double dividend reconsidered', *AERE Newsletter*, **21** (2), 11–20.

Jayaweera, D. S. (1999). 'Effective steps towards traffic calming in developing countries: a case study for the Metropolitan Region of Colombo in Sri Lanka'. Unpublished Ph. D. Thesis, Massachusettes Institute of Technology.

Jayewardene, P. and Perera, V. (1991). *Sri Lanka: The Rural Electrification Problem*, Report, Power and Sun (Pvt) Ltd, Colombo.

Jefferson, M. (2005). 'Renewable energy: how are we doing?', in Flin, D. (ed.), *Renewable Energy 2005* (London: Sovereign Publications), pp. 14–17.

Jenkins, T. N. (1996). 'Democratising the global economy by ecologising economics: the example of global warming', *Ecological Economics*, **16** (3), 227–39.

Jepma, C. and Munasinghe, M. (1998). *Climate Change Policy* (Cambridge: Cambridge University Press).

Jevons, S. (1865). *The Coal Question* (London: British Museum Archive).

Jodha, N. S. (1995). 'Environmental crisis and unsustainability in Himalayas: lessons from the degraduation process', in Hanna, S. and Munasinghe, M. (eds.) *Property Rights in a Social and Ecological Context* (Stockholm and Washington, D.C.: Beijer Institute and the World Bank), pp. 183–99.

Jodha, N. S. (2001). *Life on the Edge: Sustaining Agriculture and Community Resources in Fragile Environments* (New Delhi: Oxford University Press).

Johannes, R. E. (1998). 'The case of data-less marine resource management: examples from tropical nearshore finfisheries', *Trends in Ecology and Evolution*, **13**, 243–6.

Johansson, P.-O. and Löfgren, K. G. (1985). *The Economics of Forestry and Natural Resources* (Oxford: Basil Blackwell).

Johnson, D. G. (1973). *World Agriculture in Disarray* (London: Macmillan Press Ltd).

Jorgensen, D. W. and Wilcoxon, P. J. (1990). 'Intertemporal general equilibrium modeling of U. S. environmental regulation', *Journal of Policy Modeling*, **12** (4), 715–44.

Jorgensen, D. W. and Wilcoxon, P. (1993). 'Reducing U. S. carbon dioxide emissions: an assessment of different instruments', *Journal of Policy Modeling*, **15** (5), 491–520.

Joskow, P. (2006). 'Markets for power in the US – an interim assessment', *Energy Journal*, **27** (1), 1–36.

Kadekodi, G. K. and Agarwal, M. M. (2001). 'Why an inverted U-shaped environmental Kuznets curve may not exist', in Munasinghe, M., Sunkel, O. and de Miguel, C. (eds.), *The Sustainability of Long Term Growth* (London: Edward Elgar).

Kahn, J. R. and McDonald, J. A. (1995). 'Third World debt and tropical deforestation', *Ecological Economics*, **12**, 107–23.

Kaitala, V. and Munro, G. R. (1995). 'The management of transboundary resources and property rights systems: the case of fisheries', in Hanna, S. and Munasinghe, M. (eds.) *Property Rights and the Environment* (Stockholm and Washington, D.C.: Beijer Institute and the World Bank), pp. 69–83.

Kay, J.J. (1991). 'A nonequilibrium thermodynamic framework for discussing ecosystem integrity', *Environmental Management*, **15**, 483–95.

Kellert, S. R., Mehta, J. N., Ebbin, S. A. and Lichtenfeld, L. L. (2000). 'Community natural resource management: promise, rhetoric, and reality', *Society and Natural Resources*, **13**, 705–15.

Keogh, R. M. (1984). 'Changes in the forest cover in Costa Rica through history', *Turrialba*, **34**: (3), 325–31.

Kessler J. J. and Van Dorp, M. (1998). 'Structural adjustment and the environment: the need for an analytical methodology', *Ecology and Economics* **27** (3), 267–81.

Knetsch, J. L. and Sinden, J. A. (1984). 'Willingness to pay and compensation demanded: experimental evidence of an unexpected disparity in measures of value', *The Quarterly Journal of Economics*, **99** (3).

Kok, M. T. J. and de Coninck, H. C. (eds.) (2004). *Beyond Climate: Options for Broadening Climate Policy* (Bilthoven: RIVM).

Koopmans, T. C. (1973). 'Some observations on optimal economic growth and exhaustible resources', in Bos, H. C., Linnemann, H. and de Wolff, P. (eds.), *Economic Structure and Development: Essays in Honour of Jan Tinbergen* (Amsterdam: North-Holland), pp. 239–55.

Koskela, E., Schöb, R. and Sinn, H. (1999). *Green Tax Reform and Competitiveness*, NBER Working Paper 6922, February, 1999.

Kramer, R. A., Sharma, N. and Munasinghe, M. (1995). *Valuing Tropical Forests*, Environmental Paper No. 13, The World Bank, Washington, D.C.

Krautkraemer, J. (1988). 'The rate of discount and the preservation of natural environments', *Natural Resources Modelling*, **2**, 421–37.

Kreimer, A. and Munasinghe, M. (1991). *Managing Natural Disasters and the Environment* (Washington, D.C.: World Bank).

Krueger, A., Schiff, M. and Valdes, A. (1991). *The Political Economy of Agricultural Pricing Policies*, vols. 1–4 (Baltimore, MD: Johns Hopkins University Press).

Krupnik, I. and Jolly, D. (2002). *The Earth is Faster Now: Indigenous Observation on Arctic Environmental Change* (Fairbanks, AL: Arcus).

Kuik, O. and Verbruggen, H. (eds.) (1991). *In Search of Indicators of Sustainable Development* (Boston, MA: Kluwer).

Kumar, K. and Parikh, J. (1998). 'Climate change impacts on Indian agriculture: the Ricardian approach', in Dinar, A., Mendelsohn, R., Evenson, R., Parikh, J., Sanghi, A., Kumar, K., McKinsey, J. and Lonergan, S. (eds.), *Measuring the Impact of Climate Change on Indian Agriculture*', World Bank Technical Paper No. 402 (Washington, D. C.: World Bank).

Kumar, K. and Parikh, J. (2001). 'Indian agriculture and climate sensitivity', *Global Environmental Change*, **11**, 147–54.

Kumarage, A. S. (1999). *Assessment of Public Investments in the Transport Sector*, Report, Appendix A1, University of Moratuwa, Sri Lanka.

Kumarage A. S. *et al.* (2000). *TRANSPLAN V2: A Regional Traffic Estimation Model*, Working paper, Engineering Research Unit, University of Moratuwa, Sri Lanka.

Kverndokk, S. (1995). 'Tradeable CO_2 emission permits: initial distribution as a justice problem', *Environmental Values*, **4**, 129–48.

Laarman, J. D. and Durst, P. B. (1987). 'Nature travel in the tropics', *Journal of Forestry,* **85** (5), 43–6.

Lancaster, K., and Lipsey, R. G. (1956). 'The general theory of second best', *Review of Economic Studies*, **24**:(7), 11–32.

Larson, B. and Bromley, D. (1991). 'Natural resource prices, export policies, and deforestation: the case of Sudan', *World Development*, **19**, 1289–97.

Lawn, P. A. (2005). 'An assessment of the valuation methods used to calculate the index of sustainable economic welfare (ISEW), genuine progress indicator (GPI), and sustainable net benefit index (SNBI)', *Environment, Development and Sustainability*, **7**, 185–208.

Lazaro, T. R. (1979). *Urban Hydrology*, (Ann Arbor, MI: Ann Arbor Science Publishers).

Lee, N. and Kirkpatrick, C. (2000). 'Integrated appraisal, decision making and sustainable development: an overview', in Lee, N. and Kirkpatrick, C. (eds.), *Sustainable Development and Integrated Appraisal in a Developing World*, Cheltenham: Edward Elgar), pp. 1–14.

Leite, C. and Weidmann, J. (1999). *Does Mother Nature Corrupt? Natural Resources, Corruption, and Economic Growth*', IMF Working Paper 99/85.

Leite, J. C. (2005). *The World Social Forum: Strategies of Resistance* (Chicago, IL: Haymarket Books).

Lele, U. and Stone, S. (1989). *Population Pressure, the Environment and Agricultural Intensification: Variations on the Boserup Hypothesis*, MADIA Discussion Paper 4, World Bank, Washington, D.C.

Leontief, W. (1970). 'Environmental repercussions and the economic structure: an input-output approach', *Review of Economics and Statistics*, **52**, 262–71.

Leontief, W. (1982). 'Academic economics', Letter to the Editor, *Science*, **217**, 106–7.

Levin, S. A. (1998). 'Ecosystems and the biosphere as complex adaptive systems', *Ecosystems*, **1**, 431–6.

Levine, M. D., Gadgil, A., Meyers, S., Sathaye, J., Stafurik, J. and Wilbanks, T. (1991). *Energy Efficiency, Developing Nations and Eastern Europe: A Report to the U. S. Working Group on Global Energy Efficiency* (Washington, D.C.: International Institute for Energy Conservation).

Li, P. and Rose, A. (1995). 'Global warming policy and the Pennsylvania economy: a computable general equilibrium analysis', *Economic Systems Research*, **7** (2), 151–71.

LIFE (1998). *Linkages Between Economic Policies and the Environment in Sri Lanka*, Lanka International Forum on Sustainable Development, Colombo.

Lind, R. C. (1982). 'A primer on the major issues relating to the discount rate for evaluating national energy options', in Lind, R.C. (ed.) *Discounting for Time and Risk in Energy Policy* (Baltimore, MD: Johns Hopkins University Press), pp. 21–94.

Little, I. M. D. and Mirrlees, J. A. (1974). *Project Appraisal and Planning for Developing Countries* (New York: Basic Books).

Little, I. M. D., and Mirrlees, J. A. (1990). 'Project apprasial and planning twenty years on, in *Proceedings of the World Bank Annual Conference on Development Economics 1990* (Washington, D.C.: World Bank).

Liverman, D., Hanson, M., Brown, B. J. and Meredith, R. Jr (1988). 'Global sustainability: towards measurement', *Environmental Management*, **12**, 133–43.

Lomborg, B. (2001). *The Skeptical Environmentalist: Measuring the Real State of the World*, (Cambridge: Cambridge University Press).

Lonergan, S. L. (1993). 'Impoverishment, population and environmental degradation: the case for equity', *Environmental Conservation*, **20** (4), 328–34.

Long, J., Tecle, A. and Burnette, B. (2003). 'Cultural foundations for ecological restoration on the White Mountain Apache Reservation', *Conservation Ecology*, **8** (1), 4.

López, R. (1993). *Economic Policies and Land Management in Ghana*, Draft report, ENVPE, World Bank, Washington, D.C.

Lovei, M. (1998). *Phasing Out Lead From Gasoline: Worldwide Experiences and Policy Implications*, World Bank Technical Paper 397, Washington, D.C.

Lovelock, J. E. (1979). *Gaia: A New Look at Life on Earth* (Oxford: Oxford University Press).

Lucas, R., Wheeler, D. and Hettige, H. (1992). 'Economic development, environmental regulation and the international migration of toxic industrial pollution: 1960–1988', in Low, P. (ed.), *International Trade and the Environment*, World Bank Discussion Paper no. 159 (Washington, D.C.: World Bank), pp. 67–88.

Ludwig, D., Mangel, M. and Haddad, B. (2001). 'Ecology, conservation, and public policy', *Annual Review of Ecology and Systematics*, **32**, 481–517.

Ludwig, D., Walker, B. and Holling, C. S. (1997). 'Sustainability, stability, and resilience', *Conservation Ecology*, **1** (1), 7; http://www.consecol.org/vol1/iss1/art7.

Luenberger, D. G. (1973). 'An approach to nonlinear programming', *Journal of Optimization Theory and Applications*, **11** (3), 219–27.

Lukas, A. (2000). *WTO Report Card III: Globalization and Developing Countries*, Trade briefing paper no. 10, CATO Institute, Washington, D.C.

Lutkepohl, H. (1991). *Introduction to Multiple Time Series Analysis* (New York: Springer-Verlag).

Lvovsky, K., Hughes, G., Maddison, D., Ostrp, B. and Pearce, D. (2000). *Environmental Costs of Fossil Fuels, a Rapid Assessment Method with Application to Six Cities*, World Bank Environment Department, Paper 78, Washington, D.C.

MA (2003). *Conceptual Framework: Ecosystems and Human Well-Being*, Millennium Ecosystem Assessment (Washington, D.C.: Island Press).

MA (2005a). *Board of Directors Statement*, Millennium Ecosystem Assessment (Washington, D.C.: Island Press).

MA (2005b). *Responses Working Group Summary*, Millennium Ecosystem Assessment (Washington, D.C.: Island Press).

MA (2005c). *Ecosystems and Human Well-Being: A Framework for the Assessment* (Washington, D.C.: Island Press).

MA (2005d). *Ecosystems and Human Well-Being: Volume 3: Policy* (Washington, D.C.: Island Press).

MA (2005e). *Ecosystems and Human Well-Being: Synthesis* (Washington, D.C.: Island Press).

MA (2005f). *Living Beyond Our Means: Natural Assets and Human Well-Being: Statement from the Board* (Washington D.C.: WRI).

Mackinson, S. and Nottestad, L. (1998). 'Combining local and scientific knowledge', *Reviews in Fish Biology and Fisheries*, **8**, 481–90.

Maddison, A. (2001). *The World Economy: A Millennial Perspective* (Paris: OECD).

McLain, R. and Lee, R. (1996). 'Adaptive management: promises and pitfalls', *Journal of Environmental Management*, **20**, 437–48.

McNeill, D. (2000). 'The concept of sustainable development, in Holland, A., Lee, K. and McNeill, D. (eds.) *Global Sustainable Development in the 21st Century* (Edinburgh: Edinburgh University Press).

McRae, R. (1994). 'Gasoline demand in developing Asian countries', *Energy Journal*, **15** (1), 143.

MDG (2005). *Millennium Development Goals Report (2005)*, United Nations, New York, www.un.org/millenniumgoals.

Madrid-Aris, M. E. (1998). *International Trade and the Environment: Evidence from the North America Free Trade Agreement (NAFTA)*, World Congress of Environmental and Resources Economics, Venice, Italy.

Mahar, D. (1988). *Government Policies and deforestation in Brazil's Amazon Region*, World Bank Environment Department, Working Paper 7, Washington, D.C.

Mahar, D. J. (1989). *Government Policies and Deforestation in Brazil's Amazon Region*, Report 8910, International Bank for Reconstruction and Development and The World Bank, Washington, D.C.

Maler, K. G. (1974). *Environmental Economics: A Theoretical Inquiry* (Baltimore, MD: John Hopkins University Press).

Maler, K. G. (1990). 'Economic theory and environmental degradation: a survey of some problems', Revista de Analisis Economico, **5** (Nov.), 7–17.

Maler, K. G. and Munasinghe, M. (1996). 'Macroeconomic policies, second-best theory, and the environment', in Munasinghe, M. (ed.), *Environmental Impacts of Macroeconomic and Sectoral Policies*, (Washington, D.C.: World Bank).

Malinvaud, E. (1979). 'Costs of economic growth', in Malinvaud, E. (ed.), *Economic Growth and Resources, Vol. 1* (London: Macmillan).

Malthus, T. (1798). *On Population* (New York: Random House).

Mangel, M. Talbot, L. M., Meffe, G. K. *et al.* (1996). 'Principles for the conservation of wild living resources', *Ecological Applications*, **6** (2) 338–62.

Mani, M. and Wheeler, D. (1998). 'In search of pollution havens? Dirty industry in the world economy, 1960–1995', in Fredriksson, P. G., *Trade, Global Policy, and the Environment*, World Bank Discussion Paper no. 402 (Washington, D.C.: World Bank), chap. 8.

Manning, I. and De Jonge, A. (1996). 'The new poverty: causes and responses', in Sheehan P., Grewal, B. and Kumnick, M. (eds.), *Dialogue on Australia's Future* (Melbourne: Centre for Strategic Economic Studies).

Marglin, S. (1963). 'The social rate of discount and the optimal rate of investment', *Quarterly Journal of Economics*, **77**, 95–111.

Markandya, A., Harou, P., Bellu, L. G. and Cistoulli, V. (2002). *Environmental Economics for Sustainable Growth* (Cheltenham Edward Elgar Publishers, for the World Bank, Washington, D.C.).

Marrs, D. (2000a). 'Sasol takes over stakes in Temane gas field', *Business Day*, 3 March, Johannesburg, South Africa.

Marrs, D. (2000b). 'Cape power station likely after gas find', *Business Day*, 3 April, Johannesburg, South Africa.

Martinez-Allier, J. (2004). *The Environmentalism of the Poor* (Oxford: Oxford University Press).

Martini, A., Rosa, N. and Uhl, C. (1994). 'An attempt to predict which tree species may be threatened by logging activities', *Environmental Conservation*, **21** (2), 152–62.

Maslow, A. H. (1970). *Motivation and Personality* (New York: Harper and Row).

Mason, B. J. (1975). *Clouds, Rain and Rainmaking*, 2nd edn (Cambridge: Cambridge University Press).

Masse, R. (2001). *Impact on Poverty and Gender of Rural Electrification Programs in Sri Lanka EnPoGen Survey of Sri Lanka* (Washington, D.C.: World Bank).

Matthews, R. N., Kropff, M. J., Horie, T. and Bachelet, D. (1997). 'Simulating the impact of climate change on rice production in Asia and evaluating options for adaptation', *Agricultural Systems*, **54** (3), 399–425.

Mauro, P. (1995). 'Corruption and growth', *Quarterly Journal of Economics*, **110** (3), 681–712.

Max-Neef, M. (1995). 'Economic growth and quality of life: a threshold hypothesis', *Ecological Economics*, **15**, 115–18.

Meadows D. H., Meadows, D. L., Randers, J. and Behrens, W. W. III (1972). *The Limits to Growth* (New York: Universe Books).

Meier, P. (1997). *Economic Analysis of the Haryana Power Sector Restructuring and Reform Program* (New Delhi: World Bank).

Meier, P. (2003). *Economic Analysis of Solar Home Systems: A Case Study for the Philippines* (Washington, D.C.: World Bank).

Meier, P. (2004). *Economic Analysis of the China Renewable Energy Scaleup Programme (CRESP).* (Washington, D.C.: World Bank).

Meier, P. and Munasinghe, M. (1994). *Incorporating Environmental Concerns into Power System Decision Making – A Case Study of Sri Lanka*, World Bank Environment Department, Paper no. 6, Washington, D.C.

Meier, P. and Munasinghe, M. (2003). *Sustainable Transport Options for Sri Lanka*, ESMAP Report 262-03 (Vol. I), Washington, D.C., www.esmap.org.

Meier P., Munasinghe, M. and Siyambalapitiya, T. (1997). 'Energy sector policy and the environment: a case study of Sri Lanka', in Cruz, W., Munasinghe, M. and Warford, J. (eds.), *The Greening of Economic Policy Reform. Vol. II: Case Studies* (Washington, D.C.: World Bank).

Mendelsohn, R. and Dinar, A. (2003). 'Climate, water, and agriculture', *Land Economics*, **79**, 328–41.

Mendelsohn, R. and Neumann, J. (eds.) (1999). *The Impact of Climate Change on the United States Economy.* (Cambridge: Cambridge University Press).

Mendelsohn, R., Dinar A. and Sanghi, A. (2001). 'The effect of development on the climate sensitivity of agriculture', *Environment and Development Economics*, **6**, 85–101.

Mendelsohn, R., Nordhaus, W. and Shaw, D. (1994). 'The impact of global warming on agriculture: a Ricardian analysis', *The American Economic Review*, **84**, 753–71.

Mendes, F. E. (1994). Uma avaliacão crítica dos custos de controle da poluição hídrica de origem industrial no Brasil. Unpublished M.Sc. thesis, COPPE/UFRJ, Rio de Janeiro.

Mercer, E. and Kramer, R. (1992). *An International Travel Cost Model: Estimating the Recreational Use Value of a Proposed National Park in Madagascar.* Paper presented at the Association of Environmental and Resource Economists Contributed Paper Session: Recreation Demand Models Allied Social Science Associations, Annual Meeting, New Orleans.

Michaels, R. (2005). *Rethinking Vertical Integration in Electricity,* Department of Economics, California State University, Fullerton, CA.

Micklethwait, J. and Wooldridge, A. (2000). *A Future Perfect: The Challenge and Hidden Promise of Globalisation* (New York: Times Books).

MIDEPLAN (1996). *Balance Seis Años de las Políticas Sociales: 1990–1996* (Santiago: Ministerio de Planificación y Cooperación).

Miguez, J. D. G. (2002). 'Equity, responsibility and climate change', in Pinguelli-Rosa, L. and Munasinghe, M. (eds.), *Ethics, Equity and International Negotiations on Climate Change* (Cheltenham: Edward Elgar Publishing), pp. 7–35.

Milestad, R. and Hadatsch, S. (2003). 'Organic farming and social-ecological resilience: the alpine valleys of Sölktäler, Austria', *Conservation Ecology,* **8** (1), 3.

MIND (2004). *Action Impact Matrix Manual* (Colombo: Munasinghe Institute for Development).

MIND (2005). *Macro and Micro Impact of the 2004 Tsunami on Affected Countries and Peoples* (Colombo: Munasinghe Institute for Development and UNDP Regional Centre).

Ministry of Plantation Industries, (2001). *Plantation Sector Statistical Pocket Book* (Colombo: Sri Lankan Ministry of Plantation).

Ministry of Transport (1999). *Bus Transport Policy Report,* Government of Sri Lanka, Colombo.

MINTRAB (2002). Ministerio del Trabajo y Previsión Social; www.mintrab.cl.

Miranda, K. and Muzondo, T. (1991). 'Public policy and the environment', *Finance and Development,* **28** (2), 25–7.

Mirza, M. M. Q. and Ahmad, Q. K. (eds.) (2005). *Climate Change and Water Resources in South Asia* (London: A. A. Balkema Publishers).

MIT (2005). *Technology Review* (Cambridge, MA: Massachusetts Institute of Technology), Mass. p. 24.

MIT (1979). *New Utility Management and Control Systems* (Cambridge, MA: MIT Energy Lab).

Moffat, I. (1994). 'On measuring sustainable development indicators', *International Journal of Sustainable Development and World Ecology,* **1**, 97–109.

Morimoto, R. and Munasinghe, M. (2005). 'Small hydropower projects and sustainable energy development in Sri Lanka', *International Journal of Global Energy Issues,* **24**, (1/2), 3–18).

Moser, C. (1998). 'The asset vulnerability framework: reassessing urban poverty reduction strategies', *World Development,* **26** (1), 1–19.

MRN (1990). *Estrategia de Conservación para el Desarrollo Sostenible de Costa Rica* (San José: Ministerio de Recursos Naturales, Energía y Minas).

Mukherjee, N. (1996). *Water and Land in South Africa: Economy-Wide Impacts of Reform,* Discussion Paper No. 12, International Food Policy Research Institute, Washington, D.C.

Munasinghe, M. (1977), *Economic Analysis of Water Supply Projects: A Case Study of an African Township,* Public Utilities Department Report, World Bank, Washington, D.C.

Munasinghe, M. (1979a). *Electric Power Pricing Policy*, Staff Working Paper no. 340, World Bank, Washington, D.C.

Munasinghe, M. (1979b). *The Economics of Power System Reliability and Planning* (Baltimore, MD: Johns Hopkins University Press).

Munasinghe, M. (1980a). 'An integrated framework of energy pricing in developing countries', *The Energy Journal*, **1**, 1–30.

Munasinghe, M. (1980b). 'Integrated national energy planning in developing countries', *Natural Resources Forum*, **4** (Oct.), 359–73.

Munasinghe, M. (1980c). 'The costs incurred by residential electricity consumers due to power failures', *Journal of Consumer Research*, **6**, 361–9.

Munasinghe, M. (1981). 'Principles of modern electricity pricing', *Proceedings of the IEEE*, **69** (3), 332–48.

Munasinghe, M. (1983). 'Non-conventional energy project analysis and national energy policy', *International Journal of Ambient Energy*, **4** (2), 79–88.

Munasinghe, M. (1984a). 'Engineering-economic analysis of electric power systems', *Proceedings of the IEEE*, **72** (4), 424–61.

Munasinghe, M. (1984b). 'Energy strategies for oil-importing developing countries', *Natural Resources Journal*, **24** (2), 351–68.

Munasinghe, M. (1984c). *Rationale and Economic Basis for a Groundwater User Charge Mechanism and Legislation*, Metropolitan Waterworks and Sewerage System (MWSS) Final Report, Manila.

Munasinghe, M. (1984d). 'Implementing LRMC-based tariff structures', in Munasinghe, M. and Runtga, S. (eds.), *Costing and Pricing Electricity in Developing Countries* (Manila: Asian Development Bank), pp. 193–212.

Munasinghe, M. (1987). 'Computer and informatics issues and policy for third world development', *Information Technology for Development*, **2** (4), 303–35.

Munasinghe, M. (1988). *Integrated National Energy Planning and Management: Methodology and Application to Sri Lanka* (Washington, D.C.: World Bank).

Munasinghe M. (ed.) (1989). *Computers and Informatics in Developing Countries* (Trieste: Third World Academy of Sciences).

Munasinghe, M. (1990a). *Energy Analysis and Policy* (London: Butterworths-Heinemann).

Munasinghe, M. (1990b). *Electric Power Economics* (London: Butterworths-Heinemann).

Munasinghe, M. (1991). 'Electricity and the environment in developing countries with special reference to Asia', in Tester, J. W., Wood, D. O. and Ferrari, N. A. (eds.), *Energy and the Environment in the 21st Century* (Cambridge, MA: The MIT Press).

Munasinghe, M. (1992a). *Environmental Economics and Sustainable Development*, World Bank Environment Department Paper no. 3, presented at the UN Earth Summit, Rio de Janeiro, World Bank, Washington, D.C.

Munasinghe, M. (1992b). *Water Supply and Environmental Management* (Boulder, CO: Westview Press).

Munasinghe, M. (1992c). 'Biodiversity protection policy: environmental valuation and distribution issues', *Ambio*, **XXI** (3), 227–36.

Munasinghe, M. (1993a). 'Environmental issues and economic decisions in developing countries', *World Development*, **21** (11), 1729–48.

Munasinghe, M. (1993b). 'Environmental economics and biodiversity management in developing countries', *Ambio*, **XXII** (2–3), 126–35.

Munasinghe, M. (1994a). 'Sustainomics: a transdisciplinary framework for sustainable development', Keynote Paper, *Proceedings of the 50th Anniversary Sessions of the Sri Lanka Association for the Advancement of Science (SLAAS)*, Colombo, Sri Lanka.

Munasinghe, M. (1994b). 'Sustainable water resources management and planning (SWAMP)', Best Treatise Award Paper, *Proceedings of the International Water Association Conference*, Dubai.

Munasinghe, M. (1995a). 'Making growth more sustainable', *Ecological Economics*, **15**, 121–4.

Munasinghe, M. (1995b). *Sustainable Energy Development* (Washington, D.C.: The World Bank).

Munasinghe, M. (ed.) (1996a). *Environmental Impacts of Macroeconomic and Sectoral Policies* (Solomons, MD, and Washington, D.C.: International Society for Ecological Economics and World Bank).

Munasinghe, M. (1996b). 'An overview of the environmental impacts of macroeconomic and sectoral policies', in Munasinghe, M. (ed.), *Environmental Impacts of Macroeconomic and Sectoral Policies* (Washington, D.C.: World Bank).

Munasinghe, M. (1997). 'Sustainable long term growth: prospects for Asian cities', *Proceedings of the APEC Seminar on Sustainable Cities*, Asia Pacific Economic Cooperation (APEC), Taiwan.

Munasinghe, M. (1998a). 'Climate change decision-making: science, policy and economics', *International Journal of Environment and Pollution*, **10** (2), 188–239.

Munasinghe, M. (1998b). 'Countrywide policies and sustainable development: are the linkages perverse?', in Teitenberg, T. and Folmer, H. (eds.), *The International Yearbook of International and Resource Economics* (London: Edward Elgar).

Munasinghe, M. (1999a). 'Is environmental economics an inevitable consequence of economic growth: tunneling through the environmental Kuznets curve'. *Ecological Economics*, **29**, 89–109.

Munasinghe, M. (1999b). 'Measuring sustainability to improve economic decision making', in Munasinghe, M., Dreyer, D. and Kurukulasuriya, P. (eds.), *Greening the National Income Accounts* (Colombo and Goethe: Munasinghe Institute for Development (MIND) and German Cultural Institute).

Munasinghe, M. (2000a). *Development, Equity and Sustainability in the Context of Climate Change*, Intergovernmental Panel on Climate Change Guidance Paper, Geneva.

Munasinghe, M. (2000b). *The Sustainomics Trans-disciplinary Framework for Making Development More Sustainable*, MIND Research Discussion Paper no.1, Munasinghe Institute for Development, Colombo.

Munasinghe, M. (2001a). 'Sustainable development and climate change: applying the sustainomics transdisciplinary meta-framework', *International Journal of Global Environmental Issues*, **1** (1), 13–55.

Munasinghe, M. (2001b). 'Exploring the linkages between climate change and sustainable development: a challenge for transdisciplinary research', *Ecology and Society*, **5** (1), 14–23; http://www.ecologyandsociety.org/vol5/iss1/.

Munasinghe, M. (2002a). 'The sustainomics trans-disciplinary meta-framework for making development more sustainable', *International Journal of Sustainable Development*, **5** (1–2), 125–82.

Munasinghe, M. (ed.) (2002b). *Macroeconomics and the Environment*, The International Library of Critical Writings in Economics (London: Edward Elgar).

Munasinghe, M. (2002c). *Analysing the Nexus of Sustainable Development and Climate Change: An Overview*, Environment Directorate, COM/ENV/EPOC/DCD/DAC (2002)2/final, OECD, Paris; http://www.oecd.org/dataoecd/32/54/2510070.pdf.

Munasinghe, M. (2003). *Sustainable Livelihoods and their Linkages with Macro-policies, Issue Paper 1, Improving Policy-Livelihood Relationships in South Asia*, Department for International Development, London.

Munasinghe, M. (2004a). 'Sustainomics', in *Online Ecological Economics Encyclopedia*, International Society of Ecological Economics (ISEE); http://www.ecoeco.org/publica/encyc.htm.

Munasinghe, M. (2004b). 'Environmental macroeconomics – basic principles', in *Online Ecological Economics Encyclopedia*, International Society of Ecological Economics (ISEE); http://www.ecoeco.org/publica/encyc.htm.

Munasinghe, M. (2004c). *Evaluation of the UNEP Dams and Development Project* (Nairobi: United Nations Environment Programme).

Munasinghe, M. (2004d). 'Sustainable development: basic concepts and applications to energy', *Encyclopedia of Energy*, **5**, 789–808.

Munasinghe, M. (2007a). 'Mainstreaming and implementing the millennium ecosystem assessment (MA) results by integrating them into sustainable development strategy', in Ranganathan, J., Munasinghe, M. and Irwin, F. (eds.), *Millennium Ecosystems Assessment: Implications for Policy and Governance* (Cheltenhan: Edward Elgar Publishing).

Munasinghe, M. (2007b). 'The importance of social capital: comparing the impacts of the 2004 Asian tsunami on Sri Lanka, and hurricane Katrina 2005 on New Orleans', *Ecological Economics*, **64** (1), 9–11.

Munasinghe, M. and Clarke, C. (eds.) (1995). *Disaster Prevention for Sustainable Development: Economic and Policy Issues: A Report from the Yokohana World Conference on Natural Disaster Reduction, May 1994* (Washington, D.C.: World Bank).

Munasinghe, M. and Corbo, V. (1978). 'The demand for CATV services in Canada', *Canadian Journal of Economics*, **11** (Aug.), 506–20.

Munasinghe, M. and Cruz, W. (1994). *Economywide Policies and the Environment: Lessons from Experience* (Washington, D.C.: World Bank).

Munasinghe, M. and Gellerson, M. (1979). 'Economic criteria for optimizing power system reliability levels', *The Bell Journal of Economics*, **10** (1), 353–65.

Munasinghe, M. and King, K. (1992). 'Accelerating ozone layer protection in developing countries', *World Development*, **20** (Apr.), 609–18.

Munasinghe, M. and McNeely, J. (eds.) (1995). *Protected Area Economics and Policy* (Washington, D.C., and Gland: World Bank and World Conservation Union (IUCN)).

Munasinghe, M. and Meier, P. (1993). *Energy Policy Analysis and Modeling* (London: Cambridge University Press).

Munasinghe, M. and Meier, P. (2003a). *Sri Lanka Electric Power Technology Assessment (SLEPTA)*, ESMAP Report 262–03 (vol. III), World Bank, Washington, D.C.

Munasinghe, M. and Meier, P. (2003b). *Sustainable Transport Options for Sri Lanka*, ESMAP Report 262–03 (vol. I), World Bank, Washington, D.C.

Munasinghe, M. and Rungta S. (1984). *Costing and Pricing Electricity in Developing Countries* (Manila: Asian Development Bank).

Munasinghe, M. and Shearer, W. (eds.) (1995). *Defining and Measuring Sustainability: The Biogeophysical Foundations*, (Tokyo and Washington, D.C.: UN University and World Bank).

Munasinghe, M. and Swart, R. (eds.) (2000). *Climate Change and its Linkages with Development, Equity and Sustainability* (Geneva: IPCC).

Munasinghe, M. and Swart, R. (2005). *Primer on Climate Change and Sustainable Development: Facts, Policy Analysis and Applications* (Cambridge: Cambridge University Press).

Munasinghe, M. and Warford, J. (1978). *Shadow Pricing and Power Tariff Policy*, State of the Art Conference on Marginal Cost Pricing, Montreal, Canada.

Munasinghe, M. and Warford, J. (1982). *Electricity Pricing* (Baltimore, MD: Johns Hopkins University Press).

Munasinghe, M., Deraniyagala, Y. and Munasinghe, S. (2002). *Interactions Between Climate Change and Sustainable Development in Sri Lanka: Analysis Using the Action Impact Matrix (AIM)*, MIND Research Discussion Paper, Munasinghe Institute for Development, Colombo.

Munasinghe, M., Gilling, J. and Mason, M. (1988). *A Review of World Bank Lending for Electric Power*, IEN Energy Series no. 2 (Washington, D.C.: World Bank).

Munasinghe, M., Meier, P. and Fernando, C. (2003). *Greenhouse Gas Mitigation Options in the Sri Lanka Power Sector*, ESMAP Report 262–03 (vol. II), World Bank, Washington, D.C.

Munasinghe, M., Menezes, B. and Preece, M. (1991). 'Rio reconstruction and flood prevention in Brazil', *Land Use Policy*, **8**(4), 282–7.

Munasinghe, M., O'Ryan, R., Seroa da Motta, R., de Miguel, C., Young, C., Miller, S. and Ferraz, C. (2006). *Macroeconomic Policies for Sustainable Growth – Analytical Framework and Policy Studies of Brazil and Chile* (Cheltenham: Edward Elgar).

Munasinghe, M. and Reid, W. (2005). 'The role of ecosystems in sustainable development', *Millennium Ecosystem Assessment Launch Conference*, New Delhi.

Munasinghe, M., Sunkel, O. and de Miguel, C. (eds.) (2001). *The Sustainability of Long Term Growth*, (London: Edward Elgar).

Munich Re (1996). *Natural Catastrophe Losses Will Continue to Increase*, Press release, Munich Re Group, March 19; http://www.munichre.com.

Muylaert, M. S. and Pinguelli-Rosa, L. (2002). 'Ethics, equity and convention on climate change', in Pinguelli-Rosa, L. and Munasinghe, M. (eds.), *Ethics, Equity and International Negotiations on Climate Change* (Cheltenham: Edward Elgar Publishing), pp. 137–58.

MWSS (1983a). *Groundwater Development MWSII Final Report (GWD)*, Metro Manila, Metropolitan Waterworks and Sewerage System.

MWSS (1983b). *MWSII Water Demand and Tariff Study*, Manila, Metropolitan Waterworks and Sewerage System, pp. 61–3.

Myers, N. and Simon, J. L. (1994). *Scarcity or Abundance? A Debate on the Environment* (New York: W. W. Norton).

Najam, A. and Cleveland, C. (2003). 'Energy and sustainable development at global environmental summits: an evolving agenda', *Environment, Development and Sustainability*, **5**, 117–38.

Nakicenovic, N., Grubler, A. and McDonald, A. (eds.) (1998). *Global Energy Perspectives*, IIASA/WEC Report (Cambridge: Cambridge University Press).

Narada, The Venerable (1988). *The Buddha and His Teachings*, 4th edn (Kuala Lumpur: Buddhist Missionary Society).

Naredo, J. M. (2001). 'Quantifying natural capital: beyond monetary value', in Munasinghe, M., Sunkel, O. and de Miguel, C. (eds.), *The Sustainability of Long Term Growth*, (London: Edward Elgar).

Nepstad, D. C., Verissinco, A., Alencar, A. *et al.* (1999). 'Large-scale impoverishment of Amazonian forests by logging and fire', *Nature*, **398**, 505–8.

Nepstad, D. C., Capobianco, J. P., Barros, A. C., Carvalho, G., Moutinho, P., Lefebre, P. and Lopes, U. (2000). *Cenários Futuros para a Amazônia. Avança Brasil: Os Custos Ambientais para a Amazônia* (Belém: IPAM/Instituto Socioambiental).

NER (1999). *Electricity Supply Statistics for South Africa 1999* (Pretoria: National Energy Regulator).

NER (2002) *Electricity Supply Statistics for South Africa 2002*, National Energy Regulator, Pretoria, South Africa.

Neumayer, E. (2001). 'Measuring genuine savings: are most resource-extracting countries really unsustainable?', in Munasinghe, M., Sunkel, O. and de Miguel, C. (eds.), *The Sustainability of Long Term Growth*, (London: Edward Elgar).

Newberry, D. (2005), 'Introduction', *Special issue on European Electricity Liberalisation, The Energy Journal*, pp. 1–10.

Nexant (2004). *Sri Lanka Energy Sector Master Plan*. Interim Report ADB TA 4113-SRI, prepared for the Asian Development Bank, April.

Niang-Diop, I. and Bosch, H. (2004). 'Formulating an adaptation strategy', in Lim, B. and Spanger-Siegfried, E. (eds.), *Adaptation Policy Frameworks for Climate Change: Developing Strategies, Policies and Measures* (New York: UNDP).

Nicholson, W. (1978). *Microeconomic Theory* (Hinsdale, IL: The Dryden Press).

Nordhaus, W. and Tobin, J. (1972). 'Is growth obsolete?', in *Economic Growth* (New York: National Bureau of Economic Research (NBER) and Columbia University Press).

Nordhaus, W. D. (1994). *Managing the Global Commons: The Economics of Climate Change* (London: MIT Press).

Nordhaus, W. D. (2000). *Alternative Methods for Measuring Productivity Growth*, Discussion Paper 1282, Cowles Foundation, Yale University, New Haven, CN.

Norgaard, R. B. (2001). 'Growth, globalization and an agenda for ecological economics', in Munasinghe, M., Sunkel, O. and de Miguel, C. (eds.), *The Sustainability of Long Term Growth*, (London: Edward Elgar).

Norgaard, R. D. (1994). *Development Betrayed: The End of Progress and a Co-evolutionary Revisioning of the Future* (London: Routledge).

North, D. (1990). *Institutions, Institutional Change and Economic Performance* (Cambridge: Cambridge University Press).

Nzomo, M. (1992). 'Beyond structural adjustment programs: democracy, gender, equity, and development in Africa, with special reference to Kenya', in Nyang'oro, J. and Shaw, T. (eds.), *Beyond Structural Adjustment in Africa – Political Economy of Sustainable and Democratic Development* (New York: Praeger).

Ocampo, J. A. (2001). 'Policies and institutions for sustainable development in Latin America and the Caribbean', in Munasinghe, M., Sunkel, O. and de Miguel, C. (eds.), *The Sustainability of Long Term Growth*, (London: Edward Elgar).

Odeh, B., (2005). Enhancement of policies and tools for sustainable development. Paper presented at the Doha Development Forum (DDF-2005), Canadian International Development Agency (CIDA), Ottawa, Canada.

OECD (1994). *Environmental Indicators* (Paris: OECD).

Olson, M. (1982). *The Rise and Decline of Nations*, (New Haven, CN: Yale University Press).

Opschoor, J. B. (1998). 'Delinking, relinking and the perception of resource scarcity', in Van den Bergh, J. and Hofkes, M. (eds.), *Theory and Implementation of Economic Models for Sustainable Development*, (Dordrecht: Kluwer Academic Press), pp. 165–72.

Opschoor, J. B. and Jongma, S. M. (1996). 'Structural adjustment policies and sustainability', *Environment and Development Economics*, **1**, 183–202.

Opschoor, H. (2001). *Environmental Economics and Policy Making in Developing Countries* (Cheltenham: Edward Elgar), pp. 23–38.

Opschoor, J. B. and Reijnders, L. (1991). 'Towards sustainable development indicators', in Kuik, O. and Verbruggen, H. (eds.), *In Search of Indicators of Sustainable Development* (Boston, MA: Kluwer).

Opschoor, J(Hans). B., Button, K. and Nijkamp, P. (eds.) (1999). *Environmental Economics and Development* (Northampton, MA: Edward Elgar).

O'Ryan, R., Miller, S. and De Miguel, C. J. (2003). 'A CGE framework to evaluate policy options for reducing air pollution emisions in Chile', *Environment and Development Economics*, **8**, 285–309.

O'Ryan, R., de Miguel, C. and Miller, S. (2005). 'General equilibrium analysis of economywide cross effects in social and environmental policies: case study of Chile', *Ecological Economics*, **54** (4), 447–72.

Ostrom, E. (1990). *Governing the Commons: The Evolution of Institutions for Collective Action*. (New York: Cambridge University Press).

Ostrom, E. (1995). *A Framework Relating Human Driving Forces and Their Impact on Biodiversity*, Working Paper W95I-12, Workshop in Political Theory and Policy Analysis, Indiana University.

Ott, H. E. and Sachs, W. (2002). 'The ethics of international emissions trading', in Pinguelli-Rosa, L. and Munasinghe, M. (eds.), *Ethics, Equity and International Negotiations on Climate Change* (Cheltenham: Edward Elgar Publishing). pp. 159–78.

Pálsson, G. (1995). Learning by fishing: practical science and scientific practice, in Hanna, S. and Munasinghe, M. (eds.), *Property Rights in a Social an Ecological Context* (Stockholm and Washington, D.C.: Beijer Institute and the World Bank), pp. 85–98.

Panayotou, T. and Hupe, K. (1996). 'Environmental impacts of structural adjustment programs: synthesis and recommendations', in Munasinghe, M. (ed.), *Environmental Impacts of Macroeconomic and Sectoral Policies*, (Washington, D.C.: World Bank), chap. 3.

Panayotou, T. and Sussengkarn, C. (1991). The debt crisis, structural adjustment and the environment: the case of Thailand. Paper prepared for the World Wildlife Fund Project on the Impact of Macroeconomic Adjustment on the Environment, Washington, D.C.

Panayotou, T. and Sussengkarn, C. (1992). 'Case Study for Thailand', in Reed, D., (ed.), *Structural Adjustment and the Environment* (Boulder, CO: Westview Press).

Parker, R., Kreimer, A. and Munasinghe, M. (1995). *Informal Settlements. Environmental Degradation and Disaster Vulnerability: The Turkey Case Study* (Washington, D.C.: IDNDR and World Bank).

Parks, P. J. and Bonifaz, M. (1995). 'Nonsustainable use of renewable resources: mangrove deforestation and mariculture in Ecuador', in Hanna, S. and Munasinghe, M. (eds.), *Property Rights and the Environment* (Stockholm and Washington, D.C.: Beijer Institute and the World Bank), pp. 75–82.

Parris, T. M. and Kates, R. W. (2001). *Characterizing a Sustainability Transition: The International Consensus*, Research and Assessment Systems for Sustainability Discussion Paper, Environment and Natural Resources Program, Belfer Center for Science and International Affairs, Kennedy School of Government, Harvard University, Cambridge, MA.

Parry, I. W. and Bento, A. M. (1999). *Tax Deductions, Environmental Policy, and the 'Double Dividend' Hypothesis*, World Bank Working Paper Series 2119, World Bank, Washington, D.C.

Pasurka, C. (1984). 'The short-run impact of environmental protection costs on U. S. product prices', *Journal of Environmental Economics and Management*, **11**, 380–90.

Patinkin, D. (1965). *Money, Interest and Prices* (New York: Harper and Row).

Pearce, D. W. and Turner, K. (1990). *Economics of Natural Resources and Environment*, (Hemel Hempstead: Harvester Wheatsheaf).

Perera, J. (1988). 'Kremlin moves to save the Aral Sea', *New Scientist*, 26 November 1988.

Perrings, C. (1987). *Economy and Environment* (New York: Cambridge University Press).

Perrings, C. (1993). *Pastoral Stategies in Sub-Saharan Africa: The Economic and Ecological Sustainiblity of Dryland Range Management*, World Bank Environment Department Working Paper 57, World Bank, Washington, D.C.

Perrings, C., Maler, K. G. and Folke, C. (1995). *Biodiversity Loss: Economic and Ecological Issues* (Cambridge: Cambridge University Press).

Perrings, C. and Opschoor, H. (1994). *Environmental and Resource Economics* (Cheltenham: Edward Elgar).

Persson, A. (1994). *Deforestation in Costa Rica: Investigating the Impact of Market Failures and Unwanted Side Effects of Macro Policies Using Three Different Modeling Approaches*, Beijer Institute Discussion Paper Series 48, Stockholm.

Persson, A. and Munasinghe, M. (1995). 'Natural resource management and economywide policies in Costa Rica: a computable general equilibrium (CGE) modeling approach', *World Bank Economic Review*, **9** (2), 656–77.

Petersen, G. D., Allen, C. R. and Holling, C. S. (1998). 'Diversity, ecological function, and scale: resilience within and across scales', *Ecosystems*, **1**, 6–18.

Petry, F. (1990). 'Who is afraid of choices? A proposal for multi-criteria analysis as a tool for decision-making support in development planning', *Journal of International Development*, **2**, 209–31.

Pettersen, S. (1964). 'Meteorology', in Chow, V. T. (ed.), *Handbook of Applied Hydrology: A Compendium of Water-resources Technology* (New York: McGraw-Hill), pp. 3-1 – 3-39.

Pezzey, J. (1992). *Sustainable Development Concepts: An Economic Analysis*, World Bank Environment Department Paper 2, World Bank, Washington, D.C.

Pigott, J., Whalley, J. and Wigle, J. (1992). 'International linkages and carbon reduction initiatives', in Anderson, K. and Blackhurst, R. (eds.), *The Greening of World Trade Issues* (Ann Arbor, MI: University of Michigan Press).

Pigou, A. C. (1932). *The Economics of Welfare* (London: Macmillan).

Pimm, S. L. (1984). 'The complexity and stability of ecosystems', *Nature*, **307**, 322–6.

Pimm, S. L. (1991). *The Balance of Nature?* (Chicago, IL: University of Chicago Press).

Pindyck, R. S. (1979). *The Structure of World Energy Demand* (Cambridge, MA: MIT Press).

Pinguelli-Rosa, L. and Munasinghe, M. (eds.) (2002). *Ethics, Equity and International Negotiations on Climate Change*, (Cheltenham: Edward Elgar Publishing).

Pradhan, A. S. and Parks, P. J. (1995). 'Environmental and socioeconomic linkages of deforestation and forest land use change in the Nepal Himalaya', in Hanna, S. and Munasinghe, M., (eds.), *Property Rights in a Social and Ecological Context* (Stockholm and Washington, D.C.: Beijer Institute and the World Bank), pp. 167–80.

Pretty, J. and Ward, H. (2001). Social capital and the environment, *World Development*, **29**, 209–27.

Posch and Partners (1994). *Sri Lanka Micro Hydro Feasibility Study: Report to the Asia Alternative Energy Unit* (Washington, D.C.: World Bank).

Putnam, R. D. (1993). *Making Democracy Work: Civic Traditions in Modern Italy* (Princeton, NJ: Princeton University Press).

Quiggin, J. (1991). 'Comparative statics for rank-dependent expected utility theory', *Journal of Risk and Uncertainty*, **4** (4), 339–50.

Quiggin, J. and Anderson, J. (1990). Risk and project appraisal. Paper presented at *World Bank Conference*, Washington, D.C.

Ranasinghe, A. P. (1989). 'Impact of fuel price changes on Transport', in Wijeratne, E. N. (ed.), *Energy Pricing Options in Sri Lanka* (New York: International Labor Organization).

Raskin, P. (2006). *World Lines: Pathways, Pivots, and the Global Future*, GTI Paper Series no.17, Tellus Institute, Boston, MA.

Raskin, P., Banuri, T., Gallopín, G., Gutman, P., Hammond A., Kates, R. and Swart, R. (2002). *Great Transition – The Promise and Lure of the Times Ahead*, Global Scenario Group, Stockholm Environment Institute, Stockholm; http://www.tellus.org/Documents/Great_Transitions.pdf.

Raskin, P., Gallopin, G., Gutman, P., Hammond, A. and Swart, R. (1998). *Bending the Curve: Toward Global Sustainability*, PoleStar Series Report No. 8 of the Global Scenario Group, Stockholm Environment Institute, Stockholm, Sweden.

Ratnasiri, J. (ed.) (1998). *Final Report of the Sri Lanka Climate Change Country Study*, Ministry of Forest and Environment, Environment Division, Colombo.

Raventós, P. (1990). *Commercial and Tax Reform in Costa Rica in the Mid 1980's* (Alajuela: INCAE).

Rawls, J. A. (1971). *Theory of Justice* (Cambridge, MA: Harvard University Press).

Rayner, S. and Malone, E. (eds.) (1998). *Human Choice and Climate Change* (Columbus OH: Batelle Press), pp. 1–4.

RDA (1997). *Colombo Katunayake Expressway*, Environmental Impact Assessment Report, Road Development Authority, Colombo.

Reed, D. (ed.) (1992). *Structural Adjustment and the Environment* (Boulder, CO: Westview Press).

Reed, D. (1996). *Structural Adjustment, the Environment and Sustainable Development* London: Earthscan Publishers.

Reilly, J., Baethgen, W., Chege, F. E., Van de Geijn, S. *et al.* (1996). 'Agriculture in a changing climate: impacts and adaptations', in Watson, R., Zinyowera, M., Moss, R. and Dokken, D. (eds.), *Climate Change 1995: Impacts, Adaptations, and Mitigation of Climate Change: Scientific-Technical Analyses* (Cambridge: Cambridge University Press).

Reinsborough, M. J. (2003). 'A Ricardian model of climate change in Canada', *Canadian Journal of Economics*, **36** (1), 21–40.

Reis, E. J., and Andersen, L. E. (2000). *Carbon Emissions from Deforestation in the Brazilian Amazon*, Documento de Trabajo No. 01/2000, Instituto de Investigaciones Socio-Economicas, Universidad Catolica Boliviana, La Paz, Bolivia.

Reis, E. J. and Blanco, F. (1996). *The Causes of Brazilian Amazon Deforestation*, Mimeo, IPEA, Rio de Janeiro.

REN21 (2005). *Renewables 2005 Global Status Report*, (Washington, D.C.: Renewable Energy Policy Network, Worldwatch Institute).

Rennie, J. K. and Singh, N. (1996). *Participatory Research for Sustainable Livelihoods* (Winnipeg: International Institute for Sustainable Development).

Repetto, R., Magrath, W., Wells, M., Beer, C. and Ossini, F. (1989). 'The need for natural resource accounting', in Repetto, R., Magrath, W., Wells, M., Beer, C. and Rossini, F. (eds.), *Wasting Assets: Natural Resources in the National Income Accounts* (Washington, D.C.: World Resources Institute), chap. 1.

Repetto, R., Dower, R., Jenkins, R. and Geochegan, J. (1992). *Green Fees: How a Tax Shift Can Work for the Environment and the Economy'* (Washington, D.C.: World Resources Institute.

Reyes, C. (2001). *Twin Girls Killed in Bulacan Fire*, Inquirer News Service, December 23; www.inq7.net/met/2001/dec/23/met_6-1.htm.

Ribot, J. C., Najam, A. and Watson, G. (1996). 'Climate variation, vulnerability and sustainable development in the semi-arid tropics', in Ribot, J. C., Magalhaes, A. R. and Pangides, S. S. (eds.), *Climate Variability, Climate Change and Social Vulnerability in the Semi-Arid Tropics* (Cambridge: Cambridge University Press).

Ricardo, D. (1817). 'Principles of political economy and taxation', in Sraffa, P. and Dobb, M. H. (eds.), *The Works of David Ricardo* (Cambridge: Cambridge University Press).

Robinson, S. (1990). *Pollution, market failure, and optimal policy in an Economywide Framework*, Working Paper 559, Department of Agricultural and Resource Economics, University of California at Berkeley, CA.

Robinson, S. and Gelhar, C. (1995). *Land, Water and Agriculture in Egypt: The Economy-Wide Impact of Policy Reform*, Discussion paper, International Food Policy Research Institute, Washington, D.C.

Robson, A. J. (2001). 'The biological basis of human behavior', *Journal of Economic Literature*, **32**, 11–33.

Rocha, S. (2000). *Pobreza e Desigualdade no Brasil: O Esgotamento dos Efeitos Distributivos do Plano Real*, Texto para discussão no. 721, IPEA.

Rodríguez, A., Abler, D. and Shortle, J. (1997). 'Indicadores ambientales en un modelo de equilibrio general computable para Costa Rica', in Calvo, W., Figueroa, E. and Vargas, J. R. (eds.), *Medio Ambiente en Latinoamérica: Desafíos y Propuestas* (San José, Costa Rica: IICE/UCRy CENRE/Universidad de Chile), pp. 95–129.

Rose, A. and Abler, D. (1998). *Computable General Equilibrium Modeling in the Integrated Assessment of Climate Change*, Fifth Biennial Conference of the International Society for Ecological Economics, Santiago, Chile, November 1998.

Rose, A., Schluter, G. and Wiese, A. (1995). 'Motor-fuel taxes and household welfare: an applied general equilibrium analysis', *Land Economics*, **71**, (2), 229–43.

Rosenberg, D. and Oegema, T. (1995). 'A Pilot ISEW for The Netherlands, 1952–1992', in *Index of Sustainable Economic Welfare* Amsterdam: Institute for Environment and Systems Analysis.

Rowe, R., Sharma, N. P. and Browder J. (1992). 'Deforestation: problems, causes, and concerns', in Sharma, N. P. (ed.), *Managing the World's Forests: Looking for Balance Between Conservation and Development* (Dubuque, IA: Kendall/Hunt Publishing Company).

Rowe, R. D., Lang, C. M., Chestnut, L. G., Latimer, D., Rae, D., Bernow, S. M. and White, D. (1995). *The New York Electricity Externality Study* (Dobbs Ferry, NY: Oceana Publications).

Ruddle, K. (1995). 'The role of validated local knowledge in the restoration of fisheries property rights: the example of the New Zealand Maori', in Hanna, S. and Munasinghe, M. (eds.), *Property Rights in a Social and Ecological Context* (Stockholm and Washington, D.C.: Beijer Instiute and the World Bank). chap. 10.

Ruggles, N. (1949a). 'Welfare basis of marginal cost pricing principles', *Review of Economics Studies*, **17**, 29–46.

Ruggles, N. (1949b). 'Recent developments in the theory of marginal cost pricing', *Review of Economics Studies*, **17**, 107–26.

Ruiz, J. and Yarur, I. (1990). Un modelo de equilibrio general para evaluación de política tributaria. Unpublished Masters Thesis, Industrial Engineering, University of Chile.

Sachs, I. (2001). 'Development thinking in the age of environment: wise use of nature for the good society', in Munasinghe, M., Sunkel, O. and de Miguel, C. (eds.), *The Sustainability of Long Term Growth* (London: Edward Elgar, pp. 162–71).

Sack, R. B., Siddique, A. K., Longini, I. *et al.* (2003). 'A four-year study of the epidemiology of *Vibrio cholerae* in four rural areas of Bangladesh', *Journal of Infectious Diseases*, **187**, 96–101.

Samaraweera, C. P. (1989). 'Determinants of petroleum demand in Sri Lanka', in Wijeratne, E. N. (ed.), *Energy Pricing Options in Sri Lanka* (New York: International Labor Organization).

Samuelson, P. A. (1954). 'The pure theory of public expenditure', *Review of Economics and Statistics*, **36**, 387–9.

Sanderson J. (2002). 'An analysis of climate change impact and adaptation for South East Asia'. Unpublished Ph.D. Thesis, Centre for Strategic Economic Studies, Victoria University of Technology, BC.

Sanghi, A. (1998). 'Global warming and climate sensitivity: Brazilian and Indian agriculture'. Unpublished Ph.D. dissertation, Department of Economics, University of Chicago.

Sanghi, A., Mendelsohn, R. and Dinar, A. (1998). 'The climate sensitivity of Indian agriculture', in Dinar, A., Mendelsohn, R., Evenson, R., Parikh, J., Sanghi, A., Kumar, K., McKinsey, J. and Lonergan, S. (eds.), *Measuring the Impact of Climate Change on Indian Agriculture*', World Bank Technical Paper No. 402 (Washington, D. C.: World Bank).

Sastry, G. S. (2005). 'A model for sustainable development of mountain regions', *Indian Journal of Regional Science*, **37** (2), 53–65.

Satake, A. and Iwasa, Y. (2006). 'Coupled ecological and social dynamics in a forested landscape: the deviations of individual decisions from the social optimum', *Ecological Research*, **21**, 370–9.

Sawin, J. (2004). *Mainstreaming Renewable Energy in the 21st Century* (Washington, D.C.: Worldwatch Institute).

Schkolnik, M. and Bonnefoy, J. (1994). *Una Propuesta de Tipología de las Políticas Sociales en Chile*, UNICEF Document.

Schlenker, W., Hanemann, M. and Fisher, A. (2003). *Will US Agriculture really Benefit From Global Warming? Accounting for Irrigation in the Hedonic Approach*, NBER Summer Research Institute, Boston, MA.

Schmidt-Traub, G. and Cho, A. (2005). *Operationalizing Environmental Sustainability at the National Level – What do we learn from the Millennium Ecosystem Assessment?*, MDG Review Report, UN Millennium Project, United Nations, New York.

Schneider, R. (1993). *Land Abandonment, Property Rights, and Agricultural Sustainability in the Amazon*, LATEN Dissemination Note no. 3, World Bank, Washington, D.C.

Schneider, R. (1994). *Government and the Economy on the Amazon Frontier*, Latin America and the Caribbean Technical Department, Regional Studies Program Report no. 34, World Bank, Washington, D.C.

Schneider, R. R. (1995). *Government and the Economy on the Amazon Frontier*, World Bank Environment Department Paper no. 11, World Bank, Washington, D.C.

Schucking, H. and Anderson, P. (1991). *Biodiversity: Social and Ecological Perspectives* (London and New Jersey, and Penang: Zed Books Ltd and World Rainforest Movement).

Schuh, G. E. (1974). 'The exchange rate and U. S. agriculture', *American Journal of Agricultural Economics*, **56** (1), 1–13.

Schutz, J. (1999). 'The value of systemic reasoning', *Ecological Economics*, **31** (1), 23–9.

Schwartz, A. L. (1996). 'Theory and implementation of numerical methods based on Runge-Kutta integration for solving optimal control problems'. Unpublished Ph.D. dissertation, University of California at Berkley, CA.

Schwartz, A. L., Polak, E. and Chen, Y. (1997). *RIOTS–Recursive Integration Optimal Control Trajectory Solver. A MATLAB Toolbox for Solving Optimal Control Problems, Version 1.0*, Department of Electrical Engineering and Computer Science, University of California at Berkley, CA.

Schwartz, J. (1994). 'Environmental benefits of phasing out lead in gasoline', *Environmental Research*, **66**, 105–24.

Sen, A. K. (1981). *Poverty and Famines: An Essay on Entitlement and Deprivation* (Oxford: Clarendon).

Sen, A. K. (1984). *Resources, Values and Development* (Oxford: Blackwell).

Sen, A. K. (1987). *On Ethics and Economics* (Cambridge, MA: Basil Blackwell).

Senanayake, M. P., Samarakoddy, R. P., Jayasinghe, R. P., Hettiarachchi, A. P., Sumanasena, A. P. and Kudalugadaaracachi, J. (1999). *Is Colombo Choking its Children: A Case-Control Analysis of Hospital Attendance and Air Pollution*, Report, National Building Research Organisation and Faculty of Medicine, University of Colombo.

Sengupta, J. K. and Fox, K.A. (1969). *Optimization Techniques in Quantitative Economic Models* (New York: American Elsevier. Inc.).

Sengupta, R. (1996). *Economic Development and CO_2 Emissions*, Institute for Economic Development 75 (Boston, MA: Boston University).

Seo, N., Mendelsohn, R. and Munasinghe, M. (2005). 'Climate change and agriculture in Sri Lanka: a Ricardian valuation', *Environment and Development Economics*, **10** (5), 581–96.

Serôa da Motta, R. (1996). *Indicadores Ambientais: Aspectos Ecológicos, de Eficiência e Distributivos*, Texto para discussão 399, IPEA, Rio de Janeiro.

Serôa da Motta, R. and Ferraz, C. (2000). 'Estimating timber depreciation in the Brazilian Amazon', *Environment and Development Economics*, **5** (1&2).

Serôa da Motta, R. and Rezende, L. (1999). 'The impact of sanitation on waterborne diseases in Brazil', in May, P. H. (ed.) *Natural Resource Valuation and Policy in Brazil: Methods and Cases* (New York: Columbia University Press), pp. 174–87.

Serôa da Motta, R., Mendes, A. F., Mendes, F. E. and Young, C. E. R. (1994). 'Perdas e serviços ambientais do recurso água para uso doméstico', *Pesquisa e Planejamento Econômico*, **24** (1).

Serageldin I. (1995). *Water Supply, Sanitation, and Environmental Sustainability* (Washington, D.C.: World Bank).

Serageldin, I., Cohen, M. and Sivaramakrishnan, K. C. (eds.) (1995). *The Human Face of the Urban Environment*, Environmentally Sustainable Development Proceedings Series No 6. (Washington, D.C.: World Bank).

Serôa da Motta, R. and Fernandes Mendes, A. P. (1996). 'Health costs associated with air pollution in Brazil', in May, P. and Seroa da Motta, R. (eds.), *Price the Earth* (New York: Columbia Press), chap. 5.

Shaw, E. M. (1983). *Hydrology in Practice* (Wokingham: Van Nostrand Reinhold).

Shepard, R. W. (1953). *Cost and Production Functions* (Princeton, NJ: Princeton University Press).

Sherman, A. and Shapiro, I. (2005). Essential Facts about the Victims of Hurricane Katrina. *Center of Budget and Policy Priorities*; http://www.cbpp.org/9-19-05pov.htm.

Shyamsundar, P. (1993). 'Economic implications of tropical rain forest protection for local residents: the case of the Mantadia National Park in Madagascar'. Unpublished Ph.D. dissertation, School of the Environment, Duke University, Durham, NC.

Siebhuner, B. (2000). 'Homo sustinens – towards a new conception of humans for the science of sustainability', *Ecological Economics*, **32**, 15–25.

Silva, A. B. O. and Medina, M. H. (1999). *Produto Interno Bruto por Unidade da Federação: 1985–1998*, Texto para discussão no. 677, IPEA, Rio de Janeiro.

Simon, H.A. (1959). 'Theories of decision-making in economics and behavioral science', *American Economic Review*, **49** (3), 253–83.

Sioshansi, F. P. (2006). 'Electricity market reform: what has the experience taught us thus far?', *Utilities Policy*, **14** (2), 63–75.

Sivagnasothy, V. and McCauley, D. (2000). 'Environmental considerations in the environmental impact analysis of the Katunayake Expressway in Sri Lanka', in Rietbergen-McCracken, J. and Abaza, H. (eds.), *Environmental Valuation: A Worldwide Compendium of Case Studies* (London: Earthscan Publications).

Sneddon, C., Howarth, R. B. and Norgaard, R. B. (2006). 'Sustainable development in a post-Bruntland world', *Ecological Economics*, **57** (2), 253–68.

Snower. D. J. (1982). 'Macroeconomic policy and the optimal destruction of vampires', *The Journal of Political Economy*, **90** (3) 647–55.

Solórzano, R., Camino, R. de, Woodward, R. *et al.* (1991). *Accounts Overdue: Natural Resource Depreciation in Costa Rica* (San José and Washington, D.C.: Tropical Science Center and World Resources Institute).

Solow, R. (1986). 'On the intergenerational allocation of natural resources', *Scandinavian Journal of Economics*, **88** (1), 141–9.

Solow, R. (1993). 'An almost practical step toward sustainability', *Resources Policy*, **19** (3), 162–72.

Sousa, T. and Domingo, T. (2006). 'Is neoclassical economics formally valid? An approach based on an analogy with equilibrium thernodynamics', *Ecological Economics*, **58**, 160–9.

Southgate, D. and Pearce, D. W. (1988). *Agricultural Colonization and Environmental Degradation in Frontier Developing Economies*, World Bank Environment Department Working Paper 9, World Bank, Washington, D. C.

Speth, J. G. (2004). *Red Sky at Morning: America and the Crisis of the Global Environment* (New Haven, CT: Yale University Press).

Squire, L. and van der Tak, H. (1975). *Economic Analysis of Projects* (Baltimore, MD: Johns Hopkins University Press).

Srinivasan, A. (2005). 'Adaptation to climate change: a critical challenge for Asian development', *What's New From IGES (IGES Newsletter)*, November 2005, p. 1.

Steiner, P. (1957). 'Peak loads and efficient pricing', *Quarterly Journal of Economics*, **71** (285), 585–610.

Steininger, K. W. (1999). 'General models of environmental policy and foreign trade', in van den Bergh, J. C. J. M. (ed.), *Handbook of Environmental and Resource Economics*, (Cheltenham: Edward Elgar), chap. 28.

Stern, N. (1989). 'The economics of development: a survey', *Economic Journal*, **99** (397), 597–685.

Stern, N. (2006). *The Economics of Climate Change: The Stern Review* (Cambridge: Cambridge University Press).

Stiglitz, J. (1974). 'Growth with exhaustible natural resources: efficient and optimal growth paths', *Review of Economic Studies, Special Symposium Issue*, **41**, 123–37.

Stiglitz, J. (2002). *Globalisation and its Discontents* (New York: W. W. Norton).

Stiglitz, J. (2006). *Making Globalisation Work* (New York: W. W. Norton).

Stryker, J. D., West, R. L., Metzel, J. C., Salinger, B. L., Haymond, P. M., Slack, A. T. and Aylward, B. (1989). *Linkages Between Policy Reform and Natural Resource Management in Sub-Saharan Africa*, Report, Fletcher School, Tufts University, Bedford, Massachusetts, and Associates for International Resources and Development.

SUMMA (2003). *Sustainable Mobility, Policy Measures and Assessment*, European Commission Project Report – Directorate General for Energy and Transport, Brussels; http://www.summa-eu.org.

Swart, R., Robinson, J. and Cohen, S. (2003). 'Climate change and sustainable development: expanding the options', *Climate Policy*, **3**, 19–40.

Takayama, A. (1985). *Mathematical Economics*, 2nd edn (Cambridge: Cambridge University Press).

Tanzi, V. (1998). 'Corruption around the world: causes, consequences, scope and cures', *IMF Staff Papers*, **98** (63), 1–39.

Tanzi, V. and Davoodi, H. (1997). *Corruption, Public Investment and Growth*, IMF Working Paper 97/139, Washington, D.C.

Tarp, F. (1993). *Stabilization and Structural Adjustment: Macroeconomic Frameworks for Analyzing the Crisis in Sub-Saharan Africa* (New York: Routledge).

Taylor, L. (1990). *Socially Relevant Policy Analysis: Structuralist CGE Models for the Developing World* (Cambridge: The MIT Press).

Taylor, L. D. (1976). *The Demand for Energy: A Survey of Price and Income Elasticities*, Report, Department of Economics, University of Arizona, Tuscon, AZ.

Tellus Institute (2001). *Halfway to the Future: Reflections on the Global Condition* (Boston, MA: Tellus Institute).

Tietenberg, T. (1992). *Environmental and Natural Resource Economics*, (New York: Harper Collins Publications).

Tietenberg, T. (1995). 'Tradable permits for pollution control when emission location matters: what have we Learned?', *Environmental and Resource Economics*, **5** (1), 95–113.

Townsend, R. E. and Pooley, S. G. (1995a). 'Distributed governance in fisheries', in Hanna, S. and Munasinghe, M. (eds.), *Property Rights and the Environment* (Stockholm and Washington, D.C.: Beijer Institute and the World Bank), pp. 47–58.

Townsend, R. E. and Pooley, S. G.. (1995b). 'Corporate management of the Northwestern Hawaiian Islands lobster fishery', *Ocean & Coastal Management*, **28** (1–3), 63–83.

Trondalen, J. M. and Munasinghe, M. (2005). *Ethics and Water Resources Conflicts, Essay 12 – Series on Water and Ethics*, (Paris: United Nations Educational, Scientific and Cultural Organisation).

Tsigas, I., Gray, D., Hertel, T. and Krissoff, B. (2001). 'Environmental consequences of trade liberalization in the western hemisphere', in Munasinghe, M., Sunkel, O. and de Miguel, C. (eds.), *The Sustainability of Long Term Growth* (London: Edward Elgar), pp. 304–28.

Tufte, E. R. (1992). *Visual Display of Quantitative Information* (New York: Graphics Press).

Turner, R. K. (1999). 'Environmental and ecological economics perspectives', in Van den Bergh, J. C. M. J. (ed.), *Handbook of Environmental and Resource Economics* (Cheltenham: Edward Elgar).

Turvey, R. (1968). *Optimal Pricing and Investment in Electricity Supply* (Cambridge, MA: The MIT Press).

Turvey, R. and Anderson, D. (1977). *Electricity Economics* (Baltimore, MD: Johns Hopkins University Press).

TWNSO (2004). *Safe Drinking Water Workshop Case Studies* (Trieste: Third World Network of Science Organisations).

UN (1992). *Rio Declaration on Environment and Development* (New York: United Nations).

UN (1993). *Integrated Environmental and Economic Accounting, Series F, no. 61* (New York: United Nations).

UN (1996). *Indicators of Sustainable Development: Framework and Methodology* (New York: United Nations).

UN (2000a). *We the Peoples: The Role of the United Nations in the 21st Century*, United Nations General Assembly Report, New York.

UN (2000). *Handbook of National Accounting: Integrated Environmental and Economic Accounting – An Operational Manual* (New York: United Nations).

UN (2003). *Handbook of National Accounting: Integrated Environmental and Economic Accounting – An Operational Manual* (New York: United Nations).

UN (2006). *Trends in Sustainable Development* (New York: UN Department of Economic and Social Affairs, Division for Sustainable Development).

UNCSD (2005). *CSD Theme Indicator Framework* (New York: United Nations); http://www.un.org/esa/sustdev/natlinfo/indicators/isdms2001/table_4.htm.

UNDP (1998). *Human Development Report* (New York: United Nations Development Programme).

UNDP (2004). *World Energy Assessment: Overview 2004 Update* (New York: United Nations Development Programme).

UNDP (2005a). *Environmental Sustainability in 100 Millennium Development Goal Country Reports* (New York: United Nations Development Programme).

UNDP (2005b). *Human Development Report 2005* (New York: United Nations Development Programme).

UNDP (2005c). *Energy Services for the Millennium Development Goals* (New York: The Millennium Development Project, United Nations Development Programme).

UNCRD (1994). 'The effects of disasters on modern societies', *World Conference on Natural Disaster Reduction*, Yokohama, Japan.

Unemo, L. (1996). 'Environmental impact of government policies and external shocks in Botswana: a CGE-model approach', in Munasinghe, M. (ed.), *Environmental Impacts of Macroeconomic and Sectoral Policies* (Solomons, MD, and Washington, D.C.: International Society for Ecological Economics and World Bank), chap. 10.

UNEP (2000). *Report of the World Commission on Dams* (Nairobi: United Nations Environment Programme).

UNEP (2005). *High-Level Brainstorming Workshop for MEAs on Mainstreaming Environment Beyond MDG 7 – Conclusions* (Nairobi: United Nations Environment Programme).

UNEP (2006). *Global Environmental Outlook Year Book 2006: An Overview of Our Changing Environment* (Nairobi: United Nations Environment Programme).

UNEP (2002). *Global Environment Outlook 3*, http://www.grid.unep.ch/geo/.

UNEP, IUCN and WWF (1991). *Caring for the Earth* (Nairobi: United Nations Environment Programme, International Union for the Conservation of Nature and World Wildlife Fund).

UNESCO (2001). *Declaration on Cultural Diversity* (Paris: United Nations Educational, Scientific and Cultural Organisation).

UNFCCC (1993). *Framework Convention on Climate Change: Agenda 21* (New York: United Nations).

University of Chile (2002). *In Native Forests: State of the Environment in Chile 2002, Country Report, Institute of Public Affairs* (Santiago: Editions LOM), pp. 127–160.

University of Moratuwa (2000). *Traffic Demand Estimation for the Proposed Colombo-Katunayake Expressway'*, Report to Board of Investment, University of Moratuwa, Colombo.

Unruh, G. C. and Moomaw, W. R. (1998). 'An alternative analysis of apparent EKC-type transitions', *Ecological Economics*, **25**, 221–9.

USAID (1995). *Integrated Resource Plan for Andhra Pradesh*, Report to Andhra Pradesh State Electricity Board, Hyderabad.

USBEA (1995). *Natural Resource and Environment Accounting*, Conference Proceedings (Washington, D.C.: US Bureau of Economic Analysis).

USEPA (1985). *Costs and Benefits of Reducing Lead in Gasoline: Final Regulatory Impact Estimate*, Report EPA-230-05-85-006, Office of Policy Analysis, Washington, D.C.

USEPA (2004). *Human Health and Environmental Effects of Emissions from Power Generation*, Report, United States Environment Protection Agency, Washington, D.C.

Uzawa, H. (1969). 'Time preference and the Penrose effect in a two-class model of economic growth', *Journal of Political Economy*, **77**, 628–52.

Van den Bergh, J. (1991). *Dynamic Models for Sustainable Development* (Amsterdam: Tinbergen Institute).

Van den Bergh, J. (1996). *Ecological Economics and Sustainable Development: Theory Methods and Application* (Cheltenham: Edward Elgar).

Van den Bergh, J. (1999). *Handbook of Environmental and Resource Economics*, (Cheltenham: Edward Elgar).

Van den Bergh, J. C. J. M and Nijkamp, P. (1994). 'Dynamic macro modelling and materials balance. Economic-environmental integration for sustainable development', *Economic Modeling*, **11** (3), 283–307.

Van Dijk, J. F. W. (1999). 'Assessment of non-wood forest product resources in view of the development of sustainable commercial extraction', in Sunderland, T. C. H., Clark, L. E. and Vantomme, P. (eds.), *Non-Wood Forest Products of Central Africa* (Rome: FAO), pp. 37–50.

Van Heerden, J., Blignaut, J., Mabugu, M., Gerlagh, R., Hess, S., Mabugu, R. and Mabugu, M. (2006). 'Searching for triple dividends in South Africa: fighting CO_2 pollution and poverty while promoting growth', *The Energy Journal*, **27**, (2), 113–41.

Van Rijckeghem, C. and Weder, B. (1997). 'Corruption and the Rate of Temptation: Do Low Wages in the Civil Service Cause Corruption?' IMF Working Paper 97/73.

Van Tongeren, J., Schweinfest, S. and Lutz, E. (1991). *Integrated Environmental and Economic Accounting – A Case Study for Mexico*, World Bank Environment Department Paper no. 50, World Bank, Washington, D.C.

Vanclay, J. K. (1993). 'Saving the tropical forest: needs and prognosis', *Ambio*, **22**, 225–31.

Vanderstraetten, M. (2001). *Development of Scientific Tools in Support of Sustainable Development Decision Making, Conference Proceedings* (Brussels: European Commission).

Walker, B., Carpenter, S., Anderies, J. *et al.* (2002). 'Resilience management in social-ecological systems: a working hypothesis for a participatory approach', *Conservation Ecology*, **6** (1), 14, http://www.consecol.org/vol6/iss1/art14.

Walker, R., Moran, E. and Anselin, L. (2000). 'Deforestation and cattle ranching in the Brazilian Amazon: external capital and household processes', *World Development*, **28**, (4), 683–99.

Warford, J., Munasinghe, M. and Cruz, W. (1997). *The Greening of Economic Policy Reform, Vol. 1 (Principles)* (Washington, D.C.: World Bank).

Warford, J., Schwab, A., Cruz, W. and Hansen, S. (1994). *The Evolution of Environmental Concerns in Adjustment Lending: A Review*, Environment Working Paper No. 65, World Bank Environment Department.

WASH (1991). *Orientation of Guinea Worm Disease: A Guide to Use in Pre-Service and In-Service Training* (Washington, D.C.: USAID).

Washington, W., Weatherly, G., Meehl, A. S. Jr. *et al.* (2000). 'Parallel climate model (PCM): control and transient scenarios', *Climate Dynamics*, **16**, 755–74.

Watkins, A., Osifo-Dawodu, E., Ehst, M. and Cisse, B. (2007). 'Building science, technology and innovation capacity', *Development Outreach*, **9** (1), 2–5.

Watson, A., Alessa, L. and Glaspell, B. (2003). 'The relationship between traditional ecological knowledge, evolving cultures, and wilderness protection in the circumpolar north', *Conservation Ecology*, **8** (1), 2.

Watson, R. T., Zinyowera, M. C. and Moss, R. H. (eds.) (1996). *Climate Change 1995: Impacts, Adaptations and Mitigation of Climate Change* (Cambridge: Cambridge University Press).

Watson, R. T., Zinyowera, M. C. and Moss, R. H. (eds.) (1998). *The Regional Impacts of Climate Change: An Assessment of Vulnerability* (Cambridge: Cambridge University Press).

WCD (2000). *Dams and Development, Report of the World Commission on Dams* (London: Earthscan).

WCED (1987). *Our Common Future* (Oxford: Oxford University Press).

Westing, A. (1992). 'Environmental refugees: a growing category of displaced persons', *Environmental Conservation*, **19** (3), 201–7.

Westra, L. (1994). *An Environmental Proposal for Ethics: The Principle of Integrity* (Lanham, MA: Rowman and Littlefield).

WHO/UNICEF (2000). *Global Water Supply and Sanitation Assessment 2000*, World Health Organization and United Nations Children's Fund, Rome, Italy.

WHO/UNICEF (2005). *Water for Life*, World Health Organization and United Nations Children's Fund, Rome, Italy.

Wijewardene, R. and Joseph, P. G. (1999). *Growing Our Own Energy: Complementing Hydro-power for Sustainable Thermal Energy and Rural Unemployment in Sri Lanka*, Sri Lankan Government Report, Colombo.

Willig, R. D. (1976). 'Consumers' surplus without apology', *American Economic Review*, **66** (4), 589–97.

Wilson, J. A. and Dickie, L. M. (1995). 'Parametric management of fisheries: an ecosystem-social approach', in Hanna, S. and Munasinghe, M. (eds.), *Property Rights in a Social and Ecological Context* (Stockholm and Washington, D.C.: Beijer Instiute and the World Bank) pp. 153–65.

Winkler, H. (2006). 'Energy policies for sustainable development in South Africa's residential and electricity sectors', Unpublished Ph.D. Thesis, Energy Research Centre, University of Cape Town, South Africa.

Winkler, H., Brouns, B. and Kartha, S. (2006). 'Future mitigation commitments: differentiating among non-Annex I countries', *Climate Policy*, **5** (5), 469–86.

Winkler, H., Spalding-Fecher, R., Mwakasonda, S. and Davidson, O. (2002). 'Sustainable development policies and measures: tackling climate change from a development perspective', in Davidson, O. and Sparks, D. (eds.), *Developing Energy Solutions For Climate Change* (Cape Town: Energy and Development Research Centre, University of Cape Town), pp. 176–98.

Withagen, C. (1990). 'Topics in resource economics', in van der Ploeg, F. (ed.), *Advanced Lectures in Quantitative Economics* (London: Academic Press), pp. 381–420.

Wood, C. and Djeddour, M. (1992). 'Strategic environmental assessment: EA of policies, plans and programmes', *Impact Assessment Bulletin*, **10**, 3–22.

World Bank (1986). *Metropolitan Manila Water Distribution Project*, Staff Appraisal Report no. 5903-PH, World Bank, Washington, D.C.

World Bank (1988). *Rio Flood Reconstruction and Prevention Project*, President's Memorandum, World Bank, Washington, D.C.

World Bank (1989). *Angat Water Supply Optimization Project*, Staff Appraisal Report no. 7801-PH, World Bank, Washington, D.C.

World Bank (1990). *Water Supply and Sanitation – FY90 Sector Review*, Infrastructure Department, World Bank, Washington, D.C.

World Bank (1992a). *Development and the Environment: World Development Report 1992* (Washington, D.C.: Oxford University Press for the World Bank).

World Bank (1992b). *Water Quality and Pollution Control Project in Brazil*. Staff Appraisal Report, World Bank, Washington, D.C.

World Bank (1992c). *The Changchun Water Supply and Environmental Project in China*, Staff Appraisal Report, World Bank, Washington, D.C.

World Bank (1992d). *The Zambia Marketing and Processing Infrastructure Project*, Staff Appraisal Report, World Bank, Washington, D.C.

World Bank (1992e). *The World Bank's Role in the Electric Power Sector – Policies for Effective Institutional, Regulatory and Financial Reform*, Industry and Energy Department, World Bank, Washington, D.C.

World Bank (1993a). *Energy Efficiency and Conservation in the Developing World*, World Bank Policy Paper, Washington, D.C.

World Bank (1993b). *Peru: Privatization Adjustment Loan*. Report No. P-5929-PE. Washington DC.

World Bank (1993c). *The East Asian Miracle*, Policy Research Report, World Bank, Washington DC, USA.

World Bank (1994a) *Global Economic Prospects and the Developing Countries* (World Bank Washington).

World Bank (1994b). *Adjustment in Africa: Reforms, Results and the Road Ahead*, Policy Research Report, World Bank, Washington, D.C.

World Bank (1994c). Chile, Managing Environmental Problems: Economic Analysis of Selected Issues, Report no. 13061-CH, 19 December, World Bank, Washington, D.C.

World Bank (1995). *Social Assessment*, Environment Department Dissemination Notes no. 36, World Bank, Washington, D.C.

World Bank (1996a). *Sustainable Transport: Priorities for Policy Reform* (Washington, D.C.: World Bank).

World Bank (1996b). *World Bank Participation Sourcebook - Annex I Methods and Tools* (Washington, D.C.: World Bank).

World Bank (1996c). *Livable Cities for the 21st Century* (Washington, D.C.: World Bank).

World Bank (1997a). *Project appraisal document*, Energy Services Delivery Project Report 16063-CE, Country Department 1, South Asia Region, World Bank, Washington, D.C.

World Bank (1997b), *Harayana Sector Restructuring Project*, Project Appraisal Document. Report no. 17234, World Bank, Washington, D.C.

World Bank (1998). *Environmental Assessment Operational Directive*, Report EAOD4.01, Washington, D.C.

World Bank (2000). *World Development Report: Attacking Poverty* (Washington, D.C.: World Bank).

World Bank (2001). *World Development Indicators* (Washington, D.C.: World Bank).

World Bank (2003). *World Development Indicators 2003* (Washington, D.C.: World Bank).

World Bank (2004). *Environmental Issues in the Power Sector: Long-Term Impacts and Policy Options for Rajasthan*, Paper, World Bank, Washington, D.C.

World Bank (2005a). *World Development Indicators 2005* (Washington, D.C.: World Bank).

World Bank (2005b). *Dynamics of the GLOBAL Urban Expansion*; http://www. citiesalliance.org/publications/homepage-features/feb-06/urban-expansion.html.

World Bank (2006). *Where is the Wealth of Nations?* (Washington, D.C.: World Bank).

Worldwatch (2003). *State of the World 2003*; http://www.worldwatch.org/pubs/sow/2003/.

Worldwatch (2001). *State of the World 2001*, http://www.worldwatch.org/node/1030.

WRI (1991). *Accounts Overdue. Natural Resource Depreciation in Costa Rica* (Washington, D.C.: World Resources Institute).

WRI (1994). 'World resources environment in the 21st Century', in Ferrari, N. *et al.* (eds.), *A Guide to the Global Environment* (Cambridge, MA, and York: The MIT Press, and Oxford University Press).

WRI (1999). *World Resources 1998–99: Environmental Change and Human health* (Oxford: Oxford University Press).

WRI, UNDP, UNEP and World Bank (2000). *World Resources 2000–2001: People and Ecosystems: The Fraying Web of Life* (Washington, D.C.: World Resources Institute).

Yang, H.-Y. (2001). 'Trade liberalization and pollution: a general equilibrium analysis of carbon dioxide emissions in Taiwan', *Economic Modelling*, **18**, 435–54.

Yohe, G. and Van Engel, E. (2004). 'Equity and sustainability over the next fifty years: an exercise in economic visioning', *Environment, Development and Sustainability*, **6**, 393–413.

Yohe, G. W. and Tol, R. S. J. (2001). *Indicators for Social and Economic Coping Capacity – Moving Towards a Working Definition of Adaptive Capacity*, Working Paper, Research Unit Sustainability and Global Change FNU-8, Centre for Marine and Climate Research, Hamburg University.

Young, C. E. F. and Bishop, J. (1995). *Adjustment Policies and the Environment: A Critical Review of the Literature*, CREED Working Paper Series no. 1, IIED, London.

Young, C. E. F. (1997). Economic adjustment policies and the environment: a case study of Brazil. Ph.D. Dissertation, University College London.

Young, C.E.F (coord); (1999). Abertura comercial, competitividade e poluição: o comportamento da indústria Brasileira. Relatório de Pesquisa CNPq 523607/96. IE/ UFRJ, Rio de Janeiro.

Young, M. D. and McCay, B. J. (1995). 'Building equity, stewardship, and resilience into market-based property rights systems', in Hanna, S., and Munasinghe, M. (eds.), *Property Rights and the Environment* (Stockholm and Washington, D.C.: Beijer Institute and the World Bank), pp. 87–102.

Zylicz, T. (1995). 'Will new property right regimes in Central and Eastern Europe serve the purpose of nature conservation?', in Hanna, S. and Munasinghe, M. (eds.), *Property Rights in a Social and Ecological Context* (Stockholm and Washington, D.C.: Beijer Institute and the World Bank), pp. 63–74.

Index

631